W9-CBA-665

About the author . . .

MARTIN RIDGE took his M.A. and Ph.D. degrees at Northwestern University and is associate professor of history at San Diego State College. He is a member of the editorial boards of *The Historian, Agricultural History,* and *Pacific Historical Review.*

Ignatius Donnelly

The Portrait of a Politician

Ignatius Donnelly

The Portrait of a Politician

By Martin Ridge

THE UNIVERSITY OF CHICAGO PRESS

39779

Library of Congress Catalog Card Number: 62–19937
The University of Chicago Press, Chicago & London
The University of Toronto Press, Toronto 5, Canada

© 1962 by The University of Chicago. All rights reserved. Published 1962. Composed and printed in the
United States of America

To

RAY ALLEN BILLINGTON

Preface

THIS is the first full-length biography of Ignatius Donnelly. He has not been neglected in American historical writing, and many gifted scholars have used his personal papers, but few have really examined the thousands of items that make up the Donnelly Manuscripts of the Minnesota Historical Society. In writing about Donnelly, most authors have emphasized what they saw as the bizarre aspects of his career until his image in American history has become that of a man uprooted, a legend without a background. He has grown increasingly unreal. His entire story needs reconstruction if the misconceptions about him are to be dispelled.

But this book was not undertaken to rescue a reputation or to correct errors of scholarship or interpretation. It began as an attempt to use one man's life to illustrate the functions and maladies of the American body politic in the waning years of the nineteenth century. Gradually, however, Donnelly's personal and human experiences assumed importance in themselves, and I grew as concerned with the individual as with his social role. As a result this book became several studies: a personal history, the story of a literary career, a political narrative, and an examination of the business and political ethics of the last century.

Donnelly's life was neither happy nor effortless. Re-creating it as biography posed problems that took a decade to resolve. To offset the difficulties encountered were the advantages of interest, encouragement, and assistance that I received. These I am pleased to acknowledge. I am especially grateful to Professor Ray A. Billington, who aroused and sustained my interest in agrarian politics. I am indebted to Professors Richard W. Leopold, Clarence L. Ver Steeg, Bert J. Loewenberg, and Tracy E. Strevey, who as teachers helped to nourish my interest in the period as well as the subject.

I was also aided by friends and colleagues past and present: Mr. Harry Heuschkel, Professors Wallace N. Jamison, Delber McKee, Ernest Osgood, Sidney Warren, George Gilkey, Abraham P. Nasatir, and John R. Adams. I owe a special debt to my department chairman, Professor John E. Merrill, for his patient reading of the entire manuscript. Without the generous aid of the staff of the Minnesota Historical Society, especially Miss Lucile Kane and Miss Kathryn Johnson, I would have floundered in the mass of Donnelliana. Because Donnelly materials are widely scattered throughout the United States, I am also indebted to more than a score of librarians and manuscript curators who searched for and provided me with helpful leads.

I wish also to acknowledge my gratitude for a grant-in-aid of research from the Social Science Research Council and for a fellowship from the American Council of Learned Societies. One allowed me to complete my research, the other permitted me to take a leave of absence to finish the manuscript. The *Mississippi Valley Historical Review, Mid-America,* and *Minnesota History* have granted permission to reprint materials which were previously published.

Miss Nevada Jenia and Miss Charlotte Jones of San Diego State College's Humanities Division typed the manuscript. I owe a debt to my charitable wife, Marcella Ver Hoef Ridge, who for a decade has endlessly heard and read about Ignatius Donnelly. For any errors in fact or interpretation, I alone am responsible.

Contents

    I. The Young Man 1

   II. Cheer for the West 14

  III. The New Republican 28

  IV. A Politician in Peace and War 43

   V. The Making of a Congressman 60

  VI. A New Congressman 73

 VII. The Trials of a Congressman 91

VIII. Rebuff and Reaction 115

  IX. The Granger 149

   X. The Greenbacker 165

  XI. The Brass Kettle Campaign 180

 XII. Atlantis and Ragnarok 196

XIII. Returning to Politics 211

XIV. The Great Cryptogram 227

 XV. The Farmers' Alliance 245

XVI. Caesar's Column 262

XVII. From the Farmers' Alliance to the
People's Party 279

XVIII. The Populist Interlude 310

XIX. The Road to Fusion 341

[ix]

xx. The Middle of the Road 366

xxi. The Last Days 393

Selective Bibliography 402

Index 415

Illustrations

		FACING PAGE
Donnelly in the 1860's	. . . .	20
Kate Donnelly	. . . .	20
The library in Donnelly's house at Nininger	. . . .	21
William D. Washburn	. . . .	52
Stephen Miller	. . . .	52
Knute Nelson	. . . .	52
Alexander Ramsey	. . . .	52
Donnelly in the 1890's	. . . .	53
The title page of *The Great Cryptogram*	. . . .	244
A page of the 1623 Shakespeare folio	. . . . .	245
An early Anti-Alliance drawing	. . . . . .	276
Donnelly as "the father of the People's party"	. . .	277

No party owns us. We adhere to principle and follow where it leads. We propose to make our life a protest against the slavish caucuses and rings which now afflict this country. We are well aware that this is not the pathway that leads to political honors or emoluments. We do not seek them.

THE ANTI-MONOPOLIST, JULY 13, 1876

The Young Man
1831–1856

By and by we shall hear of Ignatius L. Donnelly.
OLIVER WENDELL HOLMES

IGNATIUS Donnelly, throughout his life, regretted that no great event occurred on the day of his birth. He would have reveled in the thought of a comet blazing in the heavens; he would have enjoyed the idea that a great issue had been decided on a field of battle; he would even have been willing to compromise with a decisive election; but, unfortunately, he had to settle for an ordinary November 3, in 1831. He was that kind of man—restless, and in all things a prisoner of his own imagination. Goethe might have described him as a man of *nature* as contrasted with his man of *talent,* for he was, indeed, a man on fire.

To his contemporaries he was unique: one saw him as a "young Falstaff, with a round chubby face, a round well developed body, and round chubby hands," but with a mind characterized by the single word—success;[1] he was self-sacrificing and honest or he was greedy and corrupt, depending upon with whom one chose to discuss him; to one newspaper man he defied analysis, being a "cryptogram and its key lost."[2] The people who knew him best recognized Donnelly as a man with many human frailties.

His life was intensely political. He seemed to live by the last

[1]Thomas M. Newson, *Pen Pictures of St. Paul, Minnesota, and Biographical Sketches of Old Settlers, From the Earliest Settlement of the City, Up to and Including the Year, 1857* (St. Paul: Brown, Treacy & Co., 1886), p. 629.
[2]Fergus Falls *Journal,* October 25, 1888.

election or for the next one. He entered politics almost as a game, but as he matured, Donnelly developed opinions and, finally, a group of political conclusions. In his early middle years, he confided to his diary:

I am not one of those who believe that politics is a mere base struggle for place and plunder—where the profoundest rascality and deepest purse always win. It is so to have lived as to make some one better for your having lived.[3]

Donnelly never abandoned the "struggle for place and plunder," but the feeling did deepen in him that one must "make some one better for your having lived." This idea, instilled by the bitterness of political defeat and tempered by his personal financial tragedies, was confirmed when he witnessed the triumph of political and economic reaction at the close of the nineteenth century. Throughout his political life, Donnelly believed that he waged a battle to improve the condition of his fellow man. No man is born with his attitude and character—Donnelly's heredity, environment, and most important, experience all helped to shape him.

Donnelly's heritage, interesting and ordinary, followed the course of many Irish-American families. Originating in Fintona, County Tyrone, the Donnellys claimed a legendary kinship to the clan of O'Neil. Somewhat humorously, Donnelly conceded that there was nothing in the records of three centuries to distinguish the family except, perhaps, their remarkable longevity—almost all the males lived at least eighty years.[4]

By 1800 Ireland had a density of population greater than any country in western Europe. Only the high food prices caused by the Napoleonic Wars kept the nation prosperous. With peace restored to Europe, the Irish felt the pinch of hard times, of a congested land, and of a predatory landlord system. When the landlords consolidated their holdings, driving out the tenant farmer, and when tax rates increased, the Irish yeoman class swelled the tide of immigrants to America.[5]

One among the many joining in the exodus from his native land

[3]Minnesota Historical Society, Donnelly MSS, Diary, December 20, 1868.
[4]Ignatius Donnelly, "A Genealogy and History of the Donnelly Family—compiled and written by Ignatius Donnelly with a survey of the History of Ireland" (MS in the possession of Mr. Philip C. Donnelly of St. Paul, Minnesota). Unfortunately this work has no pagination.
[5]William F. Adams, *Ireland and Irish Immigration to the New World from 1815 to the Famine* (New Haven: Yale University Press, 1932), p. 34.

was Philip Carroll Donnelly. Twenty years old, slight, moderately tall, with reddish hair, Philip Donnelly suffered the hard voyage to America.[6] Enrolling in a Pittsburgh, Pennsylvania seminary, he studied for the Roman Catholic priesthood. Why Philip Donnelly abandoned his studies remains a mystery. His children believed that he lacked funds, or that the seminary, like so many small colleges of that day, failed. But as his son Ignatius was fond of pointing out, "It was a day of small things . . . fortunately for me."[7]

In Philadelphia, Philip Donnelly worked for one of his uncles, who outfitted him with the pack of an itinerant peddler. Before long he owned a small shop in the city where he equipped others to sell notions to the German, Dutch, and Scotch-Irish farmers who lived in the back-country. On June 29, 1826 he married Cathrine Gavin, a second generation American of Irish extraction whose family had acquired from Philadelphia's Quakers the characteristics that made them prosper in a world of hardship. Her conscious austerity cloaked a volatile Irish disposition. Although economy was her favorite virtue, she insisted upon living well. In her home, she exercised an inflexible discipline. Her daughters, who had something of their father's wit, slyly remarked that their mother broke so many pairs of spectacles because of the hard looks she darted through them. She was proud of her oratorical ability and expressed her ideas with the striking gestures that were common to the best speakers of that day.[8]

These traits were to stand Mrs. Philip Carroll Donnelly in good stead. Her husband, always adventurous, decided to study at the Philadelphia College of Medicine. To keep Philip in school and their family prosperous, Mrs. Donnelly became a pawnbroker.[9] Although difficult for a woman of her nature, it proved to be most satisfactory for the family's welfare. By the time Philip Donnelly was admitted into the Society of Physicians there were five Donnelly children.[10] With his practice but two years old, and his wife six months pregnant, Dr. Philip Donnelly contracted typhus from a patient and died. Although only thirty-one years old at the time of her husband's death, Cathrine Donnelly never remarried. She de-

[6]Donnelly, "Genealogy and History."
[7]*Ibid.*
[8]*Ibid.*, also Donnelly MSS, Sarah Donnelly to I. D., April 26, 1870.
[9]Samuel H. Perkins, *In the Matter of the Estate of Philip C. Donnelly, Decs'd in the Accounts of Cathrine Donnelly, Adm'x* (Philadelphia: Duross, n.d.), p. 3.
[10]Donnelly MSS, genealogical material.

voted her life to her children, attempting to secure for them the best possible status in the world.

The passing of Philip Donnelly had no marked effect upon his youngest son. Ignatius Donnelly remembered his father as a scholarly man with an insatiable desire for learning. Late in his life, he wrote that his father had been a great reader of the works of Francis Bacon. If this were true, Philip Donnelly left his son an interesting heritage because no more zealous Baconian ever dwelt in the United States than Ignatius Donnelly. He knew also that his father had abandoned Roman Catholicism and this may have influenced his rather unconventional religious thinking.

Donnelly grew to manhood in Philadelphia. Although no longer the nation's largest commercial city, it was entirely urban.[11] When Donnelly was a youth, it presented the fascinating paradox of the antique and the modern. The pioneer militia system was still in effect even though the frontier had long since vanished. And, although the city was notoriously provincial, its intellectuals closed their soirées to all except the most distinguished Europeans but walked in the city's streets wearing the badge of democracy in their business and political life.[12]

It was a city torn by prejudice, riot, and hatred, as the earlier settlers, for the most part Protestants, felt the pinch of economic competition from the Irish and German Catholic immigrants in the years following 1825. When most of the immigrants joined the Democratic party, tensions increased.[13] The native Americans contended that the Irish, ignorant of American ideals, voted as their priests told them. Unscrupulous politicians exploited these feelings of diffidence with half-truths and outright lies, and eventide in the City of Brotherly Love became a time of fear. Nativism and bigotry reached a climax in the Kensington riots, when mobs, surging through the streets, burned and desecrated churches.[14] Ignatius

[11]J. Thomas Scharf and Thompson Wescott, *History of Philadelphia 1609–1884* (Philadelphia: T. H. Everts & Co., 1884), I. 617; also Roy F. Nichols, *The Disruption of American Democracy* (New York: Macmillan Co., 1948), p. 25.

[12]Oscar Handlin (ed.), *This Was America* (Cambridge: Harvard University Press, 1949), pp. 179–93.

[13]Ray A. Billington, *The Protestant Crusade* (New York: Macmillan Co., 1938), p. 198.

[14]Hugh J. Nolan, *The Most Reverend Francis Patrick Kenrick, Third Bishop of Philadelphia, 1830–1851* (Washington, D.C.: Catholic University of America Press, 1948), pp. 288–342.

Donnelly never forgot this aspect of his youth. Twenty-five years after the riots, he told a Fourth of July audience:

I can recollect that in my boyhood Philadelphia was afflicted with many riots; riots between whites and blacks, between natives and foreigners, between the different churches and different fire companies. All that has passed away. The public schools have cured it all. They have humanized the new generation.[15]

This environment had a double effect on Donnelly: he ignored his Catholic middle name, Loyola, but became fiercely proud of his Irish national origin. "If an Irishman is hung for murder," Donnelly chided critics, "his nativity is freely admitted; but if he distinguishes himself in an honorable walk of life, then it is discovered that he is Scotch-Irish."[16]

Donnelly's schooldays were some of the happiest in his life. Despite their Roman Catholic heritage, the Donnellys educated their children in the public schools. Ignatius attended the Ringgold Grammar School in the Third Ward of Moyamensing, then a Philadelphia suburb and later a subdivision.

Attending high school was undoubtedly the greatest single experience in Donnelly's youth, not only because it lifted him from the ranks of the average citizen, but also because he studied at the Central High School. Directed by Alexander D. Bache, later president of Girard College, it was superior to many of the denominational colleges of the era, with a curriculum including mathematics, physics, natural science, chemistry, French, Latin, Greek, and drawing. When Bache went to Girard College, John S. Hart assumed the leadership of Central High School. In Philadelphia, attending the Central High School meant more than just gaining an education. The institution had a reputation as an "immensely aristocratic place, where all the well-bred, patent-leathershod silver watch boys" studied under "the most aristocratic individual in this country, not excepting the President of the United States, John S. Hart, LL.D!" The title made people shiver with respect.[17]

Some of Donnelly's experiences with John S. Hart, reconstructed from his notebooks, indicate that Hart presented a detailed description of the life and times of the leading figures of English literature.

[15]Donnelly MSS, Scrapbook, galley proof of speech delivered at Red Wing, Minn., July 4, 1871.
[16]Donnelly, "Genealogy and History."
[17]Scharf and Wescott, *Philadelphia,* I, 1928–31.

Edmund Spenser was Hart's favorite author; Donnelly's reading ranged from Chaucer's *Canterbury Tales* to Richard Hakluyt's *Voyages*. Hart quoted extensively, probably from memory, and he expected his better students to acquire the habit. But Hart was more to his students than an English teacher. He fascinated them with his enthusiasm for language, constantly reiterating: "Chaucer, Spenser, Shakespeare and Milton are the four great landmarks in English literature. . . . [Of other writers of] modern or ancient times there may be some doubt but these four are past controversy. They are the Gods of our language, the deities of the English language."[18]

Hart also insisted that all his students acquire the habit of reading public documents. Donnelly became a collector,[19] and at the time of his death, his library contained more than one hundred bound volumes of documents on thousands of subjects. A decade after Donnelly graduated, Hart recalled him clearly in a letter describing his "harum-skarum" schoolboy days. "I have been pleased, in particular, to notice," he wrote, "that you have continued to cherish & cultivate that tenacity of purpose which marked you."[20]

Donnelly owed a great deal to John S. Hart. The teacher stimulated his interest in reading good prose as well as poetry. Hart drilled his charges in writing and rhetoric. Under this influence Donnelly, who displayed a natural talent for writing both verse and prose, edited a small newspaper called *The Minute Book*. In the single issue found among his papers and manuscripts was a sonnet entitled "Life" by the editor, Ignatius L. Donnelly. *The Minute Book* may have continued to be issued, but Donnelly quickly lost interest in it.[21]

Not all of Donnelly's school courses were as interesting or as rewarding as English literature. Fragmentary records indicate that his mathematics grades were mediocre and, although he exhibited an interest in natural science and geography, he did not perform well in these fields. He was unable to master German syntax, yet he read the language well enough to have his set of Goethe rebound in expensive worked covers when he left Philadelphia for the West. He could speak German haltingly, probably mixing into his speech a

[18]Donnelly MSS, English lesson book.
[19]*Ibid.*, Rev. J. B. Fisher to I. D., June 25, 1866.
[20]Donnelly MSS, J. S. Hart to I. D., January 2, 1862.
[21]Minnesota Historical Society Library, "A Scrapbook Relating to the Affairs of Ignatius and Eleanor Donnelly: 1886–97."

good deal of the Pennsylvania Dutch idiom that was common in the streets of Philadelphia.[22]

Among Central High School's meaningful contributions to Donnelly's life were the work habits he acquired. He would wake up to jot down ideas if they occurred to him in his sleep.[23] Words and phrasing fascinated him and, even in his political speeches, he frequently relied on verse.

Donnelly's poetry permeated his early diaries, letters, and notebooks. Of the several poems he wrote for publication,[24] one had genuine worth and importance. *The Mourner's Vision* was written shortly before his eighteenth birthday. It had taken almost two months to complete,[25] and he sent a copy to the popular New England author, critic, and sage, Oliver Wendell Holmes, seeking his advice. Holmes was a willing critic; he read the poem, saw something in it that stirred him, but realized also that the style reflected Donnelly's eclecticism. In his characteristic manner Holmes assumed the role of mentor.

I will give you then a little of the advice which you have courted, with a free tongue but kind spirit. You have the inward adjustments which naturally produce melody of expression and incline you to rhythmical forms, of which you will easily become a master. You are a bright scholar, who has read a good many books and perhaps have a little too much fondness of ornamenting your own composition with phrases borrowed from what you have read—very fairly credited to your sources to be true, but perhaps a little too freely interspersed. You have a quick eye and a smart wit of your own—dangerous gifts, which like young colts must be bitted and broken before they can become trusted servants. Whether you have the higher requisites which make up the true poetical character or not, I dare not undertake to decide on the strength of a school exercise. . . .

Seventeen years old! What a blessed reach of future lies before you, with talents and ambition to urge them on to excellence!! But you must remember that you are in your pupilage now, and that what you write as a boy will be judged of by the public without those allowances which friends and a limited circle of acquaintances know how to make. No judicious friend would advise you to print this gay production of your boyhood, or youth, if you choose to call it so. . . . No sir, I hope you are man enough to know that if at your age you have done well, in a few years you can do much better; that study, reflection, the natural ripening of

[22]Donnelly MSS, German lesson book. I am indebted to Professor Lynwood G. Downes of the University of Minnesota for a thorough analysis of Donnelly's German studies.

[23]*Ibid.*, November 22, 1869.

[24]Quoted in Alexander N. DeMenil, *The Literature of the Louisiana Territory* (St. Louis: St. Louis News Co., 1904).

[25]Donnelly MSS, Scrapbook; Duluth *Minnesotian*, January 20, 1872.

the crude juices will do for you what they have done for all the great minds that have born fruit worth gathering. Be patient—do not listen to partial friends,—choose subjects worthy of sincere effort, whether grave or gay,—subdue the rank luxuriance of your infancy and language by studying the pure models and by and by we shall hear of Ignatius L. Donnelly.[26]

Donnelly was a young man in a hurry, far from certain that he wanted his own "dangerous gifts . . . bitted and broken." Despite the advice, he published the poem. In a brief preface apologizing for the errors and conceding that the poem was a foolish thing to publish even at his young age, he expressed the hope that his friends and readers would refrain from telling him so.[27]

The Mourner's Vision, because it characterized superbly the growing feeling among the young intellectuals in the United States about freedom and democracy, was not without historical and political significance. Composed just after the European Revolutions of 1848, it put into words what many an American schoolboy believed, and aside from a strident American nationalism, expressed a poetic damnation of the suppression of freedom in Europe and a warm faith that it would be redeemed.

> Alas! a nation's wrecked hopes, and the might
>   That stirred the strong arm for that nation's sake;
> Alas! the brave ones striving for the Right
>   Who bade that Lazarus of Truth awake;
>   All, all were following in that banner's wake;
> And all went down before the dastard blow,
>   When Russian lightnings bade the broad night quake,
>   And left me friendless in my grief below,
> To grope alone through memory's valley'd wastes of woe.
>
> Oh! Austria the vile, and France the weak,
>   My curse be on ye like an autumn storm,
> Dragging out tear drops on the pale year's cheek,
>   Adding fresh baseness to the twisting worm;
>   My curse be on ye like a mother's, warm,
> Red reeking with my dripping sin and shame;
>   May all my grief back-turned to ye, deform
> Your very broken image, and a name
> Be left ye which Hell's friends shall hiss and curse, the same.

Donnelly, in the spirit of the Young America movement which captured the hearts of the nation's youth, felt that the United States

[26]MS in the possession of Mrs. Henry Woltman, printed in *American Literature*, XIII (March, 1941), 59–61.

[27]Ignatius Donnelly, *The Mourner's Vision* (Philadelphia: King & Baird, 1850), Preface.

would spread democracy throughout the world. Like so many other young zealots who expressed the spirit of the times, he eagerly joined the Democratic party to see that all wrongs were righted.

Never able to divorce himself from poetry, Donnelly scribbled verses into his diary periodically during most of the years of his life, but he was rarely again tempted to publish his works. On one occasion he consented to publish some poems, but only to help his younger sister, Eleanor C. Donnelly, later a leading Catholic poetess, secure wider circulation for her poetry.[28]

A graduate of the Central High School was ill-suited to earn his livelihood in the family pawnshop. Because the law was recognized as the profession of distinction, Donnelly decided to become a lawyer. He secured a clerkship in the office of Benjamin Harris Brewster, a rising member of the Philadelphia bar and destined to become the attorney-general not only of Pennsylvania but also of the United States. Scion of a wealthy New Jersey family, Brewster had earned a reputation at fashionable Princeton College as a brilliant essayist, a correct, original and profound thinker, as well as a polished speaker. Dignified and erudite, always dressed in faultless taste, he was punctiliously old-fashioned in his manners, especially to women.[29]

Brewster's law offices were in his home, where he lived in the comfort that characterized the substantial wealth of Philadelphia. Donnelly respected Brewster as an attorney and as an individual, but the environment awed him. He was extremely sensitive to the surroundings and experienced deep feelings of insecurity, especially in his associations with his fellow students. After three years, he explained his feelings to Brewster in a letter of resignation.

I would ask that my having written this letter be not known to the gentlemen of the office. Goldsmith's schoolboy was able to read the day's disasters in his tutor's face;—I could go beyond him, for in the visages of my fellow students I could always *detect* your state of feeling toward me;—were it otherwise, the one became a boorish and overbearing the other distant and cold. I lived with them, as it were, *per gratia*. The bond of connection has never been a pleasant one,—and I sever it without regret—but for yourself, accept, sir, my reiterated apology for that in which I have offended you, and believe me when I say, that the honor of that intimacy you were pleased to extend to me shall live with me as one of the proudest memories; that your counsels and your precepts shall come before me in after years and that if accident of fortune can be waived aside

[28] Allen Johnson, and Dumas Malone (eds.), *The Dictionary of American Biography* (New York: Charles Scribner's Sons, 1930), V, 369.
[29] Scharf and Wescott, *Philadelphia*, II, 1550–51.

from the path of any man, the day will come when some small part of the pride I see in my tutor will be returned to him by his student.[30]

Judged from his case book and court docket, Donnelly was not a successful attorney in Philadelphia. Much of his practice dealt with collecting judgments and satisfying personal disagreements. His fees were small. His records disclosed more than 150 entries in the four years from 1852 to 1856. A typical client employed Donnelly in twenty-nine separate matters and was reluctant to pay a fee of $150.[31] An easy creditor, Donnelly could write a client: "If you have the slightest wish ever to pay me call and see me," he wrote. "If you tell me you are unable to pay me I will make you a present of the money and shake over it. But do not let me suppose that you intend to deceive me."[32]

Donnelly was drawn quickly into politics, probably through the efforts of Benjamin Harris Brewster. A Democrat, because the Irish invariably joined the party, Donnelly regarded the Whigs as aristocratic and hostile toward the immigrant. Furthermore, the rise of prejudice in the form of the American party, or Know-Nothings, made the Democratic party all the more appealing; it alone stood out firmly against the anti-Catholic, antiforeign ideas circulating in the country.

Among Donnelly's earliest political writing was a criticism of Horace Greeley, the editor of the New York *Tribune*. After Greeley appeared in Philadelphia, Donnelly analyzed him from the point of view of phrenology, a popular scientific fad. Despite the limitations of the pseudo-science which fixed character traits by headshape, Donnelly accurately described Greeley as having:

The characteristics common to the heads of visionary, theoretical reformers: that of largeness, fulness or overplus of brains with the front deficient in the development of those organs of judgement necessary to restrain and direct the active forces of the general intellect;—leaving to the mind its activity, its ambition, its perception, but depriving it of its practicality and its clear every day view of an every day world.[33]

Objecting to Greeley's oratorical gestures, Donnelly was disgusted with his manner of employing a silk handkerchief to wipe his face as if attempting to do the entire job with one stroke. He especially disliked the constant swinging of the right arm as if trying to bring it down to make a point which never came.

[30]Donnelly MSS, I. D. to B. H. Brewster, December 30, 1852 (copy).
[31]*Ibid.*, Letter Book 2, I. D. to D. Van Sloan, April 20, 1857.
[32]*Ibid.*, I. D. to Conray, February 8, 1856 (copy).
[33]*Ibid.*, Manuscript of speech December 15, 1852.

On July 4, 1855, Donnelly made his political debut by delivering a speech on immigration before a Democratic County Assembly in Independence Square. He argued that American institutions were viable enough to absorb all the oppressed of Europe and blend them skilfully into a unified democratic whole, and that therefore immigrants were not to be feared. They were the new topsoil, that would revitalize America. These people, he felt, who brought with them the love of liberty, would help keep the flame of freedom burning brightly.[34] The speech was an immense success. Donnelly was so delighted with its reception that he spent almost two dollars for newspaper copies of it.[35] When the speech came to the attention of Senator John C. Breckinridge, that shrewd political warrior informed the young Philadelphian that he was appreciated by his party. Highly susceptible to flattery, Donnelly took Breckinridge as his model.

In 1855 the Democratic organization selected Donnelly to run for the state legislature. He withdrew from the race the day before the election, pointing out that he had failed to receive the indorsement of the Liquor League, a powerful influence in Philadelphia proper. Furthermore, when the Whig candidate took a staunch anti-Know-Nothing position, Donnelly decided to support him.[36]

In a letter to Breckinridge in June, 1856, Donnelly promised to abandon his personal affairs and do everything possible to help the Democratic national ticket of Buchanan and Breckinridge.[37] When Breckinridge suggested that he write editorials or make speeches, Donnelly was delighted. He was, he wrote Breckinridge, "anxious to show in every way my esteem for yourself personally and my pride in our past intercourse, limited as it has been."[38] Shortly thereafter, in a caustic essay on the "Composition of the Republican Party," he asserted that it was "a collection of philanthropists, learned schoolmasters, *eery haired* abolitionists, licentious amalgamationists, and fanatics of all kinds." The Democratic party, he insisted, with its great standard-bearers, had nothing to fear. "Where are all the isms that year after year have risen up against the Democracy?" he asked rhetorically. "In their grave." He predicted that the Republican party would deteriorate after the election. "The

[34]Minnesota Historical Society Library, Donnelly scrapbook, clipping from Daily *Pennsylvanian*, undated.
[35]Donnelly MSS, Ledger, July 5, 6, and 7, 1855.
[36]*Ibid.*, I. D. to J. C. Breckinridge, December 17, 1855.
[37]*Ibid.*, I. D. to Breckinridge, June 18, 1856.
[38]*Ibid.*, I. D. to Breckinridge, August 30, 1856.

abolitionists will be as before exalting the black over the white. The Know-Nothing will be once more holding his midnight council over the Irish and the Dutchman. The Yankee adventurer will return again to his peddling or his lecturing."[39] Two years later Donnelly voted Republican!

On Allhallows Eve, 1854, his mother's birthday, Donnelly met Katherine McCaffrey, his beloved Kate. Of average height, she had brown hair, a full forehead, and wide blue eyes. She could sing beautifully, and there was always pride in her bearing. Although she discarded her dignity when she lost her temper, Katherine Mc-Caffrey was never without a twinkle in her eyes. To Donnelly, she had a "pleasing countenance and a comely figure."[40]

The McCaffreys, like the Donnellys, were of Irish extraction. Petty merchants, they were intensely devout Roman Catholics. Kate's religion was an integral part of her existence. She clung to it tenaciously; throughout her life it was her shield and her solace. Donnelly's religious unorthodoxy troubled her. When she visited a married sister in Stark County, Ohio, he wrote to her explaining, half in jest, the complexity of their relationship. He spoke not only of the intimacy of romantic love but also of their religious feelings.

> You tell me "to continue to go to church." Dear, I have intended to do so. I intended to have told you so, and then thought, no, I will not, for then she will think I merely do so to win her applause. I go dear to be with you. I would go, if I felt confident that you would never know whether I went or staid. I go through a sense of faithfulness which to me is more binding than all law. I go, though my family leave me Sunday after Sunday the sole tenant of the pew.[41]

Donnelly's mother disapproved of Kate McCaffrey. She would have preferred a better match; perhaps the daughter of Benjamin Harris Brewster would have pleased her. But by July, 1855, Donnelly determined to marry Kate, even if it meant breaking with his family. They were married in September, despite the unrelenting opposition of his mother. Kate too was hostile toward her mother-in-law. For fifteen years, the women did not speak to each other![42] Although Donnelly had his share of the family pride, he deplored what he termed "the most ludicrous affair imaginable," the "pawn-broker's shop and the market stall holding a heraldric disputation."

[39]*Ibid.*, rough draft of editorial.
[40]Ignatius Donnelly, *In Memoriam* (St. Paul: Wm. L. Banning, 1895), pp. 19, 20, and 21.
[41]Donnelly MSS, I. D. to Kate McCaffrey, July 1855.
[42]*Ibid.*, Diary, April 3, 1869.

He reminded his sisters, who had sided with their mother in the controversy, that those who had risen by gradations from the "*Kerne* of Ireland," had little to fling in the teeth of others for their humble origin.[43] Not even the birth of Donnelly's first son, Ignatius Carroll Donnelly, resolved the family quarrel.

After his marriage, Donnelly supplemented his income by participating in co-operative building association schemes. Irish and German immigrants, eager to obtain homes, invested in the associations. Donnelly served as a consultant who knew the law, could draw up contracts, and advise the association on business practices. By 1856, he was an officer in five associations.[44]

When he decided to move to the West, before any of the projects were completed, he was suspected of misappropriating the funds and seeking to defraud the immigrants who had purchased shares in the Union Land and Homestead Building Association.[45] His cousin, John Duross, accused him of outright fraud, contending that Donnelly had purchased the land and sold it to the association at a large profit.[46] The allegation was untrue, but when Donnelly attempted to resign from the association his letters were refused.[47] Eventually, he compelled the association directors to examine his record books and attest to his honesty.[48]

Although Donnelly had learned about the intricacies of speculative real estate—all of which proved to be of immense value when he settled in the West—he was disappointed by his experience with the building association directors. To add to his personal concern, as he prepared to leave Philadelphia, was a persistent rumor that he had misused funds left in trust for his youngest sister. His embittered mother, still resenting his marriage, refused to deny the scandalous charge. This rumor, and a taint of scandal resulting from the allegations of the building association directors, left Donnelly with lasting personal scars.

[43]*Ibid.*, I. D. to Eleanor C. Donnelly, March 9, 1863.
[44]*Ibid.*, Ledger, index.
[45]*Ibid.*, J. Welch to I. D., April 22, May 13, 1856.
[46]*Ibid.*, J. Duross to I. D., August 10, 1861.
[47]*Ibid.*, Letter Book 2, I. D. to Union Land & Homestead Building Association, December 11, 1856. See also, Letter Book 2, I. D. to J. Duross, December 15, 1856, and J. Duross to I. D., May 2, 1856.
[48]*Ibid.*, I. D. to F. Taggart, March 21, 1857.

Cheer for the West

1856–1858

Why should we weep to sail in search of fortune?
Cheer for the West, the new and happy land.

IGNATIUS DONNELLY

As EARLY as 1852, Donnelly wrote to a friend in Chicago concerning opportunities in the prairie city for an energetic lawyer. But the response was so unsatisfactory that he gave up the idea of moving.[1] When he courted Kate, however, he promised that they would make their home in a western state where they would grow up with the country. In 1856 he decided to move to the West.

To some extent his decision was prompted by his Philadelphia experience. The city had long been known as the "Gateway to the West." Through its harbor had passed a host of immigrants who filled in the valleys of the Appalachians and later settled in the heart of the continent. The city shared the early nineteenth-century spirit of expansionism. What Donnelly did not see and hear of the adventures of men who profited from the West, he found in books. In the novels of James Fenimore Cooper especially, he saw an inspiring image of western life. Even though he realized that the days of Natty Bumppo were past, Bumppo remained for Donnelly, as he did for several generations of young Americans, a "beau-ideal of a hero."[2] Furthermore, since neither his wife nor his mother appre-

---

[1]Donnelly MSS, J. Leonard to I. D., April 15, 1852.
[2]*Ibid.*, Diary, n.d., p. 115.

ciated the demands of the other upon him and he proved unable to quiet their mutual hostility, he felt compelled to separate them. Even more important than the family squabble was a growing awareness of his sharply circumscribed financial future if he remained in Philadelphia. Without substantial investment capital or established business connections, even a young man with his education faced a long hard struggle to achieve wealth and recognition. Politics, a field which proffered social advancement as well as psychological satisfaction, was not as rewarding as it appeared to be. Although party leaders welcomed talented young men, politics was so well organized in the Keystone State that competition for preferment was extremely keen.

Perhaps Henry Adams was justified in believing that the "convincing reason for staying in the East was that he had there every advantage over the West." The grandson of one president and the great-grandson of another might well feel that "one's position in the East was the best in the world for every purpose that could offer an object for going westward."[3] But as an immigrant's son, whose status dictated a hard struggle for success, Donnelly preferred to risk the uncertainties of the West, which frightened young Adams, to the certainties of the East which frightened him.

"Every man goes [West] on his own hook," Donnelly wrote self-assuringly; "if you tired of your trade you could pre-empt 160 acres." Only the timid will remain "in this God-forsaken mountainous state where every man is trying to put down his neighbor."[4] The West Donnelly visualized in 1856 was entirely different from the way it had been a generation earlier. No one need swing an ax as did Fenimore Cooper's Aminadab to travel twenty miles in one day. No one need grow gray from privation or sacrifice his life for his children. A new force had been harnessed. "There is such an invention as steam —steam on the prairie, steam on the mountain—steam on the hills and steam power over gorges—hissing, screaming, jumping along the valleys and over the bridges."[5] Steam made life's burden bearable; steam would subdue the West!

After visiting his sister-in-law in Ohio, he lost interest in settling in the older Middle West. It "has had its day, and the chances are

[3] Henry Adams, *The Education of Henry Adams* (Boston: Houghton Mifflin Co., 1918), p. 52.
[4] Donnelly MSS, Letter Book 1, I. D. to H. Hunseiker, March 3, 1857.
[5] Minnesota Historical Society Library, Donnelly scrapbook, clipping from Daily *Pennsylvanian*, December 31, 1856.

all past."[6] He looked to the areas just being opened for settlement, such as the upper Mississippi Valley, even though many of the published accounts of the region were hair-raising.

Boosters of Michigan reported that Illinois was a pest hole[7] and a Minnesota editor informed a gullible public that the territory's "coldest day last winter froze the mercury (but then that was owing to exposing the thermometer to the cold weather!),"[8] but Donnelly traveled through the West before deciding where to settle. Having no interest in slavery, he ruled out Kansas, where open warfare jeopardized investments, and turned to Iowa and Minnesota. Transportation by stagecoach, more than any other factor, dissuaded Donnelly from moving to Iowa. The journey from Iowa City to Newton, less than one hundred miles, "was accomplished in two days of the most execrable traveling. I paid six dollars for my ticket and three dollars additional for six meals," he complained. "The dinners I received for my fifty cents were miserable beyond description. Molasses supplied in place of butter, doughy cakes substituted for bread, ham was the unchanging article of meat, and everything else was in like manner meager and mean." Indignantly, he noted in his journal, "With all this there was the most uncompromising impudence."[9]

In contrast to his discouraging Iowa experience, Donnelly's riverboat voyage from Davenport, Iowa, to St. Paul, Minnesota, was inexpensive and comfortable. The sheer beauty of the upper Mississippi River Valley impressed him enormously. "The blue water hemmed in by walls equal on both sides . . . [while] far along the western bluff the deep shadows of the declining sun and the eastern side yellow hills lit up with glory" was a sight he wished always to remember. To his diary he confided: "What a beautiful land has the red man lost and the white man won."[10]

St. Paul, Minnesota, with its narrow streets, appeared humble, but the city had little humility about it. In the 1850's, it was a typical, robust city behind the frontier. On its sidewalks buckskin-clad traders elbowed their way past finely clothed eastern travelers. The

[6]Donnelly MSS, Letter Book 1, I. D. to Mary Faiver, May 6, 1857.

[7]Henry C. Hubbart, *The Older Middle West, 1840–1880* (New York: Macmillan Co., 1936), p. 36.

[8]D. S. B. Johnston, "Minnesota Journalism in the Territorial Period," Minnesota Historical Society *Collections*, X, 249.

[9]Donnelly MSS, Diary, no pagination.

[10]*Ibid.*

hotels, though small and uncomfortable, boasted steam heat and menus difficult to rival in a seaboard city. Only its Yankee residents saved St. Paul from being another "river town." They believed in temperance, supported the Maine law, kept the Sabbath, and so, whether money was borrowed at 3 or 5 per cent per month, little of it changed hands on Sunday.

Minnesota was enjoying an economic boom. "Fortunes seemed to be dropping out of the skies, and those who would not gather them were but stupids or sluggards."[11] Merchants stockpiled goods, holding them for higher prices. The prospects for the harvest were excellent. In St. Paul, where the streets were crowded with immigrants infected with Minnesota fever, the one shrine at which all investors worshiped was the new townsite. In fact, so much of the territory had been laid out for towns that a member of the legislature facetiously submitted a resolution setting aside at least one-third of Minnesota's land for agricultural purposes![12]

In this speculatively infectious environment, Donnelly quickly formed a partnership with John Nininger, a former Philadelphian who had lived in the West for several years and had acquired extensive landholdings and broad real estate experience.[13] Nininger was preparing to develop a townsite, to be called Nininger City, on the Mississippi River seventeen miles south of St. Paul. Nininger's ancestry was German and his wife accepted the Donnelly-Nininger partnership with cynical good humor, pointing out that "two heads are better than one—even if one should be a 'Sour Kraut' and the other a 'Paddy.' "[14] The men understood each other's talents and limitations; Nininger assumed responsibility for the "outdoor business," the purchases, "the sales generally," and all other activities that called for experience. The office work, the correspondence, the accounts, the advertising, "the writing generally," were Donnelly's obligation.[15] The men realized that establishing a town required social prestige. This was easily arranged when Nininger's brother-in-law, Minnesota's former governor Alexander Ramsey, placed his name on the list of sponsors. Hopefully, Donnelly sent John C.

[11] William Watts Folwell, *A History of Minnesota* (St. Paul: Minnesota Historical Society, 1926), I, 363.
[12] *Ibid.*, p. 362.
[13] J. F. Williams, *History of Dakota County and the City of Hastings* (Minneapolis: Tribune Publishing Co., 1881), p. 436.
[14] Donnelly MSS, C. Nininger to I. D., February 26, 1857.
[15] *Ibid.*, undated, articles of agreement.

Breckinridge the title to a lot, but the vice-presidential candidate returned it.[16]

The partners also persuaded several wealthy men to participate in the project. One of these was George Robertson, a New York businessman. Fascinated with the town planting idea, Robertson, a born promoter with limitless enthusiasm, invested his talents and forty thousand dollars.[17] Another participant, Major George B. Clitherall of Washington, D.C., promised to work for any legislation that would help the town.[18] John Arnold, a St. Paul real estate developer, joined in the scheme by trading St. Paul lots for land in the new town.[19]

After launching the project, Donnelly returned to Philadelphia where he began his work for the new community by establishing a newspaper, the *Emigrant Aid Journal*. Although the first issue of the newspaper was to be printed in Philadelphia, later issues were to be published in Nininger City. Aided by a German-speaking friend, Philip Rohr, he prepared a bilingual edition of the *Emigrant Aid Journal* especially designed to attract German settlers to the town. Donnelly had hoped to begin publication by October, 1856, but the newspaper did not appear until December.

While Donnelly wrote the *Emigrant Aid Journal*, George Robertson arranged for him to present a speech in New York City in the hope that the report in the New York newspapers would give Nininger City national publicity. At the same time, Major Clitherall placed articles discussing Nininger City as a "city with a future" in many newspapers throughout the country.[20] The investors also circulated thousands of postal cards describing the advantages of Minnesota and the special merits of Nininger City. A large number of broadsides were displayed, both in St. Paul and in the East. Promotional material was even sent to Scotland, where Robertson had business connections, in the hope of attracting settlers. Distributing advertising material so rapidly that he constantly complained of a shortage, Robertson claimed that the Nininger City promotional material was part of the flood of propaganda that caused the British

[16]*Ibid.*, J. C. Breckinridge to I. D., September 15, 1856.

[17]Dudley S. Brainard, "Nininger, a Boom Town of the Fifties," a paper read at the annual luncheon of the Minnesota Historical Society on January 11, 1932.

[18]Donnelly MSS, G. Clitherall to I. D., December 8, 1856.

[19]*Ibid.*, P. Rohr to I. D., March 4, 1856.

[20]Minnesota Historical Society Library, Donnelly scrapbook, restricted collection, clipping from *Real Estate News Letter*, May, 1857.

Parliament to fear for the future of western Canada, which, adjacent to Minnesota, was dangerously close to American influences.[21]

To help immigrants who could not afford to move to Nininger City, Donnelly established the Emigrant Aid Association. Prospective settlers were to pay twenty-five one-dollar instalments to purchase membership in the society. A member was entitled to a free ticket to Nininger City, a brief period of support, and a sufficient number of tools to help him become self-sustaining. A ticket from the East to Minnesota, even at its cheapest, cost more than fifteen dollars, and the association was obviously more a publicity device than a long-range immigration scheme.[22]

George Robertson conceived a scheme almost as novel as the Emigrant Aid Association. Contacting his good friends in Scotland who operated a transatlantic shipping line, he not only persuaded the firm's representatives to sell "Glasgow to Nininger City" tickets, but also to send one of its members to Nininger City to build a hotel. Robertson shared Donnelly's hope that the plan would make the as yet unchartered city a leading terminus in the West.[23]

Although "hot house" techniques for town planting generated enthusiasm among the investors, John Arnold, the St. Paul partner, advised Donnelly to concentrate his propaganda on the regions nearest the town. Land could always be more easily sold to people who knew its real value. Arnold emphasized that, for the most part, the settlers who moved into new communities were people already near or on the frontier. The appeal abroad netted a very limited return.[24]

Donnelly worked as hard to develop Nininger City as to advertise it. He prepared plans for a hotel, and the large share owners were asked to subscribe one thousand dollars each toward its construction. The community had to rely on the surrounding countryside for trade, and Donnelly hoped that it would develop into a major river port; so he arranged to have a road built into the back-country. He also contracted for a boat to carry passengers and goods into the town from up and down river. To persuade craftsmen to settle in Nininger City, Donnelly paid for his house in town lots and building materials.[25] When some of the original investors began holding land

[21]Donnelly MSS, G. Robertson to I. D., November 27, 1856, February 23, 1857.
[22]*Emigrant Aid Journal*, December 1, 1856.
[23]Donnelly MSS, Letter Book 1, I. D. to G. Robertson, March 2, 1857.
[24]*Ibid.*, J. Arnold to I. D., June 10, 1856.
[25]*Ibid.*, Letter Book, unnumbered, I. D. to J. Nininger, August 20, 1856.

without making improvements, creating a highly speculative situation, Donnelly boldly threatened to enforce the terms of their sale contracts, which stipulated that $250 per lot should be spent on improvements within a two-year period.[26]

Eager as Donnelly was to reduce his liabilities, he willingly sacrificed his own profits to prevent speculation from damaging the town. He had hoped, on returning to Philadelphia, that he could rapidly liquidate his eastern holdings and move to the West with considerable capital. Unfortunately, business conditions deteriorated in the fall of 1856, and Philadelphia investors were hesitant about real estate ventures. It proved almost impossible for him to sell land, especially at a time when rumors reflecting on his honesty were current in Philadelphia.

To add to Donnelly's increasing anxieties were the actions of his older brother, John Gavin Donnelly. Ignatius had been persuaded by his mother to send John, a ne'er-do-well, to work as a carpenter in the construction of his home in Minnesota. No sooner had John Donnelly arrived in Nininger City than he became a center of controversy. Pleading with John to behave, Donnelly urged him to support Nininger City, not to sabotage the project. Angered by the reprimand, John abandoned Minnesota, and his return to his home community caused a furor. "Hell," he openly proclaimed, "is better than Nininger City."[27] Donnelly found no way to silence him.

But John Donnelly was one of the least of the difficulties. Nininger City had been platted only three miles from the struggling community of Hastings, which had been established a few years earlier and had a population of almost two thousand when Donnelly and Nininger formed their partnership. At the outset, Hastings had caused Donnelly little concern. In a pamphlet privately circulated among the investors in Nininger City, he explained that Hastings lacked "inspired leadership."[28] But when Minnesota, fast moving toward statehood, planned to establish permanent county seats, the Hastings–Nininger City rivalry assumed genuine importance. If Hastings became the county seat, it would be almost impossible to replace it as the county's leading city.

The settlers of Nininger City, realizing that they were too few in number to capture the courthouse, concentrated on gaining votes

[26]*Ibid.*, Letter Book 1, I. D. to J. Nininger, November 17, 1856; Ignatius Donnelly, *Statement of the Basis of the Organization of the City of Nininger, Minnesota* (Philadelphia: John Duross, 1856), p. 7.

[27]*Ibid.*, I. D. to J. Nininger, October 13, 1856.

[28]Donnelly, *Organization of Nininger*, pp. 3–4.

Donnelly in the 1860's—a youthful member of Congress. (U.S. Signal Corps Photograph.)

Kate Donnelly (assumed)—a photograph taken in the 1870's. (Minnesota Historical Society.)

The library in Donnelly's house at Nininger.
(Minnesota Historical Society.)

for either West St. Paul or Empire City, both of which were at least fifteen miles away. "If Hastings carries the election without strong resistance," Donnelly warned his Minnesota associates, "it will be a direct injury to all our interests. I hope nothing will be left un-done."[29] When West St. Paul and Empire City divided a majority between them, Hastings won by a plurality.

The loss of the county seat scarcely tempered the Hastings–Nininger City rivalry. After the election, even the most trivial considerations bothered Donnelly. Especially annoying was the fact that the Nininger City postmaster had to ride to Hastings to pick up the mail.[30] Soon the contest between the two communities reached the proportions of a standing joke everywhere in Minnesota. "Competition is an excellent thing in its legitimate track, but not when it leads to such petty jealousy and bickering as now exists between those thriving towns below us," jibed the St. Paul *Times*. "Fie, fie, children!" its editor quipped, "don't blubber over the natural and healthy effects of trade, wipe your weeping eyes, throw no more cats at each others balloons."[31] Good-naturedly, Donnelly reprinted the *Times* article in the *Emigrant Aid Journal*, but too much time, energy and money had been invested in the town for him to take the issue lightly.

At the masthead of the *Emigrant Aid Journal*, he placed the motto: "'Dost thou know how to play the fiddle?' 'No,' answered Themistocles, 'but I understand the art of raising a little village into a great city.'" Donnelly, who also thought he understood this art, felt that its secret was hidden in the influence of the press. In an editorial in the first issue of the newspaper, he wrote, "To the new town the newspaper becomes an agent in its efforts, a herald in its prosperity and a stay in its adversity."[32] Donnelly foresaw the day when the *Emigrant Aid Journal* would be the representative paper of the West.

Like the other Nininger City investors, Donnelly was apprehensive about reports that the Mississippi River would be late in opening for boat traffic. Soberly he observed that the spring of 1857 would be a turning point in the life of the town; "it will decide whether we are able to carry the contest by *coup de main* or whether we are to struggle for it through months and years."[33] But

[29]Donnelly MSS, Letter Book 1, I. D. to M. E. Ames, March 11, 1857.
[30]*Ibid.*, Postmaster J. Campbell to I. D., November 21, 1856.
[31]Quoted in the *Emigrant Aid Journal*, August 29, 1857.
[32]*Ibid.*, December 1, 1856.
[33]Donnelly MSS, Letter Book 1, I. D. to G. Robertson, March 24, 1857.

when the river ice broke early, more immigrants than ever before arrived at St. Paul. The entire West appeared to be deluged with settlers. The levees all up and down the river were crowded with passengers and piled high with freight. For Minnesota, it was a stampede that rivaled California in 1849.[34]

In the late spring, after Donnelly and his family had separated themselves from the tide of immigrants which spread over Minnesota, he joined the ranks of the "land sharks." In every way he tried to promote Nininger City as the best place in the Northwest to live. Intruding into conversations, he told uninterested listeners that Nininger City would soon be linked by railway to St. Peter, a town likely to replace St. Paul as the territorial capital. In a short time, he acquired so bad a reputation along the river that professional boatmen saw little difference between the gambler "Bill Mallen on the boat with his marked cards, and Ingeneous Doemly, with his city lots on paper selling for a thousand dollars each"; both were sharks, ready to devour unsuspecting travelers.[35] Donnelly, however, felt that he had more to offer.

In Nininger City the settlers attempted to re-create the way of life they had known in the East. Even when water was still being hauled in large barrels from the river by yoked cattle, the towns-people enjoyed a lively lyceum season,[36] and an Atheneum Association was one of the earliest community projects. By September of 1857, the town opened a public school.

Undoubtedly, Nininger City was an exceptional "paper town." Donnelly's friend Philip Rohr, who had supplied the German translations for the first issue of the *Emigrant Aid Journal*, was a noted musical impresario. Highly popular among German musicians throughout the country, Rohr planned to make Nininger a cultural center. At one time, the son of William Lloyd Garrison, George T. Garrison, worked in the offices of the *Emigrant Aid Journal*.[37] The newspaper set a standard far above that of conventional western journalism.

In the late spring and early summer of 1857, Nininger City reached an apex. More than one hundred houses had been built, and the townsite appeared covered with new construction. Never

[34]Johnston, "Journalism," X, 311.
[35]George Byron Merrick, *Old Times on the Upper Mississippi* (Cleveland: Arthur H. Clark, 1909), p. 139.
[36]John H. Case MSS, "A History of Nininger," no pagination.
[37]*Ibid.*

would the prospects seem brighter for the founders of the new town. In the summer of 1857, at twenty-six years of age, Ignatius Donnelly walked the porch of his half-completed home, considering himself a millionaire and wondering what the future held in store for him. As he surveyed the development of Nininger City, he brushed aside as groundless rumors spread by eastern newspapers that land and railroad speculation had brought the nation to the verge of financial disaster. When the Ohio Life and Trust Company failed, and panic crashed like a thunder clap over the false calm of western prosperity, it seemed incredible to Donnelly that the nation could slip into a depression when the whole Middle West was being overrun with a network of railroads and dotted with cities.

The fortune which he held in his hand in the summer of 1857 vanished during the last week of August; real estate transactions in Minnesota had practically ceased, personal notes due accumulated in enormous sums, and public confidence collapsed as gold became almost unobtainable. As eastern banks called in their western paper, money of any kind became scarce in Minnesota. Local banks failed. The business life of the territory struggled through a tragic readjustment.[38] One of the earliest depression casualties was the proposed Nininger, St. Peter, and Western Railroad. Hope for its success had rested on securing a land grant from the national government, but Congress, torn by the slavery controversy and half-convinced that railroad speculation had precipitated the panic, temporarily halted the land grant program.

Somewhat pathetically, the *Emigrant Aid Journal* attempted to minimize the impact of the panic on the shocked people of Nininger City by contending that it was localized in the financial centers of New York and Philadelphia. But almost immediately foreclosure and bankruptcy notices appeared in the columns of the paper. Hardship spread rapidly through the town because most of the investors drew money from speculative sources. The time had come for the newspaper to be a stay to the townspeople in their adversity.

In the early days of the panic, Donnelly hoped to salvage something from his Philadelphia investments. He was astonished to learn that all the city's banks had suspended payment and that some of the oldest and most respected were closed. Donnelly's business informants wrote him that not only was Philadelphia wrapped in

[38]Sidney A. Patchin, "The Development of Banking in Minnesota," *Minnesota History* (August, 1917), II, 136.

gloom, fearful of every new financial report, but also that everybody was "wishing for an earthquake and hell to pay generally."[39]

Despite the obvious loss of a personal fortune, Donnelly retained an expansive optimism, and showed no inner trepidation or concern. Nininger City had almost one thousand people. He was confident that in 1858 the unhappy and unfortunate people of the East would go west to make a new start in life.

The West, he felt, was basically sound from the financial point of view. Land was still increasing in value, despite the fact that there was no money to buy it.[40] No man in the East, he believed, could boast of a future to equal that of a man in the West with similar talents, health, and skills. Not that a westerner could expect to capture success without exertion, but simply that exertion paid better in the West. Less competition in enterprise, a labor shortage, and an abundance of personal opportunity, made the new states the best place to live.[41]

Despite Donnelly's offer to give added security in land and pay higher interest rates, his personal credit failed on September 18, 1857.[42] Money, in that day of stress, became one of his symbols of success. As he confided to a friend from Central High School of Philadelphia, "Money makes the man, the want of it the fellow."[43] But Donnelly refused to forfeit his confidence in himself or the country. Although steadfastly insisting that it would be as hard to pull him down as it would be to "shake the devil off his feet," he did not relish the choices which the depression had forced upon him.[44] He hated to sell the notes of his friends when he knew that they would be protested. He hated to admit that he was unable to continue to improve the town, when he so desperately wanted to continue the work. And he hated most intensely being unable to secure for his wife all the things he had promised her. But the alternative—returning to Philadelphia—was even more unpalatable. He resolved never to retreat to his native city.[45]

Fortunately for Donnelly, although heavily in debt, he managed to trade his personal notes for those of his creditors and achieve a

[39]Donnelly MSS, G. Burns to I. D., September 30, October 14, 1857.
[40]*Ibid.*, I. D. to J. Simonton, September 5, 1857.
[41]*Ibid.*, I. D. to J. Walsh, September 16, 1857; and I. D. to G. Burns, September 5, 1857.
[42]*Ibid.*, Baird & King to I. D., September, 1857.
[43]*Ibid.*, Letter Book 2, I. D. to G. Burns, October 9, 1857.
[44]*Ibid.*, I. D. to G. Burns, December 10, 1857.
[45]*Ibid.*, I. D. to A. Kilpatrick, December 23, 1857.

balance. Gradually, he consolidated some of his town lots into large tracts suitable for agricultural purposes. Viewing the hardship around him, Donnelly never wanted to force the small investors in Nininger City to pay their debts or to keep up their improvements, but John Nininger demanded that all their legal obligations be fulfilled. He even threatened to sue Donnelly if he did not comply with the letter of his agreements.

During the winter of 1857, there were indications of an economic revival in Minnesota. The harvest had been abundant and agricultural products were plentiful. Moreover, a level of stability had been reached when the few business and banking houses of St. Paul, which managed to survive the holocaust that burned out so many financial empires, banded together to guarantee their own city scrip. With confidence in their currency restored, Nininger City investors attempted to hang on until spring. Even dour John Nininger believed that perhaps the worst had been passed and that European capital would again be flowing to America for investment.[46]

Isolated from urban society for the first time in his life during the winter of 1857, Donnelly was too restless to devote himself exclusively to reading and writing letters. He assumed active leadership of Nininger City's community life. Early in March a group of farmers and merchants from the surrounding countryside gathered in his home to establish the Dakota County Agricultural Society.[47] Highly enthusiastic after the meeting, Donnelly wrote a letter to Governor Henry Hastings Sibley inviting him to speak at the first Dakota County Fair, which was to be held at Nininger City later that year. Donnelly enjoyed the Agricultural Society, and even though he knew almost nothing about farming, he lectured to the membership on the significance of agriculture.[48]

Delighted when he saw the steamboat *Grey Eagle* pass Nininger City, a signal of the return of the shipping season and the close of winter, Donnelly still hoped for a quick end to the depression. But trade did not revive in 1858. He was forced to write to his creditors pleading for time, asking them to trust him, extend his notes on added security in land, or extract slight compensation from a bankrupt.[49] Carefully, through the shrewd use of his limited resources, he

[46]*Ibid.*, J. Nininger to I. D., March 11, 1858.
[47]*Emigrant Aid Journal*, March 10, 1858.
[48]*Ibid.*, March 24, 1858.
[49]Donnelly MSS, Letter Book 2, I. D. to R. Smith, April 8, 1858.

managed not only to repay all of his Philadelphia indebtedness, including a one-thousand-dollar cash note, but also to retain his large home which he optimistically appraised at ten thousand dollars.[50] Candidly, however, he conceded that he had been only as honest as his welfare would allow. Although he never repudiated an obligation, he insisted that "self-defense is the first instinct of nature and the first duty to ourselves. A man who would take the clothes off his back to give his creditors would only be kicked for his pains."[51]

By the summer of 1858, Donnelly began making adjustments in his life to suit his new condition. Kate had given birth to a second child, a girl they named Mary. Of necessity, although he had already come to dislike the profession, Donnelly returned to the practice of law, while he labored to liquidate his vast real estate holdings before they were sold under the tax collector's hammer. Most of his legal work was done for former governor Ramsey.[52]

His friends looked to Donnelly as a bulwark of stability in uncertain times. Having realized that he would have to live through the depression years, Donnelly's vigorous self-confidence returned and he actually enjoyed the stresses and strains of a tight economy. Excited by the threat of lawsuits and close bargains, he overcame his "blues." "For my part," he confided to one of his close friends, "I rather like this walking on volcanoes."[53] His haunting fear of failure left him when he discovered that there was not an important man in St. Paul whose negotiable paper had not been protested. Having defaulted meant little in the West!

Pride prohibited Donnelly's confessing his troubled financial condition to his Philadelphia relatives. Resolutely, he contended that he had withstood the debacle successfully.

I was naturally careful [he wrote to his father-in-law] and in good times bought but little that I did not pay for in full or trade for; with the credit I had I could have been in debt half a million, but I anticipated the revulsion, although like a good many others I did not anticipate that it would have occurred so soon. I had sold considerable property to parties who were deemed good, and on my faith in their solvency I traded off their notes and mortgages, for land, & endorsed them. When they came due the parties had failed, the holders of the notes & mortgages did not wish to look to the land, and came down on me on my endorsements. In-

[50]*Ibid.*, I. D. to G. Burns, May 8, 1858.
[51]*Ibid.*, Letter Book 3, I. D. to M. Faiver, February 8, 1859.
[52]*Ibid.*, A. Ramsey to I. D., December 14, 1858.
[53]*Ibid.*, Letter Book 2, I. D. to G. Burns, May 31, 1858.

stances of this kind gave me considerable trouble, but by one shift or another I have contrived to reduce my entire liabilities to about $4000, while I have notes and mortgages of others in the amount of $23000 and property worth at least $40000 and in good times esteemed at twice that.[54]

Much of this was true, especially the portions describing the process by which Donnelly had managed to scale down his debts, but his business papers indicate that he was far too optimistic in assessing his financial worth. Perhaps the greatest truth in the letter came later when he added, "[I have] a fund of experience, a knowledge of business, a knowledge of mankind, and cool firm reliance in myself, that I would not trade for $500,000."

As he considered his future, Donnelly realized that his problems demanded his soberest judgment. He realized that Minnesota was passing rapidly through a period of great change. When he looked out at the river where huge quantities of grain and potatoes were being carried to southern markets, he knew these were the products of skilled farming on improved lands. The fact that Minnesota would soon cease to be a frontier state meant a great deal to him. Should he remain or move to newer lands farther west?

Many of his friends had given up the quest for fortune in the West. Fatalistically Donnelly decided that the panic had been the best experience for him. It had "laid bare the monetary and moral character of men. . . . Millionaires became beggars; men as honorable as Brutus put their property out of their names and fell back on all that common sort of roguery; first class per[sons] became as [Benjamin] Franklin says, 'the mere waste paper of mankind.' "[55] What if the state, too, had proven a *fizzle?* Would mankind be any different elsewhere? He decided that he had too much grit in his character to quit Minnesota in defeat.

[54] *Ibid.*, I. D. to McCaffrey, January 1, 1858.
[55] *Ibid.*, Letter Book 3, I. D. to G. Burns, January 7, 1859.

The New Republican
1857–1859

We are not a party of spoils, but of principles; and so that those principles triumph in important struggles, we can afford to bear disappointment in lesser ones. Let not our enemies, however, suppose that we have gone the way of other "isms." We are not dead but sleeping.

IGNATIUS DONNELLY

WITHIN one year of the day that Donnelly had written his editorial damning the Republican party in the election of 1856, he was no longer a Democrat. If he hoped to win public office, his decision required courage because both Nininger City and Dakota County, heavily settled by Irish and German Catholics, were Democratic strongholds. Throughout his life Donnelly insisted that his shift in political affiliation was based on his aversion to slavery.

But in large measure he was influenced by his Minnesota friends and business associates, especially Alexander Ramsey. A brilliant Pennsylvania Whig politician who had served in Congress, Ramsey accepted an appointment as Minnesota's first territorial governor in 1849, rather than remain a petty officeholder in his home state. Although he was soon replaced by a Democrat, Ramsey, aloof, calculating, and unafraid to make enemies, determined to rule Minnesota politics. In a rare display of humor, he best illustrated his political acumen when he pointed out that he "was half-Scotch and half-German; because the Scotch were respectable and the

Germans numerous."[1] He was known as Bluff Aleck, but it was not a term of affection.

Ramsey's political contact with Donnelly came through Dr. Thomas Foster, a physician turned journalist who was his aide and who performed the tough jobs that the former governor could not do for himself. Living near Nininger City, where he managed Ramsey's business affairs and represented him in Dakota County politics, Foster soon became Donnelly's close friend. Although his fealty to Ramsey was unquestioned, Foster thrived on political intrigue and, longing to play the role of a venerated political preceptor, decided to make Donnelly his protegé in the Ramsey state-wide organization.

In the autumn of 1857, Foster took Donnelly to the Republican territorial convention. Donnelly, who remained in St. Paul one day,[2] just long enough to be elected secretary of the convention, was immediately aware of the marked cleavage within the party. Its reform element, almost slavishly patterned along the line of the New England Whigs, eagerly pressed for both temperance reform and stricter suffrage laws. These had proved powerful issues in forming the Republican party, but in Minnesota they were equally effective in alienating Irish, Scandinavian, and especially German immigrants who were sensitive to criticism of their voting practices and cherished their *läger bier*.[3] Ramsey's followers, already gaining ascendancy in the party, wanted to play down the emotion-charged suffrage and temperance questions to win the support of the territory's immigrant population.

After the convention, Donnelly and Foster organized a county-wide Republican gathering at Hastings. As Ramsey's agent, Foster dominated the proceedings. The handful of delegates indorsed the party's platform and dutifully nominated Donnelly for the territorial senate, but, unable to take the nomination seriously, he did not canvass the county and except for a few brief notices in Republican newspapers, no mention was made of him. Even the *Emigrant Aid Journal* maintained a discreet silence. In fact, Donnelly did not even bother to mention the election in his diary, the declining fortunes of Nininger City probably stifling any enthusiasm for a campaign.

With all of Minnesota, Dakota County went Democratic. Don-

[1] Donnelly, "Genealogy and History."
[2] St. Paul *Pioneer and Democrat,* September 8, 1857; St. Paul *Minnesotian,* September 11, 1857.
[3] William James Ryland, *Alexander Ramsey* (Philadelphia: Harris & Partridge Co., 1941), p. 45.

nelly could take some satisfaction in the election's outcome because he was defeated by only three hundred votes, a good showing and a tribute to his popularity among the newer settlers. But the Republican organization, keenly disappointed, charged that the Democrats had counted the votes of Indians and half-breeds in outlying districts. For a decade, Republican politicians insisted that they had been "counted out" by Democratic election judges and defrauded by the votes of "moccasin Democrats." Donnelly, however, made no such allegations. He told a friend that he would spend the icy winter in political retirement.[4]

But when Ramsey called Dr. Foster to St. Paul to undertake the editorship of a new Republican paper, the *Minnesotian,* Donnelly suddenly found himself the leader of the Republican party in Dakota County.[5] Foster, now in a position to give fresh impetus to Donnelly's career, urged him to write political editorials on matters of general significance. Almost immediately, Donnelly wrote what proved to be the parting shot of the 1857 campaign. In an unsigned editorial that bristled with platitudes, he exhorted the Republicans to keep faith in their principles, develop political mindedness, and be active citizens.[6]

Whether purposely or because his restless energies demanded activity, Donnelly followed his own advice. In the winter and early spring he lectured before lyceum groups on non-political subjects such as Minnesota's "Indian Mound Builders."[7] And in February, 1858, he journeyed to St. Paul, where he presented a highly successful address in the hall of the House of Representatives on the means of encouraging emigration to Minnesota.[8] As Nininger City's leading citizen, he served as president of the Town Council, even though the community was predominantly Democratic.

At the Dakota County Republican convention in the autumn of 1858, he was again indorsed as a candidate for the senate. In a letter to Ramsey pointing out that the party had gained strength, Donnelly optimistically suggested that they might win.[9] Financially embarrassed by the continuing depression, Donnelly was too poor

[4]Donnelly MSS, Letter Book 2, I. D. to G. Burns, October 22, 1857.
[5]*Emigrant Aid Journal,* November 7, 1857.
[6]St. Paul *Minnesotian,* December 28, 1857.
[7]St. Paul *Pioneer and Democrat,* February 13, 1858. See also *Emigrant Aid Journal,* January 20, 1858.
[8]*Ibid.,* but see also St. Paul *Minnesotian,* February 13, 1858.
[9]Donnelly MSS, J. H. Stevens to I. D., September 24, 1858.

to campaign. He was even dunned for his five-dollar assessment to cover the cost of printing ballots.[10]

His main campaign effort, a letter to the *Minnesota Staats-Zeitung*, a leading German-language newspaper, was as much an effort to publicize himself as an attempt to destroy the popular image of the Democratic party. In straightforward prose, he argued that any German who came to America in the spirit of the Revolution of 1848 should certainly understand that slavery was immoral. After denying charges that the Republicans were hostile toward the German immigrant, he invited them to join the party. Entitled *An die Deutschen von Minnesota* and signed *Mitburger*, the article won Donnelly many lasting friends.[11] It did not, however, win him the election.

Following the defeat of the Republican candidates in 1858, Ramsey and his associates, raising large sums of money, began revitalizing the party's organization. The Republican Central Committee leased a suite of rooms in St. Paul's business district to provide a place where young men could gather, talk politics, read Republican newspapers, hold meetings, and map strategy for the next election.[12]

As an active member of the Ramsey clique and the leader of the Dakota County organization, Donnelly visited frequently in St. Paul, where he attended social gatherings that generally turned into serious political discussions. By this time, his every instinct and interest focused on politics. He determined to win a political office. His name was repeatedly mentioned as a possible candidate for the post of attorney general.[13] He even enjoyed the criticism of the St. Paul *Times,* the newspaper of the party's reform wing, when it predicted that Donnelly's name would be among those on the ticket put forth by the Ramsey machine.[14]

His political activities offered Donnelly an excuse to escape the drab life of Nininger City. The small town, no longer striving to maintain even the appearance of a rising community, was settling into the doldrums of failure. With the coming of winter both Kate and Ignatius suffered a sense of remoteness and isolation. Eager to escape, they looked forward to participating in the gay life of St.

[10]*Ibid.,* E. F. Parker to I. D., October 1, 1858.

[11]*Minnesota Staats-Zeitung,* October 9, 1858.

[12]Hastings *Independent,* October 18, 1858, and St. Paul *Minnesotian,* October 29, 1858.

[13]Donnelly MSS, I. D. to G. Burns, January 22, 1859.

[14]St. Paul *Times,* January 18, 1859.

Paul. Kate would have preferred to live permanently in the capital city, an idea which also appealed to Donnelly. But political necessity dictated that he remain in Dakota County. St. Paul could not provide all the candidates for major public offices.

To make life easier for Kate while he tried to win nomination for a state-wide office at the Republican convention of 1859, Donnelly suggested that she visit Philadelphia; he was hard-pressed financially, and he wanted her to secure a loan. The thought of returning to the East for four months without her husband frightened Kate, but she was beginning to resign herself to the necessary hardships of being married to a politician. The trip proved to be a financial failure, however, as Kate was too proud to admit that her husband needed money, and refused to borrow in his name.[15] At this time Donnelly was desperate for funds, and to secure a one-thousand-dollar loan, he was willing to submit his St. Paul real estate holdings as collateral.[16]

Donnelly waged his campaign to gain state-wide recognition by writing a series of letters in the St. Paul *Minnesotian* addressed to the foreign-born citizens of Minnesota. These were the people he felt he understood best and could most influence. He was also well aware that his strength within the party would increase if he could command the loyalty of even a fragment of this group. The letters expanded the same themes that he had employed in *An die Deutschen von Minnesota*. If the immigrants would only rid themselves of the "fascination of names," or "to use the phrase lately coined by [Oliver Wendell] Holmes, to *depolarize* all words to which tradition or long usage have given undue significance," and look at the facts, they would easily understand that the Republican party was genuinely the more democratic.[17] Adroitly blending moral and economic causes in one letter, he wrote:

Laboring men of the old world! You are many of you at the foot of the ladder which all mankind are compelled to climb; you are clambering the rungs which the overthrow of the old world's aristocratic notions has left open to you. Which party will help you up? That which stands committed to the South and slavery, that which would reduce and has reduced labor to the degradation of bondage, which presents to it no destiny but shame and humiliation? Or that party, which with no dark record in the past, with no principle but those which the Declaration of Independence has set forth, with Equality, Liberty, Humanity, for all men, strives by doing

[15]Donnelly MSS, K. D. to I. D., June 17, 1859.
[16]*Ibid.*, I. D. to O'Bryant, June 22, 1859 (copy).
[17]St. Paul *Minnesotian,* June 15, 1859.

the unalterable justice to the black, to advance the dignity and promote the welfare of the white race.[18]

He failed to maintain this high-level argument, gradually slipping into distortions, half-truths, and ultimately outright falsehoods in his statements regarding slavery. He was quickly caught up and failed to substantiate his assertion that there was an expanding class of white slaves in the South.[19] But since his goal had been to achieve publicity, Donnelly could disregard the accompanying embarrassment.

On July 9, 1859, the Dakota County Republican party held its convention under the control of Donnelly's tightly disciplined organization. Even the Hastings *Independent,* the county's leading Republican newspaper, complained that the meeting had been "packed." Its editor, Columbus Stebbins, denounced Donnelly for suppressing platforms and ignoring resolutions so that he could gain a vote of confidence that would advance his personal ambition.[20] Paying no attention to Stebbins' criticism, Donnelly joined the ranks of the enthusiastic Republicans gathering in St. Paul for their state convention and confident that the Democrats would be defeated. In the crowded clubrooms of the party's headquarters, in the lobby of the St. Paul Hotel, and in the shaded parlor of Alexander Ramsey's large home, Republican politicians bargained and argued for their candidates. Shrewdly, Donnelly refused to allow his name to be put forth as a tally clerk; he made it quite evident that he intended to be a candidate and was therefore ineligible.

Months earlier Donnelly had written to a friend, "I will be a candidate before the Republican State Convention in July for Representative for Congress. I may not succeed but a cat can look at a king, the old adage says."[21] He was, however, prepared to accept whatever position Ramsey would offer. Carefully and prudently Ramsey prepared a slate of candidates, which he planned to head by running for governor of the new state. The two congressional candidates, William Windom and Cyrus Aldrich, were selected on the basis of geography and necessity. Windom was a popular young politician who lived in the southern part of the state. Regional pride dictated his choice. Aldrich represented Republican business interests in the newly established city of Minneapolis. In addition, he

[18]*Ibid.,* July 19, 1859.
[19]St. Paul *Pioneer and Democrat,* June 17, 1859.
[20]*Ibid.,* July 14, 1859.
[21]Donnelly MSS, Letter Book 3, I. D. to J. H. Stevens, May 9, 1859.

was a personal friend of Abraham Lincoln, a rising star in the Republican galaxy. For treasurer, Ramsey selected an amiable German banker, Charles Scheffer, who was held in high esteem among German-born voters. Donnelly was his choice for lieutenant governor. None of the men was above criticism. Because he was handsome, Windom was labeled a dandy. Aldrich drank, and was prone to make intemperate speeches. Scheffer was a poor public speaker, and Donnelly was virtually unknown. Yet as a group, with Ramsey as their leader, they satisfied the requirements of geography, special interests, and nationality prejudices which could win an election.

Ramsey's was not the only slate submitted to the convention. Donnelly found four candidates opposing him for lieutenant governor and trailed Henry A. Swift, a well-known pioneer settler, on the first ballot. But he doubled his vote on the second tally to win the nomination.

The St. Paul *Pioneer and Democrat*, Minnesota's leading Democratic newspaper, feigned shock at his selection over Swift. To pass over a man of Swift's quality for a "prodigy" (Donnelly was only twenty-eight years old), "a blatant writer and dysenteric scribbler," the Republican party had sacrificed its integrity to satisfy the whims of Alexander Ramsey.[22] Despite this criticism, Donnelly was not the real target of Democratic wrath. He and his fellow candidates, the paper later noted, were merely puppets. "Behind all these," wrote the editor, "kept out of sight by the screen . . . sits . . . [sinister] Alexander Ramsey, laughing up his sleeve at the quarrels and jealousies of the competing candidates."[23]

The Republican convention recognized Donnelly's role as party spokesman when it selected him to write its appeal to the state's voters. Democratic politicians gave considerable thought to Donnelly's handiwork: *An Address to the People of Minnesota in Regard to the History, Principles, Aims and Objects of the Republican and Democratic Parties.* Almost fifty pages in length, much of it set in elite type, filled with rhetorical questions cleverly and skilfully contrived, the pamphlet circulated widely in the outlying districts of the state where farmers read it during the months before the election. Its salient points were the essence of the Republican national program: opposition to slavery, a relic of barbarism; the proscription of no man for his national origin or religion; the free and uncorrupted use of

[22]St. Paul *Pioneer and Democrat,* July 21, 22, 1859.
[23]*Ibid.,* December 6, 1859.

the ballot box; and the Homestead Law.[24] In the everyday language of the period, it was summarized crudely as "land for the landless" against the Democrats', "niggers for the niggerless."

No sooner had Donnelly won the nomination for lieutenant governor than he proudly sent newspapers reporting the convention to his wife in Philadelphia. Worried by their financial condition, Kate replied, "Does the office pay—I wish it would as that is my great anxiety." A shrewd politician, she noted that Donnelly would have a chance to "become acquainted with wire pulling & to be able to obtain influence to answer [his] purposes again." There was also the possibility of becoming governor should Ramsey abandon the office for some reason. But Kate's fears were evident when she reiterated, "Give me particulars concerning salary—if there is any—money is my weak point."[25]

The response to his nomination among Republican newspapers was Donnelly's first shock of the campaign. He anticipated that Dr. Foster's *Minnesotian* would proclaim him to be "a young man of thorough education and strong mind—an orator and a writer—one of the most able young men in Minnesota,"[26] but he was disturbed when the leading Republican county newspapers criticized his candidacy. Columbus Stebbins of the Hastings *Independent*, who had denounced Donnelly's manipulation of the Republican convention in Dakota County, was equally critical of the behind-the-scenes dealing at the state level.[27] Only after Donnelly made peace with Stebbins, convincing the editor that he would stand by Republican principles, did Stebbins agree to support him.[28]

The editor of the Faribault *Central Republican,* a fire-eating frontier journalist, "Awful" Orville Brown, belonged to the reform wing of the Republican party. His hatred for Ramsey led him to oppose practically the entire slate.[29] As he had in the case of Stebbins, Donnelly won Brown's support by committing himself to political honesty. But Donnelly's most caustic critic within the party was Abraham Van Vorhes of the Stillwater *Messenger*. The newspaper had a wide circulation in a predominantly Republican county, and Don-

[24]Donnal V. Smith, "Influence of the Foreign Born of the Northwest in the Election of 1860," *Mississippi Valley Historical Review,* XIX (1932), 191–95.
[25]Donnelly MSS, K. D. to I. D., July 26, 1859.
[26]July 22, 1859.
[27]Hastings *Independent,* July 28, 1859.
[28]Donnelly MSS, I. D. to C. Stebbins, July 28, 1859 (copy).
[29]Faribault *Central Republican,* July 27, 1859.

nelly needed its indorsement. Not part of the Ramsey group, Van Vorhes minced no words in focusing his attention on Donnelly. Van Vorhes did not like the candidate, did not like the manner of his selection, and disapproved of what he termed the "Mutual Admiration Society" within the party which sacrificed men of capacity and qualification to personal interest. Furthermore, Van Vorhes doubted whether Donnelly possessed even a tithe of the many virtues and party claims which Dr. Foster attributed to him. A pungent satirist, Van Vorhes dubbed Donnelly "Ignis Fatuus." Minnesota's unsophisticated farmers probably missed the double intent, but Donnelly's short, fat, figure made the name effective.[30]

The leading Democratic newspapers quickly picked up the name when they realized that Donnelly was sensitive to sarcasm. When "Ignis Fatuus" was worn out, the *Pioneer and Democrat* switched to "Ignatius the Lyre," or "Ramsey's organ."[31] In one way Donnelly benefited from this attention because the more sharply he drew the fire of the Democratic press the stronger it made him among the rank-and-file members of his own party. Eventually even Van Vorhes came to his defense.

The Republican newspaper reaction to Donnelly's nomination reflected the feelings of disappointment among the party's rank-and-file workers. It was contended that Donnelly's best friends became hesitant and reluctant to support him after the nomination because he was a stranger even to them.[32] Many factors contributed to making Donnelly the weakest candidate on the ticket. He was unknown in the outlying counties; his name was Irish; his religion was said to be Roman Catholic; and the combination of facetious sobriquets coined by the press made him appear ludicrous. There was so much adverse publicity about his nomination that Thomas Adams, an influential Massachusetts Republican and a member of the Republican National Committee, wrote Ramsey:

> I cannot say that I am at all pleased with your ticket. . . . Your candidate for Liet. Gov., you know was a rampant Loco Foco in Philadelphia and I have no doubt he changed for place and position, you had better taken tried men instead of pandering to the Irish or German votes.[33]

Nativism and religious bigotry were significant emotional issues in the election of 1859. Most Republican newspaper editors, such as

[30] Stillwater *Messenger,* July 26, 1859.
[31] August 7, 1859.
[32] Minnesota *State News,* January 21, 1859.
[33] Minnesota Historical Society, Ramsey MSS, August 5, 1859.

Columbus Stebbins, pleaded with their readers to judge each party by its platform and the men who defended it unequivocally, rather than accept the scurrilous half-truths which circulated to discredit men of principle.[34] But this did not reduce the undercurrent of strong Know-Nothingism among Republicans. The most influential Republicans, such as Dr. Thomas Foster and Thomas Newson of the St. Paul *Times,* could never resist the temptation to condemn an Irish Catholic twice: once for being born, and the second time for any offense he had committed.[35] The congressional candidate, William Windom, frequently accused of having been an active member of the Know-Nothing party, found it very difficult to disprove the allegations.[36] Both parties published tracts on nativism in what became a most acrimonious argument.[37]

Donnelly reacted more keenly to the nativist issue than did any of the other candidates. He was outraged when a man had the effrontery to ask for a bribe to silence a rumor that he was a Catholic priest in disguise.[38] Scandalous rumors and stories concerning him persisted, and Foster decided to deny them in print. Unfortunately, slipping into untruths as blatant as those he sought to counteract, Foster flatly denied that Donnelly was of Roman Catholic background or Irish extraction.[39]

Angered by the accounts of the campaign in the copies of the *Minnesotian* sent to her by Donnelly, Kate reminded him that his "name Ignatius & Donnelly proclaim both [his Irish and Catholic past] and denying looks like cowardice & lays you open to attack."[40] In another letter she stated, "If you are defeated I shall blame it on the *Minnesotian.* . . . Every word in relation to 'foreign,' 'Irish,' 'Catholic,' either for or against you will put your foot in it—say nothing and be deemed wise." She deplored Donnelly's all-too-ready admission that he was generally unorthodox in his religion:

I do not think it well to be so brazen and barefaced about ones [*sic*] religious beliefs especially when so infidel in its tendency—for many will think—this man would not feel bound by any oath he would take—its [*sic*] merely his word of honor. I feel sorry hubby for you to be so eager

[34]Hastings *Independent,* April 21, 1859.
[35]St. Paul *Pioneer and Democrat,* August 7, 1859.
[36]*Ibid.,* August 28, 1859.
[37]Christopher Columbus Andrews, *Know-Nothingism* (St. Paul, 1859); see also Donnelly's *Address to the People of Minnesota . . . Parties.*
[38]Donnelly MSS, Pears to I. D., August 18, 1859.
[39]St. Paul *Minnesotian,* July 22, 1859.
[40]Donnelly MSS, K. D. to I. D., July 20, 1859.

in showing that you are not a Catholic by exceedingly infidel doctrines you utter. You may find it worse to get along as an infidel than as a Catholic.[41]

Kate was disgusted with the campaign's nativistic emphasis: "Why don't you fellows harp more upon the *free soil* question," she wrote, "rather than waste your time talking foreign & Catholic business—*free soil* is what the west will swallow."[42]

But the religious issue persisted. The St. Paul *Pioneer and Democrat*, realizing the vote-pulling power that Donnelly might exert among the Catholic Irish, attempted to shame him in the eyes of the voters. Addressing itself to Donnelly, it said:

Were you not a resident of Philadelphia, in the years 1842–'43–'44, and did you not witness . . . those 'Foreign Born Citizens' shot down in the streets by the progenitors of your party—by those who are now your allies? And for what? Because they were 'Foreign Born!' Did you not witness the burning of Catholic churches, by an unprovoked mob of foreign haters, led on by men who are now the leaders of your party? Perhaps you witnessed these sad and terrible scenes with regret—you were a Democrat—and deplored as all good Democrats the occurrence of all such outrages.

Would it not be better, the paper suggested, to return to your "first love" rather than to act as a "stool pigeon for those who, you must know, hate your Irish antecedents, and if I understand rightly, your Catholic proclivities."[43]

Donnelly responded to the *Pioneer and Democrat* by writing a final letter "To the Foreign Born Citizens" in which he explained that studying the issues had forced him to conclude that the Democratic party, "the memory of whose past I honored, had ceased to be identified with the cause of freedom, the welfare of the country, or the advancement of the masses." It had become the "fag-end of a degenerating organism." He concluded with a peroration:

I did not join the Republican party for success alone. I could have found that among the Democracy, by whom I was honored by the offer of high office. I became a Republican upon sober, solemn, honest conviction. I saw two paths: One led along the line defined by the founders of the government; it was rough and stormy, but it pointed to the perpetuity of freedom and the safety of our institutions. The other lay before me broad and crowded and full of prosperity, but it went downward to darkness and ultimate disaster to the country. I chose the rough and stormy

---

[41]*Ibid.*, K. D. to I. D., August 23, 1859.
[42]*Ibid.*, K. D. to I. D., September 10, 1859.
[43]Quoted in Hastings *Independent*, August 3, 1859.

path. I proclaimed myself a Republican in the midst of the most Democratic County in our State.[44]

The Republican National Committee, looking to the possibility that the presidential election of 1860 might be settled in the House of Representatives, was determined to win Minnesota, especially the two congressional seats. It appointed Michigan's Senator Zachariah Chandler to work with the Ramsey organization and allocated five thousand dollars to pay for the publication of campaign literature in Swedish, Norwegian, and German.[45] Several distinguished Republican leaders headed by Carl Schurz, Schuyler Colfax, and Francis Blair, Jr., were scheduled to present speeches, and Horace Greeley began sending copies of the New York *Tribune* into Minnesota at a reduced rate. "All political eyes are now turned to Minnesota," Ramsey was cautioned; "it is of the greatest importance to the Republican cause that we secure the state."[46]

Although the Minnesota campaign was lavishly financed at the outset, and the State Central Committee chairman, Daniel Rohrer, boasted to Donnelly that he had more money than time,[47] Senator Henry Wilson of Massachusetts warned Rohrer that "the truth is that not one in ten of our money men is with us [in working for a Minnesota victory]. They could raise $80,000 to get a tariff through Congress but they will not give a dollar to carry your state. Indeed most of them might give money to defeat us."[48] Fear that Minnesota's Republican congressmen might be hostile to a high tariff eventually led to a shortage of eastern money. As a result Donnelly was assessed one hundred dollars to cover campaign expenses and the State Central Committee incurred a three-thousand-dollar campaign debt.[49]

In planning the campaign, Ramsey and Donnelly agreed to divide the issues, Ramsey undertaking to discuss the state-wide questions with which he was most familiar and Donnelly confining himself to the broad national questions. But unlike Ramsey, who had been nominated before the convention accepted its platform and therefore did not feel bound by it, Donnelly indorsed the Republi-

---

[44]St. Paul *Minnesotian,* August 4, 1859.

[45]Ramsey MSS, T. Adams to A. Ramsey, June 15, 1859, and R. Morgan to A. Ramsey, June 15, 1859.

[46]*Ibid.,* L. Clephan to A. Ramsey, August 15, 1859.

[47]Donnelly MSS, D. Rohrer to I. D., September 9, 1859.

[48]Minnesota Historical Society, State Central Committee Papers of the Republican Party of Minnesota, H. Wilson to D. Rohrer, September 10, 1859.

[49]Donnelly MSS, D. Rohrer to I. D., September 27, 1859.

can program of frontier reform, lower salaries for state officials, and a balanced budget. He was committed also to a complicated proposal calling for the state to repudiate or scale down its obligations to railroad creditors who were suffering because of the bankruptcy of Minnesota railroads to which the state had "lent its credit." Privately Donnelly was undecided about the railroad question. An earlier Democratic legislature, eager to encourage railroad development, had voted to lend state credit so that the builders could borrow money. But Minnesota's constitution limited indebtedness to one quarter of a million dollars. The railroad debts amounted to $2,275,000. Although many Republicans favored honoring the moral obligation, even if the legislature's action was of doubtful legality, the politicians had hit upon it as a lively campaign issue.

Unfamiliar with both the politics and finances of the railroad bond question, Donnelly was more than willing to center his speeches on Democratic leadership and its failures. He filled his daybook with excerpts from the speeches of Senator Stephen A. Douglas of Illinois, the leading western Democrat, and arranged them to prove that the senator had been inconsistent and shallow. Donnelly hit hard at Douglas' lack of concern for slavery. Following Lincoln's argument, Donnelly held that slavery was a moral issue that had to be decided before the nation could progress. Donnelly leaned heavily, too, on the minority opinion in the Dred Scott case, copying and abstracting portions of Justice Curtis' statement.

Donnelly joined Ramsey and several other Republican orators at Red Wing, an important river settlement twenty-five miles south of Hastings, for the first major political rally of the campaign. Before a town hall crowded to capacity, as martial music filled the air, and with cannons firing to excite the audience, the Republican politicians denounced the "moccasin Democrats" who had stolen the previous election.[50] When Donnelly spoke, he electrified the audience. Although he had not yet reached his throbbing prime as an orator, there were flashes indicating his potential genius. He proved remarkably adept at the political art of making the average citizen feel comfortably *au courant* with the complicated and capricious scheme of national affairs.

No one with Donnelly's natural oratorical flare had been seen in Minnesota politics. Even Thomas Newson, the reform-minded editor of the St. Paul *Times*, which was generally hostile to any Ram-

[50]St. Paul *Minnesotian,* August 27, 1859.

seyite, concluded that "however much our opponents may be disposed to make game of him, he is at least a tolerable match for their heaviest guns."[51] After four speeches, the arresting sweep of Donnelly's arm, his coolness before antagonistic critics, and his amazing ability to breathe life into topics which the average voter found dull, inspired Thomas Foster to issue a challenge in his behalf to debate any Democrat, anywhere, on any subject of the campaign.[52] Abraham Van Vorhes was so highly impressed with Donnelly's Stillwater speech, that he offered to wager a hatful of Democratic Minnesota shinplaster against a Wright County war land grant that no Democrat would dare debate him.

Donnelly was emerging as spellbinder, stump speaker, and crackerjack political fighter. He was tireless. Journeying day after day with a Republican campaign caravan, he spoke repeatedly to large and enthusiastic audiences. People in outlying districts, learning from the newspapers that he was unusual, turned out to hear him, and local party leaders were interested in talking to him during the evenings after the rallies. Youthful and vigorous, Donnelly was fascinated with political table talk in the taverns of the small towns he visited. Not only did he thrive on the excitement of the campaign, but he proved more than capable of sustaining himself through the discomfort of irregularly spaced meals and poor sleeping accommodations.

Throughout the campaign, Donnelly wrote to Kate, sharing with her his successes and describing the conditions which he encountered. Her wit and talent for dramatizing the trivial made his journey more bearable. "I am sorry to know that you are sun-burned," she wrote; "you should not mar *your* beauty by such lighthouses as the sun builds on your nose or it may mar your political prospects among the yankee temperance people."[53] Donnelly enjoyed the joke.

The colorful rallies and high enthusiasm died on election day. Donnelly waited for the returns from heavily Democratic Dakota County. Out of more than two thousand votes cast he trailed by less than sixty. But throughout the state the Republicans mounted a huge majority. The Democratic party, rent by the schism between its western and northern supporters of Stephen Douglas and its southern and eastern portion headed by President Buchanan, went down in a crashing defeat.

[51] August 30, 1859.
[52] St. Paul *Minnesotian*, August 27, 1859.
[53] Donnelly MSS, K. D. to I. D., August 27, 1859.

Donnelly at twenty-eight years of age was lieutenant governor of the State of Minnesota. Each mail delivery to Nininger City brought requests for assistance and patronage as well as offers of continuing friendship and congratulations. Donnelly had not yet learned what public officeholding meant in terms of power and influence. While he waited eagerly for Kate's return from Philadelphia, he determined to assume the role of a sagacious and practical liberal leader.

CHAPTER IV

A Politician in Peace and War

1859-1861

> Hi, diddle, diddle! the Dred Scott riddle!
> The delegates scatter like loons!
> The Dug swears to see the sport
> And the southerners count their spoons.
> HASTINGS INDEPENDENT, MAY 31, 1860

WHEN Donnelly left Nininger City to assume the responsibilities of the lieutenant governorship, he faced serious problems as a politician and legislator. The rules of the Minnesota Senate had been rewritten by the retiring Democratic officeholders so that significant legislation required a two-thirds vote for approval. With unashamed amusement the shrewdest Democratic senators waited to see how the youthful Donnelly would promote Ramsey's program under the handicap. Unaware of Donnelly's legal training, the Democrats anticipated a brash politician who, they felt confident, could be harassed and controlled. Many Republican senators doubted Donnelly's ability to cope with the legislative puzzle. Carefully studying the senate's new rules, Donnelly conscientiously turned to his legal authorities and diligently combed books treating of parliamentary procedure. His education in the law offices of Benjamin Harris Brewster was evident in the thoroughness of his preparation.

The Democrats were surprised when, challenging the validity of a vote on the basis of the rules, Donnelly read a two-thousand-word opinion which traced the procedural practices of legislative bodies in English and American history, drawing from Hansard's *Parliamentary History,* Jefferson's *Manual,* the decisions of John C. Calhoun while presiding in the United States Senate, and Cushing's *Rules of Order.* Simply and logically Donnelly contended that the previous lieutenant governor had erred in accepting permanent rules; each legislative body, by tradition, established its own rules. Donnelly reopened the question precisely where his predecessor had closed it.[1] Embarrassed Democratic senators had not prepared a defense of the rules, and Donnelly's statement went unchallenged. The Republicans won actual as well as nominal control of the legislature.

The Republicans were as pleased as the Democrats were chagrined by Donnelly's successful handling of the rules problem. The Minnesota *State News* wrote, "We have read the decision by which he set aside the arbitrary action of his predecessor. . . . So convincing is it that even political adherents of the late President [of the Senate] are constrained to admit that the latter was mistaken in his course."[2] But St. Paul's *Pioneer and Democrat* sarcastically belittled it as too much effort in such a small matter.

The President of the Senate decided a knotty point to the perfect satisfaction of one party at least. The messenger boy submitted to him the question, whether it was not the duty of the fireman to bring up the water for the use of the Senate. The decision was that the fireman was obliged to bring all the water necessary to kindle his fires! Exit the messenger boy scratching his head.[3]

Nevertheless, this decision earned Donnelly a lifetime reputation as a distinguished parliamentarian. Two decades later, he received a letter from a Minnesota railroad commissioner concerning a ruling of the Board and seeking his advice on how to deal with it. At the time of the request, every member of the railroad commission was his political enemy, but they were reminded of this early action on his part and expressed their faith in his ability and equity.[4]

While Donnelly mastered the rule question in the senate, the Republican party faced the serious problem of enacting its legislative program. Even if the Republican members of the state legislature

[1]St. Paul, *Minnesotian and Times,* January 15, 1860.
[2]January 21, 1860.
[3]February 10, 1860.
[4]Donnelly MSS, W. R. Marshall to I. D., January 4, 1878. The author was a former governor and several members of the commission had also held high positions in the state government.

had wished to forget their campaign promises, economic pressure prevented them from doing so. To restore Minnesota's credit (its scrip was worth sixty-five cents on the dollar), the Republican legislature approved a drastic cut in the salaries of state officials.[5] The governor's annual salary was reduced from $2,500 to $1,000 and his personal secretary was allocated only $400. The lieutenant governor was placed on per diem while cabinet officers were cut from $1,000 to $800 per year.[6] Despite these efforts the *Pioneer and Democrat,* noting that the Republicans enacted less legislation than the Democrats, pointed out that their legislature had spent more than the preceding one.[7]

With retrenchment accomplished, the Republicans systematically organized townships on the frontier, passed a new election law which called for registration prior to voting, and began working on relief legislation to cope with the depression.[8] Although indorsing the entire program, Donnelly figured prominently only in the isssue of emergency relief. He spoke out as favoring the reduction of interest rates, the scaling-down of debts, and the enactment of a more satisfactory bankruptcy act. Perhaps it was because his own financial position was so precarious that he understood and sympathized with the debtor and bankrupt. Hostile to the proposed emergency legislation, the Minneapolis *State Atlas,* a Republican newspaper controlled by Congressman Cyrus Aldrich, warned, "If Lieut. Gov. Donnelly, by his persistent efforts and exertions in behalf of such legislation, has entitled himself to a crown of glory, let it be placed upon his head."[9] The *Pioneer and Democrat* described Donnelly's demand for interest control as class legislation, designed to destroy the men of worth in the community, and warned the legislature against passing *"ex post facto* legislation for any imaginary 'relief' to debtors."[10] But Donnelly stood his ground. This was his first act in defense of the economically prostrate; he never repudiated it.

Committed to the Republican platform, Donnelly avoided the railroad bond issue. Prior to the election the *Minnesotian* had indorsed the platform, but after the victory, Dr. Foster called off his

[5]H. P. Hall, *H. P. Hall's Observations: Being More or Less a History of Political Contests from 1849 to 1904* (St. Paul, 1904), p. 170.

[6]John B. Sanborn, "The Work of the Second State Legislature, 1859 to 1860," Minnesota Historical Society *Collections,* X, 625.

[7]February 3, 1860.

[8]Sanborn, "Second State Legislature," pp. 619–33.

[9]March 3, 1860.

[10]February 10 and 3, 1860.

attack on the credit of the state and advocated paying the bonds.[11] Ramsey expressed the same opinion in his inaugural message to the state assembly. When the legislature ignored his suggestion by passing the bond repudiation measure, Ramsey acted independently to satisfy his program. The state being the holder of the first mortgage on the lines, the governor foreclosed the mortgages, sold the charters of the lines, and bought them all in again for the state. Through this action, he virtually counteracted the will of the legislature and guaranteed the eventual payment of the bonds.[12] The bond question had been buried alive, only to be exhumed by politicians, including Donnelly, before elections and legislatures for the next two decades.

As the legislative session drew to a close, the Republicans inventoried their leadership. The Stillwater *Messenger*, which had originally disapproved of Donnelly's nomination, observed, "No man in Minnesota occupies today a more promising and enviable position than Governor Donnelly."[13] Praising Donnelly highly, the Minneapolis *State Atlas* concluded that "aside from the Stay Law question, the Lieut. Gov. is 'good for any amount,' and we cheerfully endorse him to the fullest extent."[14] Even the Democratic newspapers mustered no criticism of his skill or impartiality as the presiding officer of the upper chamber.

Unfortunately for Donnelly, his financial problems increased during his term of office. His per diem allowance, which scarcely maintained the family, left unpaid the debts incurred in the Nininger City debacle. Desperate, he offered 20 per cent interest in an effort to raise $5,000, even committing his home as security.[15] He continued trying to borrow money throughout the spring and early summer of 1860, but he was unsuccessful.

Unable to pay board and room for his family, Donnelly lived alone in St. Paul during the session. He hated the enforced separation. Unhappily he wrote Kate, "Dollars like figures are stubborn things and will not be stretched."[16] She was soon disgusted with a political office that was rich in prestige but poor in monetary compensation. Donnelly shared her view during the early summer.

[11]Sanborn, "Second State Legislature," pp. 619–33.
[12]William W. Folwell, "The Five Million Loan," Minnesota Historical Society *Collections*, XV, 203.
[13]March 27, 1860.
[14]March 17, 1860.
[15]Donnelly MSS, I. D. to J. Persch, March 19, 1860 (copy).
[16]*Ibid.*, I. D. to K. D., May 12, 1860.

"What a miserable thing this dignity without money is!" he observed.[17]

After the legislature adjourned, Donnelly made a strenuous effort to collect some of the debts owed him. He also entered into partnership with two brothers who lived in Hastings, establishing the law firm of Hayes, Donnelly, and Hayes,[18] an arrangement which was to last for several years, although Donnelly did little more than allow his name to grace the office door and the shingle. He handled very few cases. When the Hayes brothers became his political deputies, his affairs with his partners were more concerned with politics than with the law.

Kate insisted that Donnelly make the best use of his landholdings either by leasing or farming them. He decided to work them himself. To his friends, the idea that Donnelly was actually trying to farm his lands was ludicrous. His short stocky body wading through the deep mud of a Minnesota spring cut a humorous figure. Donnelly, who had no practical experience in agriculture and relied upon others for labor and skill, gradually acquired a genuine understanding of the farmers' problems. For the first time he realized the labor involved and appreciated the risks undertaken by the men who tilled the soil.

When the Dakota County Agricultural Society invited him to present a lecture, he avoided discussing farm problems or methods of successful farming. His theme was the cultivation of the farmer's mind. The farmer, he contended, must be literate before he could be a respected member of society; he must read the best newspapers and books. Why not, he asked, devote one acre of your land to the cultivation of your mind and call it the "Mind's Acre"? His speech sparkled with quotations from David Owen, Emerson, and Humboldt. Praising the tilling of soil as the highest calling of man, he concluded that no task "in the world is so well adapted to the broadest development as agriculture."[19] The speech expressed explicitly Donnelly's Jeffersonianism. It was not simply because he spoke to farmers that he employed the theme; he actually believed it! The basic points in this speech he later repeated again and again when talking to Minnesota farmers who were suffering from the impact of industrialization.

[17]*Ibid.*
[18]Hastings *Independent,* July 5, 1860.
[19]*Ibid.,* September 21, 1860.

Shortly after the legislative session ended, Ramsey, active in national politics, found it essential to travel in the East. Since the telegraph had not yet reached Minnesota and communication was slow, Ramsey asked Donnelly to serve as acting governor in his absence. As Ramsey interpreted the state's constitution, when the governor was not able to fulfil his functions, the lieutenant governor acted for him.

Donnelly welcomed Ramsey's call to assume control of the government.[20] It was no secret that Ramsey had sent for Donnelly to "run the machine" while he was away.[21] Ramsey, whose trip to the East was linked with his vice-presidential aspirations, believed that he was a logical running mate for any eastern presidential candidate. His position in the West was strong, and his party affiliations in Pennsylvania were excellent. Although Donnelly doubted Ramsey's ability to capture the vice-presidential nomination, anything that took the governor out of the state was to Donnelly's economic and political advantage.[22]

To his surprise, Donnelly discovered that the machine ran itself! With the legislature no longer in session, there were few administrative problems. To avoid boredom, Donnelly spent hours in the state library reading for recreation and information. His files and notebooks fattened with proverbs and quips intended for political speeches and lectures.

His reading included Burton's *Anatomy of Melancholy* and the historical works of Schlegel and Guizot. As was almost inevitable during the year before the Civil War, Donnelly read extensively on government and revolution. He re-examined the *Federalist Papers*, but perhaps the most significant aspect of this reading was his interest in the works of Edmund Burke. From the *Reflections on the French Revolution*, Donnelly mustered conservative arguments against the destruction of organized government. In Burke, too, he found many rhetorical gems, especially observations concerning freedom and liberty.[23]

Donnelly viewed the governorship with a light heart, once he discovered that it offered little challenge. In one of his routine letters

[20]Donnelly MSS, A. Ramsey to I. D., April 24, 1860.
[21]*Ibid.*, A. Hayes to I. D., May 3, 1860.
[22]*Ibid.*, I. D. to K. D., May 12, 1860.
[23]*Ibid.*, a large package of notes filed at the beginning of the box containing his papers for May, 1860.

to Ramsey, reassuring him that all was going well in the state, Donnelly added, "I have drawn your salary in advance for a year, and I am consequently flushed with funds."[24] Ramsey, probably ignored Donnelly's joke.

But Donnelly's acting governorship caused the first rift in the Donnelly-Ramsey friendship. Prior to leaving Minnesota, Ramsey had asked attorney-general Gordon Cole for a ruling regarding an acting governor. In Cole's opinion, Donnelly had no right to serve. But Ramsey simply filed the opinion and requested Donnelly to come to St. Paul. Scarcely a week after Ramsey's departure, the state auditor sought Donnelly's signature for one of the few bills in need of approval. As acting governor, Donnelly signed the measure. The same day he called at the treasurer's office to draw his per diem allowance, thirty-six dollars for the week. A deputy treasurer informed him that in consequence of an opinion by the attorney-general on file in the governor's office, he had no right to per diem funds! Furious, Donnelly stamped into the office of the auditor, demanded the copy of the measure which he had signed, and tore off his signature. Angrily he prepared to return to Nininger City. Cole, afraid to face Bluff Aleck's wrath, reconsidered his opinion. Donnelly drew his per diem and signed the measure. But it was a hollow victory. Donnelly never forgave Ramsey for having subjected him to this embarrassment.[25]

Large political problems loomed on the horizon in 1860. In the spring the Democrats faced the problem of nominating a presidential standard-bearer. The rift between Stephen A. Douglas and President Buchanan had become irreparable. The President had done all within his power to break Douglas' hold on the party leaders in the Middle West. When the Democratic convention assembled in Charleston, South Carolina, Douglas was by far the strongest candidate, but he lacked the two-thirds vote necessary to win the nomination. An open split occurred when the anti-Douglas men withdrew before nominating a candidate. Later the Douglasites assembled in Baltimore to nominate the "little giant" for the highest office in the land.[26]

The Republicans welcomed enthusiastically the news of this Democratic crisis. Minnesota's leading Republican newspapers

[24]Ramsey MSS, I. D. to A. Ramsey, May 12, 1860.
[25]St. Paul *Pioneer*, September 19, 1867.
[26]Nichols, *American Democracy*, pp. 270–305.

grasped every opportunity to satirize their opponents. The Hastings *Independent* reprinted, with obvious relish, a parody of familiar nursery rhymes.

> Sing a song of Charleston!
> Bottle full of Rye
> All the Douglas delegates
> Knocked into pi!
> For when the vote was opened
> The South began to sing
> "Your little Squatter Sovereign
> "Shan't be our King!"

> There was a little Senator
> Who wasn't very wise,
> He jumped into convention,
> And scratched out both his eyes
> And when he found his eyes were out,
> With all his might and main
> He bolted off to Baltimore
> To scratch them in again.[27]

And Abraham Van Vorhes aptly characterized the Democratic position when he wrote Donnelly, "Haven't the Democracy holed themselves beautifully, and then drawn the hole in after them?"[28]

The Minnesota Republicans who convened in a party conference at St. Paul favored New Yorker William A. Seward for President. There were many reasons for this selection, but the two most obvious were Seward's leadership as an aspirant and Ramsey's hope that he would win the vice-presidential nomination, or at least a cabinet post, if an eastern Republican won the election.

When the Republicans gathered in their national convention at the "Wigwam" in Chicago, Minnesota voted for Seward, "first, last, and all the time," until it was obvious that Lincoln had received the nomination. Ramsey then made a trip to Springfield, Illinois, to make his peace with Lincoln and place the Minnesotans back in good standing.[29] His loyalty to Seward, however, remained unshaken, and in the fall of the year, Seward went to Minnesota to campaign for Lincoln.

Seward's visit was undoubtedly the high point of the presidential campaign in Minnesota. The fact that the New Yorker had been a leading contestant and, even in defeat, had magnanimously agreed

[27]May 31, 1860.
[28]Donnelly MSS, A. Van Vorhes to I. D., May 8, 1860.
[29]Stillwater *Messenger,* May 22, 1860.

to campaign in behalf of the victor, gave him great prestige. Traveling with a comfortable entourage, Seward arrived in St. Paul for a great mass meeting after making a leisurely trip up the Mississippi River. His visit was marked by a celebration, and the Republican clubs were active in stirring up excitement. Seward, an astute politician who knew the nature of his audience, made his speech a powerful appeal: it was the people of the Northwest who would be the arbiters of the destiny of the nation. A free Minnesota, a Republican state, would mean a free nation and a Republican nation. As an out-of-state speaker, Seward was the best in the country, and he doubtless helped carry the state.[30]

The party organization in Minnesota, although prepared for an easy victory, feared a last-minute upset. As early as March, newspapers insisted that Donnelly would put on the Republican harness and not cease his labors until the presidency had a Republican occupant.[31] Following the convention in Chicago, a number of Lincoln clubs, "Wide Awakes," were started to counter the influence of the Douglas organizations, "Little Giants." Donnelly received many invitations to repeat his anti-Douglas speech of the previous campaign or present a new one.

Because of the seriousness of his financial problems, Donnelly could not afford to campaign. In the preceding election, outside money in large amounts had been used, but in 1860 the State Central Committee was not only without funds but also deeply in debt. Speakers were asked to pay their own campaign expenses. Donnelly, having earned a reputation as the most effective public speaker in the administration, was the sole exception. He learned from Daniel Rohrer of the State Central Committee that Alexander Ramsey had agreed to pay for his campaign if he traveled with the governor.[32] Donnelly accepted readily, pledging himself to accompany Bluff Aleck in a tour of the crucial districts.

Early in October, when political enthusiasm should have reached its height, Minnesota's politics was in the doldrums. The Minnesotans seemed to be observers rather than participants in the election. One of Donnelly's friends noted sarcastically, "The wide awakes are getting rather sleepy."[33] Even Dr. Thomas Foster, who usually had

[30]Theodore C. Blegen, "Campaigning with Seward in 1860," *Minnesota History,* VIII (1927), 150–51.
[31]Stillwater *Messenger,* March 27, 1860.
[32]Donnelly MSS, D. Rohrer to I. D., September 5, 1860.
[33]*Ibid.,* H. Lindergreen to I. D., October 3, 1860.

no problem stirring political controversy in the columns of the *Minnesotian,* asked Donnelly to write articles on any non-political subject he found of interest.[34] Evidence of widespread apathy among the voters caused Alexander Ramsey increasing anxiety. Fearful that the regular Republican voters would not vote and that the Democrats might rally at the last moment, Ramsey wrote to Donnelly insisting that he must come to St. Cloud for a great mass rally. "You will please come prepared," wrote Ramsey, "to take in hand, and put on any glove that may be cast down to us on the way."[35] Donnelly was ready. He knew that Ramsey, who had been working for the Republican National Committee, was unprepared to defend the local administration. The St. Cloud rally was carefully staged. Donnelly spoke in English and Treasurer Scheffer in German. Much of the enthusiasm of the fiery campaign of 1859, with its torch parades, band music, and cannons, was momentarily recaptured.

The Republican St. Cloud rally brought out the final Democratic effort. On the eve of the election, Democrat Willis A. Gorman, one-time territorial governor, challenged Donnelly to a debate at the last Republican meeting of the campaign. Enthusiasm had waned during the campaign, and many Republicans feared that a few well-directed questions at this last meeting might prove disastrous. But Donnelly was unconcerned. He knew Gorman too well—his old-style southern oratory, and especially his hot temper. "Get him mad and he will be likely to hang himself."[36]

The Donnelly-Gorman debate, although well attended, proved a disappointment to both the Republicans and the Democrats. Gorman did not become excited, but Donnelly had an easy time promoting the Republican cause. Pointing to Minnesota's bumper harvest and the state's need for investment capital, Donnelly suggested that the Republican party promised new enterprise, subsidies, and profits. The rival Democratic presidential candidates—Douglas and Breckinridge—Donnelly observed, reminded him of a story of a man who asked a boy for directions. " 'Well,' said the youth, 'if you take this road you will wish you were in hell. If you take this road, you will wish that you took the first.' " This, Donnelly insisted, was the choice that the Democrats offered.[37]

Very few Minnesotans viewed the national scene with alarm. The

[34]*Ibid.,* T. Foster to I. D., October 3, 1860.
[35]*Ibid.,* A. Ramsey to I. D., October 22, 1860.
[36]*Ibid.,* A. Van Vorhes to I. D., October 29, 1860.
[37]*Ibid.,* Daybook.

William D. Washburn, lumberman, miller, lawyer, and politician—in the 1880's. (Minnesota Historical Society.)

Stephen Miller, Minnesota's governor at the close of the Civil War. (U.S. Signal Corps Photograph.)

Knute Nelson in 1892: the first Norwegian-born U.S. citizen to serve as governor, congressman, and U.S. Senator. (Minnesota Historical Society.)

Alexander Ramsey during his senatorial term in the 1870's. (U.S. Signal Corps Photograph.)

Donnelly in
the 1890's.
(Minnesota
Historical
Society.)

southern threats of secession, the evident dissolution of the Democratic party, and the possibility of revolution failed to frighten Donnelly. But after Lincoln's election, he had cause to reconsider. An old friend, George Burns, wrote him disturbing news of treason openly discussed in Washington society. Burns worried about Lincoln as a leader. "Do you think," he inquired of Donnelly, "Lincoln is the man for the emergency? Oh! for a Jackson, Clay, or Webster now!" Burns could not understand Donnelly's lack of actual knowledge of the progress toward disunion. Did not Donnelly realize that industry had been paralyzed since the election, that there were bread lines forming in the large eastern cities, and that the southern leaders had assumed a "no compromise" attitude. "I am thoroughly convinced," he lamented, that "*if Lincoln is ever inaugurated at Washington* . . . civil war, or separate confederacies, are the only alternative." Give up all hope of securing a settlement through any of these union-saving projects, he advised. "The South don't want to be saved—won't be saved, and is thoroughly satisfied it is *not* to *her* interest to be saved."[38]

Donnelly could not accept so pessimistic an interpretation of the secession movement. The thought of destroying the cornerstone of the dream was preposterous to a Minnesotan who had grown up in the spirit of the Young America ideal. He would have thought differently, no doubt, had he been educated to an awareness of the deep feelings and fears among southern leaders. But lacking this knowledge Donnelly focused his attention on the ordinary affairs of his life.

When the state legislature once more convened, Donnelly cultivated the genteel manners of the professional politician, finding comfortable seats for the ladies who visited the chamber and performing courtesies which made them his personal friends.[39] Asked by Governor Ramsey to present a dispatch from Senator Morton S. Wilkinson of Minnesota in reference to the Peace Convention to be held in the border states, Donnelly did no more than place it before the chamber. Whether he had no faith in the possibilities of such action, or whether he shared Ramsey's view that this was not a constitutional means of solving the problem of secession, is not known; but Minnesota sent no delegates. Even the usually vitriolic *Pioneer and Democrat* noted his tone of objectivity, commending his readiness "to impart the reasons for a parliamentary rule, or his construc-

[38]*Ibid.*, G. Burns to I. D., February 5, 1861.
[39]St. Paul *Pioneer and Democrat*, January 10, 1861.

tion of it. . . . He is governed by the *law*, rather than by the authority of an officer."[40]

Donnelly's personal reading reflected the influence of the changing national scene upon him. On the eve of the conflict he began reading military science and the lives of military heroes. Since his obligations in the Senate were never time-consuming, his afternoons could be spent in the state library reading Schlegel's *Caesar* and *Alexander*, Gibbon's *Manual for the Artillerist*, and most important, at least from the point of view of the notes which were taken, biographies of Napoleon.[41] The more he read about Napoleon the more he respected his strength and vitality, even though he disagreed with the imperial ideal. In later life, Donnelly kept a large bust of the Corsican in his library.

In the midst of the increasing unrest, Alexander Ramsey visited Washington, the political fulcrum of the nation. He summoned Donnelly to St. Paul, trusting him to act discreetly and avoid controversy.[42] Reluctantly, Donnelly again accepted the acting governorship. Aside from national problems, there were indications on the frontier that the Sioux Indians might attack.[43] Fear of an Indian uprising had already caused Donnelly to consider how to raise troops in an emergency when the electrifying news of the shelling of Fort Sumter reached Minnesota.

In Donnelly's mind there was no doubt that the free West would fight to preserve the Union.[44] The attack upon a federal garrison in Charleston harbor by the South Carolinians released the spring of contained patriotism among the settlers of Minnesota. And in Washington Ramsey hastened to the offices of Simon Cameron, Secretary of War, tendering his former Pennsylvania colleague a thousand men for national defense. After Ramsey put the offer in writing, Minnesotans were Lincoln's first volunteers.[45]

The President ordered the nation to arms by issuing a proclamation calling for 75,000 men to "maintain the honor, the integrity, and the existence of the National Union."[46] Ramsey telegraphed the Ad-

[40]*Ibid.*, March 3, 1861.
[41]Donnelly MSS, large package of notes dating from this period.
[42]*Ibid.*, S. Jennison to I. D., April 8, 1861.
[43]*Ibid.*, I. D. to K. D., April 14, 1861.
[44]Hubbart, *Middle West*, p. 166, contends that such a doubt did exist on the part of many living in the Middle West.
[45]Folwell, *Minnesota*, II, 77.
[46]Roy P. Basler (ed.), *Collected Works of Abraham Lincoln* (New Brunswick: Rutgers University Press, 1953) IV, 332.

jutant General of Minnesota, William H. Acker, to issue a proclamation in Ramsey's name calling for recruits. He sent a copy to his secretary, Samuel P. Jennison, which came into Donnelly's hands. Donnelly was angered by what he considered a slight. "Ramsey may explain his conduct," Donnelly wrote Kate, "but it looks very much like a hoggish dread that I might gain a little bit of credit."[47] Donnelly then issued the proclamation himself, signing it "Governor *ad interim.*"

Ramsey may have doubted the legality of recruiting men without the actual governor's permission; he may have been genuinely excited by the turn of affairs and distrusted Donnelly's ability to cope with the situation; or it may have been as Donnelly believed, a fear that he would gain too great a reputation by raising the army. But Donnelly was never satisfied with whatever explanation Ramsey gave him. Years later, when he and Ramsey were political rivals, he justified his actions by writing sarcastically:

Filled with the spirit which prompted Artemus Ward to offer all his brothers-in-law, and all his wife's cousins on the altar of his country, the Governor rushed wildly to the White House and tendered a regiment for the war; and the act was heralded here as one unprecedented in patriotism. At the same time he telegraphed me: "issue a proclamation calling for troops in my name!" I was Governor to do the work; I was not Governor to take the honors. I declined the modest suggestion and issued the proclamation in my own name.[48]

Following Lincoln's proclamation, "Save the Union" war rallies were held in St. Paul and party lines were dropped, but it was with the greatest reluctance that the *Pioneer and Democrat* abandoned calling it a Republican war.[49]

Unfortunately, Minnesota was in no position to send much of the aid Ramsey had so readily promised. As early as June of 1860, Donnelly had inquired about the condition of the state arsenal, only to discover that Minnesota had only one cannon. In theory, Minnesota should have been one of the states best prepared for a military crisis. Located on the Indian frontier, with a high ratio of men to women, and with a model militia act, the state should have been able to muster almost 25,000 men. In reality Minnesota could gather only 150 officers and 200 men. Most of these were organized into volunteer companies whose military experience consisted of drilling and

[47] Donnelly MSS, I. D. to K. D., April 17, 1861.
[48] St. Paul *Pioneer,* September, 1867.
[49] April 20, 1861.

parading on national holidays. Self-trained, they lacked equipment which should have been supplied by the federal government and they had no discipline. Furthermore, their uniforms, designed for parades, were inappropriately gaudy and far from durable.[50] Even worse, the men in two of these three drill companies were doubtful of the right of the federal government to take them into national service and many of them refused to leave the state.[51]

Ramsey spent the autumn of 1861 in Washington, leaving Donnelly to struggle with the problems of mobilizing an army. When a plan to form a truly national army on the basis of congressional districts had been rejected, the country once more fell back on the faulty and inefficient system of state regiments. Only the appointment of general officers and the disposal of troops once they had been mustered into service was left to the Washington command. To save the Union, the war was waged as a confederacy. This meant that officers, to a large extent, would be politically influential citizens rather than trained military personnel. The governors of the various states were given a powerful weapon of patronage—the high-paying commission. Recognizing this, Ramsey insisted that Donnelly help organize the Minnesota regiments and assist in the selection of officers, but Ramsey made the final decisions and left those who were disappointed looking to Donnelly for satisfaction.[52]

Ramsey enjoined Donnelly to work hard at the task of recruiting troops, but in no event was he to make any promises of appointments. Many Minnesota politicians believed that Ramsey was using the appointments to guarantee his election to the United States Senate.[53] Despite Ramsey's admonition to commission no one without specific permission, Donnelly worked hard for his friends. He tried to secure a lieutenancy for Dr. Thomas Foster's oldest son, and he did succeed in commissioning his law partner, O. T. Hayes, as a company-grade officer, but for the most part he was unsuccessful. Eager to help his friends, Donnelly, who never failed to comply when he was asked to write a letter of commendation for an office-seeker, was especially careful to send out notes of regret if the candidate proved unsuccessful.

Procuring regiments proved more formidable in life than in the

[50]John D. Hicks, "The Organization of the Volunteer Army in 1861 with Special Reference to Minnesota," *Minnesota History*, II (1918), 328–29.

[51]Donnelly MSS, S. Miller to I. D., April 24, 1861.

[52]*Ibid.*, I. D. to K. D., April 24, 1861; see also Ramsey MSS, A. Ramsey to I. D., telegram.

[53]St. Paul *Pioneer*, September 19, 1867.

military histories and biographies that Donnelly read. Mobilization found him trying to bring order out of chaos. Fortunately, Ramsey made an excellent choice of colonel for the Minnesota First Regiment—Willis Gorman. Although Gorman was a leading Democrat, he had fought with distinction in the Mexican War and was undoubtedly one of the few trained officers in the state. Even though they had been political opponents, Donnelly worked well with Gorman as Minnesota's troops neared combat readiness.[54] Taxing his physical strength and organizational ability to send Gorman what he needed, where he needed it, Donnelly was in daily communication with the colonel until the First Minnesota went east to join the army before Washington.[55]

At the outset of mobilization, Ramsey contended that he sought the best possible man for each command, but after the appointment of Willis A. Gorman, he was forced to abandon this policy. A storm of criticism arose over Gorman's commission; Democrats, regardless of their qualifications, should not have received awards at the expense of deserving Republicans. But Ramsey, determined to do his best, wrote Donnelly to keep close watch on Adjutant General John B. Sanborn and to prevent him from commissioning for political reasons alone.[56] Within a matter of weeks Ramsey, having exhausted the supply of trained officers, abandoned this policy and decided to select officers on the same basis that he would draw up a slate of candidates. "Be prepared to discuss the appointments of field grade officers with a view to politics and geography," he wrote Donnelly on the eve of the drive to raise the Third and Fourth Minnesota regiments.[57]

When Ramsey returned to Minnesota, Donnelly happily relinquished control of the state to its legal governor. The *Pioneer and Democrat* noted that he had worked with the "same careful industry and graceful ability, that have won for him so much credit in every other station in which he has been placed."[58] And the St. Paul *Press* praised the manner in which he had "discharged the laborious and responsible duties of the office with fidelity, impartiality, and discretion."[59]

At the outset of 1861, Kate Donnelly, disgusted with the lieuten-

---

[54]Donnelly MSS, W. Gorman to I. D., June 19 and 21, 1861.
[55]Ramsey MSS, S. Cameron to I. D., telegram, June 22, 1861.
[56]Donnelly MSS, A. Ramsey to I. D., September 24, 1861.
[57]*Ibid.*, A. Ramsey to I. D., October 8, 1861.
[58]November 5, 1861.
[59]November 11, 1861.

ant governorship that required so much hard work and provided so little money, hoped that Donnelly would secure some good administrative appointment that was well paid. Your wife "wants the 'Almighty Dollar' more than she wants glory," she pleaded; "money to live on and glory to die on."[60] As a result, Donnelly considered taking command of a regiment because the salary was $2,500.[61] Ramsey refused to take him seriously: he insisted that he would not consider appointing anyone but a military man to command a Minnesota regiment, but Donnelly distrusted his motives. "The old 'cuss' fears that anyone might interfere with his plans for the U.S. Senate in the future," Donnelly wrote Kate, adding that "if it turns out that he does not appoint me I will make him regret it."[62]

Donnelly continued to seek an appointment as one regiment after another was raised and sent into combat, but his requests were rejected. He may have been responsible when the Fifth Minnesota was openly proclaimed an Irish Regiment. It was hoped that men from St. Paul and Minneapolis who had not joined earlier regiments would now enlist to serve under leaders of their own nationality, background, and religion.[63] Donnelly exhibited a keen interest in the Fifth Minnesota and selected the officers carefully, but his opportunity to become a military leader never materialized, as Adjutant General John B. Sanborn was given the command of the regiment.

Denied an active command, Donnelly joined the home guard in Nininger City, where his short stocky figure was a topic of amused discussion among his friends. With charitable wit the Hastings *Independent* observed: "Some doubts being expressed as whether Mr. Donnelly could take the thirteen [sic] [thirty] inch step, he replied that 'on advance he might find it difficult in performing it, but on the retreat he was certain he could attain it with ease.' "[64]

After the initial impact of war, politics regained its hold on the men of Minnesota. As early as March, 1861, Henry C. Simpson, editor of the Lake City *Journal*, wrote a strong editorial favoring Donnelly as a candidate for governor if for some reason Ramsey did not seek re-election.[65] This preliminary "puff" proved embarrassing because although many of Donnelly's intimates hoped for this, they

[60]Donnelly MSS, K. D. to I. D., February 16, 1861.
[61]*Ibid.*, I. D. to K. D., April 24, 1861.
[62]*Ibid.*, I. D. to K. D., June 26, 1861.
[63]Folwell, *Minnesota*, II, 96.
[64]Hastings *Independent*, June 6, 1861.
[65]March 16, 1861.

wished to keep their plans a secret.[66] Nothing more was heard of the idea following the initial article, but Donnelly cautiously began to assess his strength by sending his law partner, A. M. Hayes, on a trip across the state to sound out the politicians on Donnelly's popularity. Hayes was to make as many friends and allies as possible, without giving the impression that they were to be used for or against any particular candidate.[67]

It soon became apparent that the anti-Ramsey elements in the party would welcome his lieutenant governor into their group. Opposition to Ramsey centered in Minneapolis, where Congressman Cyrus Aldrich was an eager aspirant for the United States Senate. Aldrich's followers planned to form a Union party in Minnesota—a combination of pro-war Democrats and conservative Republicans— which they hoped would defeat Ramsey.[68] Aware that Ramsey was a powerful adversary, Donnelly was reluctant to combine against him. "Do you think you have strength enough to butt old 'Aleck,'" wrote one of Donnelly's political informants. "I should hate to have you fail—it would injure you materially hereafter."[69] But as late as August, 1861, he still flirted with the idea of joining Aldrich's Union party.

When the Republican convention gathered in St. Paul on September 4, 1861, Donnelly was renominated for lieutenant governor by acclamation. Within ten days, Ramsey called a caucus of candidates to map the strategy for a short but intensive campaign. Donnelly was assigned the orator's role.[70] Meanwhile, except for the Aldrich faction's unsuccessful attempt to place a Union ticket in the field, the campaign moved on against little opposition. The Democrats being still too disorganized to launch a real campaign, the entire Republican ticket was re-elected. Donnelly had much to think about after this victory. His discussion with Aldrich had convinced him that he must advance politically or perish.

[66]Donnelly MSS, N. Tefft to I. D., March 20, 1861.
[67]*Ibid.*, A. Hayes to I. D., June 1, 1861.
[68]*Ibid.*, M. Coloney to I. D., June 19, 1861.
[69]*Ibid.*, G. Potter to I. D., July 30, 1861.
[70]*Ibid.*, A. Ramsey to I. D., September 13, 1861.

The Making of a Congressman
1862–1863

> Try the rough waters as well as the smooth.
> Rough waters can teach lessons worth knowing.
>
> EMERSON

FROM the day Fort Sumter was fired upon until the last second of New Year's Eve, the year 1861 had been one of unrelenting pain and anxiety for all concerned with the war. The great Army of the Potomac, assembled to march upon Richmond and crush the Confederacy, had bogged in the mud and by the end of January, 1862, the disgust of the men, including the Minnesota First Regiment, was profound.

The year had also been one of phenomenal progress. Once the certainty of war was apparent, business conditions began to improve rapidly and the country experienced a boom comparable to that of 1856. Never had so great an expansion of internal industry accompanied such a mighty war. Prosperity was evident on the farms as well as in the cities. Despite the heavy drain on manpower, the annual production of agricultural commodities increased enormously. Women, children, and machines replaced men in the fields, and with the war well under way the farm economy was better off than ever before—prices were high, and production was soaring.[1]

[1] Lester B. Shippee, "Social and Economic Effects of the Civil War with Special Reference to Minnesota," *Minnesota History*, II (1918), 397.

For Donnelly the year 1862 began with no more auspicious event than the inauguration of the Republican legislature. There were few problems during this session, and Donnelly's role was chiefly that of a charming host to the visitors to the Senate chamber. During the session he said little regarding legislation and supported the regime which, in turn, merely supported the war. His financial position improved slowly. Kate and the children were able to visit the capital more frequently and to remain longer. When they were in St. Paul, the family enjoyed the society of the city, particularly that of the Republican leadership. And, at the end of the legislative session, there was now no criticism of Donnelly's behavior. Even the *Pioneer and Democrat* referred to him as "our amiable Lieutenant Governor."[2]

While placidity ruled the surface of political affairs within the Republican party of Minnesota, its depths were troubled by faction. Aldrich's failure to defeat Ramsey in the gubernatorial contest continued to cause the congressman concern. He knew that Bluff Aleck, determined to rule Minnesota politics, wanted to be one of Minnesota's United States senators, not only to satisfy his personal ambitions, but also because, as Harlan P. Hall, one of Minnesota's cleverest newspapermen noted: "There was then a commissioner of Indian affairs in St. Paul to whom various Indian agents were tributary; there were many Indian and mail contracts; there was government pine almost *ad libitum,* and, in fact, all the necessary adjuncts to make a United States Senator very valuable to his friends."[3] Because the stakes were high, the struggle for control of the party machinery that could deliver the nomination was intense.

Both Ramsey and Aldrich were quick to seek Donnelly's help. As president of the Senate, Donnelly's patronage power had been slight, but he had used it well, acquiring a small and loyal group of followers. Early in January, 1862, Donnelly received a letter from David Heaton, state senator from Hennepin County and editor of the Minnesota *State News.* Heaton, who represented the Ramsey faction in Aldrich's home district, was working hard gathering support for Ramsey in the senatorial contest. "The Governor *will be the Senator,*" Heaton assured Donnelly; aiding him would have its merits.[4] Within a week, however, Donnelly received word from H. G. Mor-

[2]March 5, 1862.
[3]Hall, *Observations,* p. 57.
[4]Donnelly MSS, D. Heaton to I. D., January 10, 1862.

rison, a local Aldrich supporter, seeking Donnelly's views on the senatorial contest and asking whether he was definitely committed to Ramsey.[5]

With a conflict brewing between Ramsey and Aldrich, Donnelly shrewdly realized that he was in a good position to satisfy his own ambitions. He had two possibilities: the governorship or a congressional seat. Why Donnelly did not press for the gubernatorial nomination is unknown, but certainly the low salary deterred him; early in the year he wrote one of his creditors: "I shall be a candidate in one of the [congressional] Districts and I think, in all human probability will be elected. If I am, I will be able to do something for you."[6]

Donnelly was not the only Republican politician staking a claim to the congressional nomination. Colonel Stephen Miller of the First Minnesota Regiment, an influential St. Cloud Republican, was also a candidate. Another eager aspirant was Jared Benson, a likely compromise candidate if Donnelly and Miller deadlocked the party caucus.

Unfortunately, one of Donnelly's best friends, Mrs. Jane Grey Swisshelm, was committed to Miller. Her newspaper, the *Democrat*, was published in St. Cloud, and for reasons of geography and local pride, she indorsed Miller. But Mrs. Swisshelm not only assured Donnelly that the paper would never attack him; she defended him against criticism from anti-Catholic Republicans by focusing attention on other issues. "The next election is not to be carried on a transubstantiation platform," she wrote. "Religion succumbs to Railroads and Rebellion and nobody cares whether a candidate is catholic, quaker, or whether he was named John Calvin or John Wesley."[7] The St. Cloud *Democrat*'s ideal slate of candidates listed Ramsey for United States senator, Miller for the House of Representatives, and Donnelly for governor.

Donnelly's fear of Miller's candidacy was closely linked with the colonel's favor in the Ramsey camp. Divided in their loyalties on the congressional nomination, some of Ramsey's followers, like David Heaton, favored Donnelly, but there were indications that Ramsey had made his decision in Miller's favor. When the St. Paul *Press*, the successor to the *Minnesotian* as the official Republican newspaper, began advocating Miller's nomination, Donnelly was alarmed. The

[5]*Ibid.*, H. Morrison to I. D., January 18, 1862.
[6]*Ibid.*, I. D. to J. Persch, March 5, 1862 (copy).
[7]St. Cloud *Democrat*, June 19, 1862.

Press was a Ramsey paper, and its editorials frequently expressed his point of view. After one of Aldrich's friends called this to Donnelly's attention, Donnelly wrote the governor that there was talk in political circles that he was supporting Miller. Donnelly expressed the hope that Ramsey would let "every tub stand on its own bottom."[8] But Bluff Aleck, who would not be hurried, denied all knowledge of the matter. "Who were the lying rogues that wrote you that I am *running Stephen?* . . . Miller writes me . . . I am running you."[9] Although Ramsey stated that he was not encouraging Miller, he did not assure Donnelly that he would not do so in the future.

As early as March 20, even before Ramsey assumed his noncommittal attitude, Donnelly wrote to Cyrus Aldrich asking if he intended to seek re-election. If Aldrich was not to be a candidate, Donnelly would like to have his support. Governor Ramsey, Donnelly stated, was assisting Colonel Miller.[10] William S. King, a young scheming politician in the Aldrich faction and postmaster of the House of Representatives, immediately answered in Aldrich's behalf. "Bill" King, not given to careless talk, explained that Cyrus Aldrich did not intend to be a candidate for re-election to the House of Representatives, and that his friends would be governed in picking his successor by their best interests. Then he came right to the point, Ramsey's senatorial ambitions. Because they viewed Ramsey as "unqualifiedly hostile in every sense of the word," Aldrich's friends would support the man for Congress whose nomination "will be most likely to weaken the chances of Governor Ramsey for the Senatorship." Not only did King fail to commit himself in favor of Donnelly, he suggested that Donnelly curb his ambition for the present. "Those who are now in positions will be out of the way," he wrote, "and you and I, young men yet you know, will be on hand for places they leave behind them."[11] King's letter was followed by one from Aldrich denouncing Stephen Miller as "the biggest humbug, on a small scale" that Minnesota had produced, but adding that he had reconsidered the political situation and decided to seek re-nomination for the House.[12]

But Aldrich was not in a position to make his own decision. Unlike Ramsey, who himself exercised political power, he was the

---

[8]Donnelly MSS, I. D. to A. Ramsey, May 6, 1862.
[9]*Ibid.*, A. Ramsey to I. D., May 7, 1862.
[10]*Ibid.*, I. D. to C. Aldrich, March 20, 1862.
[11]*Ibid.*, W. King to I. D., March 31, 1862.
[12]*Ibid.*, C. Aldrich to I. D., April 15, 1862.

spokesman for a group of wealthy and prominent men in Minneapolis who viewed Ramsey, to some extent, as the representative of the rival community of St. Paul. To protect the interests of Minneapolis, a rival candidate had to be placed in the contest. Another consideration which Aldrich could not ignore was the ambition of the young men within his organization. Bill King was eager for advancement, and there were many others. These young men understood the fundamental political axiom of machine politics: the politician who will not risk to gain, will lose what he considers certain. Because of these pressures, and perhaps because he hoped that he could defeat Ramsey, Cyrus Aldrich returned to the senatorial contest.

Aldrich again extended his offer of friendship to Donnelly.[13] But it was not a specific pledge of support for Congress; in fact, both Aldrich and King informed him that they would not assist him until he had convinced the Minneapolis and Hennepin County Republican groups of his strength and loyalty. Within a matter of days, H. G. O. Morrison, an Aldrich supporter, asked Donnelly for a "*sort of confidential letter*" that he could show Aldrich's friends promising the aid of the Donnelly faction in securing the senatorship for Aldrich. He followed this request with an invitation for Donnelly to come to St. Paul to have a personal talk with the intimate coterie of Aldrich backers.[14] After they decided to accept Donnelly, King wrote: "Now Governor if you do allow Stephen [Miller] to beat you, I will swear a d——n sight harder at you than I ever did before."[15] Donnelly was also assured that Abraham Van Vorhes would support him in the columns of the Stillwater *Messenger*. From the point of view of powerful allies, Donnelly's position was completely changed.

Only the question of tactics remained to be solved in order to bring the campaign to a successful close. If Donnelly could retain the friendship of both sides in the Ramsey-Aldrich struggle, he would be assured of election. But Dr. Thomas Foster, his friend and political preceptor, disapproved of any alliance with Aldrich. Although serving as an army medical officer, he had learned of Donnelly's machinations within the party and pleaded with him "never to quarrel politically [with Ramsey]—for with all his faults not to say meannesses, he has no salient point to attack before the *people*,

[13]*Ibid.*, W. King to I. D., May 9, 1862.
[14]*Ibid.*, H. Morrison to I. D., May 16, May 19, 1862.
[15]*Ibid.*, W. King to I. D., May 16, 1862.

and his assaliant [*sic*] is always worsted."[16] In public Donnelly avoided the senatorial issue; he neither attacked Ramsey nor indorsed Aldrich.

Just before the county conventions and caucuses began, Donnelly made a major speech at an Independence Day celebration in Plainview. His address was probably a variation of one that he had given before, entitled "War and Patriotism." Three months earlier David Heaton had cautioned Donnelly about this speech. He was to be careful not to be too critical of Seward, who had a great many friends and admirers; to save a few kind words for Abraham Lincoln, "[who guides the] old ship like a brave and prudent captain"; and, no matter how well he spoke of the Germans and the Irish, to end up praising the sons of New England in the great West, for "you know how sensitive the *American* is & particularly now."[17] The Plainview speech was tailored to gloss over issues. Donnelly spoke at Plainview because it was sponsoring the largest Fourth of July celebration in the state. He even took Kate with him, something he rarely did during a campaign. Donnelly was seeking the best possible state-wide publicity.

Donnelly was knowledgeable enough as a politician to anticipate the newspaper reaction to his campaign. The first indorsement came, of course, from David Heaton's paper. This was followed by Abraham Van Vorhes' Stillwater *Messenger*, Bill King's *State Atlas*, and finally Columbus Stebbins' Hastings *Independent*, which provided a rather reluctant indorsement because once more its editor disapproved of Donnelly's methods of seeking election. There was half-hearted opposition from the St. Paul *Press*, and from Mrs. Swisshelm's St. Cloud *Democrat*.

During the last week in July the various counties in Minnesota selected and instructed their delegates to the congressional district convention. It was evident almost immediately that Donnelly had won the largest number of delegates. David Heaton, always cautious, warned Donnelly to organize the convention in advance, pick a good temporary chairman, and be especially careful about the committee on credentials.[18] But Colonel Stephen Miller, realizing that he had been defeated, withdrew from the contest and urged his friends to sponsor Donnelly. When the convention assembled, he

[16]*Ibid.*, T. Foster to I. D., June 20, 1862.
[17]*Ibid.*, D. Heaton to I. D., April 16, 1862.
[18]*Ibid.*, D. Heaton to I. D., July 27, 1862.

was the unanimous choice of the delegates on the first formal ballot.[19]

Following his nomination, Donnelly made a powerful speech in which he identified himself with the Radical Republican cause.

There has been too much tenderness—too much faltering and hesitation. Our people have been slow to realize the magnitude and desperate earnestness of the rebellion—slow to meet it with an equal earnestness.

We must teach this generation and all posterity that insurrection against just and beneficent government is the most hideous of crimes, and deserves the most terrible of punishments. We must strip the olive branch of its leaves and scourge these men into obedience. . . . Where the wrath of the nation falls it must fall as of old fell the wrath of God, in fire and ashes.[20]

When Donnelly spoke out boldly on the war issues, the St. Paul *Press*, even though it had been cool to his nomination, proclaimed, in typical frontier rhetoric, "Like Minnesota, Governor Donnelly is young and vigorous—a fit representative of the intelligence, enterprise and energy of our people."[21]

Having won the enthusiastic indorsement not only of the convention but also of the newspapers, Donnelly prepared for a vigorous campaign. He had to overcome both Republican political apathy due to the war and a strong opponent. The Democrats had nominated a former Indian agent, Major William J. Cullen, to oppose him. A wealthy Democrat who supported the war, Cullen hoped to revitalize his party and make more than a token campaign. Well aware that there was little sympathy for the Negro in Minnesota, Cullen played on the theme of using them to fight the war. In audacious speeches, he yelled that *"he was for putting down the rebellion if it took every nigger in Africa."*[22] Willing to campaign everywhere, Cullen readied himself to talk to voters in every county in the district. He scored his most successful jab at Donnelly when he challenged him to enter the army with him as a private—with the condition that the defeated man was never to seek or accept any promotion.[23] Donnelly's counter offer—whoever was defeated should enter the army—was hardly as effective.[24] Nothing came of either challenge; the campaign was interrupted by war with the Sioux.

The Indian attack had come suddenly but not without warning or

[19] St. Paul *Pioneer and Democrat*, July 31, 1862.
[20] Faribault *Central Republican* and Minneapolis *State Atlas*, August 6, 1862.
[21] July 21, 1862.
[22] Donnelly MSS, T. Barrett to I. D., August 7, 1862.
[23] St. Paul *Pioneer and Democrat*, August 9, 1862.
[24] St. Paul *Press*, August 10, 1862.

provocation. Having depleted their food supplies in the hard winter of 1861, the Sioux gathered at the Indian agency in the spring of 1862 seeking their annuities in foodstuffs and cash. The food was available in the storehouses of the Indian traders, but federal funds had not yet arrived to pay for distributing it or to make up the cash portion of the payments. During the summer the desperate Indians remained near the agency, kept alive by a mere trickle of supplies. On August 15, Chief Little Crow, deeply resentful of this maltreatment, warned that the food would be taken if it was not distributed. When alarmed Indian agents pleaded with the traders to dispense the food, the spokesman for the Indian traders replied callously, "If they are hungry let them eat grass."

Two days later an isolated farmhouse was attacked. On the following day the Indians returned to the agency, killed the men, stuffed grass into the mouth of a trader, plundered the stores, and commenced an orgy of savagery.[25] As fear and panic spread over the state, Alexander Ramsey acted with genuine courage. After ascertaining the number of men available, he turned the command of the forces over to his old political foe but personal friend, Henry Hastings Sibley. A former Indian trader and territorial governor, Sibley was the best qualified man in Minnesota to drive the Indians out of the state. When Ramsey summoned volunteers, Major Cullen, abandoning the campaign temporarily, raised a troop of frontier guards.

Donnelly joined Sibley's forces at Ramsey's request, but he went unarmed and strictly as the non-combatant liaison between Sibley and the governor. Since Sibley's forces did little more than pursue the Indians, Donnelly saw no actual fighting, but his reports to Ramsey were so brilliantly written that the governor released them to the press. As Sibley's army advanced, Donnelly described the evacuation of New Ulm.

Never, perhaps, was a more melancholy cortege seen in the world than the one which stretched along the road from New Ulm to Mankato. There were mothers there [who] wept over children slaughtered before their eyes; strong men who in a moment had been stripped of their worldly wealth, of home, of wife, and of family; who had escaped into the grass with the death shrieks of [their] parents, brothers, and sisters, ringing in their ears. All bowed down by an overwhelming grief and by an anxiety which no words can describe, but which in two cases had produced *actual insanity*.[26]

[25]Folwell, *Minnesota*, II, 109–46.
[26]St. Paul *Press*, August 28, 1862.

Donnelly's reporting of the Indian war produced a critical response from both Republicans and Democrats. His former rival for lieutenant governor, Henry Swift of St. Peter, after reading Donnelly's account of the New Ulm clash, wrote him a confidential letter correcting some of his inaccuracies. But Swift was more disturbed because Donnelly gave so much credit—in error—to Democrats. "For God's sake," he noted, "don't build up your enemies *at the expense of truth and friends.*"[27] Meanwhile the Democratic camp found another cause for censure. A contributor, writing to the St. Paul *Pioneer and Democrat* under the *non de plume* Zebulon Sawyer, lampooned Donnelly's role in the campaign. It described him as traveling in a buggy, well stocked with food, drink, and a feather bed. Sawyer contended that Donnelly wrote home for supplies not because Sibley needed them but because he had been forced to throw away such items as water-soaked casks of liquor and spoiled biscuits.[28] When some of Donnelly's friends protested against this gross insult, they provided the *Pioneer and Democrat* with an opportunity to restate the accusations while facetiously expressing its chagrin.

At the very moment when the bloody tomahawk was raised, the leaders of both parties asked: should the soldier have the vote? The Republicans insisted that it was the very minimum of justice to allow the men who were fighting for their country to have a chance to decide its policies. The Democrats, fearing a "Republicanized Army," expressed doubt that giving the franchise to the men would be constitutional or feasible. But since the Republicans controlled the state government, a special session of the legislature was summoned to authorize voting by the troops. Donnelly actively supported it. The soldiers' votes would "place my election beyond doubt," he wrote his wife, "and would require but a short canvass on my part."[29]

The law passed, and Donnelly launched a campaign to win the soldier's vote by asking President Lincoln's permission for his canvassers to work among the men of the Minnesota regiments and reminding the President that the administration's cause as well as a Republican victory in Minnesota was at stake. Without the military vote, Donnelly informed Lincoln, the state would definitely be lost

[27]Donnelly MSS, H. Swift to I. D., September 3, 1862.
[28]September 14, 1862.
[29]Donnelly MSS, I. D. to K. D., August 28, 1862.

to the party.[30] The apathy among the enlisted men and the shortage of voting commissioners worried Donnelly, but he assured his wife that Republican canvassers would be at work with the army.[31]

There was more to winning this election than intrigue and electioneering techniques. Donnelly appealed directly to the people, explaining the basic philosophy of government and society. At the Dakota County Fair, where he presented his major political speech of the campaign, the war was the fulcrum upon which his lever rested. "The theory of our government is the absolute equality of all of its members," he told the audience, "without regard to all accidents of birth, education, wealth or intelligence." The right to govern was the property of the entire people, and all but the wildest vagaries were entitled to exist unchecked among them. The chief danger to free government consisted of efforts to curtail freedom of expression as was done in the South. Two societies have grown up in America: one based on free thought and free labor, the other on a diametrically opposed fundamental premise and conclusion. For the benefit of all mankind, free government must triumph.[32] It was upon this argument that Donnelly sought election to the House of Representatives.

On the eve of the election Donnelly returned to his home at Nininger City, tired but sanguine of success. As thoughts of greatness swelled his ego, he began to study his geneaology. At this he was to work off and on for years, until he had traced, with a degree of accuracy, the ancestry not only of his own parents but also that of his wife's parents. He enjoyed this antiquarianism, found relaxation in it, and liked writing to publishers for their latest and best works on Ireland.[33]

Congratulatory messages began arriving in Nininger City even before the election. After the victory a letter arrived from Dr. Thomas Foster that was filled with paternal affection and happily proclaimed his part in pushing Donnelly into his first position of prominence. Foster was genuinely delighted. "My 'protege' [*sic*]," he wrote, "has proved himself able to walk alone—proved it to all the world."[34] But the letter that gave Donnelly the greatest satisfac-

[30]Library of Congress, Lincoln MSS, I. D. to A. Lincoln, October 7, 1862.
[31]Donnelly MSS, I. D. to K. D., October 8, 1862.
[32]Hastings *Independent*, November 5, 1862.
[33]Donnelly MSS, E. C. Donnelly to I. D., November 29, 1862; D. Appleton & Co., to I. D., December 4, 1862.
[34]*Ibid.*, T. Foster to I. D., December 25, 1862.

tion came from his mother. Her pride in his accomplishment had finally overcome her resentment, and she acknowledged that "it was a good day that you left this City: you could never get up for envy and malice would have entrameled [*sic*] you."[35] That was quite an admission from stern old Cathrine Gavin Donnelly, yet she failed to mention his wife or growing family! Flushed with success, Donnelly wrote his sister that there was only one aim in his life—election to the United States Senate. But, as he was soon to learn, a Senate seat was not easily won.

The contest between Aldrich and Ramsey remained to be decided. Even before the election Ramsey's close friend William R. Marshall, who controlled the St. Paul *Press*, launched a vigorous campaign to discredit Aldrich among the people. He turned the task of character assassination over to his brilliant young editor, Joseph Wheelock. That he proved capable of accomplishing all that was expected of him, and more, contributed to making Wheelock the dean of Minnesota's newspaper editors.[36]

In mid-September, Wheelock launched his full-scale assault on Aldrich's reputation. Pursuing a systematic policy of name-calling, publishing half-truths, and reprinting outright slander copied from small newspapers, Wheelock embarrassed Aldrich and escaped lawsuits. Searching Aldrich's past in quest of facts which could be used against the congressman, Wheelock finally hit upon the perfect incident. Aldrich had been a collector of funds for the federal government and, after a change in regulations, had refused to surrender certain fees. When litigation ensued, nothing came of it, but technically Aldrich was a defaulter.[37] To add to his handicap, Aldrich could not deny intemperance. His excessive drinking in Washington was too well known to hide. By early December, weeks before the state legislature convened to select a new senator, David Heaton wrote Donnelly that Aldrich had been destroyed as a candidate.[38]

During the castigation of Aldrich, Donnelly remained firmly in his camp, working closely with H. G. O. Morrison to gather support and plan strategy.[39] He was unhappy to find Aldrich's strength waning in the face of Wheelock's withering criticism. Aldrich con-

[35] *Ibid.*, C. Gavin Donnelly to I. D., November 23, 1862.
[36] Richard Eide, *North Star Editor* (New York: King's Crown Press, 1944).
[37] Minnesota *State News*, October 25, 1862.
[38] Donnelly MSS, D. Heaton to I. D., December 3, 1862.
[39] *Ibid.*, H. Morrison to I. D., November 25, 1862.

fided in Donnelly, relying on him to strengthen the backbone of his dismayed followers.[40] When some of Aldrich's friends began to feel that he was no longer an acceptable candidate and discussed the possibility of finding a compromise candidate satisfactory to both Aldrich and Ramsey, Donnelly assured Aldrich that he would not be such a candidate. "You will find me as true as steel,"[41] he wrote to Aldrich, and the congressman's friends emphasized that Donnelly was "all right."[42] There is no doubt that Donnelly supported Aldrich when the legislature assembled.

The Republican senatorial legislative caucus convened on the evening of January 12, 1863. On the first ballot Aldrich received fourteen votes; Ramsey received nineteen votes; and thirteen votes were scattered among other candidates. On the second ballot Ramsey's vote rose to twenty, but Aldrich's vote remained at fourteen. This stalemate lasted until the twenty-fourth tally, when Ramsey somehow acquired three more votes—none from the Aldrich block. At this point a recess was called. When the caucus reconvened, Ramsey gained three more votes; Aldrich lost three votes, and with them his chance for the United States Senate.

A pro-Aldrich newspaper queried, "Who were the new converts? and what were the influences that brought conviction to their innocent minds?"[43] Aldrich in no way blamed Donnelly for his defeat.[44] His friends, however, placed the blame directly on Donnelly, charging him with changing sides on the critical vote. Donnelly never denied the accusation. The cry was raised that he had been "carrying water on both shoulders" in the senatorial contest, but this is not quite accurate. Donnelly probably did turn to Ramsey but only after twenty ballots, when Aldrich's cause seemed lost. He must have felt that he had betrayed Aldrich, however, because he had no ready reply to a friend who wrote: "Why I did not know that you were such a daring young man [as to carry water on both shoulders]. You might have got wet, and taken cold."[45] Donnelly's friends could joke about his behavior, but he had made a life-long enemy of Bill King.

Donnelly made still another poor decision before he went to Washington. He opposed giving the St. Paul *Press* the state print-

[40]*Ibid.*, C. Aldrich to I. D., December 18, 1862.
[41]*Ibid.*, I. D. to C. Aldrich, December 21, 1862 (copy).
[42]*Ibid.*, C. Aldrich to I. D., December 28, 1862.
[43]Stillwater *Messenger*, January 20, 1863.
[44]Donnelly MSS, C. Aldrich to I. D., January 21, 1862.
[45]*Ibid.*, N. Tefft to I. D., April 16, 1864.

ing contracts, despite the fact that Joseph Wheelock had enlisted his aid and promised to support him in future campaigns. One of his friends, James Heaton Baker, cautioned Donnelly, "Remember your friends—for there lies the strength of a politician. Loyalty to friends is to a politician what *hair* was to Samson—stick to the press!"[46] When the *Press* failed to receive the contract, Wheelock never forgave Donnelly and throughout his life never ignored an opportunity to attack him. Alexander Ramsey, who was vitally interested in the *Press*, refused to participate in the argument. Eventually he arranged a merger of newspapers involved, so that the *Press* gained the printing contract. It was Ramsey's turn to make friends through Donnelly's mistakes.

Donnelly became Minnesota's fourth congressman. He had fought his way through the political maze; behind him lay the broken friendships and disillusioned allies that haunt the memory of every public man. He hoped his future would be compensation enough for the struggle he had waged—the national scene lay before him with all its problems and possibilities.

[46]*Ibid.*, J. Wheelock to I. D., December 18, 1862; J. Baker to I. D., December 21, 1862.

CHAPTER VI

A New Congressman
1863-1864

> *One never expected from a Congressman more than good intentions and public spirit.*
>
> HENRY ADAMS

DONNELLY'S election to federal office increased greatly his role in state politics and intra-party affairs. Patronage and political friendships assumed greater importance. He was besieged with requests from politicians who were seeking positions. Harassed by demands for jobs, Donnelly solved the problem by drawing up lists of names of men deemed worthy of appointment to positions of trust. Ramsey, confronted with the same problem, suggested that they share in all appointments, especially since Donnelly's closest friends were members of Ramsey's organization.[1] Donnelly agreed and the policy worked to the advantage of both men.

As a congressman, Donnelly had political obligations both to individuals and to the state party organization. He could not refuse the Republican State Central Committee's invitation to campaign in favor of Colonel Stephen Miller, the party's gubernatorial candidate. Despite the physical strain involved in a speaking tour, Donnelly willingly undertook to repay Miller for his faithfulness during the congressional race.[2] Traveling at his own expense in a two-week-long canvass of the critical districts of the state, Donnelly rapped the Democratic party for its "secession sympathiz-

[1] Donnelly MSS, A. Ramsey to I. D., May 23, 1863.
[2] *Ibid.*, W. Wilson to I. D., September 18, 1863; I. D. to K. D., September 27, 1863.

ing politicians,"[3] while reassuring Republican partisans of the certainty of the colonel's election. Miller's clear-cut victory gave Donnelly another close tie with state politics.

His political debts repaid in the autumn of 1863, Donnelly was eager to leave Minnesota for Philadelphia and Washington. Hopeful of silencing the disparaging rumors and false charges which had gained currency since he moved to Minnesota in 1856, Donnelly asked a friend to place an announcement in the Philadelphia press to the effect that Ignatius Donnelly was to be in the city.[4] Although he was eager to confront his accusers, nothing came of his efforts; the rumors persisted.

Washington, D.C., where Donnelly arrived on Thanksgiving Day, had been at war too long.[5] It was a gay, callous city—a political community filled with intrigue for place, contaminated with jealous rivalry, rife with bitter faction, and ever alert to schemes, plans, and rumors. Money, much of it lavishly spent for dinners, dances, and merrymaking, set the tone of the community. One observer thought Washington's citizens had decided to profit from and enjoy the war even if they could not win it.[6]

New congressmen not only failed to attract favorable notice in Washington, but even senior members of the House of Representatives were viewed with disdain. Henry Adams, writing with the familiarity of an insider, noted:

> Newspaper-men as a rule had no great respect for the lower House; Senators had less; and Cabinet officers had none at all. Indeed, one day . . . a Secretary impatiently broke out: "You can't use tact on a Congressman! A Congressman is a hog! You must take a stick and hit him on the snout!"[7]

Little wonder then that the Washington newspapers made no mention of Ignatius Donnelly.

The nature of Washington society upset his personal life. He lacked the money to buy or rent a large house. To have Kate with him in a hotel, he would have been forced to send his children to a boarding school. For his wife, this was impossible. She decided to take the children to Philadelphia, where she could live with her parents.

---

[3] St. Paul *Press*, October 17, 1863.
[4] Donnelly MSS, I. D. to McDevitt, October 10, 1863 (copy).
[5] *Ibid.*, Diary, November 24 to 27, 1863.
[6] Margaret Leech, *Reveille in Washington, 1860–1865* (New York: Harper & Bros., 1941), p. 232.
[7] Adams, *The Education of Henry Adams*, p. 261.

Donnelly disliked the separation,[8] and it proved even more painful when he learned that his children had contracted dysentery. The death of the youngest while Donnelly was en route to Philadelphia left him deeply grieved.[9]

Although three of Donnelly's children survived, he felt the loss most keenly.[10] He refused to accept social invitations in the months that followed. Kate grew concerned with the implications of this isolation. "I wish sometimes that you had gone around Washington where you were invited so as to obtain more personal influence," she wrote; "You are in the whirl there yet not of it & may lose opportunities by non acquaintance with the ropes."[11]

While Donnelly struggled to master the intricacies of congressional life, he was increasingly aware of the close relationship between state and national politics. At the suggestion of David Heaton, Donnelly favored Schuyler Colfax for Speaker of the House of Representatives, but Aldrich and William S. King advocated Elihu Washburne of Illinois. Washburne and Aldrich were close friends. Furthermore, the Illinois congressman's brother, William Washburn (he retained the original family spelling), lived in Minneapolis. Very wealthy, a lumberman and miller, Washburn was emerging as one of the most ambitious and influential politicians in the city. Many Minneapolis Republicans, learning of Donnelly's support of Colfax, were genuinely disappointed.[12]

Donnelly soon discovered that King's interest in the speakership involved not only loyalty to William Washburn but also his hope of remaining postmaster of the House.[13] But in the wake of the sharp criminations following Aldrich's defeat in the senatorial contest, King had alienated Donnelly. This triggered so bitter an intra-party feud in Minneapolis that even Congressman William Windom, notoriously cautious about party protocol, suggested reconciliation to both King and Donnelly.[14] Windom favored giving King the postmastership.

From the very outset of his break with King, Donnelly's friends, especially those close to Ramsey, wanted King ousted. "He dares

[8]Donnelly MSS, K. D. to I. D., November 29, 1863.

[9]*Ibid.*, Diary, January 27, 1864.

[10]*Ibid.*, M. Faiver to I. D., February 7, 1864.

[11]*Ibid.*, K. D. to I. D., April 25, 1864.

[12]*Ibid.*, H. Morrison to I. D., November 13, 1863.

[13]*Ibid.*, H. Fletcher to I. D., August 8, 1864.

[14]*Ibid.*, W. Windom to I. D., June 4, 1863; W. Windom to I. D., September 17, 1863.

you to oppose him and courts your opposition," warned Rochester editor David Blakely; "securing the Postmastership will only put money into his hands."[15] Governor Stephen Miller was equally adamant: "They won't be conciliated and ought to be destroyed."[16] Even Donnelly's law partner and campaign aide, A. M. Hayes, insisted, "King and all that crowd *secretly hate you*."[17]

Yet there were reasons to appease King. Having gained control of the Minnesota *State News*, King had a monopoly over the Republican newspapers in Minneapolis.[18] Perhaps even more important was Donnelly's awareness that he owed his success to the fact that he was a compromise between powerful rivals. Accommodating the Minneapolis Republicans might not be too high a price to pay if King would promise to be more co-operative.

When Donnelly indorsed King for the postmastership many of Donnelly's friends were dubious of King's assurances. "If he redeems the promise," wrote a supporter from Minneapolis, "I shall be both glad and disappointed."[19] King did not redeem any pledge made to Donnelly. In fact, claiming that Donnelly had done for him what he had done for Aldrich, King became even more antagonistic than ever.

At the time when Donnelly lived in Washington the Minnesota First Regiment's enlistment period was almost over. The War Department, seeking to retain seasoned soldiers, offered a bonus of $400 to the men of the First as enlistment bounty. But Donnelly knew that the men could obtain $600 if they could re-enlist at home. He promptly organized a movement to send the First Minnesota home.

In a carefully worded letter to Secretary of War Edwin Stanton, Donnelly requested that the men be sent back to Minnesota. This regiment, he pointed out, had been the first unit tendered the national government at the outbreak of the war, and although originally recruited for only ninety days, it had re-enlisted as a body for three years when requested to do so. The First Minnesota had served in every major engagement, suffered heavy casualties, and had an unblemished reputation. Allowing these men to return to Minnesota would not only boost their morale but enliven the spirits of the peo-

[15]*Ibid.*, D. Blakely to I. D., October 23, 1863.
[16]*Ibid.*, S. Miller to I. D., November 20, 1863.
[17]*Ibid.*, A. Hayes to I. D., December 21, 1863.
[18]*Ibid.*, G. Keith to I. D., November 17, 1863.
[19]*Ibid.*, H. Fletcher to I. D., December 21, 1863.

ple at home. Donnelly discreetly omitted mentioning the enlarged bounty.[20]

When Secretary of War Stanton agreed to release the men for re-enlistment in Minnesota, the congressional delegation planned a celebration for the soldiers. Vice-President Hannibal Hamlin and Secretary Stanton were guest speakers at a banquet arranged by Ramsey, Wilkinson, Windom, and Donnelly. Although each man spoke briefly, Donnelly proved to be the orator of the day and was so dramatic and effective that he was reported in both the Washington *Chronicle* and Chicago *Tribune.*[21]

When the committee appointments for the House were announced, Donnelly found that he was a member of the Select Committee for the Pacific Railroad. There was high interest in railroads in Minnesota but much difference of opinion about whether to support a state-wide network or a transcontinental system. Each town's citizens wanted it to be a railroad terminal. Most people, realizing that a transcontinental system was a long-range project, concentrated on securing the local route. Realistically, Donnelly favored a state-wide system that could be integrated with a transcontinental. His attitude raised a storm of protest among the rival towns. But Donnelly introduced legislation providing a land grant to finance the construction of a state-chartered line.

The defeat of his People's Pacific Railroad Bill left him disappointed because he had hoped to sponsor at least one piece of successful legislation. In a long letter to the St. Paul *Press,* Donnelly explained that the setback was caused by a combination of such diverse factors as the fears of the Canadian Grand Trunk Railroad Company, Chicago's jealousy of a new terminal at the head of Lake Superior, the hostility of the Central Pacific, and the general objection in Congress to giving land grants to state-chartered lines.[22] Since the last of these reasons would probably prove the most effective, Donnelly began working for enactment of the Northern Pacific Bill which would accomplish everything he wanted but under a federally chartered line. Because the Northern Pacific measure favored St. Paul by connecting with the St. Paul & Pacific Railway rather than the Lake Superior & Mississippi Railroad, Donnelly tried to keep peace between the lines, but his major concern was that the terminal should stay in Minnesota.

[20]*Ibid.,* I. D. to E. Stanton, January 12, 1864 (copy).
[21]Quoted in the St. Cloud *Democrat,* February 13, 1864.
[22]June 3, 1864.

The influential Faribault *Central Republican,* whose reform-minded editor decried the railroad rivalry as petty selfishness, asked why Donnelly concerned himself with which town should get a railroad while the fate of the nation was so precarious.[23] In fact, nothing would have pleased Donnelly more than to participate in the serious councils that argued out the political strategy of the war, but he was a junior congressman. He was, however, granted time for two major speeches. Both earned him recognition and distinction as an orator.

His first speech, dealing with immigration and presented on February 27, 1864, was in response to President Lincoln's appeal for a systematic policy. Donnelly, who had been thinking about attracting settlers to Minnesota, was quite familiar with the subject, but he did spend a good deal of time gathering additional statistics. As a new proposal, he advocated the creation of a federal immigration bureau to protect the unsuspecting aliens from abuse and to encourage immigration from Europe. A thoroughgoing Jeffersonian, Donnelly refused to see the immigrant as labor for growing industries and wanted the newcomer to take up farming.

With nearly one billion [acres] of unsettled lands on one side of the Atlantic, and with many millions of poor oppressed people on the other, let them organize the exodus which needs must come, and build, if necessary, a bridge of gold across the chasm which divides them, that the chosen races of mankind may occupy the chosen lands of the world.[24]

It was on this note, one so dramatic and reminiscent of his address to the Democratic rally in Philadelphia, that Donnelly closed his speech.

The newspaper reception of this first speech was almost entirely favorable. The Washington *Chronicle* praised Donnelly for his "marked ability in the presentation of his facts and figures, and rare discretion and common sense in his comments."[25] Most Minnesota Republican papers applauded his statesmanship, but the Democratic St. Paul *Pioneer* made light of the speech. Facetiously the *Pioneer's* editor reported that the speech had been specifically called to Lincoln's attention. The President then observed that there was "a fellow out in Illinois, who stole a blind horse and sold

[23]February 17, 1864.
[24]*Congressional Globe,* 38th Cong., 1st sess., p. 857. I have preferred, however, to use the pamphlet version of the speech which corrects the spelling and punctuation errors appearing in the *Globe.*
[25]Quoted in the Hastings *Independent,* March 17, 1864.

him to the owner by means of making him up with a glass eye."
Then he added, "Every member of Congress from the West for the
last twenty years has been making the same speech."[26]

The *Pioneer* was undoubtedly right, but its comment did not detract from the quality of Donnelly's address. Sixteen pages in length,
it was presented entirely from memory. Years later he explained the
purpose of such speeches.

> Go into the Hall of the House. There is the Hon. Blank of Kansas, or
> Oregon, or Maine reading a written speech on the great question of the
> day. True, nobody listens to him; and if you undertake to follow him you
> find that speech is but a compilation of the thoughts of others on the same
> subject. But Blank prints five thousand copies of that speech, at his own
> expense, mark you, and sends them all over his district. They penetrate
> into remote forests;—into little villages;—into scattered farm houses;—
> they reach people who have no books, no libraries, perhaps no newspapers; good, honest laborious people who want to do right, if they can only
> understand what right is. They read that speech;—spell it out by the light
> of the tallow candle or the wood fire;—to them it is a *great* speech; read
> in the mighty capital of the nation, as they think, while statesmen and
> patriots hung trembling upon every word. In short it is to them a *valuable
> means of education upon the great questions which most nearly concern
> their welfare.*[27]

But in 1864 personal recognition was Donnelly's goal as much as
political education of the people back home.

Donnelly's second speech, dealing with reconstruction policy, was
much more effective. Compared with other discussions of the subject, Donnelly's views were intelligent, restrained, and tolerant. Although he adopted an ultra-radical Republican position, the
speech provided a historical and philosophical basis for Republican
policies rather than the conventional flood of abuse, irrational scorn,
and unremitting rage. Making the peace, not waging the war, offered the real challenge. "The struggle will pass," he warned,
"from the field of battle to the arena of politics; to that terrible
arena where death can be inflicted and no sword be lifted, where a
nation can perish and no blood mark the spot where it fell."[28] The
only genuine problem of legislative concern, as Donnelly saw it, was
the prevention of another civil war.

He unhesitatingly confessed his frontier scorn for the dangerous
myth of state sovereignty.

[26]March 27, 1864.
[27]St. Paul *Dispatch*, February 23, 1870.
[28]*Congressional Globe*, 38th Cong., 1st sess., pp. 2035–39.

We who come, Mr. Speaker, from the far West have not that deep and ingrained veneration for State power which is to be found among the inhabitants of some of the older states. We have found that State lines, State names, State organizations, are in most cases the veriest creatures of accident. To us there is no savor of antiquity about them. Our people move into a region of country and *make* the State. We feel ourselves the off-shoots of the nation. We look to the nation for our protection.

The United States Congress should never be reduced to a Polish Diet; state rights must be curtailed.

Donnelly regretted that President Lincoln's plan for reconstruction fell short of a proper goal. Too much of it depended upon contingencies: a successor might repeal it or the Supreme Court might annul it. The nation's welfare could not be trusted to individual loyalty oaths as the President suggested. Lincoln's was a charitable view, not a practical one. Donnelly indorsed the more stringent measures advocated by Henry W. Davis of Maryland. If these were not adopted, Donnelly said, "I am for an amendment of the Constitution to prohibit slavery as soon as it is attainable. I am for any and every measure which will add in this respect to the security of the people."

But Lincoln was not a target for Donnelly's criticism. With a keen eye for the picturesque, Donnelly insisted that the President was not to be underrated. "He is a great man," Donnelly told the House. "Great not after the old models of the world, but with a homely and original greatness. He will stand out in future ages in the story of these crowded and confused times with wonderful distinctness." To Donnelly, Lincoln's only shortcoming was his desire to patch up rather than rebuild the government.

Angry Minnesota Democrats criticized the speech and the St. Paul *Pioneer* devoted five days of editorial comment to it. In a series of misinterpretations and distortions the paper denounced Donnelly as unfit to serve the state in the House of Representatives. Shall we send back to Washington, the editor asked, a man who looked upon his state as "the veriest creature of accident," a man who had no respect for its boundaries, its name, or any of its institutions.[29] To the *Pioneer*, Donnelly was worse than the ordinary abolitionists— worse even than the treasonous William Lloyd Garrison. After almost a week of castigation the paper's tirade concluded:

To call it a speech is hardly a proper use of terms, for from beginning to end it does not display a single element of even passable statesmanship.

[29]September 9, 1864.

It is the old spirit of the fanatic and his monotonous one idea. It is a rodo-montade, full of empty bluster and boasting, of passionate adjurations, of morbid sentimentality, and of rhetorical pyrotechnics. It goes up like a rocket and comes down like a stick.[30]

Donnelly probably ignored the criticism but welcomed the publicity; he was increasingly concerned about his renomination. William D. Washburn was threatening to reclaim Aldrich's seat for Minneapolis. Two of his brothers, Washburn could justly boast, were forces to be reckoned with in Republican caucuses; he hoped to be the third to gain recognition. Donnelly's political informants noted that tact and discretion characterized the "Washburn boom."[31] By mid-March, 1864, a whispering campaign recounting the most scurrilous stories about Donnelly was well under way. Even to the most loyal Donnelly supporters, the stories were a little "stagger-ing."

It is charged that double dealing & treachery of the meanest kind has marked your whole political career in Minnesota, that in the late senatorial contest you deceived & betrayed both the friends of Gov. Ramsey & Col. Aldrich; that you did the same thing in the controversy between the *Press* & *Union* for the printing . . . & further that to conceal your perifity [*sic*] you told falsehoods until you have become the very synonym for liar.
Furthermore it is alleged . . . you fled in disgrace [from Philadelphia] having been engaged in swindling operations involving many poor and honest people, among others your own mother, who was defrauded out of 4000 dollars. That during the past winter you have been twice arrested on criminal charges, that you are in so much disgrace that you can have scarcely any influence in Congress favorable to your district or the State. . . .[32]

There was no way to reply to such accusations.

Donnelly's shrewdest advisers were also his boldest supporters. "Do not . . . allow your fears, or desires for success lead you to make extravagant promises," warned George Keith, a federal ap-pointee in Minneapolis. True, the contest would be a severe one; Washburn had unlimited funds if he cared to use them, but it was *"brains versus money,"* as Keith saw it, and in such a case money had much to fear.[33] Furthermore, Governor Stephen Miller, who had an intense dislike of the Minneapolis politicians who were

[30]September 14, 1864.
[31]Donnelly MSS, G. Keith to I. D., January 13, 1864; H. Fletcher to I. D., January 20, and February 23, 1864.
[32]*Ibid.*, H. Fletcher to I. D., March 1, 1864; D. Blakely to I. D., March 13, 1864; and W. L. Wilson to I. D., May 30, 1864.
[33]*Ibid.*, G. Keith to I. D., January 13, 1864.

Donnelly's rivals, assured him of the support of the state office-holders. Even more important, Donnelly had persuaded Alexander Ramsey to write to the leaders of his organization expressing the hope that Donnelly would be re-elected to Congress.[34]

Unfortunately for Donnelly, Ramsey did not ask the St. Paul *Press* to indorse his candidacy. This meant that Donnelly lacked the support of a Republican paper in St. Paul and Minneapolis. In a direct appeal to the *Press,* he wrote both Joseph Wheelock and Fred Driscoll, who shared control of editorial policy, asking for an indorsement of his renomination. Wheelock, in whom the loss of the state printing contract two years before still rankled, flatly refused. The *Press,* he said, would not abstain from criticism.[35] Donnelly hoped for more from Driscoll because it had been his newspaper which had been favored for the state printing against Wheelock. But Driscoll brazenly replied that "in all candor I *cannot favor your renomination.*" Donnelly could take small comfort in his assurance that the "*Press* will *not* be used to *benefit* or *injure* individual ambitions or interests, whatever may be the private opinions of the proprietors.[36]

While Donnelly failed to win the support of St. Paul's major Republican newspaper, George Keith had approached William S. King's brother Dana, the editor of the Minneapolis *State Atlas.* Dana King, a heavy investor in McLeod County real estate, especially in the town of Greenleaf, wanted the Federal Land Office moved there. He asked Keith if Donnelly would promise to move the land office and put him in charge of it if he would support his candidacy in the *State Atlas?* Keith promptly outlined to Donnelly the possibilities implicit in King's proposal. First, it offered newspaper support in Hennepin County. Second, it might lead to a division of the King brothers, and, third, it could result in a means of controlling William S. King.[37]

Donnelly accepted King's proposition. The *State Atlas* performed an editorial somersault early in April of 1864. By May it was the most rabidly pro-Donnelly organ in Minnesota.

Dana King's defection provoked a sharp clash with his brother. Dana was removed from the editorship of the newspaper, lost his temper, and told his brother that William Washburn was a "thick-

---

[34] *Ibid.,* H. Fletcher to I. D., March 12, 1864.
[35] *Ibid.,* J. Wheelock to I. D., February 17, 1864.
[36] *Ibid.,* F. Driscoll to I. D., February 11, 1864.
[37] *Ibid.,* G. Keith to I. D., March 28, 1864.

skulled brainless Ass."[38] By early summer the *State Atlas* was again advocating Washburn for Congress.

Donnelly's friends, however, were far too skeptical about the Kings to believe William King's repudiation of Dana. After some inquiry, they agreed that the entire episode had been a carefully contrived scheme. Dana, they wrote Donnelly, was secretly editing the *State Atlas,* guaranteed of victory regardless of who was elected to Congress.[39]

But Donnelly was still committed to giving Dana King the land office at Greenleaf. Unable to make a final decision, Donnelly honored part of his promise by naming him chief of the McLeod County land office, but he hesitated to shift the headquarters to Greenleaf.[40] After a year in office King resigned in disgust. "I trusted your honor," he wrote to Donnelly, "while all my friends denounced you, and finally denounced *me* for laboring *for* you, and trusting you. . . . The result shows that . . . while your enemies charge you with being a *knave,* they, with equal good reason, charged me a fool."[41] Dana King had obviously been sincere. Donnelly's equivocation had led to duplicity!

An incumbent congressman usually has an easier campaign during a presidential election year. As a supporter of the administration, he has the advantage of nationwide publicity; as an opponent of the regime, he can ignore his local antagonist and focus attention on national issues. Although 1864 was a presidential election year, it offered no advantage for Donnelly. An opponent of Lincoln's reconstruction policy, his radical label prevented his association with the President's Union party. Furthermore, Donnelly's closest friends were convinced that Lincoln was unfit to cope with the problems facing the nation. State Treasurer Charles Scheffer wrote: "I hope for the sake of the Union, that Lincoln will not be renominated. He is honest and upright no doubt, but we need a great leader in these hard times & not one who must be pushed by the people."[42] Lincoln's renomination weakened Donnelly's candidacy by embarrassing the less well known Radical Republicans.

Donnelly needed something that would increase his prestige, something that would make his renomination a credit to the state,

---

[38] *Ibid.,* H. Fletcher to I. D., May 17, 1864.
[39] *Ibid.,* B. F. Baker to I. D., May 26, 1864; H. Fletcher to I. D., June 9, 1864.
[40] *Ibid.,* J. Wilson to I. D., August 27, 1864.
[41] *Ibid.,* D. King to I. D., June 10, 1865.
[42] *Ibid.,* C. Scheffer to I. D., February 1, 1864.

something that would remove the life-and-death power over his nomination from the hands of the local politicians. He needed an issue that would rally the independent newspapers to his side and win over the people to such an extent that the politicians would hardly dare refuse to return him.

By chance he hit on such an issue when on February 7, in a House chamber that was nearly empty and before a gallery of less than thirty, Donnelly presented a brief, general statement on Indian reform. There was no gallery reaction, but his correspondence carried a surprise. Governor Stephen Miller, who had read the speech, informed Donnelly that the Indian Office's corrupt practices supplied money to Donnelly's political opponents. Pitying the Indians, whose interests needed protection, Miller suggested that Donnelly look into Indian affairs.[43] Donnelly recognized that the nation's Indian policy was confused if not corrupt. This was an era when an Indian agent who received a salary of $1,500 a year could retire at the end of four years in office with a $50,000 bank account.[44] Appointment to an Indian agency was more lucrative than the Liverpool consulship!

Following Miller's suggestion, Donnelly quietly investigated Minnesota's Indian affairs. To his surprise, he found that a treaty had been negotiated with the Chippewa tribe. This treaty, as ratified by the Senate, included a very modest sum of money which the Indians and their lobbyist, former United States Senator Henry M. Rice, accepted. Interestingly enough, when the treaty was submitted to the House, the financial request had been increased tenfold over the amount voted in the Senate. Already suspicious, Donnelly was convinced of fraud because, even though the tribe lived in his district, he had not been asked to support the bill.

His findings led him to write to Thaddeus Stevens, chairman of the House Ways and Means Committee, explaining in detail the "overcharges of the grossest kind." To an itemized list of costs Donnelly added, in a most acrid style, his suggestion for effecting substantial economies. Stevens killed the appropriation measure in the committee. The Secretary of the Interior withdrew the treaty, and Donnelly published his letter to Stevens, circulating it throughout Minnesota.[45]

[43]*Ibid.*, S. Miller to I. D., February 13, 1864.
[44]Ellis Paxson Oberholtzer, *A History of the United States since the Civil War* (New York: Macmillan Co., 1917), I, 371.
[45]Donnelly MSS, May 2, 1864 (copy).

Episcopal Bishop Whipple and Roman Catholic Bishop Grace wrote approvingly of Donnelly's stand against the fraud-ridden Indian Office.[46] Donnelly replied forcefully to Whipple: "I shall continue to strive to do right though it lead to shades of private and obscure life. I fear that I have lopped one branch from a great Upas of fraud and corruption."[47] Bishop Grace received similar assurances. More interesting reactions came from thoroughly excited politicians who reluctantly admitted that popular sentiment was completely on Donnelly's side.

But Donnelly discovered that he had made enemies among men he could ill afford to antagonize. One of these was the highly influential Minneapolis Republican John S. Pillsbury, a personal friend of Chippewa Indian agent Ashley C. Morrill, who was reputedly responsible for the estimates submitted to the House by the Secretary of the Interior. Pillsbury insisted that Morrill was free from the taint which infected most Indian agents.[48]

Pillsbury's actions probably troubled Donnelly a good deal, but he was concerned with the newspaper reaction to his sensational disclosures. Joseph Wheelock of the St. Paul *Press* could scarcely believe that Donnelly had accomplished anything, but he could not deny that a fraud of the worst type had probably been averted. In reviewing the matter Wheelock damned with faint praise by concluding that Donnelly would have made a better case if he had known a little more geography and a good deal more about Indians; but he added that he hoped Donnelly would press to the bottom of the matter to see if there were genuine fraud and corruption in the Indian Office.[49]

Nettled by Wheelock's editorial, Donnelly wrote an open letter to the *Press* demanding to know why the newspaper doubted his honest attempt to prevent a fraud. He emphatically denied that the letter to Thaddeus Stevens had been a "secret circular" designed to embarrass the Indian Office. In reply to the suggestion that there be a full investigation Donnelly promised to "rip open this whole Indian system and let the light of day into its dark places."[50]

Wheelock's answer to Donnelly's letter was an invitation to

[46]*Ibid.*, Bishop Whipple to I. D., May 17, 1864; Bishop Grace to I. D., May 18, 1864.
[47]Minnesota Historical Society, Whipple MSS, I. D. to Bishop Whipple, May 25, 1864.
[48]Donnelly MSS, E. Clark to I. D., June 7, 1864.
[49]St. Paul *Press*, May 22, 1864.
[50]*Ibid.*, May 30, 1864.

Morrill to write a defense of the Indian Office. On June 1, the *Press* published an invective-laden editorial rejoicing in Morrill's ability to clear himself of Donnelly's accusations. When the full facts were known, Wheelock asserted, "Our young Representative . . . will hasten to atone for the injury he has inflicted."[51] But on June 5, without even waiting for a comment from Donnelly, the editor harshly criticized him for blocking the treaty. "Mr. Donnelly shows either an astounding ignorance or an astounding disregard of the wishes of his constituents," Wheelock charged, "when he congratulates himself on having defeated the fulfillment of a treaty whose object was to relieve them of these vexatious neighbors."[52]

But almost every newspaper in Minnesota took issue with the *Press*. The Hastings *Independent* praised Donnelly for reprinting the circular; the St. Cloud *Democrat* heartily indorsed his courage; and the Faribault *Central Republican* joined in the chorus denouncing the *Press* as being both unjust and fallacious in its charges. The Chippewa were not a menace; they had not attacked the frontier posts as had the Sioux a few years earlier.

The sharp debate in the Republican newspapers helped Donnelly's cause. Colonel D. A. Robertson, an influential Democrat, informed him by confidential letter that the St. Paul *Pioneer* would publish anything Donnelly wanted in print.[53] For two weeks the various county newspapers criticized the "dictatorial," "arbitrary," and "faction-led" policies of the St. Paul *Press*. The attack was led by W. B. Mitchell, editor of the St. Cloud *Democrat*, a close friend of Governor Stephen Miller and one of Donnelly's federal appointees.

It was soon evident that Wheelock had blundered in attacking Donnelly on the Chippewa treaty. As Mitchell wrote to Donnelly; "The fact is, the *Press* has done you an immense amount of good. . . . The *people* have become aroused, to canvass the matter, and are firmly impressed with the belief that you are their champion."[54] The support for Donnelly was so complete that even the usually cautious Republican German-language newspaper the

[51] *Ibid.*, June 1, 1864.
[52] *Ibid.*, June 5, 1864.
[53] Donnelly had appointed D. A. Robertson's son to West Point. Robertson had pledged support to Donnelly, even offering to talk with St. Paul Bishop Grace about helping Donnelly with Irish voters. Donnelly MSS, D. A. Robertson to I. D., April 8 and June 10, 1864.
[54] *Ibid.*, W. Mitchell to I. D., June 17, 1864.

Minnesota *Staats-Zeitung* entered the argument in his behalf.[55] By July 1, Mitchell decided to drop the issue since, as he put it, he saw "no glory in kicking a dead dog."[56]

Thoroughly discredited, Wheelock capitulated completely. He wrote Donnelly a personal letter explaining that the *Press* was not against his candidacy for Congress and asking that he not confuse disagreement on the Chippewa affair with opposition. Only complete defeat could have forced a man of Wheelock's unyielding temper into such abject surrender.[57]

While the newspapers debated in public, Governor Stephen Miller patiently undertook the difficult task of healing the wounds caused by Donnelly's exposé. The governor visited his friend John S. Pillsbury to discuss the Indian episode. Pillsbury told Miller that Morrill was "one of the purest men he ever knew and would not wrong a living being out of a dollar." But Miller advised Pillsbury to try to grasp Donnelly's motives—he was attacking the general corruption of the Indian Office. When the governor left Minneapolis, Pillsbury was undecided.[58] "Honest John," as Pillsbury came to be called in Minnesota politics, remained uncommitted for twenty days. Finally, he wrote Donnelly that, although he disapproved of the Indian affair, he would support Donnelly's candidacy for Congress.[59]

Cheered by the news, Donnelly prepared to return to Minnesota in time for the county indorsing conventions. On July 23 in St. Paul's International House, he awaited the outcome of the various caucuses. Hennepin County, as the stronghold of the opposition, concerned him most. Donnelly had heard that William King was hurrying from Washington to participate in the caucus. But even without King there had been a hopeless division among the delegates. King then arranged for a conference with Donnelly.[60]

The St. Paul *Press* sneered, King "sent for Hon. Ignatius Donnelly, who went up on the afternoon train and held a lengthy interview with King in the office of the Minneapolis *Atlas*." The result was an agreement in which Donnelly "pledged to surrender the entire control of the patronage and politics of Hennepin County into the

[55] *Ibid.*, C. Scheffer to I. D., June 25, 1864.
[56] *Ibid.*, W. Mitchell to I. D., July 1, 1864.
[57] *Ibid.*, J. Wheelock to I. D., July 1, 1864.
[58] *Ibid.*, S. Miller to I. D., June 23, 1864.
[59] *Ibid.*, J. Pillsbury to I. D., July 10, 1864.
[60] *Ibid.*, D. King to I. D., July 25, 1864.

hands of Mr. King," who, in turn, was to allow a straight Donnelly ticket to pass the convention.[61] Wheelock may have been guessing, but the hot-tempered King sent a rebuttal letter to the St. Paul *Pioneer* denying that there had been any deal. The *Press*, King wrote, hated Donnelly because it "could not bend and prostitute him to every unworthy purpose" it had in view.[62]

When the Second Congressional District convention gathered in St. Paul, the delegates renominated Donnelly with a minimum of enthusiasm. In his brief acceptance speech, he tried to close the rift between the factions. If any unkind word had been said in the heat of battle, he withdrew it; if anyone had been offended, he apologized; he wished to be a friend and servant of all the people. He closed by coupling this plea for unity with further platitudes urging moderation in the times ahead.

The St. Paul *Press* accepted Donnelly's candidacy only because he was a Radical Republican and not on the grounds of his Indian record, which it termed "merely a clap trap appeal to popular prejudices without a shadow of foundation."[63] The attitude of the *Press*, plus Wheelock's candid letter, led Donnelly into one of the major blunders of his career. A few days after the nomination he wrote a private letter to Joseph Wheelock suggesting that they declare a moratorium on their argument until after the election. "The judicial and electoral tickets are both at stake and this is no time for those who support the government to be divided by collateral issues," he warned. "I would therefore earnestly request, for the sake of the entire ticket, that you will defer all further discussion upon this question [Indian affairs] until after the election, when if you desire, I will be glad to renew an investigation into the whole subject."[64]

This letter offered Wheelock an opportunity for revenge. Even though it was a private letter, Wheelock published it. The implication was obvious: Donnelly was not a man of high principle, but a meager politician seeking sanctuary behind the cloak of party necessity.

Bluff Aleck, William Windom, and the venal *Press* have captured Donnelly, asserted the Democratic St. Paul *Pioneer*. What, it asked,

[61]July 29, 1864.
[62]St. Paul *Pioneer*, August 3, 1864.
[63]August 3, 1864.
[64]St. Paul *Press*, August 6, 1864.

could have caused Donnelly to suffer such humiliation?[65] William King's *State Atlas* demanded to know why Donnelly was trying to "hush up" the Chippewa scandal? Was it really, as the *Press* had claimed, nothing more than a "clap trap" appeal? Or had Donnelly blundered? The *Atlas* asked its readers to face the facts. Donnelly was either a "Fool or Knave!"[66] "God pity him," thundered the editorial page of the Faribault *Central Republican;* "may the people lay him aside as the child throws away the rattle-box."[67]

With mock sanctimoniousness, the *Press* defended Donnelly. "We agree to disagree for the present, in order to prevent all risks of disturbing the harmony of the party," its editor asserted.[68] Feigning innocence, it failed to understand all the hullabaloo, especially among Republican papers which should have appreciated Donnelly's good sense. The editor of the St. Cloud *Democrat,* feeling discretion the better part of valor, remained silent.

Donnelly realized that he had committed an error. He had embarrassed his closest friends in an attempt to win the half-hearted support of the *Press,* a very high price to pay. Wheelock, in publishing the personal letter, had proven that he rejected all offers of friendship.

But the political blunder lost its personal significance when he heard from Kate, who had been expecting a child and had remained in Philadelphia, that she had had a miscarriage. He considered returning to the East. But despite her weakened condition and her distress, Kate Donnelly stubbornly insisted that Donnelly continue his campaign.[69] But she admitted, "It is hard to be a politician's wife for she has to bear the responsibilities of the family."[70]

Saddened as he was, Donnelly was also a seasoned politician. He mapped out a comprehensive campaign that would take him into every area of his huge district. From September 28 to November 7 he planned to make at least one speech every day. He anticipated meeting local party leaders, listening to their political small talk, and making notes for future campaigns. His most important conference, however, was held in Minneapolis, where he joined Governor

[65] St. Paul *Pioneer,* August 7, 1864.
[66] Minneapolis *State Atlas,* August 10, 1864.
[67] Faribault *Central Republican,* August 10, 1864.
[68] St. Paul *Press,* August 13, 1864.
[69] Donnelly MSS, K. D. to I. D., September 1 and 14, 1864; C. McCaffrey to I. D., September 28, 1864; and K. D. to I. D., October 2, 1864.
[70] *Ibid.,* K. D. to I. D., October 19, 1864.

Stephen Miller for a dignified political dinner at the home of John S. Pillsbury.[71]

Donnelly received very little support from the Republican newspapers during his campaign. The St. Paul *Press*, scarcely reporting his meetings, did nothing to defend him from the vicious criticism of the *Pioneer*. In fact, Donnelly's name appeared less in the Republican St. Paul newspapers during the campaign month of October than during any previous month of his public life. Only the St. Cloud *Democrat* loyally defended Donnelly during the campaign. "He is always in his place, always sober, alert and ready," wrote Jane Grey Swisshelm in a signed editorial. "A first class parliamentarian, an able and ready debater, and an enthusiastic, backbone Republican," he deserved to be supported.[72]

When the polls closed on November 8, Donnelly could contemplate his exchange with Wheelock; he could reflect on the hundreds of miles he had traveled by buggy and riverboat—some of it with swollen ankles too tender to be placed in any position without pain; and he could ponder the health and happiness of his beloved Kate. Was it worth it? Later, when he received a copy of the Hastings *Independent* discussing the election results and his victory, he could take pleasure in having finally carried his home county—even if by the slim margin of three votes. Lincoln lost it by two.[73]

[71] *Ibid.*, Diary, September 16 to November 7, 1864.

[72] Arthur J. Larson (ed.), *Crusader and Feminist: Letters of Jane Grey Swisshelm, 1858–1865* (St. Paul: Minnesota Historical Society, 1934), pp. 275–76.

[73] Hastings *Independent*, November 17, 1864.

The Trials of a Congressman
1865-1868

Washington destroys a man's Republicanism, the
waste, extravagance, idleness and corruption is shocking and the great men of the nation dwindle into pyg-
mies as you draw near them.

IGNATIUS DONNELLY

As a REPRESENTATIVE to the United States Congress, Ignatius
Donnelly was so disgusted with a father who tried to buy his son a
post at West Point that he asked a Minnesota clergyman, John
Mattocks, to serve as an examiner for all future applicants from
Minnesota. "The nation," said Donnelly, "is entitled to the services
of the ablest young men of the rising generation."[1]

But, indignant as Donnelly was with office peddling, he himself
stooped to selling government secrets to a speculator. Before Donnelly arrived in Washington in December, 1864, John Persch, a
wealthy Philadelphia businessman, suggested that he send him information about government policies affecting the stock exchange.
Donnelly ignored Persch for a year but the speculator pleaded that
with advance knowledge about gold or tobacco, twenty or thirty
thousand dollars could be made. Shortly before his second term,
Donnelly began co-operating with Persch. Donnelly devised a complicated code to transmit confidential data. But Donnelly soon complained, "I have not received a sixpence. On the contrary my good
name has been bandied about and my influence has been impaired

[1]Donnelly MSS, I. D. to J. Mattocks, March 8, 1866 (copy).

here by the report that I was making money in gold operations."[2] One week later, apparently because Persch's reply fell short of Donnelly's expectations, Donnelly ended the arrangement.[3]

It is ironic that Donnelly participated in a dishonest scheme at the same time that public opinion, reacting to the agitation of the reform newspapers, was demanding that he pursue his initial charges regarding the Chippewa. In answer to the demand, he submitted a speech on Indian policy for inclusion in the *Congressional Globe*. Donnelly's proposals were naïve if not utopian. The Indian, guarded by the army and controlled by honest agents, would be educated until he could homestead land and cease to be the object of special legislation.[4] When copies of this message were circulated in Minnesota, there was a favorable response, especially from humanitarians who had been associated with Indian affairs.[5]

But when Donnelly tried to be more practical, he encountered unexpected difficulties. The Speaker of the House named Windom chairman of the Chippewa Indian investigating committee. During the autumn of 1865 Windom traveled to Minnesota to hold hearings. The St. Paul *Pioneer* demanded that Donnelly return,[6] and the Faribault *Central Republican* called on him not to be intimidated,[7] but Donnelly remained in Washington. Finally, he did succeed in having the Indian agent Morrill replaced by one of his political allies. But Donnelly did not realize that he was the butt of ridicule among experienced politicians who felt that he had been misled by the commissioner of Indian Affairs and had frittered away his time.[8]

In spite of having stumbled into the Chippewa affair, he emerged with a reputation of being friendly toward the Indian. Furthermore, in the public mind he remained the hero who had thwarted the fraudulent treaty. The only unfortunate aspect of the episode had been his inept handling of the newspapers. Years later, Donnelly believed that the Indian affair had not worked out badly.

[2]*Ibid.*, I. D. to J. Persch, February 23, 1865 (copy).
[3]*Ibid.*, I. D. to J. Persch, March 4, 1865 (copy).
[4]*Congressional Globe*, 38th Cong., 2d sess., Appendix, pp. 61–65.
[5]Donnelly MSS, J. Brown to I. D., March 12, 1865; S. Lowry to I. D., February 24, 1865.
[6]August 5, 1865.
[7]August 9, 1865.
[8]Minnesota Historical Society, Sibley MSS, R. McLaren to H. Sibley, March 19, 1866.

Important as the Indian matter was to Donnelly, it was insignificant when compared to the political crisis at the close of the Civil War. Radical Republican legislators, determined to provide political equality for the Negro, openly opposed Lincoln's reconstruction program. The President, a remarkably powerful adversary, strengthened by his immense personal popularity with the people, had not only won re-election against the wishes of many politicians, but also had recast the Republican party into the Union party in the election of 1864. Nevertheless, the radicals in the House stood foursquare behind Thaddeus Stevens, the aging, embittered, clubfooted leader of their cause.

When the House adjourned in the spring of 1865, the reconstruction issue remained undecided. Lincoln prepared to be magnanimous; the radicals prepared to impose a Carthaginian peace when the fighting stopped. Lincoln's assassination delayed the showdown. Since Congress was not in session, President Andrew Johnson was free to formulate a program. Only a handful of radical leaders remained in Washington to oversee the President; the others went home.

Donnelly returned to Nininger City determined to put politics out of his mind. He planted trees, fancied himself a scientific gentleman-farmer, and began repairing his large house. Because of the cost and the work involved, Kate opposed finishing what she termed their "big barracks of a house" and improving the Nininger land. She suggested buying a house in Hastings or in St. Paul,[9] but Donnelly wanted to make his home one of the rural show places of Minnesota. He looked forward to owning a handsome estate where he could entertain his Washington friends in fine country style.

Political issues, however, intruded upon his pleasant summer. Stephen Miller's refusal to seek renomination for governor led to the selection of William R. Marshall, banker, railroad executive, and publisher. Marshall, typical of the newer political leaders of the postwar era, was a businessman. Representing an interest rather than a party, he was more at ease with a successful financier or merchant, Republican or Democrat, than with an ardent partisan. Donnelly underestimated the potentialities of this type of leadership.

Except for the fact that the ballot carried a constitutional amend-

[9]Donnelly MSS, K. D. to I. D., March 15, 1865.

ment on Negro suffrage, Donnelly would have ignored the campaign. There were few Negroes in Minnesota in 1865, but he had persuaded the Republican convention to favor their enfranchisement. A spiritless campaign, he feared, would result in a vote so light that the amendment would be defeated. During the second week in October, he began his speaking tour in support of Marshall and Negro suffrage.

When the St. Paul *Pioneer* published repeated and abrupt assertions impugning his honesty, Donnelly, increasingly sensitive to name-calling politics, filed a ten-thousand-dollar libel suit.[10] He was represented by John B. Brisbin, a leading Democrat who knew that the *Pioneer* had sent a special agent to Philadelphia and who had been assured by its editors that the story "was all moonshine." Because the newspaper's actions indicated premeditated malice, Donnelly had a foolproof case. "I am glad I have brought this suit," he wrote Kate. "If I had not my reputation would have been assassinated."[11]

His personal triumph was offset by the state's rejection of the suffrage amendment. Shortly after the election, Donnelly speculated on what he believed to be the real question.

> I challenge the history of the past to produce a single instance where a revolution has occurred under equal laws in the attempt of any class to rise above the level of common rights to oppress any other portion of the population. The selfishness of human nature is not capable of any such effort. But I likewise challenge the historian to point to a single community where unjust laws did not sooner or later result in wars and turbulence—in the effort of one class to perpetuate and the other to resist injustice—both attempts springing from deep seated sentiments of the human heart.
>
> If it is true as argued by some that the history of the world shows that the negro [sic] belongs to an inferior race, that he is unfitted to compete with the white man in the desperate struggle for life, the more reason is there why he should be protected by equal laws.[12]

He remained inflexible on the subject of Negro rights.

His firm support of Radical Republicanism in the new session meant that Donnelly would clash with President Andrew Johnson. A Tennesseean with a deep-seated hatred for the wealthy planter class of the South, Johnson was mistakenly regarded as a mem-

[10] Quoted in the St. Paul *Press*, October 22, 1865; Hastings *Independent*, October 26, 1865.
[11] Donnelly MSS, I. D. to K. D., October 26, 1865.
[12] *Ibid.*, Diary, January 14, 1866.

ber of the radical group. They had hoped that he would call a special session of Congress to deal with reconstruction, but they were sorely disappointed. Johnson launched a program of executive reconstruction quite similar to Lincoln's except for a class bias.

Lacking his predecessor's mandate, Johnson turned for support to conservative Republicans and to War Democrats. His faction in Minnesota was led by Senator Daniel Norton, a War Democrat who had gained his post as a result of a Republican intra-party squabble between Congressman Windom and Senator Morton S. Wilkinson. When the break came between Johnson and the radicals, Norton realized that his only hope of retaining office rested in an alliance with the President.

As the most vigorous Radical Republican in Minnesota, Donnelly was the most vulnerable. He alone had stumped the state for Negro suffrage and had indorsed the Wade-Davis Manifesto. With suffrage defeated and Norton in the Senate, the President's cause seemed to be gaining strength. "I hear it also rumored," wrote one of Donnelly's frightened followers, "that Mr. Norton is to control all the patronage of the state and that you are to have nothing to do with it."[13] Donnelly's anxiety was justified. Norton, writing to William King, confided, "*strictly enter nos* [sic] our friend I. D. is in very hot water."[14]

None of Donnelly's friends underestimated the seriousness of his position. Postmaster William B. Mitchell, Radical Republican editor of the St. Cloud *Democrat,* wrote Donnelly, "Specific word has been sent to me [by Postmaster General Alexander Randall] that unless I came out for Johnson & the Anti-Republican nominee for Congress this fall, I was a 'dead duck.' "[15] Donnelly, given this opportunity to test his judgment of men, could take pride in the friends who rallied to his defense in the face of almost certain dismissal from office.

Although deeply involved in partisan activities, Donnelly's day-by-day congressional life dealt with essentially economic matters. The business of government for him was business—big business. Minnesota businessmen demanded that he be the agent of his constituents. He was subjected to the power of pressure groups. On occasion some of their proposals were dishonest, such as James L.

---

[13]*Ibid.*, H. Wait to I. D., April 4, 1866.
[14]Minnesota Historical Society, King MSS, D. Norton to W. King, March 7, 1866.
[15]Donnelly MSS, W. Mitchell to I. D., August 9, 1866.

Fisk's offer to share half of his portion of the congressional monetary appropriation with Donnelly if he could secure passage of a bill to provide military protection for a wagon road from Minnesota to Montana.[16] But most of the business community was more reputable.

Railroads were of paramount interest in Minnesota, and St. Paul businessmen demanded that Donnelly secure federal aid for the state's roads. "Are you on the Committee on Public Lands?" inquired Jacob H. Stewart, a leading St. Paul politician and railroad executive. "The reason I ask is that from all indications nearly all our RR Cos. will ask an extension of and such additions to their lands . . . and I am sure that you can in no way serve the state and your personal rising reputation as by taking an active part."[17] Stewart's associate, William L. Banning, a St. Paul banker who later became one of Donnelly's intimate friends, spared no words in telling him that the railroads needed a man on the proper congressional committees.[18]

After learning of his post on the Committee on Public Lands, Stewart requested that Donnelly help the Lake Superior & Mississippi Railroad increase its land grant from two to six sections and urge an extension of the time limit for the road's completion. As, Stewart pointed out, the line ran from St. Paul, in the heart of Donnelly's district, to Duluth, in its northeastern extremity. To overcome any hesitation on Donnelly's part, Stewart added:

> This is, of course, on the *Masonic Square*. I hold for you 50 shares of $100 each, of Capital Stock of the Lake Superior RR co. 5 pr ct cash I have already paid up on it and I will agree to keep it up to par for you and subject to your order. . . . I will pledge myself to you that your 50 shares within the year 1865 will *nett* [sic] to you $5000 *cash* if you desire to dispose of them.[19]

Perhaps in an era when Washington society did not destroy a man's republicanism, Donnelly would have refused the stock. But whether he accepted or rejected it, he could not deny assistance to the road. It was sorely needed for Minnesota's economic development.

Within a short time Banning arrived in Washington with specific suggestions. As a result Donnelly introduced time-extension and

---

[16]*Ibid.*, J. Fisk to I. D., December 23, 1865, February 27, 1866; Diary, February 18, 1866; J. P. Wilson to I. D., January 29, 1866; W. Mitchell to I. D., March 20, 1866; Circular, February 12, 1866; *Congressional Globe*, 39th Cong., 1st sess., p. 446.

[17]Donnelly MSS, J. Stewart to I. D., November 24, 1864.

[18]*Ibid.*, W. Banning to I. D., November 26, 1864.

[19]*Ibid.*, J. Stewart to I. D., December 3, 1864.

land-grant legislation on behalf of the Lake Superior & Mississippi.[20] In the 1865–66 congressional session Banning asked him to protect the railroad from a potential competitor by preventing a Wisconsin railroad from gaining additional land subsidies.[21] Donnelly did his best for the company.

One year later, Banning again appealed for help. Afraid that the Northern Pacific Railroad would duplicate the Lake Superior & Mississippi route, he wanted Donnelly to introduce legislation that would extend the line's land grant as far south as Sioux City, Iowa; it could then connect with the Union Pacific.[22] After talking to T. C. Durant of the Union Pacific and C. P. Huntington of the Central Pacific, Banning assured Donnelly that he would be supported in Congress. Because Banning realized that the farmers in northern Minnesota would be highly critical of Donnelly if he took any action hostile to the Northern Pacific, the management of the Lake Superior & Mississippi promised to persuade the Minnesota legislature to petition him for the extension.[23] By way of gratitude for his aid, the company's official gave him ten thousand dollars' worth of paid-up Lake Superior & Mississippi stock.[24]

Banning's fears proved groundless. Jay Cooke and Company, financial agents for the Northern Pacific, bought control of the Lake Superior & Mississippi. Donnelly escaped being caught between the irate farmers and the St. Paul railroad investors. The smaller line became an essential portion of Cooke's contemplated integrated railroad system covering the Northwest and Canada.[25]

Although Donnelly worked for all the Minnesota lines,[26] he had a special interest in William B. Le Duc's Hastings Dakota & Western Railroad. The road received its land grant and charter through Donnelly's efforts. Le Duc was overwhelmed by Donnelly's effectiveness as a legislator. "What would you most desire in connection with the organization?" he wrote exuberantly to Donnelly; "I will be very glad to help you to anything in my power."[27] This was

[20]*Congressional Globe*, 38th Cong., 2d sess., pp. 202, 296.

[21]Donnelly MSS, W. Banning to I. D., March 5, 1866.

[22]*Ibid.*, W. Banning to I. D., February 4, 5, 1867.

[23]*Ibid.*, W. Banning to I. D., March 7, 1867.

[24]*Ibid.*, R. Lewis to I. D., October 2, 1867; W. Banning to I. D., January 25, 1868.

[25]John Harnsberger, "Railroads to the Northern Plains: 1870–1872," *North Dakota Historical Quarterly*, Summer, 1959, pp. 53–61.

[26]Donnelly MSS, E. Rice to I. D., January 23, 1865; *Congressional Globe*, 39th Cong., 1st sess., pp. 2208–11; St. Cloud *Democrat*, March 10, 1866.

[27]Donnelly MSS, W. Le Duc to I. D., July 5, 1866.

Donnelly's first piece of legislation that applied directly to Dakota County. The people of Hastings were so impressed with it that all political opposition to Donnelly virtually ceased.

Because the Hastings Dakota & Western investors were his friends, Donnelly even prevented the surveying and the withdrawal of the land grant until they could buy up speculative townsites along the right-of-way.[28] To help Le Duc buy iron rails, Donnelly took him to the Cambria Iron Works in Philadelphia and to Jay Cooke.[29] When financial assistance was needed Donnelly saw Oakes Ames of Massachusetts, rapidly emerging as one of the most influential men in railroading, and asked him to participate in the project.[30] Although Donnelly refused a block of twenty-five shares in the Hastings Dakota & Western, the company eventually gave him twenty-five hundred dollars' worth of stock.[31]

Accepting money from railroads bothered Donnelly. When the St. Paul & Pacific retained him as legal counsel for the road, he was sensitive about his status, signing the bank drafts given him by E. B. Litchfield, "Rcd. the within sum a/c for salary as attorney for said Co. in all matters wherein the United States Govt. is not a party."[32] Several months later, Donnelly resigned, informing Litchfield, "The matter has given me no little uneasiness of conscience." He conceded that the railroad had not asked him to use his position to benefit it, but he confessed, "I have been laboring under the fear and dread I might instinctively be willing to do more for your company as attorney than I would if I did not hold that relation to it." He even offered to return one thousand dollars or perform some actual service for his retainer.[33] Deeply involved in the dubious practices of railroad land-grant legislation, Donnelly recognized the implications of his letter to Litchfield. There is no indication that he returned the money or was less friendly to the railroad.

Donnelly knew that the Committee on Public Lands was disposing of millions of acres of the public domain. "Just think of it," wrote one political supporter from the less settled part of the state, "10 sections on each side of these Minnesota Roads per mile with in-

[28]*Ibid.*, W. Le Duc to I. D., December 19, 1866.
[29]*Ibid.*, Diary, April 24, 25, 1868.
[30]William K. Rogers MSS, W. Le Duc to I. D., June 10, 1868.
[31]Donnelly MSS, C. Lange to I. D., May 13, 1867; W. Le Duc to I. D., June 17, 1867.
[32]*Ibid.*, Diary, November 9, 1867.
[33]*Ibid.*, I. D. to E. Litchfield, April 3, 1868 (copy).

demnity for 20 miles on either side." The poor settlers would lose out because of the withdrawal of such colossal amounts of land. As for the railroads—"Good God what do they want," he queried, "the country not only to build the Roads but to secure to them the entire advantages to be derived therefrom."[34]

When similar charges were made by Congressman John A. Kasson of Iowa, Donnelly defended the system.

It is then to us simply a question of the administration of this great public donation so set apart for the good of mankind. And I say, speaking here as a western man, and responsible to my constituents for what I say, that railroads are as important to that country as population.[35]

How could people live well, he asked, without material progress, the symbol of which was the railroad? Land, he insisted, was of little value unless utilized. A few acres of land, in contrast to the great expanse of the West, was a paltry price to pay for an end to isolation, an outlet to markets, and a degree of comfort in travel that befitted the nineteenth century. In 1866, the idea of land monopoly was far from Donnelly's mind.

Of the many local projects Donnelly sponsored during his second term, none was more complex than the Meeker Dam and River Improvement scheme. The project grew from the desires of many Minneapolis businessmen, under the leadership of Bradley B. Meeker, to make the Mississippi River navigable between St. Paul and Minneapolis. Donnelly, familiar with the local geography, introduced the conventional river and harbor bill.[36] To quiet any rivalries from towns above Minneapolis, he introduced a companion measure providing for improved navigation on the upper Mississippi River.

When the first measure passed into committee, it was opposed by Illinois congressman Elihu B. Washburne, who denounced it as one of needless waste and extravagance. Notorious as the "Watchdog of the Treasury," Washburne frequently scrutinized river and harbor bills even though he represented a river constituency. B. B. Meeker informed Donnelly that Minneapolis politicians openly stated that Washburne, always hopeful of helping his brother William, sought to discredit Donnelly in Hennepin County.

Outraged by opposition based upon political ambition, Meeker told Donnelly, "If [you] should get the grant, the *Devil in Arms*

[34] *Ibid.*, H. Wait to I. D., April 6, 1866.
[35] *Congressional Globe*, 39th Cong., 1st sess., p. 3464.
[36] *Ibid.*, p. 578.

could not prevent your carrying Hennepin County" in the convention.[37] Meeker later showed Donnelly a letter from Cyrus
Aldrich. "You have been humbugged & bamboozled," Aldrich had
written Meeker, scoffing at his reliance on Donnelly; "put not your
trust in princes."[38] Donnelly must secure the dam, Meeker insisted;
not only was the project at stake but also his political future. "It is a
big game," Meeker pleaded, "and you can realize more . . . from
its success . . . besides conferring a lasting substantial good upon a
large community and many personal friends."[39]

Donnelly shifted his legislative tactics because of Washburne's
intervention. Instead of seeking a land grant to pay for the dam and
river-improvement project, he secured a substitute proposal for a
cash appropriation to run a preliminary survey.[40] He knew that, in
most cases, preliminary surveys were followed by appropriations
large enough to complete the original proposals. By the end of the
session Donnelly had acquired an intense dislike of Washburne.

Even though he was a hard-working congressman, always alert
to any measure that would help his district and hardly less influenced by the corrupt times in which he lived than other legislators, he was no mere party hack serving only as an agent for
special interest groups. In his own mind he was a delegate to
Congress, charged with a responsibility for greatness as meaningful
as that held by James Madison or John Quincy Adams. This feeling
inspired Donnelly to flashes of the originality so characteristic of
his later life, breaking the traditional congressional mold to introduce new legislation. One highly original idea, which undoubtedly
stemmed in part from his concern for the freed Negro, called for
the creation of a National Bureau of Education to guarantee equal
educational opportunity to all citizens without regard to race or
color. His resolution, greeted with instant approval, was adopted in
the House by a vote of 113 to 32.

The nationwide response to the resolution indicated that he had
captured the popular imagination. The New York *Tribune* noted
that the bill had been introduced by a Minnesotan named Donnelly, "A smooth faced auburn haired young man—the youngest
member of the House, and his speech for the Education Bureau bill
was an ardent and intelligent argument."[41] Favorable comments ap-

[37]Donnelly MSS, B. Meeker to I. D., March 13, 1866.
[38]*Ibid.*, C. Aldrich to B. Meeker, March 30, 1866.
[39]*Ibid.*, B. Meeker to I. D., April 21, 1866.
[40]*Ibid.*, B. Meeker to I. D., June 26, 1866.
[41]Quoted in the Hastings *Independent*, June 28, 1866.

peared in the Chicago *Tribune,* the Philadelphia *City Item,* and many other newspapers in the North and West. Welcoming the idea, professional educators unanimously indorsed Donnelly's proposal at educational association meetings in Illinois, Indiana, and Michigan.[42]

But he was probably somewhat disappointed with the education bill when it finally emerged from committee. Filled with idealism, Donnelly had written in his diary, "I dream of that great institution of learning which dwelt in the imagination of Bacon."[43] The chairmanship of the education bill committee was given to James A. Garfield, who presented a conservative proposal. Nevertheless, even in this form, the Bureau of Education had a hard time passing the economy-minded House. Although the appointment was beyond his political influence, Donnelly tried to have his former teacher, John Hart, named first commissioner.[44] He was, of course, unsuccessful; Henry Barnard received the post.

The discussion of the Bureau of Education measure had not subsided when Donnelly introduced an even more original piece of legislation: a bill to encourage the growth of forests on the western plains.[45] Speaking in support of the measure, Donnelly explained the purpose trees would serve:

I. An interruption of the great winds which now sweep with unbroken force over those regions. . . .

II. The production of flocks of insectivorous birds, which by destroying the larvae of the grasshopper will put an end to that pest which now consigns vast regions to desolation.

III. A supply of wood for fuel and for building purposes, and for the thousand minor uses for which it is employed by civilized man.

Our government has paid as high as $150 per cord of wood at its military posts on the great plains. A civilized people cannot like the savage use the dry manure of the buffalo for fuel, nor can any frontier population afford to consume for fuel an article almost as scarce and as valuable as gold.[46]

The Timber Culture Act of 1873 was, in some measure, an outgrowth of Donnelly's tree-planting scheme.

The St. Paul *Press,* however, dubbed the forestry plan impractical

---

[42]Donnelly MSS, M. Bateman to I. D., July 3, 1866.

[43]*Ibid.,* Diary, April 8, 1866.

[44]Donnelly MSS, J. Hart to I. D., January 2, 1866. See also Cornell University Collection, Donnelly Papers, I. D. to J. Hart, June 30, 1866, and March 27, 1867.

[45]*Congressional Globe,* 39th Cong., 1st sess., pp. 2821, 2874.

[46]*Ibid.,* 40th Cong., 2d sess., p. 475.

and charged Donnelly with performing a pre-election publicity stunt. When Judge Edmunds, commissioner of the General Land Office, declared that "The western plains and plateaus can only be rendered habitable by planting forests," Donnelly was vindicated. The St. Cloud *Democrat* could not resist the temptation to jab at Joseph Wheelock's skepticism by insisting that vegetation could even be grown on the *Press* "with a little irrigation—say, soaking the head overnight."[47]

Neither as interesting as his educational measure nor as original as the tree-planting idea, Donnelly's most typical political speech was made during the debate on the Freedman's Bureau bill. Introducing an amendment providing for a commission to assure educational opportunity to freed Negroes, he presented a powerful indictment of the South as a cesspool of ignorance. If the White South and the free Negro were left without adequate guarantees of education, Donnelly predicted that ignorance would triumph through a corrupted ballot box. The best laws and the best constitutions were not enough to save people unable to understand them. Re-education in the South was the only solution.

Slated as a short speech, his address outran the time allotment because he was repeatedly interrupted by antagonistic congressmen who baited him on the Negro suffrage issue. How, he was asked, could he favor granting the franchise to Negroes when every word he had uttered on education emphasized their lack of preparation? Angrily he responded that he was in favor of assuring the right to vote and providing the means of gaining knowledge rather than ignoring the means and denying the right forever.

But would he vote to grant the franchise to the Negro in Minnesota, queried a War Democrat? "I am proud to say," he boldly replied, "that I not only voted for it, but that I drew the resolution [granting Negro suffrage] which was passed by the Republican State convention in Minnesota, indorsing the doctrine; and that I canvassed two-thirds of the territory of the State in behalf of it, and thank God, I am ready to do so again tomorrow."[48] Reprinted as a pamphlet, the speech, including the interruptions, defined Donnelly's Radical Republican position.

When the congressional session ended, Donnelly could afford to take his family to Cape May for a brief vacation before returning to Minnesota. There were even a few luxuries. But the craving for

[47]June 7, 1866.
[48]*Congressional Globe*, 39th Cong., 1st sess., pp. 586–90.

social life and leisure was soon satisfied. While at Cape May, resting in the quiet evening, he analyzed the historical significance of the Congress in which he had served.

> I am convinced that a purer, more patient more moderate, and at the same time abler and more patriotic body of men never convened in any age than that Congress which has just adjourned. Assembling almost in an hour of triumph no clamor for revenge escaped them. No cry for blood or confiscation was heard, all they asked were those measures essential to the future security of the nation. With all this moderation they exhibited a heroic determination to do right which neither the threats nor blandishments of extensive power could shake for one instant. They were indeed worthy representatives of that quarter of a million of heroic men whose dust now sanctified the southern land. There is scarce anything more magnificent in history than the final action upon the Civil Rights Bill, when it was passed over the President's veto by the vote of every man elected from a northern state.
>
> Congress stood like a mighty sea wall between the peace and prosperity of the nation and the rising waves of rebellion, swelled into new fury by the breath of executive favor.[49]

Donnelly took pride in his ardent Republicanism, even though he had not figured prominently in the national debate.

When he returned to Minnesota, the people, excited by news of the conflict between Johnson and the radicals, were eager to learn how their congressman had fared in the struggle. Huge audiences greeted him as he toured the Mississippi River towns south of St. Paul. The politicians, especially, wanted to see him. Since President Johnson had turned Minnesota's patronage into Daniel Norton's hands, the senator had dismissed Republican officeholders and replaced them with Democrats. Although Norton took pains to explain that his actions were entirely impersonal,[50] each dislodged officeholder convinced Republican voters that Johnson was a tyrant. As public indignation mounted, Donnelly's prestige increased.[51]

Inspired by the enthusiasm and size of his audiences, Donnelly became intemperate and vituperative in his condemnation of the President. Kate Donnelly disapproved. "It is too bombastic," she warned; "you are losing your modesty cloak."[52] But his tour could not be interrupted, and the tempo of the argument could not be slowed.

The county conventions and party caucuses were held on Sep-

[49]Donnelly MSS, Diary, July 29, 1866.
[50]*Ibid.*, D. Norton to I. D., September 7, 1866.
[51]*Ibid.*, I. D. to K. D., August 27, 1866.
[52]*Ibid.*, K. D. to I. D., August 25, 1866.

tember 15, 1866. With the exception of Ramsey County, where a favorite son was proposed, Donnelly controlled the delegates. "I am out of the woods," he wrote to Kate; "my nomination is certain, and I think it will be by acclamation. Wabasha, Dakota, Carver, Wright, Anoka [delegates] . . . are instructed for me, while I am second if not really first choice of Goodhue."[53] For once, his confidence was justified and he won renomination easily.

But for the first time since the war, with the slavery issue dead, the Homestead Law an established fact, and state sovereignty an almost bankrupt concept, the Democrats prepared for a vigorous campaign along traditional lines. Their St. Paul convention nominated Colonel William Colville, a War Democrat, who had been elected state attorney-general by the Republicans because of his outstanding reputation. A volunteer during the Civil War who had been wounded at Gettysburg, no taint of Copperheadism touched him. Moreover, he was an active Protestant.[54]

Donnelly's hopes for an easy canvass faded when a group of Democrats bought the St. Paul *Pioneer*. The campaign was scarcely under way when its editor launched a war of vilification against him. Donnelly had been a nativist the day before yesterday and was a Jesuit today, the paper told its readers. While he remained in his "bombproof office in Washington, Colonel Colville gave his very blood on the battlefield of Gettysburg." Do not be deceived by his name, it warned the Irish of St. Paul. "Any Irishman in Minnesota, who votes the radical ticket and for Ignatius Donnelly, is unworthy of the land of his birth." On election eve the tide of abuse reached its crest when the *Pioneer* denounced "Donnelly's Nigger Bureau, Nigger Schools, and Nigger Bounty of $300." He was accused of bankrupting the taxpayers of Minnesota to educate the "Nigger" and the "poor white trash."[55]

Donnelly was defended by the Republican newspapers, and himself campaigned tirelessly, traveling in an open buggy until the first snow, and then by sleigh. Even after he had been ill and forced to

[53] *Ibid.*, I. D. to K. D., September 16, 1866. H. L. Gordon, a young Wright County delegate, told Dr. Thomas Foster that he had been offered $500 to vote against Donnelly. Foster gave young Gordon a gun, and took the $500. Following Donnelly's nomination, Foster placed an advertisement in the St. Paul *Press* inviting someone to come into party headquarters to claim the money! Minnesota Historical Society, Gordon MSS, H. Gordon to W. Folwell, March 10, 1908; I. D. to H. Gordon, January 10, 1893.

[54] St. Paul *Pioneer*, September 28, 1866.

[55] *Ibid.*, October 3, 13, 16, 17, 18, November 18, 1866.

remain in bed for a day, Donnelly refused to abandon his canvass of the district. He knew that farmers and lumbermen living in the outlying areas waited all year for a chance to talk to their representative. He stubbornly insisted on fulfilling all his scheduled engagements.

The campaign reached a climax on November 3, when Donnelly spoke at Ingersoll Hall in St. Paul. He accepted a challenge to debate with his personal friend but political foe, Colonel D. A. Robertson, a vigorous and dynamic Democrat who had planned a surprise. Well aware that Donnelly had been using only one speech during most of the campaign, Robertson secretly had a stenographer record it. He rewrote Donnelly's anecdotes to prove the Democratic argument. Aside from this theatrical bombshell, he had an assortment of valid questions: the Know-Nothing charge, the salary grab, and the tariff. He ignored the war issue, slavery, and reconstruction.

Donnelly had few misgivings in debating with Robertson. He had known the colonel for years; he expected a colorful evening. As always, he was thoroughly prepared. His speech had been outlined, and its significant portions were written out in their entirety. He was completely confident.

Then Robertson began his speech. One after another he told Donnelly's favorite stories, explaining to the delighted audience the source of his wit. On the speaker's platform, Donnelly tilted his chair back and forth, keeping his eyes fixed on the ceiling.

When Donnelly came forward to speak, one hand on his coat lapel, the other raised in recognition, he admitted good-naturedly the origin of Robertson's humor. But, he added, if he could not tell the stories to better point, Colville should be sent to Washington! Following his prepared text, he answered the charge of Know-Nothingism and denied that he had voted for the salary grab. The tariff issue, new to him, required further study. When Republican policy was established, he would take his stand for or against it. During the speech, he repeated the same stories that Robertson had told. They had a devastating effect upon his listeners. While the audience howled its approval, Donnelly bowed slightly toward the downcast Robertson.[56] He noted in his diary, with legitimate pride, that even the St. Paul *Press* declared his speech "the greatest effort of campaign oratory ever made in St. Paul."[57]

[56]St. Paul *Press*, November 4, 1866.
[57]Donnelly MSS, Diary, November 3, 1866.

On election night he sat in the Hastings telegraph office waiting for the special returns to be sent to him. Certain of victory before midnight, he returned to Nininger City for the quiet of his own home. Like the majority of Radical Republicans he had escaped President Johnson's purge. Unlike the other congressmen who returned to Washington in December, 1866, Donnelly's hostility had not been sharpened to the point of a desire for vengeance.

He was troubled by their insistence upon Johnson's impeachment because it was based on an oversimplification of the process of government. He knew that "the choice of measures is too often the choice of evils"; and he was well aware that "there is some merit upon both sides of every question." But on what basis should the President be assailed or defended? Donnelly willingly conceded to Johnson what he claimed for himself, "the widest latitude of opinion and the greatest freedom in its expression." In his diary he concluded: "If impeachment was born of any spirit of persecution I should oppose it. Upon no such basis shall I sustain it."[58]

Despite his qualms of conscience, which he ultimately stilled, Donnelly was not a silent member of the radical group. He delivered an impassioned speech supporting Thaddeus Stevens' reconstruction bill. "The purpose of government is the happiness of the people, therefore the happiness of the *whole* people," he told the members of the House. "A Government cannot be half a republic and half a despotism. . . . It must become either all despotism or all republic."[59]

After enacting the essentials of the radical reconstruction program and repudiating the presidential view, Congress adjourned on March 30, 1867. It had legislated a wider suffrage, re-established military rule in the South, and fearful that Johnson would undermine the program through non-enforcement, its members planned to reconvene on the first Wednesday in July. Donnelly did not look forward to a hot July session gathered to punish the President or pass additional legislation to enforce the radical program.

As he journeyed to Minnesota, his thoughts, however, centered on his lifelong ambition—a United States senatorship. Political geography outlawed the possibility of two senators from central Minnesota. Could he afford to wait until Ramsey secured a cabinet post or the vice-presidential nomination? Each term in Congress had been harder to win. A single defeat could relegate him to political

[58] *Ibid.*, Diary, February 15, 1867.
[59] *Congressional Globe*, 39th Cong., 2d sess., pp. 559–61.

oblivion. Hopefully, he had shared his thoughts with his friends, who were astonished by his candor but unenthusiastic.[60] Nevertheless, convinced that his one opportunity for the Senate within the foreseeable future would come in 1868 when Ramsey's term expired, he began formulating plans to prevent Bluff Aleck's renomination.

His first move, to capture control of the state party organization, required that Governor William R. Marshall be replaced by someone more sympathetic to his cause. Donnelly needed both a strong candidate and a lively issue to oppose Marshall. He decided to indorse Charles D. Gilfillan, who had almost defeated Marshall at the party's 1865 nominating convention. Gilfillan also provided the political issue when he discovered, while checking the state auditor's reports for 1859–60, that the governor was a heavy investor in the controversial Minnesota railroad bonds.[61]

It was soon evident that Donnelly, unable to transfer his popularity to Gilfillan, had misjudged the temper of Minnesota's politicians. Even the enthusiastic public response to the bond issue failed to counteract the effectiveness of the state's largest newspapers. The Minneapolis *Tribune*, a newly organized daily controlled by William S. King but in part financed by William D. Washburn, indorsed Marshall, violating assurances given Donnelly that it would be neutral. Even worse, Joseph Wheelock won Marshall the support of St. Paul's reformers when the *Press* denounced Gilfillan as "the most corrupt politican in the state" and a man "not disdaining to roll for weeks in the gutters of debauchery."[62]

When Gilfillan was overwhelmed at the state convention, the St. Paul *Press* sarcastically noted that Donnelly went home sick. He had "bearded the Marshallites in their own cave," reported the Democratic St. Paul *Pioneer*, and he had been forced to return home "to save Dakota County." Governor Marshall's victory was complete! Donnelly had suffered humiliation and disgrace.[63]

In his first furious reaction to the outcome of the convention, Donnelly rejected an invitation to campaign on behalf of the state ticket; he was "too busy thrashing wheat"—his business came first.[64]

[60]Donnelly MSS, W. L. Wilson to I. D., March 15, 1867; T. Newson to I. D., March 4, 1867; A. Hayes to I. D., March 17, 1867.
[61]*Ibid.*, C. D. Gilfillan to I. D., July 29, 1867.
[62]St. Paul *Press*, August 21, 22, 1867.
[63]*Ibid.*, August 27, September 5, 1867.
[64]Donnelly MSS, T. Foster to I. D., September 24, 1867; W. Snider to I. D., October 2, 1867.

But under the prodding of Dr. Foster, when his temper had cooled, he realized that he would have to campaign if he wanted to retain his political influence. "It is a cheap victory; and you will have the credit with the party," Foster chided; "Wheat or no wheat —thrashing or no thrashing—this is your opportunity."[65]

Donnelly finally consented to make speeches in the larger towns only. Huge audiences greeted him. The *Press* in commenting on his successful reception in St. Paul's Ingersoll Hall criticized his bond views as "double distilled nonsense" but acknowledged his courageous stand on Negro suffrage and Radical Republicanism.[66] A week before the election he agreed to share a speaker's platform with Marshall, closing (publicly at least) the breach opened at the convention. Unity among the Republicans was essential, as the election results proved, because the Democrats, led by conservative Judge Charles E. Flandrau, had been highly effective in criticizing excesses in both Minnesota and Washington. Flandrau reduced the Republican majority of ten thousand votes by almost 50 per cent.

Shortly before the election, after Donnelly agreed to campaign for Marshall, Ramsey hinted that he would renew his alliance with Donnelly if he would forego his senatorial ambitions for the time being.[67] But Donnelly rejected the peace offer. He remained an avowed candidate for the Senate.

The Gilfillan fiasco had confirmed his belief that it was impossible to campaign successfully without the support of a metropolitan newspaper. In January, 1868, he became the silent partner of Harlan P. Hall, who established the St. Paul *Dispatch*. A cheaply produced evening tabloid, the paper faced intense competition not only from Democratic rivals but also from the owners of the St. Paul *Press* who sought to ruin it by publishing a special evening edition. But the *Dispatch* persevered and, for the first time since the *Minnesotian,* Donnelly could count on the support of a friendly newspaper in the Twin Cities.

When Donnelly returned to Washington in the winter of 1867, the political patronage at his disposal was virtually nil. Almost one year before, Alexander Ramsey, recognizing that Donnelly was his most serious rival, had arranged a compromise with Daniel Norton to strengthen his hold over Minnesota patronage. In exchange for sustaining a few of the President's appointments, Ramsey was granted

[65] *Ibid.*, T. Foster to I. D., September 29, 1867.
[66] St. Paul *Press*, October 22, 1867.
[67] Donnelly MSS, W. Mitchell to I. D., October 10, 1867.

a larger voice in the selection of state officeholders. Donnelly's radical followers were to be ignored.[68]

In an effort to bring the patronage issue before the voters, Donnelly published his correspondence with Ramsey regarding the creation of Minnesota's new land districts. The senator had refused to select appointees in advance, even from a list of known Republicans. Donnelly replied that when he controlled patronage in the pre-Johnson days, he had always given Ramsey's wishes paramount consideration. Ramsey, Donnelly charged, was co-operating with Norton and the President to undermine Minnesota's Republican party.[69]

In the eyes of the St. Paul *Press*, Donnelly's patronage pamphlet was an open declaration of war against Ramsey. It unleashed a new storm of denunciation charging that Donnelly had determined on a rule-or-ruin policy for the party. "The truth of the whole matter is this," fumed the *Press*; "Mr. Donnelly lives in the delusion that it is among things possible that he may become the next United States Senator." Whipped into near frenzy the editor concluded, "Every energy for good or evil of which he is possessed has, for the last year, been bent to compass this result."[70] Meanwhile, Governor William R. Marshall, still smarting under Donnelly's unsuccessful effort to oust him, declared that Donnelly must not be renominated because nothing but defeat would quench his thirst for power.

Ramsey's friends "are badly frightened," Donnelly was told, "and are moving heaven and earth to defeat you. Prepare for death or victory."[71] But Donnelly's advisers were equally apprehensive. As a radical he was at war with the President and Senator Norton; he was locked in a life-and-death struggle with Ramsey and Marshall, who controlled most of the state and federal patronage; and William Washburn of Minneapolis was again emerging as a candidate for the House of Representatives. As Donnelly's intimate friend, W. L. Wilson, lamented, he had too many enemies.[72]

During the spring of 1868, in the midst of the patronage exposé, Donnelly wrote a personal letter to Charles Folsom, editor of the Taylors Falls (Minn.) *Reporter*, discussing the problems he faced in seeking special legislation. Referring to personal opposition, Don-

[68]St. Paul *Pioneer*, March 20, 1867.
[69]Donnelly MSS, Scrapbook.
[70]March 20, 1868.
[71]Donnelly MSS, D. Basset to I. D., April 15, 1868.
[72]*Ibid.*, W. L. Wilson to I. D., April 21, 1868.

nelly named Elihu Washburne as being particularly hostile. But he went on to add: "I am at a loss to account for the actions of Mr. Washburne. I should regret to think that his continual opposition . . . is due to a desire to utterly impair my ability to serve my constituents." Donnelly professed to believe that this did not seem possible, "But the fact remains that he seems determined to resist in every way, every measure which I deem important to my constituents."[73] Since this was a personal note to Folsom explaining his failure to secure passage of a river-improvement bill, Donnelly probably felt that it called for candor. Folsom published the letter!

The St. Paul *Press* reprinted it and a copy was sent to Washburne. Whether Washburne deemed Donnelly's criticism serious, whether he personally disliked Donnelly, or whether he saw an opportunity to assist his brother gain a congressional seat, is not disclosed in Washburne's papers, but he was prompted to reply. In a letter to the St. Paul *Press* he denied working against Minnesota's interest. Rather, Washburne stated, because of Donnelly's character, he felt compelled to examine such legislation with great care. Donnelly, Washburne asserted, "left Philadelphia under suspicious circumstances" in the dead of night. Given a pass as a bribe, he had voted against rate regulation for the Union Pacific. Washburne presented himself as the true friend of Minnesota, not "*Jesuitical*" and an "office beggar" such as Donnelly, who had changed his name.[74] Washburne's letter could not have been written without a thorough knowledge of the false charges and vilifying rumors that had circulated *sub rosa* in Minnesota political circles for a decade. Washburne's Minnesota connections had provided all the material for his defamatory letter.

Incensed by the attack, Donnelly's followers urged him to come home and deal with Washburne. The St. Paul *Dispatch* contended that Washburne's unorthodox and unethical letter was an outrageous effort to influence the congressional election.[75] The county newspapers rallied to Donnelly's defense. "We deny [Washburne's] right to appeal to the sympathy of Minnesota upon the plea of protecting her interests," argued the editor of the Winona *Republican*,[76] while the Wabasha *Herald*, a strong Donnelly supporter, told its readers that "Mr. Washburne comes to scratch with an answer

[73]Taylors Falls *Reporter*, March 28, 1868.
[74]St. Paul *Press*, April 29, 1868.
[75]April 23, 1868.
[76]April 29, 1868.

wholly uncalled for, drumming up old exploded and forgotten slanders against Mr. Donnelly, and tries to injure him."[77]

Because of the shocking nature of Washburne's letter, Donnelly was dumbfounded and offended. "Who have I injured. . . . What men have I attacked," began an angry entry in his diary, vowing "eternal war with all assassins of reputation."[78] When the shock of the affront receded, he decided to reply to Washburne's charges from the Hall of the House of Representatives.

Washburne had never been a popular member of the House. His constant harping on economy, especially at the expense of other people's legislation, his air of superior virtue, his magisterial tone, and his frequent lectures to the House on its obligations assured Donnelly a sympathetic audience. Even intensely hot weather and a lack of formal business to transact did not dissuade members from attending on the day of Donnelly's scheduled rebuttal. Anticipating forensic fireworks, every member was in his seat and the gallery was completely filled.[79]

For a full hour Donnelly answered Washburne's assertions in detail. During this hour the genteel schoolboy from Central High, the amateur poet, the reader in the office of Benjamin H. Brewster were forgotten. Donnelly had become the "stump speaker" of Minnesota politics, the spellbinder, and the seasoned western frontier politician. His humor was as broad as his epithets were vindictive.

But he says I am an "office-beggar!" "An office-beggar!" and this from a man bearing the name he does! *Et tu Brute!* "An office-beggar!" But Mr. Speaker, the charge comes from such a quarter that I cannot fail to notice it. Why sir, the gentleman's family are "chronic office-beggars." They are nothing if not in office. Out of office they are miserable, wretched God-forsaken—as uncomfortable as the famous stump-tailed bull in fly time. [Laughter] Why this whole trouble arises from the persistent determination of one of the gentleman's family to sit in this body. Why Mr. Speaker, every young male of the gentleman's family is born into the world with "M.C.," franked across his broadest part. [Laughter] The great calamity seems to be that God, in his infinite wisdom, did not make any of them broad enough for the letters "U. S. S." [Laughter]

Although called to order three times by the Speaker, he was permitted to continue.

[77] April 30, 1868.
[78] Donnelly MSS, Diary, April 3, 15, 17, 18, 19, 28, 1868.
[79] George W. Julian, *Political Recollections, 1840–1872* (Chicago: Jansen, McClurg & Co., 1884), pp. 366–67.

I stand here reiterating the declaration I then made, that if any where on God's earth, down in the mire of filth and nastiness, the gentleman can pluck up anything that touches my honor, let it come. I shall meet it on its merits. I have gone through the entire catalogue; I have analyzed the contents of the gentleman's foul stomach. I have dipped my hand into its gall; I have examined the half digested fragments that I found floating in the gastric juices; but if it is possible for the peristaltic actions of the gentleman from Illinois to bring up anything more loathesome, more disgusting than he has vomited over me in that letter, in God's name, let it come.

As Donnelly's hour drew to a close, he should have resumed his seat, but his time was extended by unanimous consent so that he could make concluding remarks.

Having answered the charges, Donnelly devoted the final portion of his speech to a vicious personal attack on Washburne. His language grew increasingly vituperative and he ended by saying:

And if there be in our midst one low, sordid, vulgar soul; one barren, mediocre intelligence; one heart callous to every kindly sentiment and every generous impulse, one tongue leprous with slander; one mouth which like unto a den of foul beast giving forth deadly odors; if there be one character which, while blotched and spotted all over, yet raves and rants and blackguards like a prostitute; if there be here one bold, bad, empty, bellowing demagogue, it is the gentleman from Illinois.[80]

Despite his coarseness, his unparliamentary language, and his indefensible bad taste, Donnelly was cheered and applauded by the congressmen.[81] William Windom demanded an investigation of the accusations contained in Washburne's letter.

The following day Donnelly noted that there was a "great sensation in town over my attack on Washburne."[82] The New York *Tribune*, attempting to be neutral, pointed out that there had been no proof in charge or countercharge, but it sympathized with Washburne because of Donnelly's acrid manner.[83] The Democratic New York *Herald*, always eager to criticize the radicals, termed the speech vulgar and ungentlemanly although it conceded there were extenuating circumstances.[84] The Speaker of the House, Schuyler Colfax, no friend to Washburne, thought the speech was more than he needed.

As a direct consequence of the episode, Donnelly put the House

[80]*Congressional Globe*, 40th Cong., 2d sess., pp. 2349–54; but I used a complete version in Donnelly MSS, Scrapbook, Daily *Globe* clipping, May 2, 1868.
[81]Julian, *Recollections*, p. 368.
[82]Donnelly MSS, Diary, May 3, 1868.
[83]May 4, 1868.
[84]May 4, 1868.

of Representatives in such a bad light that it withdrew the tenth article of impeachment which accused President Andrew Johnson of improper language. It was clear that a governing body which countenanced such a speech could hardly indict the President on the same charge.[85]

At first the Minnesota newspapers received only brief telegraphic reports quoting the most potent portions of the speech, but these caused a furor. The pro-Ramsey St. Paul *Press* joined with its Democratic rival to condemn Donnelly. In fact, each tried to outdo the other in its criticism. The St. Paul *Pioneer*, echoing Chicago papers, termed him "the nastiest and most foul mouthed wretch who ever had a seat in the American Congress."[86] And the *Press* reprinted an item from the *Nation* pointing out that Donnelly's obscenity was "of that revolting kind which has nothing to recommend it even to the most degraded beings except its filth."[87]

Harlan P. Hall's St. Paul *Dispatch* attempted to vindicate Donnelly's act by placing the responsibility on Elihu Washburne for his unprovoked and dastardly attack on Donnelly in a Minnesota newspaper.[88] But Hall regretted that the speech had been made. "I fear the tilt with Washburne on Saturday has hurt you," he wrote Donnelly. "Not that it will change any of your friends but your enemies can use it to influence the lukewarm."[89] Years later Hall reflected in a book of political recollections, "I have always felt that if merciful Providence had intervened and prevented his speaking longer [than his allotted time], his political future, and indeed all his life would have been different."[90]

The Hastings *Independent*, the Rochester *Post*, the Winona *Republican* and the Goodhue *Republican* saw nothing wrong in giving an alien congressman a good drubbing. Strong language was no novelty on the frontier. Newspaper opinion was clearly tabulated when the St. Cloud *Journal* noted that "all the Republican papers in Minnesota, with the exception of the St. Paul *Press* and the Minneapolis *Tribune* . . . sustain Mr. Donnelly in his caustic reply to Washburne."[91]

The temper of the argument changed when complete texts of the

[85]Oberholtzer, *United States*, II, 114.
[86]May 6, 1868.
[87]May 15, 1868.
[88]May 7, 1868.
[89]Donnelly MSS, H. Hall to I. D., May 6, 1868.
[90]Hall, *Observations*, p. 77.
[91]Donnelly MSS, Scrapbook, complete set of clippings.

speech became available. A reader quickly discovered that the St. Paul *Pioneer* and the St. Paul *Press* based their editorials on the overly sensational telegraphic dispatches with the result that they had garbled, distorted, and prejudiced the account. The *Press*, refusing to concede this, alleged that the complete text was an expurgated version.[92] Copies of the complete text, however, were printed in pamphlet form and widely circulated in the state. Some of Donnelly's friends were reassured. There was also confidence that William Washburn had been discredited as a candidate. But W. L. Wilson, on whom Donnelly relied for an honest opinion, reluctantly admitted his pessimism.

I know you will be told differently but I am your friend, convinced of what I say, speaking the truth in kindness, & I assure you I am right. I say to you what I have not allowed myself to express to any other living man. I too endeavor to create the impression that you have received no detriment, but in my heart I feel it is not so, as manifestly do many others of your friends. With mere political men you may not have suffered much, but you have fallen in the esteem of the cultivated, refined & religious people who largely make up the Republican party. . . . If you had stopped speaking when the hammer fell [at the end of the first hour], you would have achieved complete triumph.[93]

Wilson may have been right, but did he really gauge the nature of the party? A letter-writer unknown to Donnelly unconsciously provided an answer. "We are frontier people," he noted, "and are inclined at all times to support those who dare protect themselves. We have a conundrum here. Why is Donnelly like a drawing of green tea—because you do not know his strength until you get him in hot water."[94]

[92] May 12, 1868.
[93] Donnelly MSS, W. L. Wilson to I. D., May 15, 1868.
[94] *Ibid.*, A. Brower to I. D., May 21, 1868.

VIII

Rebuff and Reaction
1868–1872

Those only deserve success who are equal to the exactions of misfortune.

IGNATIUS DONNELLY

THE NEWS of President Johnson's acquittal from the impeachment charges virtually stunned Donnelly's followers. Not only had Johnson's vindication killed their hopes for a quick return to public office, but it had ended the possibility that they could use patronage as a weapon in the forthcoming election. Even though the President had been too weakened to harass them, Donnelly's radical supporters found little ground for optimism.

Events in the House of Representatives provided some encouragement when Congressman Francis Thomas, chairman of the committee appointed to investigate Washburne's charges against Donnelly, began taking testimony. After investigators had uncovered no evidence of dishonesty in Philadelphia, Washburne refused to testify or repeat his allegations under oath. In fact, he withdrew his remarks referring to Donnelly's role as a congressman and apologized.[1] Highly pleased, Donnelly urged Francis Thomas to expand the inquiry and clear his reputation, but since the House had no interest in charges that did not reflect on its own proceedings, the case was closed.[2] The Thomas Committee issued a brief report, exonerating Donnelly and labeling false many of the rumors that had been current for years.[3]

[1] *Congressional Globe*, 40th Cong., 2d sess., p. 2756.
[2] Donnelly MSS, I. D. to F. Thomas, May 28, 1868 (copy).
[3] 40th Cong., 2d sess., *House Documents*, No. 48 (serial 1358).

"We always knew Elihu to be a conceited, overbearing, big-bellied and muddle-headed, lying pomposity," spat the St. Paul *Dispatch* in reporting the findings.[4] But the St. Paul *Press*, by judicious use of scissors in editing the copy, concluded that Washburne had simply let Donnelly "off the hook"[5]—a rather strained interpretation in the light of the facts, but one to which the editors adhered.

Equally worthwhile as a by-product of the Thomas Report was Washburne's retreat on all Minnesota legislation. Unable to make any effective display against Donnelly yet loath to withdraw his professions of friendship for Minnesota, Washburne voted affirmatively on the river-improvement schemes. The Meeker Dam project passed the House, along with other bills dealing with the Mississippi and Minnesota rivers.[6]

Before Donnelly left Washington at the close of the session, his support of the Alaska Purchase bill led him into argument with a third Washburn brother. Cadwallader C. Washburn of Wisconsin, an ardent conservative, sharply criticized Secretary of State Seward's proposed treaty. "It was a Walrussia," he snapped, and should not be taken over by the United States "in the present financial condition of the country."[7] Washburn's opposition seriously jeopardized the House appropriation for the purchase.

Donnelly's vigorous rebuttal stemmed as much from his antipathy to Cadwallader Washburn as from his expansionist zeal. Scoffing at his opponent's pusillanimous jeremiads, Donnelly put into words the sentiments of most westerners. In a spirit reminiscent of his youth and the Young America Movement, he insisted that the benefits of the American system of government should be extended to the peoples of the New World from the Isthmus of Panama "to the extremist limits of human habitation under the frozen constellations of the North." For "nothing less than a continent can suffice as the basis and foundation for that nation in whose destiny is involved the destiny of mankind," he told the House. "Let us build broad and wide those foundations; let them abut only on the everlasting seas."[8]

During July's hot final days, Donnelly returned to Minnesota prepared to campaign for re-election to the House while working

[4] St. Paul *Dispatch,* June 3, 1868.
[5] St. Paul *Press,* June 4, 1868.
[6] Donnelly MSS, B. B. Meeker to I. D., June 20, 1868; *Congressional Globe,* 40th Cong., 2d sess., pp. 2830–35.
[7] *Congressional Globe,* 40th Cong., 2d sess., p. 135.
[8] *Ibid.,* p. 3360.

for the senatorship. On August 1, the day he was scheduled to speak in St. Paul, every seat in Ingersoll Hall was occupied, men lounged in the aisles, scores of people had to be turned away at the entrance because of lack of space, and a large crowd milled about in the street outside. While a band blared martial music, Donnelly came forward on the platform, his eyes rested for a moment on the audience with affectionate familiarity, and he raised his left hand to his heart. His friends thundered applause, their hats and caps sailed into the air; they stamped their feet until the building shook. The greeting lasted for five minutes. Although the speech was merely a reply to Elihu Washburne and an open challenge to Ramsey and the St. Paul *Press*, the audience was so deeply moved and so completely captivated by his personal magnetism, that he was interrupted by yells and whoops typical of western camp meetings. At one point the intrepid Joseph Wheelock became so incensed that he attempted to debate Donnelly from the press gallery, but he was shouted down after a caustic reply from Donnelly.[9]

The following day the Democratic St. Paul *Pioneer* confessed, "There is no way to present the scene to our readers." It was "the liveliest political meeting ever held" in the city. Senator Ramsey was urged to take heed of Donnelly's strength if he expected to win. "Dignity is played out," it warned; "last evening Donnelly intruded so far into Ramsey's special thing as to quote German poetry."[10]

Ten days after this tumultuous reception, Donnelly began a pre-convention tour of his district. He was deeply impressed by the loyalty and confidence of the crowds that greeted him.[11] When Kate pleaded that he cancel an engagement because one of his farm tenants had gone berserk and threatened to destroy the harvest, Donnelly replied: "Do not worry. If we lose the entire crop, it will not ruin us." Then he added, "I have had immense and enthusiastic meetings everywhere. I think I am sure of the nomination on the first ballot—still we must prepare for the worst."[12]

Although the campaign enthusiasm continued, Donnelly grew increasingly apprehensive about the Scandinavian vote. He had failed to gain control of the *Svenska Amerikanien*, and its editor, Hans Mattson, had sided with Ramsey.[13] Newcomers to the political scene and highly susceptible to flattery, the Swedes were solidly

[9]St. Paul *Dispatch*, August 3, 1868; Hall, *Observations*, p. 78.
[10]St. Paul *Pioneer*, August 2, 1868.
[11]Donnelly MSS, Diary, August 10, 11, 12, 1868.
[12]*Ibid.*, I. D. to K. D., August 13, 1868.
[13]*Ibid.*, A. Johnson to I. D., June 30, July 28, 1868.

Republican, and were likely to vote as a bloc. Donnelly's sympathizers did not disguise their anxiety: "The infernal Swede Colonel Mattson is pitching into you and giving you fits generally," wrote an alarmed politician; "he has a big influence with the Swedes and Norwegians of this country. His motto is anybody to beat Donnelly."[14]

There were too many Republicans in St. Paul for a party caucus, and the first test of Donnelly's strength had to wait until the city's Republican primary. After forces led by Governor William R. Marshall had taken possession of the polling place in the First Ward, Donnelly's men opened their own polling place on the sidewalk. But Harlan Hall, who captained the Donnelly men in the Second Ward, later explained that "the ballot box, the palladium of our liberties," was guarded by fifteen Donnelly stalwarts. The Democratic St. Paul *Pioneer* reported that fights, ejected judges, and rioting took place in almost every ward.

When they learned they had won, the *Pioneer* reported that "even the drenching rain did not quench the triumphant Donnellyites. They thronged the streets, whooping, yelling, hurrahing for Donnelly till a late hour."[15]

When the Congressional District Executive Committee gathered to discuss convention procedure, Donnelly's cause suffered a drastic defeat. Three of the five committeemen violated all precedent by agreeing to serve as a credentials committee for the convention. Because Washburn and Ramsey forces had prepared rival delegations from several counties, but were far short of a majority, Donnelly feared the committeemen would bar his delegates. The committee chairman, T. M. Metcalf, one of Donnelly's closest friends, denounced the majority decision as a fraud. He promised to issue admission tickets to anyone who applied. The legitimacy of delegates, Donnelly's followers insisted, should be determined by the convention itself. The committee majority replied that only tickets validated by the secretary would be acceptable for admission. Donnelly delegates ignored the majority and applied only to Metcalf; the opposition applied to Metcalf and to the secretary for a counter-signature.[16]

On the morning of September 3, when the convention assembled, the anti-Donnelly forces were thoroughly intrenched in Ingersoll

[14]*Ibid.*, V. Kennedy to I. D., August 20, 1868.
[15]St. Paul *Pioneer*, August 28, 1868.
[16]St. Paul *Dispatch*, September 4, 1868.

Hall. Anticipating serious opposition, Donnelly's delegates gathered at the St. Paul Armory, a short distance from the convention hall and formed two lines for the march to Ingersoll Hall. Leading one column was William L. Banning, St. Paul banker and railroad executive; the other column was led by General William G. Le Duc. In line, also, were General John T. Averill, Harlan Hall, and Ossian E. Dodge, St. Paul's leading impresario. At Ingersoll Hall, Banning and Le Duc encountered a police guard at street level who refused them entry because their tickets had not been countersigned, but Averill, Dodge, and Hall, discovering that the police did not dare to stop them, urged the column to advance. Banning and Le Duc refused. Prior to leaving the Armory, Donnelly had insisted that there be no bloodshed. "The chances for a fight and the political opportunities of a lifetime vanished together."[17]

Returning to the Armory, Donnelly's followers nominated him by acclamation and, to avoid any suspicion of irregularity, indorsed the Republican presidential candidate, Ulysses S. Grant. To discredit the rump gathering in Ingersoll Hall they offered to submit the issue to the people through a direct primary—a proposal that was immediately rejected by the Ramsey forces at Ingersoll Hall.[18]

When the Ingersoll group decided to select a candidate, William Washburn received thirty-one votes, General Lucius Hubbard fifteen, and Christopher Columbus Andrews thirteen.[19] The leading contender, Washburn, withdrew his name from candidacy in favor of Lucius Hubbard, who had been indorsed by the St. Paul *Press*. Probably anticipating that a split in the Republican vote would assure a Democratic victory, Washburn could afford to contradict Donnelly's charge that he was an "office beggar." Hubbard was nominated on the second ballot.

General Hubbard, completely honest and aware that his candidacy jeopardized the election, pleaded that both men withdraw to save the party. When Donnelly declined, the St. Paul *Press* called his refusal stubbornly selfish.[20] The St. Paul *Dispatch*, hammering at the theme that Ramsey had manipulated the convention, refused to criticize Hubbard.[21] Too many of Hubbard's personal friends were

---

[17]Hall, *Observations*, pp. 85–87. Hall thought that "if they had fought their way into the hall, as they could, the trend of politics for the last quarter century [1875–1900] would have been different."
[18]St. Paul *Press*, September 4, 1868.
[19]Hall, *Observations*, p. 88.
[20]St. Paul *Press*, September 18, 1868.
[21]St. Paul *Dispatch*, September 4, 1868.

Donnelly partisans. Failing in his first attempt, Hubbard next suggested that a committee of five men be selected to determine which candidate actually represented the party. Two were to be chosen by Hubbard, two by Donnelly; the four were to select the fifth.[22] Completely confident of the merit of his position and his strength with Hubbard's friends, Donnelly replied: "I cheerfully accept the proposition. . . . I . . . cordially unite with you in the just and generous sentiments you have expressed, and in your desire to see the unfortunate situation which now divides our party satisfactorily adjusted."[23]

Donnelly's acceptance resulted in a hurriedly called meeting in the editorial office of the St. Paul *Press.* Present were Cyrus Aldrich; William Washburn; Fred Driscoll, co-editor of the *Press;* Joseph Wheelock; General Lucius Hubbard with his political adviser, General S. P. Jennison; and Cushman K. Davis, a brilliant young lawyer whom Donnelly had persuaded to enter politics. The caucus lasted from early afternoon until late evening. Hubbard must have been told that the party leaders would not accept the terms of his proposal to Donnelly. Threatening to call another convention, they may even have told him that losing the congressional seat to a Democrat was preferable to a Donnelly victory. Learning that he had been merely a cat's paw, General Hubbard telegraphed Donnelly that he could dispense with the committee and himself withdrew from the campaign.[24]

The St. Paul *Press,* erasing the image of Hubbard as its candidate, termed him a weak, unconscious politician easily deceived by the unscrupulous Donnelly. Wheelock brushed aside all pretense of party legality when the *Press* designated a new chairman for the District Executive Committee and issued the call for another convention which would follow a series of caucuses.[25]

"The mock convention," according to the St. Paul *Dispatch,* was composed of Ramsey's federal officeholders, Marshall's state officeholders, and Washburn's lumbermen. Without enthusiasm, the convention nominated General Christopher Columbus Andrews. Harlan Hall, who had an intense dislike of the acutely self-centered, pompous Andrews, called him a "johnny-come-lately Republican," a tool of Washburn and the St. Paul *Press,* and an outright liar.[26]

[22]Donnelly MSS, L. Hubbard to I. D., September 14, 1868.
[23]*Ibid.,* I. D. to L. Hubbard, September 21, 1868 (rough draft of reply).
[24]*Ibid.,* L. Hubbard to I. D., September 28, 1868.
[25]St. Paul *Press,* September 29, 1868.
[26]St. Paul *Dispatch,* October 9, 1868.

Despite the burgeoning social and economic problem of postwar America, no national issues were discussed during the election campaign. Eugene Wilson, the Democratic congressional candidate, shrewdly avoided risking a debate. Donnelly's campaign was based on his record as a Radical Republican and his reputation as a friend of internal improvements and the railroads. Andrews asserted that he was a war veteran, a Republican, and the party's real choice.

At the outset of the campaign the St. Paul *Dispatch* was embarrassed because eastern newspapers and even the Democratic St. Paul *Pioneer* blamed Donnelly for the schism. But after Hubbard withdrew from the contest, the *Dispatch* reprinted articles from the New York *Tribune*, the Cincinnati *Chronicle*, the Chicago *Journal*, and the Chicago *Republican* calling on Andrews to retire from the race to save the party.[27]

As Donnelly toured the state, making speeches, there were increasing indications of the desperation of his Republican opposition. Armed with pikes, lumberjacks from the Washburn camps and mills broke up his meetings. The St. Paul *Pioneer*, commenting on the episodes, was unwilling to state whether Washburn's pikemen acted on orders or out of a sense of loyalty. It left this problem to its readers to answer.[28]

The foreign-born voters appeared to be the decisive factor in the election. The *Pioneer* scoffed at Donnelly's efforts to gain a following among Irish Democrats, but one week before the election it alleged that Donnelly's forces had successfully invaded the Irish areas using hard cash to win votes.[29] There is no indication in Donnelly's extensive correspondence to substantiate the accusation. Donnelly's real anxiety stemmed from the Scandinavian defection. It was openly admitted that Hans Mattson was raising "the very devil" among voters who had formerly been solidly for Donnelly.[30] No one in Donnelly's camp had sufficient influence or prestige to offset Mattson. Unable to speak either Swedish or Norwegian, Donnelly could make no personal effort to stop the trend. If Donnelly were defeated, lamented the St. Paul *Dispatch*, the Scandinavians would be sorry when they realized that they had been duped.[31]

The morning edition of the St. Paul *Press* on election day was, save for the advertising, devoted to an attack on Donnelly's

[27] *Ibid.*, October 21, 1868.
[28] St. Paul *Pioneer*, October 25, 1868.
[29] *Ibid.*, October 30, 1868.
[30] Donnelly MSS, H. Bevan to I. D., October 10, 1868.
[31] November 4, 1868.

character and career. He was charged with selling out to the Union Pacific, providing a railroad to Hastings to undermine St. Paul, being a Jesuitical Democrat rather than a Republican, favoring mob rule and violence, and having a five-thousand-dollar slush fund provided by his dishonest railroad friends to corrupt the election.[32] It was a fitting climax to an election fought to determine whether Andrews or Donnelly would serve best to make the label Republican a euphemism for entrepreneur.

Democrat Eugene Wilson won the election with 13,506 votes to Donnelly's 11,265 and Andrews 8,595.[33] Donnelly's almost three-thousand-vote majority among Republicans proved he was the party's choice. His friends, especially Harlan Hall, were indignant at the distribution of the immigrant vote. "You certainly have this consolation," Hall insisted, "that you have had the unanimous support of all the intelligent Republicans in the District and the vote which has defeated you has been the Scandinavians who know nothing of our matters but were controlled by a few bought leaders."[34] In his memoirs, Hall observed that "the beginning of the evolution of Ignatius Donnelly from Republican member of Congress to the position of a private citizen, and thence to the leadership of the People's Party might be dated from this campaign."[35] But Hall was surely mistaken. No single defeat could have initiated the subtle and lengthy process of change.

Donnelly exorcized the feelings of anger and remorse that welled up in him at the election's outcome. "Keep up the brave heart and you shall be a Senator yet," he wrote Kate cheerfully.[36] As the outspoken candidate of the railroads, Donnelly was confident of success.[37] He felt betrayed and disappointed when Oakes Ames wrote that the Union Pacific's Board of Directors refused to enter the contest in Donnelly's behalf.[38]

Pessimistic, Kate wrote her husband that the political experts predicted his defeat. The New York *Herald* proclaimed that Ram-

[32]November 3, 1868.

[33]*Minnesota Legislative Manual*, 1869, p. 93. For a slightly different count St. Paul *Pioneer*, November 24, 1868.

[34]Donnelly MSS, H. P. Hall to I. D., November 8, 1868.

[35]Hall, *Observations*, p. 76.

[36]Donnelly MSS, I. D. to K. D., November 19, 1868.

[37]*Ibid.*, I. D. to K. D., December 27, 1868.

[38]*Ibid.*, O. Ames to I. D., December 26, 1868; Harvard College [Photostat copies in Minnesota Historical Society], William K. Rogers MSS, I. D. to W. Le Duc, December 8, 1868.

sey would retain office "because he was the best politician."[39] Living among schemes, reports, and rumors and mentally folding and unfolding a map of Minnesota starred with the names of friends and enemies, Donnelly replied: "I hope to win, yet constantly keep my mind prepared for defeat. You must do the same."[40]

Gravely determined and keeping his own counsel, Alexander Ramsey returned to Minnesota to direct his senatorial contest. Aware that Donnelly was courting the aid of former Senator Morton S. Wilkinson, Ramsey could count on William Windom, who had just been named senator by Governor William R. Marshall to fill the vacancy created by the sudden death of Daniel Norton. This weakened Donnelly's candidacy because Windom had a large following. More important, Wilkinson was a less reliable ally. So great was his own desire to return to the Senate that Wilkinson saw himself as a compromise between the rivals.[41]

On the eve of the Republican senatorial caucus, the St. Paul *Press* became increasingly vituperative. Kate, vexed by its sarcasm and abuse, had come to hate Alexander Ramsey. "Beat him no matter what happens," she wrote; "he would break the party to break you —in this case party be hanged, I would stand at nothing to beat him."[42]

But Ramsey had all the power in his hands: the state and federal officeholders, the intrenched party machinery, and the support of William Windom. At the very last moment Wilkinson, arguing that he had a better chance of defeating Ramsey, forced Donnelly to withdraw his name. Although betrayed, Donnelly urged his followers to support Wilkinson.[43] With no votes to spare, Ramsey won on the first ballot.

After his re-election to the Senate, Ramsey was willing to make peace with Donnelly. With his future secure for six years, he was once again concerned with the Republican party's future. Foster relayed Ramsey's views and pleaded with Donnelly to "meet the old man half way," but for Donnelly the chasm between them could not be bridged; future years would see it deepen.[44]

Donnelly's initial bid for the senatorship had failed. He had offered energy, efficiency, and his powerful oratory, but there was

[39]Donnelly MSS, K. D. to I. D., December 27, 1868.
[40]*Ibid.*, I. D. to K. D., January 13, 1869.
[41]*Ibid.*, K. D. to I. D., December 25, 1868; H. Wait to I. D., January 9, 1869.
[42]*Ibid.*, K. D. to I. D., January 10, 1869.
[43]*Ibid.*, M. Wilkinson and I. D. to Delegates, January 14, 1869 (copy).
[44]*Ibid.*, T. Foster to I. D., January 24, 1869.

no ideological difference between Donnelly and Ramsey—no real issue divided them. His campaign reflected the depth of his personal ambition. He assumed that his friends would identify his craving for power with an urge to improve mankind, but other than his opposition to slavery, his indorsement of public education, and his support for Negro suffrage, he gave little evidence of political or moral courage. He was almost indistinguishable from a typical Grant Era Republican.

In fact, this was clearly demonstrated in the months that followed when he became the chief lobbyist for the Lake Superior & Mississippi Railroad.[45] General John C. Frémont easily recruited him to lobby for the proposed Atlantic & Pacific Railroad which was seeking a land grant comparable to the Union Pacific's. Donnelly was promised fifty thousand dollars in cash and two hundred thousand dollars' worth of company stock. For political reasons, the stock was to be held in trust until he wanted it. Frémont, however, involved the railroad in a colossal fraud that forced it into bankruptcy, and Donnelly received nothing for his services. Much to his chagrin, the case against Frémont came to light years later when Donnelly was vigorously denouncing railroad abuses of the public welfare. The episode became a skeleton in his closet,[46] but his actions at the time were no different from those of a score of legislators who were to participate in the Crédit Mobilier.

When Congress adjourned in the spring of 1869, Donnelly returned to Minnesota to care for his farms. During his first visit to St. Paul, his friends staged an impromptu rally beneath the balcony of the Merchants Hotel. "In a vein of cheerful philosophy and good sense," according to the St. Paul *Press*, Donnelly renounced the vanity of human wishes. Cautiously tempering its own attitude, the paper added: "For a young gentleman of energy and ability, such as Mr. Donnelly is conceded to possess, the world always has a sphere and a future. . . . He will be wanted bye and bye."[47] But the St. Paul *Pioneer*, confident of its own insight, noted that while he spoke as a private citizen "the old fire was there, though smoldering, and

[45]*Ibid.*, R. Lamborn to I. D., February 23, 1869; W. Banning to I. D., April 3, 7, 1869.

[46]Allan Nevins, *Frémont: The West's Greatest Adventurer* (New York: Harper & Bros., 1928), II, 674–84; Donnelly MSS, W. Schmoele to I. D., August 19, October 9, 1869; I. D. to J. Frémont, May 29, 1870 (copy); I. D. to J. Frémont, July 2, 1870 (copy); W. Schmoele to I. D., August 24, 1871; I. D. to A. Ferris, September 3, 1871 (copy).

[47]April 28, 1869.

not flashing as it did during the canvass last fall." "Beware," its editor warned Minnesota's politicians; "see a few months hence whether he is without power or patronage, see how his enemies will wish he was in that condition, the prairies will be on fire for Donnelly before the harvest ripens."[48]

While Donnelly, retired from politics, was reading in his excellent library in the "shades of Nininger,"[49] Windom and Ramsey wanted to know his plans. Both agreed he could be valuable either in the House or as governor, but they wanted a straightforward statement.[50] Harlan Hall urged Donnelly to seek the governorship. He could promise Windom's aid because the senator wanted the support of the St. Paul *Dispatch*. With this combination, victory would be assured.[51]

Incapable of making a decision, Donnelly procrastinated. Assuming he would run for the House, General John Averill, acting with Donnelly's tacit consent, sought out Horace Austin from southern Minnesota as "our kind of man" for governor. At the same time Hall's *Dispatch* called upon Minnesota Republicans to draft Donnelly for governor. The St. Paul *Press* exploded a bombshell in the Donnelly camp by suggesting that General Averill seek the governorship himself because it would eliminate all hard feelings stemming from the previous contest. Averill declined, favoring instead someone from southern Minnesota—obviously Austin. The same day the *Dispatch* indorsed Averill for state treasurer.

Donnelly's inability to formulate a slate of candidates caused embarrassment and confusion among his friends. Averill, having found Austin and withdrawn from the gubernatorial contest, was unacceptable for treasurer in St. Paul where Donnellyites believed only a German could be elected. Groping for a solution, Averill invited Donnelly to St. Paul to select a ticket.[52] The meeting went badly. Reluctantly, Averill withdrew in favor of Emil Munch, and Donnelly announced that he was not an active gubernatorial candidate but would accept a draft.[53]

Every newspaper in St. Paul and Minneapolis except the *Dispatch* predicted defeat for Donnelly's slate at the state convention.

[48] April 28, 1869.
[49] St. Paul *Dispatch*, May 11, 1869.
[50] Donnelly MSS, J. Averill to I. D., May 30, 1869.
[51] *Ibid.*, H. Hall to I. D., June 3, 1869.
[52] *Ibid.*, H. John to I. D., August 20, 1869; T. Howard to I. D., August 20, 1869; S. Daughty to I. D., August 25, 1869; J. Averill to I. D., August 29, 1869.
[53] St. Paul *Dispatch*, September 1, 4, 1869.

Averill's friends were openly hostile and Donnelly came near charging the general with duplicity when Austin won a two-to-one victory on the first ballot. One summer of ineptitude had almost dissipated a decade of hard work. Not only had Donnelly's political organization begun to disintegrate, but he was obviously guilty in the public eye of selfish office-seeking at the expense of Averill.[54]

Disgusted with the convention's outcome, Donnelly refused to campaign for Austin. Since he was preparing to practice law, he wrote Fred Driscoll of the St. Paul *Press* that taking time off might be detrimental to his prospects.[55] Harlan Hall disagreed with this decision and felt too much was at stake for Donnelly to play Achilles before Troy.

Virtually retired to Nininger City, Donnelly looked seriously at the state of agricultural prosperity. More than eight years had elapsed since he had depended on farming for a livelihood. The Civil War agricultural boom was over; farms were already being abandoned as uneconomical because of competition from newer lands. Dakota County's population was no longer increasing rapidly. Eastern Minnesota was old land; the frontier had moved farther west. His own financial condition reflected the changing times. Wheat prices were low and costs of farming were high because new labor-saving devices forced mechanization on the owners of older lands. Many farmers in the Middle West, and Donnelly was one of them even though he did not work his own land, felt they were not making money fast enough.[56]

Donnelly decided to express his views publicly at the Dakota County Fair, on the causes for declining agricultural profits. Much to the astonishment of the audience, he entirely ignored the forthcoming election but called attention to the impact of high tariff on farm profits. Governor Marshall, also scheduled to speak, discarded his prepared address to debate the tariff issue. Neither as effective a speaker nor as well prepared, Marshall could only charge inconsistency. Provided time for a rebuttal, Donnelly ridiculed Marshall's ignorance and explained the evolution of his own thinking.

The Republican party was committed to a policy of protective tariff, and as a representative of that party, I voted and advocated it; and when the South went out we passed the laws. The war broke out and we needed the tariff. But the war is ended, and the necessity is passed. I am

[54]Mankato Weekly *Record*, September 18, 1869.
[55]Donnelly MSS, F. Driscoll to I. D., September 24, 1869.
[56]*Ibid.*, Sara Donnelly to I. D., October 26, 1869.

now a farmer myself, and dependent upon the products of my farm for support, and reflection has taught me the injustice done to the producer of the West by the present tariff system.

As for inconsistency, Donnelly quoted the adage, "The wise man changes his mind—the fool never."[57]

Two weeks later, Donnelly published an open letter citing his congressional votes to prove that he had been a moderate protectionist.[58] When Horace Greeley's New York *Tribune* condemned him as a free-trade demagogue who had caused a Republican congressional defeat in Minnesota, Donnelly replied in a letter to the editor denying that he advocated free trade. He favored a tariff for revenue and true protection, not inequitable taxation and the prohibition of imports.[59] During the late autumn of 1869, Donnelly's good friend Ossian E. Dodge suggested he become a professional lecturer. Dodge was convinced that Donnelly's ability and reputation would assure him as much as one hundred dollars for a single speech. He proposed a lecture on the highly controversial Riel Rebellion in western Canada, an uprising sparked by French-speaking Roman Catholics.[60] Since Donnelly had already gone on record opposing the movement of British troops across the United States to put down the rebellion, he agreed to defend his views publicly. This speech initiated his career as a professional lecturer.

In Donnelly's mind the Riel Rebellion was closely associated, at least philosophically, with the Fenian movement for Irish independence. He had no interest in Fenianism's selfish, violent schemes.[61] Even though he realized that his views might hurt him politically, he had written a candid letter to the editor of the Chicago *Irish Republic,* a radical nationalistic paper, explaining that the Irish would fail to enlist the sympathies of the average American because "to the mass of the American people . . . the Irish people have no love for any other liberty than Irish liberty and hostility to no oppression save English oppression."[62] Therefore, when Donnelly spoke in St. Paul in support of Louis Riel, he was not simply expressing Anglophobia or sympathy for the Irish cause, which he

---

[57] St. Paul *Pioneer,* October 14, 1869.

[58] *Ibid.,* October 26, 1869.

[59] Donnelly MSS, I. D. to editor of New York *Tribune,* December 23, 1869; also clipping.

[60] *Ibid.,* O. Dodge to I. D., November 17, 1869.

[61] *Ibid.,* J. Griffin to I. D., June 7, 1866. Donnelly marked the letter unanswered.

[62] *Ibid.,* I. D. to *Irish Republic,* December 30, 1867.

linked with the Canadian question. It was his sincere conviction that political and religious freedom could not be defended in terms of one race, one creed, or one nationality; it was universal.

Delighted with response to the speech, Ossian Dodge hailed it as a genuine triumph and urged Donnelly to compose one on the tariff. On January 6, 1870, he presented a three-hour tariff discussion before a large audience at Ingersoll Hall. Congratulatory letters and speaking invitations from Democrats and Republicans all over the state flooded his mail. The St. Paul *Press* conceded that he had breathed life into a subject usually as dead as dust, and that even his statistics became entertaining.[63]

Aside from personal experience, Donnelly's tariff views were based on material gathered from government documents, newspaper clippings, pamphlets, and speeches printed in the *Congressional Globe*. He kept a file of the tariff statements made by leading public figures. Little of the information came from orthodox economic studies, but he read widely in free-trade pamphlets. The more he read the greater became his conviction that the tariff was the product of a disagreeable corruption, and his own Washington experience reaffirmed his belief.

Donnelly was moving toward a crisis in his social thinking. On the flyleaf of his 1870 diary he wrote:

> Poverty is a horrible thing. No man ever sucked the sour lemon, Poverty, that did not puck his mouth for ever after. Seneca praised the beauties of poverty, but Seneca had a large income. . . .
> The beauties of Poverty! It is nothing but unsatisfied wants, restricted capabilities, undeveloped virtues. . . .
> A poor man is nearest barbarism for he is denied the advantage of civilization.[64]

Donnelly had never known the fruits of poverty. Along with his denunciation of the tariff as an instrument of special interests, this was a new kind of social concern. It deviated from the traditional values of freedom of speech, religion, and the ballot which he had espoused. It is ironic that he assumed these views, unable to detect the sharp and hidden conflict encompassed by his personal financial ambition and his emerging social consciousness, at a time when he was preparing to leave for Washington as a railroad lobbyist.

To mask his activities, Donnelly became the Washington correspondent of the St. Paul *Dispatch*. Harlan Hall hoped that the

[63] January 7, 1870.
[64] Donnelly MSS, Diary, flyleaf.

weekly articles would combine descriptions of Washington social life with political reporting. But Donnelly's new social awareness gave the articles a tone of political urgency. He saw the tariff as a crossroad in American politics. "The Republican party of the nation must choose between the people and the capitalists," he insisted; "*if they take the side of the latter they must not expect the former to sustain them. A party cannot live upon the memory of the past.*"[65]

Even when Donnelly described Washington's social scene he wrote in so vitriolic a manner that his complete disgust with the superficiality and vulgarity of the Grant Era was obvious.

A carpet extends from the curb to the door. You enter. Stairs, hall, rooms, are packed with moving, jostling, surging, struggling people. Here a lady expostulates with a gentleman immediately behind for standing on her train, while he, good man, assures her he is straddling it, and the man who has fastened her to the spot is several feet distant in the crowd! In one of the rooms near the door stand the host and hostess, smiling away . . . like clock-work, and mechanically shaking hands with everybody in the pump handle style. Then there are the young ladies who sweat and pant in the dancing room, with the half developed young men; and flounce and jump and chassez with as much earnestness as if it were their business in life, and each stood at the end of the cotillion to cry out, "lead your partners to their graves." Then there are the weak men who haunt the punch room, and ever anon dart in, as if to say, "really is this what you have here?" as if they had never been there before! And there are the sensible men who nose out the supper room, and who, selecting some quiet corner, near the tables, guzzle and are silent. But the great clatter, jangle and chatter goes on, a thousand interests, wishes, vanities, mingle together in one stupendous buzz and burr, while the mechanical host and hostess stand smiling away and working their pump handles, and the streams struggle in and out of the door. . . . And this is a Washington party.[66]

As Donnelly contrasted this degenerating urban society and its accompanying national corruption with the simplicity and struggle of the depression-afflicted Minnesota farmers, he was groping for a new ideological identity, for a cause as meaningful as abolitionism.

Most of Donnelly's lobbying activities were in Jay Cooke's interests.[67] The Philadelphia banker's plans required federal government permission to mortgage the Northern Pacific's land to finance the

[65] St. Paul *Dispatch*, March 1, 1870.

[66] *Ibid.*, February 14, 1870.

[67] Donnelly MSS, I. D. to K. D., March 1, 1870. At this time he broke with General Le Duc over the Hastings Dakota & Western's land grant. Offered 10,-000 acres, Donnelly replied, "If he brought me a gift of one million dollars as a gift, I would make him a present of *one hundred* thousand!"

road's construction and a federal appropriation to improve the harbor of Duluth, Minnesota. Acting for Cooke, William L. Banning employed Donnelly to lobby for the Duluth Harbor measure. "Our friends will give you all the help *they can*," Banning wrote Donnelly; "but *you* must work the business up and then *call on them and direct them how to help you*."[68] As part of the Cooke organization, Donnelly was confident of his success.

When Cooke expressed concern about Donnelly's abilities, Banning replied that no matter what representations "may be made by certain political enemies at Washington & elsewhere in regard to his influence," Donnelly was reliable. "During the hot political contests in this State in the past three years, Mr. Windom, Governor Marshall, Ramsey & Donnelly have at times crossed each other's paths and it may be have not the most kindly feelings in all respects toward each other." Nevertheless, he concluded, "None of them can, however, I am sure be more effective than Donnelly in the actual business of getting our bills through."[69]

Early in March, Donnelly suggested seeking a half-million-acre land grant to underwrite the project. If the measure could pass the Senate, he was confident the House would accept an identical bill. This would avoid the complications in a joint House-Senate committee. If it failed, a cash appropriation could be requested.[70] Cooke approved the scheme over the protests of Alexander Ramsey, who was also in Cooke's employment.

Having decided upon the plan, Donnelly set about winning friends. He sought control of the Washington *Chronicle* by giving D. C. Forney 640 acres of Minnesota land.[71] Forney used not only his newspaper to support Cooke's projects but also his personal influence with legislators, especially Iowa's Senator James Harlan.[72]

The Cooke enterprise afforded the young lobbyist the economic opportunity of a lifetime. "I am to get 15 per cent of the grant if I get it through," he wrote Kate. "The grant is for 5,000,000 acres—15 per ct. will am't to 75,000 acres. . . . 75,000 will be worth at least $2.50 per acre or $187,000."[73] Donnelly planned to retain 10,000 acres of iron and copper lands in northern Minnesota. Two days

[68]*Ibid.*, W. Banning to I. D., February 1, 1870.
[69]Historical Society of Pennsylvania [Photostat copies in Minnesota Historical Society], Jay Cooke MSS, W. Banning to J. Cooke, February 24, 1870.
[70]*Ibid.*, I. D. to Jay Cooke, March 5, 1870.
[71]Donnelly MSS, Diary, March 9, 1870.
[72]*Ibid.*, D. Forney to I. D., July 10, July 19, 1870.
[73]*Ibid.*, I. D. to K. D., March 9, 1870; Contract, March 15, 1870.

before the Senate committee hearings on the bill, he was so excited that he was almost afraid to think what success would mean.

Jay Cooke and Donnelly, supported by a battery of railroad experts and engineers, presented the Duluth Harbor plan to the Senate Committee on Public Lands. Maps were scrutinized, costs estimated, and arguments heard. Donnelly had arranged with a friendly member of the committee for an immediate vote on the proposal. The measure was approved.

Thrilled, he wrote his wife: "You can readily see that with Jay Cooke & the whole Northern Pacific Rd at my back the passage of the bill . . . is almost certain . . . worth nearly $200,000. Think of that."[74] Banning, sharing Donnelly's enthusiasm, urged him to press the matter to completion not only for a fortune but also for a United States senatorship![75]

After two days of vigorous debate the Duluth bill passed the House. Donnelly had been active on the floor during the period, sending telegrams to Cooke almost every hour.[76] The House and Senate measures, however, were not identical. Ramsey had persisted in seeking a substitute money bill. Just as Donnelly feared, the measures were sent to a joint committee. When Congress adjourned, only Cooke's Northern Pacific land mortgage scheme had been approved.

For Kate and Ignatius, the eventual defeat of the harbor bill was a major disappointment. Their many hopes and dreams based on its success were shattered. To compound their unhappiness, Kate underwent abdominal surgery and, although she recuperated rapidly, she was never wholly free of physical discomfort, if not pain, for the rest of her life.[77]

During the spring of 1870, while Donnelly lived in Washington working for Jay Cooke, he reassessed his political future. Although eager to seek re-election to Congress, he was reluctant to fight for his former position in the Republican party. In early March he wrote his closest friends that he was considering running again but as an independent.

Harlan Hall considered the idea basically unsound. General John Averill appeared a strong possibility for the regular Republican nomination. Hall could see some merit in opposing a sworn enemy,

[74]*Ibid.*, I. D. to K. D., March 19, 1870.
[75]*Ibid.*, W. Banning to I. D., March 25, 1870.
[76]*Ibid.*, series of telegrams, I. D. to J. Cooke, May 26, 1870.
[77]*Ibid.*, K. Ferris to I. D., July 7, 1870; E. Donnelly to I. D., July 8, 1870.

but a division between friends was pointless.[78] Dr. Thomas Foster pleaded with Donnelly not to ruin himself. "It is the greatest hardship of my career in politics," he wrote, "that I can see no recourse finally for my polished God-son, politically, but refuge in the folds of the Democratic church, and consequently political annihilation forever in Minnesota."[79] From each of his best friends, George Keith, T. M. Metcalf, and W. B. Mitchell came the same kind of response.[80]

Unable to recruit his Republican friends, Donnelly turned to the Democrats; their reaction was almost negative. A few politicians favored Donnelly to oust Windom but for no other reason.[81] This was small encouragement. Nevertheless, Donnelly unhesitatingly determined on a congressional campaign as an independent.

On August 20, 1870, shortly before the congressional nominating conventions, Donnelly spoke to a large audience gathered at Ingersoll Hall. His aim was to win Republican support for his cause. To Donnelly the issues upon which the Republican party had been founded—slavery, the homestead, and foreign policy—were no longer significant. The time had come to seek a new program. If the party hoped to benefit the common man, tariff reform would determine this new direction.

The tariff was more than a question of taxation. "I think we are taxed heavily enough, but we do not complain of that *per se*, for we know that the government must be supported." But, he added, "we do complain that we are robbed to make others rich; that the farmer of the West is plundered in order that the manufacturers of the East may amass fortunes." Protect American labor he argued. "Lay your taxes on your imports and graduate the tariff so that it will cover the difference between the cost of labor in the United States and its costs in England," and the cost of transportation. This would provide the American workingman adequate natural protection from foreign competition. A higher tariff, he told his audience, enriched the manufacturers at the consumer's expense.

Could manufacturers who argued for a tariff to protect American labor be believed, he asked, when they encouraged all possible immigration, even orientals. With outright demagogy, playing on the apprehensions of the workingmen in his audience, he warned

[78] *Ibid.*, H. Hall to I. D., March 18, 28, April 22, 1870.
[79] *Ibid.*, T. Foster to I. D., May 16, 1870.
[80] *Ibid.*, G. Keith to I. D., April 25, 1870; H. Johns to I. D., April 25, 1870; T. Wilson to I. D., June 13, 1870; T. Metcalf to I. D., June 14, 1870.
[81] Donnelly MSS, S. Mayall to I. D., July 27, 1870.

that the industrialists would introduce a new form of slavery that would force the *"two dollar a day man, be he Yankee or Irish . . . to retire before the one dollar a day man, with his yellow face and busy fingers."*[82]

Within one week the Hall-Donnelly partnership dissolved. Donnelly angrily noted in his diary, "Hall sold me out for $6,000 & takes the *Dispatch* over to the support of Averill."[83] On September 1, General Averill received the Republican nomination for Congress by acclamation. Ironically, Averill insisted upon and received a low tariff platform.[84]

Donnelly, meanwhile, preparing for his candidacy as an independent, asked his friends to circulate petitions calling on him to make the canvass as a People's party candidate. The day before Averill's nomination, two influential Democrats, Sam Mayall and George L. Becker, telegraphed Donnelly that the forthcoming Democratic convention would indorse him for Congress.[85]

Following his nomination by the self-styled People's party, Donnelly's name was presented to the Democrats. With an obvious lack of enthusiasm the delegates indorsed the man who had been the party's most vigorous and outspoken critic. In appearing before them, Donnelly, repenting nothing, stated with incredible boldness, "I am before you at the solicitation of my fellow citizens, and if a platform is demanded, I plant *myself on the platform of Ignatius Donnelly.*"[86] The Republicans, he warned the delegates, would try to "distract and divide" the people by talking of slavery and reconstruction. Then, because he tended more and more to personalize and dramatize issues so that differences of opinion became sources of personal enmity, he concluded:

I know full well what I have to encounter in this contest. Thousands upon thousands of dollars will be spent to defeat me. I may not be sustained by a single newspaper. I have no money to spend; I can only appeal, to the people, and ask them, if they believe I am with them to sustain me. They are my only hope and reliance. I shall go among them, like Peter the Hermit, and preach a crusade against this rich powerful and omnipresent combination. I expect to triumph. I may go down in

[82] *Ibid.,* Scrapbook, "The Unjust Tariff."
[83] *Ibid.,* Diary, August 26, 1870.
[84] St. Paul *Dispatch,* September 2, 1870.
[85] Donnelly MSS, telegrams, S. Mayall to I. D.; G. Becker to I. D., August 31, 1870.
[86] Minnesota Historical Society Library, Ignatius Donnelly, "To the Voters of the 2nd Congressional District," (n.p., n. d.).

the fight, but if I do, the next blast of the trumpet will see me on my feet again, ready for another contest.[87]

"Donnelly is home at last," sneered the St. Paul *Press;* "like Judas Iscariot he has gone to his place." His political philosophy "is Ignatius Donnelly, first, last and all the time. He knows no party save Ignatius Donnelly, no principles save Ignatius Donnelly, no religion save Ignatius Donnelly."[88]

William Marshall told Jay Cooke that Donnelly had been nominated by the Democrats. "Didn't you tell me," Marshall wrote, that Donnelly "had recanted his free trade notions."[89] But William L. Banning asked Cooke not to surrender the influence of the Northern Pacific into the hands of William S. King and William Windom, who would use it to satisfy their own ambitions.[90] In a long letter to Cooke, Donnelly defended his position.

I am as you are probably aware a candidate for Congress in this district, running on a People's Independent ticket. I will certainly be elected by a large majority, if the laborers of the Northern Pacific Railroad, mainly un-naturalized foreigners, are not induced to vote against me in a body by the contractor. I understand that they are now being organized and drilled for that purpose.

I need not say to you that I am a friend of the Northern Pacific Railroad Company.

I drew most of the original bill under which it took its first land grant. I was a member of the committee on Pacific RR'ds at the time and materially contributed to the passage of the bill, through the committee and its subsequent passage through Congress; and on all subsequent occasions I have labored earnestly and I think efficiently in behalf of the Company.

If I am returned to Congress I shall go there as the firm friend and advocate of the Northern Pacific RR.

I do not ask you to exert the influence of the Company in my favor, as it is manifestly improper for these public enterprises to tamper in politics or become the instruments of factions. I simply ask that it shall not be exerted against me.[91]

In reply to Donnelly's request, Cooke placed formal advertisements in the St. Paul newspapers explaining that the Northern Pacific was not supporting either candidate.[92] The railroad, however, was being constructed by contractors directly controlled by William S. King. Cooke did nothing to restrain King.

[87] *Ibid.*
[88] St. Paul *Press*, September 16, 20, 1870.
[89] Cooke MSS, W. Marshall to J. Cooke, September 17, 1870.
[90] *Ibid.*, W. Banning to J. Cooke, September 23, 1870.
[91] Donnelly MSS, I. D. to J. Cooke, September 23, 1870.
[92] St. Paul *Pioneer,* October 4, 1870.

Although Donnelly campaigned energetically, he had difficulty presenting the tariff issue effectively. At the time of his Dakota County Fair pronouncement almost one year earlier, wheat was selling for sixty cents a bushel. In October, 1870, the price had risen to more than one dollar a bushel. His strongest argument, the declining condition of agriculture, seemed meaningless as wheat prices climbed. He was campaigning against a non-existent depression.

Furthermore, Donnelly overestimated the value of the Democratic indorsement. The party regulars, who hated him, refused to raise money in his behalf. His cause suffered a severe setback when the official Democratic organ, the St. Paul *Pioneer*, declined to aid him despite General Henry Hastings Sibley's personal appeal to the paper's owner, H. L. Carver.[93] The attitude of the *Pioneer* encouraged increasing defections among workers.

The irate secretary of the District Congressional Committee charged that the convention had been "manipulated in the interest of the Lake Superior Railroad Company." The "general interests of the party were [being] sacrificed to aims petty and personal." Donnelly, the secretary wrote, had been "a constant persistent, and foul mouthed vilifier of Democratic men and measures for fifteen years; and only recants after . . . he has been cast out of the Republican party." The St. Paul *Pioneer* published the statement under the heading, "Let the Experiment in Prostitution be Fully Tried."[94]

Donnelly was defeated by 2,600 votes out of a total of almost 32,000 cast. Sam Mayall blamed the election's loss on the defection of one-third of the St. Paul and Minneapolis Democrats, but the Dakota *Union*, a pro-Donnelly Democratic paper, attributed it to William S. King, who controlled the votes of the Northern Pacific Construction Company's laborers.[95] Both analysts were probably correct.

Disheartened and embarrassed, Donnelly was reluctant to return to Washington as Cooke's lobbyist, because he would be forced to associate with Ramsey, Windom, King, and Averill. He asked Banning to explain his attitude to Cooke and to arrange for his final payment. A short time later, seeking to dispose of his Lake Superior & Mississippi Railroad stock to Cooke, Donnelly wrote the banker

[93] Henry A. Castle, "Reminiscences of Minnesota Politics," Minnesota Historical Society *Collections*, XV, 557.

[94] St. Paul *Pioneer*, October 24, 1870.

[95] Donnelly MSS, S. Mayall to I. D., November 12, 1870; Dakota *Union*, November, 1870.

explaining that he was "willing to take what you paid the St. Paul *Press* for the stock—viz. 20 cts. on the dollar." Closing his letter on an embittered note, he placed the responsibility for his defeat on Northern Pacific's labor gangs.[96] But Cooke denied that he had either bought stock or allowed the Northern Pacific to interfere in the election.[97]

Several months later Donnelly wrote Cooke, "I find myself after years of Congressional labor to create and develop the R. Rd System of our State, left comparatively poor, and with no opportunity to sell the stock I hold for even 20 cents on the dollar." Reproachfully, Donnelly concluded, "I have not only not been benefited a farthing by the construction of the road, but the men employed upon it were the principle means of my defeat last fall."[98]

"I beg you to feel," Cooke answered, "that . . . those who are really the Northern Pacific Co. have nothing to do with political matters." And he added, with a sincerity bred of confusion: "What those people connected with the Construction Co. did I am not aware of. It is enough to puzzle a dozen Philada. lawyers to keep track of the various influences pro & con in Minnesota."[99] Donnelly never believed him.

Having lost his political income, Donnelly turned to his farms. He had been interested in scientific farming for years. Concerned with the methods of computing profits, he had studied not merely acreage yield, but also seed, labor, and equipment costs. In 1869, he contacted Oliver Dalrymple, the best known, large-scale farm operator in the Northwest, to compare Dalrymple's costs and profits with those of a Dakota County farmer.[100] Throughout the spring of 1871, he filled his diary with accounts of experiments with fruit trees, garden crops, and machinery.

But wily Dr. Foster, who refused to allow Donnelly to sink into political oblivion, wanted him returned to power. He urged Donnelly to write a public letter defending the Grant administration. The St. Paul *Pioneer* would criticize it, the St. Paul *Press* would be

[96]Donnelly MSS, I. D. to J. Cooke, February 15, 1870 (copy, but obviously improperly dated).

[97]*Ibid.*, J. Cooke to I. D., February 21, 1871. Ellis P. Oberholtzer, *Jay Cooke, Financier of the Civil War*, II, 175, states that Donnelly was defeated through the railroad's influence, but offers no evidence. He probably relied on Donnelly's letter to Cooke.

[98]Cooke MSS, I. D. to J. Cooke, July 29, 1871.

[99]Donnelly MSS, J. Cooke to I. D., August 5, 1871.

[100]*Ibid.*, O. Dalrymple to I. D., November 3, 1869; A. Poor to I. D., November 4, 1869.

forced to defend it, and the Republicans would welcome his return to the party.[101] Donnelly rejected the advice; nevertheless, Foster began inserting brief items favorable to Donnelly in his newspaper, the Duluth *Minnesotian*. Harlan Hall, sharing Foster's personal feelings, reprinted them in the *Dispatch*.

Late in June, 1871, the *Minnesotian* in a friendly puff, noted that Donnelly, retired from politics to the "Shades of Nininger," was raising wheat instead of "Old Ned."[102] But Foster was wrong; Donnelly had accepted an invitation to present a Fourth of July speech at Red Wing, Minnesota. In an attempt to gauge the political temper of the people, he made a dramatic and stirring appeal for an end to "bloody shirt" oratory.

The war is past, and the wrath and hate which grew out of it should perish with it. We should cease to regard the South as a foreign country inhabited by our enemies. . . . Our government must rest upon the love of the people; and it can only be secured by justice, fair play, and generosity. Let us supplement universal suffrage with universal amnesty. If they have wrath and revenge in their hearts, let them spit it out through the ballot box.

The South's problems could be resolved. And, he insisted, "The cure for the Ku Klux is the school house."

But the central focus of the Red Wing speech was the emergence of monopolistic influences in the United States, especially that of the railroads. They "have in their employment one million men," he told his listeners; "Gen. Washington's army during the great revolution did not exceed twenty thousand." The railroad companies had enough political power to decide a presidential election! "Railroads like fire and water are good servants, but bad masters," he warned. "We do not attempt to do away with fire and water, but we keep them in subjugation." The railroads, furthermore, "were created to transport the commerce of the country, not to rule its politics or corrupt its laws. If they can't behave themselves we must put them in irons."

During his congressional term, Donnelly would have ridiculed anyone in the House who spoke as he did at Red Wing, but his own experiences as a lobbyist and his knowledge of the inner working relationship of the railroads and the government, convinced him that the gains produced by America's railroad development were not offset by their social costs. The solution to the problem of

[101]*Ibid.*, T. Foster to I. D., November 19, 1870.
[102]Duluth *Minnesotian*, June 24, 1871.

monopoly, he concluded, was political. "Join hands and stand shoulder to shoulder . . . against these new and powerful enemies," Donnelly pleaded. "If your politics are right, everything else will be added unto you; if they are wrong, you stand a fair chance to have everything else taken away."[103]

Several hundred copies of the speech were printed and distributed to leading men in Minnesota. If Donnelly had hoped for a vigorous and courageous response to the Red Wing plea, he must have been keenly disappointed. There was almost no reaction.

A short time later, when Dr. William W. Mayo, the politically minded Rochester physician, urged him to re-enter political life, Donnelly replied in disgust: "As I feel now, I will stick to my farm and my books, and let the dirty angels of corruption stir the nasty pool of politics to its depths." He was certain, he grumbled to Mayo, that "the fragments that come to the top will probably be equally foul whether labeled 'Republican' or 'Democrat.' "[104]

After the cool reception of the Red Wing address, he wrote Dr. Foster that his political life was finished. Why "it would be sheer madness for me to butt my head against a combination that can spend $100,000 in a single canvass." And, he added, with a piety induced by his recent political hardships, "To preach Republican principles, public virtue and private honesty . . . is to use the ritual of Christ in the foul service of some African idol."[105]

Impatient and pragmatic, Foster refused to acknowledge this argument, insisting that Donnelly go to the Republican convention and vote with the machine.[106] But "I owe something to the thousands of Republicans who followed my banner last fall," Donnelly replied. "My candidacy was based on the corruption and injustice of the 'Ring.' Can I now fall into line, take up their banner, and shout their war cries?" With even deeper anguish he added, "Why should I forge fetters for the limbs of my friends?"[107]

"You are resting in an atmosphere of hallucinations," Foster answered coldly. "You are 'played [out]' completely as you stand though your self-love wont let you admit it." Consider advice and counsel. "You may rage and bust the air, but in that line of conduct you are powerless except to hurt yourself. I wont disguise from you,"

[103] Donnelly MSS, Scrapbook, galley proof of the speech.
[104] *Ibid.*, W. Mayo to I. D., July 22, 1871; see indorsement.
[105] *Ibid.*, I. D. to T. Foster, July 28, 1871 (copy).
[106] *Ibid.*, T. Foster to I. D., August 6, 1871.
[107] *Ibid.*, I. D. to T. Foster, August 11, 1871 (copy).

Foster stated with unreserved candor and without a trace of sarcasm, "my knowledge that the course I advise is humiliating to a man of your splendid greatness. But there is no other way. 'Stoop to conquer!' "[108]

Donnelly succumbed to the demands of ambition. He wrote an open letter to the St. Paul *Dispatch* denying that his campaign for Congress in any manner repudiated his career as a Radical Republican. The St. Paul *Pioneer* criticized his action, and he was defended by the St. Paul *Press* just as Foster had anticipated.[109] Delighted, Foster urged Donnelly to go to the convention and reinstate himself completely.[110]

The Republican convention delegates were amazed at how easily Donnelly could revive his friendships after the bitterness of the preceding campaign. Called upon to address the convention so that his recantation would be public, Donnelly good-naturedly proclaimed that he had returned like a "drowned gopher." Insisting that he had not differed on issues, he avoided serious discussion of his defection:

Why, fellow citizens they stole my thunder; they elbowed me off my own platform; they crowded me out of my own bed. I could establish no line of demarkation. I had no territory I could call my own. At length, convinced that the Republican party agreed with me on every issue, except the vital one—the propriety of sending me to Congress—I concluded to come back into the happy family—and here I am!

This was no recantation at all, but it was greeted with laughter and cheers. As for the sin of bolting the organization, Donnelly claimed:

My defence will have to be that of the boy who went fishing on Sunday. A preacher saw him sitting on the river's bank. "My son," said he, "don't you know you are committing a great sin fishing on the Sabbath day?" "Wal," said the boy, "it can't be no great sin for I hain't ketched nuthin."[111]

Wholly disarmed, the convention delegates welcomed his return to the party. Even more interesting, his effectiveness among the delegates was so great that they accepted a low tariff platform, indorsed the graduated income tax, and passed a resolution that agricultural interests were paramount in Minnesota.

[108]*Ibid.*, T. Foster to I. D., August 15, 1871.
[109]St. Paul *Dispatch*, September 4, 1871; St. Paul *Pioneer*, and St. Paul *Press*, September 5, 1871.
[110]Donnelly MSS, T. Foster to I. D., September 6, 1871.
[111]Pieced together from September 20, 21, 1871, issues of the St. Paul *Press*, St. Paul *Dispatch*, St. Paul *Pioneer*, and Minneapolis *News*.

The following day, in an angry editorial, the St. Paul *Press* insisted that the Republican party did not favor agriculture over industry; did not desire so low a tariff as the convention platform implied; and, most important, opposed revising the income tax to base it on the theory of direct taxation of those who had the greatest capacity to pay.[112] Commenting on the convention and the outraged St. Paul *Press,* the Minneapolis *News* said, "This brilliant master stroke may do much to restore Donnelly's lost *prestige* as a politician, and may prove a *coup de grace* to the Ramsey protectionist ring." And, concluded the *News,* "It is a little remarkable that a political corpse, which they [his enemies] esteemed Donnelly to be, should suddenly come to life. . . . The day of miracles has not passed for Donnelly."[113]

The Republican State Central Committee, ignoring the *Press's* criticism, invited Donnelly to campaign for Horace Austin, who was seeking a second term as governor. Donnelly declined because he had opposed Austin during the previous election. Only after Austin acknowledged that Donnelly's help was absolutely necessary to win did he agree to speak on major issues in his former congressional district. No doubt he contributed to Austin's victory.

In the summer of 1871, when his political fortunes seemed lowest, Donnelly prepared two lectures which he hoped to present during the winter lyceum season. Arranging for his own tour because he refused to pay a commission to the American Literary Bureau, he announced that he was accepting invitations after the election. His two speeches "Six Years in Washington" and "American Humorists" were written to conform to Donnelly's criteria of a good lyceum speech:

Avoid those topics which may conflict with the political or sectarian views of our audience, for although our own sincerity may be undoubted, we have no right to call the world together to assault its convictions, while the occasion permits no opportunity of reply. Neither should the lecturer except incidentally attempt to instruct his audience; the task is a difficult one, and it may chance that many among his hearers may know more of the matter than he does himself. But while he avoids didactical dryness on the one hand he should not rush into trifling frivolities on the other,—or he will again underestimate the average intelligence of mankind, and lessen the public estimate of his own. He should strive to . . . teach without pedantry, to please without wearying and to enliven without becoming himself ridiculous.[114]

[112]St. Paul *Press,* September 22, 1871.
[113]Minneapolis *News,* September 30, 1871.
[114]Donnelly MSS, manuscript copy of speech.

In large measure, Donnelly achieved this delicate balance. His lecture on humor, spiced with Josh Billings, Artemus Ward, and Petroleum V. Nasby stories, became part of a repertoire that he used for twenty years. Political cartoonists later recognized Donnelly's reputation as a humorist by caricaturing him as wearing the cap and bells of a jester. "Six Years in Washington" was not so successful. Based on his experiences, it lost its appeal as the characters and events faded into the past, but when it was first presented even the St. Paul *Pioneer*, which later denounced it as too partisan, reported "Not another man in Minnesota, and but few in America, could draw such an audience as filled the Opera House last evening."[115] Because he had the intellectual endowment and oratorical ability, Donnelly turned to public lecturing when his other sources of income diminished.

As Donnelly toured Minnesota's lyceum circuit, he watched closely a significant change in national politics. For three years there had been steadily increasing opposition to Grant's Republican regime. Several factors contributed to the decay of Grant's image as a silent, dignified, powerful general into that of a bungling, inept, impressionable, vulgar President. His economic policies, especially the tariff, met increasing criticism. The reconstruction program stirred resentment because of its lack of results. And his patronage distribution surrendered the nation's civil service into the hands of corrupt politicians.

The first successful challenge of what was termed "Grantism" took place in Missouri where B. Gratz Brown and Carl Schurz broke with the Republican party regulars. Missouri's "Liberal Republicans" demanded civil service reform, honest administration of the public lands, a general political amnesty, and tariff revision.[116] By 1871, the Missourians had withstood a presidential purge and were in open war with the administration.[117]

Liberal Republicanism spread rapidly as rival factions within the Republican party divided on the Missouri platform. When Horace Greeley's New York *Tribune* abandoned Grant in shocked indignation, the Liberals gained a powerful national newspaper. In January,

[115] St. Paul *Pioneer*, January 5, 1872.
[116] Fred E. Haynes, *Third Party Movements since the Civil War, with Special Reference to Iowa* (Iowa City: State Historical Society of Iowa, 1916), pp. 10–12.
[117] Earle Dudley Ross, *The Liberal Republican Movement* (New York: Henry Holt & Co., 1919), pp. 2–32.

1872, the Missourians issued a call for a mass convention to gather at Cincinnati, Ohio, on the first Monday in May.

Most politicians assumed Donnelly would lead the Minnesota Liberal Republican movement. No other major figure in the state had clashed with the orthodox leadership, called attention to the evils of emerging industrialism, and depicted the vulgar commercialization of the Grant regime. His mail from politicians asking him to go to Cincinnati or suggesting a Liberal Republican–Democratic coalition in the next election gradually increased. In response Donnelly patiently explained that he had attempted coalition with the Democrats before, that the Democrats had proved corrupt and treacherous, and that there was a distinct possibility that Grant could be defeated. But he insisted that he had withdrawn from politics and was devoting himself to farming and lecturing.[118]

He also rejected overtures from the regular Republican organization, repeating that lecturing was now his profession. This reply did not satisfy Dr. Thomas Foster who understood Donnelly well enough not to underestimate Liberal Republicanism's magnetic effect upon him. Scrutinizing his every political move, Foster urged him to attend the regular Minnesota Republican convention as a Dakota County delegate, to accept any position offered, and to be demonstrative. "Take it and stump the State for Grant. . . . 'A word to the wise.'" And, he concluded, "If you are a party man, the only way is to be a *hell* of a party man."[119]

Donnelly knew each of the self-appointed Minnesota delegates to the Cincinnati convention. Politicians Morton S. Wilkinson, Aaron Goodrich, and Samuel Mayall as well as professional reformers Dr. W. W. Mayo, Judge Thomas Wilson and John X. Davidson made up the Minnesota group. Harlan Hall, who hoped to attend as a delegate, was forced to sit in the press gallery when the delegation's size was limited.

Although the Liberal Republicans had a distinguished group of potential candidates, they selected Horace Greeley whose antislavery views and Civil War pacifism made him unpopular with both Republicans and Democrats. But the real liability of Greeley's candidacy was his die-hard protectionism. His nomination, which compelled the subordination of the tariff issue, was evidence of the triumph of manipulators over the genuine reformers at Cincinnati.[120]

[118]Donnelly MSS, W. Osborn to I. D., April 11, 1872.
[119]*Ibid.*, T. Foster to I. D., April 16, 1872.
[120]Ross, *Liberal Republican Movement*, pp. 85–105.

That the Democrats would accept the Liberal Republican nominee as their standard-bearer in 1872 was virtually a foregone conclusion, but Greeley's candidacy almost jeopardized the scheme. Only in desperation, since no hope of victory existed without a coalition, could the Democrats be induced to indorse Greeley.

Dr. W. W. Mayo, Harlan Hall, and Morton Wilkinson, asking Donnelly to search his soul on the reform issue, urged him to act on his principles. After a late May visit to St. Paul, where he read exchange newspapers in the office of the *Dispatch* and argued with Hall, Donnelly was in a quandary. He disagreed so violently with Greeley on the tariff that he could not honestly support him. "I have no love for Grant and less for Greeley," he recorded in his diary, "and my mind is in a perturbed state."[121] On June 11, Harlan Hall and Morton Wilkinson again met Donnelly in St. Paul to plead Greeley's cause. Outwardly, Liberal Republican popularity was increasing—everywhere in the country orthodox Republicans were worried, and copies of the Republican newspapers proved it. The Red Wing speech, Donnelly was probably reminded, had been Minnesota's first call for a Liberal Republican party.

But even before Donnelly discussed political matters with Hall and Wilkinson in St. Paul, Dr. Foster had warned: "I trust you are not wavering in the faith and thinking of backsliding. Recollect, if you fall from grace this time, you will place yourself in an unfortunate position with everybody." Foster added that he and William Banning, having thoroughly discussed Donnelly's situation, agreed that the only profitable course for Donnelly was to "continue on and *zealously* in the *regular* Republican line—that any other course was death and destruction without benefit of clergy."[122] In mid-June Foster wrote again. "I am an old politician, your political Godfather, and you never yet lost by taking my advice." Knowingly and affectionately Foster went on, "From your very nature, sanguine, impressed with your own powers, pugnacious, disposed more to push enemies than to heed friends, you are not always the best judge of the course best for *yourself* to take. Let me be your mentor on this occasion." The only way to regain the political future which had been lost was to campaign for Grant. "Even silence," Foster insisted, would do no good. This election, Donnelly was told, could make him a power again.[123]

[121]Donnelly MSS, Diary, May 29, 1872.
[122]*Ibid.*, T. Foster to I. D., May 5, 1872.
[123]*Ibid.*, T. Foster to I. D., June 13, 1872.

Donnelly addressed the Knights of the Quill, Minnesota's association of newspaper editors, on June 25. It was a hot day and not all the editors were present, but it was the proper time and place to take a stand. The speech, entitled "The Necessity of a Reform in the Civil Service of the United States," surveyed all the reform measures. Warning that a protective tariff was depressing the middle class and reducing the farmer to peonage and serfdom, he told his audience that the so-called protection for business against competition should be abolished.

Donnelly expressed his deeply felt fear for democracy in the new economic order. Even the best laws, enforced by the most diligent police power, would fail to protect free institutions if the country's property were unequally distributed. He voiced a Jeffersonian ideal when he insisted, "Where there is no great aristocracy on the one hand and no vast pauper population on the other, but where each man has something at stake in the continuancy of good government; then the ballot box represents the virtue, intelligence, and honesty of the people." Donnelly challenged the editors to assume the vanguard of the reform movement.

> You have the ear and to a great extent the confidence of the people; you are perpetually talking to them in their workshops and at their firesides; you are bringing to them fact, incident, argument, inspiration. . . . It is as possible to measure your influence for good or evil as it is to measure the effects of the sun's rays upon our planet. It is not too much to say that the newspapers of the United States hold the destinies of the people of the United States in their hands.[124]

Three weeks later he sent the St. Paul *Dispatch* a copy of a letter addressed to Major John Kennedy, chairman of the Republican District Committee, in which he refused to be a Republican candidate for any office. Not that he had withdrawn from the party, but he could neither indorse nor support a party committed to a high tariff. He was not a Democrat; he was a reformer. The Democratic St. Paul *Pioneer*, welcoming Donnelly into Greeley's camp, praised him for repudiating Republican protectionists and refusing to support Grant. The Northfield *Standard*, expressing orthodox Republican sentiments, pronounced: "Too much ambition had made him mad"; and the traditionally pro-Donnelly Hastings *Gazette* was pessimistic: "Mr. Donnelly's political course for the past five years has been a series of blunders any one of which would have proved fatal to a

[124]St. Paul *Dispatch*, June 28, 1872.

man of less genius." But its editor added, "The present disaster will be found a Waterloo. No one regrets this more than ourselves."[125]

Minnesota's Republicans never worried seriously about the Liberal Republican–Democratic coalition. They ignored the reform issue, concentrated on rebuilding Grant's image of military glory, and talked about slavery. Even more significantly, they worked to consolidate their hold on the Scandinavian vote where native language newspapers and speakers were more important than the tariff, civil service, and reconstruction. Traveling on the frontier, Donnelly sensed apathy, if not hostility, among the Scandinavians. Here he felt was Grant's strength. After a day in Wilmar, he noted that it was like being in a jail. A "dull miserable town—about 2/3 Scandinavian. . . . [I] rejoiced to get off from miserable God-forsaken Swede accursed Wilmar."[126]

To generate enthusiasm for the Liberal Republicans, he invited Lyman Trumbull and J. R. Doolittle to canvass Minnesota. He also wrote Greeley urging the editor to wage a more aggressive campaign, to criticize Grant's mistakes, and to denounce especially the President's attitude toward abolitionism. Accustomed to vigorous western politics, he was disgusted when Greeley replied, "Let us have patience, God reigns and whatever is best will be."[127] He marked the letter "unanswered."

In Minnesota there was disagreement among the Liberal Republicans and Democrats on the best means of selecting a state ticket. Dr. Mayo favored a single convention under the title "Liberal." If two conventions were held, Mayo believed the weakness of the Liberal Republicans would be so apparent that the movement would be discredited.[128] On July 25, Donnelly attended a joint meeting of the Democratic and Liberal Republican State Central Committees in the office of Democrat Sam Mayall. Both parties rejected Mayo's plan. Neither wanted to lose its identity. The Democrats, aware that they controlled the bulk of the votes, wanted to select the candidates,[129] since they feared that Donnelly would seek a nomination.

But he was not a contender for office. As the temporary chairman of the Liberal Republican convention, Donnelly made a stirring appeal to the delegates, pointing out that the convention's purpose was

[125]*Ibid.*, July 15, 1872; St. Paul *Pioneer*, July 16, 1872; Northfield *Standard*, July [20], 1872; and Hastings *Gazette*, July 20, 1872.
[126]Donnelly MSS, Diary, August 21, September 1, 2, 1872.
[127]*Ibid.*, H. Greeley to I. D., August 29, 1872.
[128]*Ibid.*, W. Mayo to I. D., July 18, 1872.
[129]*Ibid.*, J. McDonald to I. D., July 30, 1872.

to put an end to political machines, to conquer the tyranny of the public officeholders, and to heal the breach which had torn the nation asunder.[130] When the delegates selected a committee to meet with Democratic leaders to choose a ticket, Donnelly served on the joint committee. After both conventions had indorsed the candidates, the Liberal Republicans joined the Democrats at the St. Paul Opera House to conclude their meetings. That evening, at a great rally planned by the Liberal Republicans, J. R. Doolittle of Wisconsin, J. B. Beck of Kentucky, and Donnelly addressed several thousand enthusiastic St. Paulites.[131]

Since he was not a candidate, Donnelly felt free to accept speaking invitations outside Minnesota. He did so for two reasons: he was interested in extending his personal reputation as widely as possible to help him in the forthcoming lecture season; and, genuinely interested in helping the Liberal Republican cause, he thought that he could be more effective outside the state, where his tariff views were not well known.

Addressing a large Irish-American audience on Chicago's southwest side, at a meeting in support of Carter H. Harrison, who was seeking election to the House, Donnelly told his listeners that the federal government under Grant was comparable to English rule in Ireland. Both, he stated, reflected not a rule of law or reason, but a military despotism pure and simple, conceived in the atmosphere of exploitation and spoliation. A Liberal Republican regime, he promised, assured a rule of humanity, not humiliation, for the South.[132]

After the successful Chicago rally, he traveled to Milwaukee where, despite inclement weather, a great crowd gathered to hear Liberal Republican speakers. Carl Schurz, the major speaker of the evening, missed his train and was several hours late. To quiet a restless audience, Donnelly presented an hour-long extemporaneous speech. When Schurz did speak, Donnelly observed, "He is not eloquent or forcible but he has *the art of stating things* with great clearness, Candor & precision." Following Schurz's address there was a torchlight procession. The Liberal Republicans, who were very numerous, enjoyed demonstrating their strength. Donnelly was favorably impressed with Milwaukee—its substantial, quiet, handsome neighborhoods and its people who shunned debt and ostentation.[133]

[130]St. Paul *Pioneer,* September 4, 1872.
[131]Donnelly MSS, Diary, September 4, 1872.
[132]Chicago *Times,* October 5, 1872; Chicago *Tribune,* October 5, 1872.
[133]Donnelly MSS, Diary, October 6, 7, 1872.

More than likely his impressions were influenced by the Milwaukee *News* report of the rally which termed Donnelly's the "Best Speech of the Campaign."[134]

As Donnelly toured the Middle West speaking in behalf of Liberal Republican candidates, the October election results indicated that Greeley would either suffer defeat or win by a very narrow margin. "Bad news," Donnelly recorded in his diary, "The Grant men have carried Penna & Ohio. . . . [I] drove home feeling depressed and disappointed." Later he added, "Found myself quoting Poe's line

> 'Whom unmerciful disaster
> Follows fast and followed faster
> Till his voice one burden bore
> NEVERMORE!"[135]

Three days later, his spirits revived, he wrote, "There is a gleam of hope yet, we have carried Indiana."[136]

When Donnelly spoke at Madison, Wisconsin, in the Assembly Hall of the State Capitol Building, a magnificent chamber almost as large as the hall of the national House of Representatives after which it was patterned, the room was crowded with "the *elite* of the city." "What a joy it is," he confided to his diary, "to find such a hall and such an audience—where one's words fall like showers of electric sparks kindling a blaze wherever they touch!" After the address, Donnelly received hundreds of people, including Wisconsin's leading jurists. He took immense pride in writing Kate that Chief Justice Dixon, "a grand man, told a friend that it was the greatest speech he had ever heard in his life." He added, that the Madison speech was "one of the greatest triumphs I have ever had."[137]

As the campaign drew to a close, Donnelly realized that he had been at least partially successful. He had made many friends who would be helpful during the lecture season. Already invitations to speak to lyceum groups in Madison, La Crosse, and Milwaukee, Wisconsin, had been received. He had enhanced his reputation as one of the Northwest's leading orators, but Liberal Republicanism was beyond salvation. Greeley was headed for certain defeat.

---

[134]Milwaukee *News*, October 6, 1872.
[135]Donnelly MSS, Diary, October 8, 1872.
[136]*Ibid.*, October 25, 1872.
[137]*Ibid.*, I. D. to K. D., October 24, 1872. Not all his speeches were so well given. Donnelly angrily noted, "Impossible to make a good impression on a cold audience or one stupified for want of ventilation—their brains grow torpid and Demosthenes would pass for an auctioneer."

Nevertheless, on election eve Donnelly spoke to St. Paul's Liberal Republicans. The St. Paul *Press* dubbed the speech the "last ripple" of the Greeley wave. Donnelly, said the *Press,* was enthusiastic, but the enthusiasm was hollow; he was confident, but his confidence was pathetic.[138] The *Press* was correct; Minnesota voted Republican by more than a twenty-thousand-vote margin.

Election day, November 3, was Donnelly's birthday. As Liberal Republicanism was passing into limbo, he meditated on the course of his life. To his diary he confided:

> I am 41 years old to-day. 20 years ago I started my career. I have not been idle. I am worth $50,000 and have established an extensive fame. If accident or disease do not carry me off I can reasonably hope for 20 more years of vigorous life—not of experiment but of position and realization.[139]

He could have added, had he been truly prophetic, that he had turned irrevocably down the road of reform.

[138]St. Paul *Press,* November 3, 1872; St. Paul *Pioneer,* November 3, 1872.
[139]Donnelly MSS, Diary, November 3, 1872.

CHAPTER IX

The Granger
1873-1875

I do not believe in leveling down to poverty but I do believe in leveling up to plenty.

IGNATIUS DONNELLY

WHEN, on January 30, 1873, Ignatius Donnelly solemnly noted in his diary: "Organized a Lodge of the Patrons of Husbandry in Hastings —Cereal Grange No. 25—I am elected Lecturer," he anticipated the beginning of a new chapter in his life.[1] The Patrons of Husbandry, popularly termed the Grange, had been established in Minnesota in 1868, with the organization of the North Star Grange by Colonel D. A. Robertson at St. Paul.[2] Within two years, there were forty granges in the state.[3] The Grange was an effort to protect the agricultural element in society from exploitation, and its rapid growth in Minnesota coincided with increasing discontent among the state's farmers. As more and more of them sought a solution to the problem of disparity between expenditures and income during the post–Civil War years, they found in the granges a congenial environment in which to air their grievances.[4]

Some farmers believed that self-help, co-operative manufacturing and marketing, and non-political organization would cure agriculture's ills; others were equally certain that state control of transpor-

[1]Donnelly MSS, Diary, January 30, 1873.
[2]Solon J. Buck, *The Granger Movement* (Cambridge: Harvard University Press, 1913), p. 42.
[3]Rasmus S. Saby, "Railroad Legislation in Minnesota, 1849 to 1875," Minnesota Historical Society *Collections,* XV (1915), 82.
[4]Buck, *Granger Movement,* p. 52.

tation and other service monopolies were the answer. This fundamental difference led to a sharp clash within the Grange when the advocates of government control endeavored to turn the organization to politics. Opponents of partisanship could point to the organization's by-laws which denied Grangers the right to discuss politics during their meetings.

For Donnelly, who was both a farmer and a politician, this difference of opinion among the Grangers was extremely important. He did not disapprove of mutual insurance companies or fraternally managed co-operatives, but he felt that the gains secured by them would be negligible when compared with results attainable through the medium of politics. Furthermore, since his own experience convinced Donnelly that organized interests—mining, banking, and railroading—were playing a large role in the politics of the post–Civil War period, he felt that the farmers should not deny themselves political expression as a group.

He wondered how vital a political force the Grange could become. Carl Schurz told him that it would "grow in importance as its basis and objective broadened."[5] No man in Minnesota was better equipped than Donnelly to undertake an issue-oriented educational campaign. To critics who condemned him for raising political issues in the organization, he replied, "You want to make a gun that will do everything but shoot."[6]

He received permission from Oliver H. Kelley, national secretary of the Patrons of Husbandry, to charge forty dollars and expenses for each lecture he would deliver. After Kelley had sanctioned the subjects he planned to discuss and the ideas he intended to express, Donnelly visited granges in Duluth, Rice, Fillmore, Mower, Olmstead, Winona, and Washington counties. Vigorously outspoken on what were considered the "live issues" of the day, he argued that the farmers needed co-operatives because the patent laws were against them. They needed competitive water transportation to force the railroads to adjust their charges to conform to popular needs. He assured Minnesota's farmers that they could take pride in having obtained legislation which fixed schedules for both passengers and freight, even though the railroad companies were fighting to have the law set aside by the state courts.

But he emphasized currency and the tariff. The Civil War greenback paper dollar had caused a depreciation of currency which had weakened the consumer's buying power. He suggested restoring

[5]Donnelly MSS, C. Schurz to I. D., April 15, 1873.
[6]Ignatius Donnelly, *Facts for the Granges* (St. Paul, 1873), p. 18.

specie payment as quickly as possible to eliminate this farmer-cheating dollar. But he reserved special attention for the tariff issue. "I was fooled," he confessed of his past opinions, "by superficial arguments . . . and believed in the so-called Protection of American Industry." Perhaps the generous people of the West could concede a tariff for revenue or one which afforded protection incidentally. "But the trouble is," he pointed out, "the manufacturers will never rest with that. They will corrupt Congress, revolutionize politics . . . to obtain the coveted prize. . . . We would be better off, safer and happier, with the whole [tariff] system swept away."[7]

In none of these speeches did Donnelly assert that he was "superior to the dictates of ambition" politically. Why all the cry, he asked audiences, against a politician who took their part? "Do offices belong only to your enemies?" Nevertheless, he said that he was not campaigning for votes and was willing to march as a "high private in the rear rank" until the evils which he had described were eliminated.[8] Donnelly's denial of self-interest, however, failed to convince the seasoned politicians, especially after he began contrasting Henry Clay's "Take care of the rich and they will take care of the poor" with his own aphorism, "Take care of the poor and the rich will take care of themselves." The St. Paul *Press* repeatedly accused him of campaigning for the United States Senate and of misrepresenting himself as a farmer.[9]

The major concern among the politicians was suggested by Frank J. Mead of the Minneapolis *Times* when he asked Donnelly about the "feasibility of the Farmers taking the field politically."[10] Although impressed by the popular reaction to his speeches, as late as June 6, in an interview for the *Times*, Donnelly stated that he was by no means certain that there would be an Independent party in the coming election. Since the Grangers were a non-political group they would act individually, but Donnelly was certain that the feeling they shared about the agricultural depression would not die before the election.[11]

Until this time, he had appealed to the Grangers to seek out candidates who were sympathetic to their cause, who could not be

[7] *Ibid.*, p. 15.
[8] *Ibid.*, p. 19.
[9] *Ibid.*, p. 16; see also, St. Paul *Press*, June 6, 1873.
[10] Donnelly MSS, Frank J. Mead to I. D., May 22, 1873.
[11] Minneapolis *Times*, June 6, 1873. Minnesota was not the first state to embark on Granger politics, and Donnelly believed that the people of the state were definitely influenced by what had been done in Illinois and what was taking place in Wisconsin.

bought off with promises of political preferment, and who were well aware of the larger issues.[12] During his state-wide tour he had spoken with a new earnestness, largely abandoning his customary humor,[13] and the response proved his effectiveness. A demand for independent political action grew in the wake of his lectures. The *Farmers' Union*, the official state Grange publication, was deluged with letters calling for a third party or for the indorsement of special candidates.[14]

On June 17, between twenty and thirty granges turned out *en masse*, several thousand strong, to parade with music, banners, and regalia, forming a colorful procession more than a mile long. After Donnelly and George I. Parsons, state grand master of the Patrons of Husbandry, addressed the enthusiastic crowd, there was much talk of a farmer party, but Donnelly still felt that the possibilities were not good.[15] The significance of the Northfield rally and of the political ramifications of Donnelly's speeches was not ignored by Minnesota's Republican leadership. In the preceding election, the 1871 platform had committed that party to legislative control over the railroads. Governor Horace Austin had advocated and secured minimum regulatory legislation, but William D. Washburn, the party's prospective candidate in 1873, appeared to disapprove of such legislation. His nomination might lead to a Republican defeat if the farmers were as thoroughly "educated" by Donnelly and other Grange leaders as they appeared to be.

A far stronger Republican candidate, one popular with the rural voters and younger members of the party, was the gifted lawyer-politician, Cushman K. Davis. He had earned a reputation as a critic of strict laissez faire by presenting a lecture entitled "Modern Feudalism," in which he advocated rigorous state control of the railroads. Convinced that Davis' nomination could probably hold every Republican-Granger vote even if the party's machinery were apathetic, an able group of Republicans, captained by the journalist Henry A. Castle and supported by Governor Austin, forced Davis' acceptance by the state convention.[16]

[12]St. Paul *Press*, June 2, 1873.
[13]Rochester *Post*, June 7, 1873. For an analysis of Donnelly's humor see Martin Ridge, "The Humor of Ignatius Donnelly," *Minnesota History*, XXXIII (1953), 326–30.
[14]Minneapolis *Farmers' Union*, June, 1873, issues.
[15]Minneapolis *Times*, June 18, 1873; see also Donnelly's Diary, June 17, 1873.
[16]Saby, "Railroad Legislation," pp. 125–26; Henry A. Castle, "Reminiscences of Minnesota Politics," Minnesota Historical Society *Collections*, XV, 561–62.

Davis' nomination had precisely the effect upon politically inclined Grangers that farsighted Republicans had anticipated. There
were two alternatives: either give up any political action in 1873 and
hope that the flood tide of enthusiasm would hold until the next election; or put up a candidate who would undoubtedly be beaten, but
whose candidacy would help in establishing a political organization.[17] Concluding that a Granger-Democratic coalition was the best
long-term objective, Donnelly decided to build a new party organization for the Grangers. At Brownsdale, where the Mower County
Grange convention assembled on July 26, a bold departure was indorsed under his auspices. Following a resolution expressing lack of
confidence in either of the older parties, a call was issued for a mass
political convention to be held September 2 at Owatonna. The
Brownsdale convention did not attack Davis' candidacy, but it severely criticized his supporters and the Republican party.[18]

After the call for a convention at Owatonna, Donnelly had to overcome the opposition of Grand Master George I. Parsons, a confirmed
Republican. Parsons, who had not been present at Brownsdale, issued an official admonitory circular reminding the local granges that
any support of the Owatonna convention would be in direct violation of Granger rules.[19] The *Farmers' Union* at first sustained the
grand master, but later reversed its policy.[20]

While the Grangers argued, Donnelly sought a political alliance
with urban labor. Speaking to the St. Paul Workingmen's Association, he insisted that railroads, like all corporations, must be the servants and not the masters of the people; as for the Republican tariff,
it had protected only the profits and not the workers in American
industry. To contain these twin evils—corporations and the tariff—
organized labor must join the farmers in political action.[21]

Meanwhile it had become apparent that the real hope of success
from the work of the Owatonna convention must lie in the realiza-
tion of Donnelly's objective, a fusion between Grangers and Democrats. Without a prior agreement with the Democrats on candidates and issues, the farmers would accomplish nothing. Democrat
Louis E. Fisher, who controlled the St. Paul *Pioneer*, insisted that

[17]Donnelly MSS, E. J. Hodgson to I. D., July 18, 1873.
[18]Austin *Transcript*, July 31, 1873; St. Paul *Pioneer*, July 27, 1873.
[19]Minneapolis *Farmers' Union*, August 16, 1873.
[20]*Ibid.*, August 23, 30, 1873.
[21]St. Paul *Pioneer*, August 27, 1873. A manuscript draft of the speech is in
the Donnelly MSS.

unless his party could name both the gubernatorial candidate and the nominee for attorney-general there would be no fusion.[22]

The day before the convention a caucus was held to designate a slate of candidates. Donnelly did not wish to place a candidate in the field against Davis. If the group decided to do so, he favored a moderate Republican such as the successful farmer, Oliver Dalrymple, who was well known and highly respected.[23] But Donnelly, unable to predict the voting strength of the Grangers, was in no position to dictate terms to the Democratic managers who knew what they could guarantee at the polls. He was fortunate in securing acceptance by the caucus of two Liberal Republican Grangers as nominees for lesser offices.[24] The following noon the Owatonna convention assembled, with Donnelly as temporary chairman. Within a matter of hours, and with machine-like precision, the predetermined slate was indorsed. A new party, calling itself the Anti-Monopoly party, was in the field.

Although he had capitulated on the selection of candidates, he did not surrender on the issues. The Anti-Monopoly party adopted a series of resolutions and pledged itself to support no man for office who violated them. Of paramount importance among these resolutions was the assertion that the state was supreme over all corporations and the demand that the state withhold or annul all corporate charters when they conflicted with public welfare. Tariffs were condemned, and support for state-constructed competitive waterways was advocated. The party also commended the Minnesota Supreme Court for its ruling in *Blake* vs. *Winona & St. Peter Railroad* in which the court upheld the state's right to determine railroad rates.[25]

Six weeks after the convention, Donnelly secured the Anti-Monopoly nomination for state senator from Dakota County. He was indorsed reluctantly by the county Democratic organization. There were even indications of a secret exchange agreement between conservative Democrats and Republicans by which the Republicans would withhold support from Davis, their gubernatorial candidate, if the Democrats would inhibit Donnelly's senatorial campaign.[26]

[22]Donnelly MSS, L. Fisher to I. D., August 8, 18, 1873.

[23]*Ibid.*, Diary, September 1, 1873.

[24]The ticket consisted of Democrat Ara Barton for governor; Republican Ebenezer Ayers for lieutenant governor; Democrat John H. Stevens for secretary of state; Republican Edwin W. Dyke for treasurer; and William P. Clough for attorney-general.

[25]Minneapolis *Farmers' Union*, September 6, 1873.

[26]Donnelly MSS, A. Barton to I. D., October 19, 1873.

Republican newspapers dubbed the Anti-Monopolists the "Potato Bug Party," implying that it was comprised of agricultural parasites, but their ridicule failed to disguise Republican concern over the causes for the new party's rapid growth.[27] In mid-June, almost four months after Donnelly began his lectures to the Grangers, swarms of Rocky Mountain locusts descended upon southwestern Minnesota devouring the crops in the fields, consuming all that was edible, and leaving in their wake ruined and despondent farmers. Naturally enough, these people were eager listeners to talk of farm improvement and ardent participants in Granger activities. But for the farmers in other parts of the state this loss meant their gain. In anticipation of a possible shortage, wheat prices rose steadily to $1.17 a bushel. Actually, until mid-September, most of Minnesota's farmers were enjoying a successful year. If economic conditions had continued to improve for them, they might have been less susceptible to Donnelly's propaganda.

But the economic outlook changed drastically just two weeks after the Owatonna convention. The Panic of 1873 brought Minnesota a series of economic crises: rapid currency depreciation, mortgage foreclosures, bank failures, and a steep price-decline. The greatest blow to the farmer was the downward march of wheat prices from more than one dollar a bushel to eighty cents by September 18. The effects of this panic were to be felt at the polling booths as well as in the market places of the state.

When the November election returns were counted, the Republican party's customary majority of twenty thousand had been reduced to less than five thousand votes. Donnelly carried Dakota County, and many other Anti-Monopoly candidates also won the election. Even where the Anti-Monopolists and Democrats were defeated, the vote was close. As an apologist for the Republican party later conceded, "A less emphatic declaration [referring to the anti-corporation plank in the Republican platform] and a nominee not known to be sympathetic with the Grangers would have lost the election."[28]

When the Minnesota legislature convened in January, 1874, it was obvious not only that Donnelly was to be the recognized leader of the Anti-Monopolists in the senate, but also that his legislative program would be the basis of most action and discussion. Thoroughly enraged by the situation, the editors of the St. Paul *Press* screamed

[27] St. Paul *Press*, September 5, 1873.
[28] Folwell, *Minnesota*, III, 85.

that Donnelly "rules the Senate with lawless license of demagogic deviltry, as the commune governed Paris, in wild defiance of law and logic and common sense."[29] Although conditions never reached the state so graphically depicted by the *Press*, there was considerable excitement during most of the session.

One of Donnelly's first moves was to call for an investigation of the Minnesota lumbering interests. For several years there had been rumors that lumber companies were pirating pine and cedar forests on state-owned lands. Almost simultaneously with Donnelly's demand for an investigation, Governor Davis suggested that unless these allegations could be disproved, formal indictments against the lumber companies should be prepared. Armed with the power of subpoena, Donnelly began an investigation of the activities of the lumberman and financier, Amherst H. Wilder. Acting on Wilder's instructions, his attorney, James Gilfillan—later chief justice of the Minnesota Supreme Court—refused to present any information until a threat of prosecution for contempt of the senate was considered. When Gilfillan did testify, he disclosed that doubt existed about the regularity of Wilder's contract with the federal government, permitting timber to be cut on Indian reservations which contained state-owned swamp and school lands. But since Donnelly was unable to subpoena the federal officials, he was unsuccessful in his efforts to prove that there had been any dishonesty or corruption on Wilder's part in gaining the contract. The Republican press ridiculed the investigations and its findings, but Wilder, with his practices exposed, voluntarily surrendered his contract. The state of Minnesota, however, neither recovered the timber which had already been cut nor received any compensation for it.[30]

As the leader of the Anti-Monopolists, Donnelly also introduced several measures aimed at placing restrictions on some of the previously unregulated activities of the great corporations in the state. The most significant of these was a bill which would have compelled all the insurance companies selling policies in Minnesota to reinvest locally all money collected in the state and to limit the interest rate on such investment to 8 per cent per annum. To prevent the establishment of high-interest subsidiary loan companies, the bill specified that no more than $3,000 in premium receipts could be loaned

---

[29]St. Paul *Press*, January 17, 1874.

[30]*Ibid.*, January 10, 13, 16, February 24, 27; Minnesota Legislature, *Senate Journal*, 16th sess. (1874), pp. 307, 313, 328–29; *Report of the Pine Land Committee to the Senate of the State of Minnesota* (St. Paul, 1874), pp. 1–12.

to any one individual or company. Donnelly was convinced that the measure would accomplish several valid purposes: it would break what many Anti-Monopolists believed to be a high-interest loan monopoly operating in the state; it would increase the amount of money available for borrowing during all seasons of the year; and it would prevent the drain of rural funds to the financial centers of the East, a matter of keen concern to the Grangers. But the Republican-controlled Senate Banking Committee, which disapproved completely of the theory behind such legislation, killed the measure, explaining that the eastern insurance companies would shun the state if the law were accepted.[31]

Railroad regulation was the most highly publicized problem before the Minnesota legislature. In 1871 two important railroad measures had been approved. One act established the office of state railroad commissioner, giving the commissioner power to subpoena both individuals and records and making it a felony to refuse to comply with his requests for information. The other measure, the so-called Jones bill, actually fixed maximum mileage rates according to established categories of freight. The railroads, however, without exception, refused to comply, and the law was tested in the courts. An appeal finally led to the Minnesota Supreme Court, which ruled in favor of the legislation, holding that the rate-making power was implicit in the sovereign power of the state, and that since the railroad commissioner determined neither the rate nor the penalties, there had been no unlawful delegation of legislative power and no usurpation of judicial function.[32] The railroads refused to conform with the law while they appealed to the United States Supreme Court.

Two different aspects of the railroad problem were placed before the legislature at the opening of the 1874 session. Governor Davis, in his inaugural address, indicated his interest in confirming the state's right to establish rates. Railroad Commissioner Alonzo J. Edgerton, in his annual report, pointed out the continued and glaring abuses perpetrated by the railroads in defiance of the Jones bill, and the inability of his office to remedy the situation under existing laws. Many of the railroad companies refused to pay gross income taxes as specified by law; many refused to comply with the Jones bill on the grounds that each railroad must itself determine what a just and

[31]Minnesota Legislature, *Senate Journal,* 16th sess., p. 19; St. Paul *Press,* January 10, 22, 1874.
[32]Saby, "Railroad Legislation," pp. 110, 141.

reasonable rate was; many wrongly used their land grants to escape taxation; and all of them relied upon extensive court action, which placed the burden of proof upon the plaintiff. The commissioner was reluctant to make suggestions, but his listing of the abuses, by their very nature, seemed to determine how the new laws should be written and what they should include.[33]

The Senate Committee on Railroads, of which Donnelly was a member, was charged with the responsibility of framing the needed legislation. But he soon refused to meet with the group, asserting that the Republican-dominated committee was determined to rewrite the laws to satisfy the interest of the railroads and not the people. For him, the basic difficulty was the problem of enforcement, which could be solved with a simple amendment to the Jones bill providing that any railroad refusing to conform to its terms would be placed in receivership until the constitutionality of the law was tested. This amendment would eliminate the most irritating of all abuses—those committed during the period of litigation. Furthermore, it would expedite judicial determination because the railroads would be eager to have the cases settled.[34]

The railroad bill of 1874 included Donnelly's receivership plan, but other provisions of the bill made it unacceptable to him. By the terms of the act, the legislature relinquished the rate-making power it had exercised under the Jones bill and delegated that power to a board of railroad commissioners appointed by the governor. This board had, under law, the power to cope with various railroad malpractices, but the burden of proof was not shifted from the plaintiff. Donnelly insisted that this was an outright betrayal of the farmers' interests. He rejected the entire idea of the rate-making commissions, placing his faith in legislative regulation. "The people elected a legislature to regulate the railroads," he argued, and any action to the contrary would not work.[35]

Donnelly disagreed with most members of the Anti-Monopoly group. They favored a bill based on the pattern set in Illinois for the establishment of a commission. His intransigeance alienated many of his associates, and when the measure came up for final adoption, Donnelly cast one of two votes registered against it. The other dis-

[33] Minnesota Executive Documents, *Report of the Railroad Commissioner for the Years 1871 to 1873* (St. Paul, 1874), pp. 10–26.

[34] Saby, "Railroad Legislation," p. 141.

[35] Ignatius Donnelly, *An Address of the Anti-Monopoly Party of Minnesota to Their Constituents* (St. Paul, 1874), p. 12.

senting vote was that of Elias F. Drake, president of the St. Paul & Sioux City Railroad, who opposed all regulatory legislation as a matter of principle.[36]

Donnelly's prediction of failure for the new act proved valid because the railroads, heavily in debt, overextended, overvaluated because of watered stock, and pressed by the financial setback of 1873, could not be substantially restricted and remain solvent. Since the commission was to determine a just rate, and since rate and profit could not be separated, rail rates actually increased in many areas under the commission system. There was no method of bringing the actual and stated liabilities into conformity. Thus the companies with watered stock demanded and received fair compensation for their stockholders. Donnelly continued to criticize the activities of the railroad commissioners. When the legislature assembled in 1875, a new law was demanded.

During the debate on railroad regulation, at a time when Donnelly was especially critical of the railroads for their legal trickery, their long and short haul discriminatory rates and their practice of corrupting legislators, he was seriously embarrassed by an exposé of part of his Washington record. His former Hastings friends, including General Le Duc, let it be known that Donnelly had been given twenty-five hundred dollars' worth of Hastings & Dakota Railroad stock for services he rendered to the company. Donnelly defended himself against the charges of corruption by pointing out that the stock had been voted to him at a public meeting of the company and that he had neither received the stock nor any money from it. He offered to withdraw from public life if it could be proved that he had made "one cent" for his services. No more had been done for the Hastings & Dakota Railroad, he asserted in a speech to the Minnesota State Senate, than would have been done for any other constituent.[37] But this was not the epitaph of the Hastings & Dakota episode; his foes frequently reminded the public of Donnelly's railroad associations. Seven years later, when Russell Sage acquired control of the Hastings & Dakota, Donnelly quietly sold the stock.[38]

As the legislative session of 1874 drew to a close, it was readily admitted by the Grangers and fusion Democrats who formed the

[36]Donnelly and Drake had argued the subject of state control and had, in a sense, agreed to disagree in a friendly manner. Donnelly MSS, I. D. to E. Drake, December 21, 1874 (copy), E. Drake to I. D., December 22, 1874.
[37]St. Paul *Press*, February 20, 1874.
[38]Donnelly MSS, Diary, December 31, 1881.

Anti-Monopoly coalition that they had failed to achieve many of their objectives. In their final caucus, they condemned the Republican majority for obstructing the cause of genuine reform, they claimed credit for the accomplishments of the session, and they created a committee under the chairmanship of William Paist, secretary of the state Grange, to prepare an Anti-Monopoly manifesto.[39] The declaration, sent to all the Minnesota granges, bore Paist's signature as secretary, but Donnelly willingly assumed responsibility for its contents and circulation.

Establishing a solid Anti-Monopoly phalanx in Minnesota proved to be an extremely difficult task. Thousands of pamphlets had to be printed and distributed, money had to be raised, and the support of influential newspapers gained, if any profits were to accrue. None of this was accomplished without intense opposition. Minnesota's conservative Democrats, far from willing to surrender their power into Anti-Monopolist hands, denied Donnelly access to their leading newspaper, the St. Paul *Pioneer,* except under limiting conditions.[40] Even those Democratic leaders who supported fusion demanded the controlling voice in the formulation of policy. As John W. McClung aptly expressed it: "We are the masters of the situation and you can win no victories without us."[41] Furthermore, many of the Grangers, decrying politics as a potential for gaining the farmer's prosperity, followed State Grand Master Parsons and the *Farmers' Union* in denouncing Donnelly and Paist for trying to make the Grange a political appendage of the Anti-Monopoly party.[42]

Realizing that without the support of a leading Democratic newspaper or a major farm journal it would be impossible to explain the Anti-Monopoly position, Donnelly and his friends established their own weekly paper. Since they lacked money for writers, office staff, and canvassers, Donnelly did most of the work himself. The first issue of the *Anti-Monopolist* appeared July 16, 1874, carrying the motto: "Speak to the Children of Israel, that They Go Forward." It was a "singular paper," the Litchfield *News-Ledger* reported, "as unlike other journals as Donnelly is unlike other men. . . . It is brimful of fight and fun, and bristles all over with invective . . . and is as dangerous a plaything as a porcupine. It is always erudite, humor-

[39]St. Paul *Press*, March 5, 1874.
[40]Donnelly MSS, I. D. to H. Lamberton, March 25, 1874 (copy); I. D. to L. Fisher, April 1, 1874 (copy); L. Fisher to I. D., April 2, 1874.
[41]*Ibid.,* J. W. McClung to I. D., May 22, 1874.
[42]Minneapolis *Farmers' Union,* June 13, 1874; see also Donnelly MSS, W. W. Mayo to I. D., April 13, 1874.

ous, sarcastic and generally logical."[43] Although the paper was a financial burden, it gave Donnelly a powerful influence in the state, especially among the rural population. He needed just such a weapon if he hoped to win all the Grangers to the Anti-Monopoly cause and break the power of Grand Master Parsons.

Parsons had done a good deal to thwart independent political action in 1873. His most telling blow, however, came on the eve of the establishment of the *Anti-Monopolist*, when he announced that he would suspend any Grange which engaged in political activity.[44] Following this virtual declaration of war, Donnelly turned Parsons' own arguments against him by accusing the grand master of using the Grange to aid the Republican party. Relying on both his friends and his newspaper, Donnelly waged a relentless war against Parsons during the summer and autumn of 1874. Two weeks before the state Grange convention the *Anti-Monopolist* discredited Parsons by quoting him as boasting: "If there be a devil—which I do not believe—and he was regularly nominated upon the Republican ticket, I would vote for him! And if there was such a character as Jesus Christ—which I do not believe—and he was now alive and nominated upon the Democratic ticket, I would not vote for him."[45]

When the Grangers assembled at their annual meeting, Donnelly and his friends were in control. Not only was Parsons replaced by Colonel Samuel E. Adams, a fusion Democrat who had collaborated with Donnelly, but a set of resolutions was adopted advocating political activity.[46] For all practical purposes Donnelly had gained control of the Grange leadership, but unfortunately for the prospects of the Grange, the ebb tide of the movement in Minnesota was already flowing. Even without the bitter disputes within the organization, the Patrons of Husbandry would probably have suffered a loss in strength through failures in its business ventures. The political disagreements accelerated the decline. There was no overnight collapse or withdrawal of membership, but within eighteen months almost one-third of the Minnesota membership had become inactive, and with this inactivity came a proportional loss of political influence.[47]

The Minnesota legislature which convened in January, 1875, faced serious problems, but these were virtually ignored because of a

[43] Quoted in the St. Paul *Anti-Monopolist*, September 13, 1874.
[44] *Ibid.*, July 30, 1874.
[45] *Ibid.*, December 3, 1874.
[46] *Ibid.*, December 23, 1874.
[47] Buck, *Granger Movement*, insert following p. 58.

contest for the United States Senate. Long before Alexander Ramsey's second term came to a close, Governor Davis, William D. Washburn, and Donnelly each prepared to dislodge him. As early as November, 1873, shortly after winning election to the state senate, Donnelly wrote to S. S. Cox seeking financial support from eastern Democrats in his fight for the senatorship. But this was hardly an opportune moment to solicit aid; the stresses of the Panic of 1873 were at their sharpest, and Cox explained that the party was "flat" from the banker August Belmont down.[48] Donnelly, however, did receive assurances of support from fusion Democrats such as Sam Mayall.

During 1874 he worked to build a combination capable of ousting Ramsey. His request for aid from Minnesota's conservative Democrats was refused. As one of his Democratic correspondents informed him: "My friend I am afraid they like you as a hewer of wood and a drawer of water but, as a judge in Israel, not at all!"[49] Nevertheless, by the time of the 1875 legislative session, it was evident that Donnelly would be the choice of the Grangers and fusion Democrats, especially since there was almost no chance of victory. Even under such circumstances, there was small enthusiasm in the Democratic caucus.

When the Republicans met to select their candidate, Ramsey controlled sixty of the eighty-four members present. Washburn's candidacy had vanished, and Davis could count on the remaining twenty-four votes. According to caucus rules and party discipline, the Davis men should have admitted defeat and supported Ramsey's nomination. Davis' friends, however, having routed the machine in the gubernatorial contest of 1873, fearful of the consequences of surrendering to Bluff Aleck, determined on a policy of anyone but Ramsey.

Voting for the senatorship, which began on January 19, disclosed that Ramsey was in control of sixty members of the legislature, Donnelly fifty-three, Davis twenty-four, with nine men scattered.[50] Donnelly's hopes faded when the Davis group refused to support him. The St. Paul *Press*, learning that Davis had spurned Donnelly, predicted Ramsey's re-election. The Republican deadlock lasted until mid-February when both Ramsey and Davis withdrew in favor of a compromise candidate, Minnesota Supreme Court Chief Justice Samuel McMillan. Ramsey had finally been beaten, but his influence

[48]Donnelly MSS, S. S. Cox to I. D., November 12, 1873.
[49]*Ibid.*, J. E. Doughty to I. D., November 29, 1874.
[50]Minnesota Legislature, *Senate Journal*, 17th sess., p. 108.

was not dissipated; President Rutherford B. Hayes appointed him Secretary of War.

Donnelly was embarrassed during the senatorial contest when a group of irate stockholders in the bankrupt Memphis, El Paso, and Texas Railroad brought suit against its directors for mismanagement and fraud. The litigation exposed many of General John C. Frémont's activities, including his Washington lobby. The St. Paul *Press*, with feigned horror, noted that Donnelly had been promised a quarter of a million dollars in company stock for his services.[51] Since defending his record called for recounting a narrative he preferred to leave untold, he secured a deposition from Dr. William Schmoele, who had been a director of the Memphis, El Paso, and Texas Railroad, that he had never received "one cent" from the company.[52] Donnelly also pointed out that he had worked for Frémont subsequent to his congressional term. The moral issues, he contended, were not the same. The legislator must ask himself, "Is such a course of action wisest and best for the people I represent?" A private citizen asks the question, "Is there anything morally wrong or personally dishonorable in the proposed measure?"[53] Even the St. Paul *Press* conceded that Donnelly had cleared himself of the charges of wrongdoing, but his motives in dedicating himself to the cause of railroad regulation were impugned.[54]

During the hectic days of the 1875 session, efforts by Donnelly to re-create the Anti-Monopoly coalition failed miserably. The old-line Democrats went back to their party, and only a handful of genuine Grangers remained loyal. The issue of railroad regulation was confused in the public attention when Republican newspapers, which

[51] February 6, 1875.
[52] St. Paul *Anti-Monopolist*, February 18, 1875.
[53] *Ibid.*, February 12, 1875.
[54] February 16, 1875. The Minneapolis *Tribune* published a little poem that had brief but significant circulation during the episode.

> Ignatius, the martyr, as he usually is,
> Is in water so hot that it fairly doth "siz"
> But he swears "you can't prove it; I got not a cent
> From the railroads to which I my influence lent."

Ironically enough there was also a rumor current that Donnelly had made vast sums of money while in Washington. In reality he was poor. Kate, who had gone east to borrow money, wrote to him with biting sarcasm: "It is really very hard that such a rich man as you are said to be should have the necessity for a couple of thousand dollars for actual payment of bills for bread and butter, but so it is. I fear your *princely style* is kept up in the Italian Court system— macaroni & lentils." Donnelly MSS, undated but identifiable as fitting here because of references to the senatorial contest.

had first indorsed the railroad measure of 1874, contended that it was confiscatory in character. In his annual message, Governor Davis betrayed the limitations of his belief in government regulation by criticizing the original railroad act, the Jones bill, as being unjust to the railroads. In the state house of representatives, it was argued that the railroads, having suffered during the Panic of 1873, were in need of assistance, not regulation.[55] Consequently, the so-called Morse bill, which restricted the powers of the railroad commission, was passed. In the senate, however, Donnelly rallied the Anti-Monopolists in an effort to check this surrender of the regulatory principle. By supporting the railroad bill of 1874, they defeated, at least temporarily, the new measure. Reluctantly—and ironically—Donnelly was advocating as better than "no law at all" a measure which he had staunchly opposed but one year before.[56] But the reaction to Grangerism had set in. The conservative-minded members of both parties worked for party discipline, and the Morse bill was forced through.

Donnelly was extremely bitter about this defeat. The new bill, severely restricting the powers of the railroad commission, did nothing, Donnelly wrote, to eliminate the vicious drawback system which gave large shippers unfair advantages; it made no allowance for determining just and reasonable rates; it provided no device for securing equal facilities; and it left to the poor farmer the expensive and time-consuming process of litigation to prove that he had been wronged. "The people ask for bread," he stormed, "and the legislature has given them a stone."[57]

[55] Rochester *Record and Union*, March 6, 1875.
[56] St. Paul *Dispatch*, March 3, 1875.
[57] St. Paul *Anti-Monopolist*, March 11, 1875.

The Greenbacker
1876–1877

---

*What the nation needs is prosperity. Money is mere
incident—a means of making exchange.*

IGNATIUS DONNELLY

THE ANTI-MONOPOLY–DEMOCRATIC coalition which Donnelly
attempted to lead during 1874–75 angered conservative Democrats.
In the spring of 1875, they decided not only to reclaim their party
but also to gain control of the coalition. Although they had lost access to their newspaper when the *Pioneer* was merged with the *Press*,
they rallied around its former editor Louis E. Fisher, determined to
elect him to a major state office. Since Fisher represented orthodox
rigid partisanship, his potential candidacy was welcomed by the
Republican press.[1]

Fisher's association with the Democratic party's conservative or
Bourbon faction, made him unacceptable to Donnelly. Aware that
the "old guard" was trying to swallow the Anti-Monopoly element,[2]
Donnelly warned that he would never indorse Fisher. Conceding
that Democrats comprised 75 per cent of the coalition, he insisted
that any attempt to develop it along conservative lines would fail.
The nomination of any Bourbon Democrat would be disastrous.[3]

At the Anti-Monopoly–Democratic joint convention, however,
Donnelly's fears were not realized. Although the conservative influ-

[1]St. Paul *Pioneer Press,* May 21, 1875.
[2]Donnelly MSS, J. Doughty to I. D., June 3, 1875.
[3]St. Paul *Anti-Monopolist,* June 10, 24, 1875.

ence increased, only Michael Doran, the candidate for state auditor, was a Bourbon. But the platform, retreating from the reform commitments of the preceding year, was conservative. Reluctantly Donnelly indorsed the candidates and the program.

One month prior to the convention, a handful of Anti-Monopoly reformers, anticipating a conservative victory and certain that continued collaboration with the Democrats meant a fatal loss of both identity and principle, asked Donnelly to repudiate the coalition.[4] Their request embarrassed him. He knew that the Anti-Monopolists were impotent without Democratic support, but he refused to criticize the extremists. When they insisted on a separate convention, he published their announcement in the *Anti-Monopolist*. But in the same edition, urging them to indorse the coalition's candidates, he pleaded that this was not the time to register a protest vote.[5] Since the irreconcilable Anti-Monopolists were few, their Owatonna convention was unimpressive. Donnelly, attending as an observer, exhorted them to continue their crusade for honest government and serious reform,[6] but persuaded them to indorse the coalition's major nominees.[7]

This effort to still criticism within his own ranks failed after the Republicans nominated John S. Pillsbury for governor. Even though the *Anti-Monopolist* denounced Pillsbury as a member of the notorious Minneapolis Millers' Association, which controlled the wheat market,[8] there was mounting dissatisfaction with Donnelly's leadership. The editor of the Minnesota *Grange Advance*, H. H. Young, protested against what he termed the "unDonnelly like" behavior which he displayed at Owatonna. As a Republican Granger, Young refused to acquiesce in this "sellout" to the Democrats.[9]

The Republican politicians greeted the Donnelly-Young clash with undisguised pleasure because they knew that it heralded the death of the Anti-Monopolist party.[10] But the division had even broader ramifications in that it drove the Grange out of partisan politics. Finally defeated on the partisanship issue, Donnelly charged that the Grange had been emasculated to save the Republican

[4]Donnelly MSS, E. Ayres to I. D., June 7, 1875.
[5]St. Paul *Anti-Monopolist*, July 12, 1875.
[6]St. Paul *Pioneer Press*, July 31, 1875.
[7]St. Paul *Anti-Monopolist*, August 2, 1875.
[8]*Ibid.*, August 30, 1875.
[9]Donnelly MSS, H. H. Young to I. D., August 14, 1875.
[10]St. Paul *Pioneer Press*, October 28, 1875.

party.[11] Not until January, 1877, was the Grange column dropped from the *Anti-Monopolist* with Donnelly's shamefaced admission that he had failed to "make the Grange great, powerful, and aggressive."[12]

Not only did he face opposition among the Grangers, but also the Democratic State Central Committee refused to help support the *Anti-Monopolist* or ask Donnelly to speak in behalf of the ticket because he would not disown and denounce the Owatonna convention.[13] Factional infighting was so keen that conservative Democrats, bolting their Dakota County convention after it indorsed Donnelly for state senator, nominated Bourbon Seagrave Smith as an independent. Eager to drive Donnelly out of public life, the county's Republican caucus indorsed Smith. Much to the chagrin of his opponents, and despite the fact that Minnesota gave Republican gubernatorial candidate Pillsbury a ten-thousand-vote majority, Donnelly won re-election.[14]

Because 1875 was a year of reaction, reformers were pessimistic about the 1876 legislative session. Donnelly, however, determined to fight for the relief of farmers and debtors. He sought legislation providing for a state commissioner of agriculture, with power to fix the standards for judging the quality of wheat. His plan would assure uniform grading in every part of the state at every season of the year, an important consideration because wheat was frequently graded down in quality during the harvest. Hostile to any governmental regulation, the Republican-controlled legislature rejected the bill.[15] During this session, Donnelly also attempted to revise the Minnesota usury law to close loopholes. Even though the idea of interest-rate control had been established years earlier, his bill, calling for stricter punishment, was defeated.[16]

Because of the frustration of his legislative program, the constant bickering among the reformers, and his inability to unite Grangers with Democrats, Donnelly finally withdrew from the coalition. The former Republican Grangers, he declared, could not reconcile themselves to the party of Jefferson Davis. Furthermore, the "bloody

[11]St. Paul *Anti-Monopolist*, July 20, 1876.
[12]*Ibid.*, January 18, 1877.
[13]*Ibid.*, November 18, 1875.
[14]*Ibid.*, October 18, 1875.
[15]St. Paul *Pioneer Press*, January 28, 1876; St. Paul *Anti-Monopolist*, March 9, 1876.
[16]St. Paul *Pioneer Press*, February 20, 1876.

shirt" had jeopardized the cause of reform from the outset. The Anti-Monopoly element must stand alone, separated from the prejudices of the past politics of the Civil War and in no way influenced by the conservatism of the monied Democrats.[17]

In the same edition of the *Anti-Monopolist* in which he confessed that the coalition had failed, Donnelly published the call for a National Greenback Labor party convention to be held in Indianapolis, Indiana, and thus created Minnesota's Greenback party. Although the paper money issue was new in Minnesota politics, it had not been slow to mature after the Civil War. The United States had been utilizing paper money since 1862, and, although the Republicans had tended to favor a quick return to specie more than the Democrats, hard times and political expediency had forced the continued circulation of the greenbacks.[18] But when the Democratic party won the congressional elections of 1874, the Republicans, in the "lame duck" session which followed, experienced what came to be called their "death bed" repentance and passed the Resumption of Specie Act. The measure provided that gold would be paid for greenbacks after 1878, that the number of greenbacks be reduced from $382 million to $300 million, and five dollars in national bank notes be substituted for every four dollars in greenbacks retired from use. This meant that $102 million in national bank notes could replace $82 million in greenbacks.

Despite this seeming introduction of more money into the economy, the nation was aware that the administration had embarked upon a deflationary policy. The Resumption of Specie Act also laid the national banks open to criticism because of a provision which allowed them to purchase interest-bearing government bonds and then use these same bonds as security for interest-bearing loans of their own currency. Western advocates of the greenback were quick to charge that this was a vast currency monopoly for which the people were forced to pay twice: once in legitimate interest and again in taxation.[19]

---

[17]St. Paul *Anti-Monopolist*, January 20, 1876.

[18]The Far West, California in particular, remained on a coin economy during most of the period. For the legislative history of the greenback see Don C. Barrett, *The Greenback and the Resumption of Specie Payment, 1862–1879* (Cambridge, Mass.: Harvard University Press, 1931) and more interesting, Robert P. Sharkey, *Money, Class, and Party* (Baltimore: Johns Hopkins Press, 1959).

[19]George L. Anderson, "Western Attitude toward National Banks, 1873–1874," *Mississippi Valley Historical Review*, XXIII (1936), 205–16.

Donnelly was not an immediate convert to "soft money." As late as 1874, lecturing before Granger audiences, he condemned the greenback as inflationary and dangerous to the welfare of the farmers. Nevertheless, as the nation sank into the long depression of the 1870's, and farm prices appeared to plunge downward faster than those of the goods and services which they purchased, Donnelly began to change his mind. In April, 1875, in an article on what he termed the "muddle of currency," he did not take exception to the principle of deflation, but to the extent and speed with which the administration was carrying it out.[20] His correspondence and his exchanges with other editors and politicians, especially J. A. Noonan of the *Industrial Age*, probably did more to change his views than anything else.[21]

When Donnelly attended the Minnesota Democratic convention in midsummer of 1875, he introduced two resolutions critical of the administration's money policy. The first called for maintaining the existing number of greenbacks in circulation while the government increased its gold reserves. The second condemned the policy of substituting national bank notes for greenbacks as subterfuge taxation of the poor. Bourbon Democrats, horrified by these proposals, mustered enough votes to defeat them. The St. Paul *Pioneer Press* rejoiced that at least Minnesota's Democratic party had not gone over to the greenback heresy as had other Democratic state organizations.[22]

As a result of these resolutions, Donnelly was severely criticized as a wild inflationist. Attempting to justify his position, he explained that he favored keeping the greenbacks in circulation until the gold reserve was increased, because the business community needed money to expand. He was not opposed to a gold-standard dollar, but he disapproved of a deflation which compelled the debtor class to pay 30 per cent more in goods and services than it had borrowed. "Who cares whether the medium of exchange is paper or gold?" he asked rhetorically. "What the nation wants is *prosperity*. Money is mere incident—a means of exchange."[23]

Despite his growing enthusiasm for the greenback cause as he understood it, Donnelly was reluctant to join the new political movement which embraced it. He feared that "Wall Street" would gobble

[20]St. Paul *Anti-Monopolist*, April 22, 1875.
[21]Donnelly MSS, J. A. Noonan to I. D., April 26, 1875.
[22]St. Paul *Pioneer Press*, July 8, 1875.
[23]St. Paul *Anti-Monopolist*, July 19, 1875.

up the movement, and his position as an Anti-Monopolist would be jeopardized.[24] When it became clear, however, during the Minnesota legislative session of 1876 that the coalition which he had forged was unable to effect reforms, Donnelly entered the Greenback party.

The Minnesota Greenback organization became the Independent Anti-Monopoly party. In recruiting members Donnelly made no direct overtures to the Democrats as he had in the past.[25] The New York *Tribune,* reviewing Minnesota's politics, sarcastically observed: "Ignatius Donnelly is going to assemble himself in a convention again. He does it every year and the result is the same—nothing; and yet he never gets discouraged." To which Donnelly retorted, "Is it not a cheerful sight in this degenerate age to see one bold man year after year proclaiming truth, even with no hope of success or reward."[26]

But Donnelly did tend to become discouraged with Greenbackism. Neither his dramatic speeches nor his editorials really strengthened the party. The state convention was comprised of a pathetically small group of reformers. Despite the poor showing, Donnelly defended the party while his own views on money matured. By the late spring of 1876, he advocated the repayment of government bonds in greenbacks. After all, he argued without subtlety, the government should not be compelled to pay a premium for gold to satisfy its creditors.[27]

On the eve of the Greenback party national convention, Donnelly favored Judge David Davis for the party's presidential nomination. In reply to a letter from Donnelly, Davis explained that he was not a candidate in the strict sense of the word. In fact, he confessed being more sympathetic to the Democratic position.[28] Disappointed, Donnelly went uncommitted to Indianapolis.

Recognizing Donnelly's national reputation as an orator and public figure, the convention delegates overestimated his political influence because he was designated the temporary chairman. His keynote speech emphasizing a centennial theme—1776–1876—stated that the founding fathers had created a nation where the man should "outweigh the dollar." It was absurd for Congress to haggle

[24]Donnelly MSS, E. Ayres to I. D., August 25, 1875.
[25]St. Paul *Anti-Monopolist,* March 9, 1876.
[26]*Ibid.,* March 23, 1875.
[27]Donnelly MSS, O. H. Page to I. D., April 10, 1876.
[28]*Ibid.,* J. Harvey to I. D., May 6, 1876.

over the future of Jefferson Davis and for the major parties to engage in this colossal diversion, while the real issues were obfuscated. The Greenbackers, he insisted, were not afraid of live issues; they were not "pampered aristocrats" like Charles Francis Adams and the hard-money liberals of New England; they were willing to deal with the real problem of economic opportunity for all classes.[29]

The platform of the Indianapolis convention reflected the complementing opinions of the various economic and geographic groups present. The midwestern farmers insisted upon an end to railroad subsidization, while eastern labor advocated a drastic change in the government's monetary policy. Both elements favored the repeal of the Resumption Act and the sale of government bonds to Americans for paper rather than to Europeans for gold. The Anti-Monopolists, who demanded the plank rejecting the substitution of silver for paper as fractional currency, tended to view the remonetization of silver as the establishment of a money monopoly which would favor the "silver interests."[30]

The Greenback Labor party's presidential nominee was kindly old Peter Cooper, the New York philanthropist who feared that he might actually be elected! Since he was eighty-five years old and no one expected him to carry on a vigorous campaign, the motives of the convention delegates had been suspect. Wallace Groom, editor of the New York *Mercantile Journal,* who was Peter Cooper's personal representative at the gathering, undoubtedly assured the delegates that Cooper would provide financial assistance,[31] but there is no proof that Donnelly's support of Cooper was insincere. There is no evidence that Minnesota's Greenback party received more than a few pamphlets from the national headquarters for use in the campaign.

When Donnelly returned from the convention the editors of the *Pioneer Press,* who had watched Donnelly's political fortunes wane, harshly insisted that the convention should have nominated him for President; after all no one else had been on all sides of all questions and all religions.[32] Increasingly sensitive to criticism, self-justification having become an overwhelming passion with him, Donnelly replied:

[29] St. Paul *Anti-Monopolist,* May 25, 1876.
[30] Chester McArthur Destler, *American Radicalism, 1865–1901* (Ann Arbor: Edwards Brothers, Inc., 1948), pp. 60–62.
[31] E. C. Mack, *Peter Cooper* (New York: Duell, Sloan and Pearce, 1949), pp. 366–68.
[32] St. Paul *Pioneer Press and Tribune,* May 20, 1876.

It seems to be the opinion of some that we are, or ought to be, simply an attached fragment, a pendent remnant, a facile tail of the Democratic party. This is a mistake. We are not and never claimed to be a Democrat, since the old Kansas-Nebraska days, twenty-five years ago. We are an Independent, and an Anti-Monopolist. We left the Republican party in the day of its power and greatness, when it had offices and wealth to bestow on those who served it faithfully; and we enlisted with the guerillas, where there was neither pay nor plunder. We cooperated occasionally with the Democrats, because of two evils they seemed to be the least; and because being a minority, they were naturally opposed to the excesses of the majority. . . .

We know it is charged that we are vacillating;—that we pass readily from party to party. . . .

Let no one accuse us of vacillation or inconsistency. No party owns us. We adhere to principle and follow where it leads. We propose to make our life a protest against the slavish rule of caucuses and rings which now afflicts this country. We are well aware that this is not the pathway that leads to political honors and emoluments. We do not seek them.[33]

In recapitulating his career, Donnelly defined his political role as that of a tribune of the people. It was this self-identification with high principle and the cause of reform that encouraged him during the campaign of 1876.

The party's convention had failed to generate enthusiasm for the Greenback cause in Minnesota. At first Donnelly had difficulty convincing many of the reform groups in the state that they should ally themselves with a party promising so slim a chance of victory. Most of the work was done by a hardened corps of newspaper editors and politicians who insisted that Donnelly lead a crusade, much as he had in behalf of the Grange only three years before, and arouse the people of Minnesota to the evils of deflation.[34] Courageously he undertook the task by planning an extensive speaking tour, a series of articles in the *Anti-Monopolist*, and the publication of thousands of handbills. With great reluctance, because defeat was a foregone conclusion, he accepted the congressional nomination for Minnesota's Second District after the Democrats spurned his offer of fusion.[35]

During the campaign Donnelly changed his mind on the remonetization of silver. Silver had been used to purchase Civil War bonds and the government should be able to repay in the same kind of money. He recognized the shallowness of his reasoning, but he was

[33] St. Paul *Anti-Monopolist*, July 13, 1876.

[34] Donnelly MSS, N. C. Martin to I. D., August 21, 1876.

[35] *Ibid.*, F. A. Davis to I. D., August 14, 1876; H. Poehler to I. D., September 29, 1876. See also St. Paul *Anti-Monopolist*, September 14, November 2, 1876.

becoming more and more a believer in a controlled currency and he felt that a return to bimetallism was one step in that direction.[36]

The Greenbackers' campaign scarcely influenced the voters of Minnesota. This election proved that Greenbackism, standing alone as an issue, was unable to attract a real following. That Donnelly received more votes in the Second District than Peter Cooper, the party's presidential nominee, did in the entire state, bears witness not only to the lack of Greenback feeling among the people, but also to the fact that his name was associated with other reform causes.

After being defeated and virtually isolated politically, Donnelly might have expected his influence in Minnesota to have reached its nadir, but this was not the case. As the self-proclaimed tribune he became the rallying symbol for all reform. Even the Republican Speaker of the House, eager to repeal a law unfair to his district, appealed to Donnelly, knowing, as he said, that it was only necessary to "call your attention to the injustice of the present law" to have your help.[37] Very few people were aware of Donnelly's hard work during the 1877 legislature. He continued his struggle for a state agricultural commissioner with the power to determine the grade for each quality of wheat. Through his efforts the legislature memorialized Congress to appropriate relief funds for Minnesota's farmers suffering from grasshopper depredation.

Donnelly's "must pass" bill in the 1877 session, one he had advocated unsuccessfully for several years, was a usury law. The St. Paul *Pioneer Press* misrepresented and misinterpreted the bill, charging that Donnelly urged a dangerous and radical innovation which would frighten investment capital from the state.[38] But on the subject of usury legislation, he had grown immune to insult or distraction. Answering rational arguments calmly, he turned invective, scorn, and ridicule upon his irrational or dishonest critics. Cajoling, pleading, reasoning in the senate, and keeping the public aware of the facts, he secured passage of his bill. Even "Honest John" Pillsbury signed it without comment.

Donnelly considered the measure a great reform. It not only outlawed interest rates in excess of 12 per cent, but also fixed a very strict punishment—forfeiture of both principal and interest—upon violators. He felt the bill would do away with Minnesota's chattel-mortgage Shylocks because it repealed a mortgage law which al-

[36] St. Paul *Anti-Monopolist*, August 24, 1876.
[37] Donnelly MSS, J. L. Gibbs to I. D., February 23, 1877.
[38] St. Paul *Pioneer Press*, February 1, 1877.

lowed a creditor to seize, without notice and without formal foreclosure proceedings, the property of his debtor. Under the Donnelly
bill, all foreclosures had to take place in court and a sixty-day notice
had to be given before any sheriff's sale could take place. "No more
thrashing machines will be sold for three dollars each!" Donnelly announced in the *Anti-Monopolist*.[39] The debt-ridden, locust-plagued
farmers in western Minnesota could be grateful to him.

Donnelly, however, had even greater cause for self-satisfaction.
The United States Supreme Court, in the so-called Granger cases,
had upheld the decision of Minnesota's Supreme Court in *Blake et
al.* v *The Winona & St. Peter Railroad*, and thus sustained the state
legislature's right to regulate intra-state commerce. "Who will talk of
communism and agrarianism now?" Donnelly asked his former
critics, reminding them of the denunciations and accusations leveled
against him in years past.[40] Two months later he added a Jeffersonian
motto to the masthead of the *Anti-Monopolist*: "Eternal hostility to
every form of oppression of the bodies and the souls of men."[41]

During the years that Donnelly associated himself with the farmer's cause, he had owned several farms and considered himself a
farmer, but he had never earned his living at the plow. In 1877,
however, Donnelly began full-scale bonanza farming at Douglas
Station, Stevens County. Two years earlier, realizing that his sons,
Ignatius and Stanislaus, were approaching manhood with no prospects of employment at home, he decided to buy land from the
St. Paul & Pacific Railroad which was trading acreage to satisfy its
bonded indebtedness. With money borrowed in Philadelphia, he
bought European-owned securities at fifteen cents on the dollar
through an Amsterdam brokerage firm. These he traded for several
thousand acres of the St. Paul & Pacific's virgin land.[42]

When he requested a name change for the town, the *Pioneer and
Press* quipped: "Douglas station, on the St. Paul & Pacific, is now the
city of Donnelly. Woe to the usurer, the wheat scalper, or grasshopper that tries to pitch his tent therein." To which Donnelly replied: "Thanks! What a paradise we could make Minnesota if we
had the power. But alas!"[43]

[39]St. Paul *Anti-Monopolist*, March 8, 1877.
[40]*Ibid.*
[41]*Ibid.*, May 10, 1877.
[42]Donnelly MSS, I. D. to Mary Donnelly, November 6, 1875; I. D. to Harry
Oyens & Sons, December 8, 1875; R. Engel to I. D., January 20, 1876; I. D. to
Henry Oyens & Sons, January 20, 1876.
[43]St. Paul *Anti-Monopolist*, February 8, 1877.

Even before Donnelly began planting wheat he discovered that the land, which he secured for less than one dollar an acre, had to be broken with a steel plow at a cost of three dollars an acre before it could be seeded. He learned how painfully expensive was the development and cultivation of the prairie. He discovered also that building materials of even the simplest type were almost prohibitive in price. This was the sod house frontier. Unlike other farmers in the region who had to pay heavy interest charges to buy machinery, Donnelly was able to trade advertising space in the *Anti-Monopolist* for it.[44] Hardly a typical prairie farmer, he made up in investment capital for what he lacked in practical knowledge.

Late in August, 1876, the dreaded Rocky Mountain locust fell upon his newly broken lands. To an experienced farmer this would have been a harbinger of disaster. Donnelly, however, was not dismayed. He prepared to plant almost three thousand seedling trees on a newly acquired Timber Culture Act claim.[45] Gradually, he became aware of the grasshoppers' presence. By late May the locust eggs were hatching in such enormous numbers that in western Minnesota growers anticipated losing the entire wheat crop. Sheet iron scoops and coal tar were used to catch and destroy the insects. By June the fields along the St. Paul & Pacific's mainline were devastated. Even the streets in the large towns swarmed with locusts, and as Donnelly noted at Willmar, "the very lawns [were] eaten bare by them."[46]

On July 3, the locusts swarmed over his farm. Like other farmers in Stevens County, he fought them by dragging ropes over his fields hoping to frighten them into flight, but he was unsuccessful. The intolerably hot days, the air filled with mosquitoes, and the sight of the helpless farmers forced to watch the locusts, like clusters of fruit on the oats and wheat, devouring their crops, left Donnelly in the depths of melancholy.[47] But the wind shifted direction. The locusts gradually swarmed in flight. By mid-August, Minnesota was virtually free from the dreaded scourge. Donnelly was among the fortunate few farmers who had not lost their entire crop.

The Minnesota farmers joined other economic groups who were suffering severely during the summer of 1877. Urban workers all

---

[44] Donnelly MSS, I. D. to J. McDonald, May 14, 1876; J. B. Bassett & Co. to I. D., May 31, 1876; R. H. Jones to I. D., June 7, 1876.

[45] *Ibid.*, Diary, April 30, May 22, 1877.

[46] *Ibid.*, Diary, June 6, 1877.

[47] *Ibid.*, A. Pettingill to I. D., July 3, 1877; Diary, July 10, 1877.

over the country were impoverished by the prolonged effects of the Panic of 1873, and the deflationary policy enforced by the Resumption of Specie Act resulted in a reduction of wages. In July, 1877, with almost three million workers unemployed, there was a series of violent strikes—strikes unprecedented in American history because workers seized whole towns, stopped trains, and betrayed a strong class hatred. In several states both the militia and the national army were used to overawe the workers and to break the strikes, but bloodshed and terrorism followed in the wake of force. The conservative newspapers of Minnesota, reflecting the business community's shock at this violence, were filled with exaggerated accounts of mob action and incendiarism.

Donnelly sharply took issue with this interpretation of the strikes. He had a politician's distrust of violence, even noting the July violence in his diary as a "horrible labor insurrection," but he could not agree with the name-calling conservative press.[48] "Whenever a man attempts to defend his rights now-a-days he is called a communist," he wrote in the *Anti-Monopolist*. "When a starving populace clamour for work or bread they are called communists." And then he added caustically, "The communists of Europe want everything in common;—the communists in America are enjoying *nothing* in common—and plenty of it." He warned the conservative politicians and newspapers to stop berating workers who wanted a living wage and farmers who wanted a fair profit. The producer was entitled to all he could get, and the function of government in a republic was to help him get it.[49]

Although strike violence never spread to Minnesota, economic conditions had serious political ramifications. There was a growing feeling among petty capitalists, promoters, and merchants that the profits gained in the new post-Civil War industrialism could be distributed more widely if the government accepted a mildly inflationary policy, perhaps even the remonetization of silver on a reasonable basis. This was clearly evident when William L. Banning, the St. Paul banker and Donnelly's friend and fellow lobbyist for Jay Cooke, persuaded the St. Paul Chamber of Commerce to pass a resolution indorsing bimetallism.[50] Horrified conservatives in both parties denounced these "silver money-maniacs" and denied emphatically that the silver dollar had been the "dollar of our fathers."

[48]*Ibid.*, Diary, July 25, 1877.
[49]St. Paul *Anti-Monopolist*, August 23, 1877.
[50]St. Paul *Pioneer Press*, April 11, 1877.

They charged that the reintroduction of bimetallism was outright debt repudiation.

Although Minnesota's conservative press expressed alarm about the inroads of the spirit of inflation in the business community, Donnelly's Greenback party did not evoke the same feeling. Having been severely drubbed at the polls, it presented no obvious threat. However, if the Democrats indorsed the greenback, as they were doing in other states, the political status quo could be upset. This dire prophecy seemed to be realized when both the Greenbacker and the Democratic conventions nominated William L. Banning for governor. The conservative Democrats, however, dominated their party's platform committee and advocated a greenback dollar redeemable in gold.[51]

The Democratic-Greenback fusion came none too soon for Donnelly. With a Democratic indorsement, albeit reluctantly given, Donnelly was re-elected despite the overwhelming defeat of Banning by John S. Pillsbury. Although Minnesota's Greenback-Democratic coalition had been routed, Donnelly was enthusiastic after surveying the national political scene in 1877. The Greenbackers had made startling gains, especially in getting Democratic support.[52] Unable to attend the Greenback national convention in Toledo, Ohio, he welcomed approvingly its platform, including many pro-labor planks. Unlike some of the more inflationist-minded Greenbackers, he did not reject the platform for its failure to espouse fiat money.[53]

In the legislative session following the election, he introduced a resolution instructing Minnesota's congressmen to support the Bland silver purchase bill. He made so careful and logical a speech in favor of his resolution that even the St. Paul *Pioneer Press* conceded its moderate tone and lucidity.[54] The resolution passed.

Although the silver question interested him, Donnelly's major energies were spent in a successful campaign in favor of state-published, free, school textbooks. The issue had interested him since 1874. At that time, it was rumored that the publishers were lobbying for increased state appropriations for books. Donnelly tried to eliminate this practice, but his bill was defeated. Perhaps his interest in what he termed the "book ring" might have waned had he not

[51]*Ibid.*, October 18, 1877.
[52]St. Paul *Anti-Monopolist*, June 17, December 20, 1877.
[53]Destler, *American Radicalism*, pp. 64–65.
[54]St. Paul *Pioneer Press*, January 17, 1878.

been informed by a school supplier that the publishers' lobby boasted of having killed Donnelly's bill.[55] As a result, he determined to crush the "book ring."

In 1875, he introduced a new textbook law but was once more thwarted by the lobby. Donnelly, shifting his legislative tactics the following year, wisely invited his friend, Senator Leinau, a conservative, honest German who was exempt from criticism, to introduce the measure. The bill gathered support when the Reverend Edward D. Neill, considered Minnesota's most distinguished scholar, testified in its favor. Donnelly defended the bill in the senate.

No sooner had it passed the senate than the St. Paul *Pioneer Press* spearheaded the attack against it by accusing Donnelly and Leinau of advocating socialism. "It is the province of the state to foster, and not to discourage private enterprise," the paper fulminated. "They should so legislate to invite capital to their borders, and not to drive it out." Donnelly and Leinau had gone too far in defining the state's powers. "The truth is that, in providing schoolhouses and teachers for the children, the state does enough. Somewhere," the *Pioneer Press* concluded, "the line must be drawn which ends the state's responsibility for the education of her citizens."[56]

The irresponsible allegations of the *Pioneer Press* overruled evidence that the state spent more on educational printing than the cost of the project. It drowned out proof that thousands of dollars could be saved. It ignored the argument that the state could solicit fair competitive bidding on high quality books.[57] Furthermore, the "book lobby" descended on the lower house like a locust plague and, whispering "communism" and "profits" into the ears of "button holed" legislators, secured the defeat of the measure by two votes.[58]

Furious, Donnelly called on the people of Minnesota to elect only legislators who would pledge themselves to a new textbook law. In 1877, both Leinau and Donnelly presented a foolproof measure providing for a commission to contract with a publisher to provide books comparable in quality to those in use. A revolving fund was to be established to maintain the supply of books. The Grange sent a special lobby to St. Paul in support of the bill.[59] No allegation of radicalism escaped even the St. Paul *Pioneer Press*. Only a "last

[55] Donnelly MSS, C. H. Roberts to I. D., November 24, 1874.
[56] St. Paul *Pioneer Press*, February 18, 25, 1876.
[57] *Ibid.*, February 29, 1876; St. Paul *Anti-Monopolist*, March 16, 1876.
[58] St. Paul *Anti-Monopolist*, March 16, 1876.
[59] *Ibid.*, February 22, March 1, 1877.

ditch fight" by the publishers' lobby held back passage of the bill until February 20, 1877.

In 1878 the publishers' lobby made an effort to rewrite the bill. Defeating their scheme became Donnelly's personal cause.[60] As the legislative session drew to a close, the St. Paul *Pioneer Press*, now committed to the idea of free textbooks, congratulated the people of Minnesota for defeating the "textbook ring." Reluctantly it conceded that to Donnelly must go the major credit for saving the bill on the legislature's final day.[61]

[60]Donnelly MSS, Diary, March 2, 1878.
[61]St. Paul *Pioneer Press*, March 8, 1878.

The Brass Kettle Campaign
1878–1880

Down with Washburn and the swindling brass kettle.

St. Paul Globe

AFTER their startling gains and successes in 1877, many Green-backers looked forward eagerly to the 1878 congressional elections. Donnelly was no exception. Because of his legislative record, his enhanced popularity, and his support of Banning in 1877, he hoped to receive serious consideration for the Democratic nomination in the Second Congressional District. He attended the Democratic convention although he had been warned that many Democrats, never having forgiven him, preferred to risk defeat with a Bourbon than win with Donnelly.[1] Spurned by the convention, Donnelly prepared to watch the election campaign from Nininger City.

However, when William Washburn defeated the incumbent Republican congressman in the Third District, J. H. Stewart, in his bid for renomination, it was immediately proposed that Donnelly run against him. William L. Banning urged him to campaign, "against the slab of lumber put up by the pine land ring," on the very day the St. Paul *Globe* observed that Donnelly was as much a resident of the Third District as the Second because he owned land in Stevens County and edited a St. Paul newspaper.[2]

Enthusiasm for Donnelly's nomination grew enormously, as the St. Paul *Globe*, leading the attack on Washburn, quoted from the

[1] Donnelly MSS, P. Rahilly to I. D., June 29, 1878.
[2] *Ibid.*, W. L. Banning to I. D., July 20, 1878; *Globe*, July 20, 1878.

Minneapolis *Lumberman,* a leading trade journal, to the effect that the district's lumbering interests were responsible for his nomination because they wanted an "able zealous advocate in National Halls." Donnelly, the *Globe* argued, "being a frontier farmer . . . knows the needs of the frontier. His sympathy and voice have been on the side of the working man. He has nothing of the cold-blooded, purse-proud aristocracy characteristic of Washburn."[3] The St. Paul *Pioneer Press,* noticing the "Donnelly wave," ridiculed the idea of his candidacy by pointing out that he could not possibly gain a single orthodox Republican or Democratic vote,[4] but Donnelly's friends informed him that the popular feeling in his behalf was astonishingly strong.[5]

Despite assurances of a "first rate chance of being elected," Donnelly was cautious.[6] The Third Congressional District, which included both St. Paul and Minneapolis, was the focal point of Minnesota's great special interests: railroads, milling, and lumbering. To win in the Third District required an intense campaign, an efficient organization, and a thick purse. "I shrink from such a gigantic campaign with such doubtful results," Donnelly confided to his diary.[7] Sharing his pessimism, Kate was certain that he could harass Washburn, even force him to spend a good deal of money, but she seriously doubted whether the Third District, carefully gerrymandered as it was, could be taken from the Republicans. Since campaigning in the Third District would be very expensive, she insisted that Donnelly have positive proof of financial support.[8]

When E. D. Cramsie, vice-president of the Minneapolis Workingmen's Union, went to Nininger City to discuss the election, he startled Donnelly by explaining that many Republicans, even Ramsey and Dr. Stewart, favored him against Washburn. Cramsie probably also reassured Donnelly that his stand in favor of the eight-hour day and against child labor guaranteed his control of the workingman's vote.[9] A few days later, Banning pledged both strong support from the St. Paul Democrats and financial help from the Democratic National Committee.[10] On the basis of these assurances, Donnelly

[3] St. Paul *Globe,* July 20, 22, 1878.
[4] St. Paul *Pioneer Press,* July 21, 1878.
[5] Donnelly MSS, W. B. McKenny to I. D., July 22, 1878.
[6] *Ibid.,* W. L. Banning to I. D., July 22, 1878.
[7] *Ibid.,* Diary, July 24, 1878.
[8] *Ibid.,* K. D. to I. D., July 25, 1878.
[9] *Ibid.,* Diary, July 24, 1878; A. E. Cramsie to I. D., August 14, 1878.
[10] *Ibid.,* W. L. Banning to I. D., July 27, 1878.

agreed to campaign if he received the nomination. At the Greenback convention, one day before the Democratic gathering, Donnelly accepted the nomination for Congress with the proviso that it be echoed by the Democrats. His hope, he told the delegates, was to bring the parties closer together on the currency issues. Furthermore, he had no wish to divide the anti-Washburn vote.[11]

The following day the Democratic convention nominated him for Congress on the first formal ballot. In his acceptance speech Donnelly forthrightly declared that he was in the fight to the bitter end, that his was a struggle to prevent the common laborer and producer from being driven into poverty, and that he was seeking to stave off an economic crisis in which a dictator might arise. Nominally, Donnelly reminded the delegates, he was not a Democrat, but if they would bury old feuds and would fight for principle, they would win.[12]

Organizing Donnelly's campaign proved difficult because the various groups refused to co-operate. Dr. J. H. Stewart's friends secretly prepared Republican ballots on which slips bearing Donnelly's name could be pasted.[13] The major organization breakdown occurred in St. Paul and Minneapolis where the Greenback-Labor party refused to co-operate with the Democrats because they distrusted them as much as they did the Republicans.[14] Donnelly tried to keep peace between the warring elements, but was never wholly successful.

Currency and the continuing depression were the two salient issues Donnelly planned to present to the people, but they were lost in the emotionally charged question of the price of wheat and how it was established. For years it had been asserted that wheat prices were low because of overproduction. Diversification of production was the solution most frequently proposed to suffering western farmers.[15] It was highly popular in the East where so distinguished a public figure as Henry Ward Beecher commented that Minnesota farmers had "too many eggs in one basket; farmers should grow something besides wheat." But as every Minnesotan realized, the prairie farmer could not plant "broom corn" or "*ruta bagas*," as

[11]St. Paul *Globe*, September 6, 1878.

[12]*Ibid.*, September 7, 1878.

[13]Donnelly MSS, E. G. Holmes to I. D., September 20, 1878; W. Wicks to I. D., September 24, 1878.

[14]*Ibid.*, J. Kessler to I. D., September 16, 1878.

[15]Henrietta M. Larson, *The Wheat Market and the Farmer in Minnesota, 1858–1900* (New York: Columbia University Press, 1926), p. 99.

Donnelly quipped, and make a profit.[16] Diversification was virtually impossible in western Minnesota. The problem as the farmers saw it was not one of production but one of marketing.

There was no grain exchange in Minneapolis. Purchases were made by the Minneapolis Millers' Association. Organized in 1867 to reduce costs and to facilitate the shipment of wheat into the Minneapolis mills, within a few years the Association's members had a monopolistic grasp on the entire wheat-producing area. What irritated the farmers was not so much the price fixing in which the Association engaged, because the price of wheat had to conform by and large to the world price, but the absolute control of grading which it practiced.[17] Because wheat was graded by weight, the difference between one grade and another being only two pounds, the farmers were angered when wheat lacking only a few ounces was graded down rather than graded up to the nearest level. They were particularly aroused when it was discovered that the weighing device, a two-quart brass kettle, could be so manipulated in the filling process that the "quality" of wheat could be altered as much as two grades. Following this disclosure, the "lying little kettle" became the symbol of monopoly's dishonesty and the corruption of the Republicans in the election of 1878.[18]

The fact that William D. Washburn was a member of the Minneapolis Millers' Association attached the twin evils of monopoly and corruption to him. "Down with Washburn and the swindling brass kettle!" boomed the *Globe*;[19] and one of Donnelly's cohorts predicted, "If the flame can be fed until election day it will be a regular Krupp gun. It is one of the most damaging projectiles that was ever shot off in any political campaign."[20] The greenback issue and the depression were virtually ignored in the Democratic newspapers; they concentrated instead on the "millers' ring."

Donnelly, realizing that the brass kettle was a good electioneering device, employed it only as a symbol of the nation's condition. He made extensive political capital of his legislative record, reminding audiences of his anti-usury bill, his textbook measure, and his hard work for farmer relief. He was surprisingly sparing in his criticism of Washburn, content to point out that as a lumberman and miller

[16]St. Paul *Anti-Monopolist*, August 22, 1878.
[17]Larson, *The Wheat Market*, pp. 91, 133, 145, 149.
[18]Hall, *Observations*, p. 228.
[19]St. Paul *Globe*, October 15, 1878.
[20]Donnelly MSS, T. G. Mealy to I. D., October 20, 1878.

who had shared in the profits of the Association, Washburn must be prepared to suffer the effects of the public indignation for the "ring's" patent dishonesty.

Donnelly focused his speeches on larger national issues. He explained and justified his view that the value of money, be it gold, silver, or paper, should rest upon the solemn promise of the government to accept it as legal tender. Elaborating his position, he denied being an inflationist, asserting that the amount of money in circulation should be adjusted to the people's needs. The Hayes administration, Donnelly cautioned, was dominated by big business and powerful financial interests. The people's rights were in genuine danger when these interests sought to return Grant to the White House to guarantee their profit taking.[21]

Donnelly felt more confident of victory when the anti-Washburn Republicans did not fade out, as he feared they might, but seemed resolved on working until the election. Enthusiastic as he became, Donnelly wrote Kate expressing his inner fear that if Washburn really began spending money, the most promising outlook could be radically altered.[22] Furthermore, it was discouraging when Harlan P. Hall, who edited the St. Paul *Globe* and was serving as the fund raiser for Donnelly's cause, produced a disappointingly small sum—$640. James J. Hill, the railroad promoter and Minnesota's most affluent Democrat, only contributed a Northern Pacific Railroad pass to the campaign. Hall was disturbed by the lack of money. "If we had $3000 we could make it for sure," he informed Donnelly. "I believe this is the year *their* money won't go around."[23]

When Donnelly was first mentioned as Washburn's possible opponent, the St. Paul *Pioneer Press* considered that his nomination would be an insult to reputable Democratic leaders. After the convention, the *Pioneer Press* professed outright amazement that the Democrats could ignore the claims of respected business and civic leaders such as General Henry Hastings Sibley, Henry M. Rice, Judge Charles Flandrau or the lumber merchants of Stillwater, Isaac Staples and E. W. Durant. The selection of a political renegade such as Donnelly was either a joke or a cruel effort to abuse Washburn in the face of certain defeat. He would not even receive the normal Democratic vote, the paper declared, because there was no en-

[21] St. Paul *Pioneer Press*, October 8, 1878.
[22] Donnelly MSS, I. D. to K. D., October 6, 1878.
[23] *Ibid.*, H. P. Hall to I. D., October 7, 1878.

thusiasm for him in St. Paul.[24] The *Pioneer Press* was correct in its analysis of St. Paul's Bourbon Democrats. They made no secret of the fact that they would have "no truck" with Donnelly and were actively working against him.[25]

Washburn and his secretary Charles W. Johnson, however, grew increasingly concerned about Donnelly's inroads among the Scandinavians. Knute Nelson, the outstanding Norwegian orator, was urged to work in Washburn's behalf. "If no break is made among the Scandinavians I shall have no apprehensions," the Republican candidate wrote Nelson. "You ought to look to it more closely."[26]

But after one month of earnest campaigning, the brass kettle issue rose on the political horizon. The Republican politicians were horrified to learn that if the kettle fraud accusation were proved to be true, even the Republican farmers would vote against Washburn.[27] The St. Paul *Pioneer Press,* in an effort to defend him, pointed out that the brass kettle was hardly a valid political issue for a congressional election. But its editors foolishly argued that the farmers had lost less being swindled by the millers than they would have if Donnelly's plan for inspectors at the grain elevators had been accepted.[28]

Washburn presented his own defense much more effectively at a Republican rally at Anoka, where he insisted that the price of wheat and its grading was determined by the world market. But more to the point, Washburn explained the attitude of American businessmen. Far from being a grasping monopolist, he argued that he helped the workingman by creating jobs and opportunities in his mills, lumber camps, and railroads.[29] Printed copies of this speech, plus proof that the Minneapolis Millers' Association purchased more wheat at top grade than at the bottom two grades combined, probably provided Washburn's most effective answer to the brass kettle question.

The *Pioneer Press,* viciously attacking Donnelly, revived all the old stories of hidden dishonesty and deceit. It even printed a purely apocryphal tale in which Anthony Trollope, the noted

[24]September 7, 24, 1878.
[25]Minnesota Historical Society, Knute Nelson MSS, C. W. Johnson to Knute Nelson, September 13, 1878.
[26]*Ibid.,* W. D. Washburn to Knute Nelson, September 24, October 11, 1878.
[27]William D. Hall MSS, F. Hale to W. D. Washburn, October 6, 1878.
[28]St. Paul *Pioneer Press,* October 14, 1878.
[29]*Ibid.,* October 15, 1878.

English novelist and traveler, referred to Donnelly as a mudslinger. The Memphis & El Paso episode was resurrected and, although the editors had previously admitted Donnelly's innocence, the documents were edited to make him appear guilty. The *Pioneer Press*, in an editorial printed as election day neared, said:

> Is there a spirit of agrarianism, he is its embodiment. Has Kearneyism a following in Minnesota, he is its prophet. Are there communists, they are for Donnelly. He reflects the bad purposes and bad passions which are either dormant or avowed in our State. The "tramps," of course, follow his banner; and the communists of society, by instinct, will give him all their support. . . . If there are those who desire a revolution in government and society, Donnelly is their representative and hope.

It accused him of being a Roman Catholic and trying to disguise the fact by never using his middle name, Loyola.[30]

Early in the campaign, the Republican Committee, alarmed by Donnelly's strength, circularized all the leading Republicans asking each to contribute to Washburn's cause. It warned that the next United States senator might be Democratic and that the loss of a single House seat might result in the enactment of a paper money bill.[31] The most seasoned Republican campaigners in Minnesota, William Windom, James Heaton Baker, and Donnelly's former foe in the election of 1868, General Christopher Columbus Andrews, answered this call.

Although the Republicans were very effectively organized in Minneapolis, Washburn confessed to Knute Nelson, "I am nervous about the frontier."[32] Controlling the rural floater vote was usually expensive, and even in this heavily financed campaign, Washburn's secretary, Charles W. Johnson, wrote Knute Nelson explaining that "we don't give money to people we don't know."[33]

Despite active Republican campaigning, one of Donnelly's friends reported: "In the American towns you will have a majority. I think nothing but lightning can stop it." Then he added, "but [I] find in the Norwegian and Swede Towns quite a number against you."[34] The Democratic party's secretary in the Third Congressional District felt that St. Paul could be "cleaned out" completely if there were

[30]October 9, 10, 29, 30, 1878.
[31]*Donnelly* vs. *Washburn*, 46th Cong., 1st sess., House Misc. Documents No. 9 (serial 1876), p. 43.
[32]Knute Nelson MSS, W. D. Washburn to Knute Nelson, October 22, 1878
[33]*Ibid.*, C. W. Johnson to Knute Nelson, October 31, 1878.
[34]Donnelly MSS, E. Meaghen to I. D., October 18, 1878; S. W. Sprague to I. D., October 21, 1878.

only a few more dollars left for a grand rally before the election. He was convinced Donnelly would carry the city.[35] Donnelly himself was pleased with the political situation, but he had been so keenly disappointed in the past that he could not overcome his inner trepidation. "There is an immense revolution & I do not see how Washburn can overcome it," he wrote Kate. "I begin to feel *certain* of election, and yet I am afraid to be too sanguine."[36]

Donnelly was defeated by 3,000 votes out of a total of 39,000 cast. He could take some satisfaction in having reduced by two-thirds the normal Republican majority of 10,000 in the Third District. His failure at the polls served, however, to compound his personal financial problems, and shortly after the election, he was forced to dispose of the *Anti-Monopolist* to satisfy his creditors.[37]

His friends, disgusted by the abundant evidence of bribery, fraud, and unlawful voting procedures, demanded that he file a "contested election" suit.[38] In the days following the election he received numerous letters citing instances of the dishonesty of election officials. Aware of the expenses involved in contesting an election, Donnelly hesitated to take definite action. He finally accepted the volunteer aid of attorney P. O. Chilstrom who offered to seek further information. Dr. J. H. Stewart, the incumbent congressman, encouraged Donnelly to file the suit by pointing out that "if a clear case is made out," Washburn would be ousted.[39] Donnelly wrote to Congressman S. S. Cox seeking advice and help. After assuring Cox that he would co-operate fully with the Democrats if Washburn was not seated, Donnelly asked Cox for financial assistance from the party. Cox reminded Donnelly that Congress usually appropriated at least a thousand dollars for the contestants if an earnest case was presented.[40] Even before Cox's letter reached him, Donnelly served formal notice that he contested Washburn's right to the seat.[41]

Gathering evidence against Washburn was not difficult, but it did take time and cost money. Donnelly, who tried to save money by doing much of the investigating himself, was forced to sell wheat at fifty cents a bushel to pay his expenses. To finance his trip to Wash-

[35]*Ibid.*, W. Tileston to I. D., October 26, 1878.
[36]*Ibid.*, I. D. to K. D., October 30, 1878.
[37]*Ibid.*, I. D. to W. B. McKenny, August 25, 1879.
[38]*Ibid.*, F. J. Mead to I. D., November 7, 1878.
[39]*Ibid.*, J. H. Stewart to I. D., December 12, 1878.
[40]*Ibid.*, S. S. Cox to I. D., December 17, 1878.
[41]St. Paul *Pioneer Press*, December 21, 1878.

ington so that he could be present for the contest, he even mortgaged some of his newly acquired land in Stevens County. The only way in which Donnelly was not sparing of funds was in the selection of his counsel—George W. Julian, a highly experienced but costly pleader.

Because his case would not be presented until the winter of 1879, Donnelly used a full year gathering evidence, selecting legal precedents, searching the body of the law for the necessary citations, and excluding peripheral material. It took him two days to write the final brief, and he explained to Kate that any shortcomings in it would have to be excused because the work was done "in the midst of threshing."[42]

When he arrived in Washington, the Democrats, who were in control of the House of Representatives, treated him "exceedingly well." He informed Kate that "Mr. Springer [the chairman of the House Committee on Elections] is earnestly my friend, so is the chairman of the subcommittee, investigating the contest, Mr. Manning."[43] Furthermore, although Donnelly had been unable to help the Minnesota Greenbackers in the 1879 autumn elections, the party's chairman, James Starkey, had written to General James Baird Weaver, a Greenback congressman and a member of the House Committee on Elections, asking him to support Donnelly's claim.[44] The only unfavorable omen was the presence of Judge Charles Flandrau, one of Minnesota's leading conservative Democrats, who had come to Washington to serve as William Washburn's attorney. This was positive proof of Bourbon Democratic opposition to Donnelly's candidacy.[45]

The brief which Donnelly submitted to the election subcommittee consisted of three parts, each with supporting documents: first, unlawful election practices; second, instances of bribery; and last, intimidation of voters. Donnelly's argument emphasized two types of unlawful election practices. The first consisted of instances of voting in unorganized counties where Governor John S. Pillsbury, in violation of the state election law, had virtually hand picked the election judges. Most of the voters in these counties were railroad employees or transients, and they indorsed Washburn almost unanimously. Donnelly asked that these votes be "thrown out" because they had not been cast according to the election law.

[42]*Ibid.*, I. D. to K. D., September 13, 1879.
[43]*Ibid.*, December 10, 1879.
[44]*Ibid.*, December 17, 1879.
[45]*Ibid.*, H. H. Finley to I. D., December 18, 1879.

The second violation of voting procedure involved an amendment to the election code passed during the 1877 legislature which provided that all ballots in cities of more than 10,000 were to be marked with the voter's number from the polling list. Because it destroyed the secrecy of the ballot, the law, immediately challenged in a St. Paul municipal election of 1878, was declared unconstitutional by Judge H. R. Brill two weeks before the congressional election. The St. Paul election officials accepted Judge Brill's ruling, but in Minneapolis there was a disagreement. Democratic City Attorney William Lochren called the local election judges together and explained the validity of Brill's decision, but he allowed each judge to use individual discretion. As a result, there was ballot numbering in precincts where the labor vote was heavy. Donnelly asked that the numbered ballots be discarded because they were illegally cast. This alone would have reduced Washburn's vote by more than half of his majority.

Donnelly's allegations of bribery were substantiated by specific instances. In case after case, he presented depositions stating that Washburn's secretary or bookkeeper negotiated for payments which ranged from outright money gifts to sacks of flour from the Washburn mills. There were illustrations of transient railroad workers who had been bribed by their supervisors with funds drawn on the account of the line's president, Washburn. Furthermore, there was evidence that in unorganized counties, an open cigar box in a freight car had served the purpose of a ballot box. Donnelly's brief, which did not specify the number of these irregularities, merely their existence, pointed to precedents in which candidates proven guilty of buying votes were automatically disqualified.

His final charge, intimidation, centered on two specific cases. The workers of the North Star Woolen Mills were voted by their employer, who told them that a Donnelly victory would not only injure the growth of Minneapolis, but also affect their job security. The second instance was that the Minneapolis Harvester Company had given men time off to vote for Washburn but not for Donnelly.[46]

Washburn's reply, which was probably written by Judge Flandrau, was as much an attack on Donnelly as it was a defense. In large measure Washburn tried to convince the conservative Democrats on the committee that Donnelly did not deserve partisan support. As for the charges, Washburn argued that the Third District had always been Republican, that much of Donnelly's case rested on

[46]*The Contested Election Case of Ignatius Donnelly versus William D. Washburn: Contestants Brief* (St. Paul: West Publishing Co., 1879), pp. 1–48.

hearsay evidence, which though admissible was of dubious worth, that Minnesota's election law concerning the voting in unorganized counties which Pillsbury had violated was improperly printed, and that the numbered ballots in Minneapolis may have been unconstitutional, but they did not affect the case in point. Furthermore, Washburn baldly asserted that the charges of bribery were ludicrous because all parties used money. And Donnelly's accusation that certain Republican officials in the unorganized counties worked for Washburn despite President Hayes' civil service directive was equally absurd because in the world of practical politics, "they all did it."[47]

George W. Julian began the argument of Donnelly's brief on January 8, with what Donnelly considered a "very able" presentation. On January 12, Judge Flandrau concluded his remarks, having consumed two whole days in a shrewd evaluation of the evidence. Presenting his own summation, Donnelly answered Flandrau point for point with a "ringing array of facts and law." Three days later, Donnelly confided to his diary, "Everything looks very favorable to success," and on January 20, he was hard at work on a synopsis of his testimony for the Democratic majority report which was to be in his favor. The report was delayed when the Democratic subcommittee chairman, General V. H. Manning, explained that one of its members, Congressman Armfield, was convinced that Washburn should be ousted, but he was not equally certain that Donnelly should be seated. Within a few days, however, Armfield was won over, and the report was prepared for publication.[48]

The news of the subcommittee's findings caused serious misgivings among conservative Republicans and Democrats. The New York *Tribune* worriedly announced that this meant handing another state to the Democrats in a Congress which might be called upon to settle a contested presidential election.[49] The St. Paul *Pioneer Press,* which had insisted on treating the election contest as a joke, was horrified with the prospect of Donnelly's return to office. The conservative Democrat, William Lochren, Minneapolis City Attorney, hurriedly left for Washington to plead Washburn's case before the Democratic National Committee.[50]

If the case of Donnelly versus Washburn had followed the tradi-

[47]*In the Matter of the Contest of Ignatius Donnelly vs. William D. Washburn. . . . Contestees Brief* (St. Paul: Pioneer Press, 1879), pp. 1–32.
[48]Donnelly MSS, Diary, January 8–25, 1880.
[49]February 12, 1880.
[50]Donnelly MSS, H. P. Hall to I. D., February 16, 17, 1880.

tional pattern, the report of Manning's subcommittee would have been submitted to the chairman of the House Committee on Elections, who, with the aid of his Democratic majority, would have promptly confirmed it. Chairman Springer would then have presented the initial report, plus its acceptance by the whole committee, to the House where, once again, the Democratic majority would have carried approval. Donnelly would have been designated the congressman from Minnesota's Third District. But this did not happen.

On March 8, when Springer was away from Washington on business, his wife opened a letter addressed to him which read: "Sir: If you will keep Washburn in his seat, in spite of the democrats, we will pay Mrs. S—— $5000. Get the thing squashed at once."[51] Because Donnelly's attorney, George W. Julian, was a personal friend of the Springer family and in the custom of calling at Springer's home almost daily, Mrs. Springer showed him the anonymous letter. Although Julian informed his client of the letter's existence, Donnelly did not understand that he was to keep it a secret. Donnelly told the story to the members of the committee who were favorable to his case and called on Mrs. Springer on March 9, to look at the letter. Convinced that it was written by either William S. King or Charles Johnson, Washburn's secretary, Donnelly telegraphed to St. Paul for copies of their handwriting.[52] Mrs. Springer, however, was sure that the message could not possibly have been written by a Republican, that it was not a bona fide bribe, whatever that meant, but an effort on the part of Donnelly's friends to insult her husband because he was not in favor of sustaining Manning's report.

Donnelly, who had two friends in Washington—Julian, his major counsel, and H. H. Finley, who was an informal counsel and congressional liaison—doubted if either of these men would resort to so low a trick. Coincidentally, Finley had written to Springer at almost the same time that the anonymous letter was mailed. When Springer returned to Washington on March 10, he was sure that Finley had written the letter. Everyone who knew about the letter agreed that the matter should be kept secret.

Donnelly was thoroughly disheartened by the episode because Springer, who had been antagonized, had used his influence with General James B. Weaver, the Greenbacker. Subcommittee chair-

[51]*Ibid.*, oversize collection, March 4, 1880.
[52]*Ibid.*, Diary, March 9, 1880.

man Manning was furious about the method of handling the affair. He was convinced that Springer either had been "bought" or was an "ass," and he swore that "there will be a committee investigation before we get through."[53] When a test of strength in the committee indicated that Weaver held the deciding vote, Donnelly enlisted the aid of Hendrick B. Wright, a leading Pennsylvania Greenbacker, who agreed to see Weaver about sustaining Donnelly's claim. On April 1, the House Committee on Elections finally voted. By a vote of eight to six, it was decided to oust Washburn, but by a vote of five to nine, with both Weaver and Springer voting against him, Donnelly failed to secure the congressional seat.

The Minnesota Greenbackers were disgusted and angry with Weaver's actions. "How can a Greenback M. C. expect any of us to hold the party together," apologized James Starkey, Minnesota's Greenback party state chairman.[54] He predicted a gloomy future if Donnelly failed to secure Washburn's place. The New York *World* explained Weaver's vote as a trade to gain Republican support for a contested election in Iowa, where Weaver hoped to elect a Greenback friend.[55] Weaver, however, had not yet heard the last of Minnesota's Greenbackers and Ignatius Donnelly. At the Greenback national convention in Chicago, the ambitious general was embarrassed by the questioning of Minnesota's delegation and made to rue the day he had cast an anti-Donnelly vote.[56]

Congressman Manning, furious at the behavior of his colleagues, wrote Springer that he would demand an investigation of the anonymous letter.[57] Before Manning could raise the issue properly, or the House take formal action to oust Washburn for dishonestly gaining his congressional seat, the Washington *Post*, piecing together information obtained from Donnelly and Manning, published a distorted version of the Springer letter with editorial comments on the Manning-Springer clash.[58] In the House, immediately following the *Post*'s report, Manning requested a point of personal privilege to present an exact statement for the record. Springer promptly defended himself, alleging that the letter had been written by H. H. Finley. On April 17, a special investigation committee was appointed to examine the facts in the Springer episode, to determine

[53] *Ibid.*, Diary, March 14, 1880.
[54] *Ibid.*, J. Starkey to I. D., April 2, 1880.
[55] Quoted in St. Paul *Globe*, April 5, 1880.
[56] Donnelly MSS, J. Starkey to I. D., June 17, 1880.
[57] *Ibid.*, Diary, April 1, 1880.
[58] April 3, 1880.

the authorship of the letter, and to rule if there had been a breach of privilege by any member of the House.[59]

Even before the investigation of the anonymous letter, Donnelly had virtually abandoned hope of victory. He feared, and with valid cause, that the Democratic National Committee was hostile to his election.[60] During much of the testimony he was both ill and depressed. He simply could not understand a world in which all his plans and labor seemed to end only in frustration, while men of lesser ability marched forward as if "God smoothed down mountains." Although a temperate man, he resorted to mixing quinine and liquor to shake off his feelings of melancholy. Disgusted with life, he read escapist novels.[61]

His pessimistic mood deepened as the investigation progressed. There were long tedious examinations of witnesses, cross-examinations, and handwriting experts who contradicted each other. Everyone conceded that the letter could in no way be attributed to Donnelly; he had nothing to gain from it. Washburn was exonerated because it lacked the deftness and subtlety of a genuine bribe. The committee pursued two alternatives: that Finley had written the letter in the hope of intimidating Springer; or that Springer had written the letter himself in the hope of escaping the wrath of his colleagues for opposing Donnelly's fair claim. Since Finley was a professional lobbyist, even the pro-Donnelly St. Paul *Globe* admitted that he might have posed as Donnelly's friend only to betray him by just such an act.[62]

As the session drew to a close, the chairman of the special committee, John G. Carlisle, stated that it was the opinion of the investigators that Finley had written the letter.[63] Under questioning from Manning, Carlisle added that it was the unanimous feeling of the committee that Donnelly had no personal connection with the letter. On the same day, two other reports were filed. One, from the Republican members of the subcommittee on the Donnelly-Washburn contest, asked that Washburn retain his place; the other, written by the Democrats, asked that he be ousted and Donnelly given the seat. No formal action was ever taken.

When Donnelly returned to Minnesota, he was utterly dis-

[59]*Congressional Record*, 46th Cong., 2d sess., pp. 2134–39, 2501.
[60]Donnelly MSS, Diary, April 1, 1880.
[61]*Ibid.*, May 17, 1880.
[62]April 6, 1880.
[63]Anonymous Letter to the Hon. William Springer, 46th Cong., 3d sess., House of Representatives Report No. 395 (serial 1983).

heartened. "I have the most unconscionable run of miserable fortune," he wrote despondently in his diary; "everything goes wrong with me. Only death spares me and mine." He contrasted his life with that of James A. Garfield who was a scant thirteen days younger and who had come to Congress the same year he had. What a difference in fortune! Garfield was receiving a magnificent ovation and the Republican nomination for President; Donnelly heard only the drone of the handwriting experts contradicting each other.[64]

The summer of 1880 was almost unbearable for Donnelly, with the burden of farming and the worry of unpaid debts. National politics seemed hopelessly confused. John Sherman's management of the Treasury Department under President Hayes had not resulted in the financial disaster which the Greenbackers had predicted but in a return to prosperity after six years of depression. Business confidence had been restored, and western farmers were blessed with unusually bountiful crops while European producers suffered unusually poor ones. Furthermore, western investment funds were easier than ever to obtain and interest rates declined.[65] The wave of Greenback popularity, which had reached its peak in the election of 1878, was beginning to recede.

Donnelly's hope of replacing Washburn hinged on a Democratic victory in 1880 or a contested presidential election in which his vote would be needed. His political position was further complicated because he could not hope for Democratic support if he continued as a Greenbacker. To make matters worse, the conservative Democrats had regained control in the Third District. They not only refused to renominate Donnelly, turning instead to Henry Hastings Sibley, but also withheld even an indorsement of his claim against Washburn. Although the Second District Democrats were willing to welcome him to their convention, he could not attend because his presence might jeopardize his Third District residency.[66] Donnelly abandoned the Greenback party after it nominated Weaver for president.[67]

When William H. English, the Democratic vice-presidential candidate, invited him to speak in behalf of the party, he accepted the

[64] Donnelly MSS, Diary, June 10, 1880.

[65] Rendig Fels, "American Business Cycles, 1865–1878," *American Economic Review*, XLI (1951), 348; and especially, Allan B. Bogue, *Money at Interest* (Ithaca: Cornell University Press, 1955), p. 82.

[66] Donnelly MSS, R. Miller to I. D., August 11, 1880.

[67] *Ibid.*, E. A. Cramsie to I. D., August 24, 1880.

offer. Campaigning for General Winfield S. Hancock, the Democratic standard-bearer, was personally distasteful to Donnelly because the candidate ignored the tariff issue, but depressed after the disappointing experiences of the past year, he was willing to abandon his ideals, accept a political position from the Democrats if one were offered to him, and return to the practice of law.[68]

The Republican victory in 1880 strangled Donnelly's hopes of victory over Washburn. The Democrats had less need of him than ever. Nevertheless, both Congressman Manning and George Julian insisted that he return to Washington to press his suit or he would fail to receive financial compensation.[69] Donnelly did receive an appropriation, but it was a thousand dollars less than his expenditures.

On November 3, Donnelly's diary reflected the pessimism which had engulfed him. "This is my 49th birthday," he wrote, "and a sad day it is. . . . All my hopes are gone, and the future settles down upon me dark and gloomy indeed." He could not see "a single ray of hope." Dejectedly he noted, "My life has been a failure and a mistake. My hopes have so often come to naught that I cease to hope. . . . Well. All I can do is to face the music and take my damnable future as it comes."[70] Many years later, looking back on the events of 1880, he concluded: "I had got down to my keel & that was pounding on the rocks. Metaphorically speaking there was nothing left to me but backbone and fists. It seemed as if all the devils in hell were let loose ag*t* me & what one didn't think of another did."[71] But, Donnelly courageously noted in his diary on the last day of the year, "we shall fight on."[72]

[68]*Ibid.*, I. D. to K. D., September 11, 1880.

[69]*Ibid.*, V. H. Manning to I. D., December 9, 1880; G. W. Julian to I. D., December 10, 1880.

[70]*Ibid.*, Diary, November 3, 1880.

[71]*Ibid.*, Diary, undated.

[72] *Ibid.*, Diary, December 31, 1880.

Atlantis and Ragnarok
1881–1883

---

*One thing is certain:—my books have lifted me out of
the dirty cess-pool of politics, nasty enough at all times,
but absolutely foul to the man who does not win.*

IGNATIUS DONNELLY

THE YEAR 1880 had been one of disaster for Donnelly; his political influence was dissipated and his economic position was poor. Farming, despite improved prices, was not rewarding enough to satisfy him. He was convinced that the Minneapolis Millers' Association had "the country by the throat" and that only a peasant could "survive their robberies."[1] His wife, who more than shared his views, pleaded with him to sell their Stevens County lands and turn his talents to better use. Reminding him that he had never really farmed before, Kate pointed out that it was too unstable and too strenuous for a man in the autumn years of his life.[2] Donnelly lacked the enthusiasm to continue taking the risks involved in working both Dakota and Stevens county lands. In December, 1880, he began selling and trading his livestock to settle his Stevens County obligations. "I shall rent all my lands next year and live like a Christian," he wrote in his diary,[3] but even this did not satisfy Kate. "Nervously depressed and morbidly wretched," Kate had set her heart on moving to St. Paul. For years she had disliked Nininger City's rural isolation and discomfort. Long into the night she would

[1]Donnelly MSS, I. D. to K. D., September 11, 1880.
[2]*Ibid.*, K. D. to I. D., September 15, 1880.
[3]*Ibid.*, Diary, December 7, 1880.

discuss with Ignatius the ways and means of making the change, but he was reluctant "to let go of a comfortable certainty for a greater uncertainty."[4]

In mid-January, 1881, Donnelly noted in his diary that he was hard at work writing a book which he called "Atlantis."[5] He began collecting notes and visiting D. D. Merrill's bookstore in St. Paul, where he bought copies of scientific magazines and works on mythology, literature, and historical geography. He wrote and did research simultaneously. Unlike professional scholars, Donnelly worked entirely alone with no exchange of views with experts in the fields in which he read. There was no scholarly correspondence, and even when he took Kate to Philadelphia for medical treatment he did not attempt to communicate with the academic world but worked in the Philadelphia Library, a solitary figure weaving his narrative.[6] By mid-March the manuscript was completed.

In writing about the fabled lost continent of Atlantis, Donnelly shared the popular intellectual interests of his day. Jules Verne's widely read romance, *Twenty Thousand Leagues under the Sea,* had been published in 1870. Verne's use of the Atlantis theme had undoubtedly influenced Donnelly's decision to explore it. For more than thirty years he had eagerly read and followed scientific news. The second half of the nineteenth century was characterized by increasing exploration of the world and analyses of existing and past civilizations. Schliemann, Morgan, Agassiz and Darwin, along with many lesser figures, were publishing information gathered in critical research in the field. As in almost every era of rapid discovery, a synthesis which would make clear to the lay public some of the implications of the new science was virtually absent. For Donnelly, with his unusual ability to perceive connections between apparent irrelevancies, to write a book which would unfold some of the speculative mysteries of science was as natural as to discuss the tariff and unravel the mystery of monopoly.

In *Atlantis: The Antediluvian World,* Donnelly attempted to demonstrate, in almost five hundred pages of material gathered from scientific treatises, literary references, legends, folklore, religion, and mythology, that Plato's fabled island of Atlantis had actually existed, that in Atlantis men first achieved civilization, that the deities of ancient mythology were the royalty of Atlantis, that the

[4]*Ibid.,* January 8, 1881.
[5]*Ibid.,* January 17, 1881.
[6]*Ibid.,* March 18, 1881.

ancient civilizations of which we have knowledge resulted from
the diffusion of Atlantean culture, and that the island sank beneath
the ocean as the result of a terrible natural convulsion.[7] To substantiate this argument, he ransacked the works of reputable scholars
such as Darwin and Fiske as well as the writings of charlatans and
pseudo-scientists and produced a mass of detailed material, much of
it of doubtful credibility. His carefully structured material, written
in an engaging and persuasive narrative, achieved a remarkable air
of authority, not only from the vast scope of his references, but also
from his reliance on simple, obvious comparisons and analogies. In
the use of his information, Donnelly combined common knowledge
with new scientific discoveries and the works of pseudo-scientists.
The style of the book, vigorous and forthright, used essentially
the same rhetorical flourishes he had employed so successfully in
political debate. Since *Atlantis* was basically a lawyer's brief in behalf of a speculative theory, Donnelly conformed to legal rather
than scientific rules of evidence. He discarded all contradictory evidence and even distorted illustrations to prove his point. But his
most serious shortcoming was in the nature of his method of analysis. Because he was not a scientist, Donnelly exercised no critical
judgment of his sources whatsoever. He simply accepted at face
value and quoted those authorities which presented evidence that
would corroborate his hypothesis, even though they might long since
have been discredited.

Donnelly went to New York with letters of introduction to all leading publishers, written by the St. Paul book merchant D. D. Merrill.
Harper and Brothers was his first choice as a publisher for his book.
Leaving the manuscript with them on March 29, he was asked to
return the following day. On his return, the editors, favorably impressed, hesitated to reply definitely, and asked him to call at ten
the next morning. When Donnelly appeared he was told that
Harper's wanted to publish the book at their own risk, provide
Donnelly with any number of copies at half the list price, and
send between fifty and a hundred to reviewers. One company
spokesman, highly enthusiastic about the book and predicting that
it would be a great success, wanted Donnelly to speak to the Geo-
graphical Society of New York. Donnelly was hugely pleased. He
had expected to pay half of the publication cost. "It is a big point

[7]Ignatius Donnelly, *Atlantis: The Antediluvian World* (New York: Harper &
Bros., 1882), p. 1.

gained," he wrote, "to have Harper Bros. take hold of Atlantis."[8]

Kate remained in Philadelphia undergoing painful medical treatment while Ignatius returned to Minnesota to look after affairs in Nininger. Donnelly himself was not well at this time. He developed a type of eczema which persisted during most of the late spring and summer, but his condition improved when his physician prescribed a cathartic.[9] These family health problems, coupled with the fact that his father had been a physician, may have contributed to his decision to send his oldest son Ignatius to medical school. But Donnelly realistically stressed other factors in his diary: "I have concluded to send him [Ignatius] to Phila & make a doctor of him;—and Stan will stay at home & study law. Neither of them are fit for hard physical work and there is not a future to clerkships."[10] On September 8, 1881, Donnelly sentimentally noted, "Today was my dear boy'[s] . . . 25th birthday, and today he left . . . for Philadelphia to study medicine at Jefferson College, from which his grandfather . . . graduated nearly 50 years ago."[11]

During the summer, as he prepared to send his son east, he became acutely aware that his children were now adults. When his daughter, Mary, announced her engagement, he was somewhat saddened. "I am very glad to know that my little girl . . . is happy. Although such things make me begin to feel old, I hope to live life over again in the happiness of my children. For their sakes I wish I was worth many millions; but then," he rationalized rather hopefully, "happiness is after all often in an inverse ratio to one's bank account."[12] In somewhat the same vein he greeted his wedding anniversary by recording in his diary: "26 years ago my dear wife and I were married. God bless her! Although we have had many ups and downs and set backs yet our married life has been happier than that of 999 out of 1000. She is a dear, good, woman, honest and true through all; a better and purer woman never lived."[13]

The first page proofs of *Atlantis* arrived at Nininger in July. As Donnelly worked on the text, correcting, adding, and deleting material, he felt the same overpowering enthusiasm but not the familiar optimism with which he usually welcomed new projects. "I

[8]Donnelly MSS, Diary, March 31, 1881.
[9]*Ibid.*, April 12, 14, 27, 1881; K. D. to I. D., May 2, 1881.
[10]*Ibid.*, Diary, June 22, 1881.
[11]*Ibid.*, September 8, 1881.
[12]*Ibid.*, August 19, 1881.
[13]*Ibid.*, September 10, 1881.

feel like a mother listening to the first cry of her first born," he confided to his diary. "It is my eldest child. It may grow up to be an imbecile but the fibres of my heart will cling to it."[14] Harper and Brothers, with the page proof in hand, were again certain that so interesting and provocative a book would have a good sale.[15]

His book in the press, Donnelly passed the winter of 1881–82 doing household chores, reading, and reflecting on his life and future. His political correspondence had dwindled to insignificance. He felt that he stood virtually alone. During the still evening of November 3, 1881, as the Minnesota sky darkened before a blizzard, Donnelly recorded: *"This is my 50th Birthday. This machine has been running on the face of the earth a half century today.* It is sad to grow old and yet one must grow old or die; and, if statistics are correct, one half of all who started in the race of life with me, in 1831, are today—nothing." Then he added, "I am in good health—a little too obese, but my hair has not yet turned gray and I am full of vigor. . . . And so, while conscious that I am growing old I still look forward hopefully."[16] But as the harsh winter settled on Minnesota, Donnelly found escape in reading archeology, Shakespeare, and French novels, and sought to control feelings of paranoia. "While I would like to be something greater and better than I am," he confessed to his diary, "with more of the comforts of life; and while I grieve sometimes over the hard fate that chains me and mine . . . to this lonely spot, nevertheless, I try to be philosophical and make the best of it. . . . We have health, domestic peace, abundance to eat and wear and a fair prospect for the future. And yet, it squeezes one's heart, to see the years slip away, while he does nothing,—is nothing."[17] On New Year's Eve, because Harper's had not yet published the book, this feeling plagued him as he reviewed the events of the year. He was pleased with the progress of his children, but he worried about the future. "My book 'Atlantis' has not been published, and my political prestige is at *zero.* . . . And so I go into the New Year . . . hoping that 'Atlantis' may be a success, that it may bring me honor, and, above all, money which I need even more than glory, and yet fearing that it may fall still born, because I am a provincial in location and a nobody in the scientific world; for mankind always look to Jeru-

[14]*Ibid.*, July 22, 1881.
[15]*Ibid.*, September 15, 1881.
[16]*Ibid.*, November 3, 1881.
[17]*Ibid.*, November 23, 1881.

salem, and think it impossible that any good thing 'can come out of Nazareth.' "[18] By late January, 1882, he even feared his political enemies were trying to prevent the publication of the book, but his irrational forebodings were dispelled when the book's advance notices were placed with the booksellers.[19]

On his publication day Donnelly, fearful of critical and harsh reviews, inscribed in his diary: "Blow wind, come rack."[20] The St. Paul *Pioneer Press* published one of the earliest notices. Anticipating the worst possible criticism, Donnelly was surprised when the paper viewed the book as "plausible, perspicuous, buttressed by many curious and recondite facts, an instance of what marvelous force may be imparted to any theory by the simple application of intellectual power."[21] This was followed by two weeks of silence from the reviewers. Looking back on his anxiety during the period, Donnelly noted, "I feared my baby stillborn; that my golden egg was addled; that the cloud of adverse fate would never lift."[22] On March 9, he braved an icy road to Hastings for his mail. In the post office he found bundles of newspapers. As he opened them searching for reviews, his excitement was intense. The Chicago *Times* printed almost two columns of complimentary review. He returned to Nininger where he shared the reports with Kate, who was as ecstatic as he was himself. When the St. Paul *Dispatch* arrived, Donnelly was virtually dumbfounded. The paper which had abused him so shamefully during the Washburn contest declared *Atlantis* to be one of the notable books of the century. Donnelly whose "feelings rose at once to 200° above the point where granite melts," began to hope the book would be so great a financial success that it would lift him "out of this slough of debt and poverty."[23]

Within a matter of days, Harper and Brothers wrote to Donnelly asking him to prepare corrections for a second edition. The company, immensely pleased with the book's reception, was prepar-

---

[18]*Ibid.*, December 31, 1881.

[19]*Ibid.*, I. D. to J. Phayre, January 30, 1882.

[20]*Ibid.*, Diary, February 18, 1882.

[21]St. Paul *Pioneer Press*, February 26, 1882. It is worth noting that Joseph Wheelock wrote H. L. Gordon: "I have cursorily run through Donnelly's book and read enough of it here within to admire the great mass of materials he collected in support of his theory, and to be amused at the characteristically illogical use he makes of them. It exhibits in an exaggerated degree the radical defects of his mental structure. He is gifted with a fine imagination without a particle of reasoning power." H. L. Gordon MSS, March 16, 1882.

[22]Donnelly MSS, Diary, March 9, 1882.

[23]*Ibid.*

ing to advertise it extensively in their other publications and to push it more vigorously. The first copies of the book sold in England indicated that it would be well received abroad.[24]

Prime Minister William Ewart Gladstone was among the earliest English readers of *Atlantis*. Having devoted time to the study of Homeric legends, Gladstone wrote Donnelly a warm and complimentary letter. Donnelly recognized the irony of receiving four closely written pages, signed W. E. Gladstone in a "square foreign looking letter with a London postmark. . . . I looked down at myself," Donnelly reflected, "and could not but smile at the appearance of the man who, in this little, snow-bound hamlet, was corresponding with the man whose word was fate anywhere in the British Empire. . . . The leg of my pants was torn; my coat was nearly buttonless . . . and I was trimming the kerosene lamps." Then he added, "I could have uttered a war hoop of exultation."[25] Following the Gladstone letter, Donnelly was convinced that either the prime minister was publicizing the book or it had been favorably reviewed in England, because Sampson, Low and Company of London ordered 250 copies for English distribution.

The presses could scarcely keep up with the sales of *Atlantis*. The book went through seven editions in 1882, which was virtually unprecedented for a piece of "non-fiction." Harper and Brothers authorized a Swedish translation in 1883,[26] and eventually the book was available in all of western Europe. By 1890 there had been twenty-three editions in the United States and twenty-six in England.

As a result of the successful reception of *Atlantis* Donnelly was elected to membership in the American Association for the Advancement of Science, although scholars never took his work seriously.[27] He was probably the most discussed literary figure outside professional and intellectual circles. The New Orleans "Mardi Gras" of 1883 was based on the *Atlantis* theme, as was the Baltimore "Oriole" pageant of the same year.[28] Thousands of people who normally did not read or hear of current books were exposed to Donnelly's work and many of them bought it. For the remainder of his life, he continued to receive occasional letters from admiring

[24]*Ibid.*, March 10, 14, 18, 22, 1882.
[25]*Ibid.*, March 26, 1882.
[26]*Ibid.*, Harper's to I. D., March 17, 1882.
[27]*Ibid.*, AAAS Announcement, August, 1882. Charles Darwin, who received a gift copy, read it with interest but in a "very skeptical spirit." March 2, 1882.
[28]*Ibid.*, Diary, February 11, September 19, 1883.

readers inclosing scraps of information which they felt might contribute to unraveling what they believed to be a scientific mystery.[29]

Although Donnelly frequently lectured on the Atlantis theme, he did not associate himself with the eccentric fringe groups which established mystical Atlantean cults based on revelations and extrasensory messages. He did not intend *Atlantis* to be the basis of a cult. It had nothing mysterious or occult in its content or method. The book's immense popularity at a later time with various cultist groups who were seeking to relate their movements to Atlantis can be attributed only to the fact that his book was the most comprehensive collection of Atlantis fact, legend, and literature compiled in English in the nineteenth century, and that it was written as a popular scientific exposition, not as a novel.[30]

He had always feared that the book's agnostic implications would raise religious prejudices against it,[31] and he was more than surprised when distinguished public figures praised it. Written in the middle of winter and in the depth of political misfortune, *Atlantis* may have provided an area for the free use of Donnelly's restless mind. It shifted, at least temporarily, his personal perspective and his interests. Certainly its popularity bolstered his self-respect in that it increased his prestige, which he felt was "below zero" prior to 1881. Somewhat bitterly he noted, when his mail increased and he was again in the public eye: "A succession of political defeats and an empty pocket would destroy the prestige of Julius Caesar."[32]

During the spring of 1882 when Donnelly was enjoying the success of *Atlantis*, Kate, suffering pain and in very poor health, pleaded with him to abandon farming. Neither Donnelly nor his sons were fit for farming, she insisted. They had not been born to the land and could not stand the isolation or the hardship.[33] "When I think of farming—I get almost sick," she wrote. "Think how hard they work—and they invariably come out in debt—& then comes borrowing next—& then misery—life is scarcely worth having. If

---

[29] *Ibid.*, J. L. Fisk to I. D., January 8, 1895, is illustrative.

[30] L. Sprague de Camp, *Lost Continents* (New York: Gnome Press, Inc., 1954), pp. 37–43. De Camp mistakenly asserts, "It remained for Donnelly to convert Atlantism into a popular cult," but he correctly assesses Donnelly's impact on the lunatic fringe who "borrowed Donnelly's material to concoct their peculiar doctrines."

[31] *Ibid.*, I. D. to K. D., March 30, 1881.

[32] *Ibid.*, Diary, April 14, 1882.

[33] *Ibid.*, K. D. to I. D., April 25, 1882.

one cannot come out clear without debt how can they expect to clear & pay interest on debt besides."[34] Kate's pleas to sell the Stevens County lands were strengthened by Donnelly's book royalties, which promised to be substantial, and by his opportunity to sell St. Paul city lots which he had owned since the Panic of 1857. By May, 1882, Donnelly, who had sold more than fifteen lots priced at three hundred dollars each, was virtually debt free.[35] Distasteful as farming was to Donnelly, he was reluctant to dispose of his lands because he hoped for a "wheat boom." Not until 1884 did he concede that he was "much better fitted to write books than to run a farm that size [3,000 acres in Stevens County]."[36]

The favorable reception of *Atlantis* stirred Donnelly into beginning a new book in May, 1882. Working ceaselessly, except for an occasional trip to St. Paul's bookstores, he finished the 450-page work in seven weeks.[37] "It grew within me from small beginnings like an inspiration," he recorded in his diary, "and I hope it may do some good in the world."[38] Almost a decade later, and still sensitive about the book, Donnelly expanded on this terse entry. "It took possession of my whole brain and being; and I could not rest until I had written it out and then the great dread of my soul," he added dramatically, "was that some accident would destroy the single copy I had & that the world would lose a revelation."[39] Only three days after completing his second book, Donnelly wrote the first page of still a third entitled, "God and the Sun," which, he stated in his diary, "came upon me in bed, like an inspiration."[40] This work was never finished.

In many ways *Ragnarok: The Age of Fire and Gravel* was a logical successor to *Atlantis*. Donnelly expounded the theory that the earth's great deposits of sand, gravel, and clay were not the results of glacial movements, as the geologist Louis Agassiz suggested, but rather had been produced by the debris of a comet which passed close to or struck the earth. The cataclysm, which occurred in prehistoric times, was remembered only in the legends of the various races of man. Donnelly linked this idea with the concept of a divine judgment of a sinful world. His title derived from a well-

[34]*Ibid.*, K. D. to I. D., May 4, 1882.
[35]*Ibid.*, Diary, May 12, 1882.
[36]*Ibid.*, I. D. to D. Sabin, March 23, 1884.
[37]*Ibid.*, Diary, May 20–30, 1882.
[38]*Ibid.*, July 8, 1882.
[39]*Ibid.*, March 18, 1891.
[40]*Ibid.*, July 11, 1882.

known piece of Scandinavian mythology. Donnelly began *Ragnarok* with the frank confession: "If I do not convince, I hope at least to interest you."[41] As in *Atlantis,* Donnelly concentrated on the popular interest in the new scientific discoveries by pointing out that "it is to be remembered that great attention has been paid during the past few years to searching for comets, and some of the results are here given."[42]

Almost everything that could be said of his method of analysis in *Atlantis* was equally true for *Ragnarok.* He spurned the scientific question of how processes took place in nature for the speculative question of why they occurred. This allowed him to use all of Agassiz's findings, but to ignore his conclusions. Donnelly's legal training was also evident when he stated: "I shall summon my witnesses that you may cross-examine them. I shall try, to the best of my ability, to buttress every opinion with adequate proofs."[43] In producing the new anthropological, geological, and biological information, he debated, reasoned, and argued with his authorities rather than testing, measuring, or computing to confirm or deny their findings. He mustered a vast array of legends and newspaper accounts dealing with the effects of comets and from them argued the plausibility of a major cosmic collision. But Donnelly, instead of stressing agnostic implications as he had in *Atlantis,* now acknowledged the guiding force of a Christian God.

In *Atlantis* Donnelly had shunned political references almost entirely, with the exception of a brief comment on the foolish idolatry involved in the worship of gold. In *Ragnarok,* however, Donnelly concluded with a cry for social justice. He warned the rich and the evil with a biblical analogy (Luke 16 : 21–31) that the millionaire with an "unexpressed belief that heaven is only a larger Wall Street, where the millionaires occupy the front benches, while those who never had a bank account on earth sing in the chorus . . . [is] but a vitalized speck . . . crawling over an eggshell filled with fire, whirling through space, a target for the bombs of a universe."[44] Criticizing the values of his materialistic generation, Donnelly pleaded: "Matter is not everything. Establish spiritual relations. . . . Take your mind off your bricks and mortar, and put out your tentacles toward the great spiritual world around you.

[41]Ignatius Donnelly, *Ragnarok: The Age of Fire and Gravel* (New York: D. Appleton & Co., 1883), p. 2.
[42]*Ibid.,* p. 88.
[43]*Ibid.,* p. 2.
[44]*Ibid.,* pp. 440–41.

. . . Widen your heart. Put your intellect to work to readjust the values of labor . . . that plenty and happiness, light and hope, may dwell in every heart."[45] Perhaps by July, 1882, Donnelly's political nature and ego were beginning to reassert themselves, and it is worth noting that he tried deftly to combine religious fundamentalism, the new science, and the emerging social gospel of reform to make his point.

Sixty days from the time he started writing *Ragnarok*, Donnelly arrived in New York, registered at the Astor House, and went to Harper and Brothers to submit his manuscript to their editors for consideration. Donnelly was pleased to learn that with *Atlantis* already in its fifth edition, much of it ordered in advance, he was a favored author.[46] When he returned, however, the editors rejected the new manuscript. It "would not sell" they insisted; "it would be denounced by scientists . . . and, in short, they feared to undertake it." Very "cast down" and highly agitated, Donnelly took a carriage, rode up Broadway to Charles Scribner's Sons where he agreed to leave the manuscript for a ten-day period. Returning to the Astor, preparing to leave for Philadelphia, and thoroughly dejected, Donnelly confessed his inability to comprehend the nation's largest city. "New York overwhelms and bewilders me with its endless roar and hurry," he wrote, just as though his whole life had been lived on Minnesota's agricultural frontier. "I got on the cars for Phila," he wrote, "& left the seething whirlpool of struggling humanity behind me."[47]

As the railroad cars rattled toward Philadelphia, Donnelly, filled with mixed emotions of self-confidence and misgiving, was wrapped in thought. "One can never read the future," he noted. "I had scarcely hoped that Harpers would publish 'Atlantis' and they did. I thought they would jump at 'Ragnarok' and they did not. I may deceive myself & the judgment of their reader may be right," he confessed, "and yet I cannot but feel that 'Ragnarok' is a plausible argument, if not a proved case, and full of the most novel matter." His faith in his judgment and workmanship was encouraged by the success of *Atlantis*. Nevertheless, as the tiresome journey drew to a close, he wrote: "But Scribner & Co. may refuse it. What then?"[48]

---

[45]*Ibid.*, p. 441.
[46]Donnelly MSS, Diary, July 19, 1882.
[47]*Ibid.*, July 21, 1882.
[48]*Ibid.*

Scribner's rejected *Ragnarok*. The publishers had sent the manuscript to a New Haven scientist who reported the theory to be absurd, "well written, but scientifically ridiculous—worthy of Jules Verne." But Donnelly refused to concede defeat. "I believe I am right & if not right plausible & that the book will be a success." Although he lacked confidence in New York publishers, having been rebuffed twice, and convinced that they would submit the text to a scientist who would "get mad at the idea of an extra-terrestrial origin of anything found on earth from the soul of man to a paving stone," Donnelly left the book with O. B. Bunce of D. Appleton. Planning to return to Minnesota, he considered going to Chicago, if D. Appleton rejected *Ragnarok*, to arrange with Jensen, McClurg and Company to print the book on shares or subscriptions.[49] D. Appleton accepted the manuscript. Donnelly insisted on an unusual royalty agreement. Since he felt that Harper and Brothers had been unfair with its flat rate of 10 per cent, Donnelly offered to accept no royalty on the first thousand books, 10 per cent on the second thousand, 15 per cent on the third thousand, and 20 per cent on all copies in excess of the first four thousand sold. In effect, Donnelly preferred to risk his initial royalty, if he could share in profits of a best seller. D. Appleton accepted the gamble.[50]

After selling *Ragnarok* and escaping from the East, Donnelly made a leisurely visit in Stevens County. "The utter rest and quiet here are in strong contrast with the horrible drive, bustle, confusion, wear and tear of New York City," he noted. "Tennyson speaks of a land where 'always it was afternoon,' here is a land where it is always the day after tomorrow." This was not a hopeful statement, as it would have been twenty years before, but rather sadness for the future of the area. "A great expanse of peaceful country, waiting for the crowding numbers and the clamorous competition of the human animal to flow in. And it will. Human nature with its beauties and its ugliness, its glories and its shames, will yet possess it absolutely; every acre will feel the plough and the hoe in it, supporting the life of that strange animal; man, who is rapidly taking possession of the whole surface of the planet."[51]

Donnelly was in Minnesota when he received the page proofs of *Ragnarok*. He was quite interested in the comments of the proof-

[49] *Ibid.*, July 31, 1882.
[50] *Ibid.*, August 7–8, 1882; I. D. to O. B. Bunce, August 8, 1882; O. B. Bunce to I. D., August 11, 1882.
[51] *Ibid.*, Diary, August 11, 1882.

reader, who enjoyed the book but who wondered how such distinguished experts as professors Dana and Le Conte would react to the second half of it, which was primarily speculative.[52] The popular response to *Ragnarok* was not as enthusiastic as it had been for *Atlantis.* Many reviewers agreed with the Chicago *Tribune*'s editor who rejected Donnelly's theory but commented that his scholarship was industrious, that he was certainly provocative, and that his reasoning would elicit considerable attention. The *Tribune,* quite naturally, was especially interested in Donnelly's assertion that the Chicago fire might have been the result of spontaneous combustion.[53] Donnelly was particularly pleased when the St. Paul *Pioneer Press* copied almost half of the *Tribune*'s three-column article. He was gratified by these reviews because he felt that they would assure *Ragnarok* a fair hearing.[54] Even though the *Pioneer Press* later criticized the book, Donnelly was not too disturbed as the sale of the book was not impaired.[55] Praise for his second book left Donnelly "strutting within like a turkey cock."[56] He probably found much satisfaction also in the fact that the Minnesota newspapers began referring to him as the "Sage of Nininger," a phrase coined by Dr. Thomas Foster years earlier, but one which had never been taken seriously.

D. Appleton informed Donnelly that *Ragnarok* sold 3,500 copies during its first five weeks on the market. Because these initial sales exceeded even the record of *Atlantis,* Donnelly believed that the book was a "great success."[57] By spring, however, the book's sales began to lag. The publishers remained optimistic since it was still being reordered,[58] and in April the entire first edition of almost 5,000 copies had been sold.[59]

Attributing *Ragnarok*'s declining sales to a lack of publicity, Donnelly expressed dissatisfaction with his publisher. He urged O. B. Bunce to have the book favorably reviewed in the company's magazine, *Popular Science Monthly,* and he was annoyed when the magazine's editor refused. Donnelly's protests brought him a copy of a letter written by E. L. Youmans, editor of *Popular Science,* in

[52]*Ibid.,* C. Becker to I. D., October 26, 1882.
[53]Chicago *Tribune,* December 3, 1882.
[54]Donnelly MSS, Diary, December 5, 1882.
[55]*Ibid.,* December 18, 23, 1882.
[56]*Ibid.,* January 27, 1883.
[57]*Ibid.,* January 19, 1883.
[58]*Ibid.,* O. Bunce to I. D., March 9, 1883.
[59]*Ibid.,* Diary, April 10, 1883.

which he discussed *Ragnarok* and explained why there would be no debate of Donnelly's theory. With a clear understanding of the distinction between science and speculation, and with ruthless frankness, Youmans wrote: "There has not been any extended attempt to refute the position of the author of '*Ragnarok*'; nor is it probable that there will be, because the minds that are taken with that work are in a very unpromising condition to reason with. The book being absurd. . . . What would you think of a man who would gravely reply to . . . the romancer Jules Verne?"[60]

Donnelly did not resent Youmans' criticism because he knew the editor was a leading advocate of the evolutionary theory but he objected to *Popular Science* ignoring his book. It was simply bad economics. Sound criticism, even if it were adverse, he was certain, would encourage *Ragnarok*'s sales.[61] Donnelly attempted to make clear that he did not expect *Popular Science* to indorse the *Ragnarok* theory. "Now I do not say that my theory is absolutely true beyond question. That can be safely asserted of few things in this world," he wrote Bunce. "But what I do claim is that it is not 'absurd and ridiculous' in itself & that it is entitled to fair consideration at the hands of thoughtful men."[62] The publishers replied that *Ragnarok*, which they had never considered a scientific treatise, would not be advertised as one. D. Appleton had published *Ragnarok* because they had faith in its market value, not in its theory.[63]

Although *Ragnarok*'s sales were slow, the book did not go out of print. In 1887 Donnelly bought the printer's plates from D. Appleton for $400 and continued publication of the book. It was sought out by a reading public interested because of the book's excitement, revelation, exotic theory, or author. Donnelly reported in 1899 that *Ragnarok* had passed through nineteen American editions.[64] It did not achieve the lasting popularity of *Atlantis*, which Harper and Brothers considered worthy of reprinting in a revised edition in 1949.

The absolute rejection of his books by America's serious scholars confirmed Donnelly's suspicions that an outsider with an idea could not gain a fair hearing in American scientific circles. "What

[60] *Ibid.*, E. Youmans to L. Hall, June 1, 1883.

[61] *Ibid.*, I. D. to O. Bunce, September 30, October 4, 1883.

[62] *Ibid.*, I. D. to O. Bunce, October 4, 1883.

[63] *Ibid.*, O. Bunce to I. D., October 17, 1883.

[64] *Ibid.*, D. Appleton to I. D., August 2, 1887. See also, Ignatius Donnelly, *The Cipher* (Minneapolis: Verulam Publishing Co., 1899), p. 374.

we call 'Science' in this country," he wrote critically a few years later, "is upheld by congeries of schoolmasters repeating what someone else has told them." The American genius, he insisted, was practical rather than speculative or philosophical. Americans had contributed virtually nothing of consequence to the thought of the world. "Agassiz was a Swiss; Darwin and Spencer are Englishmen. Take out of American scientific books what was produced on the other side of the Atlantic and there will be but little left." Then he concluded, with a bitterness born of his own experience and his resentment against American scientific provincialism: "Neither will an American Scientist accept any American thought until it has the brand of foreign approval."[65]

On November 3, 1883, Donnelly's birthday, he could reflect on an eventful year. His son, Ignatius, had returned from Philadelphia to establish a medical practice in St. Paul. His daughter, Mary, was happily married. His books were acknowledged to be highly successful, and he was again considered one of Minnesota's distinguished personages. His newly acquired fame seemed more enduring than the reputation which his political life had afforded. But his age disturbed him. "*Today I am 52 years old!* Alas and Alas! How time creeps on. Is there no way to put a break [*sic*] on this great wheel & let the world drift by you?" He had no fear of death's pain, but a great sense of the finiteness of man. "It hurts one to think of how little a space he occupies in the universe;—how for a few short years he has a chance at sunshine and the air & then is not." But the awareness of scientific knowledge, intruding into his thoughts, led him to query: "But if dust cannot perish why should the consciousness, as much greater than dust as dust is greater than nothing. . . . If matter is indestructible, why should its twin brother life . . . be destructible?" Wordsworth, he felt, was right: " 'Our life is but a birth and a forgetting.' " Then, as he prepared to face his fifty-third year, he made his realistic appraisal of man's hopes for eternity. "And so our hurt vanity finds compensation in the hope that though we may be whisked away from the sunshine here we may reappear elsewhere, under a brighter sun and in a fairer world:—"[66]

[65] Donnelly MSS, Diary, 1887–1889, undated.
[66] *Ibid.*, November 3, 1883.

CHAPTER XIII

Returning to Politics
1881–1885

Donnelly is still seeking his lost Atlantis, which sunk beneath the waves in the tempest of clouds and fire in 1868. . . . For he is his own Ragnarok too—or would be if his dream could come true. There is a pleasant suggestion of allegory in the part he assigns to comets in the phenomena of physical disturbance. For that is the part he always assigned himself in the phenomena of political disturbance.

ST. PAUL PIONEER PRESS

FOLLOWING the contested election debacle of 1880, Donnelly believed his political life was at an end. He sat in Nininger, almost a recluse, watching the consolidation of power by Minnesota's conservatives. This political development stemmed from the new economic order which was evident in Minnesota by 1880. Farmers felt themselves to be better off because of increased purchasing power and even more because of the rapid appreciation of rural land values as the state's best lands were filled in. More significant still, the tenth census disclosed that agriculture in Minnesota produced only 40 per cent of the state's annual income, manufacturing providing a larger portion.

The large cities, St. Paul and Minneapolis, having more than doubled in size during the 1870's as they became the processing, marketing, and shipping centers of the northwest, grew increasingly similar to eastern cities with large immigrant populations dominated by political machines. The Irish immigrants in the Twin Cities were controlled by Democratic politicians subservient to wealthy party leaders allied with eastern conservatives. The most influential leaders were James J. Hill, the builder of the Great Northern Railroad, and Patrick Kelly, a St. Paul merchant. Both not only made substantial financial contributions to the national Democratic party, but also helped to underwrite the Minnesota organization's deficit. These men had assumed control from the "old moccasin Democrats" just as Washburn and Pillsbury had replaced Ramsey. The Republicans retained direction of the state's affairs because of the rural immigrant voters, particularly the Scandinavians, who constituted an almost impregnable bloc dominating each congressional district. The Democratic leaders almost refused to challenge the Republican rural hegemony, just as the Republicans virtually conceded a surrender of the Twin Cities. But the philosophy of leadership in both conservative elements was essentially the same.[1] The manifest horror of the urban Democratic leadership when Donnelly, welding together rural and urban voters, contested Washburn's election, proved the Democrats preferred a conservative Republican to an erstwhile Anti-Monopolist. In this political climate Donnelly had almost no political correspondence and entertained very few politicians who were not intimate friends.[2]

In the summer of 1882, a liberal Democrat living in the newly redistricted Third Congressional District asked Donnelly to consider seeking the Democratic nomination to oppose Republican Congressman Horace Strait. The new district, which did not include St. Paul or Minneapolis, was largely rural and had been drawn to assure a Republican majority of almost 10,000 votes. State Democratic party leaders in the Twin Cities had written off all hopes of defeating the Republican incumbent, but liberal Democrats living in the Third, sanguine of an upset, were willing to co-operate with independents. Donnelly, enjoying the first pleasures of authorship, was unwilling to return to public life. "Count me out," he answered, explaining that he had "no stomach for fights." He saw no sense in trying to woo Republican votes when Strait would have an easier

[1] Horace Samuel Merrill, *Bourbon Democracy of the Middle West, 1865–1896* (Baton Rouge: Louisiana State University Press, 1953) is an interesting treatment of the general movement in the Middle West as a whole.

[2] Donnelly MSS, H. Hall to I. D., February 5, 1882. Hall, having lost interest in the farmers after the "brass kettle" campaign, told Donnelly they could "freeze and starve" as far as he was concerned.

time buying conservative Democratic support. Donnelly insisted that 1882 was the year he would avoid politics.[3]

After the congressional nominating conventions, Dr. Albert A. Ames, the Democratic mayor of Minneapolis, requested Donnelly's help.[4] Ames, who had been selected to oppose William D. Washburn, realized that the Democrats lacked strength in the smaller towns and among the farmers. He understood, also, that as the mayor of the state's largest city, he was at a disadvantage in rural areas. Donnelly's popularity in the farm districts, especially among the English-speaking element, was still worth courting. Lacking enthusiasm for a campaign, Donnelly explained that he was too busy writing to play politics. But Ames, a shrewd and persuasive political boss, would not accept the refusal. He visited Donnelly in Nininger. Insisting that his support was indispensable, Ames pleaded that Donnelly devote his attention only to the campaign's final week. To help defray expenses, Ames offered him twenty-five dollars! After learning that a Minneapolis crowd shouted itself hoarse calling for him by name, Donnelly succumbed to the flattery and reluctantly consented to make seven speeches against Washburn.[5] Gratified with the warmth of his reception after being on the sidelines for three years, he was deeply moved by his audiences' enthusiastic reception as he castigated Washburn.[6]

Although enjoying this resurgence of his political influence, he tried to adhere to his self-imposed commitment to eschew active politics. Invited by the president of the Illinois Anti-Monopoly League to attend the convention in Chicago, Donnelly answered that as an "Anti-Monopolist [he was] willing to march in [the] rear ranks as [a] high private but [that he] could not lead off." He explained that he was "out of politics—[and] in the literary field."[7] Late in the summer of 1883, replying to an admirer urging his return to public life, Donnelly openly confessed his disillusionment by stating that the "people must help themselves," that he "had spent years and thousands of dollars in their behalf," and that he

[3] *Ibid.*, J. M. Bowler to I. D., July 29, 1882.
[4] *Ibid.*, A. A. Ames to I. D., October 4, 1882.
[5] *Ibid.*, J. Willis to I. D., October 16, 1882; see also Diary, October 16, 1882.
[6] *Ibid.*, I. D. to K. D., November 4, 1882; St. Paul *Globe*, November 5–7, 1882.
[7] Donnelly MSS, E. L. Brown to I. D., January 15, 1883; see indorsement. It is interesting to note that although Donnelly considered himself an Anti-Monopolist, he would have nothing to do with the Greenback party. He marked unanswered a request to attend the party's caucus in 1883. See J. Starkey to I. D., January 28, 1883.

had had "no reward but suspicion, distrust & polit[ical] ostracism."[8]

Absorbed in his books and enjoying his family, Donnelly re-mained aloof from public life, but his interest in Minnesota affairs was undiminished. His son Ignatius C. Donnelly, practicing medi-cine in St. Paul, informed him of growing evidences of despair among the laboring population for whom there was no employment during the winter of 1883–84.[9] He read widely in national newspapers to keep abreast of the changing economic pattern in the nation. Of special interest was the increasing number of references to agricul-tural discontent and unrest. By the spring, he could not remain quiescent. Donnelly could not, with a clear conscience, refuse Lyman Loring's invitation to speak to the convention of the newly formed but highly active Minnesota Farmers' Alliance: "Farmers in this State need your abilities; you who so well know the wrongs they are enduring, who have felt so long for them to give voice to their grievances, and assist them in their endeavors to fully protect themselves from monopolies."[10] But Donnelly was unwilling even to think of creating a political organization as he had among the Grangers in 1873.

Early in May, without Donnelly's knowledge or consent, George Gillitt, editor of the Republican Hastings *New Era,* began a move-ment aimed at nominating Donnelly to oppose Horace Strait, an ineffective representative who had alienated many Republicans by seeking a sixth term.[11] The *New Era's* call for Donnelly to challenge Strait was echoed during the following weeks by independent and Democratic newspapers. At Gillitt's request he went to Hastings to discuss the formation of a People's party ticket against Strait. Don-nelly repeated that he was devoting his time to literature, that he had withdrawn from politics, and that he had "no stomach for a fight." "Unless the *people* were greatly in favor of change," Don-nelly insisted, he would not consider seeking a public office. Two days later, he returned to Hastings to confer with General Adams, publisher of the Democratic Hastings *Union,* who was filled with enthusiasm and who insisted that the Democrats would nominate Donnelly for Congress if he wanted to campaign. "All Hastings seems to be in my favor," he noted with surprise. "Has the political tide turned at last? Has my time come?" His trepidation,

[8]*Ibid.,* M. P. Finnegan to I. D., August 23, 1883; see indorsement.
[9]*Ibid.,* I. C. D. to I. D., January 16, 1884.
[10]*Ibid.,* L. Loring to I. D., March 9, 1884.
[11]*Ibid.,* G. Gillitt to I. D., May 2, 1884.

after years of being vanquished, was obvious when he added, "I hope it & yet I fear it."[12]

Unimpressed with the sudden outpouring of newspaper publicity, Kate retained a critical view of political realities. "Do not lose your head," she prudently warned. "Remember Strait has money— [he] owns Scott county." The Third District, she shrewdly observed, was cut out to beat Donnelly; it was strongly Norwegian. She reminded him, also, that because party lines were always more tightly drawn in a presidential election year, "these very fellows who are wanting you now will go back on you." This cry for Donnelly, Kate feared, was simply an effort to frighten Strait into yielding concessions to a few influential Democrats.[13]

Conservative Democrats in the Third District who loyally supported the state's Democratic leaders warned Donnelly that he would not receive their support. Before meeting with Third District party officials, he wrote a score of letters to political friends asking for their advice. When he met the District Congressional Committee, he forthrightly and independently explained that he "would not make the run unless all the Dem[ocrats] cordially supported" him. He did not try to influence them. The decision, he insisted, was theirs to make.[14]

Meanwhile, George Gillitt's brother Harvey began working for a People's party slate among discontented Republicans. They all agreed that a regular Democrat could not defeat Strait, and although they were unenthusiastic about Donnelly, they were willing to accept him for one term. The Gillitts were convinced that Donnelly had an excellent chance to win. In mid-July Harvey Gillitt sent out a circular, written by Donnelly, calling for a People's party mass convention to meet at Glencoe, August 20, 1884, to nominate a candidate to oppose Strait.[15] This would coincide with the regularly scheduled Democratic convention; and the Farmers' Alliance was to gather at Glencoe a day earlier.

The organization Democrats disapproved of participation in the Glencoe mass convention. W. H. Mitchell suggested that Donnelly visit Minneapolis and discuss his plans for the campaign with the party's state leadership.[16] At this meeting State Senator Michael

[12]*Ibid.*, Diary, May 8, 1884.
[13]*Ibid.*, K. D. to I. D., May 7, 16, 1884.
[14]*Ibid.*, O. M. Hall to I. D., May 13, 1884; Diary, June 26, 1884.
[15]*Ibid.*, H. Gillitt to I. D., July 9, 12, 1884.
[16]*Ibid.*, W. Mitchell to I. D., July 14, 1884.

Doran, who usually spoke for the conservative wing of the party, said that Donnelly's candidacy would not be opposed if he agreed to indorse the Democratic platform and speak on behalf of Grover Cleveland. Donnelly probably accepted, even though he still had to win his own nomination.[17]

In a statement published July 31, Donnelly explained that he was not a candidate for the congressional nomination in the traditional sense. "But . . . I have been labored with so often, that I have constructively consented to make the fight, provided I am the candidate of all three conventions at Glencoe." The St. Paul *Pioneer Press*, angrily disbelieving Donnelly's "reluctance" and insisting that the Alliance and the People's party were trying to foist him on the Democrats, regretted that distinguished and deserving Democrats were being set aside to advance a cast-off Republican. A few days before the convention, the *Pioneer Press*, in an effort to prevent Donnelly's nomination, predicted that if he tried his "old games among Republican farmers" he would "promptly [be] relegated to the cool shades of literary seclusion which he has been enjoying for some years with great advantage to himself and to the public at large."[18]

On August 19, the Alliance convention indorsed Donnelly over Strait thirty-two to one. The following day the People's party, tailored for the purpose, nominated Donnelly without opposition. The conservative Democrats, however, made a determined effort to keep Donnelly off their ticket. O. M. Hall of Red Wing supported William M. Campbell of Litchfield against Donnelly. Campbell, closely linked with James J. Hill, was so notorious a railroad lawyer that a citizens' protest had convinced Governor Lucius Hubbard that he should not appoint him to the Minnesota Railroad Commission. To defeat Campbell, Donnelly, handshaking and probably reassuring the Democrats of his earlier pledge, made four speeches. He managed to defeat Campbell thirty-two to twenty-seven.[19]

Donnelly campaigned enthusiastically: the conservative Democrats were not actively working against him; he was greeted by unusually large audiences; and for the first time he seemed able to

[17] St. Paul *Pioneer Press*, April 21, 1885.
[18] *Ibid.*, July 31, August 16, 1884.
[19] Donnelly MSS, J. J. Thornton to I. D., May 17, 1885; Diary, August 21, 1884.

penetrate the Scandinavian bloc.[20] The Hastings *New Era* appealed to the reform-minded Republicans at the outset by charging that "Mr. Donnelly opened his campaign with ringing speeches; Mr. Strait opened the campaign with a corkscrew."[21] The St. Paul *Globe,* amazed by the genuine and fervent enthusiasm of Donnelly's audiences, predicted, as much in actual belief as to bolster party spirit, that Donnelly would "bury Major Strait so deep that no political Gabriel . . . [would] ever arouse him into life again."[22] Conceding that Donnelly was carrying on a lively campaign, Strait accused him of using tricky words and with playing unfairly on the prejudices of farmers.[23]

Late in September the *Pioneer Press,* previously scoffing at Donnelly's campaign as being "fun for the boys," grew alarmed that he might be about to unseat Strait and became increasingly vituperative. Conservative Democrats were told that Donnelly had refused to indorse Cleveland, the Democratic presidential aspirant. The paper conceded that Strait, obviously not a great statesman, had alienated many Republicans, but argued that even he was more worthy of support than the demagogic Donnelly.[24] Since Strait was not an effective speaker—Donnelly had referred to him as a "tongueless wirepuller"—the congressman tried to enlist Cushman K. Davis, James Heaton Baker, William Le Duc, and even Alexander Ramsey to campaign on his behalf.[25]

Donnelly criticized Strait as a tool of the Northern Pacific Railroad because he had voted against federal reclamation of the railroad's land grant.[26] Strait replied that Donnelly had been guilty of providing the Northern Pacific with its huge holdings. Only the distressed financial condition of the railroad and the state's need of transportation, Strait said, motivated his decision to support it. Donnelly rejected this argument. In the 1860's, when Minnesota was a frontier and he was a member of Congress, the railroads had needed subsidies, but in 1884, he argued, assistance was unnecessary. Don-

---

[20]*Ibid.,* C. Bush to I. D., August 29, 1884; F. Whitlock to I. D., September 2, 1884; Diary, September 6, 1884.
[21]*Ibid.,* Scrapbook, October, 1884; see *Temperance Review,* October 3, 1884.
[22]September 17, 1884.
[23]St. Paul *Pioneer Press,* September 17, 1884.
[24]*Ibid.,* September 21, 22, 1884.
[25]Donnelly MSS, R. Johnson to I. D., September 24, 1884; I. D. to J. H. Baker, September 27, 1884 (copy).
[26]St. Paul *Pioneer Press,* August 26, 1884.

nelly could point to James J. Hill who had built the Great Northern Railroad without federal aid.[27] Railroad regulation, railroad corruption, and the railroad abuses of the farmers were the basic issues of the campaign. Northern Pacific responded to Donnelly's attack by allowing the district manager at Willmar to run a special election-day car so that the railroad's crews could vote against him.[28]

Although Minneapolis and St. Paul were not in Donnelly's district, their newspapers commented so extensively on the Strait-Donnelly contest that it became the leading news item in the state. Since Donnelly was supported by the *Budstikken,* the largest and oldest Norwegian paper in the state, even the Scandinavians followed the campaign carefully.[29] It was obvious to most observers that Donnelly's appeal was proving unusually strong. St. Paul's Roman Catholic bishop, John Ireland, believed that Donnelly would be elected.[30] And James Heaton Baker, who was stumping the district in Strait's behalf, admitted that Donnelly was making a good fight.[31]

In mid-October, afraid that Donnelly might win, the *Pioneer Press* published a special supplement for the Third District, alleging that he had worked with Finley in writing the Springer letter. The paper falsely contended that this was the finding of the Carlisle investigating committee.[32] Donnelly immediately threatened a libel suit.[33] In response the *Pioneer Press* mockingly asserted that he was either joking or seeking to coerce the editors. Nevertheless, within ten days the paper beat a retreat, conceding that it had misrepresented the facts but insisting that this had been done merely to be facetious. The newspaper claimed that Donnelly had become unusually sensitive.[34] On election eve, safe from retaliation or contradiction before the voting, the *Pioneer Press* issued its final blast, charging that Donnelly had plagiarized another author in writing *Atlantis.*[35]

Cleveland won the presidency, but the Minnesota vote was strongly Republican. The *Pioneer Press* was certain, as the large Republican tally was being recorded, that Donnelly would be deluged

[27]*Ibid.,* October 4, 6, 1884.
[28]Donnelly MSS, J. Spicer to I. D., October 3, 4, 1884.
[29]*Ibid.,* G. Johnson to I. D., October 9, 1884.
[30]*Ibid.,* J. Ireland to I. D., October 14, 1884.
[31]St. Paul *Pioneer Press,* October 15, 1884.
[32]*Ibid.,* October 15, 1884.
[33]St. Paul *Globe,* October 17, 1884.
[34]St. Paul *Pioneer Press,* October 24, 1884.
[35]*Ibid.,* November 2, 1884.

by a majority of at least 6,000 votes. Donnelly, however, running well ahead of Cleveland in the district, was defeated by less than 1,000 votes out of a total of more than 32,000 cast. His show of strength was so phenomenal that he appeared to be Minnesota's foremost Democrat. "I beg of you not to be downcast," his wife told him, "as you know you scarcely expected to win against such odds. I am glad," she added, that "you made the canvass as it shows you how popular you are with the people and you have reason to be proud . . . [that] you have shown you are not a dead man for it has taken a big lot of money to defeat you." Convinced that Cleveland would be obligated to give Donnelly federal patronage, she suggested that he go to New York, visit the President-elect, and seek the most lucrative position possible—a lifetime judgeship or the United States surveyor general office for Minnesota.[36]

In an effort to secure a voice in patronage distribution, Donnelly wrote to William F. Vilas, Wisconsin's leading Democrat, a railroad lawyer, and the obvious midwestern candidate for a cabinet post in the Cleveland administration. Donnelly offered to prepare a petition signed by Minnesota's Democratic candidates requesting that Cleveland appoint Vilas to the cabinet. Expressing regret at Donnelly's defeat, Vilas thanked him for the indorsement.[37] A short time later Donnelly sent Cleveland a letter praising Vilas and suggesting a cabinet position for him. The letter was signed by the defeated Minnesota candidates.[38]

Donnelly knew Vilas as a low-tariff Democrat and a brilliant orator but seemed unaware of his intimate association with the party's conservative wing. In July, at the Democratic National Convention in Chicago, Vilas was allied with James J. Hill and Patrick Kelly in gaining Cleveland the presidential nomination.[39] Late in December Patrick Kelly, speaking for Minnesota's Bourbons, informed Vilas that they were urging his appointment to the cabinet.[40] Kelly, already quoted in the *Pioneer Press* as boasting that he and Michael Doran controlled Minnesota's patronage,[41] undoubt-

[36]Donnelly MSS, K. D. to I. D., November 8, December 14, 1884.

[37]William F. Vilas MSS, I. D. to W. F. Vilas, November 19, 1884; Donnelly MSS, W. F. Vilas to I. D., December 13, 1884.

[38]Donnelly MSS, I. D. to G. Cleveland, November 27, 1884 (copy). Donnelly had written Cleveland earlier with a proposal that Cleveland denounce as vicious the contract immigrant labor system being introduced into the country. Cleveland MSS, I. D. to G. Cleveland, November 17, 1884.

[39]St. Paul *Pioneer Press*, July 8, 9, 1884.

[40]William F. Vilas MSS, P. Kelly to W. Vilas, December 30, 1884.

[41]St. Paul *Pioneer Press*, November 29, 1884.

edly felt influential enough to guarantee Cleveland's approval. The President-elect made Kelly, who was Minnesota's state party chairman as well as Minnesota's national committeeman, a welcome visitor at Albany. Cleveland most assuredly knew that Kelly had matched James J. Hill's five-thousand-dollar contribution to Cleveland's campaign.[42]

Donnelly naïvely assumed that his support for Vilas and his near victory in the congressional race would insure him a share of patronage distribution. He prepared lists of possible appointees and wrote letters polling party workers for suggestions. But he became increasingly conscious of the sensitivity of Third District Democrats to the emerging domination of Kelly and Doran.[43] Frankly astonished as well as disappointed, Donnelly lamented that he had hoped for reasonable preferment after Cleveland's election, but "I find that Pat Kelly and Michael Doran are giving symptoms of combining against me, and I find myself as completely ostracized under the Democratic rule as I have been for nineteen years under the Republican Administration."[44] His concern must have deepened when Vilas visited St. Paul as Kelly's guest to discuss politics with leading Twin Cities conservatives, at a meeting to which Donnelly was not invited. Shortly thereafter, Kelly went to New York to urge Vilas' case before Cleveland.[45]

Determined to seek patronage without Kelly's aid, Donnelly borrowed money from friends who hoped for postmasterships and joined the crowd of politicians and office-seekers in Washington following Cleveland's inauguration. He held high hopes of success because Vilas was named postmaster general in the new administration. He gave no sign of pessimism even after Patrick Kelly, when he prepared to leave Washington, was quoted as saying, "I got all I wanted; and isn't that enough I'd like to know?"[46]

Aware that Kelly had gained control of Minnesota's patronage, Kate wrote Ignatius suggesting that he relax, allow Kelly to be blamed by dissatisfied office-seekers, and seek the best position offered to him even if it meant going abroad. "I feel we should be

[42]*Ibid.*, December 10, 1884.

[43]Donnelly MSS, W. P. Christensen to I. D., November 27, 1884; E. Stringer to I. D., December 22, 1884; J. Spicer to I. D., December 29, 1884; L. L. Baxter to I. D., January 19, 1885.

[44]*Ibid.*, Diary, December 30, 1884.

[45]St. Paul *Pioneer Press*, February 22, 1885; Minneapolis *Tribune*, February 1, 1885.

[46]St. Paul *Pioneer Press*, March 11, 1885.

meek until we are able to show our claws," she wrote. Ignatius was reminded that Kelly, beaming with the news of Cleveland's victory the night following the election, remarked to Donnelly, "Pick any foreign mission you please and you shall have it." Kate recognized that it would be difficult for her husband to forego his fight for patronage, but she implored him to do so and accept a living. "I hate politics," she concluded; "it is a low trade—no honor or honesty—or gratitude or even decency."[47]

In Washington Donnelly spent hours in Vilas' office seeking a conference. Finally the postmaster general came out, greeted him with enthusiasm, apologized for the tedious delay, and invited Donnelly to dine with him. After a pleasant meal, Vilas offered to make a special appointment with the President so that Donnelly could meet him. Immensely pleased, Donnelly felt that the probability of gaining a post had been increased.[48] The St. Paul *Pioneer Press*, commenting on Donnelly's efforts in Washington, doubted that he could secure the surveyor generalship or a foreign post. The paper pointed out that he had not been pro-Cleveland during the campaign. Facetiously, the newspaper noted that many Democrats and Republicans would have liked to see Donnelly abroad, but not at the expense of an appointment.[49]

Donnelly may have followed Kate's suggestions, but more than likely he was advised by Vilas that he had to have Kelly's indorsement before he could secure a position because Donnelly finally asked Kelly to write Secretary of the Interior L. C. Q. Lamar requesting his appointment as surveyor general. Kelly declined to make the request. He explained that the appointment would bring more dissatisfaction and trouble than he cared to encounter; for the sake of party harmony, he should withdraw his application. Not, however, entirely hostile, Kelly offered: "I will be glad to assist you in obtaining a mission abroad should you desire it."[50] Donnelly was powerless. Kate suggested that he agree to step aside if Kelly and Hill would appoint the friends who had relied on Donnelly for positions.[51] Donnelly probably realized that to accept Kelly's proposal would mean to surrender any claim that he had on the administration into Kelly's hands.

[47]Donnelly MSS, K. D. to I. D., March 11, 13, 1885; see St. Paul *Pioneer Press*, April 26, 1885.
[48]*Ibid.*, Diary, March 11, 12, 13, 1885.
[49]St. Paul *Pioneer Press*, March 18, 1885.
[50]Cleveland MSS, I. D. to P. Kelly, April 2, 1885.
[51]Donnelly MSS, K. D. to I. D., April 12, 1885.

While Donnelly considered alternatives, Kelly and Doran consolidated their power at a meeting of the Minnesota State Central Committee. By unanimous resolution the group authorized Kelly and Doran to act for the party on all matters relative to federal patronage and requested the heads of federal departments to recognize no other indorsements for office. All applications were to be submitted to Kelly and Doran for approval.[52] Kelly, Doran, and Hill, determined to make the party a church which would admit of no dissent, were ready to excommunicate anyone who deviated from its established dogma or ritual. Even the cynical *Pioneer Press*, reputedly owned in part by James J. Hill, referred to the "Kelly-Doran office-broking agency." The shocked Minneapolis *Tribune* indignantly claimed that they were named the "proconsuls of the province of Minnesota." This was the first instance in American history, the *Tribune* asserted, when a state central committee had formally recognized absolute "boss" control of patronage.[53]

Newspaper accounts of the State Central Committee's actions reached Donnelly shortly after he had learned from his close friend and political aide, Patrick Rahilly, that Michael Doran refused to help Donnelly secure any position.[54] Donnelly decided that his only hope of gaining influence was to discredit Kelly and Doran in the eyes of the people. When a *Pioneer Press* reporter asked Donnelly for his reaction to Minnesota's political news, Donnelly replied: "It was unjust and unfair. . . . I asked for a local office with a salary of about $2000, an office that has been sometimes filled, before now, by comparatively obscure men." Explaining that he had reason to aspire to "something higher and more lucrative than the office of surveyor general," he expressed surprise at the intense opposition to him. "I have done nothing to provoke it," he insisted; "the excuses given me are flimsy." Kelly, Donnelly added, refused him the surveyor generalship but suggested a foreign mission. "In other words I was not a good enough Democrat to fill a small office, but I was good enough a Democrat to represent the party and the nation at some foreign court with twice or three times the salary and ten times the conspicuosity."

In response to the reporter's obvious question of why there was a

[52]St. Paul *Pioneer Press*, April 15, 1885; St. Paul *Globe*, April 15, 1885; Minneapolis *Tribune*, April 17, 1885.
[53]St. Paul *Pioneer Press*, April 22, 1885; Minneapolis *Tribune*, April 17, 20, 21, 1885.
[54]Donnelly MSS, P. Rahilly to I. D., April 14, 1885.

vendetta against him, Donnelly lashed out: "Michael Doran and Patrick H. Kelly are simply the mouthpieces of Jim Hill. Jim is the *deus ex machina*, the colored gentleman under the woodpile: the new leader of the reformed Democracy in Minnesota. Jim doesn't approve of my granger legislation in the past, or my granger proclivities in the present, or my granger possibilities in the future. . . . Jim is a great man." Then Donnelly added angrily, Hill "has taken a contract to stamp me out, and the cowardly creatures who worship his millions are ready to join in the work." Conceding that he had "neither money nor newspaper, nor patronage, and it is a very unequal contest—one man against a gang of millionaires," Donnelly warned the Minnesota Democratic party that "if those who flee from the corruption of Republicanism are met at the threshold of the Democratic camp" by James J. Hill, Patrick H. Kelly, and Michael Doran, "the Republicans will hold the state and congressional districts for another generation."[55]

Thoroughly embarrassed by Donnelly's denunciation, Michael Doran acidly told a *Pioneer Press* reporter in St. Paul, "Mr. Hill isn't in politics," even though this statement was an outright lie. Doran then went on to charge that Donnelly "had never identified with the Democratic party," had "never represented the party or worked for it," and had never even said he was a Democrat. Doran charged Donnelly with breaking his promise to campaign for Cleveland and the Chicago platform. He had even refused to allow speakers from the state committee to campaign for Cleveland in the Third District.[56]

"Donnelly pretended that it is a small favor he is asking," Kelly told a *Pioneer Press* reporter, "but that is not the case. He does not want the office merely for the salary it will bring him. He would like to use it for his personal aggrandizement." Sheepishly Kelly admitted that he "volunteered to sign his [Donnelly's] papers for the Swiss mission," but he insisted that he had done it only to let Donnelly "down easy." Kelly's friends had already given him "a gavel rap over the knuckles on account of it."[57]

In Washington, Cleveland was hard put to explain Minnesota's patronage, admittedly a national scandal. "I never knew anything

[55]St. Paul *Pioneer Press*, April 19, 1885.
[56]*Ibid.*, April 21, 1885. For Hill's role in patronage see, Horace S. Merrill, "Ignatius Donnelly, James J. Hill, and Cleveland Administration Patronage," *Mississippi Valley Historical Review*, XXXIX (1952), 516.
[57]St. Paul *Pioneer Press*, April 22, 1885.

about it beforehand, so this thing is the first notice I have had of it. Those people are so far off," the President complained, ". . . you see they are over a thousand miles off, and we don't know much about them. They all come down here and claim to be simon pure, but how can we tell?" Office-brokerage "is not my way of doing things," Cleveland indignantly insisted. The mails were open and free to everybody, so anyone could send in an application, stated the President. He concluded that all applications would receive fair consideration.[58]

Before the President's statement was made public, Donnelly sent Vilas a scorching letter recapitulating the entire patronage squabble, charging Hill with buying influence, denying that he had opposed the administration, and pleading that it was utterly unfair to refuse him a minor post because a national committeeman would not indorse him. Donnelly sent a copy of the letter to the *Pioneer Press*.[59] Vilas, following Cleveland's line, answered by acknowledging Donnelly's service to the party but explained that he was determined to avoid quarrels which he did not understand.[60] Donnelly then sent Vilas a packet including news clippings and portions of letters expressing the shocked response among Democrats to Kelly's job selling.[61] Vilas pleaded innocence; Kelly's announcements did not affect him.[62]

On May 1, Donnelly took Cleveland at his word and appealed to him directly. In a packet containing Minnesota newspaper clippings, copies of his letters to Kelly, and Kelly's answers, Donnelly sent a letter charging that Minnesota's responsible Democrats were scandalized. On the letter which Kelly had written refusing to indorse Donnelly for surveyor general but suggesting a foreign post, Donnelly underscored in red pencil the foreign mission offer and wrote at the bottom: "How can a man be worthy of a mission abroad and not be worthy of a little place at home?" In asking for the President's objective consideration Donnelly stated: "I am so firm in my own honesty and my popularity with the Democrats of the Northwest that I would be glad if you would send some reliable agent to Minnesota to enquire as to the facts."[63]

Either the scandal or the information in Donnelly's letter convinced Cleveland that he should rebuke Kelly and consider Don-

[58] *Ibid.*, April 27, 1885.
[59] Donnelly MSS, I. D. to W. F. Vilas, April 23, 1885 (copy).
[60] *Ibid.*, W. F. Vilas to I. D., April 25, 1885.
[61] *Ibid.*, I. D. to W. F. Vilas, April 27, 1885 (copy).
[62] *Ibid.*, W. F. Vilas to I. D., April 27, 1885.
[63] Cleveland MSS, I. D. to G. Cleveland, May 1, 1885.

nelly's case more carefully. Two weeks later, Vilas informed Donnelly that the first assistant postmaster was to rely on his opinions for appointments in the Third District.[64] Determined to fight Kelly, Doran, and Hill, Donnelly visited every cabinet officer he could, recommending his friends for positions and opposing conservative candidates.[65] Donnelly wrote Minnesota's Republican Senator Dwight M. Sabin, reminding him of his offer to give a thousand dollars and stand on his head to see Kelly beaten, and asked him to help him secure the surveyor generalship by seeing or writing Cleveland. Sabin, who was quite ill, proved to be of no assistance.[66] The *Pioneer Press*, trying to explain Donnelly's persistent quest for the surveyor generalship, pointed out that the office controlled the Minnesota pine lands and that he was probably still as interested in digging out fraudulent entries as he had been in Granger days.[67]

Donnelly's influence with Vilas waned quickly. The postmaster general, who remained Cleveland's primary patronage dispenser, refused to urge the appointment of Donnelly's friends. Angrily Donnelly wrote Vilas asking him to withdraw all of Donnelly's indorsements on file in the Post Office Department. "I shall announce to the public," Donnelly stated boldly, "that the stepping stone to favor is to know my enemies."[68] By the end of June, Donnelly had only the faintest hope that Secretary of the Interior L. C. Q. Lamar would help him. In disgust and despair, he noted in his diary: "The R.R. & robber interest is all against me & it is very potent. Vilas who professed great friendship is a cold-blooded, servile politician & trickster & the tool of Kelly."[69]

Although Donnelly failed to secure the surveyor generalship, his bitter struggle embarrassed the administration and prevented Cleveland from making any appointment. The *Pioneer Press* noted that Donnelly "stuck in a peg which those who detest him most cordially" were unable to pull out. The paper added that a scheme to consolidate the Minnesota and Dakota districts was being given serious consideration primarily as a device to avoid the painful necessity of choice among Minnesota candidates.[70]

Donnelly continued to write to Cleveland asking for genuine civil

[64] Donnelly MSS, W. F. Vilas to I. D., May 14, 1885.

[65] St. Paul *Pioneer Press*, May 19, 1885.

[66] Donnelly MSS, I. D. to D. Sabin, May 19, 27, 1885; F. Norris to I. D., June 18, 1885.

[67] St. Paul *Pioneer Press*, June 12, 1885.

[68] Donnelly MSS, I. D. to W. F. Vilas, June 16, 1885 (copy).

[69] *Ibid.*, Diary, June 29, 1885.

[70] St. Paul *Pioneer Press*, August 1, 1885.

service leadership. "For the sake of the Dem[ocratic] party & good government," he entreated, "call a halt in this Kelly business. Do not use your power to build up a disreputable boss in this Northwestern Country." He urged the President to hold the balance evenly between differences. "You were elected as a protest against Bossism and corruption," Donnelly pleaded; "you should not give a few mean, base, greedy grasping men power to enrich themselves at the expense of the people & the cost of the party's future."[71]

When Kelly and Doran recommended that William M. Campbell, who had opposed Donnelly within the party for the Third District nomination, be appointed Minnesota's United States marshal, he again protested to Cleveland. This was more than merely a repudiation of the district convention and a reflection upon him. "Campbell is a noted lobbyist . . . in the interest of the Rail Road Companies in their efforts to corrupt legislation by buying up members of the State Legislature," Donnelly stated.[72] But the protests were in vain; Cleveland appointed Campbell.

On New Year's Eve, 1885, Donnelly evaluated the hectic and disappointing events of the year. Because of the expenses of trips to Washington, his financial affairs were in a nearly chaotic condition. He had even been forced to assign his book royalties to his sons to escape liens levied against him. "I had built up hopes that I would get an office—the Surveyor-Generalship of Minnesota and help myself & the boys financially," he wrote in his diary, "but my enemies Hill, Kelly, Doran & their string of base fellows, attacked me and defeated me."[73] As he looked forward to 1886, he prepared to live in terms of his response to a suggestion that he yield to the Twin Cities conservatives. "It is not in Mr. Kelly's power to destroy me," he wrote. "My influence does not depend upon office holding or office giving. If it had the Repub[licans] would have obliterated me long ago." Proudly he declared, "I feel that I have more influence today in the N[orth] W[est] than I have ever had before; an influence based on the fact that I have persistently fought the Rings & the Robbers to my own great detriment and injury." Courageously, he added, "I can live without office. . . ."[74]

[71]Donnelly MSS, I. D. to G. Cleveland, October 21, 1885 (copy).
[72]Cleveland MSS, I. D. to G. Cleveland, November 3, 1885.
[73]Donnelly MSS, Diary, December 31, 1885.
[74]*Ibid.*, I. D. to W. Deacon, August 26, 1885 (copy).

XIV

The Great Cryptogram

Great Scott!—Confusion!—O immortal Will,
What's this a darn'd American has found—
That all your reputation is worth nil,
That you've a base impostor been all around?
LONDON STRAND JOURNAL

"IN THE winter of 1878-9," Ignatius Donnelly wrote, "I will reread the Shakespeare Plays, not, as heretofore, for the delight which they would give me, but with my eyes directed to discover whether there is or is not in them any indication of a cipher."[1] His interest in the authorship of Shakespeare's plays, however, originated much earlier. In January of 1873, imprisoned in Nininger City by a severe Minnesota blizzard, he noted that he was preparing a lecture on the authorship of the plays,[2] but his enthusiasm for the project probably waned with the coming of the spring thaw and the return to active political life.

In the next five years, he occasionally read books and articles concerning Shakespeare's life and the English political and intellectual environment of his times. The more knowledge he gained of Shakespeare's humble origin, his lack of formal education, and his career, the more Donnelly became convinced that the actor's name had been used to cover the work of some brilliant Elizabethan personality. To Donnelly, Francis Bacon appeared to be the logical author because of the sequence of events in his life, his experience, and his

---

[1] Ignatius Donnelly, *The Great Cryptogram* (Chicago: R. S. Peale & Co., 1887), p. 516.
[2] Donnelly MSS, Diary, January 7–13, 1873.

genius. But, as Donnelly confessed, one consideration troubled him: "Would the writer of such immortal works sever them from himself and cast them off forever?"[3] Not until he learned of Bacon's interest in ciphers did he turn to a careful study of Bacon's life. The quest for the cipher became Donnelly's recreation while he was writing *Atlantis* and *Ragnarok*. And it may have occurred to him that just as in *Atlantis* and *Ragnarok* he had attempted to provide the reading public with an interesting solution to scientific problems, so in discovering a secret message hidden in Shakespeare's works he could provide the answer to the most popular literary puzzle of the age.

Donnelly bought Bacon's works as well as significant Shakespeariana while he worked on what he first termed "my essay on Bacon & Shakespeare."[4] Evidence that he was influenced by his reading appeared in *Atlantis*, where he referred to Francis Bacon as a "profoundly wise and great man" and in *Ragnarok*, where he expressed doubt that Shakespeare had written the plays.[5] He was fortunate in being able to use a bibliography of the Bacon-Shakespeare controversy which was prepared by W. H. Wyman.[6]

Concentrated work on the cipher did not begin until Donnelly finished writing *Ragnarok* and secured a facsimile of the 1623 Shakespeare folio. In his enthusiasm, Donnelly even carried the folio to Stevens County, prepared to study it at night during the period of the wheat harvest. On September 23, 1882, he recorded cautiously: "I have been working . . . at what I think is a great discovery I have made, to wit: a cypher in Shakespeare's Plays . . . asserting Francis Bacon's authorship of the plays." But Donnelly admitted confusion, conceded that there appeared to be three arithmetic cipher systems which turned up key words such as "Bacon," "Francis," "William," "Shake," and "Speare." "I am certain there is a cypher there, and I think I have the key," he noted; "all this cannot be accident."[7]

Deeply involved in attempting to decipher the plays during the ensuing months, he resented intrusions upon his privacy, especially the "dirty little business troubles" stemming from his indebtedness.[8]

[3] *The Great Cryptogram,* p. 505.
[4] Donnelly MSS, Diary, December 28, 1881.
[5] *Atlantis,* p. 283; *Ragnarok,* p. 114.
[6] W. H. Wyman (compiler), *The Bibliography of the Bacon-Shakespeare Controversy, with Notes and Extracts* (Cincinnati: Cox & Co., 1884), it appeared first in 1882.
[7] Donnelly MSS, Diary, September 23, 1882.
[8] *Ibid.,* December 23, 1882.

Unlike *Atlantis* and *Ragnarok,* which were written in isolation from the scholarly world, his Shakespeare studies were a vital part of the Baconian cultist movement. Corresponding with people in England and America who believed that Bacon was the author of the plays,[9] he was reluctant to abandon his own skepticism. It was years before he accepted his own findings.[10] In his diary, recording each new discovery and each change of system, he noted: "I have at last, I think, got the whole key," or, "It is very difficult to find sequences . . . [but] it seems to be a system."[11] On one occasion, feeling quite optimistic, he wrote Kate that he had checked the cipher's findings against Green's *History of the English People* and discovered that they agreed.[12]

By December, 1883, deciphering the plays had become Donnelly's consuming passion. "I think about it all day & dream about it all night," he wrote; "it is hideously complicated & perplexing."[13] In January, 1884, he began to correspond with Appleton Morgan, a railroad executive who had written *The Shakespeare Myth.*[14] Replying to Morgan late in May, obviously convinced that he had solved the puzzle, Donnelly stated that he could prove beyond question that Bacon was the author of the plays.[15] By this time, tired of working at the cipher's mathematics, and increasingly impatient to publish his work, he noted that despite the very hot weather, he was busy "licking into shape the vast mass of materials" which he had accumulated and was busy writing *The Great Cryptogram.*[16] A few months later when Morgan visited Donnelly, the cipher was explained to him. Amazed by the work, Morgan confessed that either a cipher existed or Donnelly had discovered a most extraordinary series of coincidences in the plays.[17]

In September Morgan released the news of Donnelly's cipher. As a news item it was picked up in the winter of 1884, and in the spring of 1885 Donnelly was interviewed by the Chicago *Weekly News* and the Washington *Post.*[18] There was a substantial amount of

[9]*Ibid.,* Mrs. C. M. Potts to I. D., May 24, 1883.
[10]*Ibid.,* K. D. to I. D., July 25, 1888.
[11]*Ibid.,* Diary, March 15, April 10, July 30, 1883.
[12]*Ibid.,* I. D. to K. D., August 6, 1883.
[13]*Ibid.,* Diary, December 14, 1883.
[14]Chicago Historical Society MSS, I. D. to A. Morgan, January 24, 1884.
[15]Donnelly MSS, A. Morgan to I. D., May 29, 1884; see indorsement.
[16]*Ibid.,* Diary, June 23, 1884.
[17]*Ibid.,* A. Morgan to I. D., see card clipped to Morgan letter, September 1, 1884.
[18]April 2, 1885; April 12, 1885.

criticism in the newspapers, especially in the St. Paul *Pioneer Press*, where Donnelly's clash with Kelly, Doran, and Hill was being aired.[19] In the months that followed, the *Pioneer Press* kept asking, where is the cryptogram?[20] The New York *Sun* devoted two columns in a Sunday edition to Donnelly's work: "A cipher which by the very unvarying application of a simple key works out of the plays a long and continuous story could not by any possibility be the result of accident; nor could it be the product of the most skillful imposture." The editors refused to believe that Donnelly was self-deluded or mistaken. "Either he has determined to throw away for the sake of shortlived notoriety a well-earned reputation, and to make himself for all time a ridiculous and despised figure in literary history, or he has in fact hit upon the proof that Bacon was the real Shakespeare."[21] Donnelly was not surprised by the world's incredulity. "I should not believe in the existence of such a cypher myself," he wrote Charlotte Porter, the editor of *Shakespeariana*, "if I had not the proofs constantly before me as I work."[22]

Having had books published by Harper and Brothers and D. Appleton, feeling that he had not been equitably treated, and hopeful of securing a larger share of the profit, Donnelly determined to offer *The Great Cryptogram* through a subscription publisher. His optimistic estimate was that the book would sell at least one hundred thousand copies.[23] In March, 1887, while negotiating with R. S. Peale and Company of Chicago to print an American edition, Donnelly wrote Sampson, Low and Company in England offering them the book if they would provide a royalty of one dollar a volume.[24] Donnelly believed that the book would be pirated unless an English publisher established the copyright. Peale not only accepted Donnelly's terms, but also promised to arrange for publication of the book in England.

To stimulate additional interest in his forthcoming work, Donnelly wrote two articles entitled "The Shakespeare Myth" which he published in the *North American Review*. In the first he summarized the circumstantial evidence that impugned Shakespeare's authorship of the plays. The second article, which reproduced a small portion of the cipher, argued that "there is no more doubt of

[19] St. Paul *Pioneer Press*, May 3, 1885.
[20] *Ibid.*, December 15, 1885.
[21] Quoted in Washington *Post*, June 15, 1886.
[22] Donnelly MSS, I. D. to Charlotte Porter, November 13, 1886 (copy).
[23] *Ibid.*, I. D. to Metropolitan Publishing Co., July 12, 1885.
[24] *Ibid.*, I. D. to Sampson, Low & Co., March 16, 1887 (copy).

the reality of the cipher than there is of the reality of the plays."
The work was incomplete, Donnelly warned his readers, because it
would take him a year longer to decipher all of the narrative. "I will
publish part of the story this year," he wrote, "and satisfy the in-
credulous of the truth of the discovery."[25]

The publisher of *The Great Cryptogram*, R. S. Peale, who was
highly enthusiastic about its prospects, felt that it would be the
"crowning work" of his life in the publishing field.[26] He was so confident of the book's success that Donnelly's contract specified an
advance royalty payment of several thousand dollars even before the
manuscript was completed. The company, preparing for an extensive publicity program, arranged to have the New York *World* devote a large portion of a Sunday edition to the book. "If the *World*
sees fit to send an intelligent, unprejudiced gentleman here," Donnelly wrote Peale, "I will reveal *part* of the cipher rule." Donnelly
feared to explain all of it because it could be pirated.[27]

To avoid any charge of complicity if Donnelly's work proved a
fraud, the editors of the New York *World* employed Professor
Thomas Davidson, a mathematician, to interview him and to test
the cipher. Although Peale had arranged for the publicity, neither
Davidson nor the *World's* staff was preparing an advertising stunt.[28]
The mathematician, who was to write an eighteen-thousand-word
article for the newspaper, went to Nininger City early in August,
1887. He was astounded by Donnelly's cipher. Peale's editor, F. J.
Schulte, noted with a sigh of relief, "I was gratified to see that the
gun so carefully loaded has been successfully discharged."[29] When
Davidson returned to New Jersey, he rechecked the system and
reported that he was "able to say that the counting proceeds according to a fixed rule. That is a crucial point, of course. . . . I am very
much impressed with your work, & have almost become a Baconian
without the cipher!"[30]

On August 28, the front page of the New York Sunday *World* was
devoted to Davidson's favorable appraisal of *The Great Cryptogram*.
The St. Paul *Globe*, commenting on the *World's* review, observed
that Donnelly had "succeeded in getting an amount of free advertis-

[25]*North American Review*, June, 1887, pp. 572–82; July, 1887, pp. 27–68.
[26]Donnelly MSS, R. S. Peale to I. D., July 9, 1887.
[27]*Ibid.*, I. D. to R. S. Peale, July 22, 1887.
[28]*Ibid.*, R. S. Peale to I. D., July 21, 1887; J. A. Cockerill to F. J. Schulte
(telegram), July 27, 1887; F. J. Schulte to I. D., July 27, 1887.
[29]*Ibid.*, F. J. Schulte to I. D., August 8, 1887.
[30]*Ibid.*, T. Davidson to I. D., August 17, 1887.

ing that the money of the Vanderbilts could hardly have purchased. To cap the climax he secures, without money and without price, two pages of a review . . . an advertisement that money could not procure, but which reckoned in column rates would have a monetary value of $2000."[31]

F. J. Schulte informed Donnelly that the company planned to "educate the general public to the Bacon-Shakespeare controversy" by providing the small newspapers of the country with articles and advertisements before Peale's canvassers entered an area.[32] The vigorous publicity campaign convinced Peale that *The Great Cryptogram* would sell more than one hundred thousand copies in the United States. He allowed Donnelly to borrow $4,000 in advance royalties beyond the specifications of their contract. Donnelly, delighted with what he felt to be more than a personal vindication, exploded in a burst of ancestral pride: "A good many people believe that the proper occupation for a person of Irish blood is digging a ditch or flourishing a shilela [*sic*]. They are presumed to know nothing about literature & to ultimately lack those qualities of patience & perseverance which are held to be the birthright of the Anglo-Saxon." Highly self-satisfied he added, "I think I have done something to dispel that prejudice."[33]

To prevent the theft of Donnelly's cipher rule when *The Great Cryptogram* was in press, Peale brought a special printer to Chicago to set up the crucial portions of the book without seeing the remainder of its contents. The first edition was set at twelve thousand copies. Two aspects of the project caused the publisher concern as he prepared to arrange for a foreign edition. Peale was surprised to learn that Donnelly had deciphered only seventeen hundred rather than seventeen thousand words of the secret story in the plays. He was disturbed also because he did not understand the cipher and feared English publishers would be reluctant to undertake an expensive work on the publisher's word alone. Peale urged Donnelly to explain the intricate rule to him or secure the indorsement of some entirely disinterested literary person. Before Peale sailed for England, Donnelly sent him a package with sufficient material to defend and explain the cipher rule.[34]

[31]St. Paul *Globe*, August 31, 1887.
[32]Donnelly MSS, F. J. Schulte to I. D., September 22, 1887.
[33]*Ibid.*, Diary, 1887.
[34]*Ibid.*, R. S. Peale to I. D., October 1, 14, 21, November 1, 1887; F. J. Schulte to I. D., October 7, 10, 15, 1887.

With the book in press, Donnelly grew increasingly apprehensive about its success. He came to doubt the subscription method, fearful that people would return their copies if the book received adverse reviews.[35] Finishing the book in midwinter proved a "terrible task" for Donnelly, who was almost overcome by the dread that the world would not accept it and that it would prove a failure. "I do not care so much for loss of glory as I do for dollars and cents," he wrote; money was "very necessary to help my children out of the slough of poverty." Under these circumstances, "authorship . . . is not a delightful occupation." He confessed that he felt "like one in solitary confinement in the penitentiary: all without is white with desolate snow, no one comes to see me from weeks end to weeks end; I work from 10 o'clock in the morning until 11 at night, with a few minutes intermission for meals & one hour's lonely walk. . . . But I am chained to the stake and cannot fly. Oh! how I shall rejoice when the great task is finished, no matter how the book turns out."[36]

In England, Peale was unprepared for the deep-rooted prejudice he encountered when he tried to sell *The Great Cryptogram.* Macmillan and Company, his first choice, "would not even consider the idea." He finally accepted Donnelly's suggestion, Sampson, Low and Company. Edwin Arnold, the editor of the London *Daily Telegraph*, told Peale that he "might as well expect the English people to give up their belief in their Constitution as their belief in Shakespeare." But Peale persuaded the editor to publish a portion of *The Great Cryptogram.*[37] Late in November, 1887, the *Telegraph* carried a two-column article on the book suggesting that Donnelly's position left room for only three possible views: he was an impostor, he had deluded himself, or he was right! Too much effort had been put into the publication to justify any moderate conclusion.[38] Two days later, the *Telegraph* hedged. "We cannot and will not yet surrender Shakespeare's glorious name and fame to the desperate ingenuity or self-deception of Mr. Donnelly," the editors wrote. If the cipher proved valid, they would insist that Bacon had worked the cipher into the 1623 edition of the plays. "No! we are not convinced!—but we are astonished," concluded the *Telegraph;* "we are uneasy, and we are a little perplexed."[39] The following day the paper published

[35]*Ibid.*, I. D. to F. J. Schulte, November 4, 1887.
[36]*Ibid.*, Diary, December 11, 1887.
[37]*Ibid.*, R. S. Peale to I. D., November 6, 8, 1887.
[38]London *Telegraph*, November 26, 1887.
[39]*Ibid.*, November 28, 1887.

two full columns of letters to the editor dealing with the Bacon-Shakespeare controversy. On November 30, the staid *St. James Gazette* denounced some of Donnelly's cipher works charging that "the absurdities involved in them are infinite."[40] The London *Strand Journal* jibed:

> Come from your grave, O "Bard of Avon," come,
> And tell this Yankee all his tall talk's a flam,
> A figment of his too "cute brain," a hum,
> The disinterment of his "cryptogram."[41]

The American reception of *The Great Cryptogram* was equally antagonistic. The *North American Review*, which had published Donnelly's "The Shakespeare Myth," followed it with an item entitled "Those Wonderful Ciphers." The author, admitting that he had not seen Donnelly's work, ridiculed all attempts to decipher the plays. "It is all the fashion nowadays to believe that something Shakespeare did or did not write contains a cipher," he noted sarcastically. "The literary man who has not his own pet Baconian cipher of Shakespearian cryptogram is a *rara avis*."[42] Critical as were the English commentators, Donnelly felt they were fair and reasonable when compared with the Americans, who seemed to be "inspired by the R[ail] R[oad] corporations," in "concerted purpose to write down the book" even before it appeared.[43]

The hostile reviews and the slow prepublication sale of *The Great Cryptogram* led Peale to withhold any further advance royalty payments. Indignantly, Donnelly protested that the publisher had promised him the money. If sales were lagging, it was as much due to Peale's canvassers as to the critical press accounts. Peale insisted that he did not take a gloomy view of the book's prospects. Even though the book had been attacked by the newspapers, he was convinced that a plan could be arranged to assure successful sales. "Whether your theory is accepted or not, will not discourage me in the sale of the book," Peale wrote. "You have written a wonderful book and I know we can sell it."[44]

With an "infinite sense of relief," Donnelly finished the last page of *The Great Cryptogram*. "It is a vast book of about 1000 pages," he

[40]Chatto & Windus MSS, University of California at Los Angeles.
[41]February 12, 1888.
[42]Arthur D. Vinton, "Those Wonderful Ciphers," *North American Review*, November, 1887, p. 555.
[43]Donnelly MSS, Diary, December 31, 1887.
[44]*Ibid.*, R. S. Peale to I. D., February 7, 1888.

recorded in his diary; "I feel like a boy let loose from school."[45] The book, in printed form, fell two pages short of Donnelly's estimate.

The Great Cryptogram was actually three books in defense of one argument. In the first section, Donnelly constructed a skilfully executed brief explaining why Shakespeare could not have written the plays and why Bacon could. He pointed out Shakespeare's lack of basic legal and literary knowledge, his illiteracy as indicated by his handwriting, his personal character, and his lack of experience. Bacon was presented as a poet, politician, traveler, and scholar, whose philosophy and experience attested to his authorship. Two hundred pages of *The Great Cryptogram* were devoted to noting parallelisms in expressions, metaphors, opinions, quotations, style, and even errors as they appeared in the plays and in Bacon's works. This first section, five hundred pages in length, was as impressive a display of Donnelly's erudition as were *Atlantis* and *Ragnarok*.

The second portion of the book explained Donnelly's personal quest for the cipher, his false leads, his knowledge of cryptography, and the highly complex arithmetic which disclosed the cipher story. The cipher numbers were based on Donnelly's observation of the irregular pagination, bracketing system, hyphenation, and italics in the 1623 Shakespeare folio, especially in *Henry IV*. Donnelly constructed a correlation among them and basic root numbers such as 505 and 523 which allowed him to count words and extract from the play's contents a series of words that comprised a narrative. But to make the system effective, he had to count backward as well as forward. The initial word "How," for example, was derived through the following series: $523 - 284 = 239 - 51 = 188 - 20$ brackets and hyphens $= 168$. Word 168 on page 74 column two $=$ How. The narrative, so tortuously extracted from the plays, unfortunately lacked romance for the average reader and was absurdly simple to the literary historian. The reader was confronted with selected deciphered passages interspersed with polemic paragraphs to set the secret story in perspective. The over-all effect of the demonstration of the cipher was bewildering and disappointing.

In the third section, actually an annotated bibliography, Donnelly discussed the history of the Baconian movement, defended the cultists who advocated Bacon's authorship, and listed other works to which they might lay claim. The book concluded with a defense of Bacon and an attack on his Whig critics.

[45] *Ibid.*, Diary, March 11, 1888.

In many ways *The Great Cryptogram* gives clues to Donnelly's thought processes and values. He could not accept the idea that the creator of Shylock was a moneylender as was Shakespeare and not a debtor as was Bacon. In a similar vein, Donnelly depicted Bacon as the courageous, honest, struggling politician victimized by office-seeking, greedy corruptionists who were eager to despoil the public treasury. Attempting to discuss Bacon's philosophical concepts, Donnelly produced an undiscriminating characterization. Throughout the book, the style is highly personal and intimate, with occasional flashes of frontier humor—For example, in describing his search for the cipher he wrote, "I was often reminded of our Western story of the lost traveler, whose highway changed into a wagon-road, his wagon-road disappeared into a bridle-path, his bridle-path merged into a cow-path, and his cow-path at last degenerated into a squirrel-track, which ran up a tree!"[46]

Despite the bizarre touches, Donnelly tackled the cipher work itself critically. The knowledge that a cipher must be systematic and capable of reproduction by anyone conditioned his thinking. It was a tremendous task, more than comparable, in Donnelly's eyes, to the translation of the Rosetta stone by Champollion le Jeune and Thomas Young. "My problem," he wrote, "was to find by means of a cipher rule of which I knew little, a cipher story of which I knew less. A more brain-racking problem was never submitted to the intellect of man."[47] Although Donnelly confided to his diary after completing the book, "I hope to be ranked by posterity with those divine lunatics Socrates & Bacon who loved mankind more than they loved themselves,"[48] he defended his delay in submitting a partially finished cipher story to the public. "I felt, at the same time," he confessed to his readers, "that I owed some duty to the nineteenth century, as well as to the sixteenth and hence my work was greatly broken in upon by public affairs."[49]

Having positively asserted that a cipher existed, he stated almost at the close of the book: "I admit . . . that my workmanship in the elaboration of the Cipher is not perfect. There are one or two essential points of the cipher rule that I have not fully worked out. I think that I see the complete rule," he added, "but I need more leisure to elaborate and verify it abundantly and reduce my workmanship to

[46] *The Great Cryptogram*, p. 566.
[47] *Ibid.*, pp. 575–77.
[48] Donnelly MSS, Diary, 1888.
[49] *The Great Cryptogram*, p. 889.

mathematical exactness."[50] Donnelly's failure to achieve precision is significant because *The Great Cryptogram* was the only book in which he tried to employ the scientific method, and it proved that he was neither mathematically minded nor accurate.

Donnelly's cryptographic work received both casual and critical appraisal. At the request of Joseph Medill, the publisher of the Chicago *Tribune*, Professor Colbert, a distinguished Chicago astronomer, read *The Great Cryptogram* and discussed the cipher rule with Donnelly. Colbert, although he felt Donnelly had taken liberties in his counting, was convinced that there was a cipher in the plays.[51] Medill, however, refused to indorse the book in the Chicago *Tribune* because he did not think Donnelly had proved that Bacon had woven the cipher into the plays.[52] Experienced military and scientific cryptographic experts considered that Donnelly did not understand the basic rules of cryptography, that he was seeking an arithmetic cipher far too unsophisticated for the Shakespearian plays, and that his system was no system at all in that it provided an unacceptable latitude of choice to the decipherer.[53] Contemporary critics hostile to *The Great Cryptogram* quickly discerned that his "master key" fitted loosely and had no difficulty in parodying his work.[54]

Donnelly sailed for England immediately after completing *The Great Cryptogram*. He planned to visit fellow Baconians and to help the sale of his book through a series of lectures and debates. His many friendships, resulting from his Shakespeare-Bacon correspondence, made it possible for him to hope for a fair hearing in English literary circles.

On arrival in England, Donnelly went to Francis Bacon's home at St. Albans to see the "high tower" where Donnelly believed the cipher had been constructed.[55] Kate, having remained in Philadel-

[50] *Ibid.*, p. 890.

[51] Donnelly MSS, R. S. Peale to I. D., February 25, 1888; I. D. to R. S. Peale, February 29, 1888 (copy); I. D. to K. D., March 11, 1888; Diary, March 12, 1888.

[52] *Ibid.*, J. Medill to I. D., December 27, 1888.

[53] William F. and Elizabeth S. Friedman, *The Shakespearian Ciphers Examined* (Cambridge: At the University Press, 1957), pp. 5–37. The authors assume that Donnelly had a mathematical turn of mind which, of course, he did not. Numbers fascinated him, but he was essentially speculative, and nonquantitative in his thought processes.

[54] See Joseph G. Pyle, *The Little Cryptogram* (St. Paul: The Pioneer Press Co., 1888) and Aldwell Nicholson, *No Cipher in Shakespeare* (London: T. F. Unwin, 1888).

[55] Donnelly MSS, I. D. to K. D., March 29, 1888.

phia, received letters describing in detail the places he visited and his thoughts about them. After sightseeing in Westminster Abbey, Donnelly reacted with characteristic ambivalence. "The Abbey is a wonderful place! Nowhere else on earth is so much history and human greatness crowded together in so small a space. I shall never forget the start it gave me when I was contemplating the flat tombstone of Dr. Samuel Johnson, the poet, critic, and linguist . . . to glance down at my feet and find I was over all that was mortal of the author of *David Copperfield* and *Barnaby Rudge*. What a world of reflection rush over the mind at the mention of Charles Dickens." But Donnelly was quick to detect what he saw as injustice within Westminster Abbey. "And this is the trouble with the Abbey," Kate learned, "as it is with the world. Wealth (too often based on villainy) shoulders merit into a corner. Hence all that makes the Abbey respectable is condensed in what is called 'The Poets Corner.' "[56]

On April 17, 1888, Donnelly presented a lecture at Westminster Hall. Arrangements had been made by Mrs. Henry Potts, an active member of the Baconian Society and one of Donnelly's staunchest advocates. A dignified if not aristocratic audience had been invited to attend.[57] Almost nine hundred people, including such distinguished literary figures as Oscar Wilde, gathered to hear him explain the cipher rule. Sampson, Low & Company were enthusiastic after the meeting, confident that sales would increase following favorable newspaper accounts.[58] In the United States, the *Irish Standard* reported that Donnelly was being lionized at London's Westminster Hall, and quoted him as "enjoying the pleasures of modern Babylon." It noted, too, that he was being subjected to sharp adverse criticism. Donnelly doubted that he could convince John Bull of Bacon's authorship."[59]

As an American politician, keenly interested in the English legislative process, he visited the House of Commons where he saw Gladstone, who reminded him of little John Quincy Adams, largely bald, quick, keen, restless, and watchful. Not having seen Thomas Parnell since his Washington days, Donnelly was surprised at how greatly the orator had aged, but still remained "clear & cool in his utterances, self-balanced, self-controlled." The facilities of the House of Commons, entirely too primitive by American standards, disappointed Donnelly. "Plain long benches of oak or walnut with green

---

[56]*Ibid.*, I. D. to K. D., April 4, 1888.
[57]*Ibid.*, I. C. D. to K. D., April 14, 1888.
[58]*Ibid.*, I. D. to K. D., April 17, 1888.
[59]Minneapolis *Irish Standard*, April 21, 1888.

cushions," he noted, "a label with a number at [the] back, No division—no tables—nothing but a pocket on [the] back of the benches in front to stick papers into." He thought the method of voting "barbarian—going out into two rooms—[a] Chinese way of wasting time. Why not an electric arrangement," he asked; "take [a] vote in a minute with perfect accuracy." The little square hall with a scarcely visible ladies' gallery disappointed him as did the Members of Parliament themselves, who appeared "very much like a lot of school boys—hesitating, halting speech—some good heads, but no orators."[60]

At the House of Lords, Donnelly was the guest of the Earl of Aberdeen, whom he had met in the United States. The Earl "was very kind and affable," Donnelly later recorded, "he took me through the library into [the] House of Lords—a very handsome chamber." But Donnelly found the formal ritual involved in the passage of legislation an anachronism. "The Queen always consents," he quipped. "I am told she has never vetoed a bill. If she did the dynasty, it is said, would not last forty-eight hours." Donnelly, however, was somewhat premature when he concluded, in 1888, "It is all ancient forms and ceremonies with a republic underneath." When the Earl of Aberdeen brought him to the floor of the House of Lords for a full view, Donnelly good-humoredly noticed "the dismay of one usher when I got out of the line of procession, he felt the British Constitution was in danger."[61]

During the evening of May 31, Donnelly debated the authorship of the plays in the University Union at Oxford. He was "received by the students with a perfect storm of applause." Donnelly's son, who sat in the gallery, was amused watching the annoyance of some of the "Dons" or professors. "There was one not far from me," he reported to his mother, "who was thoroughly disgusted with the whole thing; yet could not help listening with rapt attention to everything that . . . [father] said."[62] When the audience was polled, as was the custom of the University, Donnelly had been routed 167 to 27. But at Cambridge, five days later, where he debated Professor Leese of Trinity College before an audience of more than five hundred, only 120 supported Leese, 101 indorsed Donnelly, and much to his pleasure, "nearly 300 were so bewildered that they refused to vote at all!"[63]

[60]Donnelly MSS, Diary, May 14, 1888.
[61]*Ibid.*, July 5, 1888.
[62]*Ibid.*, I. C. D. to K. D., June 9, 1888.
[63]*Ibid.*, J. Fearon to I. D., June 1, 1888; W. Smith to I. D., June 8, 1888; *The Cipher*, p. 357.

Never had the Baconians attained a more attentive hearing. Donnelly received invitations directed through Dr. R. M. Theobald, president of the Baconian Society, to visit many social and professional groups, including a dinner given by the distinguished Royal College of Surgeons. Even a few outstanding public figures, such as John Bright, openly accepted *The Great Cryptogram*.[64] When the London *Literary World* devoted a full page to the book without a sneer or a distortion, Donnelly believed that "the thick clouds are beginning to break."[65]

He had anticipated that *The Great Cryptogram* would encounter intense opposition in England. Markedly different from his usually sensitive and impetuous reaction to unfavorable comments was his genuine tolerance of the first criticism leveled against him. "I expect a good deal of abuse," he informed Kate; "it is like drawing a man's back teeth when he thinks they are sound, to ask him to give up his prejudices."[66] But as the criticism in both England and America grew increasingly personal, Donnelly lashed out at what he felt were unfair, irrational, and abusive attacks upon him.[67] Quite familiar with his vituperative rejoinders, Kate warned him to focus his replies on the issues and, above all, avoid personal comments. When he ignored her injunctions, she wrote, "I am sorry whenever I see anything you write that is too decidedly vicious as to your critics. You must remember," she added, "that you were years making up your mind positively & you, I may say, have taken the world's belief by storm and want it to bow down at once to your opinion."[68]

Despondent over the apparent rejection of his book and the depressing London weather, Donnelly cursed his fate. "I had hoped that the ill fortune which had pursued me for twenty years—since 1868—would have lifted and left me," he confided to his diary, "but my book is a failure; and my political prospects are dark for there is no hope for a poor man accomplishing anything among the base & sordid politicians of Minnesota. It would seem as if my hopes rose high only to be crushed." Even the thought of his contemplated trip to Ireland did not stimulate or encourage him. "I go disheartened in the midst of wretched weather—cold, raw, and continually raining, to visit the poor oppressed, God-forsaken land of my ancestors,

[64] Donnelly MSS, Dr. Squire to I. D., June 26, 1888; A. Skirrow to I. D., June 15, 1888.
[65] *Ibid.*, Diary, May 17, 1888.
[66] *Ibid.*, I. D. to K. D., April 28, 1888.
[67] Minneapolis *Irish Standard*, June 23, 1888.
[68] Donnelly MSS, K. D. to I. D., May 24, July 25, 1888.

where the Pope has joined with the Orangemen to keep the miserable inhabitants in continued misery." He could "take no pride, no
pleasure in the visit. I shall behold the spot where the people of my
blood, my ancestors, for generations led lives of savages and peas-
ants, in mud hovels, without comfort, pleasure or enlightenment;
and I shall feel that the curse which overshadowed them has descended upon their representative, and that despite profound
thoughts and superhuman industry I can make no headway toward
fortune." Ireland was an "accursed land" with an "accursed people."
He even dreaded the thought of returning to the United States, "a
land where nearly every newspaper has a sneer or insult for me;
where the rich are growing richer and the poor poorer; where
corporations and capitalists are grinding the face of labor; where the
sum of human misery is increasing every day;—and God looks on
and permits it all." He had longed for an opportunity to right the
wrongs of the past decades. "With wealth," he lamented, "I could
have done something for mankind; but my book is howled down by
a corrupt press; I am poor and powerless:—I can only grind my
teeth and cry to heaven."[69]

Despite his despair, Donnelly enjoyed his trip to Ireland. On the
way he visited the Scottish home of the poet Robert Burns, and
later he overcame his gloom long enough to praise the United States
to his Irish relatives. But he was eager to leave the British Isles and
be free from rain and fog. "I wouldn't give Minnesota for the whole
British Empire," he had written Kate months earlier. "Thank God
for Columbus and the land of sunshine."[70] Preparing to sail aboard
the "Umbria," Donnelly, once again an Irish-American Anglophobe,
expressed his relief that he would "soon leave this prejudiced,
bigotted, class-ridden, semi-aquatic country."[71]

Although *The Great Cryptogram* failed to sell, Peale was still
willing to push the book in the market. He was certain that the
author could do more to sell it to potential buyers than anyone else.

[69]*Ibid.*, Diary, July 15, 1888. It is worth noting the extent to which Donnelly
denounced the papacy for "selling out" Ireland in the hope of re-establishing
Roman Catholicism in England. The Irish "are the last remnant of the human
race that clings to the Popedom with unshaken and unquestioning faith; and
he would trade off those who love him to the Tories of England in the hope
that he can buy back with their tears and misery Westminster Abbey and
St. Paul Cathedral. It is simply horrible. Fancy the Savior consigning the people of Nazareth to centuries of wretchedness that he might induce the High
Priest to let him preach in the Temple of Jerusalem!"
[70]*Ibid.*, I. D. to K. D., May 4, 1888.
[71]*Ibid.*, I. D. to K. D., August 2, 1888.

"I believe you have got to start out as Christ did with his Apostles," Peale insisted, "and spread the thing throughout the country by your personality. You be Christ, & I'll furnish the apostles." Since the newspaper criticism had hurt the book, only a lecture series defending it could produce a market.[72]

When Donnelly returned from Europe, Peale conceded that interest in the book had died out. The publisher retained his faith that Donnelly would "receive justice" and that the book would be ranked "where it belongs, among the wonders of the world," but he was hopeful that Donnelly would produce a plan to increase sales. "I am not going to do any *squealing* because it was not a success. I went into it with a good deal of faith, & my faith grew as we went along, until the long delay occurred in bringing the book out," he wrote. "However, I am willing to stand by our original contract, which leaves me in the hole just $8194.37." But this did not include Donnelly's personal note for $4,000 which had been paid as advance royalties.[73] The publisher, who grew steadily more pessimistic, by January, 1889, saw no hope for the book unless Donnelly took to the lecture circuit and canvassed the country. He offered Donnelly the chance to buy the plates, stock, and copyright.[74]

In England, however, the debate stirred by *The Great Cryptogram* continued in the columns of the *Literary World*.[75] Answering his critics with letters to the editor, Donnelly reviewed the books of his reviewers. He unsuccessfully urged the Earl of Verulam, the heir to Bacon's estate, to grant permission to sink a "hole two feet square and six feet deep," convinced that important Baconian manuscripts had been secreted away in a manner disclosed in the cipher story.[76] As the months passed, and no forceful literary person undertook to defend and expand on Donnelly's position, interest waned.

Donnelly refused to concede that *The Great Cryptogram* was dead. He had always doubted Peale's bookkeeping accounts of the sales, even to the extent of employing the Pinkerton Agency to check on the publisher's agents, records, and staff.[77] When Peale suggested that the book be dumped at cost to a book syndicate, Donnelly refused to agree and charged him with misrepresenting

[72]*Ibid.*, R. S. Peale to I. D., May 23, 1888; F. J. Schulte to I. D., August 8, 1888.

[73]*Ibid.*, R. S. Peale to I. D., September 17, 1888.

[74]*Ibid.*, R. S. Peale to I. D., January 29, 1889.

[75]January 11, 1889.

[76]Donnelly MSS, I. D. to Earl of Verulam, February 15, 1889; I. D. to Raylor, Hoare & Rox, April 29, 1893.

[77]*Ibid.*, I. D. to K. D., May, 1888.

the subscription method. The polite correspondence between Donnelly and Peale ceased. Peale wanted Donnelly to repay his loan; Donnelly wanted possession of *The Great Cryptogram*.[78]

When Donnelly refused to allow Peale to discount the book, when he made no effort to repay his loan, and when he continued to denounce Peale as misrepresenting the subscription method of selling books, the publisher angrily wrote Donnelly: "Before I took your book, I questioned you on the one point on which the sale of the book would depend. That point was, as to the INTRICACY of the cipher. You stated that it would be so plain and simple that a CHILD would understand it. Those," Peale insisted, "were your precise words. Now what were the facts—The most learned mathematician in all Chicago, after spending six weeks in study, was obliged to interview you personally before HE could understand it."[79]

Crimination and recrimination led Peale to sue Donnelly for nonpayment of his debt. Donnelly entered a countersuit for breach of contract, but the publicity was humiliating. "There it was in the paper with headlines & caricature—my enemies rejoicing," Donnelly wrote in his diary, "I cursed the evil spirits that are pursuing me & swore at the damnable subtlety of Francis Bacon which . . . covered me with ignominy."[80] To settle the Peale obligation, Donnelly traded the publisher St. Paul city lots in exchange for the plates for the book. Morbidly, he noted, "I will . . . put them in my garden, and build a little house to cover them. . . . The little building will be my monument of colossal failure." "Everytime I look at it," he concluded bitterly, "I shall think of wrecked hopes and ruined ambitions."[81]

Although *The Great Cryptogram* had not sold widely, it attracted so much attention that Donnelly was in demand as a lecturer. In the autumn of 1889, he joined Reverend William L. Davidson on the Chautauqua circuit and sought to use *The Great Cryptogram* as a study text.[82] In 1891, Donnelly had a series of debates scheduled with Professor J. C. Freeman of Wisconsin. Although Donnelly disliked Freeman and thought him a conceited prig, he could not afford to ignore the offer of a hundred-dollar-a-night fee with the

[78]*Ibid.*, R. S. Peale to I. D., May 25, 1889; I. D. to R. S. Peale, May 28, 1889; R. S. Peale to I. D., June 11, 1889.

[79]*Ibid.*, R. S. Peale to I. D., December 5, 1890.

[80]*Ibid.*, Diary, May 18, 1892.

[81]*Ibid.*, December 22, 1892.

[82]*Ibid.*, W. L. Davidson to I. D., August 7, 1889; R. S. Peale to I. D., August 27, 1889; I. D. to W. L. Davidson, September 4, 1889.

opportunity for an unlimited number of engagements.[83] Despite the bold, aggressive, and engaging appearance which Donnelly presented to his audiences, the nature of professional debating distressed him. His opponent's jokes about the cipher "made chits for the girls and the addle-pated business men laughed." Angrily and in self-pity, he denounced his own role in life. "To be made the laughing stock of school-girls! I feel like Falstaff, when he threatened to take his brains out and butter them and feed them to a dog for his breakfast."[84]

The failure of *The Great Cryptogram* left Donnelly feeling angry and afflicted, but it did not destroy his faith that a cipher existed. "I stand astounded before the stupidity of mankind," he wrote in 1890 of the world's rejection of his work.[85] "I wish there were two of me," he once wrote, "so that one could attend to politics while the other worked out the Baconian cipher."[86] In his available free time, he continued to labor at the cipher, determined to vindicate himself in the eyes of the literary world. It was his great fear, he confessed, that because "the full cipher rule eludes me and I may never be able to convince the world that I am right . . . [that I] will go to the grave ridiculed and despised. . . ."[87]

In 1899, in the waning years of his life, Donnelly privately printed *The Cipher in the Plays and on the Tombstone,* his final contribution to the Bacon-Shakespeare argument. It analyzed the inscription on Shakespeare's tombstone, applied the cipher rule to some portions of the sonnets, turned again to the plays, and ended with the assertion that the Rosicrucian Society had been charged with keeping the secret of the cipher and of Bacon's authorship. Viewed as the work of a crank, it was stillborn as it came from the presses. The literary public, determinedly skeptical, rejected Donnelly's hypothesis of a secret conspiracy and ignored his plea "to patiently advance through the thistles and cockle-burrs, and help us settle the great, and enduring controversy, as to whether the immortal plays were written by the play-actor of Stratford, or the greatest intellect that ever appeared on this theater of human action—the transcendent Francis Bacon."[88]

[88] *Ibid.,* J. Freeman to I. D., March 23, 1891; J. Shearer to I. D., April 13, 1891.

[84] *Ibid.,* Diary, April 28, 1891.

[85] *Ibid.,* section on bills and notes, 1890.

[86] *Ibid.,* Diary, November 7, 1890.

[87] *Ibid.,* December 22, 1892.

[88] *The Cipher,* Preface.

THE GREAT CRYPTOGRAM:

FRANCIS BACON'S CIPHER in The SO-CALLED SHAKESPEARE PLAYS.

By IGNATIUS DONNELLY, Author of "Atlantis: The Antediluvian World," and "Ragnarök: The Age of Fire and Gravel."

"And now I will vnclaspe a Secret booke
And to your quicke conceyuing Discontents
Ile reade you Matter, deepe and dangerous,
As full of perill and aduenturous Spirit,
As to o'er-walke a Current, roaring loud,
On the vnstedfast footing of a Speare."
1st Henry IV., Act I, Sc. 3.

·Chicago;
·New York and London·
R. S. Peale & Company.
1888.

The title page of *The Great Cryptogram*. (San Diego State College Audio-Visual Services.)

A page of the 1623 Shakespeare folio, showing Donnelly's work in deriving the cipher. (San Diego State College Audio-Visual Services.)

CHAPTER XV

The Farmers' Alliance
1885-1888

*There are really but two parties in this state today—
the people and their plunderers. The only issue is:
Shall the people keep the fruits of their own industry
or shall the thieves carry them away?*

IGNATIUS DONNELLY

WHEN Milton George, editor of Chicago's *Western Rural*, announced that the Minnesota chapters of the National Farmers' Alliance would hold their initial convention at Rochester, Minnesota, on
December 8, 1881, no one anticipated significant results. Minnesota
farmers were enjoying almost unprecedented prosperity. The Alliance, which stressed class action on the part of the farmers against
concentrated capital and monopoly, appeared to be as outdated as
the defunct Grange. The Rochester meeting brought delegates from
the eighty chapters who lived in more than a score of Minnesota
counties.[1]

The Alliance grew very slowly, barely doubling the number of its
chapters during its first three years. But in 1884, as Minnesota's
wheat prices declined sharply to their lowest levels since 1869, as
investment money sought regions paying higher returns, and as
farm critics began discussing the need for diversification in the
wheat belt, many farmers turned again to political action. Believing

[1]John D. Hicks, "The Origin and Early History of the Farmers' Alliance in
Minnesota," *Mississippi Valley Historical Review*, IX (1922), 204; *The Great
West*, February 14, 1890.

as they had in Granger days that food handlers were taking the lion's share of the market price of the commodity, they were eager to reduce the cost of transportation, storage, and marketing. The Alliance, committed to a policy of political action for the farmers' benefit, suddenly became a vital organization. Despite the dedication of its members and the principles which it had advocated, the Alliance lacked both effective leadership and a specific program. Consequently, the organization turned to Ignatius Donnelly for leadership.

More than any other public figure in Minnesota, he was identified with the agrarian cause. As one Alliance member wrote, pleading with him to attend their annual convention in 1884: "Farmers in this state need your abilities."[2] When Donnelly joined the Alliance, although he was reluctant to lead it politically because he was still smarting from the debacle of his 1880 contested election, the Alliance chapters eagerly indorsed him for Congress against Strait in the Third District. Even after his defeat, influential Alliance leaders asked that he associate himself with the organization. "The farmers will not be satisfied without a speech from you at the [annual] meeting," Donnelly learned from state Alliance secretary George Haigh, "but it is your large experience in legislative affairs that we desire at this time."[3]

The Minnesota Alliance convened in St. Paul in early February, 1885, obviously to coincide with the state legislative session. Donnelly participated actively in the discussions, and presented the keynote speech. He denounced the "Millers' Ring" and urged the Alliance to press for legislation which would declare combinations such as the Millers' Association to be in restraint of trade. Something was wrong with Minnesota's marketing system, he insisted, when a farmer could haul wheat by wagon into Canada and make a larger profit than by selling it at his local grain elevator. Reminding his listeners that the Alliance was nonpartisan, he recommended seeking candidates who would serve the producers' cause. During the legislative session, he represented the Alliance before committees considering railroad and warehouse bills.[4] As a result several Alliance-sponsored measures were enacted by the legislature.[5]

[2]Donnelly MSS, L. Loring to I. D., March 9, 1884.

[3]*Ibid.*, G. Haigh to I. D., January 25, 1885.

[4]St. Paul *Pioneer Press*, February 5, 6, 1885; St. Paul *Globe*, February 6, 1885.

[5]Donald F. Warner, "Prelude to Populism," *Minnesota History*, XXXII (1951), 130.

The Alliance gained new members during 1885 as a result of successful lobbying and the steady decline of the farmers' economic status. By February, 1886, the St. Paul *Pioneer Press*, taking cognizance of the increased prominence of the Alliance not only within Minnesota but also throughout the country, noted that it was evidently an attempt to establish a third party representing agricultural interests. The coming annual meeting of the Alliance, the *Pioneer Press* predicted, "promises to be one of the most important and interesting that has ever been held."[6]

Donnelly arrived in Minneapolis to attend the 1886 Alliance convention shortly after he had suffered his patronage defeat at the hands of Minnesota's conservative Democrats. Despite his political impotence, the convention selected him to draft the Alliance program. Presented with an exceptional opportunity to serve as the recognized spokesman for the organization, his report, dramatically delivered, expressed views as much his own as the Alliance's. Donnelly's resolutions urged that the Alliance remain political but nonpartisan, that it continue to indorse means and measures but not parties. There were only two real parties, the plundered and the plunderers, and the Alliance should seek the support of all labor in its quest for social justice. For a state legislative program he proposed closer grain inspection, elected railroad and dairy commissioners, a maximum annual interest rate of 8 per cent, and the passage of a law declaring it a felony for a judge to accept favors from railroads. Donnelly suggested as a national program the Alliance advocate a tariff for revenue, bimetallism, a shorter lifetime for agricultural machinery patents, the operation of the railroads at a fair profit, and federally financed agricultural experiment stations and institutes. When he finished his speech, the Alliance members, eagerly accepted his proposals just as they were presented.[7]

The St. Paul *Pioneer Press* solemnly declared that he had devoured the Alliance, having taken "it by storm with a dazzling display of skyrockets and Roman Candles."[8] The paper contended that he was using the Alliance to gain public office, possibly the governorship. Two weeks later at an Alliance rally at Herman, Minnesota, Donnelly took time in his speech to respond to the charge. "The newspapers are concentrating their fire upon . . . [me] just as they

[6]St. Paul *Pioneer Press*, February 23, 1886.
[7]Minneapolis *Tribune*, February 26, 1886; St. Paul *Pioneer Press*, February 23, 26, 1886.
[8]St. Paul *Pioneer Press*, February 27, 1886.

did in the old Grange days," he observed. "I ask nothing of the association but the privilege of advocating its principles. The members
of the Alliance are not responsible for me, nor I for them," he insisted. "I work with them simply because they are working for the
people. When they cease to do so, I will leave them." Then he concluded, "No man or organization owns me. I will think my own
thoughts, and . . . it is not in the power of the newspapers, rings or
railroads to deny me a hearing."[9] The *Pioneer Press* grudgingly admitted that Donnelly was serving the Alliance, but it refused to
acknowledge that he had prevented the immediate formation of a
Farmer-Labor party through a union of the Alliance with the Minnesota Knights of Labor.[10]

In the early summer of 1886 a group of anti-Bourbon Democrats
met in St. Paul to discuss plans to replace Kelly and Doran as the
party's Minnesota leaders. Donnelly suggested that they assume a
strong anti-monopoly position and associate themselves with the
Farmers' Alliance. He was convinced that a combination of Republican farmers and the reform Democrats could sweep the state and
enact significant legislation. All the politicians present agreed that
the Democratic party in Minnesota would fail, even supported by
federal patronage, if Kelly, Doran, and Hill retained control. Against
Donnelly's advice, they summoned a mass meeting for July 1.[11]

Although more than five hundred invitations were extended,
scarcely more than one hundred Democrats attended the July 1 conference. Aside from Donnelly, Dr. Albert A. Ames of Minneapolis
was the only well-known politician present. In a lively speech, Donnelly attacked Kelly and Doran for their crude patronage policies
but reminded his listeners that they had not come "to make war on
two insignificant men." The genuine question was, "Shall the government be run in the interests of Jim Hill and the railroads, or in
the interest of the people?" Manipulators and political bosses, he insisted, had to be driven out. When Donnelly proposed Ames as a
possible gubernatorial candidate, he was greeted with a storm of applause. The meeting adjourned, its members determined to capture
control of the Democratic party at its September convention.[12]

Following the July conference, the conservative Democrats tried

[9]*Ibid.*, March 19, 1886.
[10]*Ibid.*, May 26, 27, 1886; Donnelly MSS, Diary, May 25, 1886.
[11]St. Paul *Pioneer Press*, June 11, 1886; St. Paul *Globe*, June 11, 1886.
[12]St. Paul *Pioneer Press*, July 2, 1886.

to make peace with Donnelly. Judge Lars M. Rand of Minneapolis, chairman of the state Democratic platform committee, asked him to draft in secret a platform for the fall convention.[13] "It seems to me," Donnelly replied, "that it would not be right for me to prepare even secretly a platform for the next Dem[ocratic] St[ate] Conven[tion] until I know what the complexion of that body is to be. . . . I will not be used as an instrument to transfer the people to the power of Jim Hill." With obvious sincerity, he concluded, "I have nothing in the world but my voice and my influence and I am resolved to use both for the benefit of my fellow men not for their injury."[14]

Throughout the summer Donnelly wrote to influential Democrats proposing that they join with him in ousting Kelly, Doran, and Hill. Without "these *incubi*," the party could combine with the Alliance and the Knights of Labor to govern the state. If the Alliance were forced "to choose between Republican thieves and Democratic thieves, they, being largely Republican, will prefer rascals of their own kidney."[15] He appealed by circular to the rank and file Democrats too. "The time has come," he wrote, "when the Democrats of Minnesota will be called upon to decide . . . between the few who seek to grasp all the power and wealth, and the many who seek to preserve their rights as American citizens and freemen."[16]

During the late spring and summer while Donnelly endeavored to unseat the Bourbon Democratic leadership, he was the key liaison between the Alliance and the Minnesota Knights of Labor.[17] The Knights had entered Minnesota city politics with an amazing display of strength and unity in 1885. By 1886 even the *Pioneer Press* conceded that the union was making significant inroads among the older parties in both the large cities and small towns of the state.[18] On September 1, 1886, at a meeting of the officers of the Alliance and the Knights of Labor, a sharp cleavage developed between the two groups. The Alliance officials favored establishing a third party which would nominate a coalition Republican and Democratic slate. The Knights, confident that Ames would secure the Democratic nomination, wanted to indorse the Democratic party. It was finally agreed that a committee led by Donnelly and J. M. McGaughey of

[13] Donnelly MSS, L. Rand to I. D., July 19, 1886.
[14] *Ibid.*, I. D. to L. Rand, July 20, 1886 (copy).
[15] *Ibid.*, I. D. to J. L. MacDonald, August 12, 1886 (copy).
[16] *Ibid.*, Diary, August 20, 1886 (pasted into Diary).
[17] *Ibid.*, C. Canning to I. D., April 24, 1886.
[18] St. Paul *Pioneer Press*, February 24, 1886.

the Knights of Labor would present a program to both party conventions and indorse the party which accepted their demands.[19]

The following day, Judge Thomas Wilson of Winona invited Donnelly to visit him at the Ryan Hotel in St. Paul to discuss a reconciliation between Donnelly and the Doran-Kelly faction. Wilson argued with him for three hours, but Donnelly refused. "He pressed me hard," Donnelly noted in his diary. His only condition, Donnelly insisted, was the removal of Doran.[20] Wilson spent several days seeking Doran and trying to convince him that some compromise was necessary to save the party. Doran, however, must have issued a counter ultimatum. Wilson once more urged Donnelly to yield, an act, he felt, that Donnelly would never regret.[21]

On the eve of the Democratic primary elections, Dr. Albert A. Ames deserted Donnelly and the reform Democrats to support Doran and Kelly. His defection confirmed Bourbon domination of Minnesota's Democratic party for at least two years. Thoroughly disgusted with Ames' deceit and corruption, Kate reiterated her pleas to Ignatius to "drop politics." "You are wasting precious time with scoundrels," she wrote; "the time is corrupt—there is no virtue."[22] Donnelly, however, was determined to fight Hill, even after the conservatives captured the Democratic Dakota County caucus and prevented his attending the convention as a delegate.

Nevertheless, he went to the Democratic convention to present the joint resolution of the Alliance and the Knights. When he approached the platform, following J. M. McGaughey of the Knights, the chairman angrily lashed out, "We are willing to listen to the representative of the Knights of Labor, but no sneak can come in under his cover." The delegates jeered and Donnelly, unable to speak, left the hall. "Such a humiliation has never before been witnessed in any public place in the Northwest," commented the *Pioneer Press*.[23] With Donnelly absent, McGaughey presented the Alliance-Knights program, which was accepted by the convention. The convention then nominated Ames for governor amid great enthusiasm. "The saloon element & railroads are triumphant," Donnelly despondently recorded, "and my star sets behind a huge black cloud."[24]

But two days later he resumed the offensive. In an interview for

---

[19] *Ibid.*, September 2, 1886.
[20] Donnelly MSS, Diary, September 2, 1886.
[21] *Ibid.*, T. Wilson to I. D., September 3, 6, 1886.
[22] *Ibid.*, K. D. to I. D., September 8, 1886.
[23] St. Paul *Pioneer Press*, September 14, 18, 1886.
[24] Donnelly MSS, Diary, September 14, 1886.

the St. Paul *Globe,* he struck back at Ames. He "came to my room at the Merchants Hotel at St. Paul and asked me to take the stump for him if he ran for governor. I told him . . . I would agree to do so . . . [but] he was to declare against bossism . . . he has failed to live up to the agreement."[25] Furthermore, Donnelly predicted that the Alliance and the Knights would support the Republicans if their convention accepted the joint program.

The Republicans, eager for votes but not for ideas, gave Donnelly a polite hearing when he presented the Alliance-Knights proposals. The chairman was somewhat rude in chuckling audibly as Donnelly denounced the railroads, but the delegates accepted the resolutions. The Republican convention thus indorsed a reduced interest rate, extensive railroad regulation, the elimination of child labor, and state industrial safety legislation. With the exception of the temperance question—the Democrats opposing all sumptuary laws and the Republicans indorsing high license fees—both political parties in Minnesota had virtually identical platforms in 1886.

The following day a conference of the Alliance and the Knights of Labor wrangled over which party to indorse. The Knights, their strength among city workers, favored Ames. The Alliancemen, except those living in areas where a fusion with the Democrats would give them power, wanted to indorse the Republican nominee, Andrew Ryan McGill.[26] There was an urban-rural division among the reformers. In the past, Donnelly had served as the nexus between the two groups, but because of his distrust of the Democrats and his dislike of Ames, he sided with the Republican Alliancemen.

He returned to Nininger to work on *The Great Cryptogram.* Democratic Judge J. L. MacDonald attempted to reconcile Donnelly and Ames, but Donnelly refused.[27] When the Republicans offered Donnelly $100 for each speech he would make in support of McGill and their ticket, Donnelly spurned the proposal.[28] He was going to finish his book.

Without his knowledge or consent a group of Alliance members in his district, four-fifths of whom were Republicans, organized a People's party and nominated him for the lower house of the state legislature. But C. P. Carpenter, who edited the Dakota County *Tribune,*

[25] St. Paul *Globe,* September 17, 1886.

[26] St. Paul *Pioneer Press,* September 24, 1886.

[27] Donnelly MSS, J. L. MacDonald to I. D., September 30, 1886 (endorsement).

[28] *Ibid.,* I. D. to A. R. McGill, October 5, 1886; Diary, October 14, 1886.

warned that the nomination might be an effort to "kill him off."[29] When it was rumored that the railroads were determined to defeat him by spending money, sending political organizers into the district, and arranging to send several hundred railroad laborers into West St. Paul to vote against him, Donnelly decided to wage a real campaign. He sought assurances from former Governor John S. Pillsbury, who was directing the Republican State Central Committee, that they would try to prevent the "running" of railroad hands into West St. Paul.[30] Donnelly held two large meetings and spoke at every schoolhouse where he could find an audience.

On election day, he went to West St. Paul and challenged the residency of every railroad worker who wanted to vote. When the laborers grew turbulent, Donnelly, supported by both of his sons who were armed with pistols, "shut them out." "It is a small office," he admitted, "but a great victory." He was deeply touched to learn that almost seven out of eight voters in Nininger and more than two out of three in Hastings indorsed him. "I am proud to think," he wrote warmly in his diary, "I stand so well among the people I have lived with for 30 years."[31]

The *Pioneer Press*, always amazed at Donnelly's political resilience, acknowledged that "it would take a universal cataclysm to keep Donnelly under."[32] But an Alliance paper observed: "Get the mops ready. Ignatius Donnelly was elected to legislature by a majority of about 800. You can almost hear the water drip as he squeezes it out of railroad stock."[33]

Minnesota Republicans elected McGill governor by less than 1 per cent of the popular vote, but lost three of the state's congressional seats. The temperance issue, Cleveland's use of patronage, and the defection of Republican Alliancemen had virtually upset the Republican hegemony. Almost every member of the Minnesota legislature was committed to enact the program which Donnelly forged at the Alliance-Knights of Labor conference. In a friendly letter of congratulation to Andrew McGill, Donnelly cautioned the governor that the Democrats "would sweep the state in 1888" if the Republican party's platform promises were not fulfilled.[34]

[29]*Ibid.*, C. Carpenter to I. D., October 11, 1886.

[30]*Ibid.*, J. S. Pillsbury to I. D., October 25, 1886; I. C. D. to I. D., October 27, 1886.

[31]*Ibid.*, Diary, November 3, 1886.

[32]St. Paul *Pioneer Press*, November 5, 1886.

[33]Fergus Falls *Journal*, November, 1886.

[34]McGill MSS, I. D. to A. R. McGill, November 8, 1886.

In mid-November, Donnelly sent a circular to all the farmers who had been elected to the Minnesota lower house inviting them to attend a pre-session meeting to discuss a legislative program. "I am not a candidate for any office," he stressed; "my constituents, however, expect *me* to do something for their relief this winter, and I am well aware that individually I am like any other member, powerless. It is only by a cordial union," he reminded them, ". . . and only by massing *our* votes . . . that *we* can obtain such reasonable and just legislation as *we* have a right to ask."[35] Through T. H. Lucas who represented the Knights of Labor element in the legislature, Donnelly was promised co-operation during the session. He was assured that their support for Ames went no further than the election.[36] Alliance President George W. Sprague disappointed Donnelly by summoning an executive committee meeting after the legislative session began. Because Sprague's action made formulating a legislative program difficult, Donnelly charged that he was "locking [the] stable door after [the] horse is stolen. The Alliance might as well dissolve," he told Sprague, "if it purposes to abdicate its function in that way."[37]

Shortly thereafter, Donnelly wrote Governor McGill concerning the role of the Alliance in political appointments dealing with agriculture and pointed out that there were two elements in the Alliance, one led by Sprague which was hostile to McGill and the other led by State Lecturer T. C. Hodgson which was friendly. Donnelly was hopeful that McGill would recognize the vital interest of the Republican Alliance and labor men by favorable appointments or at least consultation.[38]

At the pre-session caucus of a hundred farm legislators which Donnelly had scheduled, he made a plea for unity of purpose, but refused to assume leadership. The St. Paul *Globe,* which had suggested that he was seeking the United States senatorship, and the St. Paul *Pioneer Press,* which had alleged that he was building his own private party so that he could be elected Speaker of the House, were surprised by his silence.[39] They were even more startled when Donnelly appeared at the Republican caucus explaining that the Republicans in his district had indorsed him. He voted in favor of

[35]Donnelly MSS, November 15, 1886, circular.
[36]*Ibid.,* J. Lamb to I. D., December 7, 1886.
[37]*Ibid.,* G. Sprague to I. D., December 20, 1886 (indorsement).
[38]McGill MSS, I. D. to A. R. McGill, December 29, 1886.
[39]St. Paul *Pioneer Press,* December 15, 1886, June 5, 1887; St. Paul *Globe,* December 15, 1886.

Cushman K. Davis, who was elected senator.[40] Donnelly also supported Republican William R. Merriam for Speaker of the House
and may have won his membership in the House Railroad, Judiciary,
and Grain committees because of this indorsement.

Although keenly aware that his influence in the legislature was
sharply limited by the division within the Alliance, his bitter clash
with the Democrats, and the deep-seated distrust of him felt by
many Republicans, he decided to fight for the reform program that
he had succeeded in placing before the voters. His first move was to
insist that the house members fulfil their platform pledges by passing a resolution petitioning Congress to approve an interstate commerce law.[41] This was practically the only proposal he urged that
passed without acrimonious debate. An anti-usury law, which had
been included in both party platforms, encountered fierce opposition. Conservative legislators echoed the cries of the *Pioneer Press*
that it would drive capital out of the state. Although Donnelly
squeezed the measure through the lower house, reminding the members of the farmers' plight, it was defeated in the senate.[42] When
Donnelly introduced a "clean elections law" calling for the registration of resident voters thirty days before the election and the Australian or secret ballot to prevent bribery and intimidation, even
though no one dared oppose it publicly, the bill was amended—his
opponents alleging that it was too complicated to implement. In its
altered form the bill was rejected.[43]

His successes were few. After a heated debate regarding punishment for conspiracy, he did manage to secure passage of the free
market bill which declared market-controlling combinations such as
the Minneapolis Millers' Association to be in restraint of trade. The
Pioneer Press accused him of playing rural against urban votes to
pass the bill.[44] Ironically it reversed the charge when Donnelly
sought employer liability legislation as a means of gaining safer
working conditions.

Since Donnelly was now particularly hostile to the railroads, he
introduced a severe regulation measure. It would have granted special shipping privileges to Minnesota grain producers. The severity
of the bill engendered immediate opposition. Fearful of an open

[40]St. Paul *Pioneer Press*, January 7, 1887.
[41]*Ibid.*, January 12, 1887.
[42]*Ibid.*, January 14, 26, February 3, March 3, 1887.
[43]*Ibid.*, January 20, February 1, March 6, 1887.
[44]*Ibid.*, January 14, 21, March 1, 1887.

fight, conservative members attempted to kill Donnelly's bill by sending it back to committee while he was out to lunch. When this ruse failed, a substitute measure was introduced.[45] To defend the substitute bill, house members charged that Donnelly's bill was "too broad Granger." They attacked Donnelly personally as seeking "all the glory of railroad legislation," and asserted that he had the idea no bill could pass without his approval. They claimed they had "to sit down on Donnelly" to pass legislation.[46] But the arguments died away when Donnelly, angered to "white heat," alleged that a house member had been "offered $250 to vote against my bill, and $250 more to vote for the substitute"; he demanded an investigation.[47]

Although the house could not deny his request, it debated the substitute measure. Donnelly reminded the members of the platform pledges which called for genuine regulation. "This ought to be called Jim Hill's legislature," he blared when passage of the substitute bill seemed inevitable. "I have been called a leader in this House," he replied to the charge that he had tried to dominate the legislature, "and during the past few days the newspapers have had a good deal to say about Donnelly's downfall. I never tried to be a leader. . . . I am here simply to look after the interests of the farmers," and he concluded, "I have no doubt that by simple neglect of duty I could have lined my pockets and gone home a richer man."[48]

Two days later the investigating committee presented sworn testimony with no denial of the fact that one member of the house had offered money to another to defeat Donnelly's bill. Despite a concerted effort to prevent the publication of the document, the report was printed. The house, however, refused to act against its members. Obviously, to impugn two members meant admitting the truth of Donnelly's charges against the majority. In an almost absurd commentary on the house's failure to accept the report, the St. Paul *Pioneer Press* concluded that the bribery charge had broken Donnelly's power in the legislature.[49]

During the difficult 1887 legislative session, Donnelly had used his limited influence as effectively as possible to enact the Alliance–Knights of Labor program. He talked, perhaps too long and too vigorously, but he avoided pet schemes and radical measures. He intro-

[45] *Ibid.*, February 3, 9, 10, 1887.
[46] Donnelly MSS, A. H. Baker to C. Lightbourne, February 22, 1887.
[47] St. Paul *Pioneer Press*, February 17, 1887.
[48] *Ibid.*, February 19, 24, 1887.
[49] *Ibid.*, February 26, 27, 1887. The defense argued feebly that it was a joke, but did not deny that the actual words had been stated.

duced only fifty-seven bills in a chamber that usually concerned itself with more than two thousand measures. Eighteen of his suggested laws were accepted entirely or in an amended form.[50] The St. Paul *Globe*, in reviewing the legislative session, believed that he had been underrated. "The simple fact that a legislature wasted a whole session in attempting to bury one man . . . does not detract from the man's standing before the people. . . . There is a well-settled popular conviction that on the issues over which the legislature quarreled Mr. Donnelly was nearer right than the legislature." The editor was convinced Donnelly was more popular with the people than he had been before the legislature convened.[51]

Minneapolis labor leaders who formed a new Union Labor party invited Donnelly to attend their first convention to discuss the failure of labor's program in the session. Donnelly, however, was reluctant to associate himself with the party because it advocated the "single tax" policies of Henry George. A Union Labor party politician arguing that the party was not radical explained that "the only flag we will follow is the Star Spangled Banner and the issue we demand is tax reform."[52] But Donnelly, although he had read *Progress and Poverty* and had a high opinion of George's literary and logical powers, doubted his panacea. "So far as they relate to the concentration of vast quantities of land in the hands of the few as in Ireland and elsewhere they are clearly right, but so far as they may attack individual right to property in a piece of land as a farm or town lot," Donnelly was too much of a Jeffersonian to accept them. He paid unconscious homage to John Locke, when he asserted that George's ideas "strike at one of the fundamentals of society and civilization, the right of a man within proper limits, to enjoy the fruits of his own labor. If that is destroyed . . . the world relapses into barbarism."

Donnelly objected to the Union Labor party embracing the single tax because he felt it unwise for workingmen "to go into vast radical abstractions about reform of the total constitution of modern society. They should, without theorizing, use the instrumentalities around them for correcting abuses." Donnelly viewed labor as entitled to seven rights:

[50]*Ibid.*, February 4, 1887; John D. Hicks, "The Political Career of Ignatius Donnelly," *Mississippi Valley Historical Review*, VIII (1921), 110; Folwell, *Minnesota*, III, 174.

[51]St. Paul *Globe*, March 3, 1887.

[52]Donnelly MSS, C. Moeller to I. D., March 12, 1887; T. Lucas to I. D., March 18, 1887; C. Moeller to I. D., April 8, 1887.

The right to the full fruits of their labor.

The right to education & the broadest enlightenment.

The right to rise and go forward.

The right to acquire all forms of property, for property is comfort, peace, plenty, & civilization.

The right to obtain from this world all the blessings, benefits, and beauties there are in it.

The right to be esteemed gentleman even while he labors with his hands.

The right to combine to reach these results.

Impatiently he advised the labor leaders to "look around" and "study the situation" but "for heaven's sake leave abstractions alone." Whenever "any law, custom or class interferes with these rights . . . take possession of the ballot box . . . and reform one abuse after another until the last vestige of injustice is wiped out."[53]

In the summer and autumn of 1887, Donnelly struggled to finish *The Great Cryptogram*. The advance royalties gave him financial freedom at a trying time because insects had again ravaged his farms and he recorded that "for the first time in 25 years our granary has not a bushel of wheat in it."[54] He attended the Alliance convention in February, 1888, to suggest that the organization adopt an official newspaper, but his mind was on his forthcoming trip to England and he seemed to overlook the deepening chasm between the Alliance and the labor group.

A short time after Donnelly's departure for England, an executive committee of the Alliance indorsed a St. Paul banker, Albert Scheffer, for governor. The decision had been made without consultation with the Knights of Labor, which found itself faced with the choice of accepting the Alliance or acting alone. Scheffer's indorsement was the result of a feeling among Fifth District Alliancemen that the Republican party would be forced to nominate the banker or lose the election. Personally ambitious, Scheffer accepted the Alliance reform program and even the Democratic party's tariff and temperance position in the hope of winning the election. The actions of Scheffer and the Alliance were closely analyzed by Minnesota's influential politicians. "Have come to the conclusion that Alliance organization is certainly on [the] wane and not near as strong or numerous as has been generally supposed," John S. Pillsbury informed Henry Hastings Sibley. "Organization somewhat divided many who are want-

[53] *Ibid.*, I. D. to C. Moeller, April 9, 1887.
[54] *Ibid.*, Diary, December 31, 1887.

ing to secure political offices and care more for this than for good or
promotion of interest of agriculture. Organization particularly con-
fined to 5th District. . . . In South & Southwest portion of state
very little dissatisfaction." Pillsbury concluded by noting that it was
"almost certain that influence of these men [Fifth District Alliance
leaders] shall not increase as time for convening legislature ap-
proaches."[55]

Among the Knights of Labor, dissatisfaction with Scheffer's indorsement increased steadily. Eric Olson, editor of the St. Paul *Labor Echo,* who had served as a member of the Alliance executive
committee, objected to being overwhelmed on the Scheffer vote. By
midsummer many of Donnelly's close friends in the labor movement
started a "draft Donnelly" campaign. "You are the only man in the
State," wrote John Lamb from Minneapolis, "in whom the people
have confidence, and who is thoroughly known."[56] By late July, the
Labor Echo virtually indorsed Donnelly against Scheffer.

As Donnelly returned from England, his son, Stan, asked that he
stay out of politics in 1888 and suggested that "some other duck fight
forlorn hopes for the dear old farmer & laboring man."[57] Kate supported her son's plea that Ignatius "not be dragged into any third or
fourth party." Since she knew her husband believed that Harrison
would defeat Cleveland for the presidency, Kate thought he should
campaign for the Republican ticket outside Minnesota.[58] But there
were other reasons for Donnelly to remain with the Republicans. His
experiences in England had upset his views on free trade; he felt
labor needed protection in the form of a tariff. Furthermore, Kelly
and Doran still controlled the Democrats. To split the Republican
vote would give them control of the state.

Nevertheless, on his return Donnelly attended the Farmer Labor
party convention and accepted their gubernatorial nomination. Several years later, he was to argue that he had done so because he was
unaware of the actual political situation.[59] This may be true. More-

---

[55] Sibley MSS, April 6, 1888. Pillsbury and Sibley, who were members of the
Board of Regents of the University of Minnesota, were vitally concerned with
the Fifth District leadership because it had advocated separating the Agricultural College from the university. Although Donnelly favored experiment stations and sometimes felt the university was a bastion of reactionary academi-
cians, at this time he did not attack it. In 1887, Sibley asked Donnelly's aid
in passing the University's budget.
[56] Donnelly MSS, J. Lamb to I. D., July 10, 1888.
[57] *Ibid.,* S. D. to I. D., August [21], 1888.
[58] *Ibid.,* K. D. to I. D., August 21, 1888.
[59] St. Paul *The Great West,* August 19, 1892.

over, Eric Olson and the labor group may even have convinced him that reform's cause could best be served by defeating Scheffer. Possibly, as the *Pioneer Press* suggested, Donnelly was rarely able to ignore a nomination.[60] But there can be no doubt of his sincere intention to campaign. The Farmer Labor party leaders promised to raise a three-thousand-dollar war chest.

Perhaps as a result of Donnelly's nomination,[61] but more than likely because Republican leaders had spent huge sums of money organizing hundreds of political clubs and had shrewdly estimated the waning strength of the Alliance, they rejected Scheffer and nominated William R. Merriam.[62] Donnelly found the selection embarrassing.[63] In 1887, he had supported Merriam for Speaker of the House. Even though Merriam was a banker, he had indorsed Donnelly's usury bill and many other reform measures. He had the reputation of advocating honest, economical government. The pro-Scheffer Fifth District Alliance leaders indorsed Democrat Eugene Wilson, the Kelly-Doran candidate.

The Republicans put pressure on Donnelly, hopeful that he would withdraw from the campaign. Congressman John Lind, having talked with Senator Cushman K. Davis and General Goff of the Republican National Committee, invited Donnelly to speak for Harrison in New York. If Harrison should win, "and your assistance would further our chances greatly, you would have the gratitude of the writer and both our Senators and the party generally," wrote Lind. "And in that event we will be in a position to see to it that your claims for recognition at the hands of the party will not be ignored." Lind closed with both an offer and plea saying that "whatever the result nationally you would still have the gratitude and good will of every Republican in our State. This would be pleasant at least and I hope of benefit to you in the future."[64] Lind's proposal was precisely what Kate Donnelly had hoped for. Donnelly would have been paid to campaign, and a Republican victory would have guaranteed a federal appointment.

"I am greatly obliged to you," Donnelly replied, "[but] I do not feel that I ought to leave Minnesota at this time. My duty is here, defending the people from the robberies of railroad corporations."

[60] St. Paul *Pioneer Press*, July 22, 1888.
[61] Warner, "Prelude to Populism," p. 133.
[62] St. Paul *Pioneer Press*, April 28, 1888; Sibley MSS, J. S. Pillsbury to H. H. Sibley, April 6, 1888.
[63] St. Paul *Pioneer Press*, September 6, 7, 1888.
[64] Donnelly MSS, J. Lind to I. D., September 21, 1888.

He had kindly feelings toward the Republican party, but he felt that it was "in the hands of men who will lead it to the devil. . . . I fear," he concluded, "the party can only be reformed from the outside."[65]

As Donnelly campaigned for governor, he had reason to reconsider his reply to Lind. The Farmer Labor party failed to raise sufficient funds to pay even the cost of printing its ballots. Although Donnelly received an excellent welcome, especially among labor groups, he undoubtedly faced intense opposition from the strong Alliance faction in the Fifth District. By October 5, Donnelly reluctantly admitted to the *Pioneer Press* that the Farmer Labor party would probably withdraw because it could not canvass the entire state. Six days later, he withdrew from the race, indorsed Merriam, and explained that had he not been tendered the Farmer Labor candidacy on his return from England, he would have attended the Republican convention to vote for Merriam. He was, he insisted, sacrificing no principles.[66] Ironically enough, he had accepted the Democratic nomination for the lower house in the state legislature! Donnelly conceded that espousing Merriam might cause his defeat. It was asking a good deal of the Dakota County Democrats to vote for a man who opposed their state ticket. Although Donnelly never acknowledged publicly that his withdrawal had antagonized labor, he was well aware that labor groups felt that he had betrayed them.[67]

His hope at this time, which he confessed to an old friend, W. D. Conner, was that there would be a Sabin-Washburn deadlock in the Republican senatorial caucus and that somehow he could emerge as senator.[68] Probably with this in mind, he accepted speaking engagements for the Republican State Central Committee to campaign for Merriam at a fee of one hundred dollars a speech.[69] It was difficult, after years of opposition, to defend the Republican party. He expressed no feelings of contrition. "I do not come back because I have had a change of front," Donnelly told a roaring crowd of three thou-

[65] *Ibid.*, I. D. to J. Lind, September 23, 1888.

[66] St. Paul *Pioneer Press*, October 12, 1888; St. Paul *The Great West*, February 12, 1890.

[67] St. Paul *The Great West*, May 23, 1890. The paper defends Donnelly, arguing that he was misled and used by self-interested labor leaders.

[68] Donnelly MSS, I. D. to W. Conner, October 20, 1888.

[69] *Ibid.*, Diary, Memoranda Section. This explains the money which Donnelly had borrowed from Merriam's bank, the St. Paul Merchants' National. Donnelly owed $700 but this was a valid debt for which he signed a note. R. Elliot to I. D., November 23, 1888. He used his speaking engagement funds to repay the obligation.

sand in Minneapolis, "if there has been any change it has been made by the Republican party." He refused to abuse the Democrats—the party was a "double yolked egg," he told his audiences; "one section contains some able patriotic men. Then there is the other portion." In Europe there was an old saying, he went on, " 'Scratch a Russian you find a Tartar.' It may with equal truth, be said, Scratch the Democratic party of this state, and you will find Jim Hill."[70]

Harrison ousted Cleveland, Merriam won a sweeping victory, but Donnelly lost by less than 150 votes out of more than 4,000 cast. Although he attributed his defeat to the railroads and the influence of W. D. Washburn, Donnelly had campaigned too vigorously for Merriam and not hard enough for himself in Dakota County.[71]

Despite his defeat, he launched his campaign for the Senate. He wrote to friendly politicians, Alliance members, and Republicans, denouncing Washburn and promising that he would remember his friends.[72] One of Minnesota's shrewdest Republicans, Knute Nelson, perhaps the state's most influential Norwegian politician, candidly replied, "The men who encourage you will do nothing for you." Nelson was convinced that "the Yankee blue blood of the Twin Cities would never tolerate that a damned Norwegian without boodle should ever aspire to the U.S. Senatorship, and you will before you are much older realize that an Irishman without boodle will be in the same fix."[73] Nelson's feeling that money would determine the outcome was widely shared. Although the newspapers did not take Donnelly seriously, he had the support of fifteen delegates on the first ballot compared to Washburn's fifty-two and Sabin's forty-three. But on subsequent tallies, Washburn quickly gathered enough votes to win.[74]

[70]St. Paul *Pioneer Press*, October 31, 1888.
[71]Donnelly MSS, October, 1888, correspondence with C. P. Carpenter; Diary, November 11, 1888.
[72]*Ibid.*, I. D. to C. H. Brush, November 23, 1888.
[73]*Ibid.*, K. Nelson to I. D., November 26, 1888.
[74]St. Paul *Pioneer Press*, January 18, 1889; Eugene V. Smalley, *A History of the Republican Party: From Its Organization to the Present Time* (St. Paul: E. V. Smalley, 1896), p. 231.

Caesar's Column
1889–1890

The fact is, my friends, that a wrong has no rights, except the right to die. . . .

IGNATIUS DONNELLY

ON JANUARY 19, 1889, the night after Washburn was elected senator, Donnelly sat in his room in St. Paul's Merchants Hotel and started writing a book foretelling the future of American civilization. It stemmed from his disgust with political dishonesty, his repugnance to the social and moral institutions that seemed to join rather than oppose corruption, his abhorrence of the prevailing social philosophy based on the survival of the fittest, and his desire to do something other than grind his teeth in defeat. The book was written not as an act of desperation but as an act of faith in the democratic principle that men could control their own destinies. He was thoroughly convinced that the decisive American response to industrialism would be made in the forthcoming decade. His ideas focused on the possibility that the American people might fail to choose wisely. Four months later, Donnelly had practically finished his first, "perhaps his last" novel, and he planned to publish it under the pseudonym Edmund Boisgilbert to free it from the criticism which his name would elicit.[1]

Caesar's Column was written as a series of letters describing the adventures of a young traveler in the United States in 1988. As a seer

[1] Donnelly MSS, Diary, May 17, 1889. Perhaps a psychologist might logically conclude that in writing *Caesar's Column* Donnelly divested himself of any desire to change society through antisocial means.

of the technological wonders of the future, Donnelly rivaled Jules Verne in anticipating airships, great metropolitan centers with incredible communication and transportation systems, and a world of abundant physical comforts. His story, punctuated by socio-political discourses, was as melodramatic as a Dumas novel, with cringing villains, wild pursuits, disguised heroes, and hairbreadth escapes. But the book did not conform to Donnelly's own definition of fiction as "a beautiful world, a world where justice ever reigns & virtue is ever triumphant without the bareness, the baseness, the treachery of this poor belly-governed debased society of ours."[2] Unlike the bland and tepid *Looking Backward* by Edward Bellamy, where the American future was roseate, where all problems facing the nineteenth century had been amicably solved, Donnelly's work depicted in a biting pyrographic style a degraded society devoid of reform's influence, with the rich in complete control, the laboring classes reduced to a horrible quasi-barbaric poverty, ending in a revolution more bloody and violent than any that had preceded it.

Throughout the narrative, Donnelly played upon the dominant fears and anxieties of the American farmer and worker regarding the future of American life. When the American laboring class of the twentieth century, obviously amalgamated with coolie immigrants, was painted with an oriental cast, when the growth of conformity was displayed as leading to a society where physical as well as intellectual homogeneity existed, and when the ruling class was identified as being composed of Jews, Donnelly was exploiting popular bogies.

In selecting the Jews as the moneylending group which came to rule, Donnelly's thinking disclosed his reliance on the Shylock stereotype as well as his acceptance of Darwinian evolution. The Christians through the centuries subjected the Jews to the "most terrible ordeal of persecution the history of mankind bears any record of," one of Donnelly's characters explains. "Only the strong of body, the cunning of brain, the long-headed, the persistent, the men with capacity to live where a dog would starve survived the awful trial. Like breeds like." As a result, he adds, "When the time came for liberty and fair play the Jew was master in the contest with the Gentile." Then, "They were as merciless to the Christians as the Christians had been to them. They said, with Shylock, 'The villainy you teach me I will execute; and it shall go hard but I will better the in-

[2]Donnelly MSS, Diary, 1889, last page.

struction.'" Although Donnelly condemned the Christian and exonerated the Jew, the impact of fastening upon the Jew as a threat to the moral, political, and economic safety of the producing classes, according to later students of anti-Semitism, was enormous in fomenting a mood that persisted into the twentieth century.[3]

In a chapter entitled, "A Twentieth Century Sermon," he portrayed the future gospel as a triumph of Herbert Spencer's interpretation of Darwin superimposed on the liturgy and terminology of the nineteenth-century church. Donnelly represented his clergyman as saying, "Let us close our ears to the cries of distress we are not able to relieve. It was said in old times, 'Many are called, but few are chosen.' Our ancestors placed a mystical interpretation on this text; but we know what it means:—many are called to the sorrows of life, but few are chosen to inherit the delights of wealth and happiness. . . . Why, then should we concern ourselves about the poor. . . . Let us leave them in the hands of nature. She who made them can care for them."[4]

In explaining the deterioration of American society, Donnelly discussed the nineteenth-century reform movements which failed to alleviate deepening social ills. He pointed out that Marxism called forth no enthusiasm from American workers, the co-operative movement provided no solution because it continued the principle of profiteering, universal education was a panacea without goals, and religion, which should have worked for good, had degenerated into a sop for the masses and a boon for the exploiters. As a result, by 1988, Donnelly wrote, reform was impossible. The only means of combatting the upas of exploitation was a massive world conspiracy of the workers led by a brilliant Jew who had been driven from his synagogue, a huge vengeful American farmer who had been victimized by usury, and a vindictive intellectual whose family name had been

[3]Ignatius Donnelly, *Caesar's Column* (Chicago: Free Speech Publishers, n.d.), pp. 36–37. See Richard Hofstadter, *The Age of Reform* (New York: Alfred A. Knopf, 1955), pp. 67–70, 79, 80: includes summaries of the work of Oscar Handlin and Daniel Bell. For an antidote see C. Vann Woodward, "The Populist Heritage and the Intellectual," *The American Scholar*, XXIX (1959–60), 55–72. It is worth noting that in the St. Paul *Anti-Monopolist*, February 17, 1876, Donnelly denounced religious bigotry and racial prejudice. "Give the Jew a chance. This is their country as well as ours, and they have a right to make all out of themselves that they are capable of without shouting 'Jew, Jew,' after them. A great nation, like all magnificent mosaic work, has room in it for all the race elements of the world. There is room here for Goth and Celt and Basque and African and Jew,—yes even for the Indians, if they can survive civilization."

[4]*Caesar's Column*, pp. 214–15.

discredited by perjured testimony. Because the evil had penetrated so deeply into world society, the triumvirate had almost no plans beyond the hellish explosion that would break the log-jam which barred the progress of mankind.

Although it touched the nerves of prejudice and anxiety dealing with race, religion, politics, and sex, producing a climax of violence unprecedented in American fiction, Donnelly's book was neither sadistic nor nihilistic in spirit. Throughout *Caesar's Column*, Donnelly's hero proclaimed the validity of God, the idea of right as distinct from power, the value of property, marriage, and justice, as well as the need to subordinate human appetite for social gain. In fact, Donnelly closed his narrative with the hero and heroine escaping to establish a utopia based on the political and social reforms advocated by the Grangers, Alliance, and the Knights of Labor. But this was almost anticlimactic. The impact of the book was in its shocking revelation not of the future but of the present. Donnelly had virtually taken off the skin and exposed the bare bones of what he felt to be the false American credo which placed its trust in progress through technology, laissez faire, and Social Darwinism.

The book was rejected by Harper and Brothers, Charles Scribner's Sons, Houghton Mifflin, and D. Appleton. O. B. Bunce, of D. Appleton, conceding that it might be a best seller, explained that the company would not publish a book of such "revolutionary not to say inflammatory character."[5] When *Caesar's Column* was submitted to A. C. McClurg, the publisher refused to acknowledge that it was fiction and attacked it as prophecy. "I do not believe that matters are now tending in the direction that you foreshadow. I believe that many men of property and influence are working earnestly toward the removal of existing evils in society, and that in a day when people so clearly possess authority and power, no such culmination of evils in society as you foreshadow, is possible. It is possible, however," he wrote Donnelly accusingly, "to make people believe that brutal and frightful remedies must be plotted. . . . I believe the effects of this book (because it is so extravagant and so unjust toward the wealthier classes) would have effect only upon those who already believe in disturbance and Anarchy." McClurg fervently hoped the book would never "see the light," and that Donnelly

[5]Donnelly MSS, I. D. to Harper & Bros., May 21, 1889; Harper & Bros., to I. D., July 12, 1889; I. D. to Scribner's Sons, July 29, 1889; Scribner's Sons to I. D., August 29, 1889; I. D. to O. Bunce, September 2, 1889; O. Bunce to I. D., September 16, 1889; Houghton Mifflin to I. D., November 21, 1889.

would abstain from committing the "great crime" of inflaming the passions of people. If Donnelly did publish it, McClurg pleaded that it be sold for more than one dollar to keep it from falling into the wrong hands.[6] "If I was to destroy the book I would not thereby arrest the evil tendencies of our age, which in my judgement, are dragging civilization rapidly and certainly to its own funeral," Donnelly replied to the horrified publisher. "Our corrupt courts and juries and debauched legislatures, our U.S. Senate filled by men who have bought their seats, our demoralized voters, our indifferent newspapers, and the increasing degradation of the laboring classes . . . and poverty among agricultural classes these, all these," he hotly declared, "would remain and continue to operate if my book never saw the light. To suppress the truth is not to arrest the consequences of evil."[7]

Donnelly finally found a publisher in F. J. Schulte and Company. Schulte, who had worked on Donnelly's *Cryptogram* for R. S. Peale, was enthusiastic about *Caesar's Column*. Only one aspect of the work, the chapter dealing with religion, troubled him.[8] Donnelly, who could balk at an editorial suggestion that "social system" be changed to "society," refused to temper the chapter. Although deeply religious, he had grown increasingly hostile to organized sects and creeds.[9] He expressed immense satisfaction at the spread of secularism and anticlericalism. "It was a black and bloody and bitter and dreadful world when the black gowns controlled it—both in Europe and America," he wrote four months after completing *Caesar's Column*. "God forbid that they should ever dominate intelligent mankind again."[10] Despite the "Sermon" chapter, Schulte predicted

[6]*Ibid.*, A. C. McClurg to I. D., December 30, 1889.
[7]*Ibid.*, I. D. to A. McClurg, December 31, 1889 (letter press copy).
[8]*Ibid.*, F. J. Schulte to I. D., January 3, 7, 30, 1890.
[9]*Ibid.*, J. C. McDonough to I. D., June 27, 1889. Donnelly indorsed the letter to the effect that to call himself a Roman Catholic would be a fraud. His Diary, 1890, expressed a crude if not vulgar manifestation of skepticism toward Christianity. "I cannot believe that the maker of the universe with its hundred million visible stars and its thousand millions of invisible suns with a billion planets and satellites, worked for twenty years at the carpenters trade in Judea; and permitted a lot of lousy Jews to murder him. The proposition is too incredible to be thought of. But this does not say that the spirit & purpose of God may not be behind this Christianity."
[10]*Ibid.*, Diary, September 20, 1889. Donnelly also noted that the "incredible yarns which constitute the great bulk of the creed" had fallen into disuse. "Now the thinking classes do not believe a word of this stuff; and the unthinking scarcely remember it anyhow." With fitting irony and Darwinian terminology, Donnelly added, "Now and then you see a spectacular theological student, but the very 'cut of his jib' proclaims that he belongs to a *genus* that is

that the book would be a financial success. The publisher allowed Thomas J. Morgan, a leading Chicago socialist who had learned McClurg had rejected a radical book, to read the page proof. Morgan was genuinely impressed; *Progress and Poverty* was hard reading, *Looking Backward* was for perusal, but he felt *Caesar's Column* held the reader's interest and asked to be reread.[11]

Major newspapers and reviewers ignored the book when it appeared early in April, 1889, but the labor and rural press gradually gave the work a hearing. *Caesar's Column* made "its own way," Schulte told Donnelly; "One purchaser brings another."[12] By June, both a hard-cover and an inexpensive paper edition were on the market, and by August 4,000 copies had been sold. The audience widened steadily until Schulte was selling 1,000 copies a week by December, 1890. By 1899, Donnelly estimated that 230,000 copies had been sold in the United States and 450,000 copies in Europe.[13] Because Edmund Boisgilbert was obviously a pseudonym, and Schulte treated it as such, the authorship of *Caesar's Column* became a leading non-controversial question among American reformers. Donnelly, aware that the mystery helped the sale of the book, waited for the most strategic opportunity to disclose his authorship.

At the time Donnelly began writing *Caesar's Column*, the Minnesota branch of the Northwest Alliance was suffering a marked decline in strength. The Republican party's rejection of Albert Scheffer and Merriam's victory discredited the Alliance almost everywhere in the state except the Fifth District where strong, politically oriented leadership retained a disciplined following. The reluctance of Minnesota farmers to join the Alliance contrasted strangely with the tremendously enthusiastic reception of the movement in the South and Midwest, especially in North Dakota. Minnesota's apathy was due to the organization's failure to cope with pressing farm needs such as inexpensive insurance, binders twine, and agricultural machines. The Alliance could not hope to win support exclusively with a political program because single candidates or parties could espouse programs with greater success.

---

fast disappearing;—he is the survival of a past age; his kind are nearly all fossils:—he is a sort of mental *gar-fish*, swimming around in the midst of a new order of things."

[11]*Ibid.*, F. J. Schulte to I. D., March 17, 19, 1890.

[12]*Ibid.*, F. J. Schulte to I. D., April 24, 1890.

[13]Donnelly, *The Cipher*, p. 374. The most recent edition, edited by Walter B. Rideout was published by Harvard University Press in 1960 as an American classic.

This was clearly recognized at a meeting of the Alliance executive committee which was attended by H. L. Loucks of the Dakota Alliance and Alonzo Wardall, the head of its insurance department. The Dakotans not only offered advice, but also prepared to integrate insurance marketing. The Fifth District Alliance leaders, realizing that insurance promised both profits and power, sought to establish a local company under their control. J. J. Furlong, president of the Austin Fire and Storm Mutual Insurance Company and an active Allianceman, was eager to establish an Alliance company. In May, the executive committee organized the Alliance Hail and Cyclone Mutual Insurance Company. The executive committee served as the board of directors, but Alonzo Wardall of Dakota was also a member.[14]

As state lecturer, Donnelly was a member of the executive committee, but he played a minor role in developing the insurance program. He contented himself with writing circulars for his deputy, John Allison, who traveled widely trying to establish new chapters. The sale of inexpensive hail insurance in the wheat belt revitalized the Alliance. Allison reported the Alliance was "catching on" because of the insurance appeal.[15] By early June, the sale of insurance had become so profitable that Alliance agents were quarreling over territories. Only the relative poverty of some of the wheat growers kept them from joining the organization to share in the program. Allison optimistically predicted that he would organize two hundred new chapters in six months.[16]

The more frequently Donnelly was called to address farmers whose excitement centered on immediate economic needs, the more deeply interested he became in the Alliance insurance program. On August 21, curious about just how much money farmers actually saved, how much money the companies really made, and how it affected the farmer's political allegiances, Donnelly wrote Alonzo Wardall explaining that he was going to push an Alliance Life Insurance program. Donnelly wanted help in sending out circulars in English, German, and Scandinavian.[17] He planned to visit as many county fairs as possible and to sell the Alliance program. In late September, Donnelly persuaded the Alliance executive committee,

[14]Donnelly MSS, Diary, March, 1889; J. Allison to I. D., March 27, 1889; J. J. Furlong to I. D., March 30, April 25, May 23, 1889.
[15]*Ibid.*, J. Allison to I. D., May 8, 29, 1889.
[16]*Ibid.*, J. J. Furlong to I. D., June 4, 1889; J. Allison to I. D., July 24, 1889.
[17]*Ibid.*, I. D. to A. Wardall, August 21, 1889.

which was flush with funds from insurance profits, to support *The Great West* as their official newspaper. The paper's owner, Dr. Everett W. Fish, an excitable, vigorous, colorful, and intemperate journalist, was eager to pump new life into the Alliance and to move his paper from Glenwood to St. Paul.[18] One month later, Donnelly issued a circular asserting that the Alliance with six hundred chapters had insured "54,000 acres against hail at 15 cts an acre while other companies charged 40 to 60 cts." Life and fire insurance programs were available at comparable savings and the Alliance planned to market coal and farm machinery at greatly reduced prices. "The Alliance is non-political and not a secret society," Donnelly wrote, "All farmers should turn out and hear the[ir] speakers."[19]

Although nonpartisanship was the official Alliance position, in late November Donnelly awakened to a scheme conceived by President George Sprague which would link the organization to politically ambitious Albert Scheffer by allowing him to underwrite the fire insurance program. To prevent this coup, Donnelly urged Alonzo Wardall to raise additional stock in an Alliance company newly organized for the purpose and to see Governor Merriam.[20] A few days later Donnelly visited Merriam and received at least minimum assurances of financial support.[21] But Donnelly lost Wardall's aid almost immediately because the Dakota Alliance seceded from the Northwest Alliance at the St. Louis convention of all Alliance organizations. The Dakotans joined the more radical and newly created Farmers Alliance and Industrial Union, the outgrowth of the coalition of southern farm leadership with those in the country who would support increased rural and industrial reform.

Donnelly warned George Sprague not to reintroduce the Scheffer issue. "I have no personal ill will toward Mr. S.," Donnelly explained, but his presence had produced "bad blood that has not yet been eliminated." He reminded Sprague of the Alliance policy of avoiding partisanship. "It is essential that the Alliance should live; it is not essential that it should insure houses from fire."[22] But unable to stop Sprague and Scheffer from forming a fire company, Donnelly moved closer to Merriam, who bought stock in *The Great West*.[23]

[18]*Ibid.*, E. Fish to I. D., December 13, 1888, January 13, 1889, February 16, 1889; Diary, September 19, 1889.

[19]*Ibid.*, mimeographed circular, October 30, 1889.

[20]*Ibid.*, I. D. to A. Wardall, November 24, 1889 (letter press copy).

[21]*Ibid.*, Diary, November 27, 1889.

[22]*Ibid.*, I. D. to G. Sprague, December 9, 1889 (letter press copy).

[23]*Ibid.*, Diary, January 15, 1890.

The newspaper attacked Sprague, accusing him of accepting a highly paid office in Scheffer's fire insurance company.[24] Although it pained Donnelly to think that he had been used to build the Alliance for Scheffer, he lacked his usual determination to fight. Almost feeling that valuable time that should have been devoted to writing was being wasted, he attended meetings at *The Great West*'s offices in St. Paul where Dr. Fish urged him to run for President of the Alliance. Donnelly, perhaps fearful of defeat, was reluctant to seek the post.[25]

On March 4, 1890, four hundred Alliance delegates convened in St. Paul where Donnelly greeted them as the convention's keynote speaker. He was witty, brilliant, and pointed in his remarks. His audience laughed, shouted, and cheered. "We are not here to wage war on any political party," he hoarsely reiterated the nonpartisan pledge, "but we are here to serve notice on all parties that if they do not work for the welfare of all people, they might as well order their coffins and fix the date for their funerals." Then, in a sense facing his opposition within the group, he added, "We are not here to take up the cause of any politician. We are not here to attach the Alliance as a tail to the political kite of a Gov. Merriam, or a would-be Gov. Scheffer." If the Alliance members wanted political action, the fight should be made to gain control of the legislature.[26]

When the convention prepared to elect officers, Donnelly charged President Sprague with accepting a two-thousand-dollar-per-year post in the Hekla Insurance Company. Furthermore, the president and secretary of the Alliance had been given stock in the company by banker Albert Scheffer, the St. Paul politician who owned the firm. Even this slashing attack did not win the presidency. Donnelly withdrew his name after an informal vote indicated that he would lose. The shrewd Fifth District politicians, arguing that Donnelly was too valuable as lecturer, convinced the delegates to vote for a coalition headed by R. J. Hall, which replaced every executive officer except Donnelly.[27]

[24]St. Paul *The Great West*, February 7, 1890.

[25]Donnelly MSS, Diary, February 28, 1890. Donnelly did enjoy writing. At this time he published an article in the New York *Sun*, March 16, 1890, explaining that the United States was a land of abundance where poverty resulted from maldistribution. His proposed solutions consisted of a graduated income tax, severe antitrust laws, and the direct intervention of government to protect the interests of laboring men.

[26]St. Paul *Pioneer Press*, March 5, 1890.

[27]*Ibid.*, March 7, 1890; Donnelly MSS, G. Day to I. D., March 17, 1890.

Donnelly's failure to capture the Alliance presidency meant that the organization would move quickly toward direct partisan activity. The vigorous and open clash among Alliance leaders did not dampen the enthusiastic feeling of many Alliance members for a third party. Comparing the movement with the Grange, Donnelly conceded that the Grange "was mild in comparison with this. It lacked the interest . . . it was better natured, men were not so much in earnest then as now." The rapid growth of Independent Alliance parties in other states, the political loyalty bred of economic interest, and the determination of the Fifth District politicians, strengthened the drive for an independent party. Politicians who had seen Donnelly fashion the Grange and Greenback movements into political machines were perplexed by his strategy at this time. The most direct politician in Minnesota seemed to be playing a cat-and-mouse game rather than assuming leadership.[28]

In the Fifth District plans were made to issue a call for a mass political conference following the district convention. Alliance President Hall at first extended and then withdrew an offer for Donnelly to address the gathering, asserting that Fish and Donnelly had used *The Great West* against him.[29] Donnelly replied with a blistering letter insisting that some of the men in the organization had already made their fortunes through the Alliance and that others may have had hopes of doing so, but *The Great West* would expose them. "As for myself," he truthfully if not self-righteously proclaimed, "I have worked eight years for the Alliance without a cent reward." He was not seeking money or petty prestige which interested some Alliance leaders. "I was a man of eminence and influence before the Alliance was born and I will be when it's dead." Donnelly asked nothing of the Alliance, "but the opportunity to serve it." Then he warned Hall, "I have fought lions in my day and I am ready now to go on the warpath against jackals,—or jackasses."[30]

Still angry, Donnelly turned to Fish urging that he use *The Great West* against his virulent opponents. "There are a dozen men who are fighting you & me," Donnelly informed the editor; "you have the ear of the multitude. These men must be *isolated* and *destroyed*." Fish, who has been described as a "vine-ripened fanatic to whom the world and the people in it were a simple study in pure black and

[28] St. Paul *The Great West*, May 2, 1890; Donnelly MSS, E. Olson to I. D., April 8, 1890.
[29] St. Paul *The Great West*, May 2, 9, 1890.
[30] Donnelly MSS, I. D. to R. J. Hall, May 28, 1890 (letter press copy).

white," needed little encouragement to strike at Hall.[31] Since Donnelly was linked to Merriam and the creation of a third party would cut into the Republican rural vote, he wrote the governor apologetically, "I regret the condition of affairs. . . . I want to help you, but do not see how I can break with the Alliance."[32]

At a meeting of the Alliance executive committee the icy hostility of Hall and Donnelly nearly broke into intemperate argument when the issue of political action was discussed. With more than a thousand chapters and a potential vote of thirty thousand, Hall pointed out that the overwhelming majority of the Alliancemen favored the establishment of a state ticket similar to those in other states. Donnelly willingly accepted the principle of political action, but insisted that it be limited to congressional and legislative races. To enter a state race would provoke divisive issues that would ruin the organization. The committee delayed action until the Fifth District convention.[33]

That the Fifth District would indorse a mass political convention was a foregone conclusion. Even Donnelly's friends who attended the meeting to prevent Hall from dominating the proceedings favored direct political action as a third party. Convinced that the Alliance was right, Fish broke with Donnelly on the question and *The Great West* indorsed the idea of an independent party.[34] As a result the Alliance executive committee summoned a mass political convention, including in its call the request for labor union support and attendance. The newspapers made much of the feeling that the Alliance wanted to nominate Republican Knute Nelson, who had expressed sympathy for the barest minimum of the reform program, but who would not think of abandoning his own party.[35]

Fearful that his influence among the farmers was weakened, Donnelly attended the Knights of Labor meetings in St. Paul believing that his strength in the new party could rest on labor support. But the noisy, argument-filled sessions proved of dubious value. Thoroughly disgusted with his role in what had happened, he tried to

[31]Warner, "Prelude to Populism," p. 135; Donnelly MSS, I. D. to E. Fish, May 28, 1890 (letter press copy).
[32]Donnelly MSS, I. D. to W. Merriam, June 1, 1890 (letter press copy).
[33]St. Paul *Pioneer Press*, June 6, 1890.
[34]*Ibid.*, June 13, 1890; St. Paul *The Great West*, June 13, 1890.
[35]St. Paul *Pioneer Press*, June 26, 1890. Perhaps to steal a march on Donnelly's opposition, Fish wrote Knute Nelson offering to support him with money and *The Great West* if he would oppose Hall. St. Paul *The Great West*, September 9, 1890.

analyze his own feelings. "I am in doubt whether it is profound phi-
lanthropy, extra mundane influences, or rank insanity [that keeps
me in the movement]. It is certainly a thankless task."[36]

At the caucus before the Alliance Labor Union party convention,
Donnelly declined to be a candidate for governor. He suggested that
his friends support a well-known farm-politician, Henry Plowman of
Otter Tail County. The caucus, however, demanded that Donnelly
submit his name.[37] Although he was not the keynote speaker, he
gained the floor before the nominations to explain that he was not
seeking an office, that he attended the meeting to help select the
best man, and that he had no intention of bolting the organization.
There was so much that the Alliance could do that he hoped that it
would not tear itself to pieces but work as an integrated force for
reform.[38]

The convention balloting for the gubernatorial nomination surprised him. The labor delegates, still embittered by his withdrawal
in 1888, voted almost solidly against him on each ballot. The first
tally gave Donnelly 172 votes, Hall 170, Nelson 56, with another 107
scattered. In the second ballot Hall led him by ten votes and lacked
only one of gaining the nomination. Donnelly gained the floor, but
instead of graciously withdrawing in favor of Hall, he suggested
a compromise candidate, Patrick Rahilly, a well-known, popular
farmer and Democratic politician. This tactic upset Hall's backers
who abandoned their candidate to make a counter offer, Sidney M.
Owen, editor of Minnesota's leading farm journal, *Farm, Stock and
Home*. Donnelly agreed, finding cold comfort in "being able to lay
out Hall when he had almost touched victory."[39]

Called upon by the convention delegates to speak after his defeat,
instead of making the anticipated genial address emphasizing the
need for harmony, Donnelly startled the gathering by lashing out at
the labor representatives. Within the Alliance proper Donnelly
noted, he had been the choice for governor; the defeat had been
caused by the labor delegates. Angrily he told the audience, "I have
labored for them in season and out of season, and I stood beside one
of them in the legislature and fought for their cause. Verily I have
my reward," he sarcastically exclaimed; "I thank them for it."[40]

[36]Donnelly MSS, Diary, July 7, 1890.
[37]*Ibid.*, July 18, 1890.
[38]St. Paul *Pioneer Press*, July 17, 1890.
[39]Donnelly MSS, Diary, July 18, 1890; see Carl H. Chrislock, "Sidney M.
Owen: An Editor in Politics," *Minnesota History*, XXXVI (1958), 113.
[40]St. Paul *Pioneer Press*, July 18, 1890.

Routed and keenly disappointed, he relied on Fish of *The Great West*. "We must either control the next annual meeting [of the Alliance]," he warned, "or organize a new society. Let it be war to the knife, and knife to the hilt."[41]

The Alliance Labor Union party ignored Donnelly. The party's central committee, dominated from the Fifth District, named the St. Paul *News* the party's official newspaper and thereby threatened *The Great West's* leadership in the Alliance. Highly incensed, not only by the convention but also by this punishment, Fish embarked on a personal vendetta. At the outset, only Sidney M. Owen, because he was not yet identified with R. J. Hall, escaped Fish's wrath. Donnelly, however, tried to gain a voice in the party's management through his friend Patrick Rahilly, who had accepted an Alliance Labor Union party congressional nomination. The attempt was not successful. Despite Rahilly's warnings that the committee needed Donnelly to campaign, the response was disappointingly negative. The party's central committee enjoyed discussing anti-Donnelly cartoons in the daily press and agreed to see Donnelly only if he consented to stump the entire state.[42] Alert to the cleavage within the Alliance Labor Union organization, Tams Bixby of the Republican State Central Committee urged Donnelly to break with the group and campaign for Merriam.[43] Donnelly refused.

Corruption within the Alliance executive committee afforded Donnelly the opportunity to strike at his enemies. The secretary of the Alliance, John Lathrop, had misappropriated funds. He had been exposed by *The Great West*.[44] At an executive meeting Donnelly demanded an accounting. Lathrop, who was a member of the Fifth District faction, was not easily confronted. Donnelly noted dramatically in his diary that Lathrop "threatened me with violence with his hand in his pocket as if he meant to draw a weapon. I went out and bought a revolver when the miscreant quieted down. He was just mean enough to shoot an unarmed man."[45] But after ousting Lathrop, Donnelly failed to secure an indorsement of Fish and left the meeting in disgust. No sooner had he departed than Hall looted the Alliance treasury by voting its funds to support the Alliance Labor Union party's campaign.[46]

[41]Donnelly MSS, I. D. to Fish, July 20, 1890 (letter press copy).
[42]*Ibid.*, K. D. to I. D., August 27, 1890; P. Rahilly to I. D., August 30, 1890.
[43]*Ibid.*, T. Bixby to I. D., August 29, 1890.
[44]St. Paul *The Great West*, August 15, 1890.
[45]Donnelly MSS, Diary, September 10, 1890.
[46]St. Paul *The Great West*, September 19, 1890.

"I feel disheartened," wrote Donnelly. "The power of the corporations is so great that it seems like insanity for one man, advanced in life and with small means to attempt to fight them." Dejected, he asked himself, "Why should any man attempt to do what God does not do, or seek to do? The whole battle seems so fruitless and hopeless!" The familiar temptation to "go home and stay home and stick to my books," once more arose. That would be the practical sensible course, he rationalized, "but that this foolish desire to help mankind pulls me away, as if I was tied to wild horses." The "compound man is a miserable man," he observed, "a single minded fool gets ten times as much comfort out of the world as a mind cut with many facets."[47]

Despite his depressing lamentations, Donnelly had already succeeded in gaining an Alliance Labor Union party nomination for the state senate.[48] After he failed to secure the Democratic indorsement and a few days before the Republican convention, he pleaded with Fish to temper his attacks in *The Great West*. Having long advocated the Alliance Labor Union platform calling for reduced interest rates, additional railroad legislation, a free grain market, prohibition of child labor, and employer liability laws, Donnelly felt Fish's continuing allegations jeopardized the program, Donnelly, and even the paper.[49] But Fish disapproved of Donnelly's tactics; he was determined to ruin Sidney M. Owen, even if it meant ceasing publication on January 1, 1891.[50]

The Dakota County Republican convention refused to indorse Donnelly's senatorial nomination even though he had appealed to Governor Merriam for support.[51] His initial reaction of disappointment and chagrin yielded to an intense belligerence and a determination to "fight it out." Optimistically, he wrote Kate, perhaps to cheer her, "The prospect of success is good. . . . In any event, I must fight or subside."[52]

During the final weeks of October, 1890, the Minnesota political campaign reached a feverish crescendo. In many districts, Alliance Labor Union and Democratic slates were consolidated in the hope of defeating the Republicans. Owen, Hall, W. W. Erwin, Minnesota's leading criminal lawyer, and James Heaton Baker toured the state in

[47] Donnelly MSS, Diary, September 18, 1890.
[48] *Ibid.*, H. Gillitt to I. D., September 9, 13, 1890.
[49] *Ibid.*, Diary, October 1, 3, 1890.
[50] *Ibid.*, October 6, 1890.
[51] *Ibid.*, October 3, 1890.
[52] *Ibid.*, I. D. to K. D., October 7, 1890.

behalf of the Alliance Labor Union cause. Owen, trying to discuss issues, focused attention on the tariff, which he felt was too high, burdensome state taxes, excessive railroad capitalizations, and high railroad rates. Merriam's Republican campaign was supported by Senator Cushman K. Davis, Congressman John Lind, and during the last week of the campaign, even Knute Nelson whose great popularity among the Norwegians and Alliancemen was undoubtedly a telling factor. The Republican speakers claimed as deep an interest in farm and labor problems as their opponents who, they charged, were merely seeking to divide the Republican farmers and workers so the Democrats could win.

In Dakota County, Donnelly campaigned for the entire Alliance Labor Union ticket, but especially for its platform. The extractions of the railroads, the millers, and the monopolies were his constant theme. Donnelly concentrated his appeal on the Irish-American farmers where he hoped to work a political revolution by persuading them to vote the straight Alliance ballot. With both a Republican and a Democrat opposing him and with the persistent rumor that railroads would send laborers into his district to vote, Donnelly was not considered a serious contender.[53]

The election proved to be the first major Republican reversal in twenty-five years. They lost control of the state treasurer's office, and the only Republican elected to Congress was John Lind. In the Fifth District, the Alliance Labor Union candidate for Congress, Kittel Halvorson, gained office. Strengthened by vigorous campaigning, a loyalty bred of the Alliance organization, and the general wave of agrarian discontent, the third party cut deeply into the normally Republican rural vote. Owen secured almost 60,000 votes, nearly 25 per cent of the total, and Merriam, with a scant 40 per cent, narrowly defeated Democrat Thomas Wilson. To the amazement of many politicians, Donnelly won his bid to the state senate. Flushed with a victory that salvaged his political fortune, Donnelly exuberantly wrote his former political crony, Dr. W. W. Mayo, "The sky is luminous with promise."[54]

A few days later he issued a press release to *The Great West* calling for his election to the Alliance presidency. The success of the Alliance program in the legislature was contingent on the fidelity of the next president. "If you have faith in me: if you believe that for a quarter of a century I have fought the battle of the people without

[53] *Ibid.*, C. Carpenter to I. D., October 28, 1890.
[54] *Ibid.*, I. D. to W. W. Mayo, November 6, 1890.

The Minnesota Don Quixote.

An early anti-Alliance drawing by Bart,
Minneapolis *Journal*, February 24, 1891.

POP.

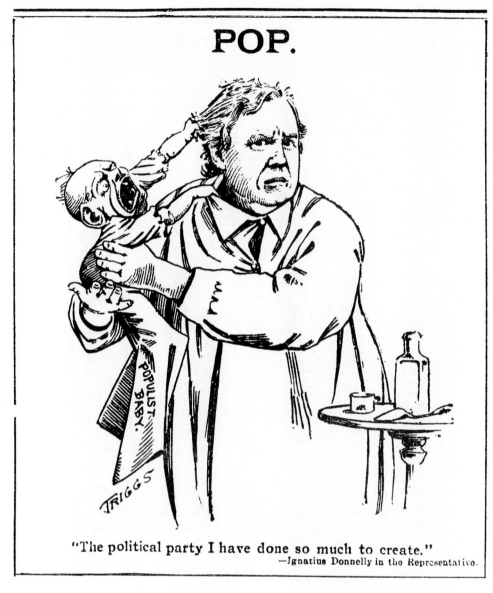

"The political party I have done so much to create."
—Ignatius Donnelly in the Representative.

Donnelly as "the father of the People's party,"
Republican Minneapolis *Tribune,* August 31, 1894.

a shade of variation or turning; if you believe the railroad corporations of this state have not money enough to buy me to desert the cause of the people," Donnelly pleaded, "then I ask you to support me." Instruct your delegates, he warned, "The Rings and Corporations will pack the hotels, and the very floor of your convention with paid agents, who will make the air sulphurous with their lies against me."[55]

But circumstances outside Minnesota played a significant part in his quest for the Alliance presidency. As early as 1888, Donnelly was recognized as the state's best known and most highly articulate farm politician. He was asked repeatedly to attend meetings of the Northwest Alliance and to discuss organization policies with southern Alliance spokesmen, especially General Leonidas L. Polk. The southerners who dominated the National Farmers' Alliance and Industrial Union, which had been formed in St. Louis, wanted to recruit Donnelly, whose reputation was enhanced by the wide circulation and exchange of *The Great West*.[56] As the National Farmers' Alliance and Industrial Union prepared to meet in Ocala, Florida, Polk urged Donnelly to attend either as a delegate or as an individual. The Alliance was working a revolution in the politics of a dozen states in the South and Midwest. The national or regional leaders who did not know him personally were eager to meet him, there were highly important policies to discuss, and the feeling was strong that he should assume a role as national lecturer.[57] The convention was scheduled for the first week in December, and Donnelly was too busy fighting for the Alliance presidency to attend, but when the annual report of Minnesota activities was presented, the delegates were told that Donnelly had written *Caesar's Column*.[58] Already well known, he was immediately projected into national leadership. Letters of congratulation and approbation soon swelled his correspondence.

The news, however, was of greater importance in Minnesota. Donnelly, whose following within the Alliance was large enough to have given him the Alliance Labor Union nomination had it not been for the labor group, won the overwhelming approval of the undecided members as the author of *Caesar's Column*. After careful planning, Donnelly went to the Fifth District convention and won

[55]*Ibid.*, November 15, 1890, circular; St. Paul *The Great West*, December 5, 1890.

[56]Donnelly MSS, E. H. Atwood to I. D., November 29, 1888; G. Sprague to I. D., February 27, 1889; L. L. Polk to I. D., May 7, 1889.

[57]*Ibid.*, L. L. Polk to I. D., October 4, November 15, 1890.

[58]St. Paul *The Great West*, December 5, 1890.

half of the delegates from the stronghold of his sharpest rivals.[59] Despite charges by Eric Olson that he had defected in 1888 and the suggestion of Sidney M. Owen that a compromise candidate other than Donnelly or Hall would be best for the Alliance, Donnelly's strength increased. In a desperate effort to thwart him, it was proposed that the very popular Scandinavian, Halvorson, oppose Donnelly for the post. Even so astute a gesture proved ineffective. Warning Halvorson to stay out of the race, Donnelly won a smashing victory. He captured the presidency with 542 votes, sweeping aside Halvorson with 105, Hall with 6, and Owen with 2 into a temporary eclipse.

When Donnelly stepped forward to speak, his hand pressed over his heart, the audience of seven hundred farm delegates—not a silk hat or a boiled shirt in evidence—shouted themselves hoarse. His address, presented with the tone and vigor of *Caesar's Column*, defended radical action. "The word radical means that which goes to the root of things," he explained to an audience that accepted him as the Sage of Nininger. "It comes from the Latin word 'radix' a root." The time for going slow had passed. "Remember the French Revolution!" Donnelly roared. "The fact is, my friends, that a wrong has no rights, except the right to die—and die at once." This was the essence of his position. He defended it by asserting that the struggle was one between classes and quoted Karl Marx to the effect that in such a battle the most violent and malignant passions of the human breast—"the furies of private interest" were aroused.[60]

[59] St. Paul *Pioneer Press*, December 13, 1890; Donnelly MSS, C. Carpenter to I. D., December 13, 16, 1890; H. Swain to I. D., December 22, 1890.

[60] St. Paul *Pioneer Press*, December 31, 1890; Donnelly MSS, I. D. to K. Halvorson, December 21, 1890 (letter press copy).

From the Farmers' Alliance to the People's Party
1890–1892

For twenty five years I have labored to make the people supreme and put down the unnatural and dangerous power of money. . . . As long as I live I cannot do otherwise,—for every man who is born brings into the world with him the ticket which tells the road he is to travel and determines his ultimate destination on the great railway of life.

IGNATIUS DONNELLY

SHORTLY after Donnelly's election to the state senate, in the hope of securing the chairmanship of the Senate Railroad Committee, he agreed to co-operate with the other Alliance Labor Union party legislators. Had it been possible, he would have formed a nonpartisan "reform bloc" which could have controlled policy; failing in this, he preferred working with the Republicans, but the Alliance Labor Union party, in which he was almost an outsider after his clash at the convention, wanted a coalition with the Democrats. Because the Republicans constituted a plurality, a Democratic–Alliance Labor Union party combination would control both houses of the legislature. The politicians in such a combination, however, had little in common except their Republican foes and the desire to share the spoils of office, principally the legislative chairmanships. Alliance legislators, such as Donnelly, distrusted the Democrats whether they were followers of Bourbon boss Michael Doran or the anti-Doran Twin Cities labor group that espoused the single tax.[1] The Alliance itself was sharply divided between Donnelly's handful of friends and the Alliance Labor Union party group led by John Hompe of the Fifth District who followed Owen's suggestion that the Alliance pursue a conservative program.[2]

At a pre-session caucus Democratic and Alliance Labor Union politicians agreed upon the division of chairmanships and the general outline of the legislation they hoped to enact. Donnelly probably committed himself to support a Democratic sponsored anti-usury measure as a *quid pro quo* to secure the coveted railroad committee chairmanship and to gain passage of a strong railroad regulatory bill. Because, under senate rules, committee posts were assigned by the lieutenant governor, a change in the rules would be necessary before the coalition's plan could be implemented. The task of divesting Lieutenant Governor Gideon S. Ives of his appointive power fell to Donnelly, probably because it would draw intense criticism from the Republican newspapers. After a sharp debate Ives surrendered his control of chairmanship appointments, but the Republicans succeeded in publicizing their protests despite Donnelly's efforts to prevent what he termed abusive language from being included in the senate record. The St. Paul *Pioneer Press*, focusing on Donnelly, its bête noire, hoped to embarrass the Democrats in the coalition by charging them with blindly following the lead of the "phosphorescent genius" into a political bog.[3]

Despite the hostile publicity Donnelly received in the Republican press and the charge that he was trying to dominate the session, he was neither the leader of the combination nor the advocate of extreme measures. He introduced comparatively little new legislation, but all of it was significant—and all provoked heated debate. He was, however, increasingly short-tempered and easily baited into angry harangues. Kate, recognizing this growing weakness in Ignatius, pleaded with him to control his temper because it sacrificed his dignity and jeopardized his health. "Get the *laugh* on your enemy" by ignoring him, she suggested; "everyone knows you can retaliate if you desire to."[4] Although the advice was easy to receive, Ignatius

[1] Carl H. Chrislock, "The Alliance Party and the Minnesota Legislature of 1891," *Minnesota History*, XXXV (1957), 302–3. Donald F. Warner, "Prelude to Populism," p. 142; and the St. Paul *Pioneer Press*, January 4–9, 1891.
[2] St. Paul *The Great West*, November 28, 1890.
[3] St. Paul *Pioneer Press*, January 15, 1891.
[4] Donnelly MSS, K. D. to I. D., January 23, 1891.

found it difficult to implement. His years of struggle for power forced him into the mold of an intense person, extremely jealous of his prerogatives, supremely assured of his own righteousness, easy to admire from a distance, but highly difficult to work with.

The earliest indication that he could not depend on the pledges of the Democratic-Alliance Labor Union coalition was a move by one Democrat and two Alliance senators, led by John Hompe and supported by all the Republicans, to discharge Hompe's moderate, rather than Donnelly's extensive, railroad bill from the railroad committee. Donnelly's measure was essentially similar to a house proposal sponsored by F. M. Currier of Blue Earth County. When Donnelly's proposal was rejected, party lines were drawn and the Currier bill was defeated.

Because the United States Supreme Court had declared the Minnesota Railroad Law of 1887 unconstitutional in its revolutionary decision, *Chicago, Milwaukee & St. Paul Railroad Company* v. *Minnesota,* the need for a new measure was urgent. The Donnelly-Currier proposals would have moved Minnesota forward two decades in the field of regulation. Hompe's bill merely restated the 1887 act in a manner acceptable to the Court. It was passed by a combination of Republican and Alliance votes.[5] Donnelly succeeded in amending the Hompe bill by fighting for a provision that rates fixed by the Railroad Commission would remain in effect during litigation contesting railroad abuses.[6] The source of Donnelly's thinking on railroad legislation was a successful Illinois law.[7] The failure of Hompe's law was evident two years later when a Republican governor asked the legislature to fulfil its obligation to the state's farmers by enacting more effective legislation.[8]

The angry argument between Donnelly and Hompe regarding railroad legislation was well under way when two usury measures were presented in the senate. The Republican-sponsored bill called for the forfeiture of principal and interest where usury could be proved. The Democratic measure ignored mandatory forfeiture. Having fathered the forfeiture provision years earlier, Donnelly favored the Republican proposal. He was immediately charged with violating his caucus pledge to support the Democratic-Alliance

[5]Chrislock, "Alliance Party," 307–8; St. Paul *Pioneer Press*, February 15, 1891; St. Paul *The Great West*, February 20, April 1, 1891; and Donnelly MSS, G. Becker to I. D., February 23, 1891.

[6]St. Paul *Pioneer Press*, March 31, 1891.

[7]*Ibid.*, March 11, 1891.

[8]*Ibid.*, January 3, 1893.

Labor Union coalition.[9] Donnelly did not reply to this allegation, probably because it was true! But since Hompe had gone over to the Republicans to kill Donnelly's railroad bill and the coalition had failed to indorse Donnelly's employer liability law, he felt justified in pushing his program alone. His two-month struggle with both Republicans and Democrats led him to confide to his diary, "Nothing but my sense of duty could spur me on to such a conflict."[10]

Taking his case to the people through an Alliance circular published in *The Great West*, he explained that, although the new Democratic bill lowered legal interest rates on general loans, it permitted any rate where contracting parties agreed, and it reduced the punishment for usury to a farce. This was a sell out! Alliance members were urged to write their legislators to retain the existing law which Donnelly had inspired years earlier.[11] Despite familiar pleas, on this occasion expressed by Hompe, that a softer law was necessary to provide investment money in the frontier counties, Donnelly's appeal seemed to be successful. The senate accepted the forfeiture clause.[12] *The Great West* claimed Donnelly had won a genuine victory.[13] The legislature, however, rejected all usury legislation in 1891.

In the midst of the railroad regulation debate, the *Pioneer Press* slandered Donnelly by publishing a letter William S. King had written to the investigating committee at the time of the Springer episode, which accused Donnelly of criminal corruption. When the editors refused to retract, Donnelly brought suit against the paper.[14] The King letter was part of a campaign of vilification mounted against Donnelly during the session. When the Democratic usury bill was defeated, the *Pioneer Press* asserted that anarchism was Donnelly's stock-in-trade. "He speculates in it just as other people speculate in wheat or town lots."[15]

Before the legislative session ended, Donnelly secured passage of a bill prohibiting the Pinkerton Police from serving as armed thugs in Minnesota and waged an unsuccessful fight for an eight-hour working day as well as a bill to tax mortgage holders. He argued

[9]*Ibid.*, February 19, March 1, 3, 1891.
[10]Donnelly MSS, Diary, March 4, 1891.
[11]St. Paul *Pioneer Press*, March 5, 6, 1891; St. Paul *The Great West*, March 6, 1891.
[12]*Ibid.*, March 13, 16, 17, 1891.
[13]St. Paul *The Great West*, March 30, 1891.
[14]St. Paul *Pioneer Press*, February 16, 17, 1891.
[15]*Ibid.*, March 23, 1891.

against increased appropriations, but the "coalition," which eventually broke up over a patronage squabble, rarely sustained him.[16] He fought so tenaciously for the farmers and laborers that Dr. W. W. Mayo accused him of seeing everything from their point of view. According to Mayo, Donnelly wanted economy for everyone except the farmers.[17]

When the legislature adjourned, Donnelly noted that he had "worked with excessive energy and persistence to accomplish reforms but was thwarted by the fools and the knaves:—and in public affairs it is hard to know which is most dangerous to society."[18] The *Pioneer Press* noted that the Donnelly-Currier bill, the mortgage tax bill, the employer liability bill, and the usury bill had been defeated by combinations of Republicans and conservative Democrats or maverick Alliance men. The Republicans, the paper boasted, had actually controlled the government. Nevertheless, the *Pioneer Press* set the tone for Republican propaganda for the next decade by contending simultaneously that the inability of the Alliance Labor Union party to effect reform, the high cost of the session, and the embittered debates proved that only the Republicans could insure stable government.[19]

The Minnesota Alliance ran no more smoothly than the affairs of the legislature. The convention that had elected Donnelly president accepted a strong state program demanding reduced interest charges, the Australian ballot, government control of railroads, the abolition of child labor, state-manufactured binders twine for grain farmers, a state-owned grain elevator at Duluth, and a tax on mortgage holders. Their national platform denounced the McKinley Tariff, alien landownership, the ineffective silver purchase law, long-term monopolistic franchises, the use of adulterants in food processing, grain speculation, and the United States Indian policy. They indorsed such ideas as equal pay for equal work regardless of sex, government arbitration of labor disputes, a graduated income tax, and local option elections for prohibition laws.[20]

To the annoyance of Fish, the convention refused to accept the platform drafted by the National Alliance and Industrial Union at Ocala, especially the highly controversial subtreasury plan. This

[16]*Ibid.*, April 16, 17, 1891.
[17]*Ibid.*, April 20, 1891.
[18]Donnelly MSS, Diary, April 23, 1891.
[19]St. Paul *Pioneer Press*, April 20, 1891; Chrislock, "Alliance Party," 310–12.
[20]*Ibid.*, January 2, 1891.

scheme, approved by Alliance leaders L. L. Polk, L. L. Livingston, and Dr. C. W. Macune, called for federally operated storage facilities for non-perishable agricultural products, where farmers could deposit their produce, receive up to 80 per cent of their local market price, and have the privilege of selling their produce within one year. The cost of storage, insurance, and handling as well as 1 per cent interest were to be charged against the farmer. If the farmer did not sell his product within one year, it was to be forfeited to the government. Behind the scheme was the idea of greater marketing flexibility, a revolution in farm credit, as well as an end to the vicious southern crop-lien and sharecrop systems. The failure of Minnesota farmers to recognize that the plan was neither so radical nor so unworkable as the conservative press insisted, led Fish to describe the Minnesota Alliance platform as tepid.[21]

Fish was also disturbed by Donnelly's reluctance to drive his opponents out of the Alliance. Instead of placating them and even allowing them to share in making policies, Fish demanded that Donnelly remain the "old Roman" and not act like a "sentimentalist." The editor was particularly outspoken because Donnelly permitted a brash, bright, teenage factory girl, Eva McDonald, the "darling" of St. Paul labor circles, to be elected state lecturer of the Alliance. She was closely associated with Twin Cities politics, linked with the Hall faction in the Alliance, and not a member of any Alliance chapter. Fish argued that her selection was both illegal and bad politics.[22] More than sharing Fish's view, Kate believed Eva McDonald's election "lowered the office. . . . I feel it is an insult." Shrewdly Kate observed, "she will be 'tanky' & troublesome & she will have a vote—& you have too many of the opposition on the executive committee."[23] Four months later, Donnelly shared Kate's conviction that Eva McDonald was both vexatious and a knave.[24]

The sharp clash between Donnelly and the leaders of the Alliance Labor Union party in the legislature confirmed his belief that they were determined to discredit him. Strongly intrenched, however, as president of the Minnesota Alliance, Donnelly insisted that the party's affiliation with the farm organization had terminated with

[21] St. Paul *The Great West,* January 11, 1891.
[22] *Ibid.,* January 11, 1891; St. Paul *Pioneer Press,* January 3, 1891, also expressed the idea that Donnelly would have trouble with Eva McDonald.
[23] Donnelly MSS, K. D. to I. D., January 8, 1891.
[24] *Ibid.,* Diary, April 23, 1891.

the election.[25] Carrington Phelps, chairman of the Alliance Labor Union party's state central committee, replied that it was not merely the peer but the superior of the Alliance because it included labor voters and had a legal existence under Minnesota law. He defied Donnelly to organize a new party.[26]

The chasm between Donnelly and the Alliance Labor group deepened when he announced that he would lead the Minnesota delegation to the Cincinnati convention of farm, labor, and reform parties. The Alliance executive committee not only named him first delegate at large but also gave him the power to approve the credentials of the other Alliance delegates. *The Great West* proclaimed that the Minnesota Alliance would urge the formation of a national party.[27] The Alliance Labor Union spokesman, Phelps, announced that a party delegation consisting of Sidney M. Owen, James H. Baker, Eva McDonald, and R. J. Hall would also attend the Cincinnati meeting.[28]

Donnelly's reputation preceded him to Cincinnati. In nearly every reform newspaper from the radical Winfield, Kansas, *Nonconformist* to Tom Watson's *People's Party Paper* in Georgia, Donnelly was heralded as the author of *Caesar's Column.* He was frequently mentioned by southerners, who favored creating a third party, as a potential presidential candidate.[29] When the Alliance Labor Union party delegates challenged his right to represent Minnesota, the convention credentials committee refused to seat them. Eva McDonald made a special effort to gain recognition as a valid delegate, but the committee denied her petition by a vote of twenty-five to one.[30]

The National Alliance Union convention assembled in Cincinnati's Music Hall beneath banners proclaiming, "UNITED WE STAND DIVIDED WE FALL," "NINE MILLION MORTGAGED HOMES," and "OPPOSITION TO ALL MONOPOLIES." Despite the great enthusiasm and cordiality among the delegates, the question of a new party divided them. Sentiment favoring the establishment of a third party

[25] St. Paul *Pioneer Press*, April 23, 1891.

[26] *Ibid.*, April 26, 1891.

[27] St. Paul *The Great West*, May 8, 1891; Donnelly MSS, A. Stromberg to I. D., May 12, 1891.

[28] St. Paul *Pioneer Press*, May 16, 1891.

[29] Donnelly MSS, M. Wilkins to I. D., February 19, 1891; St. Paul *The Great West*, March 20, 1891; St. Paul *Dispatch*, May 9, 1891.

[30] St. Paul *The Great West*, May 22, 29, 1891.

had motivated the Kansans to call for the Cincinnati convention, but the influential Alliance leaders, such as L. L. Polk, James B. Weaver, C. W. Macune, and Jerry Simpson, who believed the timing to be inopportune, wanted to delay action until 1892.[31]

Before the lines of division were clearly drawn and before the convention was fully organized, while committees were being selected, Donnelly, gaining recognition from the temporary chairman, suggested that to save time, a National Committee be created. Instantly there was an uproar; delegates leaped to their feet demanding to be heard. Down the aisle toward Donnelly strode James B. Weaver, his moustache quivering with fury, his eyes flashing, demanding to be heard. Pointing his long arm at Donnelly, Weaver hotly denounced the proposal as a parliamentary maneuver designed to pledge the convention to the idea of a new party. Bolt upright in his seat, his lips turned in a smile, Donnelly retorted by asking Weaver if he thought "5000 people had traveled thousands of miles to get there, at their own expense, simply to pass a few resolutions and go home." The chairman ruled his motion to be out of order, but it was obvious that the vast majority of delegates supported his move to form a third party.[32]

Acknowledged for his literary distinction and his years of work for reform he was named a member of the convention's resolutions committee. The committee members elected him chairman, and he met with Robert Schilling, Milwaukee's veteran labor leader, and Kansas Congressman Jerry "Sockless" Simpson to draft a report. Determined to resolve their differences, the men locked themselves in a room at the Emory Hotel. "We had a stormy time," Donnelly recorded. Simpson who opposed immediate political action "almost came to blows" with Schilling. Donnelly was not favorably impressed with Simpson, "a curious character, keen and smart with many original ideas but neither profound nor wise." The committee, arguing until four o'clock in the morning, adjourned to meet at ten. By noon they had agreed upon a compromise. As Donnelly later explained, it was agreed to establish a People's party national committee organization which would attend a proposed Alliance

[31]Stuart Noblin, *Leonidas La Fayette Polk: Agrarian Crusader* (Chapel Hill: University of North Carolina Press, 1949), p. 269; Kansas City *Star*, May 23, 1891; St. Paul *Pioneer Press*, April 20, 1891.

[32]John D. Hicks, *The Populist Revolt* (Minneapolis: University of Minnesota Press, 1931), p. 213; St. Paul *Pioneer Press*, April 20, 1891; Minneapolis *Representative*, June 16, 1897; Donnelly MSS, Diary, May 19, 1891.

and reform convention in February, 1892, at St. Louis. If the St. Louis meeting, which was to be the response to a call for all reform elements, did not support a third party, the National Committee would summon a convention to nominate a presidential candidate.

Donnelly had formulated the compromise which proved satisfactory to both groups. At three o'clock in the afternoon, surprisingly fresh and clearheaded after his hectic night, he went before the convention, explained the compromise in a ringing speech, and, with a voice that could be heard in every corner of the hall, he read the platform which reiterated indorsement of the Ocala resolutions of the previous year. He apologized for the document's brevity and its failure to embrace proposals dear to many elements present, but in a crisis, he urged shortening the creed to lengthen the party's lists.[33]

Following Donnelly's speech, "fatigue, foreboding, quarrels vanished," among the delegates, "as if struck out by lightning. Breathless and hushed the listening hundreds," heard him conclude, "We think we have performed work which will affect the politics of this country for the next fifty years."[34] A wildly enthusiastic thirty-minute demonstration followed. Flags were massed, delegates with state banners and placards marched through the aisles, Texas rebel yells rent the air, Northern blue and Confederate gray shook hands beneath a waving American flag, while men and women shouted and clapped their approval. "The audience," Donnelly wrote, "was crazy with excitement, many of them in tears."[35] The convention adopted the platform with scarcely a dissenting vote. Named to the newly established National Committee, he was to organize Minnesota's People's party.

Donnelly was the hero of the convention. Having "found the third party advocates an unorganized mob, state delegations acting independently and all looking for a leader," commented the Kansas City *Star*, "leadership was thrust upon him and he brought order out of chaos."[36] The *Pioneer Press*, infuriated by his leap to national prominence, editorialized: "Donnelly may be fairly recognized as

[33]Hicks, *Populist Revolt*, p. 215; St. Paul *The Great West*, May 29, 1891; Donnelly MSS, Diary, May 19, 1891.
[34]St. Paul *Pioneer Press*, May 21, 1891.
[35]St. Paul *The Great West*, May 29, 1891; Donnelly MSS, Diary, May 19, 1891.
[36]Kansas City *Star*, May 23, 1891.

the leading spirit of the convention of cranks and adventurers, of political charlatans and their ignorant dupes."[37] *The Great West,* proclaiming his triumph, hailed him as the "Grand Old Man from Dakota County." Throughout the nation, Fish observed, Donnelly was being considered as a presidential candidate. He was acknowledged the "father of the People's party," his oratory had overwhelmed the convention, and although he was cool toward the subtreasury plan, he had a courageous record on the issues of transportation and finance.[38]

Having reclaimed the initiative, Donnelly summoned a meeting of the political leaders of the Minnesota Alliance and its executive committee at the Merchants Hotel in St. Paul. Over the strenuous protests of Eva McDonald, Eric Olson, John Hompe, and R. J. Hall, the Alliance withdrew its indorsement of the Alliance Labor Union party and accepted the People's party as its political vehicle.[39] Donnelly compromised with the opposition to the extent of appointing Carrington Phelps to the People's party central committee because James H. Baker and Sidney Owen pledged that the move would prevent an Alliance Labor Union party convention in 1892. Later, Donnelly, who had no confidence in Phelps, admitted that he would have preferred no truce with the old group,[40] but having forced them to accept Fish as a committee member, he may have thought that a generous gesture was required.

When the news of Donnelly's action regarding the Alliance Labor Union party spread through the Alliance, one of his followers who missed the significance of his tactics wrote: "You must have the disposition of a 'Christ' to hug your enemies to your heart as you have."[41] Fish objected even more vigorously to Donnelly's policy; "A man who cannot crush cannot survive," he warned. "These men are after your scalp—use you to boost themselves—and lose no moment to lie . . . and misrepresent you." Refusing to associate with Owen, who "could knife you & me & is doing it every hour," Fish continued to be critical of Hall and Phelps.[42]

To escape from the heated controversies and the petty squabbles of political life, Donnelly relaxed with what he termed literary

[37]St. Paul *Pioneer Press,* May 22, 1891.
[38]St. Paul *The Great West,* June 6, 12, 1891.
[39]*Ibid.,* July 10, 1891; St. Paul *Pioneer Press,* July 8, 1891.
[40]St. Paul *Pioneer Press,* July 8, 1891; Donnelly MSS, I. D. to M. Cutter, July 9, 1891.
[41]Donnelly MSS, W. R. Hally to I. D., July 13, 1891.
[42]*Ibid.,* E. Fish to I. D., September 17, 1891.

pursuits. Encouraged by the success of *Caesar's Column*, he wrote *Doctor Huguet*, a fantasy dealing with the race problem in the South. Written during his spare moments in the autumn of 1890, the book pleased him because it read smoothly. He experienced a great sense of relief after he returned the final proofs to F. J. Schulte. When writing, Donnelly always feared he would never live to complete the manuscript.[43]

Published in September, 1891, *Doctor Huguet* received very unfavorable reviews.[44] Donnelly, unable to fix the tone of the book, had devoted an entire chapter to a discussion of the intellectual and literary attitudes of Elizabethan England in a work that was otherwise a straightforward narrative. Even *The Great West's* complimentary review conceded that the first thirty pages were dull.[45]

Despite its structural and stylistic failings (much of it sounded like a cross between a political speech and a sermon) and its forced passages touching on Baconianism, *Doctor Huguet* was a book with a daring if not satirical twist. The story dealt with a brilliant young southern physician, infatuated with an intelligent and beautiful woman who encouraged him to enter politics to serve mankind but persuaded him to keep secret his views on racial equality because they were too radical.[46] When Doctor Huguet considers entering political life, the author, through the Faustian contrivance of a transfiguration, places Huguet's soul and mind in the body of the coarsest, most brutal and evil Negro in his community. The Negro assumes possession of Huguet's body and status. The narrative recounts the steady success of evil in the person of Huguet's body, and the failures of brilliance, honesty, and courage in the form of Huguet's soul and mind locked in the body of the black man. Only in the field of religion is the transformed Huguet able to find outlet, but the white community apprehensively views him as a threat to public safety. His worst foe is his own body, protected by status, although propelled by evil. The transformation is reversed when the Negro slays his own form and Huguet's soul and mind are freed to reclaim possession of his own body.

As a fantasy, *Doctor Huguet* was a startling book. With great

[43]*Ibid.*, Diary, May 17, 1890, July 16, 1891; I. D. to K. D., June 12, 1891.
[44]*Ibid.*, F. J. Schulte to I. D., September 9, 1891.
[45]St. Paul *The Great West*, September 18, 1891.
[46]Donnelly believed that the Negro was capable of a healthy life in American society, but he had his doubts about the Indian who seemed disinterested in assuming the customs and responsibilities of the white. *Doctor Huguet*, p. 214.

sympathy for the southern intellectuals and the impoverished Negroes who were struggling to achieve a *modus vivendi,* Donnelly struck hard at the opaque discipline of the southern mind in dealing with race, its inability to apply standards: good or evil, moral or immoral, legal or illegal, and the willingness of a group of intelligent people in the South to compromise their principles to gain political power. Written forty years too late to fit into the radical antislavery literature and published at a time when the Negroes' struggle for legal and personal status was practically at a standstill, *Doctor Huguet* was not destined for popularity. The book trod too heavily on the manners and mores of too large a segment of the population. Apart from a few courageous Alliance leaders who sought to merge white and Negro Alliances and who openly dared to identify the race issue as a device for keeping conservatives in power, and a handful of educators who accepted Donnelly's faith in education as the answer to the most pressing problem in the South, he had few supporters.

In 1899, Donnelly announced that the book had passed through five editions, but the number printed was probably quite small. Occasionally *Doctor Huguet* kindled a flame in the heart of a reader. Burton O. Aylesworth, president of Drake University, wrote Donnelly that the book "assaults prejudice like a tempest. . . . Every black man has been something other than he was, since I read Dr. Huguet. . . . I am not the same myself!"[47] The feelings of at least one Negro concerning the book were expressed by a Little Rock, Arkansas, physician who wrote Donnelly, "Any white man who can afford to speak out in such unmistakable terms for a race who have so little with which to reward him, is to be praised by every colored man."[48] In many ways *Doctor Huguet* constituted a restatement of Donnelly's position as a Radical Republican during the Civil War, coupled with the People's party attitudes.

Donnelly's law suit against the *Pioneer Press,* the consequence of the paper's publication during the legislative session of William S. King's letter in the Springer episode, came to trial in mid-October, 1891. The *Pioneer Press* editors pointedly asserted that the real significance of the case was Donnelly's political future. The paper retained Judge Charles Flandrau, who argued that King's letter had been published in 1884, that it had been given to the paper by the plaintiff, that it was not published with malicious intent, and

[47]Donnelly MSS, B. Aylesworth to I. D., February 4, 1892.
[48]*Ibid.,* J. H. Smith to I. D., March 29, 1892.

that, so far as the newspaper knew, the statements made in the letter were true. Cyrus Wellington, Donnelly's attorney, contended that the letter, originally sent to the congressional committee as a handwriting sample, contained scandalous allegations which the *Pioneer Press* knew to be entirely untrue. Wellington produced evidence that the editors had admitted they were in error but refused to retract the letter. Because Donnelly's income derived from the sale of books and from public lectures, Wellington asked one hundred thousand dollars in damages as a result of income loss.[49]

Judge Flandrau, attempting to prove that Donnelly had no reputation to destroy, sought to sustain King's allegations. General Le Duc willingly testified that Donnelly had accepted Hastings & Dakota stock while in Congress. But under cross-examination, he confessed that it was for service other than securing the land grant. Le Duc also admitted personal hostility toward Donnelly stemming from his opposition to Le Duc's giving control of the Hastings & Dakota to Oakes Ames.[50]

William S. King, the major witness, stated that Donnelly had tried to buy his brother Dana's vote in a party caucus, that he had heard from others that all he had written in the letter was true, that he had seen a letter from Donnelly to one Charles Clark referring to five hundred dollars Donnelly had paid for a senate vote, and that Colis P. Huntington had sent King a twenty-five-hundred-dollar negotiable instrument to be given to Donnelly. King's allegations were successfully impugned by Wellington. Dana King, mentally ill, was not able to testify; Charles Clark was dead and there was no Clark letter to substantiate the charge. As for the Huntington draft, King had no copy of it, could give no explanation of why Huntington should have sent him a negotiable instrument intended for Donnelly. In cross-examination, King forgot details and contradicted himself. Furthermore, Wellington impugned King's personal character as a witness by pointing out that he had fled to Canada to avoid testifying in a law suit in 1874, that he remained away until he was exempt from prosecution, and that he had been indicted for perjury.[51]

Testifying in his own behalf, Donnelly denied all the charges against him. He knew nothing of a Huntington draft. Under oath he recapitulated the story of his congressional work for the railroads,

[49]St. Paul *Pioneer Press*, October 21, 1891.
[50]St. Paul *The Great West*, October 30, 1891.
[51]St. Paul *Pioneer Press*, October 22, 1891.

denying any technical wrongdoing or even doubtful conduct. He had not sued the *Pioneer Press* in 1884 when the letter first appeared because he had been too poor for a contest.[52]

At the close of the hearing, the presiding judge directed the jury as to the law, pointing out that none of the allegations had been proved, and that Donnelly had indeed been injured. Cheerfully, Ignatius wrote to Kate that he hoped for at least a fifty-thousand-dollar settlement.[53] The jury, however, awarded only one dollar and court costs![54]

Donnelly was crushed, boasted the *Pioneer Press*; his reputation was worth one dollar! The paper claimed that the jurors had actually believed King, but legal technicalities necessitated their decision. *The Great West,* in Donnelly's defense, pointed out that the small judgment stemmed from Donnelly's having given the letter to the paper ten years earlier. Nevertheless, Fish cried, the settlement was grossly unfair.[55] But Donnelly's prestige had been dealt a severe blow. Herman E. Taubeneck, chairman of the People's party National Committee, confided to Eva McDonald that "the $1.00 verdict in the Pioneer suit had completely queered Donnelly's chances for the presidential nomination."[56]

Although keenly disappointed, ten days after the humiliating settlement Donnelly, feeling as young, strong and vigorous as he had at twenty, noted in his diary a "fierce determination not to be suppressed or trampled underfoot, but to fight the good fight for truth and right, as long as God gives me life."[57] He was resolved to strengthen the Alliance, despite the waning interest among Minnesota farmers because of an excellent harvest and sharply increased wheat prices. In announcing the annual meeting he rallied the members. "Our enemies expect that by telling us we are dead we will die," he wrote. "They think that because the pressure of want has been lessened . . . we will give up our principles and submit to any injustice."[58] Donnelly also fought to retain control of the organization. As in the preceding year, he called for instructed dele-

[52]*Ibid.,* October 24, 1891.

[53]Donnelly MSS, I. D. to K. D., October 23, 1891.

[54]St. Paul *Pioneer Press,* October 25, 1891. The court costs ran in excess of $4000; St. Paul *The Great West,* July 8, 1892.

[55]St. Paul *The Great West,* October 30, 1891.

[56]Dollenmayer MSS, E. McDonald Valesh to A. Dollenmayer, November 24, 1891.

[57]Donnelly MSS, Diary, November 3, 1891.

[58]St. Paul *The Great West,* December 4, 1891.

gates who would prevent the Alliance from becoming the tail of the Democratic kite. "*The Alliance*," he emphasized, "must stand alone or go down."[59] *The Great West*, meanwhile, warned that the Hall clique and Eva McDonald were preparing to oust Donnelly and reject the People's party.[60]

When the Alliance convened in Minneapolis, Donnelly presented a vigorous two-hour speech on the state of the organization and its program. He acknowledged that the number of active chapters had declined to three hundred and seventy-seven, a result of naming Eva McDonald state lecturer rather than naming an active Allianceman to the post, but he predicted renewed vitality and growth in 1892. "The real issue in our politics today," he jabbed at gold standard politicians, "is whether the dollar or the man shall rule this country." The time had passed when men served the state, he said. "Government was made for man—not man for government." The federal government must establish postal savings banks so that there would be no profit and no gambling with the people's money. He decried the expenditure of a million dollars for a new state office building in marble, by a legislature that would not build a grain elevator for the state's farmers. Nevertheless, he was not pessimistic. "The thinking part of mankind goes forward, dragging the conservative part along by the heels," he said, "but they go forward and the history of man's advance along the pathway of time, is recorded in the broad tracts [*sic*] the conservative leaves in the mud."[61]

The *Pioneer Press* labeled Donnelly a dictator when he retained the presidency of the Alliance and replaced Eva McDonald with Dr. Fish.[62] Aside from the Alliance presidency, the key issue of the convention was the subtreasury plan. Donnelly and Fish favored the entire Cincinnati platform, including the subtreasury; their opponents, who realized that fusion with the Democrats was impossible if the subtreasury was accepted, fought the scheme. Donnelly pushed the subtreasury plan through the convention.

As the Alliance president, he was selected to head the Minnesota delegation to the forthcoming St. Louis convention.[63] But he had been too moderate for his dynamic and excitable lieutenant, Dr.

[59]Donnelly MSS, circular, December 15, 1891.
[60]St. Paul *The Great West*, December 25, 1891.
[61]*Ibid.*, January 8, 15, 1892.
[62]St. Paul *Pioneer Press*, January 6–8, 1892.
[63]*Ibid.*, January 7, 8, 14, 1892.

Fish. When Donnelly allowed James H. Baker to be selected as a convention delegate, Fish fumed in angry criticism of Donnelly's inability to remain implacably hostile to a foe. Enemies, the editor insisted, should be crushed. Unless Donnelly could force himself to be merciless to their opposition, Fish threatened to sell *The Great West* and to give up the fight.[64]

The creation of a People's party National Committee at the Cincinnati convention permitted the advocates of independent political action to plan for the St. Louis convention. Donnelly learned that C. A. Powers of Terre Haute, Indiana, had joined National Committee Chairman Herman E. Taubeneck in assuming that the southern Alliances would oppose political action as a third party. Convinced that the southern Alliance group would dominate the convention unless the People's party men planned a strategy in advance, Taubeneck hoped to distribute pro-third-party men in as many northern delegations as possible.[65] As part of preconvention strategy Donnelly attended a meeting, sponsored by Frances Willard, of the Women's Christian Temperance Union in Chicago where he joined Weaver in drawing up a program to be submitted at St. Louis. Donnelly spoke out boldly against the saloon, and prudently in favor of woman suffrage on a municipal basis.[66]

On Washington's birthday, as temporary chairman Colonel Ben Terrell of Texas let fall the gavel to call the St. Louis convention into session, a huge audience sat beneath the dazzling lights of an electric chandelier in Exposition Music Hall. On the stage were more than three score of the leaders of the reform movement. The Associated Press, reporting for Republican and Democratic newspapers, referred to the participants as "the greatest gathering of the representatives of disaffected political elements that the world has ever seen."[67] For more than a day, while Colonel L. L. Polk, Mrs. Mary E. Lease, Torrence V. Powderly of the Knights of Labor, and Donnelly, presented speeches, the credentials committee attempted to provide a legal basis for representation. On Donnelly's motion, Frances Willard and the Women's Christian Temperance Union delegates were seated.[68]

[64]Donnelly MSS, E. Fish to I. D., January 9, 1892.

[65]*Ibid.*, C. A. Powers to I. D., January 3, 17, 1892; H. Taubeneck to I. D., July 7, December 4, 30, 1891, January 14, 1892; M. Rankin to I. D., September 4, 1892.

[66]*Ibid.*, F. Willard to I. D., December 8, 1892; St. Paul *The Great West*, February 5, 1892.

[67]Quoted in *The Great West*, February 26, 1892.

[68]The most complete description remains Hicks, *Populist Revolt*, pp. 205–37.

Although about eight hundred delegates gained approval, the fierce arguments before the credentials committee vouched for the fact that the third-party question sharply divided the members. The election of L. L. Polk as permanent chairman was a victory for the delegates who favored independent political action. But the opposition to a new party by southern Alliance leaders who were fearful of splitting the white vote was so strong that the People's party National Committee decided to avoid an open clash which would have threatened the show of unity. The third-party issue, therefore, was dropped while a resolutions committee drafted a platform.

Divided as the delegates were on tactics and such major issues as fiat currency, the subtreasury, and government ownership of railroads, they were all acutely aware that they lived in an America where, both in the city and on the farm, people could and did starve and where men and women could wander hungry and desperate without any hope of public assistance. The vividness of their speeches and immense popularity of *Caesar's Column* among the delegates indicated that big business and all the machinery of a technological age haunted their thoughts with an apocalyptic image that seemed destined to be ghastly reality—a society from which had disappeared not only the early nineteenth-century political relationship between man and the state, but also the sense of humanity which had antedated the social application of Darwinian evolution.

When Donnelly came before the convention to present the platform preamble which he based on earlier convention calls and manifestoes, he focused on the very essence of the movement.

We meet in the midst of a nation brought to the verge of moral, political and material ruin. Corruption dominates the ballot box, the legislatures, the Congress, and touches even the ermine of the bench. The people are demoralized. Many of the States have been compelled to isolate the voters at the polling places in order to prevent universal intimidation or bribery. The newspapers are subsidized or muzzled; public opinion silenced; business prostrate, our homes covered with mortgages, labor impoverished, and the land concentrating in the hands of capitalists. The urban workmen are denied the right of organization for self-protection; imported pauperized labor beats down their wages; a hireling standing army, unrecognized by our laws, is established to shoot them down, and they are rapidly disintegrating to European conditions. The fruits of the toil of millions are boldly stolen to build up colossal fortunes, unprecedented in the history of the world, while their possessors despise the republic and endanger liberty. From the same prolific womb of governmental injustice we breed two great classes—paupers and millionaires. The national power to create money is appropriated to enrich bondholders; silver, which has been accepted as coin since the dawn of history, has been demonetized to add to the purchasing power of gold by decreasing the value of all forms of property as well as human labor, and the supply of currency is purposely abridged to fatten usurers, bankrupt enterprises and enslave industry. A vast conspiracy against mankind has been organized on two continents and is taking possession of the world. If not met and overthrown at once it forbodes terrible social convulsions, the destruction of civilization, or the establishment of an absolute despotism.

In this crisis of human affairs the intelligent working people and producers of the United States have come together in the name of peace, order and society, to defend liberty, prosperity and justice.

We declare our union and independence. We assert one purpose to support the political organization which represents our principles.

We charge that the controlling influences dominating the old political parties have allowed the existing dreadful conditions to develop without serious effort to restrain or prevent them. They have agreed together to ignore in the coming campaign every issue but one. They propose to drown the cries of a plundered people with the uproar of a sham battle over the tariff, so that corporations, national banks, rings, trusts, "watered stocks," the demonetization of silver, and the oppression of usurers, may all be lost sight of. They propose to sacrifice our homes and children upon the altar of Mammon; to destroy the hopes of the multitude in order to secure the corruption funds from the great lords of plunder. We assert that a political organization, representing the political principles herein stated, is necessary to redress the grievances of which we complain.

Assembled on the anniversary of the birth of the illustrious man who led the first great revolution on this continent against oppression, filled with the sentiments which actuated that grand generation, we seek to restore the government of the republic to the hands of the "plain people," with whom it originated. Our doors are open to all points of the compass. We ask all men to join with us and help us.

In order to restrain the extortions of aggregated capital, to drive the money changers out of the temple, "to form a [more] perfect union, to establish justice, insure domestic tranquility, provide for the common defense, promote the general welfare and secure the blessings of liberty for ourselves and our posterity," we do ordain and establish the following platform.[69]

After the reading of the platform, which was shorter than the preamble, reiterating and strengthening the Ocala demands by calling unequivocally for government ownership of railroads, the audience's thundered applause was interrupted by shouts for Donnelly. The crowd surged forward and many people on the platform surrounded him attempting to shake his hand. L. L. Livingston of Georgia, recognizing in Donnelly's preamble a moral commitment

[69]Donnelly MSS, February 24, 1892; see also Hicks, *Populist Revolt*, pp. 435–37.

to a third party, moved for the adoption of the platform without mention of the preamble, but the followers of Tom Watson, Livingston's Georgia rival, saw through the ruse and called for its inclusion.[70] After approving the preamble and the platform overwhelmingly the convention adjourned.

By prior arrangement, and with the vast majority of the delegates remaining in their seats, the group reconstituted itself a mass meeting of individual citizens. Weaver, who was named chairman, promptly appointed a committee to meet with the executive committee of the People's party. The two committees merged. The remaining consideration was a suitable date for the People's party nominating convention. Donnelly favored arranging for an early convention, but Weaver suggested that the convention be delayed until both Republicans and Democrats, disillusioned with their parties, would turn in hope to the People's party. Despite Donnelly's warning that this policy could be "suicidal," in that it left the initiative with the older parties, Weaver's proposal was adopted. July 4 was set as the convention date.[71]

When Donnelly returned from St. Louis he began converting the Minnesota Alliance into the People's party by asking each chapter to ratify the St. Louis platform.[72] *The Great West* announced that he was seeking the People's party gubernatorial nomination and that he planned to make sixty-five speeches prior to the state convention to develop the issues of the campaign.[73]

Through the newspaper and in his speeches, Donnelly elaborated upon both the St. Louis platform and his ideas for progressive state government. He reiterated his opposition to Henry George's single-tax plan because it would injure the farm owner.[74] Donnelly examined the status of railroad regulation in detail; as early as 1889, he had anticipated that the United States Supreme Court would reverse the Granger rulings. He explained that the Court's recent decisions, based on a revolutionary application of the Fourteenth Amendment in *Chicago, Milwaukee, & St. Paul Railroad Company*

[70]C. Vann Woodward, *Tom Watson: Agrarian Rebel* (New York: Rinehart & Co., 1938), p. 202. Southern white supremacists were duly shocked when Donnelly, sounding like Doctor Huguet, boldly asserted, "The new order of things would wipe out the color line in the South."

[71]Fred E. Haynes, *James Baird Weaver* (Iowa City: State Historical Society of Iowa, 1919), pp. 308–9; Hicks, *Populist Revolt*, p. 229.

[72]St. Paul *Pioneer Press*, March 16, 1892.

[73]St. Paul *The Great West*, April 1, 1892.

[74]*Ibid.*, April 15, 1892.

v. *Minnesota* were the worst since Dred Scott. The Court had construed an amendment intended to guard the rights of Negroes as individuals to protect the intrenched interests of business corporations from legitimate regulation for the public weal. The Court, Donnelly contended, was "the last ditch of Plutocracy in the country, packed by the great railroad corporations, in consideration of immense largesses given to corrupt the presidential elections." Respect nothing that does not warrant respect, he told his listeners; "judicial wigs and gowns are no more to me than so much horse-hair and dry goods."[75] The fact that the Court had upset legitimate efforts to control the railroads convinced Donnelly that public ownership achieved through purchase at a fair price was the only solution to the problem of railroad regulation.

At the outset of the campaign Donnelly did not discuss silver currency or the increasing rate of land mortgages. Touring western Minnesota, he saw farmers burning straw in their stoves instead of coal, and his "blood boiled" to think that "33 cts is stolen off the price of every bushel of wheat" to pay speculators and processors. Confirmed in his conviction that it was "God's work to expose and resist such robberies," he became more and more vituperative.[76] In the smaller towns extraordinary crowds gathered to hear him, people having come from twenty-five and thirty miles away, but in St. Paul Donnelly was denied the use of a hall and Robert Schilling, who shared Donnelly's podium, was showered with rotten eggs by unruly Republicans.[77]

A rumor that Donnelly was seeking the People's party nomination for the presidency gained currency when Jerry Simpson indorsed him.[78] Even after learning that he was not a potential candidate, Simpson wrote him expressing his conviction that Donnelly's "great ability" and years of service had earned him the honor.[79] When *The Great West* denied any presidential aspirations on Donnelly's part, it tacitly voiced preference for the ticket of Weaver and Polk.[80]

After attending a People's party National Committee meeting at Omaha, Nebraska, Donnelly issued the call for the Minnesota convention explaining that labor groups would be welcomed. Denying

[75]St. Paul *Pioneer Press*, January 10, 1889; St. Paul *The Great West*, March 30, 1890, April 8, 1892.
[76]Donnelly MSS, Diary, June 15, 1892.
[77]St. Paul *The Great West*, June 24, 1892.
[78]St. Paul *Globe*, March 18, 1892.
[79]Donnelly MSS, J. Simpson to I. D., April 21, 1892.
[80]St. Paul *The Great West*, May 13, 1892.

that there was anything secret about the People's party, he charged that such allegations were a pretext to introduce religious bigotry into the campaign. He was not amused when the Democratic St. Paul *Globe* called him "the absolute dictator of the People's party." Some men, he thought, would be flattered by the statement; he was not. "I have not the first element of a 'boss.' And, if I had, the People's party would not stand any such dictator for twenty-four hours."[81]

As Donnelly organized the People's party, Phelps of the Alliance Labor Union party issued a call for a rival convention. Phelps, who opposed the subtreasury and government ownership of railroads, counted on the support of John Hompe and James H. Baker. An April meeting of the Alliance Labor Union party's executive committee offered to make peace with Donnelly, if they could gain representation at the People's party Omaha convention. But Donnelly ignored the proposal. *The Great West* ridiculed the idea of uniting with a group basically hostile to the essential program of the new party.[82]

Early in April, 1892, the Republican newspapers prophesied that the People's party and the Democrats would be forced into a merger, but Michael Doran tartly answered that "the Democratic party will not fuse with a lot of ———— cranks."[83] Fish labeled the Republican statement an "awful lie," asserting that "no man in the People's party even *considers* the matter."[84] He published a letter from party chairman Herman E. Taubeneck stating that "fusion means confusion" and that "the very moment we use them [votes or offices] as trading stock . . . we will sink into oblivion."[85]

But Donnelly learned secretly from Taubeneck that plans had been made for the Democrats to replace their presidential electors with People's party electors in states where the combined vote might upset the Republican majority. It was hoped that this would force the election into the House of Representatives by preventing Harrison from winning a majority of the electoral votes.[86] This information, plus the knowledge of planned mergers between the Democrats and the People's party in other states may have led Donnelly to send Fish, protesting and reluctant, to discuss fusion with Minne-

[81]*Ibid.*, June 10, 1892, quoting the St. Paul *Globe*.
[82]*Ibid.*, April 29, 1892.
[83]St. Paul *Pioneer Press*, April 5, 1892.
[84]St. Paul *The Great West*, April 15, 1892.
[85]*Ibid.*, April 29, 1892.
[86]Donnelly MSS, H. E. Taubeneck to I. D., June 16, 1892.

sota's Democratic Congressman J. N. Castle and with the editor of the St. Paul *Globe*. Fish later explained that he had undertaken the mission to sabotage it. Rumors of a Democratic-People's party merger persisted until late in October when the Democratic leaders grudgingly yielded to orders from Cleveland's managers in New York and accepted the People's party electors. The People's party executive committee, using the lame excuse that it lacked lawyers, indorsed two Democrats for state judgeships.[87]

Shortly before the Omaha convention, Donnelly heard from Lester C. Hubbard, editor of the Chicago *Vanguard*, urging him to support Judge Walter Q. Gresham for the People's party presidential nomination. Donnelly was later reassured that Gresham, definitely seeking the nomination, was willing to accept the St. Louis platform except for the subtreasury plan. Gresham's advocates wanted Donnelly to meet Taubeneck in Chicago for a party caucus, or pledge Minnesota to Gresham. Although Donnelly telegraphed to Chicago that Gresham was highly respected, he added, "I cannot speak for delegation until we meet in Omaha."[88]

Perhaps in the hope of dramatizing its work, the People's party convened July 2 at Omaha's Coliseum so that it could present its program on the anniversary of the Declaration of Independence. Ten thousand delegates and spectators crowded the circular auditorium which had been decked with flags, banners, and evergreen. The hot Nebraska sun which shone through the building's many windows rivaled the warm enthusiasm demonstrated on the convention floor.

While the credentials committee wrestled with the problem of bogus reform organizations and contested delegations, Donnelly, as the party's most distinguished orator, was called upon to sound the keynote for the convention. "There is not a single president of a railroad company," he roared to the cheers of the crowd; "there is not a single representative of any of the rings which are robbing or sucking the life blood out of the American people." What a contrast, he pointed out, existed between this convention and the Democratic and Republican meetings, which were in the hands of monopoly. "I want it understood that I am not saying anything

[87]St. Paul *The Great West*, January 12, 1894; Minneapolis *Farm, Stock and Home*, May 1, 1893; St. Paul *Representative*, April 19, 1893.

[88]Donnelly MSS, L. C. Hubbard to I. D., June 17, 1892; A. Frain to I. D., June 20, 1892; I. D. to A. Frain, June 22, 1892. There was a rumor that Gresham had been converted to the People's party position after reading *Caesar's Column*. See Hicks, *Populist Revolt*, p. 233.

against the rank and file of either of these parties," he added hastily bringing shouts of "good" from his audience. But, "this battle in which we are employed is the battle of mankind. This continent is the last great camping ground of the human race. If liberty fails here," he warned, "it fails forever. Every oppressed nation in the world is looking upon this convention to discover whether the . . . stars and stripes shall float across the country steadily rising generation after generation to higher levels of culture and civilization, or if it shall float a solemn mockery above a land cursed as Europe is cursed—the middle class driven off the land, while concentrated in the hands of a few is the wealth provided by the toiler." If the party failed, he said, reiterating the jeremiad of *Caesar's Column,* the American people faced a future as drab as that of the starving Oriental.[89]

Despite a half-hearted effort to nominate Gresham, originating with the leadership of the Knights of Labor, and without the late L. L. Polk to offer a genuine alternative, the selection of Weaver was a foregone conclusion. An effort on the part of a few Minnesotans who were eager to prevent Donnelly from seeking the gubernatorial nomination urged that he receive a place on the national ticket. The pro-Donnelly Alliance delegates, however, "did not favor chasing rainbows"; they were certain he would be Minnesota's governor.[90] Had a southerner such as Polk been nominated, perhaps Donnelly or Dakota's Senator James H. Kyle would have been a logical vice-presidential candidate. Weaver's nomination dictated a southern running mate. General James G. Field of Virginia was the obvious choice.

More enthusiasm was displayed for the People's party platform than for the candidates. Although the platform committee proposed no basic changes in the long-standing demands for the subtreasury, bimetallism, public ownership of transportation and communication, and the elimination of alien landownership, land monopoly, and land speculation, it proposed several resolutions which touched off heated debate. Of particular concern to Donnelly was the resolution supporting the boycott against the Rochester ready-made clothing companies. "If this resolution was simply to express our prejudice as a class, I would not support it," he told the convention, but "it is a declaration that free men will not clothe their limbs in the goods of manufacturers of this slave-making oligarchy." To

[89] St. Paul *The Great West,* July 8, 1892.
[90] *Ibid.*

loud cheers from labor delegates, he added his familiar cliché, "It is war to the knife and knife to the hilt." Calling for the withdrawal of opposition based on the mere word "boycott," he demanded and received a rising vote of support for the boycott resolution.[91] As at St. Louis, when Donnelly read his platform preamble, now presented in an expanded version, the delegates were wildly enthusiastic.[92]

Returning to Minnesota he faced the final organized opposition of the Alliance Labor Union party which had held its convention July 7 with the intention of forcing Donnelly into a conference. Their convention had conditionally nominated James H. Baker for governor, but it had appointed a committee led by W. W. Erwin to attend the People's party state convention.[93] The group realized that every Alliance chapter in the state, even those in the Fifth District, had indorsed the People's party. Erwin had no bargaining power.

Perhaps because of their weakness, or their nuisance value, or the fear that he would be accused of "bossism," Donnelly allowed W. W. Erwin to attend the convention and address the delegates. One of the finest public speakers in Minnesota, Erwin began pleading for unity, asking the convention to temper its stand on the subtreasury, but before he could finish speaking shouts of "liar" from the delegates interrupted him and in the ensuing uproar the Alliance Labor Union committee left the hall. Defeated on the state level, the Alliance Labor Union party withdrew its gubernatorial candidate, but continued to oppose the People's party in local races.[94]

The People's party convention nominated Donnelly for governor by acclamation. This harmony did not survive the indorsement of Owen for the United States senatorship. Determined to keep Owen, whom he viewed as a traitor, off the ticket, Fish demanded that Owen subscribe to the Omaha platform. Owen refused to accept the subtreasury scheme, and over groans and shouts of no fewer than one-fifth of the delegates, he was rejected as a candidate.[95] The alienation of Owen's friends was matched by the convention's refusal to honor Donnelly's request that a temperance plan be in-

[91]Quoted in Eric Goldman, *Rendezvous with Destiny* (New York: Alfred A. Knopf, 1952), p. 47.
[92]St. Paul *The Great West*, July 8, 1892.
[93]St. Paul *Pioneer Press*, July 8, 1892.
[94]Donald F. Warner, "Prelude to Populism," p. 145.
[95]St. Paul *The Great West*, July 22, 1892.

cluded in the platform, an action which resulted in the formation
of a Prohibition party that further split the reform vote. Aside
from the Omaha platform, the convention turned more sharply
radical in demanding direct government by referendum rather than
legislative action.[96]

Although Donnelly was confident of victory, 1892 was a presidential election year, and party feelings, sometimes weakened during off-year contests, were usually revitalized by national issues.
Even though the Democrats nominated an ineffective campaigner,
Daniel Lawler, he was a St. Paul Roman Catholic who appealed
for votes on a religious education question. The Democrats were
certain Lawler could cut deeply into precincts where Donnelly's
very name would otherwise have attracted votes. Furthermore, and
even more important, the Republicans were so frightened that they
turned to the most effective Scandinavian "vote-getter" in Minnesota, Knute Nelson. Although Nelson began his career as a political
maverick demanding social legislation, he had become increasingly
conservative and less flexible in his thinking on economic and social
issues. His selection was an open admission that the Republican
party could no longer count on Minnesota's Scandinavian vote
without paying more than lip service to their politicians. It was no
secret by 1892 that Nelson was a rather poor reformer, but he was an
excellent Norwegian! Nelson, however, appealed to the voters on a
platform favoring a low tariff, railroad regulation, and state industrial supervision.

Donnelly began campaigning by challenging Nelson and Daniel
Lawler to debate the issues in a "good natured, courteous and in-
cisive manner." He planned seventy-five speeches throughout the
state, promising to make the coming campaign "the liveliest ever
seen in Minnesota."[97] Scoffing at charges that he was ill and would
withdraw, that he had parted association with Fish, and that he was
working for fusion, Donnelly stated that he was in the race to advocate the Omaha platform. After Nelson refused to debate Donnelly
in Austin, Minnesota, when both men were in the town to make
political speeches on the same day, the Democratic St. Paul *Globe*
pointed out that Nelson had suffered a setback.[98] However, he

[96] St. Paul *Pioneer Press*, July 14, 15, 1892.
[97] St. Paul *The Great West*, August 19, 1892.
[98] St. Paul *Globe*, September 1, 1892. Knute Nelson did not lack for courage.
After a fight on the hustings, *The Great West* headlined: "Knute slugs a
farmer," October 28, 1892. Donnelly had his troubles too. When a heckler
interrupted a speech to ask about the *Pioneer Press* libel suit he spat back,

scored a coup at Donnelly's expense by releasing a letter Fish had written to him in 1890 offering complete support if Nelson would accept the Alliance indorsement for governor.[99]

In the midst of the campaign, Donnelly published *The Golden Bottle*, a political tract "intended to explain and defend in the thin disguise of a story, some of the ideas put forth by the People's party."[100] In that the book depicted America under People's party direction, it was a utopian novel presenting an alternative to *Caesar's Column*. The story was a fantasy concerning the adventures of a Kansas youth, Ephraim Benezet, who secured a bottle of liquid which would convert base metals into gold. In discussing the social and political impact of this power—the power to create money by fiat—Donnelly described the impoverished condition of western farmers, the high interest rates, the harassment of debtors, and the corruption within the banking system. Developing his plot, Donnelly emphasized many of the prevailing fears of rural America, just as he had in *Caesar's Column*. He focused particular attention on the migration of farm families to the cities as a result of mortgage foreclosures. Urban working conditions, especially sweatshop situations in the clothing industry, destroyed the moral vitality of women. Prostitution and delinquency in American cities were the by-products of rural depression. Donnelly stressed also the dishonesty of the American newspaper editors who, lacking honor and integrity, interpreted the news to satisfy the economic interests of their employers.

In tracing the rise of Benezet, armed with the power to create money, to the presidency of the United States, Donnelly extolled temperance, woman suffrage, a general rise in the status of women, the nationalization of railroads, the elimination of slums, and the advantages of a broad educational system. The key which would unlock the door to these treasures for the American people was a flexible monetary system allowing full development of economic opportunity, unrestrained by the predatory banking interests.

In the final portion of the book, Donnelly treated America's role in the world. He reaffirmed his faith that it was America's destiny to

---

"That dollar did not represent the value of my reputation, but the amount of injury which the Pioneer could inflict upon any man's reputation." *Pioneer Press*, November 6, 1892.

[99] St. Paul *The Great West*, September 9, 1892.

[100] *The Golden Bottle* (St. Paul: D. D. Merrill, 1892), p. 3.

extend the "doctrines of the Revolution of 1776 . . . over all the continents and all the islands." Benezet, in his inaugural address, boldly proclaims that the progress of the United States has been limited by the flood of impoverished immigrants from Europe. Europe's debauched aristocracy has survived in the industrial era because it could export labor. "Our country was the safety-valve which permitted the discontent of the Old World to escape. If that vent was closed, every throne in Europe would be blown up in twenty years." In language reminiscent of *Caesar's Column*, Benezet adds: "For the people of the Old World, having to choose between death by starvation and resistance to tyrants, would turn upon their oppressors and tear them to pieces."[101]

The world struggle conceived by Donnelly in 1892 was broader than the one for political democracy that characterized the Young America Movement of the Jackson era. "There can be no peace so long as a single toiler is denied the fruits of his own industry," Benezet tells his listeners. "For the first time, the great republic cries out to the humble of the world 'The blessings we enjoy should be yours, it is better to die fighting than live as slaves.'"[102]

Although Donnelly carefully pointed out that the People's party opposed war, Benezet precipitates a war with all of Europe and summons the oppressed masses to overthrow their governments. Leading an army of Negroes and whites who fight as brothers in the common cause of liberty, Benezet, accompanied by generals conveniently named Weaver, Field, Taubeneck, and Schilling, liberates all of western Europe.[103] The German Kaiser William could only be humbled by military defeat. The Russian tsar's assassination by nihilists who have infiltrated the Russian officer corps breaks the fanatical loyalty of the peasant soldiers and allows Benezet to succeed where Napoleon failed. With autocracy overwhelmed everywhere in Europe, Benezet establishes a United States of Europe and eventually a Universal Republic for the world, startlingly similar to the League of Nations. Significantly, nationalism and national self-determination were a vital aspect of the new order. Benezet encouraged the Jews to establish a national state in Palestine.[104] The

[101] *Ibid.*, pp. 201–3.

[102] *Ibid.*, pp. 204–5.

[103] Donnelly enjoyed himself sprinkling the book with names of friends whom he made heroes and thinly disguised the names of enemies whom he painted as venal.

[104] It is interesting that *The Golden Bottle*, written in the heat of the campaign, was virtually devoid of anti-Semitism.

offices of the world organization which were located in the Azores—
the mountain tops of "Atlantis"—were as oriented to economic
problems as to world peace.

The fantasy ends as a dream. Benezet is awakened to the truths of
the People's party, especially the money issue. Even as he is forced
to leave his farm, a victim of mortgage foreclosure, he prepares to
work for the utopian world which the People's party program could
produce. Donnelly used the proceeds from the sale of the book to
help finance the People's party campaign.[105] Although published in
both hard covers and in a paper cover edition, *The Golden Bottle*
saw only one printing.

The publication of the book marked a change of emphasis in
Donnelly's campaign. He began discussing the mortgage question as
it related to grain prices. His speeches pointed to the obvious disparity between the prices farmers received and the world market
price. The producer, he insisted, was being robbed for the benefit of
the middle man. If elected, he promised legislation which would
redistribute the profits in grain production.

Even more significant, for the first time Donnelly made the
demonetization of silver—the "Crime of '73"—a genuine campaign
issue. In a signed article, he publicly defended the theory of a
conspiracy on the part of English bankers, including the Jewish
House of Rothschild, who were interested in having American bonds
repaid in gold so that they could make enormous profits and who
secured the demonetization of silver by corrupting the American
Congress. Although the conspiracy idea had already gained wide
circulation in the wheat and silver states after the publication of
Mrs. S. E. V. Emery's sensational book *Seven Financial Conspiracies,* Donnelly felt compelled to document his acceptance of
the theory by references to *Banker's Magazine* and the *Congressional Record.*[106] Incredible as the conspiracy concept appeared to
many people even at that time, to Donnelly it probably had unusual plausibility. His own experience in Congress and as a lobbyist
in the Grant Era strengthened his conviction that Congress could
be manipulated. If millions of acres of land could be given to railroad entrepreneurs, there was nothing startling in the idea that
silver could be demonetized to satisfy the wishes of private
bankers, especially if the silver producers manifested no opposition.

In mid-October, Donnelly assessed his political campaign. He

[105] Donnelly MSS, circular, August 10, 1892.
[106] St. Paul *The Great West,* October 14, 1892.

had encountered tremendous enthusiasm. Never before had he been able to raise campaign funds so easily. "Men rush up . . . and thrust $5.00 bills in my hands," he wrote Kate, but "I will be glad when the fight is over, no matter how it ends." Donnelly had already completed more than one hundred and fifty speeches since he began his drive for the governorship.[107] The campaign, however, had been complicated by Fish, who continued to attack the opponents of the subtreasury plan. Donnelly begged Fish "to let S. M. Owen alone until after the election at least. Every attack you make on Owen loses me votes," he told the editor, "and I trust you will not continue them unless you want to see me defeated." The Republicans, he concluded, were "tickled" by Fish. Donnelly was reluctant to order a special ten-thousand-copy edition of *The Great West* if it would serve to "stir up dissension in our ranks."[108]

The national People's party organization had not been of assistance to Donnelly early in the campaign. Weaver failed to raise money in the silver mining states. Taubeneck was always short of campaign funds. Despite Weaver's personal courage—he carried his canvass into Georgia where he was virtually mobbed—the candidate disappointed Taubeneck because of his lack of organizational ability.[109] Late in October, Weaver, with Mrs. Mary E. Lease, famous for her speeches telling Kansas farmers to "raise less corn and more hell," toured Minnesota. Having committed himself to the silver cause, Weaver's speeches centered on the conspiracy theme.[110] Donnelly appreciated Weaver's help, but he realized that he needed labor support in the Twin Cities. Torrence V. Powderly of the Knights of Labor, who could not campaign in Minnesota because of illness, wrote an open letter to Minnesota's workingmen asking them to turn out for Donnelly. Powderly reminded the labor organizations that when the controversial boycott provision came before the Omaha convention, "Donnelly took the floor and electrified that vast audience by his eloquent plea for justice." Labor had no truer friend, stated Powderly; "I never listened to anything so forcible, so sweeping, so keen and so fair."[111]

The Republicans concentrated their attack upon Donnelly because Lawler was unlikely to penetrate the Scandinavian strong-

[107]Donnelly MSS, I. D. to K. D., October 16, 1892.
[108]*Ibid.*, Diary, October 16, 1892.
[109]*Ibid.*, H. E. Taubeneck to I. D., July 27, August 4, October 1, 1892.
[110]St. Paul *The Great West*, October 28, 1892.
[111]Donnelly MSS, November 1, 1892 (copy).

holds. A Chicago Norwegian-language newspaper, widely circulated in Minnesota during the campaign, repeated the exploded charge that Donnelly had been bribed by the Union Pacific Railroad and called him the pope's candidate.[112] Threatened lawsuits were futile against this type of vilification. Not as vicious, but equally damaging, were the charges in the Republican newspapers that the People's party was "destructive, chaotic and socialistic." The *Pioneer Press* had a more valid contention when it insisted that farm prices were not as low as Donnelly made them out to be. Minnesota wheat was selling for more than ninety cents a bushel in Chicago. To elect a People's party candidate, the newspaper argued, would mean another turbulent legislature that would upset the finances of the state.[113] So violent had the campaign become that on the eve of the election, *The Great West* prepared a special edition naming Donnelly "The Great Commoner" and Knute Nelson a "claim jumper," and the St. Paul *Pioneer Press* drafted an entire issue charging that Donnelly and Michael Doran had secretly agreed to allow Doran to enter the United States Senate if Donnelly won the governorship.[114]

The very vigor of his campaign had impressed Donnelly. "I rejoice to think that I am so near the end of my work. . . . I have conversed with 10,000 persons, wrote a novel, prepared two 'broadsides' of eight pages each; carried on a large correspondence and supervised the whole campaign. I hope to win," he wrote, "& yet nothing is certain." He was keenly aware that 1892 was a "presidential year & the Republicans have a majority of 11,000 over the Democrats and 40,000 over the Alliance on the vote two years ago." Rationalizing, he confessed, "I may have spent all my immense labor for nothing; but I felt it was my duty to make the fight in the interests of the country and mankind." Still horrified by the terrifying prospect that man would lose not only his heritage but also his humanity, he added, "I believe in *Caesar's Column*, and I would avert these results if possible." Then sloughing off his mood, Donnelly concluded, "I have had a grand campaign; tremendous meetings—great enthusiasm. I shall have done some good even if I am beaten."[115]

In many parts of the nation the People's party gained congres-

[112]St. Paul *The Great West*, September 16, 30, 1892.
[113]St. Paul *Pioneer Press*, July 23, September 30, 1892.
[114]*Ibid.*, November 3, 1892; St. Paul *The Great West*, November 4, 1892.
[115]Donnelly MSS, Diary, November 3, 1892.

sional seats or came close to upsetting the established political power structure, but the 1892 showing was considerably weaker than it had been two years before. Donnelly ran a poor third gaining scarcely 40,000 votes to Lawler's 94,000, and Nelson's 109,000 —the Prohibition ticket drawing off 11,000 reform votes. In the Fifth District, John Hompe had defected with his Alliance followers to work for the Republicans.[116] The Norwegian clergy, devoting a pre-election Sunday to Nelson's cause, stuffed the pews with Republican literature. There were also charges of wholesale use of money to buy votes.[117] But Donnelly suffered his greatest losses in the urban counties. The working men in Minneapolis and St. Paul had refused to support him. Despite his efforts and his convictions, he was unable to serve as the bridge between the rural and urban reform groups.

In disgust, he returned to his beloved and intriguing cipher "worth more than all the governorships in the world," and in his diary he wrote, "Beaten! Whipped! Smashed! . . . Our followers scattered like dew before the rising sun."[118]

[116] St. Paul *Pioneer Press*, October 14, 1892.
[117] Donnelly MSS, H. G. Day to I. D., November 25, 1892.
[118] *Ibid.*, Diary, November 10, 1892.

The Populist Interlude
1893–1894

---

*Whenever the prosperity of a people is attacked their
liberty and morality are both assailed.*

IGNATIUS DONNELLY

FOLLOWING the defeat of the People's party, Donnelly broke with
Fish. *The Great West* attributed the election loss to Donnelly's
pleas for harmony as well as his kowtowing to Minneapolis labor
groups, which had produced three thousand rather than thirteen
thousand votes. Because of the vigor of Fish's criticism, *The Great
West* was dropped as the official organ of the Alliance and Fish
resigned from the executive committee. He suggested that Owen
and Donnelly join him in withdrawing from the leadership of the
People's party. Without their personal animus, Fish was certain the
party would increase in strength.[1] The editor resented Donnelly's
charge that *The Great West* had devoted too much effort to national
affairs, but he did not loose his spleen on him even after Donnelly
appealed for funds so that the Alliance could secure a new paper.

In January, 1893, the Minnesota Alliance convened in Minneapolis. H. L. Loucks and General Weaver attended the session,
making pro-silver speeches and unsuccessfully urging the delegates to merge with the National Farmers' Alliance and Industrial
Union. The small delegations indicated that Alliance membership
had declined drastically. Donnelly, defending his election record
against *The Great West*'s charges, easily won re-election to the

[1] St. Paul *The Great West*, November 25, 1892; St. Paul *Pioneer Press*,
November 18, 1892.

[310]

presidency.[2] The Alliance platform reflected the impact of the election. Significantly, it omitted the subtreasury scheme, which linked the thinking of most Alliancemen with its "father," Dr. C. W. Macune, and was dropped when he withdrew from the Alliance movement during the campaign alleging "bossism" on the part of Loucks and Taubeneck. Macune joined Ben Tillman in subscribing to a fusion policy in the South.[3] Even without the subtreasury, the Alliance program of government ownership of railroads, unlimited coinage of silver, a graduated income tax, a referendum on prohibition, initiative, referendum, and woman suffrage, was a retreat from the Omaha platform.[4]

Although Donnelly wanted to retain his influence within the Alliance, his political prestige was low and he seemed prepared to abandon public life. "I do not expect to be a candidate again for any office," he told a *Pioneer Press* reporter. He added that at the close of the forthcoming 1893 legislative session, he wanted "to separate from all members of the senate on terms of kindness and good will."[5]

The desire to retire peacefully from politics at the close of the session did not overcome his determination to strike down as many as possible of the mélange of predatory institutions existing in Minnesota. His was one of the few dissenting voices to charge that special interests were at work in a bill permitting the state to fulfil private pledges to build a Minnesota exhibit at the Chicago World's Fair.[6] He voted with the minority who favored a state inheritance tax.[7] True to the People's party belief in direct democracy, he favored annual rather than biennial sessions.[8] He denounced, as a relic of barbarism, a measure which sanctioned the whipping of inmates in the state reformatory.[9] An Alliance-indorsed bill calling for a state-owned grain elevator had his hearty support.

Unlike conservative Alliance leaders, who were embarrassed because they had opposed the subtreasury scheme as dangerously

[2] St. Paul *Pioneer Press*, January 5–6, 1893.
[3] St. Paul *The Great West*, November 4, December 9, 16, 1892.
[4] *Ibid.*, January 13, 1893.
[5] St. Paul *Pioneer Press*, December 16, 1892.
[6] *Ibid.*, January 27, 1893; Donnelly MSS, S. M. Owen to I. D., January 28, 1893.
[7] St. Paul *Pioneer Press*, February 8, 1893.
[8] *Ibid.*, February 17, 1893.
[9] *Ibid.*, March 8, 1893.

paternalistic, and who seemed afraid to antagonize small grain elevator operators to please farmers,[10] Donnelly sincerely believed in state ownership of such vital public facilities. Since principle had actuated him to work for a state grain elevator, he angrily denounced Nelson's hamstringing of the project,[11] and he deeply regretted the state court's ruling it unconstitutional.

During the first month of the session, Donnelly introduced a resolution to be sent to the United States Congress demanding an investigation of price-fixing by the distributors of anthracite coal. Because of excessively high coal prices in Minnesota, an *ad hoc* senate committee was established under his chairmanship to determine if any state legislation would be applicable. He began taking testimony from coal dealers who explained that the supply of Minnesota hard coal was handled by a single individual, John J. Rhodes. Summoned to testify under oath before the committee, Rhodes was taciturn and hostile. Insisting that his business was private, Rhodes denied any knowledge of combinations to fix prices, restrain trade, or control the market. When questioned about his business records, he stated that he knew all of his customers so well that he kept no books. If they accepted Rhodes' testimony, the committee's investigations were at an end.

Rather than admit defeat, Donnelly sent a senate officer to Rhodes' offices and seized his books. The committee's action was taken without a court order. Minnesota's attorney-general, Henry W. Childs, warned that Donnelly's actions were illegal. When Rhodes asked for his records, Donnelly pointed out that he had perjured himself before the committee by denying the existence of any business accounts, but even more important, the seized materials presented positive proof of criminal conspiracy and price-fixing. Donnelly was preparing to turn his evidence over to the Hennepin County prosecutor.

Failing to regain his books from the senate, Rhodes sought a writ of mandamus. Reluctantly Attorney-General Childs, charged with defending the state's interests, prepared to defend the committee. He conceded that the evidence had been secured improperly, but asked the court to examine the motives of the plaintiff in secreting documents which had been requested by a legal body. A legal impasse followed. Donnelly asked the Hennepin County Grand Jury

[10]Chrislock, "Sidney M. Owen," pp. 117–18.
[11]St. Paul *Pioneer Press*, April 2, 19, 1893; St. Paul *Representative*, May 10, 1893.

to indict Rhodes for conspiracy, antitrust combination, and price-fixing. Rhodes brought suit against the committee for $50,000.[12]

The sensational disclosures of the committee restored Donnelly's influence throughout the state and substantiated his earlier allegations that the people were in the clutches of a predatory, merciless, corrupt gang of monopolists. The Minneapolis *Tribune,* congratulating him on his successful exposé, claimed that his prestige was so great that no measure could pass the legislature without his approval.[13] Public opinion was so thoroughly aroused that a citizens' committee organized a mass meeting to protest "coal combines" at Market Hall in St. Paul. Almost three thousand people shouted for Donnelly to address them. Having lost St. Paul in the preceding election, Donnelly greeted the crowd saying, "I am the most popular man in Minnesota—between elections." His vigorous condemnation of price-fixing and his demands for enforceable anti-monopoly legislation won prolonged applause. In reporting the meeting the *Pioneer Press* grudgingly admitted the existence of the combine, but condemned Donnelly for raising a fuss over an issue on which nothing could be done.[14]

Unable to secure action against Rhodes, the senate acceded to Donnelly's request for a resolution empowering Governor Nelson to appoint a commission to deal with the coal combine on an interstate level.[15] Nelson, finding himself forced into the role of reformer and realizing the incendiary nature of the anti-monopoly issue, decided to broaden the approach by calling an interstate Anti-Trust Conference to be held in Chicago. The governor invited Donnelly to join him in representing Minnesota.[16] Donnelly thanked Nelson publicly "for this mark of confidence." He hoped that a large convention, with delegates from many states would do a great deal of work, but he confessed a lack of optimism and a fear that the conference would serve to "whitewash all the villanies [sic]."[17] Privately, Donnelly wrote Henry D. Lloyd, People's party leader in Illinois, "Can you get all the People's party men together on Sunday afternoon" before the session. "Notify Genl. Weaver, Des Moines, Iowa—he is one of the Iowa delegates. Wire Gov. Waite, Denver, Colo. & suggest him to notify his delegation. Also Gov.

[12]St. Paul *Pioneer Press,* January 27, March 15, 16, 17, 19, 21, 1893.
[13]Donnelly MSS, F. N. Stacy to I. D., March 21, 1893.
[14]St. Paul *Pioneer Press,* March 14, 1893.
[15]*Ibid.,* March 20, 1893.
[16]Donnelly MSS, K. Nelson to I. D., May 19, 1893.
[17]St. Paul *Representative,* May 24, 1893.

Shortridge, Fargo, N.D. same request. . . . I fear the convention will be literally packed with tools of the Rings," he wrote. "I see John Sherman is to be present. That means the RRds. are scared." Donnelly cautioned Lloyd, "We must be prepared, if the convention is packed, to split it up & have a conference of our own that will mean something and do something."[18]

As permanent chairman of the Anti-Trust Conference, Nelson attempted to set the tone for the meeting by explaining that "what is needed is a law which will enumerate the acts of a trust which are illegal. It ought to prescribe a short and simple form of indictment. . . . The law should be made to clearly define what is a monopoly of trade."[19] Donnelly, Lloyd, and Weaver, however, demanded more immediate and more drastic action. In an impassioned speech, Weaver condemned trusts and urged direct political action through support of anti-monopoly politicians. "I am a radical in my views," said the erstwhile presidential aspirant, "but conservative in my method."[20] When Donnelly gained the floor, "a bundle of manuscripts in his hand and fire in his eyes," he read a set of resolutions calling upon the federal government to take possession of the anthracite fields by right of eminent domain, pay the owners a reasonable compensation, and operate the fields as a public trust. His resolutions also called for legislation which would allow the nationalization of all monopolies and the elimination of legal exemption for trusts and combines—in effect, by statute restrict the United States Supreme Court's interpretation of the due process clause in the Fourteenth Amendment.[21]

When Donnelly's radical proposals were defeated by a vote of forty-four to thirty-one, Lloyd, Weaver, and more than twenty-six delegates withdrew from the conference. In a separate meeting they denounced the majority, approved of Donnelly's resolutions, and accepted a suggestion from Weaver that they indorse bimetallism. Returning from Chicago, Donnelly blasted Nelson's convention as a "humbug" where "a lot of harmless, perfunctory, milk-and-water resolutions" had been adopted.[22] So that no one should misunderstand the meaning of his Chicago resolutions, Donnelly later ex-

[18]Henry D. Lloyd MSS, I. D. to H. D. Lloyd, May 30, 1893.
[19]St. Paul *Representative,* June 7, 1893.
[20]St. Paul *Pioneer Press,* June 7, 1893.
[21]*Ibid.,* June 7, 1893; St. Paul *Representative,* June 7, 1893.
[22]St. Paul *Pioneer Press,* June 7, 1893.

plained that there were two ideas put forth—"first, that a combine to rob the people had no right to the protection of the laws of the land; and . . . second . . . that there is no warrant in any constitution, state or national, which authorizes the courts to set themselves up above the congress, or the legislative branches." The People's party interpretation of the "theory of our government [is] that its [power] should rest with the great mass of the people, and not with a few lawyers." Or, more candidly, he added, "The principal object of government is the protection of human beings, not property." Donnelly not only considered the Supreme Court's actions in holding a corporation to have the rights of a person dangerous, but also ludicrous. Consider, he wrote, the bench will soon declare that "corporations have the right to marry and rear children."[23]

The coal exposé lingered in the courts for months. Prices did not decline, despite the extreme economic unrest in 1893. In reply to criticism that he had failed to get results, Donnelly angrily noted that he had no power to bring about change. If he were a dictator for one year, he intemperately announced, the monopolists would take "balloons for a new planet." The anthracite coal combine, tenaciously maintaining its control, refused to sell anthracite to a cooperative, except through the Rhodes agency where it was assured a 100 per cent profit.[24] The Grand Jury permitted Rhodes to escape a perjury indictment by denying that the senate had a right to administer oaths. Since the Grand Jury also refused to view unlawfully gathered evidence, it refused to bring an indictment for conspiracy. Rhodes won his case against the senate with a settlement compensation of thirty-five hundred dollars, but the judgment was vacated on appeal.[25]

While Minnesota was being rocked by Donnelly's disclosures about the coal combine, he suddenly found himself opening still another investigation. At his suggestion, Senator Henry Keller introduced a resolution on March 1 for a general investigation of tax evasion through unlawful exemption. Two days later a small sum of money was allocated to defray expenses, and the scope of the investigation was restricted to pine lands and school lands. Within a matter of days, as news of Keller's activities escaped the committee

[23] St. Paul *Representative*, June 28, October 18, 1893.
[24] *Ibid.*, October 25, November 15, 1893.
[25] *Ibid.*, June 7, 1893; January 10, 1894; St. Paul *Pioneer Press*, January 4, 9, 1894.

chamber, rumors spread over the state that colossal timber frauds had been uncovered.[26] On April 10, when the Keller committee submitted a report, Donnelly, who had served as minority party representative, told the senate that the findings of the investigation indicated a scandal that "will shake the state from center to circumference."[27] The Keller report, which discreetly omitted any names, although it was common knowledge that lumbering activities involved Minnesota's wealthiest and most socially prominent people, presented a mass of quickly gathered evidence that school and swampland pine reserves had been plundered.

Fifth District Congressman Loren Fletcher, a lumberman, immediately denounced this effort to malign and damage the reputation of men who had built Minnesota by subjecting them to investigation by a "rat-headed gang of reformers."[28] Thoroughly incensed by Fletcher's sanctimonious attitude and the personal attack, Donnelly seized the initiative in the senate by castigating Fletcher ruthlessly, suggesting that anyone who defended thieves was capable of theft.[29] Donnelly became the center of the stormy controversy when the *Mississippi Valley Lumberman,* a leading trade journal, called the Keller report "peculiarly Donnellian . . . the work of that dishonest political juggler."[30]

Because of the sensational results of the coal exposé neither the governor nor the legislature could allow this first pine land report to be pigeonholed. Using all his influence and prestige, Nelson, who saw an opportunity to make as well as wreck political fortunes, forced Minnesota's Republican legislators to accept a resolution introduced by Donnelly calling for a full-scale investigation. The governor was given the power to establish a joint house and senate commission which could investigate and bring suit against offenders. Five thousand dollars was allocated to the commission.[31] Although Donnelly stated that he did not wish to serve on the commission, he was not only appointed to it but was elected chairman.[32] All pine land sales were suspended during the investigation.

[26] St. Paul *Pioneer Press,* March 12, 1893.
[27] *Ibid.,* April 10, 1893.
[28] Minneapolis *Tribune,* April 12, 1893.
[29] St. Paul *Pioneer Press,* April 13, 1893.
[30] Quoted in Folwell, *Minnesota,* III, 505.
[31] Donnelly's resolution did not receive consideration, but a request from Nelson was approved. The governor, granted ten thousand dollars to survey the state's pine reserves, released a portion of it to the commission.
[32] St. Paul *Representative,* April 19, 1893.

With both time and money available, the commission employed as its investigator Harris Richardson of the St. Paul law firm of Warner, Richardson, and Lawrence. Under Donnelly's general direction and prodding—the actual investigation was painstakingly and courageously accomplished by Charles F. Staples—the commission checked the accounts of the state auditor whose office was charged with control of Minnesota's timber lands, combed the records of the surveyor-general, and sent its own timber scalers into the field to measure lumber. Patiently information was gathered, rumors of pine theft sifted, and legal briefs drawn up.

As evidence accumulated, some lumbermen came forward and simply paid their lawful obligations. The first case successfully prosecuted was against C. A. Smith and Company, a partnership in which former Governor "Honest John" Pillsbury was a silent but embarrassed partner. But even before the Smith case, Donnelly warned that the commission was unearthing vast frauds that touched major leaders in both Republican and Democratic parties.[33]

After twenty months of investigation, the commission submitted a report to the governor. The state auditor's office procedures were condemned as inconceivably bad. The land accounts were "not even an apology for records." The auditor had permitted land to be sold without any knowledge of its timber value. He had, in fact, actually accepted the judgment of the lumbering company doing the cutting. There was evidence that lumber companies kept as employees men who were official timber scalers for the surveyor-general. Even worse, the auditor had sold hardwood lands without the legal right to do so and even sold the land without holding a public auction. There had been timber cruising on state school lands—companies cutting school land lumber adjoining their holdings. It was surmised that there had not been a valid pine sale since 1885. Incredible, too, was the discovery that the state treasurer had permitted cutting prior to payment; some obligations were already eight years outstanding!

The commission reported that it had collected $30,526.29 without suit from two companies and one person. There were six lawsuits pending with the certainty of recovering $157,284.28. Briefs were in preparation against seventeen other legal entities in amounts totaling $205,076.44. But, in Donnelly's language, this was "a mere bagatelle" saved from school lands compared with the saving result-

[33] *Ibid.*, November 1, 1893, January 3, 1894; St. Paul *Pioneer Press*, December 8, 1894.

ing from frightened lumbermen who now filed honest reports. The commission estimated that the stopping of hardwood sales by the auditor during the two-year period probably saved enough to pay for the cost of the investigation. The commission asked that their task be continued by a new body because the work had only begun. At the close of the report Donnelly demanded new legislation for the lumber industry. "Close the doors absolutely," he begged, "and let the rascals find some other victims than the children of the State."[34]

David M. Clough, the Minneapolis lumberman who succeeded Nelson as governor, ignored the report and did not press for a new commission to continue the investigation and prosecution of timber violators. The legislature, however, guided by Charles F. Staples and Harris Richardson, enacted the first partially successful regulatory legislation. Unfortunately for Minnesota's treasury, without Donnelly in the legislature to demand prosecutions for triple indemnity and complete restitution, an amendment to the regulatory bill was quietly added authorizing the state auditor to compromise existing claims. Behind this act, and actually in violation of its spirit, State Auditor Robert C. Dunn settled the pending suits for one-tenth of the state's claims. Governor Clough did not attempt to complete the legal briefs which the commission had begun. The "lumber barons" of Minnesota were far too influential in the 1890's to fall victim, even to an irate public.[35]

In the 1893 legislature, Donnelly heralded the first dawn of Minnesota's Progressive Era. He was broadly humanitarian not in the emotional but in the historical sense in his opposition to corporal punishment in the Minnesota penal system. His concern for more direct popular government and his scathing comments regarding the Supreme Court's interpretation of the Fourteenth Amendment were indicative of a rejection of the idea of government for the people rather than by the people. Most important, Donnelly's muckraking investigations, albeit they were sensational, intimating or es-

[34]Ignatius Donnelly, *Report of the Pine Land Investigating Committee to the Governor of Minnesota filed with the Governor December 21, 1894* (St. Paul: Pioneer Press Printing Co., 1895). Personally Donnelly favored closing the forests to private companies and creating a state monopoly.

[35]Donnelly MSS, I. D. to Warner, Richardson & Lawrence, April 2, 1894. Folwell, *Minnesota*, III, 514, refers to the amendment as "a noble and convenient act of grace." Folwell also refused to publish the names of the plunderers because "by making liberal benefactions to churches, communities, and colleges [they] have brought forth fruit meet for repentance!"

tablishing conspiracy, were coldly rational in that the quest for evidence and their findings disturbed primarily the thoughts of men rather than their emotions. The pine land investigation reports did not ask Minnesotans to feel that there was sin in the world; it asked them to pass legislation protecting the public interest. Furthermore, the clear-cut acceptance of paternalism, where the public interest demanded it, was never more clearly evident.

During the early months of 1893, when Donnelly was beginning his investigations, he was actively rebuilding the waning influence of the Alliance. His state lecturer, L. C. Long, even encouraged Eva McDonald, who had married labor leader Frank Valesh, to remain in the movement. Donnelly began publishing the *Representative*, a weekly newspaper, which he hoped would provide for open discussion of Alliance and People's party issues without fear or favor. He willingly sought a compromise with Owen's friends, contending that internecine warfare had defeated People's party programs and candidates. "We must have peace," he joked, "even if we have to fight for it."[36]

As Donnelly sought agreement with Owen, he found himself at war with his friend Fish. The editor of *The Great West* grew increasingly hostile and more personal in his criticism of Donnelly's leadership when the *Representative* appeared. In late April, Fish denounced Donnelly as an egomaniac, expressing regret that he had ever supported him.[37] The *Pioneer Press* enjoyed the spectacle of Fish repeating all of the familiar anti-Donnellyisms while Ignatius accused Fish of accepting Republican bribes. Threats and counterthreats of libel suits were hurled, but there was no formal legal action.[38]

Fish vindictively denied that he had written *Donnelliana*, a highly laudatory campaign biography prepared under his name in 1892, to which was appended a collection of Donnelly's more well known sayings and platform jokes. The editor charged that Donnelly had written the book himself. Although Donnelly refused to acknowledge authorship of the work, it had been compiled by him and his son-in-law George Giltinan, and rewritten and edited by Fish. That Donnelly had exercised the author's prerogative re-

[36]Donnelly MSS, L. C. Long to I. D., January 28, March 22, 1893; St. Paul *Representative*, April 19, 1893.

[37]St. Paul *The Great West*, April 28, 1893.

[38]*Ibid.*, May 5, 19, 24, 1893; St. Paul *Representative*, May 10, 17, 1893; St. Paul *Pioneer Press*, May 13, 1893; and Donnelly MSS, E. Fish to I. D., May 13, 1893.

garding content is certain; he signed the contract, and the manuscript eventually returned to his possession.[39] In fact, F. J. Schulte who had published Donnelly's first novels objected to a portion of the book which he termed an "anonymous slander." After a sharp quarrel, Schulte refused to print parts of the original manuscript.[40]

As the Fish-Donnelly argument reached a climax, the editor hinted that he was preparing a *Donnelliana* of a different type. He filled *The Great West* with letters from angry subscribers demanding that Donnelly withdraw from the People's party leadership. In an open letter to party chairman Taubeneck, Fish called for Donnelly's expulsion from the National Committee because he favored fusion.[41] Although Donnelly replied to Fish's attack with equally vitriolic rejoinders, the *Representative*'s primary argument was that success for the program was possible only through a reconciliation of the Donnelly, Owen, and R. J. Hall factions.[42]

While Donnelly was struggling to retain a voice in the People's party and carrying out his senate investigations, the United States was swept into the most serious depression of the nineteenth century. Declining economic conditions in Europe, the opening of vast new agricultural areas, and the completion of the nation's basic railroad network, plus unrestrained speculation and consolidation in industry, combined to produce a sharp money panic, business failures, unemployment, and the lowest agricultural prices since the Civil War. Cleveland, re-elected to the presidency in 1892, was in large measure convinced that agitation for unlimited coinage of silver had disturbed popular confidence in the economy. Launching a program to increase the federal government's gold reserve, he also determined to repeal the Sherman Silver Purchase Act, which permitted the government to pay its obligations in coin—gold or silver. He was eager to reassure the business community that there would be no devaluation of the dollar.

[39]St. Paul *The Great West*, September 11, 1891, May 24, 1893; St. Paul *Representative*, June 14, 1893; Donnelly MSS, F. J. Schulte to I. D., August 7, 1891; December 7, 1891; contract for book, February 13, 1891; Diary, August 31, 1891. It is worth noting that Kate interceded with Donnelly on behalf of his sisters who pleaded that Donnelly exclude the fact that his father had been a Mason. "They are women," she wrote, "religious Catholic women. . . . This point is vital in their social relations." Donnelly omitted the item. Donnelly MSS, K. D. to I. D., November 23, 1891.

[40]Donnelly MSS, F. J. Schulte to I. D., December 21, 1892.

[41]St. Paul *The Great West*, June 2, 9, 16, 23, July 7, 1893.

[42]St. Paul *Representative*, June 7, 1893.

Because of Cleveland's decision the battle was joined between those advocates of currency manipulation favoring a cautious expansion of the economy through a balanced budget, relatively high interest rates, and the gold standard; and those advocates of manipulation favoring a more dynamic economy through inflation. This was not, as it had on occasion been described, a struggle between conservative Republicans and Democrats who opposed juggling the financial policies of the government and a group of radicals subscribing to currency manipulation. It was really a question of whether the manipulation would be on behalf of those who stood to gain through lower prices, "tight money," and high interest rates, and those who stood to gain through increasing prices, "soft money," and low interest rates.

Since a return to bimetallism was the most obvious means of expanding the economy, the producers of silver, many of whom shared little with the inflationists other than an interest in silver prices, became deeply involved in the politics of currency manipulation. A National Bimetallic Coinage Association with a headquarters in Washington, D.C., began promoting the return to silver as early as 1886 when the price of silver dipped because of increased production. The nature and size of the investment in silver dictated that its producers would not surrender their largest potential customer —the United States government—without a struggle. The production of silver was related to the mining of such other metals as lead, copper, and gold. The value of these holdings had grown until by 1890 three times as much money was invested in silver as in iron mines. The dollar output value of the silver mines, even in depressed times, exceeded one-fourth the dollar output of coal, the life-blood commodity of the industrial era.

Not only were thousands of people involved in silver production, but also after 1890 virtually every silver-producing state had entered the union prepared to exercise its influence in behalf of bimetallism. The growing political importance of the silver states was evident in the passage of the Sherman Silver Purchase Act by a strictly Republican Congress in 1890. More significant was the rapid penetration of silver advocates into all parties by 1892, especially the People's party. By 1894, through non-partisan organizations such as the American Bimetallic League, the National Bimetallic Union, and the Pan-American Bi-Metallic Association, a flood of pamphlets and news releases, many crudely anti-Semitic and anglophobic in character, repeated the conspiracy theory of the role of Anglo-Jewish bankers in the silver demonetization and demanded absolute unlimited coinage.[43]

The People's party was peculiarly vulnerable to silver propaganda. It was committed in theory to an expanding economy based on managed currency; it was centered in areas already anglophobic and apparently latently anti-Semitic; and more important, it lacked the financial support which organized silver producers could provide. Although Weaver had failed to raise a large war chest during his swing through the silver states in 1892, the thought of using silver as the device to gain power captured the imagination of Weaver and many of the more pragmatic People's party politicians. By the time Cleveland determined on the repeal of the Sherman Silver Purchase Law, a complex three-way struggle was in progress among Democratic, Republican, and People's party politicians as to which could capture the other in the net of silver.

At an all-day meeting of Alliance and People's party leaders in St. Paul in July, attended by Weaver and Senator William A. Peffer of Kansas, the silver question was given a complete airing. Weaver asked all the delegates who were present to denounce Cleveland's attempt to repeal the Sherman Law and to support the American Bimetallic League. In echoing Weaver's pleas, Peffer suggested that silver was becoming the key question of the day. Donnelly, who had been named vice-president of the American Bimetallic League, explained that he was prepared to promote the silver cause in Minnesota and had the power to appoint local co-ordinators.[44] A few days later, Donnelly was told by an optimistic Taubeneck that the People's party could benefit from the silver element. Taubeneck wanted a meeting of the party's executive committee to map strategy for an August conference of the American Bimetallic League.[45]

The Chicago conference of the American Bimetallic League was held just prior to the opening of the special session of Congress

---

[43]Except for some educated guesses in Hofstadter's *Age of Reform,* no adequate socio-political history of the silver movement exists. It is interesting to notice that the government's obligation to repay in gold became a moral issue among non-economic groups in society, especially Eastern established churches. It is somewhat ironic that the "Bible belt" of Bryan's strength reflected an ambivalence that warrants additional analysis.

[44]St. Paul *Representative,* July 12, 1893.

[45]Donnelly MSS, H. Taubeneck to I. D., July 8, 1893.

summoned by Cleveland to repeal the Sherman Silver Purchase Law. Weaver was selected to preside over the giant protest meeting,[46] and although a substantial number of Democrats and Republicans attended, the most aggressive speeches were made by members of the People's party. Governor Davis H. Waite retained for himself the sobriquet "Bloody Bridles" when he shouted, "If it is forced upon us . . . it is better, infinitely better, rather than that our liberties should be destroyed by tyranny . . . that we should wade through seas of blood—yea, blood to the horses bridles."[47]

In large measure Donnelly set the tone of the conference when the delegates demanded that he address them. He spoke for an hour, reiterating a theme he had created in the *Representative*, which denounced the demonetization of silver as one of the most iniquitous actions of the age. Emphasizing the role of conspiracy in the "Crime of '73," he asserted that the Constitution would not be "blotted out or become a weapon in the hands of the European Rothschilds." The people were aroused, he insisted; Democrats, Republicans, Prohibitionists, the People's party were "singing the same song." He confessed that he preferred fiat money, but since this was unattainable in the immediate future, he believed the forces of reform should unite behind silver, since to do otherwise would result in a victory for plutocracy.[48] As a member of the resolutions committee, in which capacity he impressed William Jennings Bryan, Donnelly helped draft the formal statement which denounced the conspiracy of 1873 and demanded the immediate opening of the mints to unlimited coinage of silver.[49] Read to the enthusiastic delegates by Donnelly, the resolutions were adopted.

The *Pioneer Press* used Donnelly's role in the convention to condemn the proceedings. Notorious to the readers of the *Pioneer Press* after *Caesar's Column* as the man who favored "gory revolution" and who even dared to praise as courageous and honest Illinois Governor John Peter Altgeld's pardoning the "Haymarket Riot anarchists," Donnelly's very presence in Chicago defined the conference as un-American and anarchistic. In the weeks that followed, the paper happily reported that St. Paul's bankers were supporting

[46]Chicago *Tribune*, August 1–4, 1893.
[47]St. Paul *The Great West*, August 11, 1893.
[48]*Ibid.*, St. Paul *Representative*, August 2, 9, 1893.
[49]William J. Bryan, *The First Battle* (Chicago: W. B. Conkey Co., 1896), p. 153; St. Paul *Representative*, August 5, 1893.

Cleveland. The *Pioneer Press* predicted that the Silver Act would be repealed.[50]

By the early autumn of 1893 as the depression deepened, business slowed, industrial production almost reached a standstill, and the number of unemployed workers mounted steadily, even the *Pioneer Press*, which rarely varied its readers' fare from attacks on Cleveland as a Democrat with praise for his hard money policies, reported a steadily increasing incidence of worker mass meetings and rioting. On August 26, Donnelly spoke to an enormous gathering of unemployed workers at Market Hall in St. Paul. Although he vigorously condemned the Cleveland administration, he truthfully and logically pointed out that the depression was world-wide in its scope. "The remedy is not to be found in violence," his listeners were told, "but in a peaceful solution of the problem."[51] To shed "a single drop of blood would disgrace our civilization," he said. The solution to the pressing economic problem was twofold. First, a return to a growing economy required more money, and silver was the easiest means of gaining it. To attack the Sherman Silver Purchase Law as causing the depression, as the gold-standard Republicans and Democrats did, was a cruel joke. Second, the immediate need was for a public works program which would give men work and income as well as getting business started. Since neither the cities of Minnesota nor the state itself had funds necessary to carry out such a program, Donnelly called for deficit spending to fight the depression. "I believe in such a crisis we have a right to shift the burden upon posterity, or in other words to borrow from the future."[52]

Government spending as a public policy, however, was too radical a doctrine for Minnesota in the 1890's. Donnelly denounced critics of government intervention who feared that free institutions would be jeopardized by trying to legislate prosperity. "What is freedom worth to a man who is dying of hunger?" asked the *Representative*. "Can you keep a room warm, next winter, with the thermometer at 30° below zero, by reciting the Declaration of Independence? Wherever the prosperity of a people is attacked," he warned, "their liberty and morality are both assailed."[53]

[50]St. Paul *Pioneer Press*, August 2, 3, 9, 13, 1893; St. Paul *Representative*, July 5, 1893. Donnelly had expressed the idea that the Haymarket trials were a travesty of justice.

[51]St. Paul *Pioneer Press*, August 22, 27, 1893.

[52]St. Paul *Representative*, August 30, 1893; St. Paul *Pioneer Press*, August 27, 1893.

[53]St. Paul *Representative*, September 13, 1893.

For both laborers and farmers, Donnelly viewed the future apprehensively. "Hang on to your land to the last gasp," he advised Minnesota's farmers. "There are no more Minnesotas on the planet; and every day the battle of life will grow fiercer."[54] Recognizing as did most public men that the frontier era was drawing to a close, Donnelly warned: "We have practically reached the limit of our available free land supply. That free-land has been the safety-valve of Europe and America. When that valve is closed, swarming mankind every day will increase the danger of explosion. Nothing can save the world but the greatest wisdom, justice and fair play."[55] The prospects of achieving a just society seemed dim indeed.

The status of the working man "is terrible," Donnelly informed readers of the *Representative*. "It is with them not a question of making money, but of avoiding starvation." An unprecedented trend in the nation's history was taking place, Donnelly noted. "Hundreds and thousands are going back to Europe; others are moving into the woods, building shanties, reverting to Indian conditions."[56] Always in the back of Donnelly's mind, surging forward when economic conditions approached alarming proportions, was his vicious anti-Orientalism. The attempt to repeal Chinese exclusion legislation during the depression winter of 1893 provoked an inflammatory anti-Chinese editorial in the *Representative*. The opponents of exclusion legislation were charged with wanting to see a "Chinaman, who can live on rice and rats, work for 30 cents a day, put down by the elbow of every American mechanic, to reduce him to the same fare and wages . . . and drive the producers off their land." Exploiting the immorality seemingly implicit in the nineteenth-century American's image of the Oriental, he added, "They can stock them [the lands of Caucasian farmers] with rat-tailed slant-eyed Mongolians, where one wife will do for a whole township, and neither public schools nor churches will be needed."[57]

When Cleveland overcame congressional opposition and succeeded in gaining the repeal of the Silver Purchase Act, wheat

[54] *Ibid.*

[55] *Ibid.*, November 15, 1893. That Donnelly had read news accounts of Frederick Jackson Turner's paper "The Significance of the Frontier in American History" given July 12, 1893, at Chicago seems highly probable. He may also have seen Turner's article, "Problems in American History," which appeared in *Aegis*, a University of Wisconsin student publication. Certainly the similarity of Donnelly's phrasing to Turner's is too striking to be dismissed as coincidence.

[56] St. Paul *Representative*, September 20, 1893.

[57] *Ibid.*, November 8, 1893.

prices slumped twelve to fifteen cents a bushel, reaching a post–
Civil War low. There was, however, no corresponding decline in the
costs of distribution, transportation, or production. Freight rates
dipped only slightly, but taxes remained firm, some even increasing
because of expanding demands for public services. Little wonder
that Cleveland's Secretary of Agriculture, J. Sterling Morton, drew
the criticism of rural politicians when he contended that the American farmers were suffering least in the depression and coupled his
statement with the charge that the leadership in the Alliances was
"farming the farmers" for personal gain.[58]

Within the Minnesota Alliance, personal squabbles frequently
attracted as much notice as issues. During December, the month
preceding the 1894 conventions, Fish enlivened his unrelenting
attack on Donnelly's leadership. Ironically, in his effort to oust Donnelly from the Alliance presidency, Fish boosted Owen. The editor
pointed to Owen's acceptance of the silver cause and blamed Donnelly for the decline in the number of Minnesota Alliance chapters
from twelve hundred in 1891 to two hundred and fifty in 1893. But
Donnelly recruited considerable popular support as a result of his
success in the legislature and his willingness to share leadership with
Owen's group. Even R. J. Hall agreed that Donnelly had worked
conscientiously to harmonize the discordant elements in the Alliance.[59]

The *Pioneer Press* doubted that Donnelly would retain his control
of the Alliance in the face of Fish's slashing attacks. Predicting a
vigorous fight on the convention floor, it expressed the belief that the
members wanted him out of the movement.[60] The *Pioneer Press's*
prediction of a hectic session was fulfilled when, after a day of political maneuvering, newspaper reporters were excluded at nine o'clock
and Fish began a two-hour tirade against Donnelly. He reiterated
his charges, both personal and political, heaped vitriol and invective
upon his former associate, and in completely unrestrained language
termed him a "fat brute." For an hour, Donnelly replied in kind.
When Fish asked for a formal investigation, Donnelly supporters
refused, turned off the lights, and adjourned the meeting.[61] Donnelly

---

[58]*Ibid.*, Carl C. Taylor, *The Farmers' Movement, 1620–1920* (New York:
American Book Co., 1953), p. 282.

[59]Donnelly MSS, R. J. Hall to I. D., December 28, 1893.

[60]St. Paul *Pioneer Press*, January 9, 1894.

[61]St. Paul *The Great West*, January 12, 1894.

retained the Alliance presidency; disgusted, Fish announced that *The Great West* would be moved to South Dakota.

The victory had probably been secured with a nod from Owen's friends on the promise that Donnelly would not seek the gubernatorial nomination. More than mere expediency dictated Donnelly's decision. Patrick Rahilly, his good friend, had written candidly to Donnelly two weeks before the convention. "The fact is Mr. Donnelly is all right to make speeches, write platforms, plead the people's cause, but when it comes to vote for him that is quite another matter."[62] But, an even more important consideration may have been Kate, who had suffered a severe stroke in November, 1893. Although she was recovering slowly, Kate may have requested, as she had so many times in the past, that he forsake political office for health reasons.

On the day of the convention Donnelly announced: "I am not a candidate for any office and *never will be*. I am growing old and the grave is not many years ahead." He proposed to spend the remaining years of his life dedicated to his conviction "that the best religion in the world is that of doing good to our fellow creatures." And he added, "If any ambitious man thinks I stand in his way, in any respect, I am ready to 'step down and out.' "[63] Despite the fact that Owen had been cool to the prospect of Donnelly's re-election as Alliance president, two weeks later the *Representative* indorsed Owen as the logical gubernatorial candidate of the People's party.[64] In the months that followed, Donnelly continued to advocate Owen as the party's best choice.

As Minnesota's People's party moved toward unity, the party's national leadership clashed on the silver issue. Weaver and Peffer, who indorsed it as the key issue, faced opposition from Congressman "Sockless" Jerry Simpson, Governor Davis H. Waite of Colorado, and Tom Watson of Georgia. Although Donnelly had welcomed Weaver and Peffer to Minnesota in July, 1893, had accepted a vice-presidency in the American Bimetallic League, publishing its attacks on the Rothschilds as Anglo-Jewish bankers, and had attended the August Silver Conference in Chicago, he refused to make silver

---

[62]Donnelly MSS, P. Rahilly to I. D., December 28, 1893.

[63]St. Paul *Representative*, January 10, 1894.

[64]*Ibid.*, January 24, 1894; Donnelly MSS, S. M. Owen to I. D., February 5, 1894; H. G. Day to I. D., February 23, 1894; I. D. to Owen, February 24, 1894 (letter press copy).

the major issue. Acutely aware that the major parties might be frightened into remonetizing silver as a technique for smashing the entire reform movement, he warned that "if silver was remonetized, there are still vastly important questions of government paper money, of an abundant currency, of land, and of transportation."[65]

Taubeneck, however, viewed the policy question from a different angle. In Washington, the advocates of silver, both Republicans and Democrats, were discussing the establishment of a silver party. "We must recognize the fact that if a new party is organized and they make the money question the great issue," Taubeneck wrote Donnelly; "we will receive no more recruits, except a few socialists and communists, and that many of our best men in the West will leave us to join the new movement. Without silver," Taubeneck's jeremiad continued, "we will simply become the forerunner of a great third party that is to be organized, as the abolition party was to the republican party."[66]

Nevertheless, Donnelly refused to remain too closely associated with the silver group in the party. "We all believe that metallic currency is a temporary expedient—a relic of barbarism," he replied to a critic who accused the party of selling out reform to the plutocratic silver interests, "but so long as either metal is to be used we insist that both shall be used because both constitute a larger and more abundant currency . . . and therefore more favorable to the mass of the population."[67] A month later he noted that the proper way to break the power of monopoly was "to divorce the idea of money totally from any metallic commodity; to make the measure of values rest entirely upon the fiat, or command, or power of government."[68] He was courageous enough to attend the American Bimetallic League conference in Des Moines, Iowa, and to tell the members not to trust everyone who shouts for "free silver" because there were equally basic reforms to be advocated.[69] For a brief period, too, he removed an advertisement of the nation's leading silver tract, W. H. Harvey's *Coin's Handbook*, from the *Representative*, explaining that "it is an *anti-fiat* or anti-greenback publication. . . . Our position—repeatedly stated—is, that we do not believe in

[65] St. Paul *Representative*, December 13, 1893; St. Paul *Pioneer Press*, November 18, 1893.
[66] Donnelly MSS, H. Taubeneck to I. D., January 29, 1894.
[67] St. Paul *Representative*, February 14, 1894.
[68] *Ibid.*, March 7, 1894.
[69] St. Paul *Pioneer Press*, March 23, 1894.

commodity money, of gold, silver, brass, lead, wheat or potatoes, but as long as gold is continued to be used, we insist that its ancient colleague silver, shall be used with it, as a matter of justice to the debtor class."[70]

Believing that "wheat at 45 cents a bushel is enough to make any man forget his [past party] prejudices and think for himself," Donnelly felt the depression, which had been attributed to Cleveland, would drive Democrats into the People's party.[71] He predicted that the Democrats, arguing among themselves about the tariff, the income tax, and silver, would split into two camps: an "eastern faction led by Bourke Cochran of New York, and the western by that splendid orator, Bryan of Nebraska." Donnelly was confident that Democratic fission would release rank-and-file western Democrats who, as good Jacksonians, would be attracted to the pure democracy of the People's party, "the masses against the classes."[72]

The business conditions, which Donnelly believed would accelerate the growth of the People's party, worsened, and 1894 proved to be unprecedented for its economic unrest. In Massillon, Ohio, Jacob S. Coxey, a successful businessman, a reformer, and People's party enthusiast, called upon the government to put unemployed men to work on public improvements and pay them in legal tender greenbacks irredeemable in gold. To dramatize both his program and the tragic nature of mass unemployment, Coxey decided to lead a "petition in boots" to Washington.[73] As men gathered, not only in Ohio but in other parts of the country, preparing to march on the nation's capital, feelings of both compassion and apprehension spread through the nation.

Donnelly insisted to Taubeneck that the People's party be free from any association with the Coxey movement.[74] "We do not like the movement of 10,000 or 100,000 men, now organized under Mr. Coxey and advancing on Washington," noted the *Representative*. "A vast array of starving men becomes a terrible thing:—once started no one can control them. . . . If they are encountered by government troops the slaughter may be terrible."[75] Donnelly be-

[70]St. Paul *Representative*, April 18, 1894.
[71]*Ibid.*, February 7, 1894.
[72]*Ibid.*, February 21, 1894.
[73]Henry Vincent, *The Story of the Commonweal* (Chicago: W. B. Conkey Co., 1894), pp. 49–53.
[74]Donnelly MSS, H. Taubeneck to I. D., March 17, 1894.
[75]St. Paul *Representative*, March 28, 1894.

lieved that any excesses stemming from Coxeyism would be charged to the People's party. It was neither Coxey, whom Donnelly trusted, nor Carl Brown of California, whom Donnelly knew as a friend, that disturbed him. But he disapproved of the idea of mass popular demonstrations by drilled men in Washington.[76] As "Coxey's army" moved toward the nation's capital, fed and urged to move on in small towns in Ohio and Maryland, Donnelly denounced the garbled and distorted news accounts of Coxey's movements.[77]

Coxey's arrest in Washington, D.C., for attempting to speak from the Capitol steps, and his plaintive protest, "Up these steps the lobbyists of trusts and corporations have passed unchallenged on their way to committee rooms, access to which we, the representatives of the toiling wealth producers, have been denied," touched Donnelly deeply. To walk five hundred miles to read a stump speech, amid jeering hoodlums and corrupt legislators, seemed "like going through a great deal to get very little." Nevertheless, to Donnelly Coxeyism was the symptom of a disease. "It represented poverty, hardship, distress, and suffering" which, of course, he attributed to the "capitalistic class of New York and London." His sympathy "went out to the poor homeless helpless wanderers." Their "wretched cry to heaven out of their misery," their "cry to Congress, the little god of this under-world of ours," Donnelly wrote, was met by "Congress increasing its police, getting ready its gattling guns; summoning its soldiers, and ransacking obsolete laws to see if the unarmed petitioners could be stopped . . . from parading the streets; from holding meetings; from assembling in the capitol grounds to present their grievances." All congressional motions to discuss Coxey's request were sent to committees without a hearing. Such a policy, Donnelly concluded, was a shabby substitute for "humane and reasonable treatment."[78]

Coxeyism, a pathetic expression of protest, in no way compared to the deep-seated anxiety and despair that led to the formation of the anti-Catholic, American Protective Association. A secret fraternal organization, the APA had grown slowly in the upper Mississippi River Valley until by 1893 its membership numbered almost seventy thousand. The enormous social tensions produced by the severity of the depression of 1893 acting on Protestant laborers, swelled the national membership to perhaps half a million with the heaviest

[76]*Ibid.*, April 4, 1894.
[77]*Ibid.*, April 18, 1894; St. Paul *Pioneer Press*, April 23, 1894.
[78]Minneapolis *Representative*, May 9, 1894.

concentrations in Michigan, Ohio, and Minnesota.[79] Organizers for the APA espoused a conspiracy theory that the depression was the result of a papal scheme to flood the nation with immigrants, gain the best jobs for Catholics, create financial disorganization by systematic attacks on the banking system, and thus pave the way to bring the papacy to America.

The depression, therefore, activated the latent anti-Catholicism which had always been a factor in Minnesota politics. Since the Roman Catholics were primarily Democrats, the APA unquestionably aided the Republican cause. The Scandinavians joined the organization in such large numbers that an APA and Scandinavian-language paper merged.[80]

As early as November, 1893, Donnelly recognized that the sudden spurt of growth of the APA among laborers constituted a threat to the People's party. He charged that the APA, big business, and Jewish gold mine operators were linked in a plot to split the labor movement and prevent a People's party victory.[81] Because of increasing religious and political tension in Minnesota, Donnelly was invited to present a public lecture on the APA.[82] On April 12, 1894, he debated Professor Walter Sems of the APA before a St. Paul audience. The *Pioneer Press*, displaying unusual impartiality in describing the meeting, reported that Donnelly had not defended Catholicism but appealed to Christian love and brotherhood. The paper noted that he drove sectarianism from the hall, calling for fair play even to the point of defending Sems from the hissing and jeering crowd.[83]

In a second debate two days later, Donnelly charged that, "This thing has been gotten up to distract the American people, so that England can force upon us a dear and scarce currency and drive wheat down to 45 cents a bushel. Who's gone into this conspiracy?" he asked rhetorically. "The great employers of labor. They've got a clause in the oath that no member of the APA shall strike with a Catholic, and there is hardly a union without a Catholic in it."[84]

[79]John Higham, *Strangers in the Land* (New Brunswick: Rutgers University Press, 1955), p. 80.
[80]Mary Callista Hynes, "The History of the American Protective Association in Minnesota" (M.A. thesis, Catholic University of America, n.d.), p. 102.
[81]St. Paul *Representative*, November 15, 1893.
[82]Donnelly MSS, F. A. Briggs to I. D., February 27, 1894; J. Furay to I. D., April 18, 1894.
[83]St. Paul *Pioneer Press*, April 12, 1894.
[84]*Ibid.*, April 15, 1894.

Replying to an admirer who approved of his position in the APA argument, Donnelly explained: "We want to hold our whole country together and save it from sectarian bitterness, anarchy and civil war. I am really alarmed today at the outlook and apprehend great danger from the unrest and discontent of the people." And he added, "We have practically got to the end of our public lands, and the real strain upon our institutions has just begun."[85]

In Minnesota the APA reached its crest of popularity at the time of the Sems-Donnelly debate. Soon the Scandinavian attitude changed and reason overcame a misplaced xenophobia, when it was realized that the APA was emphatically anti-immigrant. The mood of religious bigotry was not so easily forgotten. It doubtless lingered in the conservative Scandinavian churches and probably flared up against the Minnesota Democrats, even, ironically enough, when they supported so vigorous a Protestant as William J. Bryan. Donnelly, explaining his opposition to the APA in a long article in the *Representative*, noted that "the founder of the society, Henry F. Bowers, of Clinton, Iowa, is an attorney, in receipt of a salary from the Chicago and Northwestern Railroad Company; and he is reported to have said that when they got the society fairly started 'there would be no more strikes!' " The editorial concluded: "The society was established to distract public attention from the economic questions of the hour; and preventing all producers uniting against a common enemy, by setting them to fighting each other over questions of the next world; or old world memories of ages past."[86]

Donnelly suffered deep personal anxiety during the winter and spring of 1894. Kate, her health seriously impaired, was moved to St. Paul, where her elder son provided her with daily medical care. In June, she suffered a fatal stroke. Donnelly, who had been a devoted husband for forty years, was wholly distracted.[87] He succumbed to a painful attack of rheumatism but was forced to take his exhausted elder son to Michigan for a rest cure and sulfur baths. The expenses of the long illness impoverished him. Many old friends, such as William L. Banning, offered aid,[88] and his bitterest enemies in the Catholic political community, Patrick H. Kelly and Michael Doran, offered financial assistance, as did the son-in-law of James J. Hill.

[85]Donnelly MSS, I. D. to J. Corey, April 14, 1894 (carbon).

[86]Minneapolis *Representative*, May 9, 1894.

[87]Donnelly, *In Memoriam*, pp. 23–25; Donnelly MSS, Diary, December 31, 1894.

[88]William L. Banning published *In Memoriam* as a private printing.

Although Donnelly later stated that he declined their offers, he confessed that he had been "profoundly touched by these manifestations of friendship, and, that . . . from that hour we never permitted an unkind word to escape from our lips or pen as to . . . these gentlemen."[89] Certainly by midsummer Donnelly was less critical of Minnesota's Democrats, but whether his policy stemmed from a desire to attract Democrats to the People's party or because of a personal *rapprochement* seems impossible to determine.

Shortly before the state People's party convention in July, the nation was severely shaken by the effects of the American Railway Union strike. Originally a controversy over the right of workers to negotiate with management without fear of reprisals, at the Pullman factory complex near Chicago, the strike spread over almost the entire Middle and Far West when the American Railway Union called for a boycott of all Pullman cars because George Pullman refused arbitration. The railroads, under contract to move Pullman cars, found their employees unwilling to operate trains with the cars attached. Although the union encouraged its members to operate mail trains, the General Managers' Association of the railway companies refused to separate the cars. As the paralysis of transportation spread, violence broke out in the railroad marshaling yards with pillaging of stalled cars and conflict between police and crowds. Much of the disorder stemmed not from union members but from hoodlums who sought to take advantage of the strike. The federal government sent in troops to pacify Pullman, Illinois by force, over the protests of Illinois Governor John P. Altgeld, and secured an injunction against Eugene V. Debs, president of the American Railway Union, because the movement of United States mail was impeded.

"Our readers know that we are not of those who advise desperate measures," Donnelly wrote when news of the injunction reached Minnesota. "In the terrible times which have been brought on this country . . . we have counseled the labor force to be patient and long enduring . . . and that the real remedy for all their grievance was . . . to unite and take possession of the government through the ballot box." He could not help regretting, "as much as any, the disturbance of business, the interruption of travel and the mails and even the ten thousand inconveniences brought on the whole people of the United States by the great strike. But," he went on, "remem-

[89]Minneapolis *Representative,* January 26, 1898.

ber that there never was any reform accomplished in this world that
did not disturb someone. As the French say, 'to make an omelet, you
must break some eggs.'" Then he concluded tersely, "The settlement
of the slavery question inconvenienced a great many people."[90]

Three days after Donnelly's editorial, the Ramsey County
People's party organization passed a resolution in support of the
American Railway Union. In Hennepin County, the People's party
organization not only indorsed the boycott but also condemned
Cleveland and called for the impeachment of Senator Cushman K.
Davis who was reputed to have refused to support a resolution
against presidential policy by saying, "You might as well ask me to
vote to dissolve this government."[91]

The party's convention gathered in Minneapolis when the Pullman strike approached its climax. Donnelly, called upon to present
the keynote speech, pointed with pride to the new unity in the party
but devoted the heart of his address to the spirit of unrest so evident
in the nation. "I do not believe the country was in as much danger in
1861, when the legions of Lee were in sight of the capitol, as it is
today," he told the attentive delegates. "Then it was a battle between sections which it was possible to unite. Today the struggle is
internecine. . . . The battle is not for the separation of sections, but
for the total subversion of the very principles upon which the government is founded." Emphasizing his and the party's rejection of
violence, he stated, "We do not believe that the path of reform is
through the torch and the rifle. We believe that it is through the
ballot box." He denied that the People's party was sectional. "We
believe in union, but not in union of conqueror and captive. We
insist that the West and the South must have a fair share of the
blessings."

In discussing the American Railway Union boycott, Donnelly
placed the responsibility entirely on George Pullman. His powerful
voice boomed: "I do not believe that working men ask anything that
is not reasonable, fair, and right. I do not believe that the men called
strikers fired the buildings or destroyed property in Chicago. Their
great leaders have appealed to the men to refrain from violence. In
their convention in Chicago," he reminded his listeners, "the

[90]*Ibid.*, July 4, 1894. Donnelly vigorously denounced employers who attempted to prevent employees from joining unions. He advocated legislation
outlawing yellow dog contracts in 1893, and was sharply critical of Twin
Cities transit magnet, Thomas Lowry, who attempted to use the yellow dog
agreement. St. Paul *Representative*, November 1, 1893.
[91]St. Paul *Pioneer Press*, July 8, 1894.

A[merican] R[ailway] U[nion] by unanimous standing vote, resolved that their only hope was the ballot box, and that they would stand by the People's party." Donnelly drew wild applause by criticizing Cushman K. Davis.[92]

The convention nominated Owen for governor. Although Donnelly had provided the voice for the convention, his influence was waning. He was unsuccessful in urging the nomination of his son-in-law, George Giltinan, for state auditor, and even though Donnelly was chairman of the platform committee, William R. Dobbyn, a Universalist clergyman who edited the urban reform paper, *Progressive Age,* and who was closely allied with Owen, provided a report that placed greater stress on woman suffrage and the nationalization of liquor than Donnelly would have preferred. Donnelly, however, managed to preserve the basic Omaha platform and to gain strong pro-American Railway Union resolutions. The defense of Debs and the presence of Jacob Coxey, who spoke in support of the People's party, agitated the *Pioneer Press* to defend its assertion that the party stood for anarchism and all that was worst in human nature.[93]

After the convention, many of the delegates remained in Minneapolis for the Minnesota Grain Growers conference sponsored by the Alliance. The meeting was the result of a movement, which Donnelly had encouraged, suggesting that farmers attempt to raise prices by controlling the flow of wheat at the grain elevators. Declining prices spurred the movement and Donnelly publicized it widely through the *Representative.* Both the millers and the railroads approved the control of the elevator operators, charging that the operators plundered the farmer as well as the carrier and processor.[94]

The conference of grain growers was marked by open disagreement. Donnelly's proposal that a major warehouse be rented in Duluth was rejected by Owen's friends who favored asking each local Alliance to build its own elevators. The program accepted by the conference of the Grain Growers Association was to integrate the Association and the Alliance so the latter would be strengthened "by giving it something to do."[95] Because neither money nor managerial skills were available in the various Alliances to implement it,

[92]Minneapolis *Tribune,* July 11, 1894; St. Paul *Pioneer Press,* July 11, 1894; Minneapolis *Representative,* July 18, 1894.
[93]St. Paul *Pioneer Press,* July 12, 1894.
[94]St. Paul *Representative,* February 14, March 21, 1894; Minneapolis *Representative,* April 4, June 27, 1894.
[95]Minneapolis *Representative,* July 18, 1894.

Donnelly accepted the program but continued to fight for a Duluth elevator. He scored a genuine success when he persuaded James J. Hill to offer the Association a warehouse at a nominal price. When it was refused, Hill cut the cost of shipping wheat by one cent a bushel—a saving of one and a quarter million dollars to northwest farmers. Hill, Donnelly pointed out, was not motivated by generosity; he perceived "as clearly as any man in the United States, that his customers are being ruined to enrich a small coterie who are no benefit to the state but who carry their ill-gotten gains . . . among the aristocracy of Europe."[96] Ironically, the reduction of railroad rates cut deeply into the People's party theme that monopoly could only be controlled through nationalization.

Knute Nelson, seeking to retain the governorship, practically ignored the Democratic candidate, George L. Becker, who carried the burden of "Cleveland's depression," and vigorously denounced the absence of a genuine state economic program in Owen's platform. Nelson could point to his administration's record in the coal conference and the pine land investigations. Nationalizing railroads and minting silver were national programs; Nelson even indorsed silver. The wheat farmer, he insisted, was suffering from overproduction and foreign competition. There were no simple legislative panaceas to cope with this problem.[97]

But the Republicans were alarmed. There had been a substantial loss of support among Scandinavian newspapers.[98] Donnelly was predicting that even a conservative estimate of the People's party strength would assure Owen one hundred thousand votes. His confidence that Owen would oust Nelson soared when silver Democrats and silver Republicans formed an independent party to indorse Owen.

As the campaign achieved great intensity, Donnelly, hammering at the financial conspiracy theme, became intemperately critical of Jewish moneylenders. He did not blame the Jews for finding themselves forced into trading in gold, but he pointed out that the anti-Semitic outbreaks in Germany resulted from the aggressive attitude of the wealthy Jews. "We do not advocate another Spanish Inquisition, but we do advocate . . . that they should get out of the gold bondage which is now destroying the human race." Despite his plea

[96]*Ibid.*, August 15, 1894.
[97]St. Paul *Pioneer Press*, July 30, 1894.
[98]Minneapolis *Tribune*, June 15, 1894.

to give them "the same chance as the Christians,"[99] Donnelly learned that he offended many Jews. In a long article the following week he explained that "he did not mean to hurt the feelings of anyone." Apologetically he wrote: "A plutocratic Jew is no worse than a plutocratic Christian—in fact he is half as bad. For the Jew, for nearly 2,000 years has been proscribed, persecuted, and hunted down; fenced into the corners of towns; hounded, pelted, and stoned by ignorant populations when the Jews were preserving the knowledge of the one true God in the midst of an idolatrous and degraded world." He pointed out the contributions of Mendelssohn, Spinoza, Disraeli, especially noting that "Karl Marx, the Jewish reformer, faces Rothschild, the Jew plutocrat."

"No, No," Donnelly wrote. "We would not persecute the Jews. . . . We are fighting Plutocracy not because it is Jewish or Christian, but because it is Plutocracy. . . . We have lots of Christian money sharks in western Minnesota who would drive Shylock to hang himself out of shame." And he closed, "We would be sorry to be understood as saying one word that would pander to prejudice against any man because of his race, religion, nationality or color."[100] Through his identification with the Minnesota People's party, Donnelly served to dissociate it from the rising tide of nativism of the 1890's. His vigorous denunciation of the APA as an economic instrument and his forthright, honest, if confused, effort to separate the Jews as a people from Jews as bankers differed strikingly from the somewhat later attitude of Georgia's Tom Watson, who moved steadily toward bigotry.

The quickening pace of the campaign brought a request for Donnelly to join Eugene Debs at a giant People's party rally in Chicago. The quiet, calm logic and forthrightness of the labor leader impressed him. As a professional politician, as a member of a party no longer new, and as a speaker trying to overcome the stigma of anarchism, Donnelly sought to create a distinctly conservative

[99] Minneapolis *Representative*, September 5, 1894.

[100] *Ibid.*, September 12, 1894. Donnelly grew increasingly sensitive about the ramifications of the anti-Rothschild material in the People's party press. He ridiculed and condemned Johnny-come-lately bullies who stupidly misinterpreted criticism of interlocking directorates of money as anti-Semitism. Apropos of this ridicule of anti-Semitism was his story of "the New York rowdy who knocked down a poor Jew, and when the Jew asked him what he did it for replied:— 'You Jews killed Christ.' 'But,' said the Jew, 'that was 1800 years ago.' 'Don't care,' said the tough, 'I only heard about it last night.'" Minneapolis *Representative*, November 13, 1895.

image for the People's party. He informed a St. Paul reporter that he had told his audience that the party was not one "of destruction, but of construction; that they were not cranks, but statesmen." He pointed out "that the Democratic party had already stolen one of our great principles, the income tax, and that the Republican party of the grand old state of Pennsylvania had so far followed in our footsteps as to demand $40 per capita of circulation where we demanded $50." He told his listeners: "We were not anarchists, and that if we obtained power we did not propose to strip the well-to-do of their possessions!"[101]

The major Republican campaign against the People's party was two-fold. First, it relied on Knute Nelson's record as an opponent of monopoly because of the coal conference and his friendship for labor because of his approval of factory legislation. Second, it attacked the People's party as comprised of anarchists who supported Debs and Coxey. The *Pioneer Press,* pointing to the 1891 legislature, argued that the People's party was radical, extravagant, and ineffective.[102] But as the People's party's show of strength far outstripped expectations, the anarchism issue, a mild resurgence of APAism, and the allegation that the People's party would reduce the cost and increase the use of liquor became more important.

Donnelly, although he had accepted the Dakota County People's party nomination for state senator, campaigned vigorously everywhere in Minnesota. He asked the voters to unite behind the entire People's party slate so that local taxes could be reduced, railroad rates adjusted, a state grain elevator constructed, and fair judges selected. Donnelly attributed the depression to the Republicans rather than to Cleveland, fearful of a swing away from the Democrats to the Republicans. Donnelly was working so hard in the southwestern part of the state, he ignored a warning that unless he devoted at least five full days to Dakota County he would lose the election.[103] The incredibly large receptions the People's party candidates received encouraged Owen to write Donnelly: "It is the rings and combinations in the state that are now trembling in their boots."[104]

The election results disclosed that Owen gained almost ninety thousand votes, thirty thousand more than he had secured in 1890,

[101] St. Paul *Pioneer Press,* October 2, 1894.
[102] *Ibid.,* October 16, 18, 1894.
[103] Donnelly MSS, H. Gillitt to I. D., October 30, 1894.
[104] *Ibid.,* S. M. Owen to I. D., October 24, 1894.

and fifty thousand more than Donnelly had tallied in 1892. The Democratic vote had declined from ninety thousand in 1892 to fifty thousand in 1894. Knute Nelson increased the Republican vote by nearly forty thousand to carry the state with almost one hundred and fifty thousand votes. Although People's party politicians found solace in their display of strength, they missed the significance of the fact that the combined People's party–Democratic vote had not increased appreciably since 1890, while Republican strength had increased almost 80 per cent. The APA had undoubtedly hurt the Democrats just as the Pullman strike and Coxey's movement had damaged the People's party. Minnesota's rural districts were probably more aroused by the fear of anarchism than by the depression. The "Cleveland" Panic of 1893 and the ensuing depression with its complex social ramifications, some of which were manifest in the election of 1894, indicate that the protest vote was sharply divided. The largest portion turned to the Republicans as the established party. A significant minority embraced the People's party, bringing it to its zenith.[105]

Aside from reporting Owen's defeat, the Republican St. Paul *Pioneer Press* crowed most wildly when it noted that Donnelly "was beaten for Senator in his own County, which he has always heretofore carried in his breeches pocket. . . . But what will Donnelly do," the paper asked sarcastically, "now that his political career has come to a sudden and final ending."[106]

"We can now look to our own affairs," Donnelly disgustedly noted in the *Representative*. "If the legislature was populistic, or if our party had a controlling voice in it, we should have been glad to have been there to help them work out great reforms for the good of the whole people." The fact that the Republicans had gained control of the legislature led Donnelly to conclude that he would have been powerless. He shrewdly anticipated that "the pine land investigations will cease; the state elevator will be heard no more; the reduction of interest on money will be dropped." Angrily he concluded: "Nothing will be done for the good of the people. And the people deserve it. And they will suffer for it."[107]

[105]It is worth noting that the People's party vote across the nation had increased almost half a million from 1892 to 1894. It is equally significant that they suffered defeats almost everywhere. Minnesota's trend reflected the Northwest; in the South, silver and the race issue were the determinants. Hicks, *The Populist Revolt*, 330–39.

[106]St. Paul *Pioneer Press*, November 8, 1894.

[107]Minneapolis *Representative*, November 7, 1894.

In analyzing the election returns, he noted that the People's party had gained in each congressional district. Largest increases had been won in St. Paul and in the two frontier districts. "We lost among the farmers of the state," he conceded. "Why they should go back on us, with wheat at 45 cents a bushel, is something no man can understand."[108] Donnelly, however, recognized two inescapable conclusions. First, "if we are to carry this country in 1896 we must satisfy the average mind that we are reasonable and right." He called upon the party to suppress the wild, the extravagant, and the fanatical men within its ranks. The justification for fanaticism was not questioned; the damage to the party by the eccentric wing was the issue. The second was his own failure to convert the Alliance into a powerful political force. As a result, he resigned from the Alliance presidency, "so that the work should go into more youthful and energetic hands." Apologetically, he added, "I have done my part. . . . God seems to have decreed that I should never possess any high position, from which I could carry out my ideas for the good of the human family."[109]

As 1894 drew to a close, Donnelly used the columns of the *Representative* to urge harmony and tolerance among the Alliance and People's party leadership. "Do not conclude because a man looks at things differently from yourself, that he is necessarily a rogue, or a part of some conspiracy," Donnelly pleaded. "Another man may be right and you may be wrong. No man has a monopoly on wisdom. Let us all throw our suggestions into the pot, and boil them with the fires of discussion, and some good thing will come out."[110]

[108] *Ibid.*, November 14, 21, 1894.

[109] *Ibid.*, November 28, 1894; St. Paul *Pioneer Press*, November 30, 1894. Although he denounced fanaticism, Donnelly did not hesitate to write in defense of the American Railway Union workers who had been blacklisted. "Men starving in the United States of America because they tried to get enough to supply themselves and wives and children, as Americans should live. It is awful. Blacklisted! Branded like Cain! So that every man that meets them on the street will slay them." Minneapolis *Representative*, December 5, 1894.

[110] Minneapolis *Representative*, December 19, 1894.

CHAPTER

XIX

The Road to Fusion
1895-1896

Let us subordinate everything to the success of the cause; but do not let us subordinate the cause to success.

IGNATIUS DONNELLY

THE ANNUAL meeting of the Minnesota Alliance, which convened at Century Hall in Minneapolis early in January, 1895, was one of the largest in several years. The prevailing spirit of harmony was strengthened when the delegates heard Donnelly reaffirm his faith in the organization and restate his conviction that its leadership should be entrusted to younger men. He was not, he insisted, a candidate for any office.[1] As the convention drew to a close, he voiced the highest praise for the newly elected officials.

That evening he returned to the Brunswick Hotel for a solitary dinner. He had relinquished control over an organization to which he had been dedicated for almost a decade. As he sat alone eating in the dining hall, L. C. Long, state lecturer of the Alliance, tapped him on the shoulder and asked him to step into the hotel parlor where many of his closest political friends had gathered. The Alliance Long stated, "was proud, in having the greatest statesman, the greatest orator, and the greatest scholar in the United States for a leader so long." Then he added, " 'The Pen is mightier than the sword' and we therefore present you with this pen that it may be used unhesitatingly against the enemies of your cause." Before Don-

---

[1]St. Paul *Pioneer Press*, January 9, 1895.

nelly could reply, Major J. M. Bowler, who had known him as a
political friend and foe for thirty-seven years, also presented him
with a gold-headed cane.

Donnelly was deeply touched. "I assure you that I have always
tried to do right," he responded. "I know I am not infallible," his
voice trembled, "but I have done my duty to the best of my judgment. . . . I am not used to a cane," he said. "But I will attempt to
use it peacefully, although if necessary, I will not hesitate to use it
on the heads of scalawags!"[2]

When the state legislature gathered to select a new United States
senator, some of the People's party leaders, eager to recruit silver
Republicans, proposed that the People's party legislators support
Republican former congressman John Lind because he had joined
the silverites. Donnelly opposed the plan. Lind was no more a
friend of the People's party program than William Washburn, Donnelly stated. "If you abandon your party," he warned, "you incite
the rank and file to do likewise." But every day they cast votes for
their own candidate, he added, they announced all over the state
and the nation that the "People's party is not dead, but a living
entity."[3]

Donnelly's view prevailed. The People's party legislators even
honored him by casting their votes for Donnelly when the official
balloting took place. He was, of course, never a serious contender
for the Senate.[4] The contest, however, was of genuine interest to
him, and he was hugely pleased to see the Republican caucus reject
incumbent Senator William D. Washburn in favor of Governor
Knute Nelson. Washburn's defeat released a burst of vindictive
animosity which Donnelly had stored for a quarter of a century
against the coterie of men he long believed had conspired against
him—Washburn, William S. King, Alexander Ramsey, and Joseph
Wheelock. All of them, he noted in an acrid article in the *Representative,* had now tasted the bitter dregs of defeat.[5]

No longer an officer of the Alliance or a member of the state
legislature, Donnelly became a full-time newspaper editor. During
the early months of 1895, the *Representative* expressed his views
on the issues that interested his readers. He devoted a series of
articles to refuting Henry George's single-tax scheme as entirely

[2]Minneapolis *Representative,* January 16, 1895.
[3]*Ibid.,* January 9, 1895.
[4]St. Paul *Pioneer Press,* January 22, 1895.
[5]Minneapolis *Representative,* January 30, 1895.

impractical. Ironically enough, Minneapolis labor groups objected to his criticism of "Georgism" while the Republican Minneapolis *Tribune* noted that "if Donnelly were so sound and logical upon other prominent questions of the day, he would be a pretty good Republican."[6] He refused to debate the issue with Henry George in 1895, not because he feared the outcome but because he simply could not afford to lecture for only fifty dollars.[7]

United States Supreme Court rulings in the midwinter and spring of 1895 provoked Donnelly's bitterest protests. He denounced the Court's failure to issue a writ of *habeas corpus* in behalf of Eugene Debs. Donnelly believed that in upholding a lower court's action in sending Debs to prison, the Court had sustained a criminal attack upon civil liberties.[8] The Court's action, coupled as it was with the Knight case which made a mockery of the Sherman Anti-Trust Law when applied to industry, led Donnelly to restate his opposition to the doctrine of judicial review.[9] The Court, the stronghold of intrenched interests, he angrily maintained, frustrated the will of the people. Although he usually expressed great trust in popular government—initiative, referendum, even proportional representation —he remained realistic enough, unlike some later Progressives, to caution supporters of direct democracy that the passage of such legislation would not issue the nation into "Elysium."[10]

The deepening of the depression and the increase in personal hardship during 1895 intensified Donnelly's criticism of shams in society. Invited to contribute an article to a publicity campaign to encourage European immigrants to settle in Minnesota, he denounced the scheme as a fraud. "I protest against inducing foreigners to share our miseries," he wrote. "They will seek a paradise, and find a hell . . . [where] our newspapers are a blazing panorama of bankruptcies, starvation and murders."[11] In a similar vein, he condemned fatuous reformers who proposed sending unemployed city workers to live off the land. Nothing would have brought Donnelly more pleasure than that every poor man should have enough land to support himself and his family. But he knew farming required "special training, and a special kind of knowledge," as well as "capital enough" to maintain a man until his crop could be har-

[6]*Ibid.*, December 12, 26, 1894; January 2, 16, 1895.
[7]Donnelly MSS, F. A. Briggs to I. D., February 11, 1895.
[8]Minneapolis *Representative*, January 16, 1895.
[9]*Ibid.*, February 20, April 24, 1895.
[10]*Ibid.*, February 6, October 9, 1895.
[11]*Ibid.*, January 30, 1895.

vested. "A human being on 80 acres of unimproved land," he pointed out, "is as helpless as if he were on 80 acres of water—in fact more so, for he could get a fishing line and probably catch something to eat."[12] Donnelly was especially annoyed when he learned of a papal decree permitting workingmen to ignore church dietary laws under special circumstances. "What is wanted is another papal decree," he noted caustically, "that the bishops and the priests shall all go to work to give the poor good laws, so that they may have plenty to eat."[13]

Maintaining the *Representative* was a heavy financial burden. Minneapolis merchants refused to advertise in the paper though they had promised to do so when they invited him to move it from St. Paul. Eventually, a large share of the paper's operating expenses was sustained when Donnelly became a business agent for H. R. Eagle and Company, which sold binders twine to grain farmers.[14] But the *Representative* never attained financial solvency. On more than one occasion, Donnelly warned his readers that unless they paid their subscriptions, he would be forced to abandon publication. From time to time, he was compelled to reduce the size of the paper, but in 1895 he steadfastly refused to turn his accounts receivable into the hands of a collection agency.[15]

The *Representative* reflected Donnelly's awareness of the momentous political changes taking place in the South and West. The stunning defeat of Bourbon Democrats, such as Minnesota's George Becker in 1894, was the first phase of a revolution that was to leave the conservative Democrats "damnably mauled."[16] The Bourbon leadership in the Middle West was under increasing criticism from the party's more liberal wing, which was using the silver issue as a device to dissociate itself from the Cleveland administration. The fight for party leadership by the liberal silverites—the second phase of the revolution—was well under way by 1895.

To capitalize on the disintegration of the Democratic party before it regained its integrity through internal realignment, required honesty, initiative, and boldness on the part of the leaders of the People's party. It was at this point that the silver mining interests

[12]*Ibid.*, April 3, 1895.

[13]*Ibid.*, July 17, 1895. Donnelly did concede that many of the good ecclesiastics were working in that direction, but he felt that "it should be universal and in all creeds."

[14]*Ibid.*, July 19, 1895; Donnelly MSS, H. R. Eagle to I. D., July 29, 1895.

[15]Minneapolis *Representative*, October 2, 1895.

[16]Merrill, *Bourbon Democracy*, pp. 238–74.

resolved upon one of the most determined promotional efforts in the nation's history. There was a marked increase in the number of silver meetings, pamphlets, and subsidized editors and politicians. The growing effectiveness of silver propaganda foretold that the coalition of silver advocates would create a new political force. The People's party leadership, attempting to absorb disgruntled Democrats and Republicans into the organization, became acutely conscious that within its own ranks were men who wished to identify the party with silver, even at the risk of being captured by the issue, a trophy of an older party which might yet accept a silver platform.[17]

General James B. Weaver, recognized leader of the silver group and titular head of the People's party, endeavored to make silver the paramount issue by proposing that a new party platform be drafted at a meeting in St. Louis in February, 1895. Donnelly did not attend the conference, but he had learned that the opposition to Weaver was well organized and determined to retain the Omaha platform.[18] Although Herman E. Taukeneck supported Weaver, the St. Louis gathering reaffirmed the Omaha stand. Thoroughly dissatisfied by the outcome of the conference, Weaver wrote Donnelly asking support for another meeting. Weaver wanted twenty party leaders to attend the conference and publish their views. He was confident that silver would be the primary concern.[19] Donnelly probably replied to Weaver in the same way that he answered General A. J. Warner, president of the American Bimetallic League, who labored continually for a party based solely on the silver issue. "Narrow Populism to free-silver alone," Donnelly wrote, "and it will disappear in a rat hole." He warned against the party representing nothing but the pecuniary interests of the silver mine owners; "it will die of universal and deserved contempt."[20] Too shrewd a politician to break with Donnelly on the silver issue, Weaver professed to agree with him that the major question was how to combine all the reformers into a solid phalanx against the plutocracy.[21]

Donnelly did not wish to rally the various reform groups by making the People's party platform a "scrap bag in which everything is to be stuck which anybody is in favor of." He wanted the platform

[17]Woodward, *Tom Watson*, p. 203; Hofstadter, *The Age of Reform*, pp. 105–6.

[18]Donnelly MSS, D. H. Waite to I. D., December 11, 1894; G. F. Washburn to I. D., December 22, 1894.

[19]*Ibid.*, J. B. Weaver to I. D., January 13, 1895.

[20]Minneapolis *Representative*, January 30, 1895.

[21]Donnelly MSS, J. B. Weaver to I. D., March 23, 1895.

to be "an engine of reform; clean cut and definite; [and] not be turned into a menagerie, a dime museum or a Chinese laundry."[22] For this reason he was unwilling to include the socialist proposals originated by the radical Chicago People's party group. The word "socialism" held no terror for Donnelly, but he believed that the people would not understand its implications, and after it was thoroughly misconstrued in the conservative press, it would lead to defeat. Actually Donnelly, increasingly cautious about the platform, was seeking to avoid "isms." "Let us be radically right, but in all things reasonable," became his position.[23]

In the sense that he was unable to formulate a substitute issue as dynamic as silver or move toward the radical left wing group, he gradually surrendered the initiative to the silverites. Furthermore, his books contributed appreciably to the excitement surrounding the silver movement. *The Golden Bottle*, although actually lampooning metallic currency of any kind, struck so vigorously at the advocates of the gold standard that the use of silver seemed a logical technique for achieving a manipulated currency. In April, 1895, Donnelly wrote what he told Henry D. Lloyd was a "pot boiler" on the financial question, *The American People's Money*. Although hopeful that Lloyd would write an introduction to the book, Donnelly confessed that it had been written at the publisher's request because there was a "demand for such stuff." "Even the philosophers," Donnelly acknowledged, "have to bow to the humors of the many-headed monster—the public."[24]

The American People's Money was not strictly a silver tract. Donnelly favored fiat currency, but this ideal solution he relegated to the distant future. In reaffirming his initial position—that if a metallic currency system were used, silver should share with gold as a basis for money as it had in the past—he presented the attitude of many old style greenbackers toward silver. Published in a twenty-five-cent paper edition, *The American People's Money* briefly rivaled in popularity W. H. Harvey's *Coin's Financial School*. By dramatizing silver, keeping it before the public as an issue, Donnelly unconsciously played into the hands of the silver element in the People's party.

In a somewhat similar manner, his attitude toward the Democrats

[22]Minneapolis *Representative*, February 13, 1895.

[23]*Ibid.*, May 1, September 4, 18, 1895.

[24]H. D. Lloyd MSS, May 26, 1895. *The American People's Money* (Chicago: Laird & Lee, 1895).

paved the way for increased co-operation. Assuming that the Minnesota Bourbon Democrats, led by Michael Doran, would remain firmly in control of the party machinery, Donnelly favored a strong anti-monopoly platform with an indorsement of silver.[25] He hoped a large number of Democrats would turn toward the People's party, but he did not anticipate the wholesale defection of Democratic leadership into the silver camp. Such men could not be expected "to meekly enter our tents to do the chores of women," he admitted. Reluctantly he was forced to concede that the People's party should work with the silver Democrats if it could be arranged "without sacrifice of pride or principle on either side."[26]

Davis H. Waite of Colorado warned Donnelly in confidence of the dangerous trend within the People's party toward silver, and fusion with the Democrats. "I hardly know what to think of Weaver," wrote Waite. Weaver is "in sympathy with Bland & Bryan . . . which is essentially a Democratic movement. He came into Colo[rado] in the pay of that outfit and undertook to stampede the Colo[rado] Pop[ulists] on the single issue of silver." Shrewdly Waite observed, "he only enthused those democrats who came over to our party in 1892 for the sole purpose of carrying us back with them to the democratic party." The fact that Weaver had personally assured Waite that he had lost confidence in the American Bimetallic League and that he was prepared to stand firm on the Omaha platform led Waite to doubt Weaver's sincerity.[27]

Donnelly, however, attempted to remain neutral. He published signed articles by Tom Watson, critical of the socialists and asking for a return to the Ocala platform. His paper also carried the pro-silver views of Herman Taubeneck. "Let the discussion go on," Donnelly urged, let each and every word be said before the convention.[28] He favored the silver and reform groups retaining their individual identity but uniting upon candidates who would root out social evils one by one.[29] Confident that the silverites among the Republicans and the Democrats would have to "fish or cut bait" at their national conventions, he remained skeptical when William Jennings Bryan explained, "I am doing what I can to get the silver democrats to capture the national convention. . . . I shall not sup-

[25] Minneapolis *Representative*, June 5, 1895.
[26] *Ibid.*, July 10, 1895.
[27] Donnelly MSS, D. H. Waite to I. D., August 22, 1895.
[28] Minneapolis *Representative*, October 30, September 4, 1895.
[29] *Ibid.*, November 6, 1895.

port a gold bug for president." Donnelly was certain both established parties would reaffirm their faith in gold despite southern and western Republicans and Democrats who advocated silver.[30]

By the time the National Committee of the People's party met to fix a date for their national convention, their very tactics made silver the issue. Eager for victory, they saw the problem as one of summoning an early convention and pre-empting the ground of silver and reform, or of waiting patiently while the Republicans and Democrats divided on the issue so that the People's party could recruit the defectors. Taubeneck, who wanted to pre-empt silver as the issue, favored an early convention.

Before the committee meeting, Donnelly engaged in a wide correspondence with members of his own party as well as with influential silver Republicans and silver Democrats to determine their views and advocate his own. He learned that the People's party men in California feared an early convention. They suspected eastern radical labor groups of wishing to foist Eugene Debs on the People's party as a presidential candidate, a policy the Californians believed would prove fatal. They were also concerned about the residue of the APA movement in the West, and the rising tide of jingo war spirit as a result of Cleveland's tough policy regarding England and Venezuela.[31] The westerners favored a July convention, hopeful that the temporary issues would have subsided. They indorsed a suggestion from Donnelly that the convention be held when a nomination could be made jointly with other advocates of silver and reform.[32] Republican silver enthusiast Senator William M. Stewart of Nevada, expanding on Donnelly's proposals, added that behind

[30]*Ibid.*, November 13, 1895; Donnelly MSS, W. J. Bryan to I. D., November 13, 1895.

[31]Donnelly had been worried about the rise of a military spirit in America. He criticized Cleveland's policy. Donnelly was not interested in a war of liberation or expansion. Domestic problems were far more serious. "It looks very much like an effort to redeem a discredited administration by a war furore," he wrote. "Olney, the Secretary of State, is at the bottom of it." The Democratic party "by getting up a foreign war that will . . . cost hundreds of thousands of lives and billions of property all in order to re-galvanize the rotten corpse Democracy in popularity." "We do not like aggressive British aristocracy any better than the rest of the people of the United States; and we have the warlike instinct as much as any of us, but we do not want to be 'played for a sucker' by Cleveland and Olney, and go into hysterics whenever they wave the American flag and play Yankee Doodle." Minneapolis *Representative*, December 5, 1894; December 11, 25, 1895.

[32]Donnelly MSS, T. V. Cator to I. D., December 17, 19, 1895; E. M. Wardall to I. D., December 19, 1895.

the brilliant oratory of the day, the silverites and the People's party could unite on candidates.[33] Bryan, who was laboring day and night to bring into existence a Democratic convention which would repudiate Cleveland and gold, wrote Donnelly favoring a People's party convention following those of the older parties so that the silverites could gain full advantage from defectors.[34] The National Committee of the People's party, in sanctioning a July convention, accepted the silverite policy of Bryan's supporters who wanted to wait until after the Republicans and Democrats had named their candidates—the identical policy Donnelly had warned against in 1892 as potentially suicidal in that it abandoned the initiative to the opposition.

Early in February, Donnelly scoffed at rumors that he was a presidential aspirant. He was pleased, however, that talk of his potential candidacy terrified his enemies.[35] Some of his friends within the Minnesota People's party insisted that they would rally other state delegations and place his name in nomination. Donnelly must have been touched to receive letters from politicians in other states offering to support him in a bid for the presidency. He replied that he would not push himself forward, there was no lack of good candidates, but if the convention wanted him, he would not hesitate to serve. Realistically, Donnelly did not anticipate gaining the nomination.[36]

In the spring of 1896, Davis H. Waite, increasingly apprehensive because of efforts to fasten on silver at the expense of the genuine issues in the platform and fearing the duplicity of the "bimetallic princes," expressed his opposition to any union with the silverites unless the Omaha platform was accepted.[37] Taubeneck, however, who was delighted with the strategy agreed upon by the National Committee, found the political picture highly encouraging. He confidently predicted that the Republican convention would "make a gold standard platform or a straddle . . . and probably nominate McKinley. This will cause a break in the Republican ranks of the West, especially in the silver producing states." Senator Henry M. Teller was nearly out of the Republican party. If Senator Fred T. DuBois of Idaho should join Teller and walk out of the Republican

[33]*Ibid.*, W. M. Stewart to I. D., December 20, 1895.
[34]*Ibid.*, W. J. Bryan to I. D., January 1, 1896.
[35]Minneapolis *Representative*, February 2, 1896.
[36]Donnelly MSS, T. S. Fisk to I. D., February 29, 1896; W. Atkeson to I. D., March 23, 1896; I. D. to H. Murphy, May 28, 1896 (rough draft).
[37]*Ibid.*, D. H. Waite to I. D., March 12, 1896.

convention, there would be "an irreparable break in the Republican ranks in the West . . . [which] . . . will give us the electoral vote of nearly all the western states."[38]

Six days before the national convention of the Republican party, Taubeneck wrote Donnelly asking him to go to St. Louis to help negotiate a basis of co-operation with the silver Republicans who would bolt their party to nominate a pro-silver candidate. Taubeneck hoped for a meeting including Teller, DuBois, and Weaver. Unable to attend the meeting, Donnelly replied that he would be with them in spirit. *"We must get together,"* he indorsed the back of Taubeneck's letter. Taubeneck was beginning to fear the effectiveness of William Jennings Bryan and Richard Bland within the Democratic party. Donnelly hoped that Taubeneck could perform the impossible task of persuading the silver Democrats to withhold selecting a presidential nominee until the People's party convention.[39]

A large lobby of Democrats led by Bryan and Bland attended the Republican convention in St. Louis, resolved to move heaven and earth to persuade the silver Republicans who bolted after McKinley's nomination to join the Democratic party and go to their Chicago convention. Bryan was rumored to have spent a week in St. Louis, pleading, cajoling, and flattering as only he could. But the silver Republicans, preferring to retain their identity, leaned toward greater co-operation with the People's party. "I think we have received the full benefit of the Republican bolt for our party in the future," Taubeneck optimistically reported to Donnelly. The silver Republicans agreed to maintain their own organization until after the People's party convention. They would then unite with the People's party to select candidates in the states west of the Mississippi River. "The Democrats are exceedingly sore, especially the silver wing of the party," Taubeneck added. "They have the arrogance to claim that the bolting Republicans ought to join them and that the Populists ought to endorse their National ticket."[40]

Perhaps Taubeneck's ability to woo the silver Republicans rested in part upon his indorsement of Teller as a presidential candidate if the Democrats accepted a platform based on silver. Taubeneck's public statement that the Democrats must take Teller because the People's party would not indorse a straight Democrat, indicated his

[38]*Ibid.*, H. E. Taubeneck to I. D., May 15, 1896.
[39]*Ibid.*, H. E. Taubeneck to I. D., June 10, 1896.
[40]*Ibid.*, H. E. Taubeneck to I. D., June 22, 1896.

growing acquiescence in the idea of fusion, but it infuriated the People's party radical wing. Robert Schilling who was "raising hell about the Teller address," explained to Donnelly that he was asked to consent, "but I refused point blank." Schilling could not understand why "the Gresham blunder at Omaha" was not enough to cure them. "You would be my first choice," Schilling confided to Donnelly, "but the d—— APA nonsense would hurt you."[41]

Throughout this political maneuvering, Donnelly remained almost silent. He had steadfastly rejected the idea of fusion. It was clearly evident after the Republican convention that the silver wing of the Democratic party had captured so many state party organizations that they would control the Democratic nomination. No one had worked harder for the presidential nomination than Bryan, who was recognized as being young, aggressive, and well suited to present the stirring call of the revitalized party. His soaring eloquence in delivering the "Cross of Gold Speech" climaxed his successful campaign for the nomination. The Democrats not only nominated Bryan, who had flirted for years with the People's party, but also accepted a platform favoring silver, disavowing the Cleveland administration's financial policies, condemning the United States Supreme Court decision invalidating the income tax, and denouncing Cleveland's action in the Pullman strike. Aside from the Democratic vice-presidential candidate, Samuel Sewall, a Maine banker and railroad executive, the People's party moderates found little to oppose in the actions of the Democratic convention.

Bryan's nomination left the People's party facing a dilemma. As Henry Lloyd explained, "If we fuse, we are sunk; if we don't fuse, all the silver men we have will leave us for the more powerful Democrats."[42] T. J. Meighan, chairman of the Minnesota Central Committee of the People's party, was unwilling to "swallow Bryan without salt," but he was reconciled to fusion in some form.[43]

Donnelly, admitting in the *Representative* that Bryan was a brilliant politician, conceded he might be ready to support him but, "Can we transfer the Populist vote to him? We fear not." In Minnesota the bulk of the party were former Republicans whose prejudices toward the Democrats were deep and strong. Donnelly doubted

[41] *Ibid.*, R. Schilling to I. D., June 22, 1896; H. E. Taubeneck to I. D., July 5, 1896.

[42] Caro Lloyd, *Henry Demarest Lloyd* (New York: G. P. Putnam's Sons, 1912), I, 259.

[43] Donnelly MSS, T. J. Meighan to I. D., July 14, 1896.

that campaign enthusiasm could triumph over these feelings. Similarly, he conceded that the Democratic platform came "very close to the Populist platform," but it was not identical. The additional question remained: "What if we put all the treasures of reform into the Democratic boat and they scuttle it? The head of the Democratic party is now in the wheat and cotton fields, but its legs are still shackled in the banking houses of New York. Where is the line where radicalism ends and compromise begins? What is the corpse and what is the man? Would it not be better to stand by our own party?"[44] "Exciting times these," he noted in his diary. "Shall we or shall we not indorse Bryan for President? I like Bryan, but I do not feel that we can safely adopt Dem[ocratic] candidates. I fear it will be the end of our party."[45] Because of this public stand, Donnelly was aligned with Tom Watson of Georgia as a Mid-Road Populist— one who refused to merge with either party.

Although Donnelly assumed a strong antifusion position in public, privately he prepared for capitulation. He wrote Thomas D. O'Brien, Minnesota's Democratic National Committeeman, suggesting a possible basis for co-operation on a state level. O'Brien was not easily lured into making positive commitments prior to the People's party convention. "I am sure you will appreciate," he cautiously informed Donnelly, "the fact that the more that is done for Bryan at St. Louis by the Populists the more kindly the Democrats of this state will feel towards that organization." To preclude Donnelly's taking offense at being ignored in the negotiations for fusion, O'Brien added, "I hope you will not permit minor questions to interfere with the great object we all have of uniting the silver forces."[46] The Democratic National Committee, which was directly concerned with securing Bryan's indorsement at the People's party convention, wrote to Donnelly one day before the meeting, inviting him to campaign in Bryan's behalf.[47]

Fourteen hundred delegates swarmed into hot and humid St. Louis to attend the convention of the People's party. There were rustic, impoverished southern Alliancemen; intellectual socialists who were unable to cope with the procedures of a mass meeting and appeared effete; old-time third-party politicians of the Granger and Greenback days looking for friends and enemies dating back

[44]Minneapolis *Representative,* July 15, 1896.
[45]Donnelly MSS, Diary, July 18, 1896.
[46]*Ibid.,* T. D. O'Brien to I. D., July 18, 1896.
[47]*Ibid.,* I. O. Wesner to I. D., July 21, 1896.

almost a quarter of a century; reformers dedicated to bizarre causes; reform press editors bent on creating a rival force in American news reporting; and newly recruited silverites who had schemed and planned and worked so hard in anticipation of the convention that they could almost savor the zest of victory in the air. In their appearance, if not in their political attitudes, the delegates presented a sharp economic and social contrast to the Republicans who had nominated William McKinley in the same hall less than six weeks earlier.

Donnelly went to St. Louis confident that he would make a noteworthy contribution to the party's final decision of the fusion issue. Many Minnesota delegates elected from Alliance strongholds had been instructed to urge his nomination as a "favorite son" candidate. Although he could not have taken the movement seriously, there is no evidence that he actively encouraged it; he was probably highly flattered, especially by the indorsement of Sidney M. Owen's friend, William R. Dobbyn, who edited the St. Paul *Progressive Age*.[48] That delegates from other states were drawn to Donnelly also encouraged him to believe that he would play as large a role in 1896 as he had in 1892.

On the eve of the convention, organized opposition to Bryan among the most distinguished figures in the party had virtually collapsed. Peffer, Simpson, and even Waite had given in to Weaver, Allen, and Taubeneck. The antifusion forces were disorganized. The huge and militant Texas delegation, which caucused the day before the convention, was unable to agree upon a candidate after discussing and rejecting Debs, Donnelly, Vandervoort of Nebraska, and their fellow Texan James H. "Cyclone" Davis.[49] Had Donnelly been energetically supported by the Minnesota delegates, he might have proved the only man around whom the radicals could have rallied in 1896, just as they had in Cincinnati in 1891. But Sidney M. Owen and William R. Dobbyn had secretly resolved to prevent Donnelly from regaining any prestige at the convention. Although he was chairman of the Minnesota delegation, his opponents succeeded in excluding Donnelly from all the convention committees. Furthermore, Owen was obviously committed to fusion. To indorse Donnelly, even tacitly, would have jeopardized Owen's position in the eyes of Minnesota's Democrats.

The antifusionists, desperately in need of a well-known figure to

[48]Minneapolis *Representative*, July 23, 1897.
[49]Woodward, *Tom Watson*, p. 295.

advance for permanent chairman of the convention, awakened Donnelly in the middle of the night to ask him to accept the position. Although the permanent chairmanship was the most strenuous post at the convention, he consented to be a candidate if the Mid-Road group wanted him to do so. In the morning, however, the antifusionist steering committee did not submit his name because the Minnesota delegation reputedly protested against his selection.[50] When the Mid-Road group indorsed an obscure Maine politician, James E. Campion, for the chairmanship, all hope of winning over the undecided delegates to the Mid-Road position was lost. Campion was no match for Senator William V. Allen of Nebraska, a dedicated Bryanite and a fusionist who had been slated for the chairmanship by the Weaver group.

Opposition to Donnelly within the Minnesota delegation exploded publicly when a group of northern Mid-Roaders decided to place his name before the convention as a presidential candidate. They printed Donnelly badges and arranged for the Indiana delegates to distribute them. An Indiana delegate walked into the Minnesota headquarters when the delegates were in caucus, and caught the eye of Donnelly, who was presiding as chairman of the delegation. Requested to state his mission, the Hoosier delegate walked to the speaker's table and opened a bundle of badges. Printed at the top of white ribbons were the words, "MIDDLE OF THE ROAD," and below them, "DONNELLY FOR PRESIDENT." When the Indiana delegate announced that his state was willing to support Donnelly, he encountered stony silence from the Minnesotans.

"I want to say to the delegates from Minnesota," said Donnelly rising to his feet, "that this action on the part of the Indiana man is entirely spontaneous and not the result of any plan or scheme of any sort. I have said that I was not a candidate and still say it. Still if the delegates from my own state see fit to give me their votes, I shall esteem it a matter to be very proud of." There was no response. The Indiana delegate folded the bundle of badges and left the room. The Donnelly boom collapsed. He had been humiliated. Only thirteen of the state's fifty-four delegates, it was later claimed, had supported him. Deeply offended, Donnelly later wrote, "and this was our reward for twenty five years of labor on behalf of reform."[51]

The Mid-Roaders finally settled on S. F. Norton of Illinois and

[50]St. Paul *Globe*, July 21, 1896; Minneapolis *Representative*, July 29, 1896.
[51]Minneapolis *Journal*, July 22, 1896; Minneapolis *Representative*, July 29, 1896.

Frank Burkett of Mississippi as their candidates for president and vice-president. With an outpouring of their pent-up enthusiasm, the Mid-Roaders attempted to stage a rally, but the Bryanites seemed to have controlled the electric lights and the effort became a grotesque display with Mrs. Mary E. Lease and "Cyclone" Davis shouting and parading in the light of flickering candles.[52] Although disorganized, the antifusion element was large enough to threaten the outcome of the convention. Fearful that the Mid-Roaders would never approve of complete fusion—nominating both Bryan and Sewall—as Weaver and Senator William V. Allen hoped, but might actually bolt the convention, the idea spread among the delegates that the rules should be changed so that the vice-presidential candidate could be nominated first. Despite an earlier public refusal by Senator James K. Jones, chairman of the Democratic National Committee, to accede to the idea of replacing Sewall with a People's party candidate, the move was made in an effort to consolidate the party through the vice-presidency.

The anti-Bryan group readily accepted the change of rules proposal, confident that Sewall would never prove satisfactory to the majority of the delegates. Support for the change came also from delegates who wished to preserve the party identity, and from some delegates who held the lingering hope that the Democrats might withdraw Sewall. Adoption of the new rules upset Democratic party plans. Senator Jones telegraphed Bryan for instructions. The candidate empowered Jones to withdraw his name if Sewall did not receive the nomination. To prevent any misunderstanding, Bryan also telegraphed Chairman William V. Allen, "I shall not be a candidate before the Populist convention unless Sewall is nominated." Allen pocketed his message. Jones released his, just about the time the vice-presidential nominating speeches were in progress. Six men were placed in nomination, but only three—Sewall, indorsed by the ultra-fusionists, Burkett, favored by the die-hard Mid-Roaders, and Thomas Watson, supported by the compromise element—received genuine attention.

Donnelly aptly expressed the majority's opinion when he thundered that he was "willing to swallow Democracy gilded with the genius of Bryan," but would not "stomach plutocracy in the body of Sewall."[53] Donnelly's indorsement of Watson probably influenced many undecided antifusionists. "I stood at the cradle of the

[52]Hicks, *The Populist Revolt*, pp. 359–62; Woodward, *Tom Watson*, p. 296.
[53]Hicks, *The Populist Revolt*, p. 364; St. Louis *Republic*, July 25, 1896.

People's party," he said, "and God forbid that I should be here to attend its funeral."[54] Watson won the party's candidacy on the first ballot, but not until the lights had been tampered with to allow for significant vote shifts.

By the next morning all the delegates knew that Bryan had wired Jones to withdraw his name unless Sewall was nominated. The St. Louis newspapers also carried a flat denial by Jones of any plans to withdraw Sewall's name from the Democratic slate because he had failed to gain the People's party nomination. William V. Allen refused to allow any discussion of Bryan's message to come before the convention.

The determined antifusionists placed S. F. Norton's name in nomination for the presidency. In nominating Bryan, Weaver told the convention, "I would not endorse the distinguished gentleman named at Chicago, I would nominate him outright, and make him our own, and share justly and rightfully in his election." Donnelly seconded Bryan's nomination in behalf of the Minnesota delegation, but he did not urge Bryan to indorse the People's party platform or even to repudiate Sewall in favor of Watson. Identity of belief was not the issue, Donnelly argued. The People's party was not merging with the Democratic party; it had simply agreed to accept the Democratic candidate on the strength of personal admiration for him as a man and the overwhelming urgency which existed to unite in some way all the reform elements.[55]

During the balloting a rumor spread through the convention hall that Bryan had wired Allen withdrawing his candidacy. Donnelly climbed on his chair, bellowed for recognition from Allen, and asked the chairman if Bryan still wished to remain a candidate after Watson's nomination. Although he was later said to have the telegram in his pocket, Allen denied knowledge of its existence.[56] Twice during the balloting the Texans caucused, threatening to bolt the convention. Henry D. Lloyd, unable to muster enough courage to disregard Clarence Darrow's advice, did not attempt to stem the Bryan tide. The desire to preserve the People's party, the first reform party to achieve national importance since the Civil War, stilled many voices and contributed to Bryan's nomination.[57] "A party which hates [the]

---

[54] St. Louis *Republic*, July 23, 1896.
[55] Minneapolis *Representative*, July 29, 1896; Haynes, *Weaver*, pp. 379–80.
[56] Minneapolis *Representative*, August 24, 1898.
[57] Woodward, *Tom Watson*, p. 301.

Democracy accepted the Democratic nominee," wrote Lloyd expressing the anguish of the antifusionists, "and a party which has no faith in silver as a panacea accepted silver practically as the sole issue of the campaign."[58]

Donnelly returned from St. Louis thoroughly disheartened. Sad, embittered, disappointed because of his betrayal at the hands of Sidney M. Owen and the fusionists within the Minnesota delegation, he filled the columns of his newspaper with accounts of how his enemies "put the cold steel" into him and "turned it around several times." The actions of Owen, he charged, were not only personally treacherous but also like those of Jerry Simpson—so eager to secure a Democratic indorsement in his home district that he wanted to accept the entire Democratic slate, even Sewall. "There were so many in our convention, who were candidates for office, or who expected to be, and hoped for Democratic endorsement," Donnelly lamented, "that they swept us on to the nomination of Mr. Bryan." Bristling with animosity, he added, "The Democracy raped our convention while our own leaders held the struggling victim."

Donnelly stated that he would support Bryan and Watson, but confessed a preference for another ticket. He regretted the foolishness of the convention delegates in urging Bryan to accept their platform. Shrewdly he predicted that Bryan would never accede to their terms. "If he even attempted to meet the People's party halfway," Donnelly quipped, "Bryan would find himself, trying to ride two horses, going in opposite directions." Reformers, however, had no choice. For the sake of the issues and the future, Donnelly urged them to stand together. Personally, after the election, he planned to retire to his library and the more rewarding domain of literature.[59]

It was absurd to reply, as did the pro-silver Duluth *Herald*, by accusing Donnelly of seeking to aid Mark Hanna and the Republicans, a stigma the Bryanites usually reserved for less well-known Mid-Roaders.[60] But Donnelly's defection was serious; his lack of enthusiasm jeopardized the carefully prepared plans of Minnesota's silverites to nominate John Lind for governor. Lind, who had entered politics as a Republican, had allied himself with William D. Washburn and served three terms in Congress, winning re-election when

---

[58]Quoted in Carl C. Taylor, *The Farmers' Movement* (New York: American Book Co., 1953), p. 306.

[59]Minneapolis *Representative*, July 29, 1896.

[60]*Ibid.*, August 5, 1896.

every other Minnesota congressional seat had been lost by the Republicans. As early as May, 1895, Lind had joined the western silver Republican group. He was in correspondence with Bryan, obviously seeking an active role in any movement of the silver forces to combine.[61] Unquestionably, Lind's action related to Nelson's triumph over Washburn in Minnesota's Senate race. Nelson's victory menaced Lind's political future within the Republican party. A Swede, Lind was distrusted by Nelson who probably recognized him as his most serious rival among Scandinavian Republicans.

During 1896, as the silver issue divided the Republicans, Lind emerged as the leader of the minority group. Behind him was the influence of Washburn's disgruntled followers, eager to defeat Governor Clough because he had defected to Nelson to gain the office.[62] As a Swede, as a Republican who had broken with his party after McKinley's nomination, and as a politician entirely separated from their intra-party squabbles, Lind was the ideal image of a gubernatorial candidate among the rank-and-file members of the People's party. Before the Democratic convention nominated Bryan and accepted silver, even Donnelly had expressed satisfaction with Lind as a potential candidate.[63]

After Bryan's nomination by the People's party, the Minnesota Democrats struck a bargain with the state's silver Republicans. They named Lind as their gubernatoral candidate, while selecting Democrats for treasurer and secretary of state. The posts of lieutenant governor and attorney-general were left open as bait for the People's party to fill if they accepted the ticket. The fusionists anticipated success at the People's party state convention, until Donnelly returned from St. Louis at odds with Owen, and apparently determined to maintain party integrity by denouncing Owen and opposing fusion.

No personal animus clouded the relationship between Donnelly and Lind, but Lind's association with Washburn made him vulnerable to criticism. The editor of the Willmar *Tribune*, Christian Johnson, strongly opposed to Lind's drive for the People's party nomination, almost pleaded with Donnelly to stop Lind. Johnson suggested that Donnelly could be nominated for governor, or at least control the convention if he wished to do so. Recognizing Donnelly's intense

[61]George Stephenson, *John Lind of Minnesota* (Minneapolis: University of Minnesota Press, 1935), p. 103.
[62]*Ibid.*, pp. 100, 107.
[63]Minneapolis *Representative,* July 1, 1896.

hatred of Washburn, Johnson pointed out that he did not propose to help elect a governor and have Washburn and the wheat ring fill all the state offices. "The more we look at this Lind wave," Johnson warned, "the more we see the fine Italian hand of Bill Washburn."[64]

After a personal conference, Donnelly was persuaded to accept Lind. He was given assurance from T. J. Meighan, chairman of the Minnesota People's party, and Thomas D. O'Brien that there would be no wholesale fusion. It is also highly probable that Lind, Meighan, and O'Brien agreed to support Donnelly rather than Owen on the issue of party fidelity at the People's party convention.[65]

When the convention assembled on August 26, Lind's nomination as well as the formation of the coalition slate was a certainty. With something of the spirit that characterized Donnelly almost a quarter of a century earlier, Lind accepted the indorsement just as he had that of the Democratic convention, not as a Democrat, or a Republican, or a member of the People's party, but as a citizen wishing to contribute to the cause of reform.[66]

But the Owen-Donnelly controversy became the prime cause of contention and excitement at the convention. An attempt was made to prevent Donnelly from addressing the convention, but the delegates, obviously sympathetic to his cause, called for him to speak. He abstained from attacking Owen before the delegates. He refused to sanction a discussion of his "betrayal" at the national convention. To raise the issue would have meant a "poll-parrot-and-monkey-time," and a vulgar washing of "dirty linen" that Donnelly feared would "tear the convention to pieces and greatly injure the party." At his request the convention dropped a motion to censure the Minnesota delegates to the St. Louis convention who had violated their instruction by opposing his candidacy. Owen, however, was not indorsed by the state convention, although he was the party's congressional candidate in its Fifth District stronghold.

Pleased with the outcome of the convention, Donnelly was full of praise for Lind as "eloquent, able, thoughtful, penetrating" and a "kind of Gothic Lincoln." Lind's nomination proved the wisdom of the People's party because it united all the voters in the state who

[64]Donnelly MSS, C. Johnson to I. D., August 7, 9, 1896; Stephenson, *Lind,* p. 109.

[65]Donnelly MSS, T. J. Meighan to I. D., August 11, 1896; J. Lind to I. D., August 11, 1896; T. D. O'Brien to I. D., August 12, 1896. See also Stephenson, *Lind,* p. 110, which explains that Donnelly met with Lind but fails to explain how Donnelly was won over.

[66]St. Paul *Pioneer Press,* August 27, 1896.

opposed the gold standard. Donnelly was confident that Lind, if elected, would "do his whole duty not only by those who voted for him but by those who did not."[67]

Early in September Donnelly went to Lincoln, Nebraska, to participate in the celebration marking the opening of Bryan's campaign as the People's party candidate. No auditorium in the city was large enough to accommodate the audience—there were nearly five thousand people present—and an open air meeting was held. Much impressed with Bryan's stamina as a campaigner, Donnelly observed that his canvass was unparalleled in the history of American statesmanship. "He shows in his face," Donnelly noted with the sympathy of a seasoned political veteran, "the wear and tear of the great ordeal he is passing through, but his voice is still clear and his energy unimpaired. His sagacity is as remarkable as his endurance." Donnelly viewed Bryan as being as much a product of the West as Lincoln, although "trained under more favorable conditions than those which surrounded the railsplitter."[68]

Prior to leaving Nebraska, he visited briefly with Bryan. Able and shrewd, perceptive enough to realize Donnelly's susceptibility to flattery, Bryan was "very kind & complimentary." Weaver and Donnelly, Bryan told him, "were the only two Populists he could depend upon." Donnelly was in good spirits when he left Bryan. The presidential candidate had held out the "dim hope" that he would get a cabinet post if the Nebraskan were elected. But Donnelly was too realistic to indulge this dream. "I have been disappointed so often," he recorded, "that I am not sanguine as to anything."[69] Two weeks after his conference with Bryan, the Democratic National Committee invited Donnelly to campaign for the ticket. Listed as a member of the People's party, he usually received a hundred dollars for each speech.[70]

At the request of Marion Butler, chairman of the National Committee of the People's party, Donnelly wrote a manifesto for the 1896 campaign which was directed at the Mid-Road group. The party had not been swallowed by the Democrats, he insisted, rather the older party had turned to them for inspiration. The People's party

[67] Minneapolis *Representative*, September 2, 1896.

[68] *Ibid.*, September 9, 16, 1896, quoting from Omaha *World Herald*, September 7, 1896.

[69] Donnelly MSS, Diary, September 9, 1896.

[70] *Ibid.*, J. K. Jones to I. D., September 23, October 19, 1896; T. D. O'Brien to I. D., October 14, 1896 (telegram).

retained its organization, it retained a major candidate in the person of Thomas Watson, and if it retained its determination the People's party could redress the "Crime of 73." "The occasion raps at the door," he wrote with genuine emotion; ". . . in the name of God, your country, your children and all the poor and oppressed of the whole world, we ask you not to forego this opportunity to do good and help mankind."[71]

The People's party found it increasingly difficult to raise campaign funds. Not only was the nation in the depths of a depression, but also the party's support of Bryan tended to channel funds into the Democratic party. Reminding the readers of the *Representative* that this was the people's battle, he pleaded for even the smallest contribution. "Who are the first ten men," he wrote, "to immortalize themselves by sending in ten dollars each."[72] Donnelly regretted that he could not afford to speak under the auspices of the National Committee of the People's party. He told J. A. Edgerton just what he explained to the Democratic National Committee. Before he could campaign, enough money had to be raised to employ an editor for the *Representative*. The People's party lacked the funds to underwrite the *Representative* during the contest.[73] The paper, which had never been self-sustaining, was proving too great a financial responsibility for Donnelly to bear. He seriously considered giving it up if Bryan lost the election.[74]

Bryan planned to campaign in Minnesota during the second week in October. Although the state had never cast its electoral votes for a Democratic candidate, there was a feeling among Minnesota politicians that the era of Republican ascendency was drawing to a close. Governor Clough, who was seeking re-election, lacked the personal magnetism and ethnic appeal of John Lind. He was also confronted with the vigorous opposition of many influential Republicans such as Charles Towne and Frank Day who controlled newspapers and advocated silver. It was hoped that Lind would draw so many Republican Scandinavian voters to the fusion ticket that, added to the normal Democratic and People's party vote, the state ticket would carry Minnesota for Bryan.

[71]*Ibid.*, M. Butler to I. D., September 18, 1896 (appended typescript).
[72]Minneapolis *Representative*, September 23, 30, 1896.
[73]Donnelly MSS, I. D. to J. Edgerton, September 30, 1896 (carbon copy); J. Edgerton to I. D., October 3, 1896.
[74]*Ibid.*, Diary, October 5, 1896.

The Democratic leadership carefully prepared for Bryan's visit. Because St. Paul's largest auditorium seated only ten thousand people, the candidate was to tour the city and speak at several halls. The best political speakers in the state were brought to St. Paul to introduce Bryan or to present speeches preceding or following his appearance. Donnelly was asked to speak at the St. Paul Auditorium.[75]

Enormous crowds, far exceeding the expectations of the Democratic committee, greeted Bryan in St. Paul. Ten thousand people filled the Auditorium and Donnelly estimated that nearly three thousand jammed the streets outside the building. In the west side of the city, in the Irish ward, there was an even larger turnout. Bryan's eloquence captivated his listeners, and Donnelly confessed that attempting to follow Bryan on the platform "was the hardest task we ever had in our life." As a speaker, Donnelly noted of Bryan, "he is a great man—a very great man—and he sweeps the minds of men along with him." He was so impressed with Bryan's speeches and the demonstrations that accompanied them that he predicted the candidate would carry Minnesota by fifty thousand votes.[76]

In a personal meeting at the Ryan Hotel, Bryan called Donnelly aside for a private discussion. For three-quarters of an hour, while Bryan relaxed on his bed, they talked about Tom Watson's relentless campaign for the vice-presidency and his determination to press for Sewall's withdrawal from the race. Donnelly showed Bryan his correspondence with Senator Marion Butler touching on the Watson matter. Bryan did not share Donnelly's concern regarding Watson. He preferred to talk of his hopes for the future if he won the election. "His purposes are pure and noble," Donnelly recorded in his diary; "if he is the choice of the people he will give the country an administration the greatest and best it has ever enjoyed." Infected with Bryan's sincerity, his apparent depth of conviction, and his approach to the issues as he talked about them, Donnelly observed, "It seems to me he has been raised up by Providence to save the country from sinking into old world conditions."[77] In commenting publicly about his Sunday afternoon with Bryan, he stressed Bryan's

[75]*Ibid.*, Stan Donnelly to I. D., October 7, 1896; E. R. Lynch to I. D., October 7, 1896.

[76]*Ibid.*, Diary, October 11, 1896; Minneapolis *Representative*, October 14, 1896.

[77]*Ibid.*, Diary, October 11, 1896.

humility, insisting that "there was no vanity; no self glorification. It was the revelation of a great philanthropic unselfish heroic soul, that was anticipating only four years of unremitting toil in the effort to lift up and benefit mankind."[78]

Two days after the St. Paul rallies, Bryan went to Minneapolis where he spoke to a large audience at the Exhibition Building. He deviated from his prepared text to answer William D. Washburn, who had written to him in a manner critical of the advocates of silver. Fastening on a few phrases in Washburn's letter implying that Bryan's audience "like others [was] dominated by human selfishness," Bryan castigated Washburn for condemning the desires of labor to share in profits of production while he condoned the efforts of "gold bugs" to retain a system which worked to their own advantage. Because he had been accused of seeking to divide the American people, class against class, Bryan told a Minneapolis audience, "I am willing to array all the people who suffer from the operations of trusts, syndicates, and combines against the few who operate them for their own benefit." No more affirmative statement could have been given to the reformers. Bryan had rallied the support of Henry George's Single Taxers, of Eugene Debs' socialist group, of Edward Bellamy's Nationalists; and after Minneapolis, Donnelly wrote, "Go on, Mr. Bryan, we are with you!"[79]

The campaign against Bryan and Lind in Minnesota, typical of the Republican national effort, produced a great outpouring of accusations of "repudiation" and "anarchism." The effort to frighten voters into retaining their Republican loyalty was well in line with Mark Hanna's Republican campaign throughout the country. Minnesota farmers reported that lending companies were threatening to withdraw all mortgage money and to foreclose all mortgages if Bryan won the election.[80] The Minneapolis *Journal* in a full page advertisement carrying the headline, "LIND'S SUCCESS VS. MINNESOTA'S CREDIT," and signed by over two score business leaders from the Twin Cities and Chicago, more than hinted that a Democratic victory spelled bankruptcy for the state and a deepening of the depression.[81] Senators Cushman K. Davis and Knute Nelson defended the

---

[78]Minneapolis *Representative*, October 11, 1896.
[79]*Ibid.*, October 28, 1896; William J. Bryan, *The First Battle* (Chicago: W. B. Conkey Co., 1896), pp. 538–54.
[80]Minneapolis *Representative*, October 7, 1896.
[81]Minneapolis *Journal*, October 31, 1896.

gold standard in a series of speeches given throughout the state. For the first time since the Civil War during a major political contest, Donnelly did not figure prominently in the newspapers.

Employed by the Democratic National Committee, Donnelly campaigned in Illinois, Kansas, and Missouri. He spoke primarily in Bryan's behalf, but he was frequently relied upon to patch up the differences among antifusionists. He did not campaign extensively in Minnesota, even though his friends insisted that he be a candidate for the state legislature. He had not opposed his nomination, but he had not fought for it. Harvey Gillitt had assured his selection by the People's party and Thomas D. O'Brien worked to secure a Democratic indorsement. One of his friends, encouraging Donnelly to remain in the contest, pointed out that party labels or indorsements had ceased to have importance for him in the eyes of the voters. Donnelly was Dakota County's favorite son.[82] In agreeing to run, he explained that he was committed to numerous engagements outside the state. He promised to speak in Hastings, as had become his custom, on the eve of the election.[83]

The night before the Hastings speech, having returned from the political hustings, Donnelly noted that he had played a "part in the greatest and most momentous campaign of this generation. I have done my best to save the Republic," he wrote in his diary, "but the question is, is it fit to be saved? Can anything but the intervention of divine Providence," he wondered somewhat pessimistically, "prevent the swarming idiots from wrecking themselves."[84]

Bryan gained six and a half million votes, but lost to McKinley, who collected slightly more than seven million, securing two hundred and seventy-one electoral votes to Bryan's one hundred and seventy-six. In Kansas, Nebraska, South Dakota, Idaho, Montana, and Washington, the fusion candidates won control of state legislatures and captured governorships. Minnesota, however, gave McKinley a sixty-thousand-vote majority over Bryan, and Governor Clough managed to defeat Lind by less than four thousand out of a total of more than three hundred thousand votes cast. Even Owen, who had a reputation as the best vote-getter in the People's party was defeated in the Fifth District, his vote lagging Lind's by six

[82]Donnelly MSS, H. Gillitt to I. D., September 24, 1896; T. D. O'Brien to I. D., September 25, 1896; J. B. Lambert to I. D., October 2, 1896.

[83]Minneapolis *Representative*, October 14, 1896.

[84]Donnelly MSS, Diary, November 1, 1896.

thousand! The Republicans gained control of both houses of the Minnesota legislature.

"Never were the circumstances more favorable," wrote Donnelly, who found the election results incomprehensible. "We had a splendid candidate and he made a gigantic campaign; the elements of reform were fairly united, and the depression of business universal, and yet in spite of all, the bankrupt millions voted to keep the yoke on their own necks!" He could only add, "I tremble for the future."[85]

When the final tabulations had been made, Donnelly discovered that he had been elected. "We shall probably poke our head out of the cyclone cellar, and anxiously inquire if the storm has blown over," he told the readers of the *Representative*. "It is well that a few specimen Populists should survive, so that people may know what the breed looked like."[86] As he had in years past, Donnelly promised to do his best for the people. "We will possess little power. There will be only 25 Populists and Democrats in the House against 92 Republicans—hardly enough for seed." With a touch of pathos and nostalgia, he noted: "There was a time, ten or twenty years ago, when we would have tried to wrest reform even from this adverse majority, and should have taken them by storm; but that day is past. We realize how powerless are the people against the Money Trust." Nevertheless, he concluded, "We shall try to vote right and to do such little good as may be incidently possible."[87]

In compliance with the newly enacted Minnesota Pure Election Law, he published his first campaign expense report. "It amounts to the enormous sum of $3.98! Of this 60 cents was for railroad fare. . . . The remainder, $3.38, was our share of the very modest assessment of the People's party county committee for incidental expenses." Although he believed in the underlying basis for the election law, Donnelly felt the Minnesota statute had been enacted more to placate the critical than to eliminate dishonesty. Facetiously, he had entitled the news item, "Extensive Corruption."[88]

[85] *Ibid.*, November 6, 1896.
[86] Minneapolis *Representative*, November 4, 1896.
[87] *Ibid.*, November 11, 1896.
[88] *Ibid.*, November 18, 1896.

The Middle of the Road
1897–1898

And today the People's party . . . [is] a demoralized mob, dragging its dirty skirts through the mire of defeat.

IGNATIUS DONNELLY

IN TERMS of the success or failure of the People's party as a political institution, one could argue convincingly that a Bryan victory would have proven as devastating as did a Bryan defeat. The fundamental question of fusion would have remained equally urgent. Unquestionably, those who had supported Bryan enthusiastically or who had won election to office because of party coalitions would have favored continuing association. Perhaps the southerners such as Watson, or the Chicago radicals such as Lloyd, would have refused to join, but they would have been isolated because they were as much in conflict with each other as they were with the fusionists. The victory of McKinley, the "Advance Agent of Prosperity" as he was dubbed during the campaign, in no way increased the centrifugal forces within the People's party. The process of disintegration, which had begun with the rise of silver sentiment among the leadership, could only have been overcome by a major reconstruction of the party's leadership and program.

In analyzing the election, searching for the party's errors, Donnelly failed to distinguish between the reasons why Bryan lost and the causes of the party's failure to retain its identity. He felt the first mistake was "watering down" the Omaha platform to make it more palatable to the Democrats. This, he insisted, lost the support of urban radicals and divided and demoralized labor. The second mistake, he observed, was the attempt to force an "unnatural marriage" of the Democratic and People's parties. They had been locked in a desperate struggle, with the southern Democrats representing the identical forces in their region that the Republicans expressed in Minnesota. The fusion policy was viewed by the southern wing of the People's party as an outrageous betrayal. Donnelly concluded that the proper solution would have been an independent slate at St. Louis. Fusion on a local basis may have offered limited possibilities, but on a national level, Donnelly sided with Tom Watson against it.[1]

Donnelly wrote to Taubeneck, no longer party chairman, suggesting that a statement be issued charging the Republicans with full responsibility to bring prosperity. Bryan's defeat should not be acknowledged as fatal to the party.[2] A short time later he wrote to Senator Marion Butler of North Carolina, who had replaced Taubeneck as chairman, pointing out that the party was disintegrating and many of its members were going over to the Democrats "body and boots." Donnelly urged Butler to summon a meeting of the National Committee at St. Louis where a definite stand could be taken on the issue of co-operation with other parties. In 1898 and 1900, Donnelly insisted, the People's party must not be an appendage.[3] Afraid that a national meeting would be dominated by the radical element, Butler rejected Donnelly's proposal. As an alternative, he suggested issuing a circular expressing the party's opinion on key questions. He invited Donnelly to contribute his views. The letter was marked unanswered.[4]

Butler's reluctance to assume leadership resulted in a move by the National Reform Press Association, primarily editors of newspapers indorsing the People's party, to halt the continuing drift toward fusion. Paul Vandervoort, president of the Association, summoned a meeting of the editors for February 22 in Memphis, Tennessee. Although Donnelly was unable to attend the conference because of the Minnesota legislative session, he wrote Vandervoort expressing his hope that the editors would defend the party's independence. "It is not dead and should not be buried," was Donnelly's plea.[5]

[1]Minneapolis *Representative*, November 4, 1896.
[2]Donnelly MSS, I. D. to H. Taubeneck, November 7, 1896 (carbon).
[3]*Ibid.*, I. D. to M. Butler, November 28, 1896 (carbon).
[4]*Ibid.*, M. Butler to I. D., December 10, 1896.
[5]*Ibid.*, I. D. to P. Vandervoort, December 29, 1896 (carbon).

The actions of the Reform Press Association persuaded Butler to canvass the party leadership regarding some type of conference. Ten days before the Memphis gathering, Butler wrote Donnelly that he would not dissociate the National Committee from the Reform Press conference. In a warm, friendly, and persuasive letter, Butler, who probably intended to placate the Mid-Roaders, told Donnelly that as he read his letter and one from Weaver, he "recalled Cincinnati as though it were but yesterday, then St. Louis, then Omaha, then St. Louis again." He recalled the number of times that Donnelly "had quieted the storms that were raging in the conventions and at the opportune time seemed to say, 'Peace, be still!' and the waves subsided." Butler "recalled that in each instance subsequent events proved the wisdom of your course and the unwisdom of General Weaver's." Weaver had written Butler, "The forces cannot be realigned now or the issues changed. . . . In this state [Iowa], our allied forces have just declared the union permanent upon the issues involved in the late struggle and there was not a dissenting voice. . . . No power can separate us." Recognizing the existence of a "little dissatisfaction here and there," Weaver concluded, "it is trifling in point of numbers and unsustained by sound tactical judgement." Butler decided that he could not follow such a man and turned to Donnelly who had opposed Weaver steadfastly from the outset.[6]

Until the Memphis conference, Butler, apparently, was not entirely committed to fusion. The decision by the Reform Press Association to urge the National Committee to call a delegate convention for July 4, 1897, or to call it themselves if Butler failed to act, opened a rift between Butler and the editors. At a meeting of party congressmen, which Butler called to discuss policy, his contention that only friction between fusion and antifusion forces would result from a convention was sustained. Therefore, the National Committee refused to sanction the July 4 conference scheduled by the Reform Press Association to meet at Nashville, Tennessee.

In much the same spirit as he had worked to preserve the party's national identity, Donnelly sought to prevent Minnesota's fusionists from succeeding as Weaver had in Iowa. Donnelly charged that Owen and the coterie of men around him who favored fusion had been discredited by their overwhelming defeat in 1896.[7] Vigorously and candidly he told a party worker that a "certain malignant, pie-hunting, shallow-pated influence is at last exposed and will hereafter

[6]*Ibid.*, M. Butler to I. D., February 13, 1896.
[7]Minneapolis *Representative*, December 9, 1896.

have no control over the actions of the party." He expressed the kindest of feelings toward the Democrats and Republicans who had worked so closely with the People's party in 1896. "We may be ready to co-operate again," he wrote, "but in the meantime, we will insist that the Populist party must live and maintain its identity and independence."[8] He called upon party members to attend the state convention, which would assemble in early January, to prevent the silver Democrats and Republicans who had played leading roles in 1896 from controlling the policy.[9] But Donnelly was only partially successful. He managed to stave off an attempt by the secretary of the State Central Committee, E. R. Lynch, aimed at complete fusion through the creation of a new party, the People's Democratic party. He failed, however, to secure a pledge against fusion in 1898.[10]

During the opening days of the Minnesota legislature, Donnelly behaved with such unusual "modesty and circumspection" that the Minneapolis *Tribune* noted his dignity and restraint. He appeared to be a man aware that life was at best but a passing show and that "soon he must lay down in his last sleep, leaving posterity to give him his rightful place in history." The calm broke, however, when Judge Hicks, who represented Hennepin County in discussing a revision of the state's election laws, spoke disparagingly of Donnelly's contest with Washburn. "It was a reminder of the old days," wrote the *Tribune*, "when Donnelly walked about with a perpetual club on his shoulder, when life was one continual fence, and when his meat and drink was warfare." After replying to Hicks, Donnelly told the house that he was known as a friend of the people; he could defend his legislative record. "The old man [Donnelly] had the best of the fight from the start," added the *Tribune*, "and when he concluded, a dozen leading Republicans came up to shake the hand of the Sage of Nininger."[11]

Although his following was negligible, Donnelly was an influential member of the legislature because of his strong views, his parliamentary skill, and power of persuasion. He lent his voice to established policies. Rarely did he fail to support education measures, but in 1897 he urged a cut in the budget of the University of Minnesota, insisting that Minnesota's immigrant farmers who were trying to

[8]Donnelly MSS, I. D. to W. A. Bentley, December 19, 1896 (carbon).
[9]Minneapolis *Representative*, December 30, 1896.
[10]Minneapolis *Penny Press*, January 5, 1897; Minneapolis *Representative*, January 13, 1897.
[11]Minneapolis *Tribune*, January 17, 1897; Minneapolis *Representative*, January 20, 1897.

scratch out a living could not afford a great research institution. Scholarship, he conceded, was fine for the Smithsonian Institution, but it was too great a luxury for Minnesota.[12] By this time he disliked and distrusted college professors, especially Shakespearean experts and economists. He had an ambivalent attitude toward higher education.[13] Privately he cherished professional education for himself and his sons. Publicly, however, and sincerely, he had written, "The purpose of our great system [of education] is not to create doctors and lawyers and professors, but the universal education of the masses. We are friendly to the university, but it will bear watching. . . . This republic of ours," he concluded, "could survive if there was not a single university in the land, but it would not endure for a single generation without public schools."[14]

Donnelly continually endeavored to enact legislation that he had favored for years. He voted for a railroad rate regulation measure which was defeated, but he no longer raged at such failures. In his opinion, public ownership was the only solution to the problem of natural monopolies such as the railroads, the telegraph, and the telephone. The salutary effects of government ownership—the purification of politics, the substantial reduction of rate litigation, the general lowering of rates, and the job security for employees—made regulation only a stop-gap measure pending the final solution.[15]

He introduced three minor bills. The first, a minimum literacy test for voting, stipulated that each voter be able to read, and to write his own name. The second, an Alliance-sponsored measure, required the establishment of grain scales at railroad stations so that grain would be weighed prior to shipment. The third, a tax relief measure for small farmers, exempted property holders from taxation on the first thousand dollars of assessed valuation. All three measures failed to pass. Somewhat saddened, Donnelly reported his ineffectiveness, noting that some legislators voted against good legislation because they were afraid of giving him publicity.[16]

[12] Minneapolis *Representative,* January 20, 1897.

[13] One professor who had Donnelly's respect was Richard T. Ely of the University of Wisconsin, and Donnelly quoted extensively from Ely to justify government ownership of railroads. Minneapolis *Representative,* April 11, 1894.

[14] Minneapolis *Representative,* February 28, 1894.

[15] *Ibid.,* March 3, 1897; Donnelly even persuaded the house to approve of a resolution favoring federal ownership of the telegraph. Donnelly MSS, I. D. to N. H. Matsinger, April 21, 1897 (carbon).

[16] Minneapolis *Representative,* March 10, 17, 24, 1897.

Foreign policy figured briefly during the session when Donnelly introduced a resolution calling on the United States Senate to reject the Olney-Pauncefote treaty. The treaty, which provided for the arbitration of Anglo-American disputes, had strong support from peace groups and was scarcely opposed in the American newspapers. Anglophobes, especially Irish-Americans, were sharply critical. They had spurred Cleveland to assume a strongly anti-English stand in the Venezuela controversy. Acutely suspicious of Cleveland, Donnelly had not been swept along in the rise of jingoism. He had not sustained the Irish-American enthusiasm for war over Venezuela, but his opposition to the arbitration treaty was essentially Anglophobic. He filled the columns of the *Representative* with quotations from Washington, Jefferson, Adams, and Blaine emphasizing distrust and hostility toward England. Donnelly's resolution was rejected in the house. The ultimate failure of the treaty in the United States Senate, where it had been indorsed by both Minnesota senators, Davis and Nelson, quite pleased Donnelly.[17]

On March 4, the Minnesota legislature devoted a full day to speeches and resolutions observing William McKinley's inauguration. Virtually ignoring McKinley, Donnelly used the occasion to launch a vicious attack upon Cleveland, asserting that he had entered the presidency a poor man but left it a millionaire. Although staunchly Republican, the conservative St. Paul *Pioneer Press* defended Cleveland, abusing Donnelly by repeating in virulent terms the exploded charges of the past and in addition calling him a dog! Donnelly threatened a suit for $50,000 if the newspaper failed to retract.[18] When the *Pioneer Press* laughed off the threat, Donnelly filed suit. The libel suit was initiated not so much for money as to force the *Pioneer Press* to mend its ways. Donnelly informed the readers of the *Representative* that even the one-dollar judgment he secured in his earlier suit against the *Pioneer Press* had cost so much in legal fees that Joseph Wheelock and Fred Driscoll had lost control of the paper.[19]

Charles Flandrau, retained by the *Pioneer Press* to defend it, was reputed to have sent out five hundred letters seeking information regarding alleged corruption on Donnelly's part. At the trial Flandrau went back for a quarter of a century, but produced only the scanti-

[17]*Ibid.*, January 27, February 3, April 14, May 12, 1897.
[18]*Ibid.*, March 17, 1897; St. Paul *Pioneer Press*, March 5, 1897.
[19]Minneapolis *Representative*, April 28, 1897.

est of hearsay evidence. Michael Doran was subpoenaed, but denied that Donnelly had ever sold his vote or his brains to the Democratic party.[20]

Donnelly's case was brilliantly handled by his son Stan. In the final statement to the jury which Ignatius made personally, and which he termed "terrific," Donnelly evened his score with Wheelock and Flandrau. "Flandrau abused me shamefully in 1891," he confided to his diary, "and I paid him back with usury. My denunciation of Wheelock as a perjurer burned like a red hot branding iron." Before the verdict was rendered, Donnelly added, "If I don't get a cent of damages I got $10,000 of satisfaction out of the scoundrels for their life-long persecution."[21] When the jury awarded him one thousand dollars and court costs, Donnelly was satisfied. "Rather a high price to pay," he wrote in the *Representative*, "for the luxury of calling a gentleman a dog."[22]

One of Donnelly's first acts as a member of the legislature was to introduce a resolution calling for a joint senate-house committee to investigate a report by the state auditor, Robert C. Dunn, to the effect that his predecessor had alienated through error school lands containing substantial iron ore deposits worth more than ten million dollars. The house approved of the resolution, and Donnelly, who was named chairman, began a preliminary survey of the facts. As thorough as he had been in the pine lands investigation, Donnelly was complimented for his intelligent, discreet, and unemotional approach to the problem. He expressed his gratitude to the legislators who supported his effort to recover the great Mountain Iron tract which was held by the Rockefeller interests.[23]

Before the joint committee even consented to investigate, a two-hour hearing took place, in which Donnelly presented the evidence that he felt justified so time-consuming and costly an investigation. Because these were school lands which only the governor had the power to alienate, Donnelly contended that no legal sale had occurred. He asked the committee to determine not only the extent of the loss but also the most advantageous means of reclaiming the iron lands.[24] To preclude abuse of the investigatory power, the committee limited the scope of the inquiry to four questions: Did the state

[20]*Ibid.*, July 6, 1898.

[21]Donnelly MSS, F. N. Dickson to I. D., June 28, 1897; J. J. McCafferty to I. D., June 28, 1897; Diary, June 25, 1897.

[22]Minneapolis *Representative*, June 30, 1897.

[23]*Ibid.*, January 13, 20, 1897.

[24]*Ibid.*, February 3, 1897.

own the land? Did it divest itself of the title? Under what circumstances had the lands been released? And, what steps could be taken by the state in defense of its right?

In a comprehensive final statement the joint committee reported that the lands in question had become part of the state school lands in 1884, that neither the state auditor nor the state land commissioner had the right to relinquish the land and their actions were therefore null and void, that the state auditor had known that the land embraced valuable mineral holdings, and that the committee was of the opinion that additional testimony would tend to establish the existence of a combination entered into to divest the state of its title. The committee recommended that a new committee be created, empowered to take legal action to force the Mountain Iron Mining Company to make restitution to the state.[25] Undoubtedly, further investigation would have embarrassed many state officials who, according to an apologist, had been "doing their best to develop the resources of the state."[26] But it was Donnelly's hope that the state would reclaim at least ten million dollars.[27] Henry D. Lloyd thought the investigation the greatest public service of Donnelly's life.[28]

Lacking emotionalism despite its sensational character, the report passed the house by a vote of ninety-six to six. The senate, however, crippled it by amendments. A substitute measure providing for an additional proceeding by a committee including the governor, state auditor, and attorney-general was finally approved by both houses. Donnelly assumed that the attorney-general would retain counsel and sue to reclaim the lands. Six months later, thoroughly disillusioned, he observed that the Rockefellers were still digging and blasting the ore out of the mines, and that nothing had been done by the attorney-general.[29] The new committee, rejecting the reasoning in Donnelly's report, denied that the state ever held title to the lands in question! The furtive corruption of state officeholders and the mining company was never tested in the courts.[30]

[25] *Ibid.*, April 14, 1897.
[26] Folwell, *Minnesota*, III, 224.
[27] Minneapolis *Representative*, April 21, 1897.
[28] Donnelly MSS, H. D. Lloyd to I. D., March 6, 1897.
[29] Minneapolis *Representative*, November 3, 1897.
[30] For an incredible "white-wash" see Folwell, *Minnesota*, III, 224. But see also, Matthias N. Orfield, *Federal Land Grants to the States with Special Reference to Minnesota* ("University of Minnesota Studies in the Social Sciences," No. 2 [Minneapolis: University of Minnesota Press, 1915]), pp. 229–34.

When Donnelly published the call of the National Reform Press Association for the Nashville, Tennessee, conference, the disagreement between Minnesota's Mid-Road Populists and the advocates of permanent fusion became glaringly obvious. William R. Dobbyn, who led the fight for fusion and contended that the People's party had almost ceased to exist, argued that to hold conferences was to maintain a legal fiction.[31] Owen never accepted Dobbyn's extremist view, although Donnelly attempted to stigmatize Owen by associating him with Dobbyn's position.

F. C. Gibbs, State Central Committee chairman, pleaded for an end to the Owen-Donnelly vendetta, because the party and the Central Committee were equally divided in loyalty between the two men. To force a choice would fragment the organization.[32] Although Donnelly expressed a willingness to forgive Owen for his personal attacks, he refused to be a pallbearer at the funeral procession while Owen led the party to the "boneyard."[33]

A stormy session of the State Central Committee provoked by the Nashville conference ended in a draw. Eager to secure indorsement not only for the Omaha platform but also for the Nashville conference, Donnelly even proposed that critics of the forthcoming meeting be charged with party disloyalty. But the Committee, although agreeable to the Omaha stand, refused to name official delegates to Nashville. It suggested that, since the conference had been called by the Press Association, all the reform editors attend.[34] Owen's *Farm, Stock and Home,* a part of the reform press, attacked the Nashville conference even before it assembled, charging its leadership had acted without justification, on the supposition that the National Committee would sell out to the Democrats.[35]

Most of the several hundred delegates and observers who gathered at Nashville were Mid-Road southerners, disgusted with Weaver and distrustful of Butler. Donnelly was as much their hero as was Tom Watson. They looked forward to seeing and hearing him.[36] But even more was expected of Donnelly. James H. Ferris, chairman of the executive committee of the National Reform Press Association, wrote him prior to the conference lamenting the party's

[31]Minneapolis *Representative,* May 26, 1897.
[32]Donnelly MSS, F. Gibbs to I. D., June 5, 1897.
[33]Minneapolis *Representative,* June 16, 1897.
[34]*Ibid.,* June 23, 1897; Donnelly MSS, rough draft of resolutions for the State Central Committee, June 17, 1897.
[35]Minneapolis *Farm, Stock and Home,* July 1, 1897.
[36]Donnelly MSS, J. H. McDowell to I. D., June 11, 1897.

dilemma. If the conference attacked the fusionists, the result would be an internecine struggle that would damage the party irreparably. If they sanctioned fusion, it meant the party's end. Could Donnelly provide a middle ground? Revealing the depth of his anxiety, Ferris later warned that even the Press Association showed indications of disintegrating.[37]

The Nashville conference was described as a "suit for divorce" between the People's party and the Democrats because the delegates were so violently opposed to fusion.[38] Donnelly served as chairman of the platform and planning committee. The only disagreement evident among the committee members was the extent of their distrust of Marion Butler. The majority believed that Butler would not issue a call for a People's party convention until after the Democrats had selected a candidate. Donnelly doubted that Butler was capable of such perfidy, but he acceded to the majority's request to prepare for a Mid-Road convention.

In a long speech expressing the views of his committee, Donnelly reaffirmed the principles set forth at Cincinnati in 1891. Because there was no single issue such as silver that would prove a universal panacea, the welfare of mankind, Donnelly declared, demanded the continued existence of the People's party. "It is the only national party. It has no fraternal blood on its garments." The most important immediate reforms, he suggested, were initiative and referendum because they would break the yoke of control exercised by "wire pullers" and "office seekers."

To assure the validity and vitality of the People's party, it was proposed that a National Organization Committee be formed, composed of three representatives from each state and presided over by a national chairman who would direct the work of the organization. An executive committee of five members would aid the chairman. To promote membership, a People's party club system would be created. The executive committee would be empowered to summon a convention or poll the party members on the issue, if it believed that the party's National Committee was not pursuing an honest policy.[39]

The Nashville delegates accepted these proposals, and a separate Mid-Road organization came into existence. Implicit in the creation of the National Organization Committee was the obligation to oversee the party's National Committee and prevent it from moving to-

[37]*Ibid.*, J. Ferris to I. D., June 16, 26, 1897.
[38]Hicks, *Populist Revolt*, p. 381.
[39]Minneapolis *Representative*, July 14, 1897.

ward fusion by threatening independent political action. Defending the decision reached at Nashville, Donnelly denied that it was an effort to overthrow the party's national organization. It was, he insisted, based on the fear that the fusionists would avoid a separate convention in 1900. As late as September, Donnelly continued to indorse Butler rather than face an open break on the fusion issue.[40]

During the wrangling within the People's party, there was a general recognition that the party's issues had lost their sting. From the earliest days of the Alliance, economic depression had been the primary reason for the party's existence. Its reform programs, its insistence that there was a financial conspiracy, and its popular appeal, constituted a response to economic hardship. The politics of the People's party was a politics of poverty, depression, and declining status. Within the context of the thinking of the People's party, neither a Cleveland nor a McKinley regime would see a return to prosperity.

At the time of McKinley's inauguration, Donnelly had sneered, "The reign of Confidence will begin. The Advance Agent of Prosperity will advance. Every man and woman will have plenty to eat and drink and wear. Hunger will depart forever from the land. . . . There shall be no more mortgages nor taxes nor sheriff's executions." Facetiously, he added, "And the Populists will hang their burning cheeks with shame."[41] But the "Advance Agent of Prosperity," entirely without his knowledge, had been just that. War between Greece and Turkey in the spring of 1897 had sent wheat prices climbing. Floods in eastern Europe and drought damage in France reduced wheat harvests by more than one-third of a billion bushels. American wheat exports rose steadily. For the first time since 1891 gold imports exceeded exports. Furthermore, there was a sharp expansion in gold production because of a new purification process, and gold prices actually declined, encouraging price increases in foodstuffs.[42]

Contributing equally to the waning strength of the People's party was the steady encroachment upon its platform, either directly or through compromise proposals, by both Republicans and Democrats. Although silver was the most dramatic illustration of this, Donnelly angrily denounced the Republicans for stealing People's party thunder by advocating initiative and referendum.[43] By autumn of 1897,

---

[40]*Ibid.*, July 28, 1897; Donnelly MSS, I. D. to J. Hanley, September 14, 1897.
[41]Minneapolis *Representative*, March 3, 1897.
[42]*Ibid.*, August 18, September 8, 1897.
[43]*Ibid.*, July 7, 1897.

he was critical of the Democrats for extolling antitrust legislation while treating the People's party as if it had "white leprosy and smallpox and cholera."[44]

The initial meeting of the National Organization Committee created at Nashville took place in St. Louis in late November, 1897. Aside from proposing a platform more radical than the accepted Omaha position—they favored direct government loans to individuals without the intervention of private banks—the committee suggested that the party hold its national presidential nominating convention in 1898 to prevent a recurrence of the events of 1896. The National Organization Committee also proposed a conference in January, 1898, to which the People's party National Committee could be invited.[45]

Although Donnelly failed to attend the St. Louis conference, the suggestion of an early nominating convention appealed to him. "Shall we burn our ships and go in for a grand battle for principle, and leave the consequences to God?" he wrote with rhetorical flourish in the *Representative*. "Or shall we wait until the tentacles of the politicians enfold us in a network of suction and there is nothing left of us but the bones."[46] An early convention, he was convinced, would save the platform and drive out the fusionists. Donnelly's enthusiastic reception of the idea was matched by other leading Mid-Road editors, and even the influential *Southern Mercury* advocated a convention as early as July, 1898.

Increasingly apprehensive after the formation of the National Organization Committee, Chairman Butler considered calling a meeting of the party's National Committee. Even before the St. Louis meeting, it was rumored that Butler was acting only out of fear that the new organization would assume leadership if he did not summon a conference.[47] Following the St. Louis proposals for an early convention, Butler, forced to take cognizance of the Mid-Road sentiment, issued a call for a meeting of his committee in the hope of placating or appeasing the National Organization Committee. Eventually, it was decided that both groups would meet at the same time in Omaha, Nebraska, in June, 1898.[48]

In a letter to Tom Watson, Donnelly expressed the hope that the

[44] *Ibid.*, September 8, 1897.
[45] *Ibid.*, December 29, 1897.
[46] *Ibid.*, December 1, 1897.
[47] Donnelly MSS, J. McBride to I. D., September 23, 1897.
[48] Minneapolis *Representative*, December 29, 1897.

party would hold an early convention. Watson was Donnelly's choice for the vice-presidential nomination. Although he had spoken favorably of Wharton Barker, a Pennsylvanian and a recent party recruit who was seeking the presidential nomination, Donnelly confided to Watson that Barker was not his preference.[49] Wrapped in one of his gloomy moods, Watson was gladdened by the "one reformer whose arm does not tire and whose heart does not fail," but confessed to Donnelly that the future did not inspire him with hope. He told Donnelly that the fusionists, consumed with "the deadly greed for office," were as eager to merge with the Republicans in Georgia as they were to merge with the Democrats in Kansas. Watson had given up; he was "practicing law and letting those fusion brethren have right of way."[50] His exchange of views with Watson indicated that Donnelly may have been actively seeking the presidential nomination. He denied this categorically in a newspaper editorial late in December, 1897, when he expressed a tinge of regret that he had been passed over for Bryan in 1896. Probably with little justification, Donnelly observed that his nomination would have held the party together.[51]

During the first week in January, 1898, Minnesota's Mid-Road group held a state-wide rally in St. Paul. Recognized as their leading spokesman, Donnelly declared emphatically against fusion but, interestingly enough, advocated John Lind for governor. Almost two months earlier, in a personal letter to Lind, Donnelly had urged him to accept the People's party nomination in 1898, confident that he would carry the state.[52] But the Mid-Roaders were in no mood for Lind, even though Donnelly did propose his candidacy as a device for stealing the best potential vote-getter in the state. Proud as the Swedes were of Lind, and much as he was admired by many of the antifusionists, the experience of 1896 was too close for them to approve the instrument of fusion.[53] The Mid-Roaders threatened independent political action unless the State Central Committee agreed to a state nomination convention by March 16, 1898.

After the January party rally, Donnelly clashed with his long-time political associate, Major J. M. Bowler. Encouraged and supported by Donnelly, Bowler had run for lieutenant governor on the fusion

[49]Donnelly MSS, I. D. to Tom Watson, December 6, 1897.
[50]*Ibid.*, Tom Watson to I. D., December 14, 1897.
[51]Minneapolis *Representative*, December 22, 1897.
[52]Donnelly MSS, I. D. to John Lind, November 8, 1897.
[53]Stephenson, *Lind*, p. 132; Minneapolis *Representative*, June 12, 1898.

ticket in 1896, but when he failed to join the Mid-Road camp, Donnelly criticized him as a fusionist. In 1897, a rumor spread that Donnelly had sold out to James J. Hill, and Donnelly accused Bowler of giving William R. Dobbyn a distorted version of the offers of aid which Donnelly had received after Kate's death. In a manner reminiscent of so many other occasions in his life, when he had believed a public justification was warranted, Donnelly published a long narrative account of his wife's death and the events which followed. He pointed to his voting record in the legislature and his stand on reform issues to repudiate charges of betrayal.[54] The fusion group, however, determined to use freight rates on Hill's railroad from the Red River Valley to the Twin Cities as a campaign issue, continued to charge Donnelly with duplicity.

F. C. Gibbs scheduled a meeting of the State Central Committee to discuss party organization and the forthcoming nominating convention. That Gibbs had joined Owen and the fusion group was obvious because he had invited Weaver and National Chairman Butler to attend the meeting and address the committee. The Mid-Roaders feared that they would be forced to accede to fusion under pressure of the "Popocrats of the Twin Cities."[55] One week prior to the State Central Committee meeting, Donnelly, warning that Gibbs and Owen were attempting to influence the committee, urged party members to instruct their State Central Committeemen to oppose the fusion clique.

When the committee gathered in Minneapolis, there were such sharp differences that they could not even agree on a method for inviting John Lind to address them. The well-contrived plans of the fusionists, however, were successful, and Donnelly observed sarcastically, "Whenever your views are so unpopular that they will not stand alone, it is good tactics to import prominent men from other regions, so that curiosity may be mistaken for enthusiasm."[56] The committee set the time for the convention as June, rather than March as the Mid-Roaders had hoped, and although the *Representative* tried to play down this defeat using the excuse that the farmers needed more time for planting, the fusionists were free to fix a date which would make co-operation with the Democrats possible.

In an interview with the St. Paul *Dispatch,* Donnelly replied to

[54]Minneapolis *Representative,* September 15, 1897; Donnelly MSS, J. Bowler to I. D., October 8, 1897.
[55]Minneapolis *Representative,* February 9, 1898.
[56]*Ibid.,* February 16, 1898.

the statements by E. R. Lynch, State Central Committee secretary, that the Mid-Roaders had been routed and Donnelly with tear-filled eyes had begged to be recognized as a proxy. "I am a fighter and not a weeper," Donnelly told the *Dispatch's* reporter. Furthermore, he declared that fusionism had been beaten at every turn. They had favored representation at the convention based on the fusion vote of 1896, but it had been fixed on the straight vote of 1894. Lynch's effort to oust him had been overruled twenty to three. "If the People's party June convention turns to fusion," Donnelly warned, "there will be two tickets in the field. The People's party must . . . not be the tail end of the democracy, or anything else."[57]

One week after the State Central Committee meeting, Donnelly married his twenty-year-old secretary, Marian Olive Hanson, in the Minneapolis Norwegian Methodist Church. Employed as a typist and stenographer in 1896, Marian Hanson had worked for the *Representative* and spent three months at Nininger City. At first, Donnelly had jestingly referred to her as his typewriter and wondered whether she was a Swede or a Norwegian. Shortly before Christmas, 1897, he noted in his diary that he was strongly drawn to her and was considering marriage. "Her very poverty endears her to me," he wrote. He had not forgotten Kate: "I revere the memory of my dear dead wife," he noted, "but life is very lonely for me. . . . I may live twenty years longer . . . and I shrink from the loneliness of a companionless existence. I am not moved by sensual considerations," he added, "but by the hollowness of the heart—the yawning abyss of solitariness."[58]

Donnelly's decision to remarry was followed by a "great row" with his children. They viewed Marian Hanson as an adventuress, simply intent on sharing Donnelly's meager estate. In an effort to gain freedom of action, yet keep the respect of his children, he wrote to his elder son, "I have reached the conclusion that it is due to the undying love I bear your mother and my affection for you, my children . . . that I should leave nothing undone that may restore peace in our family, even though it be at the risk of further personal abasement on my part. I ask you, therefore, to call the family together and read them . . . this communication." He asked his children only to be civil and formal in a matter of common courtesy. It had been four years since Kate's death. Did his children wish to consign him "to a life of dangerous solitude" in his old age, he asked. Did they know

[57]St. Paul *Dispatch*, February 18, 1898.
[58]Donnelly MSS, Diary, September 1, 1896, December 18, 1897.

anyone, "who would be willing to share my small income and my isolated life; and nurse me, if need be, through the infirmities that accompany advancing years." Reminding them that poverty was no crime, he pointed out that Kate was even poorer than Marian Hanson at the time he married her. Apologetically he wrote that Kate had asked him "not live alone in . . . old age." "I loved her living and I loved her dead, and I shall continue to love her as long as life beats in my heart," he wrote in full emotion. "And I love her children and my children and their children and I desire while I live, to have them around me." He closed his letter, "I ask nothing of any of you but love and peace. Be just, be generous. Do what your hearts prompt you to do, and what your conscience tells you is right."[59]

Donnelly was not immediately successful with his children. His daughter remained aloof for a brief period. Gradually a formal, perfunctory, common courtesy came to exist. Following their wedding, when Marian went to Philadelphia to visit his sisters, she was greeted with kindness and generosity. The tall, frail, blonde Norwegian immigrant girl was not only the wife but also the devoted admirer of the aging Sage of Nininger.[60]

One week before Donnelly's wedding, a terrific explosion sank the United States warship, "Maine," in Havana harbor. Although Donnelly had favored aid to the Cuban rebels, even at the risk of war with Spain, he shared the anti-imperialist views of Weaver and Watson.[61] Shrewdly analyzing the influence of the business community, which was enjoying its first economic upturn, Donnelly could not believe that McKinley would go to war. Commenting on the President's ultimatum, Donnelly wrote, "Wall Street will see to it that the Spanish Affair Begins and Ends in Nothing more Serious than a Fist Fight."[62] "If war breaks out, despite the plutocrats, and continues for six months," Donnelly observed on the very eve of hostility, "our government will be forced to issue greenbacks, and give the country good times." Angrily he concluded, "It is a crying shame that we can only loosen the grip of the money-power, on the throats of the people, by murdering tens of thousands of innocent producers."[63] The

---

[59]*Ibid.*, December 24, 31, 1897. See also S. Donnelly to I. D., February 1, 1898; I. D. to I. C. D., rough draft, February 9, 1898.

[60]In a personal interview with the author, Marian Hanson, her eyes twinkling, said: "I married him because I loved him! He was like an eagle on a mountain!"

[61]Haynes, *Weaver*, p. 386; Woodward, *Tom Watson*, pp. 334–35.

[62]Minneapolis *Representative*, June 23, 1897, April 13, 1898.

[63]*Ibid.*, April 20, 1898.

failure of Congress to enact a graduated income tax, once the war had begun, confirmed Donnelly's suspicion that the monied class was resolved to profit from the conflict. "This is a bondholder's war," he wrote caustically, "Let the poor devils foot the bill."[64]

Although he willingly agreed that all citizens should support the government during the war, he feared that the hysteria associated with war would destroy the liberties of the people and stamp out the public's interest in the great domestic issues. "Do not let us enslave ourselves under the pretense of liberating others," he warned. "The citizens of this country have been suffering wrongs as grievous as those inflicted upon Cuba by the Spaniards."[65]

Angered by the conduct of the war, he deplored the expenditure of one and a half million dollars a day. "It would have been cheaper to have bought Cuba outright from Spain. It would have saved many millions of dollars and many thousands of lives. But then," he wrote bitterly, "there is the glory, and the Taxes."[66] He told an English friend, "We have nothing in our newspaper now but War—War—War, pictures of ships and portraits of military and Naval heroes."[67]

The possibility of peace found Donnelly growing narrowly isolationist, asking the American people to stop their "philanthropic regard for other nations" and turn their attention to their own affairs. "A naked semi-savage in Cuba chewing a banana," he crudely observed, "is not as sad a sight as a civilized American citizen killing himself for lack of employment."[68]

Donnelly did not find the Spanish-American peace terms reassuring. In discussing the acquisition of islands in the Pacific and the Caribbean, he noted that "it is something new to spread our banner over distant islands, swarming with ignorant and half savage races." Convinced that it would be impossible to extend the franchise immediately to the newly gained regions without "jeopardizing the fate of the Republic," he commented soberly, "New and serious questions open before us."[69] Not only was he worried about the political future but also he shared the alarm of many anti-imperialists that coolie laborers on the islands would make a few nabobs rich by competing with American workers.[70]

[64]*Ibid.*, May 4, 1898.
[65]*Ibid.*, April 20, May 11, 1898.
[66]*Ibid.*, June 1, 1898.
[67]Donnelly MSS, I. D. to C. Potts, July 30, 1898.
[68]Minneapolis *Representative*, August 10, 1898.
[69]*Ibid.*, August 17, 1898.
[70]Donnelly's anti-imperialism was neither so sharp nor so pointed as S. M. Owen's in *Farm, Stock and Home* which was both more isolationist and more

The Spanish-American War did not force a moratorium on the squabbling factions within Minnesota's People's party. Central Committee Chairman Gibbs appealed for co-operation with the Silver Republicans and Democrats in the forthcoming state elections. Donnelly answered with a circular distributed by Henry Fay which summarized the Mid-Road position. Warning party members that the Democrats might reverse their position on silver, that plans had already been made to betray the party at the Minneapolis state convention, and that even the election of John Lind as governor without a People's party legislature would be meaningless, the circular asked the people to have enough courage to oppose fusion and face being termed bolters or the hirelings of Republican boss Mark Hanna.[71] But Donnelly's efforts to gather support for the party's convention were not entirely successful. Many of his friends were too poor to attend. Dr. Christian Johnson lamented that the Democrats, exercising terrific pressure, were promising state jobs to delegates if they favored the fusion ticket and elected John Lind.[72]

In a letter to the Minneapolis *Times*, F. C. Gibbs accused Donnelly of being a wire-puller and attempting to be a party boss. He charged that James J. Hill and the Great Northern Railroad controlled the *Representative* because railroad lands were advertised in the paper.[73] Donnelly conceded that he advertised railroad lands and that advertisements paid the cost of operating the paper, but he denied that Hill or anyone else dictated the paper's policy. What other paper, Donnelly challenged, really tackled the problem of the railroad monopoly. While the Minneapolis *Times* and the other newspapers railed against Hill, they were silent on the Supreme Court decision which made state regulation impossible. The *Representative*, he insisted, never deceived the people with demagogic allegations; it always urged the only honest solution—government ownership.[74]

Two weeks before the June 15 convention, the entire front page of the *Representative* carried a plea for antifusion delegates to spurn John Lind and retain the party's integrity. Donnelly denied that he was seeking office. "We were acting governor 40 years ago during the Civil War," he wrote; "and we have no ambition for place now."

economically oriented toward McKinley's behavior. It replied specifically to statements that the new possessions would provide opportunities for jobs for American labor. *Farm, Stock and Home*, August 1, 1898.

[71]Donnelly MSS, April 21, 1898, rough draft.
[72]*Ibid.*, C. Johnson to I. D., May 3, 1898.
[73]Minneapolis *Times*, May 16, 1898.
[74]Minneapolis *Representative*, May 18, 1898.

Somewhat saddened, he confessed, "We would like to be United States Senator . . . [but] we give up."[75] A week later, apparently aware that he could not control the convention, he indicated that he would not give up his opposition to fusion. He asked the party faithful to prepare to "go it alone," rather than accept a fusion with men who pretend that they all think alike "when they do not."[76]

Three Minnesota political conventions assembled on June 15. The Democrats nominated only state Supreme Court judges. The Silver Republicans selected John Lind as the gubernatorial candidate. By prearrangement with the fusionists, both conventions waited for the People's party to complete the coalition slate. The People's party convention, however, did not prove easy to manipulate. Donnelly and the Mid-Roaders offered sharp opposition from the outset. When he spoke in favor of T. J. Meighan for convention chairman because Meighan opposed fusion, he was interrupted by shouts from delegates demanding to know how Donnelly won election to the legislature, if not by Democratic party indorsement. After a fight over contested delegates, Meighan's defeat indicated the temper of the convention.

Following one of Donnelly's speeches, although he had not mentioned Sidney M. Owen by name, the editor of *Farm, Stock and Home* came before the convention to reply to charges which he claimed had been hurled against him. He denied that he had ever committed any act to damage the party; he was tired of being maligned; and he offered to show up the real traitor. Encouraged by shouts of approval and a cry of "Show him up" from State Chairman Gibbs, Owen, trembling with excitement blurted, "I am going to have my say and cut deep."[77] Donnelly, he charged, was no man to speak of party loyalty because he had been bought by Republican Governor Merriam. Donnelly had killed every cause he embraced, shouted Owen over the catcalls of Donnelly's friends who attempted to drown him out. To end the furor, Donnelly arose, asked his supporters to allow Owen to speak, and requested that the same courtesy be extended when he wished to reply.

Owen's attack became increasingly vitriolic. Donnelly was the "Benedict Arnold of Populism." Owen was disgusted with those who sought to appease and conciliate Donnelly. "What are you going to do to conciliate me!" he demanded. "If we want to be successful," he

[75] *Ibid.*, June 1, 1898.
[76] *Ibid.*, June 8, 1898.
[77] Minneapolis *Tribune*, June 16, 1898; St. Paul *Pioneer Press*, June 16, 1898.

added, "let us get rid of him; I believe his present name is not his right name, but a paraphrase of a more euphonious title more befitting his character—Ignominious Donkey."[78]

Donnelly later published as much of Owen's speech as he could, convinced that his opponent, in betraying his inner feelings, had disclosed himself to be more savagely hungry for power than even his followers had imagined. Owen's name-calling spree had resulted in his own embarrassment. It was no longer possible for him to play the role he had assumed since his selection as the compromise candidate in the struggle between Donnelly and Hall. Although almost ten years younger than Donnelly, Owen faded from active politics. The remaining years of his life were anticlimactic.[79]

The Minneapolis *Tribune* correspondent described Donnelly as he rose to reply to Owen's attack. "He stood facing the multitude for a moment with a great frown upon his face, looking like the lion defeated but still belligerent and terrible. . . . Then as the cheering continued," the reporter added, "he smiled, a passing acknowledgement." Although most newspapers reported that Donnelly's rebuttal was as acrid as Owen's speech, Donnelly held that he had merely stated the facts of the preceding decade without embellishment or invective. He did not deny that he had supported Republicans in 1888, but he pointed out that the People's party was not then in existence. How could Owen condemn him for failing to support a party that did not exist! As for backing out of the Farmer Labor gubernatorial candidacy, the exploded allegation, Donnelly explained that the party had lacked even minimum funds and Eric Olson had been its exclusive advocate. Donnelly denied that he had taken money in 1888, which was false in that he had been paid to campaign for Merriam. He added that if he had been seeking economic rewards, an impoverished political party was not where he would turn. Regarding Owen's charge that Donnelly had displayed continued hostility toward him, Donnelly reminded the delegates that in 1890, Owen refused to allow him to campaign in the Alliance party's behalf when Owen was the gubernatorial candidate.

Owen was the real traitor to the party, Donnelly insisted. He had refused to allow the former Greenbackers to speak for him in 1890. Later, he opposed going to Omaha and did his utmost to sabotage the People's party. He supported the defunct Alliance party until James H. Baker was withdrawn as a candidate. Although Owen

[78] *Ibid.*
[79] Minneapolis *Representative,* June 22, 1898.

might deny these charges, Donnelly angrily shouted, there were many men present prepared to gainsay him. Others would bear witness to Owen's betrayal of the party's principles. In 1894, as a member of the platform committee, Owen had opposed silver, blandly asserting, "We are not all agreed upon it." "In 1896, at the national convention, he spoke against initiative and referendum," Donnelly continued, "and subsequently Owen had the effrontery to deny it until sworn testimony contradicted him. *Farm, Stock and Home*," Donnelly charged, "has been filled with articles denying that party affiliations had meaning. How could Owen have the temerity to accuse Donnelly of disloyalty? Owen opposes everything the People's party favored—silver, the greenback, initiative, and referendum!"[80]

Aside from the personal clash—Donnelly and Owen nearly came to blows after their verbal spree—the convention faced the fusion issue. Contending that principles were more important than party, Owen urged that they join the Democrats who accepted the key planks in the People's party platform. Donnelly warned that the party's rank and file were disillusioned Republicans who would never be a tail to the Democratic kite. The only fusion possible, he suggested, would be a nonpartisan mass convention. He preferred losing with the People's party, but if all party labels were dropped, he would go along to keep peace.[81] Despite Donnelly's eloquent pleas and last-minute attempt to filibuster, the delegates voted for fusion 569 to 396.

The Mid-Roaders walked out to organize a new convention. They nominated old-time Alliance leader L. C. Long for governor and Kittel Halvorson, the durable Fifth District Scandinavian politician for lieutenant governor. The convention indorsed Donnelly as the party's candidate for the United States Senate. The Omaha platform, somewhat updated, was approved. Donnelly denied that he was the spirit behind the bolt. It was the whole party, he insisted, that had rejected fusion. With enthusiasm that belied his sixty-seven years, Donnelly wrote: "Now the People's party lives, now it will grow as it grew in 1892. . . . For we are the true reform party of the age and the rest are all bogus."[82]

While Donnelly ripped into John Lind as a lawyer and a phony soldier (Lind had enlisted as a quartermaster during the Spanish-American War) the Mid-Roaders hoped that Lind would reject the

[80]*Ibid.*; Minneapolis *Times*, June 16, 1898.
[81]Minneapolis *Times*, June 16, 1898.
[82]Minneapolis *Representative*, June 22, 1898.

nomination.[83] They even prepared a circular for the friends of the *Representative* claiming that Lind's actions would rally the entire party behind L. C. Long and the Mid-Road ticket.[84] When Lind accepted the triple nomination, the Mid-Roaders suffered a major setback. Dr. Christian Johnson, whose opposition to Lind verged on the fanatical, dejectedly informed Donnelly that there was so much disgust among the rank and file that the party should abandon the state contests and try to win local offices if it could not count on at least forty thousand votes.[85]

Because of the state convention, Donnelly had been unable to attend the Omaha conference of the party's National Committee and National Organization Committee. The struggle within the National Committee as to whether it would yield to the Mid-Road demands of the Nashville group was not easily resolved. After a sharp argument in the credentials committee, the fusionist group and Marion Butler retained control. But the need for conciliation was so evident that a committee of six—three pro- and three antifusion delegates—was appointed to formulate a procedure for the party acceptable to both elements. The result, termed the "Omaha Contract," was accepted by the gathering. The Mid-Roaders considered it a victory because the party's National Committee consented to schedule the party's convention at least thirty days prior to the Democratic convention. The National Committee also agreed not to interfere in national, state, or local elections except to indorse straight People's party candidates.[86] But a score of southerners, who distrusted Butler and rejected the Omaha agreement, issued a call for a party convention to be held at Cincinnati on September 4, 1898, to reaffirm their principles and to select a presidential slate for the election of 1900.

The schism within the Minnesota People's party dictated that Donnelly reject the Omaha Contract. Marion Butler and Minnesota's fusionists represented the same position. To support Butler's stand at Omaha would have vitiated Donnelly's effort to build a new Mid-Road party. Justifying his behavior, Donnelly contended that Butler had broken the pledge by indorsing fusionists.[87] Butler's opposition to the straight People's party slate in Minnesota during the summer

[83]*Ibid.,* June 29, July 6, 1898.
[84]Donnelly MSS, circular, July 6, 1898.
[85]*Ibid.,* C. Johnson to I. D., July 29, 1898.
[86]Hicks, *Populist Revolt,* pp. 384–85; Minneapolis *Representative,* July 29, 1898.
[87]Donnelly MSS, H. Tracy to H. B. Fay, July 20, 1898.

of 1898 provoked Donnelly to write, "The only way you can cure that dog [Butler] is to cut his tail off close behind his ears." Later he wrote, "Butler deserves better to be hung by the neck to the nearest tree than to longer be trusted with power by the honest Populists of the United States."[88]

The Socialists made a half-hearted effort to capture the Mid-Road convention. F. R. Gordon suggested that Donnelly bring Eugene Debs to the Cincinnati convention and declare in favor of a co-operative commonwealth.[89] "I suppose all Populists and all intelligent men are in the broad sense of the word 'Socialists,'" Donnelly replied; "that is to say they believe that the safety and prosperity of the individual is to be found in the development of all the powers of society. . . . The People's party is an outgrowth of the same sentiment which gave our country the post office and the public school system." Donnelly willingly agreed that "all classes of reformers [should be] working together for the same end"; but he feared that "if we made the coming battle under the standard of Socialism, our whole campaign would be taken up explaining to the people what Socialism meant." Affably he concluded, "Why therefore cannot the Socialists come in and assist the Populists just as the abolitionists of 1860 aided the Republican party."[90]

Trying to gather support for the September convention, Donnelly did write to both Henry D. Lloyd and Eugene Debs inviting them to attend, even in a Socialist capacity.[91] Neither Lloyd nor Debs wanted to go to Cincinnati, but Debs, approaching the prime of life and devoting himself to uniting the Socialists, responded by sharing the views of a new American radicalism toward the Mid-Roaders. "The tendency is toward Socialism," he wrote, "and I think it is far better to unite those who grasp the true principles than to seek a union of elements who are at all the intermediary stages between capitalism and Socialism and who in this state are as difficult to harmonize as if they still adhered to the old parties." But since the request to attend the Cincinnati convention had come from Donnelly, who during the grim days, had stood shoulder to shoulder with him in Chicago, Debs added kindly, "but coming from you, the invitation is a strong incentive to my going and while un-

[88] Minneapolis *Representative*, July 27, August 3, 1898.
[89] Donnelly MSS, F. R. Gordon to I. D., July 26, 1898.
[90] *Ibid.*, I. D. to F. R. Gordon, July 30, 1898 (carbon).
[91] Lloyd MSS, I. D. to H. D. Lloyd, August 11, 1898.

able to promise, if conditions are favorable I will do myself the pleasure of meeting you when the convention assembles."[92]

Donnelly was delighted with the plan of some Minnesota delegates to present his name as a presidential candidate. Aware that little prospect existed for his election, Donnelly confessed that the nomination would raise his spirits and probably help the sale of his books. "Think of a man with $23 in the bank," he noted wryly, "running for the presidency."[93]

The convention which assembled in Cincinnati's Lyceum Hall, a convention which Donnelly realized needed a desperate remedy, was sparsely attended. Tom Watson was unable to attend, and the only prominent members were Jacob S. Coxey and Donnelly. Most of the delegates were aging radicals dating from Granger and Greenback days. Entirely absent was the blazing intensity of endeavor which had characterized the stormy meetings in 1891, 1892, and 1896. Donnelly, selected unanimously as both temporary and permanent chairman, dominated the meeting. In a long, turgid platform statement of party history and principles he offered little to inspire the convention. Free silver was abandoned in favor of "legal tender paper money" and the antimonopoly stand was reaffirmed. Of more than passing interest was the great emphasis which he placed on initiative, referendum, recall, and direct primaries. It was predicted that direct primaries would eliminate party bossism. Recall was urged as a party mechanism as well as a political program, to keep party officials loyal to party principles. Greatest faith was placed in direct democracy. All legislation, the platform urged, should be submitted to referendum. Challenging as initiative, referendum, and recall might be to young intellectual progressives, it was not the same genre of reform that silver or the subtreasury had been. Even Donnelly's rhetoric could not make it exciting to a generation jaded by listening to Bryan's "Cross of Gold Speech," the People's party platform preamble, and the denunciations of the "Crime of '73."

The decision to nominate a slate for the national election in 1900 led to a walkout of almost half the delegates. Those who withdrew charged the majority with attempting to push through nominations without the consent of the rank and file. The bolters, however, were viewed by the majority as obstructionists, knowingly or

[92]Donnelly MSS, E. Debs to I. D., August 17, 1898.
[93]*Ibid.*, Diary, August 10, 1898.

foolishly working for Marion Butler. One month after the convention, Donnelly contended that both allegations were without basis in fact. The slate selected was submitted to a party referendum and the bolters indorsed it.

In the balloting for the presidential nomination, Donnelly lost by nine votes through the defection of ten Minnesota delegates led by Eric Olson, who had never forgiven him for the fiasco of 1888. He was, however, the unanimous choice for the vice-presidential nomination. Reluctantly, Donnelly accepted the nomination. He favored a southerner for second place, preferably Tom Watson, but when Watson's friends asserted that the Georgian would not consent, Donnelly agreed to take the place to dispel the charge that he was "sulking in his tent." Insisting, however, that a party referendum be held, Donnelly expressed his willingness to withdraw for the welfare of the party. In his diary, he was more pragmatic. Without any hope of victory, Donnelly took solace in accepting the nomination as a "good advertisement" for his books and lectures and thus increasing the "supply of bread and butter" on his table.[94]

Ironically, the convention organized as a protest to bossism and dictation by monied interests, nominated Wharton Barker for president after promises that he would finance the campaign. If Wharton Barker did not fulfil this pledge, Donnelly felt that he would be of little use because he was neither an effective speaker nor a brilliant writer.[95] Following his nomination, Barker disappointed the Mid-Roaders by professing to be as poor as the others. Because Coxey was too radical and Watson too disheartened, the responsibility to lead was thrust upon Donnelly.[96] But he realized that he was too old and too impoverished to assume the obligation.

In Minnesota, desperate for support, he turned to William H. Eustis, the Republican opponent of John Lind, in the hope that Eustis would encourage the Mid-Road People's party to draw votes from Lind. But Eustis refused to help the People's party even to secure enough names for its petition to gain a place on the ballot.

---

[94]*Ibid.*, September 9, 1898; Minneapolis *Representative*, September 14, October 5, 1898; Hicks, *Populist Revolt*, pp. 386–87.

[95]Donnelly MSS, Diary, September 9, 1898.

[96]*Ibid.*, W. Barker to I. D., September 12, 1898. Barker's selection left Tom Watson embittered and thoroughly disillusioned. He wrote Donnelly, "No party ever did its educational work better than ours. Where we missed was on organization. Had we all concerted & supported a daily newspaper, a first class magazine, and a central library bureau, all working in unison with a central committee of organization which was honest, competent, ineligible to office, all hell couldn't have resisted us." *Ibid.*, T. Watson to I. D., September 24, 1898.

Although he anticipated a close race, his followers assured him that they would carry the Twin Cities and win.[97]

On October 12, Donnelly announced that he would not seek re-election to the state legislature, using the face-saving excuse that he was too busy planning his vice-presidential campaign. Privately, he confessed to his sister, Sarah Donnelly, that he could not run for the office because of the intense opposition to him among the Irish Catholics in Dakota County after his marriage to Marian.[98] More than likely, also, since he earned his living through lecturing, he could not afford even a modest campaign.

As the election campaign drew to a close, the *Representative* displayed an almost pathetic quality. It attacked Lind, accusing him of representing the old Washburn clique, being devoid of principle, hiding behind a patriot's uniform, and seeking office as his Scandinavian birthright. Lind's popularity and evidence that he would win drew the comment that his personal victory would mean nothing for the cause of reform. A vote for the Mid-Road slate, Donnelly pleaded, was not a vote for a hollow phantom, but a symbol of faith in a genuine reform party.[99]

Elected governor by twenty thousand votes, Lind failed to carry any other fusion candidate to victory. Most of the ticket was overwhelmed by a crushing fifty thousand vote Republican majority. As Donnelly had predicted, Lind's victory was entirely personal. The Mid-Road ticket, led by L. C. Long, suffered an ignominious defeat, failing to win even 3 per cent of the popular vote. Significant and perhaps indicative of both the disinterest and disillusion with politics after the turbulence that marked the elections since 1890, more than eighty thousand voters, who had voted in 1896, ignored the contest in 1898.

In the first post-election issue of the *Representative,* Donnelly expressed his satisfaction that fusion candidates other than Lind had been completely routed. If Lind made a good governor, Donnelly promised to sustain him. He held no personal malice toward Lind, even though opposing him during the election, and angrily denounced the nativists who were indignant because a naturalized citizen had been elected governor.[100] Donnelly, who had long suf-

[97]*Ibid.,* W. Eustis to I. D., September 21, 1898; I. D. to W. Eustis, September 27, 1898; E. Twitchell to I. D., September 28, 1898.
[98]*Ibid.,* I. D. to Sarah Donnelly, October 31, 1898; Minneapolis *Representative,* October 12, 1898.
[99]Minneapolis *Representative,* November 2, 1898.
[100]*Ibid.,* November 9, 1898.

fered Protestant ire as a Roman Catholic and now Catholic ire because he married a Protestant, had genuine sympathy for Lind.

In a comforting letter to L. C. Long, admitting that the future did not look encouraging, Donnelly concluded: "We have the consolation of knowing that all those in this state who were instrumental in breaking up our party got nothing for it, and the Democrats, who have been behind the movement to slaughter the People's party, are themselves defeated all over the Union."[101]

[101] Donnelly MSS, I. D. to L. C. Long, November 10, 1898.

CHAPTER
XXI

The Last Days
1899–1901

We must keep a stiff upper lip and fight it out to the end. We could get nothing from any other course even if disappointment induced us to take it. For my part, "sink or swim live or die," I shall stand by my principles till the infernal regions are turned into a skating rink.

IGNATIUS DONNELLY

IN MARCH, 1899, Donnelly decided to publish privately his last book, *The Cipher in the Plays and on the Tombstone*. He had tried for more than a year to find a publisher but had encountered universal opposition. His extravagant claims that Bacon was the author of Marlowe's works and even Cervantes' were simply too incredible. But having worked on the book for eight years and having committed himself publicly about its contents, he felt obligated to publish it. Hopeful that the new book would "carry conviction with it," he asked Sampson, Low and Company to handle the English edition but they refused.[1] Minnesota reviewers treated the book kindly, the sole exception being the Minneapolis *Journal,* whose editor later conceded that he had not read it.[2]

The Cipher neither sold well nor engendered the furious controversy that marked the publication of *The Great Cryptogram.*

[1]Donnelly MSS, I. D. to Sampson, Low & Co., October 24, 1898.
[2]Quoted in Minneapolis *Representative,* November 23, 1899.

Donnelly, who interpreted public apathy as acceptance, believed that he would reclaim his financial investment.[3] The book also was given away as a bonus to new subscribers of the *Representative*. As in the case of *The Great Cryptogram*, he did not claim that his arithmetical workmanship was perfect. In fact, he later conceded that he lacked a consistent rule for fixing the order of the cipher words in all of his cipher work.[4] Donnelly asked W. Waldorf Astor, who had indorsed the Baconian cipher, to underwrite the cost of publishing a proposed new book, "Ben Johnson's Cipher," in the summer of 1900. Astor refused, and the manuscript was never published.[5]

After the election of 1898, Donnelly urged Milton Park, National Committee chairman for the Mid-Road People's party, to rebuild public confidence in the organization. He suggested forming clubs and supporting a reform newspaper, rather than scheduling conventions that people could not afford to attend. The defeat of the fusion candidates would encourage many fusionists to return to the Mid-Road position.[6] In Minnesota, the People's party was planning a precinct-by-precinct rehabilitation in an effort to eliminate the bickering and schism that had always weakened the organization.[7] The passage of Minnesota's direct primary law encouraged the Mid-Roaders because they felt that the Democrats would no longer be able to manipulate the party through the fusionists at party conventions.

William Jennings Bryan may have shared this view of the direct primary. He attempted to persuade Donnelly to accept fusion. Bryan must have been astounded when Donnelly suggested the Democrats indorse the People's party ticket.[8] Donnelly, however, believed that Bryan would fail to secure the Democratic nomination in 1900. Given the choice between joining the People's party or serving as a tool of the eastern conservatives, Bryan, Donnelly felt, would accept the latter. Because of the imperialism issue, Donnelly had lost all respect for Bryan. "Four years ago he [Bryan] claimed that . . . [silver] was the supreme issue, and that mankind must not be sacrificed on a cross of gold." Now, Donnelly

[3]Donnelly MSS, I. D. to I. C. D., December 27, 1899.
[4]*Ibid.*, I. D. to A. Walker, January 13, 1900 (carbon).
[5]*Ibid.*, W. Astor to I. D., August 27, 1900.
[6]*Ibid.*, I. D. to M. Park, December 16, 1898.
[7]*Ibid.*, H. B. Fay to I. D., December 30, 1898.
[8]*Ibid.*, I. D. to C. H. Hopkins, January 25, 1899.

noted, "he throws the cross of gold in the ditch, and is terribly interested in a lot of savages on the other side of the globe."⁹

Not that Donnelly indorsed imperialism! The *Representative* vigorously condemned McKinley's use of the army in the Philippines. Although denying that he was a "carping critic" or that he favored "kindling a fire in the rear of a government when it is engaged in carrying on a foreign war," Donnelly refused to be silent regarding news of American atrocities, demanding that "our government should not violate the laws of civilized warfare and indulge in an indiscriminate slaughter of men, women, and children."¹⁰ He fervently hoped that many sincere and honest Americans would shrink from the implications of imperialism, ignore the older parties which were willing to compromise with the issue, and look to the passionately anti-imperialist wing of the People's party for leadership.¹¹

But he did not consider imperialism, per se, the issue of the age. Compared to economic exploitation and its social application—"reducing the value of man and all of his products"—"the Philippines is a mere bagatelle."¹² He was appalled by the vicious attacks on human rights everywhere in the world. Angrily he observed the hypocrisy of "Democrats . . . howling about Republicans shooting negroes in the Philippines and the Republicans objecting to Democrats shooting negroes in the South. This may be good politics," he added, "but it is rough on the negroes."¹³

In a similar vein, he deplored the wave of anti-Semitism that spread over Europe and the United States toward the end of the nineteenth century. "The Jews are not all plutocrats," he wrote, horrified by the aftermath of the Dreyfus episode; "a large majority of them are the poorest people in the world. The half-starved workers of the sweatshops of London, Berlin and New York are mostly Hebrews." To Donnelly it was "inexplicable that a Christian people, worshipping a Jew, the son of a Jewess, should entertain such terrible bigotry against the people of his race." It is all wrong, he wrote; "Live and let live should be the motto of the world."¹⁴ Six months earlier, he had condemned "beard pulling" episodes in

⁹*Ibid.*, I. D. to J. D. Scott, May 24, 1900 (carbon).
¹⁰Minneapolis *Representative*, June 1, 1899.
¹¹*Ibid.*, May 3, 1899; Donnelly MSS, W. Barker to I. D., July 30, 1899.
¹²Minneapolis *Representative*, November 16, 1899.
¹³*Ibid.*, June 15, 1899.
¹⁴*Ibid.*, July 27, 1899.

which elderly Jews had been abused in New York City. "Let us suppress the cannibals of all races," he pleaded, "and lift up the wretched of all races."[15]

Ironically when wars, famine, and crop failures in the world sent wheat prices skyrocketing, Donnelly admitted no moral twinge at American farmers profiting through the despair of others. "We did not make it," he declared, "and we are not responsible for it."[16]

The advent of agricultural prosperity which some politicians attributed to the increase in the world's gold production, Donnelly greeted with undisguised cynicism. Even reluctant to concede that there was a genuine McKinley prosperity, Donnelly contended that if more gold had caused it here was positive proof that a handful of men, by denying the nation additional currency as silver, had plunged the people into a quarter-century-long depression.[17] By continued reliance on a metallic currency, he believed, their greed and selfishness would bring an end to the temporary business boom.

But Donnelly was having a difficult time differentiating between his position and that of the energetic young progressives in the Democratic party. The *Representative,* its columns filled with criticism of great trusts, was scarcely different from many Democratic reform newspapers. It was inconceivable to Donnelly that the Democrats and the Republicans could advocate reform. He ridiculed the Democrats as a bogus antitrust party. Nevertheless, the persistent Democratic emphasis on reform forced him to assume a more radical position. When the Democrats spoke of monetary reform, they meant silver, Donnelly stated. The People's party meant fiat currency. When the Democrats talked about antitrust legislation, they meant regulation, but the People's party meant government ownership.[18]

His increasing drift toward socialism led to glaring and evident inconsistencies in his position. This was especially obvious in his rejection of conservationism, a main plank in the progressive platforms of the era. Donnelly brushed aside the testimony of experienced timber-culture specialists who expressed alarm about watershed damage and the potential disaster implicit in denuded forest lands. To him, conservation was a Cleveland scheme; a conspiracy intended to pave the way for large landed estates for a nobility

[15] *Ibid.,* January 18, 1899.
[16] *Ibid.,* July 20, 1899.
[17] *Ibid.,* June 1, 1899.
[18] *Ibid.,* September 28, 1899.

of the future. He remained blind to the paradox of his position. Donnelly, in one breath, could argue for the full use of state power for social welfare, and express complete trust in the state even to the extent of advocating public ownership of basic industries, but when it was a question of trusting it to administer public lands for the benefit of the people, Donnelly retained his Jeffersonian diffidence and his Lockean ideals. "The finest crop land can raise is not trees, but a lot of rosy cheeked, fat, healthy, white children of the best races of the world." He had asserted earlier and frequently reiterated that "the best use that can be made of the public lands is to let the people have them in tracts of 160 acres each."[19]

Straddling two economies—the agrarian and the industrial—he sought the best of both. With an almost desperate nostalgia Donnelly wished for a return to a laissez faire agricultural economy that he conceived as having existed during his young manhood. The merits of such a system vindicated his quest for fortune and justified his later political career. Yet while he clung tenaciously to this agrarian laissez faire myth, he demanded government ownership of natural monopolies because private industry, which polluted water, corrupted politics, and brought periodic unemployment, placed the true cost of its operations on society. The social cost of the agrarian society—the destruction of the public domain—Donnelly regarded as opportunity; the social cost of industrial capitalism—the evils of unrestrained exploitation of resources—he found abhorrent.

By 1900 Donnelly was a frustrated and exasperated by-stander in the political scene. Irritated because the People's party held no promise of growth unless the Democratic party dissolved, he wrote his old friend Lemuel H. Weller of Wisconsin that the Democrats were "too abominably dishonest to quarrel over any question of principle."[20] After watching John Lind and William Jennings Bryan trying to win People's party votes for fusion in Minnesota's primary election, he confided to Weller, "I am falling back on the new beatitude of the darkey preacher, 'Blessed am dey what specs nothin' for dey aint gwine to be disappointed.'"[21]

The Republicans renominated McKinley; the Democrats again favored Bryan as their standard-bearer, and a handful of fusionists meeting at Sioux Falls, South Dakota, indorsed Bryan and selected

[19]*Ibid.*, May 12, 1897, January 18, August 24, October 21, 1899.
[20]Donnelly MSS, I. D. to L. H. Weller, January 4, 1900.
[21]*Ibid.*, I. D. to L. H. Weller, January 11, 1900.

Minnesota's Republican former congressman Charles A. Towne for vice-president. But the Mid-Roaders squabbled. Although Barker and Donnelly retained the party's nomination through a party referendum, the National Reform Press Association insisted that there be a new party convention in 1900.[22] Donnelly's fears that an effort would be made to drop the Barker-Donnelly ticket were probably justified because of the general dissatisfaction regarding Barker, who had proved so ineffective. The Mid-Road convention, held in May at Cincinnati, after balking somewhat at Barker, finally indorsed him.

Even though the delegates were aware that Donnelly's health was failing, he had not an enemy in the hall and his nomination was approved unanimously.[23] He appeared to the delegates just as he had for almost four decades, a short compactly built man, an Atlas without the world on his back, his shoulders stooped from the long hours of study and writing. His skin still had a glow of health and he looked like a successful merchant with plenty of leisure. Only his massive head set squarely on his body, as if nature had omitted a neck, made him striking. His light blue eyes retained their dreamy quality and his voice, pleasant to the ear, was well modulated though usually at higher than normal pitch when he was engaged in animated discussion. Talking to friends without effort, interested in what he was saying, apparently more at home in private conversation than on the rostrum, his conversation with the delegates was intimate. His humor ranged from the dirty political sneer to a warm self-indulgent laughter. The cut of his dark clothing intensified his corpulency, and his full chin and heavy jaw denoted his bull-dog tenacity.

But this appearance was deceiving; the winter and spring of 1900 had proved unusually hard on Donnelly. He worried about the *Representative,* no longer self-sustaining and in part underwritten by Hill's advertising subsidy. In February Donnelly wrote his elder son for medical advice. "I sleep from eight to ten hours every night; have a good appetite, and my mind seems just as bright as ever, but I have a feeling of weakness, especially in walking." Explaining that he customarily walked an hour every day, he added, "I find sometimes my feet dragging." With his irrepressible good humor, he closed, "I feel indignant when my hair is not gray, and I eat and sleep like a plowman, to have my cowardly legs going back on me. I

[22]Minneapolis *Representative,* May 25, 1899.
[23]Hicks, *Populist Revolt,* p. 400.

am reminded of the Irish soldier who said, 'his heart was as brave as a lion, but his cowardly legs ran away with him.' "[24]

In the following months he was ill with the grippe. His weight declined sharply and Donnelly confessed to his diary that his health was failing. Because he was already under treatment as a diabetic, it was difficult to build him up physically.[25] At the beginning of the summer, Donnelly, complaining that he was unable to campaign as vigorously as before, envied Bryan his endurance.

On July 4, 1900, at a patriotic rally, Donnelly had a novel sensation. "When I came to speak," he wrote in his diary, "my powers went back on me. I made a faux pas of it. For the first time in my life I made a dead failure of it. But my nerve held and I waded through it." Several hours later, he attempted a second address and confessed: "Again did I make a poor speech. I felt greatly ashamed of myself."[26]

Placed under doctor's care when he returned home, the initial diagnosis was heat prostration.[27] Later, it was determined that he had suffered a mild stroke, an acute congestion of the speech center of the brain. It was a danger signal, Donnelly's son informed him.[28] The news that he was ill, unable to speak, was a genuine blow to the handful of dedicated People's party leaders. At first he refused to answer his mail, but by August he offered to withdraw his name from the People's party ticket. Much ill-feeling and recrimination followed among Donnelly's friends and those of Wharton Barker. Donnelly, however, was not a part of it. He knew that his newspaper would die after the election and with it the Mid-Road party in Minnesota.

"I am 69 today," he wrote, three days before the election. "I begin to feel very old, although I preserve my youthful appearance remarkably:—my hair is not yet gray; but my legs are weak. I drag my feet when I walk." Sadly he observed, "My ill fortune pursues me. If I had not had a partial stroke of palsey [sic], I would have made the whole U.S. ring with my appeals for the Mid-Road ticket."[29]

Shortly after midnight on January 1, 1901, Donnelly suffered a fatal heart attack. His obituary was printed in newspapers all over

[24]Donnelly MSS, I. D. to I. C. D., February 2, 1900.
[25]*Ibid.*, Diary, May 24, 1897.
[26]*Ibid.*, July 4, 1900.
[27]*Ibid.*, J. C. Cummings to I. D., July 17, 1900; I. D. to J. Parker, July 24, 1900.
[28]*Ibid.*, I. C. D. to I. D., November 11, 1900.
[29]*Ibid.*, Diary, November 3, 1900.

the world. The cultists commented on his contributions to the Shake-speare-Bacon argument as well as *Atlantis* and *Ragnarok*. The rural and radical press noted that he was a man who had risen from the kerne of Ireland to become a hero of the cause of reform. The large daily newspapers in the Twin Cities called attention to the fact that his pall-bearers included some of the most distinguished business and political leaders of Minnesota—some of whom had been his bitterest political enemies!

In the years following his death, Donnelly's image as a hero of the Populist Movement began to emerge. His name became a synonym for reform. Much of the legislation which he advocated was even-tually enacted into law by both the federal and state government. Certainly the evils that he described so graphically were steadily at-tacked in the twentieth century. In assessing his role in the reform movement there was a tendency to overlook his few successes and to single out the bizarre drama that usually surrounded his social criticism.

Among Americans who sought a sympathetic understanding of the plight of the farmer and laborer at the close of the nineteenth century, Donnelly was held in high esteem. In fact, he almost at-tained the status of what folklorists term the "clever hero." His enemies were characteristically the great, the strong, and the cruel. He was the protagonist of democracy, the avenger of evil, and the agent of a kind of comic justice. Donnelly was viewed as a leveler who attempted to reduce those who arrogated too much power or special privilege to themselves.[30]

But to some scholars of religious liberty, urbanization, and au-thoritarianism in American life, he was scarcely a hero. His political novels were interpreted as having imperialistic, nativistic, anti-Semitic, and demagogic tendencies. He appeared not as the forerun-ner of the politically liberal left, but of the potentially authoritarian right. But both his critics and supporters overlooked the highly sensitive, human, troubled man lost in the thicket of endless political intrigue and based their judgments on a colorful, flamboyant image-figure that did not really exist.

In a psychological sense, Donnelly was a true rebel. He was never without a feeling of alienation from the group, even when he seemed most identified with his environment. He experienced the stimulation that came of an intellectual awareness of rejection. The

[30]Orrin E. Klapp, "The Clever Hero," *Journal of American Folklore*, LXVII (1954), 30, describes the attributes of this type of hero.

revolt of son against mother, of citizen against city, of lawyer against legal system, of Catholic against Church, of politician against party, of author against critic, were all within his compass. These feelings, channeled into a drive for success and recognition which manifested itself in a hunger for power, made Donnelly an instrument for social change. Because his nature was strong, misfortune, the poison of the weak, seemed to be his tonic.

To the very end of his life, even though his decisions were not based on theoretical study but on facts that forced him into action, Donnelly knew why he wanted to live, and so his life was bearable and he was never entirely embittered. And after all, it is the way in which a man accepts his fate, the way in which he faces his environment, that affords him the opportunity—under both pleasant and trying circumstances—to add genuine meaning to his life.

Selective Bibliography

MANUSCRIPTS

Personal Papers

DONNELLY MSS. The Donnelly Papers, located in the Minnesota Historical Society, St. Paul, Minnesota, consist of 95 boxes. The largest number of items are letters received. In many instances, he made notations of his answers as indorsements upon letters. In the later years of his life, typed and letter press copies of his outgoing mail make it possible to reconstruct his significant correspondence. In addition there are more than 200 books, diaries, ledgers, memorandum books, scrapbooks, political notebooks, and bound volumes of documents. The material probably represents the most extensive collection of personal papers for the study of the Populist Movement in Minnesota and the Middle West. The collection includes Donnelly's manuscript drafts for his books, articles, and speeches as well as his letters to Baconian enthusiasts and scientific cultists. A family genealogy is in the possession of Mr. Philip Donnelly of St. Paul, Minnesota. In addition to the extensive holdings of the Minnesota Historical Society, there are other Donnelly materials of importance in the following libraries: University of California, Los Angeles; Yale University; Georgetown University; Chicago Historical Society; Holy Cross College; The Johns Hopkins University; Cornell University; New York Public Library; The University of Rochester; Haverford College; Historical Society of Pennsylvania; Allegheny College; and the State College of Washington.

ADAMS, CHARLES P. MSS. Minnesota Historical Society.

ANDREWS, CHRISTOPHER C. MSS. Minnesota Historical Society.

AUSTIN, HORACE. MSS. Minnesota Historical Society.

BAXTER, LUTHER L. MSS. Minnesota Historical Society.

BRACKETT, GEORGE A. MSS. Minnesota Historical Society.

CASE, JOHN H. MSS. Minnesota Historical Society.

CHATTO & WINDUS. MSS. University of California, Los Angeles.

CHUTE, RICHARD. MSS. Minnesota Historical Society.

CLEVELAND, GROVER. MSS. Library of Congress.

COOKE, JAY. MSS. Historical Society of Pennsylvania [Photostatic copies in Minnesota Historical Society].

COUNTRYMAN, LEVI N. MSS. Minnesota Historical Society.

[402]

DAVIS, CUSHMAN K. MSS. Minnesota Historical Society.
DOLLENMAYER, ALBERT. MSS. Minnesota Historical Society.
FOLWELL, WILLIAM W. MSS. Minnesota Historical Society.
FOSTER, THOMAS. MSS. Minnesota Historical Society.
FRIDLEY, ABRAHAM M. MSS. Minnesota Historical Society.
GORDON, HANFORD L. MSS. Minnesota Historical Society.
HALE, WILLIAM D. MSS. Minnesota Historical Society.
HEATON, DAVID. MSS. Minnesota Historical Society.
KING, WILLIAM S. MSS. Minnesota Historical Society.
LE DUC, WILLIAM G. MSS. Minnesota Historical Society.
LINCOLN, ABRAHAM. MSS. Library of Congress.
LIND, JOHN. MSS. Minnesota Historical Society.
LLOYD, HENRY D. MSS. State Historical Society of Wisconsin.
LYND, JAMES W. MSS. Minnesota Historical Society.
McGILL, ANDREW R. MSS. Minnesota Historical Society.
MITCHELL, WILLIAM B. MSS. Minnesota Historical Society.
NELSON, KNUTE. MSS. Minnesota Historical Society.
NEWSON, THOMAS M. MSS. Minnesota Historical Society.
PETTIT, CURTIS H. MSS. Minnesota Historical Society.
RAMSEY, ALEXANDER. MSS. Minnesota Historical Society.
REPUBLICAN PARTY STATE CENTRAL COMMITTEE. MSS. Minnesota
    Historical Society.
RICE, HENRY M. MSS. Minnesota Historical Society.
ROGERS, WILLIAM K. MSS. Harvard College [Photostatic copies in
    Minnesota Historical Society].
SIBLEY, HENRY H. MSS. Minnesota Historical Society.
STEVENS, JOHN H. MSS. Minnesota Historical Society.
VALESH, EVA M. MSS. Columbia University (Oral History).
VILAS, WILLIAM F. MSS. State Historical Society of Wisconsin.
WASHBURN, CADWALLADER C. MSS. State Historical Society of Wiscon-
    sin.
WASHBURNE, ELIHU. MSS. Library of Congress.
WELLER, LEMUEL H. MSS. State Historical Society of Wisconsin.
WHIPPLE, HENRY B. MSS. Minnesota Historical Society.
WINDOM, WILLIAM. MSS. Minnesota Historical Society.

Unpublished Dissertations and Theses

BUCKNER, PHILIP F. "Silver Mining Interests in Silver Politics, 1876–96."
    Master's thesis, Columbia University, 1954.
CRAWFORD, PAUL. "Ignatius Donnelly, Agrarian Agitator." Ph.D. disserta-
    tion, School of Speech, Northwestern University, 1950.
EIDE, RICHARD B. "The Influence of Editorship . . . on the Growth of
    the St. Paul *Pioneer Press,* 1849–1909." Ph.D. dissertation, Uni-
    versity of Missouri, 1939.
GALVIN, EUCHARISTA. "The Influence and Conditions Affecting the Settle-
    ment of Minnesota, 1837–1860." Ph.D. dissertation, University of
    Chicago, 1929.

HECK, FRANK H. "The Civil War Veteran in Minnesota Politics." Ph.D. dissertation, University of Minnesota, 1938.

HENDRICKS, GEORGE. "Rise of the Republican Party in Minnesota." Master's thesis, University of Minnesota, 1922.

HOLBROOK, FRANKLIN F. "The Early Political Career of Ignatius Donnelly, 1857–1863." Master's thesis, University of Minnesota, 1916.

HYNES, MARY C. "The History of the American Protective Association in Minnesota." Master's thesis, Catholic University of America, n.d.

JOHNSON, DOROTHY E. "Attitude of the Germans in Minnesota toward the Republican Party in 1865." Master's thesis, University of Minnesota, 1945.

KARSTAD, RUBY G. "Political Party Alignments in Minnesota, 1854–1860." Master's thesis, University of Minnesota, 1940.

LUTZKY, SEYMOUR. "The Reform Editors and their Press." Ph.D. dissertation, University of Iowa, 1951.

MOORE, EDMUND A. "The Political Career of Ignatius Donnelly, 1863–1873." Master's thesis, University of Minnesota, 1925.

NYDAHL, THEODORE (ed.). "The Diary of Ignatius Donnelly, 1856–1880." Ph.D. dissertation, University of Minnesota, 1944.

RIDGE, MARTIN. "The Making of a Tribune." Ph.D. dissertation, Northwestern University, 1951.

SCHEIDLER, L. J. "Silver and Politics, 1893–1896." Ph.D. dissertation, University of Indiana, 1936.

SILVEUS, MARIAN. "The Antecedents of the Campaign of 1896." Ph.D. dissertation, University of Wisconsin, 1933.

SMITH, PAUL S. "Party Politics in Minnesota, 1865–1871." Master's thesis, University of Minnesota, 1918.

WRIGHT, GRACE ANNE. "William Windom: Public Servant." Master's thesis, University of Wisconsin, 1911.

PRINTED MATERIAL

Newspapers

Austin (Minn.) *Transcript,* 1872–73
Chicago (Ill.) *Times,* 1872
Chicago (Ill.) *Tribune,* 1872, 1882
Duluth (Minn.) *Minnesotian,* 1869–74
Faribault (Minn.) *Central Republican,* 1858–65
Fergus Falls (Minn.) *Journal,* 1880, 1884–87
Freeborn County (Albert Lea, Minn.) *Standard,* 1869
Glencoe (Minn.) *Register,* 1869
Hastings (Minn.) *Dakota Union,* 1867–86
Hastings (Minn.) *Gazette,* 1866–1880
Hastings (Minn.) *Independent,* 1857–66
Kansas City (Mo.) *Star,* 1891
Lake City (Minn.) *Journal,* 1861
Lake City (Minn.) *Leader,* 1871

London (England) *Telegraph,* 1887–89
Mankato (Minn.) *Record,* 1859–79
Mantorville (Minn.) *Express,* 1869
Milwaukee (Wis.) *News,* 1872
Minneapolis (Minn.) *Chronicle,* 1866–67, 1883–96
Minneapolis (Minn.) *Farm, Stock and Home,* 1890–1900
Minneapolis (Minn.) *Farmers' Union,* 1867–74
Minneapolis (Minn.) *Irish Standard (Northwest Standard),* 1885–1900
Minneapolis (Minn.) *Journal,* 1896–99
Minneapolis (Minn.) *State News,* 1855–63
Minneapolis (Minn.) *Penny Press,* 1893–97
Minneapolis (Minn.) *State Atlas,* 1860–69
Minneapolis (Minn.) *Times,* 1872–73, 1890–1900
Minneapolis (Minn.) *Tribune,* 1867–1900
Nininger City (Minn.) *Emigrant Aid Journal,* 1856–58
New York (N.Y.) *Tribune,* 1869
Northfield (Minn.) *Standard,* 1872
Red Wing (Minn.) *Argus,* 1868–90
Red Wing (Minn.) *Grange Advance,* 1873–80
Rochester (Minn.) *Post,* 1872–73
Rochester (Minn.) *Record and Union,* 1875
Rochester (Minn.) *Federal Union,* 1873
St. Cloud (Minn.) *Democrat,* 1858–66
St. Cloud (Minn.) *Journal,* 1866–76
St. Louis (Mo.) *Republic,* 1892–96
St. Paul (Minn.) *Anti-Monopolist,* 1874–78
St. Paul (Minn.) *Broad Axe,* 1891–1900
St. Paul (Minn.) *Dispatch,* 1868–83, 1886–97
St. Paul (Minn.) *Globe,* 1878–1900
St. Paul (Minn.) *The Great West,* 1889–94
St. Paul (Minn.) *Minnesotian,* 1856–59
St. Paul (Minn.) *Minnesotian and Times,* 1859–60
St. Paul (Minn.) *Minnesota Monthly,* 1869–70
St. Paul (Minn.) *Minnesota Staats-Zeitung,* 1858–60
St. Paul (Minn.) *Pioneer,* 1862–74
St. Paul (Minn.) *Pioneer and Democrat,* 1855–62
St. Paul (Minn.) *Pioneer and Press,* 1875
St. Paul (Minn.) *Pioneer Press,* 1876–1901
St. Paul (Minn.) *Pioneer Press and Tribune,* 1876
St. Paul (Minn.) *Press,* 1861–75
St. Paul (Minn.) *Times,* 1856–59
St. Paul–Minneapolis (Minn.) *Representative,* 1891–1901
St. Peter (Minn.) *Tribune,* 1869
Stillwater (Minn.) *Messenger,* 1859–65
Taylors Falls (Minn.) *Reporter,* 1868
Wabasha (Minn.) *Herald,* 1859
Washington (D.C.) *Chronicle,* 1870
Washington (D.C.) *Post,* 1880, 1886
Winona (Minn.) *Republican,* 1856–76

Periodical Articles

ACKERMAN, GERTRUDE W. "Volunteer Guards in Minnesota," *Minnesota History*, XVI (June, 1935), 166–77.

ANDERSON, GEORGE L. "Western Attitude Toward National Banks, 1873–1874," *Mississippi Valley Historical Review*, XXIII (September, 1936), 205–16.

BARNES, JAMES A. "Myths of the Bryan Campaign," *Mississippi Valley Historical Review*, XXXIV (December, 1947), 367–404.

BLEGEN, THEODORE C. "Campaigning with Seward in 1860," *Minnesota History*, VIII (June, 1927), 150–71.

———. "The Competition of the Northwestern States For Immigrants," *Wisconsin Magazine of History*, III (September, 1919), 3–29.

———. "James W. Taylor," *Minnesota Historical Bulletin*, I (November, 1915) 153–219.

BRAINARD, DUDLEY S. "Nininger, A Boom Town of the Fifties," *Minnesota History*, XIII (June, 1932), 127–51.

CASTLE, HENRY A. "Reminiscences of Minnesota Politics," Minnesota Historical Society *Collections*, XV (1915), 553–98.

CRAY, LORIN. "Memorial of Gen'l James Heaton Baker," Minnesota Historical Society *Collections*, XV (1915), 753–54.

CHRISLOCK, CARL H. "The Alliance Party and the Minnesota Legislature of 1891," *Minnesota History*, XXXV (September, 1957), 297–312.

———. "Sidney M. Owen: An Editor in Politics," *Minnesota History*, XXXVI (December, 1958), 109–26.

CURTI, MERLE E. "Young America," *American Historical Review*, XXXII (October, 1926), 34–55.

DEMEULES, DONALD H. "Ignatius Donnelly: A Don Quixote in the World of Science," *Minnesota History*, XXXVII (June, 1961), 229–34.

DONNELLY, IGNATIUS. "Delia Bacon's Unhappy Story," *North American Review*, CXLVIII (March, 1889), 307–18.

———. "The Shakespeare Myth," *North American Review*, CXLIV (June, 1887), 572–82; CXLV (July, 1887), 57–68.

DORPALEN, ANDREAS, "The German Element and the Issues of the Civil War," *Mississippi Valley Historical Review*, XXIX (June, 1942), 55–76.

DOWNES, LYNWOOD G. "The Soldiers Vote and Minnesota Politics, 1862–1865," *Minnesota History*, XXVI (September, 1945), 187–210.

ENGBERG, GEORGE B. "The Knights of Labor in Minnesota," *Minnesota History*, XXII (December, 1941), 361–90.

———. "The Rise of Organized Labor in Minnesota," *Minnesota History*, XXI (December, 1940), 372–94.

FELS, RENDIG. "American Business Cycles, 1865–79," *American Economic Review*, XLI (June, 1951), 325–48.

FITE, GILBERT C. "Republican Strategy and the Farm Vote in the Presidential Campaign of 1896," *American Historical Review*, LXV (July, 1960), 787–806.

FLANAGAN, JOHN T. (ed.). "Letter from Holmes to Donnelly," *American Literature*, XIII (March, 1941), 59–61.

FOLWELL, WILLIAM W. "The Five Million Loan," Minnesota Historical Society *Collections*, XV (1915), 189–214.

GILFILLAN, CHARLES D. "The Early Political History of Minnesota," Minnesota Historical Society *Collections*, IX (1901), 167–80.

GILMAN, RHODA R. "Ramsey, Donnelly, and the Congressional Campaign of 1868," *Minnesota History*, XXXVI (December, 1959), 300–308.

GLADDEN, WASHINGTON. "The Embattled Farmers," *Forum*, X (November, 1890), 315–22.

HALBO, PAUL S. "Wheat or What? Populism and American Fascism," *The Western Political Quarterly*, XIV (September, 1961), 727–36.

HANDLIN, OSCAR. "American Views of the Jews at the Opening of the Twentieth Century," *Publications* of the Jewish American Historical Society, XL (June, 1951), 323–44.

HARNSBERGER, JOHN. "Land, Lobbies, Railroads and the Origin of Duluth," *Minnesota History*, XXXVII (September, 1960), 89–100.

———. "Railroads to the Northern Plains, 1870–1872," *North Dakota Historical Quarterly*, XXVI (Summer, 1959), 53–61.

HICKS, JOHN D. "The Organization of the Volunteer Army in 1861, with Special Reference to Minnesota," *Minnesota History Bulletin*, II (February, 1918), 324–68.

———. "The Origin and Early History of the Farmers' Alliance in Minnesota," *Mississippi Valley Historical Review*, IX (December, 1922), 203–26.

———. "The People's Party in Minnesota," *Minnesota History Bulletin*, X (November, 1924), 531–56.

———. "The Political Career of Ignatius Donnelly," *Mississippi Valley Historical Review*, VIII (September–June, 1921), 80–132.

HIGHAM, JOHN. "Anti-Semitism in the Gilded Age: A Reinterpretation," *Mississippi Valley Historical Review*, XLIII (March, 1957), 559–78.

HEWITT, WARREN F. "The Know Nothing Party in Pennsylvania," *Pennsylvania History*, II (April, 1935), 69–85.

JOHNSON, HILDEGARD BINDER. "The Election of 1860 and the Germans in Minnesota," *Minnesota History*, XXVIII (March, 1947), 20–36.

JOHNSTON, DANIEL S. "Minnesota Journalism in the Territorial Period and Minnesota Journalism from 1858 to 1865," Minnesota Historical Society *Collections*, X (1905), 247–351; XII (1908), 183–262.

KLAPP, ORRIN E. "The Clever Hero," *Journal of American Folklore*, LXVII (January–March, 1954), 21–34.

KUHLMANN, CHARLES B. "The Influence of Minneapolis Flour Mills upon the Economic Development of Minnesota and the Northwest," *Minnesota History*, VI (June, 1925), 141–54.

LIBBY, ORRIN G. "A Study of the Greenback Movement, 1876–84," *Transactions* of the Wisconsin Academy, XII (1899), 530–43.

McGRANE, REGINALD C. "Ohio and the Greenback Movement," *Mississippi Valley Historical Review*, XI (December, 1924), 526–42.

MERRILL, HORACE S. "Ignatius Donnelly, James J. Hill and Cleveland Administration Patronage," *Mississippi Valley Historical Review*, XXXIX (December, 1952), 505–18.

NAFTALIN, ARTHUR. "The Tradition of Protest and the Roots of the

Farmer-Labor Party," *Minnesota History*, XXXV (June, 1956), 53–63.

O'LEARY, PAUL M. "The Scene of the Crime of 1873 Revisited: A Note," *Journal of Political Economy*, LXVIII (August, 1960), 388–92.

PATCHIN, SIDNEY A. "The Development of Banking in Minnesota," *Minnesota History Bulletin*, II (August, 1917), 111–68.

REZNECK, SAMUEL. "Distress, Relief, and Discontent in the United States During the Depression of 1873–78," *Journal of Political Economy*, LVIII (December, 1950), 494–512.

RIDGE, MARTIN. "The Humor of Ignatius Donnelly," *Minnesota History*, XXXIII (Winter, 1953), 326–30.

——. "Ignatius Donnelly and the Granger Movement in Minnesota," *Mississippi Valley Historical Review*, XLII (March, 1956), 693–709.

——. "Ignatius Donnelly and the Greenback Movement," *Mid-America*, XXXIX (July, 1957), 156–68.

——. "Ignatius Donnelly: Minnesota Congressman," *Minnesota History*, XXXVI (Spring, 1959), 173–83.

ROE, HERMAN. "The Frontier Press of Minnesota," *Minnesota History*, XIV (December, 1933), 393–410.

RUGGLES, CLYDE O. "The Economic Basis of the Greenback Movement in Iowa and Wisconsin," *Proceedings of the Mississippi Valley Historical Association*, VI (1913), 142–65.

SABY RASMUS. "Railroad Legislation in Minnesota 1849–1875," Minnesota Historical Society *Collections*, XV (1915), 1–188.

SANBORN, JOHN B. "The Work of the Second State Legislature, 1859–1860," Minnesota Historical Society *Collections*, X (1905), 619–33.

SHIPPEE, LESTER B. "Jane Grey Swisshelm: Agitator," *Mississippi Valley Historical Review*, VII (December, 1920), 206–27.

——. "The First Railroad between the Mississippi and Lake Superior," *Mississippi Valley Historical Review*, V (September, 1918), 121–42.

——. "Social and Economic Effects of the Civil War with Special Reference to Minnesota," *Minnesota History Bulletin*, II (May, 1918), 389–412.

STEPHENSON, GEORGE M. "Nativism in the Forties and Fifties with Reference to the Mississippi Valley," *Mississippi Valley Historical Review*, IX (December, 1922), 185–202.

UNGER, IRWIN. "The Business Community and the Origins of the 1875 Resumption Act," *The Business History Review*, XXXV (Summer, 1961), 247–62.

VINTON, ARTHUR D. "Those Wonderful Ciphers," *North American Review*, CXLV (November, 1887), 555–62.

WACK, HENRY W. "Personal Recollections of a Great Baconian: Hon. Ignatius Donnelly," *American Baconiana*, I (November, 1923), 1–14.

WARNER, DONALD F. "Prelude to Populism," *Minnesota History*, XXXII (September, 1951), 129–46.

WELLS, ORVILLE V. "The Depression of 1873–1879," *Agricultural History*, XI (July, 1937), 237–49.

WILCOX, BENTON H. "An Historical Definition of Northwestern Radicalism," *Mississippi Valley Historical Review*, XXVI (December, 1939), 377–394.

WOODWARD, C. VANN. "The Populist Heritage and the Intellectual," *The American Scholar*, XXIX (Winter, 1959–1960), 55–72.

ZORN, ROMAN J. "Minnesota Public Opinion and the Secession Controversy," *Mississippi Valley Historical Review*, XXXVI (April, 1961), 435–56.

Government Publications

Minnesota Executive Documents, *Report of the Railroad Commissioner for the Years 1871 to 1873* (St. Paul, 1874).

Minnesota Executive Documents, *Report of the Pine Land Investigating Committee to the Governor of Minnesota, filed with the Governor December 21, 1894* (St. Paul, 1895).

Legislative Manual of the State of Minnesota [1874–98] (St. Paul, 1874–99).

Journal of the [Minnesota] *Senate* [1859–99] (St. Paul, 1859–99).

Journal of the [Minnesota] *House* [1859–99] (St. Paul, 1859–99).

Congressional Globe, 38th, 39th, 40th, 41st Congresses.

House Executive Document No. 76, 38th Congress, 1st session, 1864. Estimate for the Chippewa Treaty.

House Executive Document No. 70, 38th Congress, 2d session, 1868. Estimate for Appropriation for the Chippewa of the Mississippi.

House Executive Document No. 458, 57th Congress, 2d session, 1903. Biographical Congressional Directory.

House Executive Document No. 9, 46th Congress, 1st session, Misc., 1879. Contested Election of Donnelly *vs.* Washburn.

House Report No. 48, 40th Congress, 2d session, 1868. Investigation of the Charges against Ignatius Donnelly.

House Report No. 1791, 46th Congress, 2d session, 1880. Donnelly *vs.* Washburn.

House Report No. 395, 46th Congress, 3d session, 1880. Anonymous Letter to Hon. William M. Springer.

Pamphlets

ANDREW, CHRISTOPHER C. *Mr. Donnelly's Opposition to the Northern Pacific Railroad*. 1868.

———. *Know-Nothingism*. n.d.

DONNELLY, IGNATIUS L. *The Mourner's Vision*. 1850.

———. *Statement of the Basis of the Organization of the City of Nininger*. 1856.

———. *Nininger City*. 1856.

———. *The Sonnets of Shakespeare: An Essay*. 1859.

———. *Address to the People of Minnesota in regard to the History, Principles, Aims, and Objects of the Republican and Democratic Parties*. 1859.

———. *Immigration*. 1864.

———. *Reconstruction*. 1864.

DONNELLY, IGNATIUS L. *Freedman's Bureau.* 1866.

———. *Homestead Law.* 1868.

———. *Address to the Republican Committee of the Second Congressional District.* 1868.

———. *The Unjust Tariff.* 1870.

———. *Facts for the Granges.* 1873.

———. *An Address of the Anti-Monopoly Party of Minnesota to their Constituents.* 1874.

———. *In Memoriam.* 1895.

Contested Election Case of Ignatius Donnelly versus William D. Washburn: Contestant's Brief. 1879.

In the Matter of the Contest of Ignatius Donnelly vs. William D. Washburn . . . Contestee's Brief. 1879.

PERKINS, SAM'L H. *In the Matter of the Estate of Philip C. Donnelly, Decs'd in the Account of Cathrine Donnelly, Adm'x.* n.d.

Books

ADAMS, HENRY. *The Education of Henry Adams.* Boston: Houghton Mifflin, 1918.

ADAMS, WILLIAM F. *Ireland and Irish Immigration to the New World From 1815 to the Famine.* New Haven: Yale University Press, 1932.

ARNOLD, W. J. *The Poets and Poetry of Minnesota.* Chicago: S. P. Rounds, 1864.

BARNES, WILLIAM H. *The Fortieth Congress of the United States.* New York: George E. Perine, 1869.

BARRETT, DON C. *The Greenbacks and the Resumption of Specie Payments, 1862–1879.* Cambridge, Mass.: Harvard University Press, 1931.

BELL, DANIEL (ed.). *The New American Right.* New York: Criterion Books, 1955.

BENSON, LEE. *Merchants, Farmers and Railroads.* Cambridge, Mass.: Harvard University Press, 1955.

BILLINGTON, RAY A. *The Protestant Crusade.* New York: Macmillan Co., 1938.

BOGUE, ALLAN G. *Money at Interest.* Ithaca: Cornell University Press, 1955.

BRYAN, WILLIAM J. *The First Battle,* Chicago: W. B. Conkey, 1896.

BUCK, PAUL H. *The Road to Reunion, 1865–1900.* Boston: Little, Brown & Co., 1937.

BUCK, SOLON J. *The Granger Movement.* Cambridge, Mass.: Harvard University Press, 1913.

CLAPESATTLE, HELEN. *The Doctors Mayo.* Minneapolis: University of Minnesota Press, 1941.

CURTISS-WEDGE, FRANKLIN (ed.). *History of Dakota and Goodhue Counties, Minnesota.* 2 vols. Chicago: H. C. Cooper & Co., 1910.

DE CAMP, L. SPRAGUE. *Lost Continents.* New York: Gnome Press, 1954.

DEMENIL, ALEXANDER N. *The Literature of Louisiana Territory.* St. Louis: St. Louis News Co., 1904.

DESTLER, CHESTER M. *American Radicalism, 1865–1900.* Ann Arbor: Edwards Bros., Inc., 1948.

DEWEY, DAVIS R. *Financial History of the United States.* New York: Longmans, Green & Co., 1918.

DONDORE, DOROTHY. *The Prairie and the Making of Middle America.* Cedar Rapids: The Torch Press, 1926.

DONNELLY, IGNATIUS. *The American People's Money.* Chicago: Laird & Lee, 1895.

DONNELLY, IGNATIUS. *Atlantis: The Antediluvian World.* New York: Harper & Bros., 1882.

DONNELLY, IGNATIUS. *Caesar's Column.* Chicago: Free Speech Pub., n.d.

DONNELLY, IGNATIUS (WALTER RIDEOUT, ed.). *Caesar's Column.* Cambridge, Mass.: Harvard University Press, 1960.

DONNELLY, IGNATIUS. *The Cipher.* Minneapolis: Verulam Publishing Co., 1899.

DONNELLY, IGNATIUS. *Doctor Huguet.* Chicago: F. J. Schulte & Co., 1891.

DONNELLY, IGNATIUS. *The Golden Bottle.* St. Paul: D. D. Merrill, 1892.

DONNELLY, IGNATIUS. *The Great Cryptogram.* Chicago: R. S. Peale & Co., 1887.

DONNELLY, IGNATIUS. *Ragnarok: The Age of Fire and Gravel.* New York: D. Appleton & Co., 1883.

EIDE, RICHARD B. *North Star Editor.* New York: King's Crown Press, 1944.

FAULKNER, HAROLD U. *The Decline of Laissez Faire, 1897–1917.* New York: Rinehart & Co., 1951.

FAULKNER, HAROLD U. *Politics, Reform, and Expansion, 1890–1900.* New York: Harper & Bros., 1959.

FISH, EVERETT W. *Donnelliana: An Appendix to Caesar's Column.* Chicago: F. J. Schulte & Co., 1892.

FITE, EMERSON D. *Social and Industrial Conditions in the North During the Civil War.* New York: Macmillan Co., 1910.

FLANDRAU, CHARLES E. *Encyclopedia of Biography of Minnesota.* Chicago: Century Publishing Co., 1900.

FOLWELL, WILLIAM W. *History of Minnesota.* 4 vols. St. Paul: Minnesota Historical Society, 1924–1926.

FRIEDMAN, WILLIAM F. and ELIZABETH S. *The Shakespearean Cyphers Examined.* Cambridge: Cambridge University Press, 1957.

GARDINER, CHARLES M. *The Grange: Friend of the Farmer.* Washington, D.C.: The National Grange, 1949.

GARDINER, MARTIN. *Fads and Fallacies in the Name of Science.* New York: Dover, 1957.

GLAD, PAUL W. *The Trumpet Soundeth.* Lincoln: University of Nebraska Press, 1960.

GOLDMAN, ERIC. *Rendevouz with Destiny.* New York: Alfred A. Knopf, 1953.

HALL, HARLAN P. *H. P. Hall's Observations.* St. Paul: n.p., 1904.

HANDLIN, OSCAR. *This was America.* Cambridge, Mass.: Harvard University Press, 1949.

HAVIGHURST, WALTER. *Upper Mississippi: A Wilderness Saga.* New York: Farrar & Rinehart, 1944.

HAYS, SAMUEL P. *The Response to Industrialism, 1885–1914.* Chicago: University of Chicago Press, 1957.

HAYNES, FRED E. *James Baird Weaver.* Iowa City: The State Historical Society of Iowa, 1919.

HAYNES, FRED E. *Third Party Movements Since the Civil War with Special Reference to Iowa.* Iowa City: The State Historical Society of Iowa, 1916.

HICKS, JOHN D. *The Populist Revolt.* Minneapolis: University of Minnesota Press, 1931.

HOFSTADTER, RICHARD. *The Age of Reform.* New York: Alfred A. Knopf, 1955.

HOPKINS, VIVIAN C. *The Prodigal Puritan.* Cambridge, Mass.: Harvard University Press, 1959.

HUBBART, HENRY C. *The Older Middle West, 1840–1880.* New York: D. Appleton-Century, 1936.

JOSEPHSON, MATTHEW. *The Politicos 1865–1896.* New York: Harcourt, Brace & Co., 1938.

JULIAN, GEORGE W. *Political Recollections 1840–1872.* Chicago: Jansen, McClurg & Co., 1884.

KELLEY, OLIVER H. *Origin and Progress of the Patrons of Husbandry in the United States.* Philadelphia: J. A. Wagenseller, 1875.

KIRKLAND, EDWARD C. *The Coming of the Industrial Age.* New York: Holt, Rinehart & Winston, 1960.

KNOLES, GEORGE H. *The Presidential Campaign and Election of 1892.* Stanford: Stanford University Press, 1942.

LARSON, ARTHUR J. (ed.). *Crusader and Feminist: Letters of Jane Grey Swisshelm, 1858–1865.* St. Paul: Minnesota Historical Society, 1934.

LARSON, HENRIETTA M. *Jay Cooke: Private Banker.* Cambridge, Mass.: Harvard University Press, 1936.

LARSON, HENRIETTA M. *The Wheat Market and the Farmer in Minnesota 1858–1900.* New York: Columbia University Press, 1926.

LEECH, MARGARET. *Reveille in Washington 1860–1865.* New York: Harper & Bros., 1941.

LLOYD, CARO. *Henry Demarest Lloyd.* New York: G. P. Putnam's Sons, 1912.

MACK, EDWARD C. *Peter Cooper: Citizen of New York.* New York: Duell, Sloan & Pearce, 1949.

MATTSON, HANS. *Reminiscences.* St. Paul: D. D. Merrill, 1891.

MERRICK, GEORGE B. *Old Times on the Upper Mississippi.* Cleveland: Arthur H. Clark Co., 1909.

MERRILL, HORACE S. *Bourbon Democrat of the Middle West, 1865–1896.* Baton Rouge: Louisiana State University Press, 1953.

NEVINS, ALLAN. *Frémont: The West's Greatest Adventurer.* 2 vols. New York: Harper & Bros., 1928.

NEVINS, ALLAN. *Grover Cleveland: A Study in Courage.* New York: Dodd, Mead & Co., 1934.

NEWSON, T. M. *Pen Pictures of St. Paul, Minnesota.* St. Paul: Brown, Treacy & Co., 1886.

NICHOLS, JEANNETTE P. and RANDALL, JAMES G. (ed.). *Democracy in the Middle West 1840–1940.* New York: D. Appleton-Century Co., 1941.

NICHOLS, ROY F. *The Disruption of American Democracy.* New York: Macmillan Co., 1948.

NICHOLSON, ALDWELL. *No Cipher in Shakespeare.* London: T. F. Unwin, 1888.

NOBLIN, STUART. *Leonidas LaFayette Polk: Agrarian Crusader,* Chapel Hill: University of North Carolina Press, 1949.

NYE, RUSSELL B. *Midwestern Progressive Politics, 1870–1950.* East Lansing: Michigan State College Press, 1951.

OBERHOLTZER, ELLIS P. *A History of the United States Since the Civil War.* 5 vols. New York: Macmillan Co., 1936.

OBERHOLTZER, ELLIS P. *Jay Cooke Financier of the Civil War.* 2 vols. Philadelphia: George W. Jacobs & Co., 1907.

ORFIELD, MATTHEW N. *Federal Land Grants to the States with Special Reference to Minnesota.* (University of Minnesota Studies in the Social Sciences No. 2.) Minneapolis: University of Minnesota Press, 1915.

POTTER, DAVID M. *People of Plenty.* Chicago: University of Chicago Press, 1954.

PRIESTLEY, DALHOUSIE. *God in Politics.* Portland: Freedom Publishing, 1893.

PYLE, JOSEPH G. *The Life of James J. Hill.* New York: Doubleday Page & Co., 1917.

PYLE, JOSEPH G. *The Little Cryptogram,* St. Paul: Pioneer Press Co., 1888.

RHODES, JAMES F. *A History of the United States from the Compromise of 1850 to end of the Roosevelt Administration.* 9 vols. New York: Macmillan Co., 1928.

RIPLEY, WILLIAM C. *Railroads: Rate and Regulation.* New York: Longmans, Green & Co., 1912.

RODDIS, LOUIS H. *The Indian Wars of Minnesota.* Iowa City: Torch Press, 1956.

ROSS, EARLE D. *The Liberal Republican Movement.* New York: Henry Holt & Co., 1919.

RYLAND, WILLIAM J. *Alexander Ramsey.* Philadelphia: Harris & Partridge Co., 1941.

SALOUTOS, THEODORE. *Farmer Movements in the South 1865–1933.* Los Angeles and Berkeley: University of California Press, 1960.

SCHARF, THOMAS J. and WESCOTT, THOMPSON. *History of Philadelphia 1609–1884.* 3 vols. Philadelphia: L. H. Everts & Co., 1884.

SHANNON, FRED A. *The Farmer's Last Frontier, 1860–1897.* New York: Farrar & Rinehart, Inc., 1945.

SHARKEY, ROBERT P. *Money, Class and Party.* Baltimore: Johns Hopkins University Press, 1959.

SMALLEY, EUGENE V. *A History of the Republican party from its Organization to the Present Time and Biographical Sketches of Leading Minnesota Republicans.* St. Paul: E. V. Smalley, 1896.

SMITH, HENRY NASH. *The Virgin Land.* Cambridge, Mass.: Harvard University Press, 1950.

STANWOOD, EDWARD. *American Tariff Controversies in the Nineteenth Century.* 2 vols. Boston: Houghton Mifflin & Co., 1903.

STANWOOD, EDWARD. *A History of the Presidency.* Boston: Houghton Mifflin & Co., 1898.

STEPHENSON, GEORGE M. *John Lind of Minnesota.* Minneapolis: The University of Minnesota Press, 1935.

STEWART, WILLIAM M. *Bondholders' Conspiracy to Demonetize Silver.* San Francisco: n.p., 1885.

SWISSHELM, JANE GREY. *Half a Century.* Chicago: Jansen, McClurg & Co., 1880.

TAUSSIG, FRANK W. *Some Aspects of the Tariff Question.* Cambridge, Mass.: Harvard University Press, 1915.

TAUSSIG, FRANK W. *Tariff History of the United States.* New York: G. P. Putnam's Sons, 1900.

TAYLOR, CARL C. *The Farmers' Movement.* New York: American Book Co., 1953.

USHER, ELLIS B. *The Greenback Movement of 1875–84 and Wisconsin's Part in It.* Milwaukee: Meisenheimer Printing Co., 1911.

VAN VLECK, GEORGE W. *The Panic of 1857.* New York: Columbia University Press, 1943.

VINCENT, HENRY. *The Story of the Commonweal.* Chicago: W. B. Conkey Co., 1894.

WEST, NATHANIEL. *The Ancestry, Life, and Times of Hon. Henry Hastings Sibley.* St. Paul: n.p., 1889.

WHEELOCK, JOSEPH A. *Minnesota.* St. Paul: William R. Marshall, 1862.

WILDMAN, MURRAY. *Money Inflation in the United States.* New York: G. P. Putnam's Sons, 1905.

WOODWARD, C. VANN. *Tom Watson: Agrarian Rebel.* New York: Rinehart & Co., 1955.

WYMAN, W[ILLIAM] H. *The Bibliography of the Bacon-Shakespeare Controversy, with Notes and Extracts.* Cincinnati: Cox & Co., 1884.

ZINK, HAROLD. *City Bosses in the United States.* Durham: Duke University Press, 1930.

INDEX

Acker, William H., 55
Aberdeen, Earl of, 239
Adams, Charles Francis, 171
Adams, Henry, 15, 73, 74
Adams, John Q., 100, 238
Adams, Samuel E., 161
Adams, Thomas, 36
Address to the People of Minne-sota . . . , 34
Agassiz, Louis, 210
Alaska Purchase Debate, 116
Aldrich, Cyrus: as congressional candidate, 33; Senate nomination sought by 64, 70–71; mentioned, 59, 61, 75, 100, 120
Allen, William V., 354, 355
Alliance Hail and Cyclone Mutual Insurance Company, 268
Alliance Labor Union party: and Donnelly, 273, 275, 276, 279, 288; fused with Democrats, 275; in legislature, 283; nominates J. H. Baker, 302; and People's party, 299; in state conventions, 273, 299; mentioned, 274, 285
Allison, John, 268
Altgeld, John P., 323
American Association for the Advancement of Science, 202
American Bi-Metallic Association, 321
American Bimetallic League, 322, 323, 328
American People's Money, The, 346
American Protective Association; *see* APA
American Railway Union, 333–35
Ames, Albert A., 213, 248, 250, 253

Ames, Oakes, 122, 291
Anatomy of Melancholy, 48
Andrews, Christopher C., 120, 186
Anthracite Coal Investigation, 312–15
Anti-Catholicism, 5, 38, 330–31
Anti-Monopolist, 160, 161, 166, 167, 168, 174, 187
Anti-Monopoly party of Minnesota, 154, 155
Anti-Orientalism, 262–65, 301, 325
Anti-Semitism: Donnelly denies, 336–37; in *Golden Bottle,* 305; in *Caesar's Column,* 263–64; mentioned, 321, 322, 395, 396, 400
Anti-Trust Conference, 313–15
APA, 331–32, 339
Appleton, D., 208
Arnold, Edwin, 233
Arnold, John, 18, 19
Atlantis: The Antediluvian World: agnosticism of, 203; analysis of, 197–98; Donnelly's anxiety about, 200–201; and literary puzzles, 228; popularity of, 209; mentioned, 235
Astor, W. Waldorf, 394
Austin Fire and Storm Mutual Insurance Company, 268
Austin, Horace, 125, 140, 152
Averill, John T., 119, 125, 131, 133, 135
Aylesworth, Burton O., 290

Bache, Alexander D., 5
Bacon, Francis, 227, 228, 393
Baconian Society, 238, 240

Bacon-Shakespeare controversy: authorship studied, 227; Bacon cursed, 243; cipher search, 228; correspondence of, 228–29; cultist, 229; debates, 239, 243; Donnelly's caution in, 240; reception of cipher, 230; Westminster Hall lecture on, 238

Baker, James H.: in campaign of 1890, 275; candidate for governor 1892, 302; delegate to Cincinatti, 285; mentioned, 72, 186, 217, 218, 288, 385

Banning, William: candidate for governor, 177; and Donnelly, 130, 180–81; railroad lobbyist, 96–97; and bimetallism, 176; mentioned, 96, 119, 134

Barker, Wharton, 378, 398

Barnard, Henry, 101

Beck, J. B., 146

Becker, George L., 133, 336, 344

Beecher, Henry W., 182

Bellamy, Edward, 263

Belmont, August, 161

Benson, Jared, 62

Bixby, Tams, 274

Blair, Francis, Jr., 39

Blake et al. v. *The Winona & St. Peter Railroad*, 154, 174

Blakely, David, 76

Bland, Richard, 350

Bland Silver Purchase Bill, 177

Boisgilbert, Edmund, 262

Bourbon Democrats, 165, 169, 185, 188, 219, 280, 344, 347

Bowers, Henry F., 332

Bowler, J. M., 342, 378

"Brass Kettle," 183–87

Breckinridge, John C., 11, 17–18, 52

Brewster, Benjamin Harris, 9, 43, 111

Brill, H. R., 189

Brisbin, John B., 94

Brown, B. Gratz, 141

Brown, Carl, 330

Brown, Orville, 35

Bryan, William Jennings: APA and election of, 332; campaign against, 363–64; defeated in 1896, 364, 366–67; and Donnelly, 360, 362; Minnesota campaign in 1896, 361–63; as People's party candidate, 360; and the St. Louis People's party convention, 353,

Bryan (*Continued*)
356; mentioned, 323, 329, 347, 349, 350, 351, 355, 394, 397

Budstikken, 218

Bunce, O. B., 207, 209

Burke, Edmund, 48

Burkett, Frank, 355

Burns, Robert, 241

Butler, Marion: as Chairman People's party National Committee, 360; on Donnelly and Weaver, 368; on Donnelly break, 387–88; leadership opposed, 387; mentioned, 362, 367, 368, 377, 379, 390

Caesar's Column: analysis of, 262–65; reception of, 267; mentioned, 278

Calhoun, John C., 44

Cameron, Simon, 54

Campbell, William, 216, 226

Campion, James E., 354

Carlisle, John G., 193

Carpenter, C. P., 251

Carver, H. L., 135

Castle, Henry A., 152

Castle, J. N., 300

Central High School, 5

Central Pacific Railroad, 77, 97

Chandler, Zachariah, 39

Charles Scribner's Sons, 206–7

Chicago *Irish Republic*, 127

Chicago, Milwaukee, & St. Paul Railroad Company v. *Minnesota*, 297–98

Chicago *Vanguard*, 300

Chicago *Western Rural*, 245

Chicago World's Fair, 311

Chief Little Crow, 67

Childs, Attorney General of Minnesota, 312

Chilstrom, P. O., 187

Chinese exclusion; *see* anti-Orientalism.

Chippewa Treaty, 84–86

Cincinnati Convention: Alliance Labor Union delegates in, 285; compromise in, 287; Donnelly in, 285–88; Ocala platform approved, 287

Cipher in the Plays and on the Tombstone, 244, 393–94

Clark, Charles, 291

Clay, Henry, 151

Cleveland, Grover: administration and Donnelly, 225–26; Minnesota pa-

Cleveland, Grover (*Continued*)
  tronage, 223–24; presidential candidate, 215–16; in Pullman Strike, 334; and Sherman Silver Purchase Act, 320–22; mentioned, 218, 220, 252, 300
Clough, David M., 318, 361, 364
Cochran, Bourke, 329
Coin's Handbook, 328
Colbert, Professor, 237
Cole, Gordon, 49
Colfax, Schuyler, 39, 75, 112
Colville, William, 104, 105
Conner, W. D., 260
Cooke, Jay: and Donnelly, 129–31, 134, 135; as financier, 97; political neutrality of, 135–36
Cooper, James Fenimore, 14, 15
Cooper, Peter, 171, 173
Cox, S. S., 162, 187
Coxey, Jacob S., 329, 330, 339, 389
Coxeyism, 329, 330
Cramsie, E. D., 181
Crédit Mobilier, 124
Crime of '73, 306, 323, 389
Cross of Gold Speech, 351, 389
Cullen, William, 65, 66, 67
Currier, F. M., 281

Dakota County: Agricultural Society, 25; County-seat election, 20–21; Fair, 69, 126; Republican convention of 1859, 33; settled, 28
Dakota County *Tribune,* 251
Dakota Farmers' Alliance, 268
Dakota *Union,* 135
Dalrymple, Oliver, 136, 154
Darrow, Clarence, 356
Darwin, Charles, 202, 210
Davidson, John X., 142
Davidson, Thomas, 231
Davidson, William, 243
Davis, Cushman K.: nominated for governor, 152; in Pullman Strike, 334–35; on rail rates, 157, 164; opposes Ramsey, 162; elected Senator, 253–54; mentioned, 120, 156, 217, 259, 276, 363
Davis, David, 170
Davis, Henry W., 80
Davis, James H., 353
Davis, Jefferson, 167, 171
Day, Frank, 361
Debs, Eugene, 333, 335, 337, 343, 348, 353, 388

Democratic-Alliance Labor Union party coalition 1891, 280
Democratic party Convention, 1860: at Baltimore, 49; at Charleston, 49; of 1886, 250
Democratic-Greenback fusion, 177
Deutschen von Minnesota, An die, 31
Dickens, Charles, 238
Dobbyn, William, 335, 353, 374, 379
Doctor Huguet, 289–90
Dodge, Ossian E., 119, 127–28
Donnelliana, 319–20
Donnelly, Cathrine Gavin, 3, 70
Donnelly, Eleanor C., 9
Donnelly-Currier Bill, 283
Donnelly, Ignatius:
  Ancestry of: 2, 3, 69, 232
  Anti-Semitism of: 262–65, 336, 337
  Appraisal of: 1–2, 318–19, 400–401
  Congressional campaigns of: (1862) 65–69; (1864) 89–90; (1866) 104–6; (1868) 117–21; (1870) 131–35; (1876) 172–73; (1878) 181–87; (1884) 214–19
  Congressional career of: and Alaska purchase, 116; and Commission of Education, 101; and First Minnesota, 76–77; and Freedman's Bureau, 102; and government secrets, 91–92; and House Speakership, 75; and Indian Reform, 81, 84, 88, 89, 91, 92; and Internal Improvements, 99; and Johnson, 95, 103; and D. King, 82; and Lincoln, 80; and Negro suffrage, 94; and personal life, 74–75; and Reconstruction Speech, 79–80; and St. Paul *Press,* 88; and Select Committee for Pacific Railroads, 77; and Steven's Reconstruction Bill, 106; and tree planting scheme, 101–02; and Washburne, 110, 111–13, 115; and West Point, 91
  Contested election of, 188–95
  Description and Personality, 1, 281, 398
  Editor, 18, 160, 319
  Farming activities, 47, 93, 136, 174–75, 182–83
  Health, 90, 199, 398–99
  Law practice, 10, 13, 47
  Lectures: "American Humorists," 140–41; Credo of, 140; "Riel

Donnelly, Ignatius (*Continued*)
Rebellion," 127–28; "Six Years in Washington," 140–41

as Lieutenant Governor: acting governor, 48–49, 54; joins Aldrich against Ramsey, 63; as administrator, 48–49; campaigns for Lincoln, 51–52; candidate for, 33–42; seeks colonelcy, 58; commissions friends, 56; debates W. Gorman, 52; debtor relief, 45; elected, 41; enfranchising soldiers, 68; First Minnesota organized, 56–57; in home guard, 58; Indian depredations described by, 67; Indian uprising feared by, 54; military appointments, 57; opposes Ramsey for Senate, 1861, 59; orders mobilization, 55; Plainview speech, 65; praised, 46, 57; Radical Republicanism, 66; railroad bond issue, 45; reading while, 48; rift with Ramsey, 49; re-elected, 59; senate rules, 44

as lobbyist: for Jay Cooke, 129–31, 136; correspondent for St. Paul *Dispatch* while, 128–29; Duluth Harbor Bill, 130–31; exposed, 163; for Frémont, 124; withdraws, 135

Marriages of: first, Katherine McCaffrey (Kate), 12–13 (*see also* Donnelly, Katherine); second, Marian Hanson, 380–81, 391

Mid-Road politics of: and Bowler, 378–79; and Bryan, 394; and Butler, 368; and Cleveland, 371; and Democratic reformers, 377; and Hill, 379; and McKinley prosperity, 376; and Nashville Conference of Reform Press Association, 374–76; and Omaha Contract, 387; and Owen at People's party convention (1898), 384–85; and presidential aspiration in 1897, 378; and vice-presidential candidate, 390

Money theories of: and conspiracy of Crime of '73, 306; and deficit spending, 324; and fiat money, 323; and inconsistencies, 169; and specie payment, 151; mentioned, 328–29

Donnelly, Ignatius (*Continued*)
and Patronage fight of 1885: and Bourbons in 1886, 249–50; and Cleveland, 224, 226; and Doran, 250; and Hill, 222–23; and Kelly, 221; loss of, 225–26; and Sabin, 225; and Vilas, 219, 221, Washington visit during, 220

and People's party: and Bourbon Democrats, 347; campaign outside Dakota County (1894), 338; candidate for governor (1892) 297, 302–09; convention of 1896, 357; and Debs, 337; defeat in 1892, 309; and Democratic National Committee, 352; father of, 287–88; favorite son candidacy in 1896, 353, 354; fusion of Minnesota Democrats and Populists prevented by, 368; fusion opposed by before convention in 1896, 351; and Jacksonian Democrats, 329; and Lind's nomination in 1896, 358; Preamble People's party platform, 295; presidential candidacy rumored, 349; role in Democratic-People's party fusion negotiations of 1892, 299–300; and St. Louis convention (1892) 294–97; and silver in 1894, 327–28; in 1895, 345; silver and Watson, 355; and Frances Willard, 294. *See also* William Jennings Bryan

Political career of (early): and attorney-generalship (1859), 31; candidate for Pennsylvania legislature, 11; candidate for territorial senate (1857), 29–30; enters politics, 10; first political speech, (1855), 11; seeks Congressional nomination (1859), 33; mentioned, 32, 34

as State Legislator: and Anthracite Coal Investigation, 312–15; defeated (1888), 260–61; (1894) 339; Democrats indorse (1873), 154; elected (1873), 155, (1875), 167, (1877), 177, (1886), 251–52, (1890), 276, (1896) 364–65; legislative control over railroad rates, 158–59, 254–55; People's party indorses for Senator (1895) 342; Pine Lands Investigation (1874), 156; Pine Lands

Donnelly, Ignatius (*Continued*)
Investigation Report (1893), author of, 318; Railroad Committee chairmanship (1891), 279; Senatorial aspirations (1888), 261; textbook fight, 177–79; usury legislation, 156–57, 173–74, 280

Views on: Altgeld, 323; British Legislative Process, 238–39; British visit, 240–41; Congressional speeches, 79; Congressmen, 100; Coxey, 329–30; education, 369–70; frontier's closing; 324–25; government ownership, 370; immigration, 11, 78, 343; Ireland, 240–41; labor's rights, 257; Lincoln, 80; New York City, 206; poverty, 128; Presidential impeachment, 106; Pullman Strike, 334; religion, 264, 266; scientific America, 209–10; secession, 53–54; socialism, 388; state's rights, 80; tariff, 126, 128–20, 258; *see also* Anti-Orientalism, Anti-Semitism

Writings of: *An Address to the People of Minnesota . . .* , 34; *The American People's Money,* 346; *Atlantis,* 197–203, 209–28, 235; *Caesar's Column,* 262–67, 278; *The Cipher in the Plays and on the Tombstone,* 244, 393–94; *Donnelliana,* 319–20; *Doctor Huguet,* 289–90; *Golden Bottle,* 304–6, 346; *The Great Cryptogram,* 231–237, 241–42, 251, 257, 393; *Mourner's Vision,* 7–8; poetry, 6, 7, 8, 9; *Ragnarok,* 204–09; 228, 235; "Shakespeare Myth," 230

Youth and education of: born, 1; middle name Loyola, 5; reasons for moving West, 14–15; at Ringgold School, 5; studies English literature, 5–6; studies law, 9–10; *see also,* Alliance-Labor Union party; Bacon-Shakespeare controversy; Greenback Labor party; Katherine Donnelly; Minnesota Farmer's Alliance; Railroad Regulation; Tariff

Donnelly, Ignatius Carroll, 12, 174, 199, 214

Donnelly, John Gavin, 20

Donnelly, Katherine (Kate): advice of, 75, 196–97, 215, 219, 258; ancestry, 12; death of, 332, 379; described, 12; illnesses, 89, 197–99, 327; opinions, 37, 57–58, 123, 131, 181, 284; mentioned, 26, 32, 35, 94, 130–31, 250

Donnelly, Marian; *see* Hanson, Marian

Donnelly, Mary, 26, 199

Donnelly, Philip Carroll, 3, 4

Donnelly, Sarah, 391

Donnelly, Stanislaus, 174, 199, 258, 372

Doolittle, J. R., 145–46

Doran, Michael: as Bourbon, 166; as candidate for State Auditor, 166; and Democratic People's party fusion 1892, 299; and Donnelly's indorsement, 215–16; and Donnelly and Cleveland, 222–23; and Donnelly reconciliation, 250; and financial aid at Kate's death, 332; shares patronage control, 219; mentioned, 248, 280, 308, 372

Douglas Station (Donnelly, Minnesota), 174

Douglas, Stephen A., 40, 41, 49, 52

Drake, Elias F., 159

Dred Scott Case, 40, 298

Driscoll, Fred, 82, 120, 126

DuBois, Fred T., 349–50

Duluth Harbor Bill, 130–31

Duluth *Minnesotian,* 137

Dunn, Robert C., 318, 372

Durant, E. W., 184

Durant, T. C., 97

Duross, John, 13

Edgerton, Alonzo J., 157

Edgerton, J. A., 361

Edmunds, Judge, 102

Election of 1856, 28

Emerson, Ralph W., 47

Emery, S. E. V., 306

Emigrant Aid Association, 19

Emigrant Aid Journal, 18

English, William H., 194

Erwin, W. W., 275, 302

Eustis, William H., 390

Faribault *Central Republican,* 35, 78, 86

Farm, Stock and Home, 273

Farmer Labor party, 258–60

Farmers' *Union,* 152, 160

Fay, Henry, 383

Federalist Papers, 48

Fenianism, 127

Ferris, James H., 374

Field, James, 301

Fifth District Alliance: in election of 1892, 309; influence appraised, 258; insurance program, 268; political action 1890, 270; favors Scheffer for governor, 257; indorses Wilson for governor 1888, 259

Fifth Minnesota Regiment, 57–58

Finley, H. H., 191, 194

First Minnesota Regiment, 60, 76

Fish, Everett W.: and Alliance, 271–72, 284, 293; and *Donnelliana,* 319; and Donnelly, 270, 272, 310, 319–20; and Hall, 273; as journalist, 269; and Owen, 275, 307, 326; and People's party, 299–300

Fisher, Louis E., 153, 165

Fisk, James L., 95–96

Flandrau, Charles: *Pioneer Press* defended by in libel suits, 290–91, 371; Washburn's counsel in contested election, 188–89; mentioned, 108, 184

Fletcher, Loren, 316

Folsom, Charles, 109–10

Fort Sumter, 54, 60

Forney, D. C., 130

Foster, Dr. Thomas: background of, 29; on Donnelly-Aldrich, 64–65; on Donnelly's ancestry, 37; on Donnelly and Republican party, 107–8, 136–39; and Liberal Republicanism, 143; and *Minnesotian,* 30; as Ramsey's agent, 29; mentioned, 36–37, 41, 45–46, 51, 56, 69, 107–8, 123, 132, 142, 208

Franklin, Benjamin, 27

Freedman's Bureau, 102

Freeman, J. C., 243

Frémont, John C., 124, 163

Furlong, J. J., 268

Garfield, James A., 101, 194

Garrison, George T., 22

Garrison, William Lloyd, 22, 80

George, Henry, 256, 297, 342–43

George, Milton, 245

Gibbs, F. C., 374, 379, 382

Gilfillan, Charles D., 107

Gilfillan, James, 156

Gillitt, George, 214

Gillitt, Harvey, 215, 364

Giltinan, George, 319, 335

Gladstone, W. E., 202, 238

Golden Bottle, 304–6, 346

Gordon, F. R., 388

Gorman, Willis A., 52, 57

Grace, Bishop, 85

Grain Growers Association, 335–36

Grange: abandons partisan politics, 166; decline of, 161; Donnelly joins, 149; Donnelly lecturer in, 148, 150; factions within, 149–50; lobbying, 178; purpose of, 149; mentioned, 151, 153

Grange Advance, 166

Granger Cases, 174

Grant, U. S., 119, 141, 145, 184

Great Cryptogram, 231, 232, 233, 234, 235–37, 241–42, 251, 257, 393

Great West, 269, 272, 274, 276, 298, 310, 320, 327

Greeley, Horace, 10, 39, 141–43, 145, 147

Greenback Labor party, 168, 170–71, 188, 194

Gresham, Walter Q., 300

"Grey Eagle" steamboat, 25

Groom, Wallace, 171

Haigh, George, 246

Hall, Harlan P.: on Donnelly defeat in 1868, 122; urges Donnelly to seek governorship, 125; on Donnelly-Washburne episode, 113; at Liberal Republican convention, 142; role in campaigns (1868), 118–19; (1878), 184; mentioned, 61, 108, 120, 126, 131, 133, 143

Hall, O. M., 216

Hall, R. J., 270–272, 274, 278, 285, 288, 326

Halvorson, Kittel, 276, 278, 386

Hancock, Winfield S., 195

Hanna, Mark, 357, 363, 383

Hanson, Marian (second Mrs. Donnelly), 380

Harlan, James, 130

Harper & Bros., 198, 206

Harrison, Benjamin, 259, 260, 261

Harrison, Carter H., 146

Hart, John S., 5–6, 101

Harvey, W. H., 328, 346

Hastings Dakota & Western Railroad, 97–98, 159
Hastings *Gazette*, 144–45
Hastings *Independent*, 33, 50, 86
Hastings *New Era*, 214, 217
Hastings *Union*, 214
Hayes, A. M., 47, 59, 76
Hayes, Donnelly, and Hayes, 47
Hayes, O. T., 47
Hayes, Rutherford B., 163
Haymarket Riot, 323
Heaton, David, 61, 62, 65, 75
Hekla Insurance Co., 270
Hicks, Judge, 369
Hill, James J., 212, 218–20, 223, 261, 383
Hodgson, T. C., 253
Holmes, Oliver Wendell, 7–8, 32
Hompe, John, 280, 281, 288, 309
House of Commons, 238
House of Lords, 239
Hubbard, Lester C., 300
Hubbard, Lucius, 119–20
Huntington, Colis P., 97, 291

Illinois Anti-Monopoly League, 213
Imperialism, 381–82, 395
Industrial Age, 169
"Ingeneous Doemly," 22
Ireland, 240–41
Ireland, John, 218
Irish Standard, 238
Ives, Gideon S., 280

Jeffersonianism, 47, 78, 144
Jennison, S. P., 120
Johnson, Andrew, 93–95, 103, 106, 113, 115
Johnson, Charles W., 185–86, 191
Johnson, Christian, 358, 383, 387
Johnson, Samuel, 238
Jones Bill, 157–58, 164
Jones, James K., 355
Julian, George W., 188, 190–91, 195

Kasson, John A., 99
Keith, George, 81–82, 132
Keller, Henry, 315–16
Kelley, Oliver H., 150
Kelly, Patrick, 212, 219–20, 221, 223, 248, 332
Kennedy, John, 144
Kensington Riots, 4
King, Dana, 82–3, 291

King, William S.: alienated by Donnelly, 71; dislikes Miller, 64; Donnelly, conference with, 87–88; Minneapolis politician, 63; railroad vote controlled by, 134; seeks postmastership of House, 75–76; mentioned, 83, 95, 135, 191, 282, 291
Knight Case, 343
Knights of Labor: and Ames, 251; and Gresham, 301; and Minnesota's reform Democrats in 1886, 249; and Scheffer, 257; strength in large cities and towns, 249; mentioned, 253, 272
Knights of the Quill, 144
Kyle, James H., 301

Labor Echo, 258
Labor rights, 257
Lake Superior & Mississippi Railroad, 77, 96–97, 124
Lamar, L. C. Q., 221, 225
Lamb, John, 258
Lathrop, John, 274
Lawler, Daniel, 303, 309
Lease, Mary E., 297, 307, 355
Le Duc, William, 97–98, 119, 159, 217, 291
Leese, Professor, 239
Leinau, Senator, 178
Le Jeune, Champollion, 236
Libel suits: with *Pioneer*, 94; with *Pioneer Press* (1891), 290–92; (1897) 371
Liberal Republican party: Cincinnati convention, 142–43; and Donnelly, 137–38, 143, 144, 145–46; and Greeley campaign, 146–47; and Carter H. Harrison of Illinois, 146; mentioned, 141
Lincoln, Abraham: on Donnelly's Immigration Speech, 78–79; greatness evaluated, 80; lack of public confidence in, 53; leadership criticized, 83; reconstruction program, 93; vote in Dakota County, 90; mentioned, 34, 50, 54, 68, 69
Lind, John: career traced, 357–58; defeated for governorship 1896, 364; denounced in 1898 campaign, 386–87; elected governor 1898, 391; machinations behind nomination of 1896, 358–59;

Lind, John (*Continued*)
nativist critics of denounced by Donnelly, 391–92; nominated by fusion slate 1898, 384; People's party considers indorsing for Senator 1895, 342; praised by Donnelly in 1896, 359; mentioned, 259, 276, 383, 397
Litchfield, E. B., 98
Litchfield *News-Ledger*, 160
Livingston, L. L., 284, 296
Lloyd, Henry D., 313, 346, 351, 356, 373, 388
Lobbying; *see* Cooke; Donnelly, Lobbying; Hastings Dakota & Western Railroad; Lake Superior & Mississippi Railroad
Locke, John, 256, 397
Lochren, William, 189–90
London *Daily Telegraph*, 233
London *Strand Journal*, 234
Long, L. C., 319, 341, 386–87, 391–92
Loring, Lyman, 214
Loucks, H. L., 268, 311
Lucas, T. H., 253
Lynch, E. R., 369; 380

McClung, John W., 160
McClurg, A. C., 265–66
McDonald, Eva, 284–85, 288, 292, 293, 319
MacDonald, J. L., 251
McGaughey, J. M., 249
McGill, Andrew R., 251–53
McKinley Tariff, 283
McKinley, William: Spanish ultimatum ridiculed by Donnelly, 381; mentioned, 349, 353, 364, 366, 396–97
McMillan, Samuel, 162
Macune, C. W., 284, 286, 311
Madison, James, 100
Mallen, Bill, 22
Manning, Van H., 188, 190, 192, 195
Marshall, William R.: 70, 93, 107, 118, 126, 130, 134
Marx, Karl, 278
Mattock, John, 91
Mattson, Hans, 117–18
Mayall, Samuel, 133, 135
Mayo, Dr. W. W., 138, 142, 143, 145, 276, 283
Mead, Frank J., 151
Medill, Joseph, 237

Meeker, Bradley B., 100
Meeker Dam, 99–100, 116
Meighan, T. J., 351, 359, 384
Memphis, El Paso and Texas Railroad (Memphis & El Paso), 163, 186
Merriam, William, 254, 259–60, 261, 269, 272, 274, 276
Merrill, D. D., 197
Metcalf, T. M., 118, 132
Mid-Road convention, 1898, 389–90
Miller, Stephen: Donnelly's congressional candidacy indorsed 1864, 81; Donnelly urged to investigate Indian fraud, 84; elected governor, 73–74; opposes Donnelly for congress, 62; Pillsbury-Donnelly peacemaker, 90; refuses renomination for governor, 93; mentioned, 65, 76, 87
Milwaukee *News*, 147
Minneapolis *Journal*, 363
Minneapolis *Lumberman*, 181
Minneapolis Millers' Association, 166, 183, 185, 196, 254
Minneapolis *State Atlas*, 45, 82
Minneapolis *State News*, 76
Minneapolis *Tribune*, 107, 313, 369
Minnesota Farmers' Alliance: and Alliance Labor Union party, 288; charges Alliance leader seeking personal gain, 271; Cincinnati platform, 293; circular for caucus in 1887, 253; conventions, (1884) 216, (1885) 246, (1886) 247, (1890) 270, (1893) 310–11, (1894) 326–27, (1895) 341; decline appraised, 257–58; and Democrats, 248; Donnelly delegate Cincinnati convention, 285; Donnelly honored for work in, 341–42; Donnelly role in, 246, 247–48; growth of, 245, 267; insurance program, 267–69; legislative program (1891), 283; and McGill, 251; and non-partisanship, 270, 272; Ocala platform, 283–84; and People's party, 288; and political action, 246; presidency of, (1890) 270–71; (1891) 278, (1892) 293, (1893) 310–11; and Scheffer, 257; mentioned, 214
Minnesota Legislature: (1887), 255, (1893), 311–19, (1897), 369–71

Minnesota Liberal Republican Convention, 145–46

Minnesota Mid-Road People's party Convention, 386

Minnesota People's party: defeat (1894), 339, 340; Democratic fusion divides in 1896, 351–52; denounced as socialistic, 308; Donnelly denies his boss rule of 1892, 299; Donnelly nominated for governor by, 302; formed, 287; gains in election of 1894, 339; state conventions (1892), 298–99, (1894), 335, (1896), 359, (1898), 384–86

Minnesota Prohibition party 1892, 302–3

Minnesota Pure Election Law, 365

Minnesota Republican Convention 1886, 251

Minnesota Staats-Zeitung, 31, 86–87

Minnesota *State News*, 44

Minnesota Union party, 59

Mississippi Valley Lumberman, 316

Mitchell, W. B., 86–87, 95, 132

Mitchell, W. H., 215

Moccasin Democrats, 30

Morgan, Appleton, 229

Morgan, Thomas, 267

Morrill, Ashley C., 85–86, 92

Morrison, H. G. O., 61–62; 64, 70

Morton, J. Sterling, 326

Mountain Iron Tract Investigation, 372–73

Mourner's Vision, 7–8

Munch, Emil, 125

Napoleon, 54

National Bimetallic Union, 321

National Bureau of Education, 100–101

National Farmers' Alliance and Industrial Union, 269, 277, 283

National Organization Committee, 375, 377, 387

National Reform Press Association, 367–68, 374–75

Nativism, 4, 36–8, 391–92. See APA

Negro; see *Doctor Huguet*

Negro suffrage in Minnesota, 93–94, 102

Neill, Edward D., 178

Nelson, Knute: and Anti-Trust Conference, 313; campaigns as liberal in 1894, 337; campaigns for

Nelson, Knute (*Continued*)
Washburn, 185–86; elected governor 1892, 309; favored by Alliance for governor 1890, 272–73; re-elected by largest Republican vote 1894, 339; relation to Lind, 358; Senator, 342; views senatorial contest 1888, 261; mentioned, 276, 308, 363

Newson, Thomas, 37, 40–41

New Ulm Massacre, 67

New York *Herald*, 112, 122–23

New York *Sun*, 230

New York *Tribune*: Donnelly's Education Bureau praised by, 100; Donnelly's Greenback party ridiculed by, 170; Donnelly's tariff views condemned by, 127; Donnelly-Washburn contests, implications of, 190; notes Washburne-Donnelly episode, 112; mentioned, 10, 39

New York *World*, 231

Nininger City: and Donnelly-Nininger partnership, 17; and Hastings, 20–21, publicity of, 18–19; speculation, 22, mentioned, 25, 30, 69

Nininger, John, 17, 25

Nininger, St. Peter, and Western Railroad, 23

Nonconformist, 285

Noonan, J. A., 169

North American Review, 230, 234

Northern Pacific Railroad, 77, 97, 217–18

Northfield *Standard*, 144

North Star Grange, 149

North Star Woolen Mills, 189

Norton, Daniel, 95, 103, 108, 123

Norton, S. F., 354, 356

O'Brien, D. O., 352

O'Brien, Thomas D., 359, 364

Ocala Convention, 277

Olney-Pauncefote Treaty, 371

Olson, Eric: 258–59, 278, 288, 385

"Omaha Contract," 387

Omaha Convention 1892, 300–302

Omaha Platform, 311, 345

Owatonna Conventions: (1873), 154–55, (1875), 166

Owen, David, 47

Owen, Sidney M.: and Alliance presidency, 278, and bimetallism, 326; defeated for governor, 339;

Owen, Sidney (*Continued*)
defeated for House, 364; and Donnelly at party convention (1898), 385; issues raised by in 1890 campaign, 276; on National Reform Press Association; 374; nominated for governor, 272; at St. Louis convention, 353; role at 1896 convention, 357; mentioned, 276, 285, 288, 302, 307

Paist, William, 160
Pan-American Bi-Metallic Association, 321
Panic: of 1857; 23; of 1873, 155, 176; of 1893, 320, 324
Park, Milton, 394
Parnell, Thomas, 238
Parsons, George I., 152–53, 160–61
Patrons of Husbandry; *see* Grange
Peace Convention, 53
Peale, R. S., 230–32, 242–43
Peffer, William A., 322
People's Pacific Railroad, 77
People's party: and American Railway Union 334–35; APA threatens growth of, 331; and Donnelly, 349, 360–61; issues lose vitality, 376; National Committee on 1896 convention, 348–49; and platform issues adopted, 376–77; St. Louis convention 1896, 352–55; silver propaganda, 322
People's party: of 1870; 133
People's party of 1884, 216
People's Party Paper, 285
People's party National Committee, 286–87, 368
People's party State Central Committee, 379
Persch, John, 91
Phelps, Carrington, 285, 288, 299
Philadelphia, 4, 14, 23–24, 78
Philadelphia College of Medicine, 3
Phrenology, 10
Pillsbury, John: and Donnelly in 1864, 87; and Farmers' Alliance in 1887, 257–58; nominated for governor, 166; re-elected governor, 177; role in lumber frauds, 317; violations of election law, 188; mentioned, 85, 90, 173, 212, 252

Pine Land Investigation: (1874) 156; (1893), 315–19
Pinkerton Agency, 242, 282
Plainview, Minnesota Speech, 65
Plowman, Henry, 273
Poe, Edgar Allan, 147
Polk, Leonidas L., 277, 284, 286, 294, 301
Popular Science Monthly, 208
Porter, Charlotte, 230
"Potato Bug Party," 155
Potts, Mrs. Henry, 238
Powderly, Torrence V., 294, 307
Power, C. A., 294
Preamble to People's Party Platform, 295
Presidential election 1860, 51–52
Progress and Poverty, 256, 267
Pullman, George, 333
Pullman Strike, 333–35; 339

Radical Republicanism, 66, 93, 290
Ragnarok: analysis of, 204–5; popular reception of, 206–9; mentioned, 228, 235
Rahilly, Patrick, 222, 273, 327
Railroad regulation: in *Chicago, Milwaukee & St. Paul Railroad Company* v. *Minnesota*, 281; and Donnelly-Currier Bill, 283; and Donnelly (1874), 158, (1887), 254–55, (1891), 280; fought in Minnesota courts, 157; issue in election 1884, 217–18; and Jones Bill, 157; and Minnesota legislature (1875), 163–64, (1891), 281, (1897), 370; and Morse Bill, 164; and rate-making commission system, 158; Supreme Court, 297–98, mentioned, 152, 158
Ramsey, Alexander: appointed Secretary of War, 163; Attorney General overruled by, 49; background of, 28; campaigns for governor, 39–40; Civil War officers appointed by, 57; controls Republican convention 1859, 33; and Cooke lobby, 130; favors Donnelly for congress 1864, 82; favors railroad bonds, 46; Lincoln visited by, 50; and Miller campaign, 63; nominated for Senator, 1862, 71; orders mobilization, 54–55; and patronage under

Ramsey, Alexander (*Continued*)
Johnson, 108–9; re-elected Senator 1868, 123; Senate seat lost, 162; and Sioux War, 67; and Seward, 50; and Swedish vote in 1868, 117–18; as Territorial governor of Minnesota, 17; Vice-Presidency sought by, 48; mentioned, 17, 34, 36, 51, 52, 54, 72, 135, 181, 212, 217
Rand, Lars M., 249
Randall, Alexander, 95
Representative, 319, 320, 325, 327, 340, 344, 347, 383, 391
Republican State Convention (1861), 59, (1886), 251
Republican Territorial Convention 1857, 29
Resumption of Specie Act, 168, 176
Rhodes, John J., 312
Rice, Henry M., 84, 184
Richardson, Harris, 317–18
Riel Rebellion, 127
Robertson, D. A., 86, 105, 149
Robertson, George, 18–19
Rocky Mountain locust plagues, 155, 175
Rohr, Philip, 18
Rohrer, Daniel, 39, 51
Rosetta stone, 236
Rosicrucian Society, 244
Rothschild, House of, 306, 323

Sabin, Dwight, 225, 261
Sage of Nininger, *see* Ignatius Donnelly
Sage, Russell, 159
St. Albans, 237
St. Cloud *Democrat*, 86
St. Louis convention 1892, 294–97
St. Paul & Pacific Railroad, 77, 98
St. Paul *Dispatch*, 108, 110, 116, 128–29
St. Paul *Globe*, 180, 183, 217, 231, 253, 256
St. Paul *Minnesotian*, 32, 35, 52; *see also* Hall, Harlan P.
St. Paul *News*, 273
St. Paul *Pioneer:* 78, 80–81, 88, 94, 104, 117–18, 121, 135
St. Paul *Pioneer and Democrat*, 34, 38, 44–45, 55, 68
St. Paul *Pioneer and Press:* on American Bi-Metallic Association Chicago Conference, 323; on *At-*

St. Paul (*Continued*)
lantis, 218; on Bourbon Democrats and Donnelly, 217; on Cleveland's silver views, 323–24; and Democrats in 1891, 280; on Donnelly and the Alliance, 247; on Donnelly's bribery charge in 1887, 255; on Donnelly in 1878 campaign, 181, 184; on Donnelly and the legislature, 254, 280; on Donnelly and Speakership of House, 253; on Donnelly's textbook measure, 178; on Donnelly's 1894 defeat, 339; on Kelly-Doran patronage, 222; People's party termed anarchists, 338; mentioned, 218, 247, 259, 283, 292, 308, 326
St. Paul *Press:* and Chippewa affair, 85–86; calls congressional caucus, 1868, 120; on Liberal Republican party's failure, 148; absorbs *Pioneer*, 165; refuses to indorse Donnelly in 1864, 82; state printing contract gained, 71–72, on tree-planting scheme, 102; mentioned, 62, 65, 77, 87, 109, 134, 140, 155
St. Paul *Times*, 21, 31, 37
St. Peter, Minnesota, 22
Sampson, Low & Co., 202, 230, 238, 393
Sanborn, John B., 57–58
Scheffer, Albert, 257, 259, 267, 269
Scheffer, Charles, 34, 52, 83
Schilling, Robert, 286, 298, 351
Schmoele, William, 163
Schulte, F. J., 231–32, 266, 289, 320
Schurz, Carl, 39, 141, 146, 150
Sems, Walter, 331–32
Sewall, Samuel, 351
Seward, William A., 50–51
Seven Financial Conspiracies, 306
Shakespeare Folio 1623, 228
"The Shakespeare Myth," 229–30; 234
Shakespeariana, 228
Sherman Anti-Trust Law, 343
Sherman, John, 194
Sherman Silver Purchase Act, 320–23; 326
Sibley, Henry Hastings, 25, 67, 135, 184, 194, 257–58
Silver: relationship to major political parties, 322

Simpson, Henry C., 58
Simpson, Jerry, 286, 298, 327
Single Tax; *see* George, Henry
Sioux, 54, 66–67
Smith, C. A. and Co., 317
Smith, Seagrave, 167
Southern Mercury, 377
Social Darwinism, 263–65
Spanish American War, 382
Spencer, Herbert, 210
Sprague, George W., 253, 269, 270
Springer Letter, 190–95
Springer, William, 188, 191–92
Stanton, Edwin, 76–77
Staples, Charles F., 317–18
Starkey, James, 188, 192
Stebbins, Columbus, 33, 35, 37
Stevens, Thaddeus, 84, 93, 106
Stewart, Jacob H., 96, 180, 182, 187
Stewart, William, 348
Stillwater *Messenger*, 35–36
Strait, Horace, 212, 217, 246
Subtreasury, 283, 284
Svenska Amerikanien, 117
Swift, Henry A., 34, 68
Swisshelm, Jane G., 62, 90

Tariff: and Anti-Monopoly party, 154;
    and Donnelly in 1869, 126–27;
    in Donnelly's Grange speeches,
    151; and Donnelly-Marshall de-
    bate, 127; Donnelly's lectures
    on, 128–29; Donnelly's reading
    on, 128; Donnelly urges as issue
    of day, 1870, 132; and Minne-
    sota Alliance 1891, 283; and
    Minnesota Republicans in 1871,
    139; mentioned, 151, 276
Taubeneck, Herman E.: denies fusion
    rumor in 1892, 299; as People's
    party National Committee Chair-
    man, 292; and silver issue, 328,
    345; and Silver Republicans and
    People's party, 350; mentioned,
    294, 307, 311, 320, 322, 367
Teller, Henry M., 349–50
Terrell, Ben, 294
Textbook ring, 177–79
Theobald, R. M., 240
Thirty-Ninth Congress, 103
Thomas Committee, 115–16
Thomas, Francis, 115
Tillman, Ben, 311
Timber Culture Act, 101
Towne, Charles A., 361, 398

Trinity College, Cambridge, 239
Trumbull, Lyman, 145

"Umbria," 241
Union Labor party, 256
Union Pacific Board of Directors, 122
Union Pacific Railroad, 97
Union party 1864, 83
United States Supreme Court, 297–
    98, 343
University Union of Oxford, 239
U.S.S. "Maine," 381
Usury legislation, 156–57, 173, 254,
    281–82

Valesh, Frank, 319
Vilas, William, 219, 220, 221, 224,
    225
Vandervoort, Paul, 367
Van Vorhes, Abraham, 35, 41, 50, 64
Venezuela Controversy, 371
Verne, Jules, 197

Wade-Davis Manifesto, 95
Waite, Davis, 313, 327, 347
Wardall, Alonzo, 268–69
Warner, A. J., 345
Warner, Richardson and Lawrence,
    317
Washburn, Cadwallader C., 116
Washburn, William D.: congressional
    aspirant 1864, 81; on business-
    man in American life, 185; elec-
    tion suit rejoinder in 1878, 189–
    90; elected U.S. Senator, 261;
    loses Senatorship, 342; as Minne-
    apolis miller and lumberman, 75;
    and Minneapolis Millers' Associa-
    tion, 183; nominated for congress
    1878, 180; on railroad regulation,
    152; mentioned, 99, 114, 119–
    20, 184, 187, 188, 212, 357
Washburne-Donnelly episode, 112–14
Washburne, Elihu, 75, 99, 100, 110,
    111–12, 115
Washington *Chronicle*, 78, 130
Washington *Post*, 192
Watson, Thomas: anti-Semitism of,
    337; Donnelly favors for vice-
    president (1896), 355, (1898),
    378; Mid-Road position taken
    by, 352; Ocala platform urged in
    1895 by, 347; as People's party
    vice-presidential candidate 1896,
    356; on Weaver and Peffer silver

Watson, Thomas (*Continued*)
    position in 1894, 327; mentioned,
    285, 297, 362, 378, 390
Weaver, James B.: on American Bi-
    metallic League Chicago Confer-
    ence, 323; on Anti-Trust Confer-
    ence, 1893, 313–14; campaigns
    for Donnelly in 1892, 307; on
    Cleveland's silver views, 322, on
    Donnelly at Cincinnati conven-
    tion, 286; on Donnelly-Washburn
    suit, 191–92, at the Farmers'
    Alliance convention of 1893, 310;
    as a Greenback congressman,
    188; at Minnesota State Central
    Committee, 379; mobbed in
    1892, 307; on People's party-
    Democratic fusion, 368; as Peo-
    ple's party candidate, 301; pro-
    poses silver in 1895, 345;
    mentioned, 294, 317, 347
Weller, Lemuel H., 397
Wellington, Cyrus, 291
Westminster Abbey, 238

Wheelock, Joseph: 70, 72, 82, 85–88,
    117, 120, 371
Whigs, New England, 29
Whipple, Bishop, 85
Wilde, Oscar, 238
Wilder, Amherst, H., 156
Wilkinson, Morton: 53, 95, 123, 142–
    43
Willard, Frances, 294
Wilson, Eugene, 121–22, 259
Wilson, Henry, 39
Wilson, Thomas, 142, 250
Wilson, W. L., 109, 114
Windom, William: 33, 75, 92, 95,
    112, 123, 125, 135, 186
Women's Christian Temperance Un-
    ion, 294
Wright, Hendrick B., 192
Wyman, W. H., 228

Youmans, E. L., 208–9
Young America Movement, 8, 116,
    305
Young, H. H., 166
Young, Thomas, 236

This book may be kept
FOURTEEN DAYS
A fine will be charged for ea
the book is kept overt

39779